FOURTH EDITION
MANAGEMENT

▲▼ ADDISON-WESLEY PUBLISHING COMPANY

Reading, Massachusetts ▲ Menlo Park, California ▲ Don Mills, Ontario ▲ Wokingham, England
Amsterdam ▲ Sydney ▲ Singapore ▲ Tokyo ▲ Mexico City ▲ Bogotá ▲ Santiago ▲ San Juan

FOURTH EDITION
MANAGEMENT

Don Hellriegel . John W. Slocum, Jr.

College of Business Administration
Texas A&M University

Edwin L. Cox School of Business
Southern Methodist University

Sponsoring Editor:	*Connie Spatz*
Production and Copy Editor:	*Jerrold A. Moore*
Text Designer:	*Margaret Ong Tsao*
Art Editor:	*Kristin Belanger*
Illustrator:	*Scientific Illustrators*
Photo Researcher:	*Darlene Bordwell*
Manufacturing Supervisor:	*Hugh Crawford*
Cover Designer:	*Mike Fender*

Photo Credits: *Part I, Darlene Bordwell; Part II, Polly Brown/Archive Pictures; Part III, Michael Heron/Woodfin Camp & Associates; Part IV, Peter Southwick/Stock, Boston; Part V, Sandra Johnson/The Picture Cube; Part VI, © 1982 Joel Gordon; Part VII, Charles Harbutt/Archive Pictures*

Library of Congress Cataloging-in-Publication Data

Hellriegel, Don.
  Management

  Bibliography; p.
  Includes index.
  1. Management.   I. Slocum, John W.   II. Title.
HD31.H447 1985   658.4   85-11113
ISBN 0-201-11542-5

To Lois and Gail

Unlike the study of chemistry, biology, or physics, the study of management cannot represent the "real world" in a laboratory setting where the student can learn through experiments and practice. It is difficult—often impossible—to create first-hand experiences in the classroom that develop the conceptual, technical, and communication skills an effective manager needs. Thus the management student faces many abstract ideas, concepts, and research findings about managing people and events in the business world. The major challenge in teaching and in studying management, then, lies in finding a counterpart to the laboratory. We believe that this can be done through effective use of real-life cases and incidents.

The primary goal of the fourth edition of *Management* is to make the learning and teaching processes simpler, clearer, and more rewarding. We believe that we achieved that goal by the way we present the concepts of management in the text, the extensive use of examples and cases to illustrate the application of these concepts in real-world situations, and the careful selection of figures, tables, and photographs to highlight, summarize, and complement the text.

Objectives

Five objectives guided us in the development of this edition:

■   Emphasizing an international theme without creating an international business management textbook;

■   Presenting concepts, models, and techniques with new and lively examples of problems that real managers have faced—regardless of industry, level in the organization, or function—and describing how those problems were attacked.

■   Integrating management concepts and practices by relating real-life incidents to the topics covered in each chapter;

Preface

- Presenting material in a manner most useful to both student and teacher, always keeping in mind the interests of our target audience: sophomores or juniors enrolled in their first management course, and the instructors who will guide their development; and

- Reflecting the latest in management thinking and practice while avoiding fads.

New to This Edition

Here is a sampling of the many significant improvements contained in this edition:

An international theme

Our emphasis on an international theme represents an increasing awareness that businesses and their managers no longer operate only within the borders of their own countries; rather, that business today involves flows of information, resources, and goods that transcend national boundaries.

- *Expanded coverage.* The previous edition's chapter on international management has been broadened substantially.

- *International focus.* Each chapter contains this special feature. It presents current articles from important and influential business publications that relate directly to the subject of each chapter.

Four new chapters

Besides significantly updating all chapters in the previous edition, we added four new chapters:

- Chapter 5, "Ethics and Social Responsibility in Management," reflects our belief that this area of concern will become even more critical to managers as they cope with the complexities of a changing world.

- Chapter 11, "Impact of Information Processing on Organization Design," focuses on ways in which technology and management-information systems influence an organization's structure.

- Chapter 18, "Control Through Staffing and Performance Appraisal," emphasizes the importance of using these two essential human-resource functions in improving managers' abilities to achieve organizational objectives.

- Chapter 20, "Career Development," discusses the factors affecting career decisions, stages in career development, and ideas for successfully managing a career.

Organization of chapters

This edition presents management from a modified functional managerial approach. The core parts of the book cover decision making and planning, organizing, leading, and controlling. We have improved the book's organization in the following ways.

■ Part III contains a new twist: we present the decision-making chapters prior to the planning chapters. In the first two parts of the text we lay a firm foundation that enables students to begin developing decision-making skills—skills that students need as they delve into the managerial functions of planning, organizing, leading, and controlling.

■ Part IV, which focuses on organization design, includes a major change: the integration of management-information systems and their influence on the design and structure of organizations.

■ Part V, the organizational behavior section of the book, contains two significant new topics: organizational cultures and individual stress.

■ Part VI, coverage of the controlling function, now follows the decision-making, planning, and organizational behavior sections, giving the student a broad base that supports this further discussion of power and how it should be used.

Features within Chapters

The learning aids described below were designed to help students grasp concepts discussed in the text.

New and better cases

Each chapter contains three types of cases and incidents, with each type serving a specific learning function.

■ Each chapter opens with a Preview Case that highlights the topics covered in the chapter. Each case is intended to spark curiosity about the way these situations evolved and why.

■ Each chapter contains one or more In Practice descriptions of how a concept, model, or technique was applied (or misapplied) in real situations. These descriptions relate directly to the topic being discussed in the text at that point.

■ One or more Management Incidents and Cases appear at the end of each chapter. These cases help students analyze and assess real-life situations by applying concepts learned from reading the chapter.

Manager's vocabulary

An understanding of certain key terms and concepts is essential to the study of management, and together they form an indispensable vocabulary for managers.

■ Within the text, key terms and concepts are identified by italic, boldface type and are defined.

■ At the end of each chapter, they are listed alphabetically in the Manager's Vocabulary section.

■ At the end of the book, they are referenced by page in the Subject Index.

End-of-chapter questions

Two sets of questions are presented at the end of each chapter.

■ Review Questions, new to this edition, help students determine whether they have adequately mastered the content of each chapter.

■ Discussion Questions can be used by students while studying or by the instructor to stimulate class discussion.

References

At the end of each chapter, complete citations of the sources used as references in the chapter are given. A number of the entries also provide guidance for where to look for further information about specific topics covered.

Supplements

Several important supplements are available to help both the student and the instructor use this edition of *Management*.

■ *Instructor's Manual*. The manual includes extensive lecture notes, highlights of major themes in the textbook, transparency masters and a list of films that supplement the material in each chapter.

■ *Student Study Guide*. This guide was prepared by Abraham Axelrud, Jonas Falik, and Suzanne D'Agnes of Queensborough Community College of the City University of New York. It provides examples, questions, and answers to enrich the learning process.

■ *Transparencies*. These visual aids present figures and tables and include much new material not used in the text.

■ *Experiential Exercises Book*. These exercises were prepared by Marshall Sashkin of the University of Maryland and the National Institute of Education and by William Morris. Exercises on perforated worksheets follow the content of the text.

■ *Test Bank and Microcomputer Testing Package*. This material is available free to adopters. The TESTGEN program is compatible with IBM and Apple equipment. It consists of a program disk and data disks containing questions from our Test Bank. In the fall of 1986, graphics will be added to TESTGEN's capabilities.

There's an Old Saying: No Man Is an Island

Contrary to stereotypes, authors don't simply go off to their own "islands" to write their books. Without the help of many individuals, the development and production of our fourth edition would not have been possible.

We would like to give our special thanks to Jeff Kerr of Southern Methodist University for his special insights on the entire manuscript. We also thank Dean William H. Mobley and Lyle F. Schoenfeldt of the College of Business Administration, Texas A&M University, and Hans Hillerbrand, Provost, and Mick McGill of Southern Methodist University, for providing assistance and the intellectual work environment that enabled us to develop this book. For prompt and accurate typing and word processing, we thank two superb secretaries: Janet Macha (Texas A&M University) and Jane Bell (Southern Methodist University). Without them, we doubt that the manuscript could have been completed.

Many first-class professionals at Addison-Wesley worked with us as a team to make this a better book. Those most directly involved, and for whom we hold deep appreciation and respect, include: Connie Spatz, our management editor, who worked with us so creatively on the numerous editorial judgments involved in each step of the process; Janice Jackson Hill, the management editor who astutely assisted in setting the basic direction for this revision; Shirley Rieger, who kept a seemingly endless flow of correspondence and feedback loops on track; Jerrold Moore, whose superb copyediting was invaluable in improving the flow and readability of the manuscript while maintaining technical accuracy; Barbara Pendergast, whose management-by-objectives throughout the production process resulted in a finished product on time; Kristin Belanger, who is chiefly responsible for this edition's superb art program; and Darlene Bordwell, who used her creative eye in selecting and obtaining the many new photos in this edition.

Finlly, we give special thanks to our families for their empathy and understanding of our need to spend so many evenings and weekends on our "authors' islands" rather than with them.

Reviewers

The intellectual stimulation and guidance provided by the many reviewers of this and the previous editions were essential to improving the fourth edition. Although there were times when all of the ideas about what to include were in conflict, the comments and suggestions of the reviewers listed below led to a substantially improved book, and we are grateful to each of them.

Achilles A. Armenakis
Auburn University

Michael B. Arthur
Suffolk University

Thomas Barry
Southern Methodist University

Curtis W. Cook
San Jose State University

James Dawson III
Tom Thumb Supermarkets/Page Drug

William A. Day
Ohio University

Bruce Erickson
University of Minnesota

Dan Farrell
Western Michigan University

Dudley Faver
Texas Tech University

David Finley
Southland Corporation

Ann Flavin
Optigraphics Corporation

Jerry K. Geisler
Eastern Illinois University

Virginia Geurin
University of North Carolina

Charles Greer
Oklahoma State University

David W. Grigsby
Clemson University

Douglas C. Hall
Boston University

James L. Hall
Santa Clara University

Robert W. Hollmann
University of Montana

Richard Huseman
University of Georgia

R. Duane Ireland
Baylor University

Lynn Isabella
Southern Methodist University

Ellen Jackofsky
Southern Methodist University

Ben L. Kedia
Louisiana State University

Bruce A. Kemelgore
University of Louisville

Jeffrey Kerr
Southern Methodist University

William R. LaFollette
Ball State University

Gary Latham
University of Washington

Donna E. Ledgerwood
North Texas State University

Jim Ledvinka
University of Georgia

Paul James Londrigan
C.S. Mott Community College

Mark Martinko
Florida State University

Mick E. McGill
Southern Methodist University

Gregory Mechler
C.A. White Trucking Company

Paul N. Myers
Arthur Young & Company

John M. Nicholas
Loyola University

Gregory Northcraft
University of Arizona

Winston Oberg
Michigan State University

David D. Palmer
University of Connecticut

David W. Pentico
Virginia Commonwealth University

Darrell Piersol
Southwest Texas State University

James C. Quick
University of Texas at Arlington

Samuel Rabinowitz
Rutgers University

V. Jean Ramsey
Western Michigan University

Mark Rigg
Southland Corporation

Daniel Robey
Florida International University

Joseph Rosenstein
University of Texas at Arlington

Marshall Sashkin
National Institute of Education

John Sheridan
Texas Christian University

Charles C. Snow
Pennsylvania State University

H. A. Sutherland
Brooklyn Union Gas

Sheila Teitelbaum
Kingsborough Community College

Mary Thibodeaux
North Texas State University

Jeff Weekley
Zale Corporation

Stuart Youngblood
Texas A&M University

Carl P. Zeithaml
Texas A&M University

College Station, Texas
Dallas, Texas

D.H.
J.W.S. Jr.

DON HELLRIEGEL

Don Hellriegel is the Jenna and Calvin R. Guest Professor of Business Administration and a Professor of Management at Texas A&M University. During his ten years at Texas A&M, he has acted as Interim Executive Vice Chancellor for Programs and as Management Department Head. In addition to his teaching responsibilities and business consulting, Dr. Hellriegel has co-written numerous books and articles on management and organizational behavior. In conjunction with his active participation in the Academy of Management, he served as Editor of the *Academy of Management Review* from 1982–1984. He is currently Vice-President and Program Chair of the Academy of Management. Dr. Hellriegel received an MBA from Kent State University (1963) and a Ph.D. in management from the University of Washington (1969).

JOHN W. SLOCUM JR.

John W. Slocum Jr. is a Distinguished Professor of Organizational Behavior and Administration at the Edwin L. Cox School of Business, Southern Methodist University. Dr. Slocum, past President of the Academy of Management, was Editor of the *Academy of Management Journal* from 1979–1981 and is a fellow in the Academy of Management and a fellow in Decision Sciences Institute. He has served as a consultant to organizations as varied as Westinghouse, NASA, Brooklyn Union Gas Company, Beatrice Foods, Holiday Inns, Inc., and Hershey Foods. He has authored or co-authored four books and more than 70 articles for professional journals. Like his colleague and co-author, Dr. Slocum received an MBA from Kent State University (1964) and a Ph.D. in organizational behavior from the University of Washington (1967).

About the Authors

Contents in Brief

CONTENTS

PART V LEADING 402

12 Individual Motivation in Organizations 404

13 Leadership   438

FOURTH EDITION
MANAGEMENT

P A R T I

MANAGEMENT:
AN OVERVIEW

The Nature of Management

LEARNING OBJECTIVES

After studying this chapter, you should be able to:

- Define the term *management.*
- Describe the eight characteristics of successfully managed companies.
- Identify three levels of management.
- Explain the importance of the four basic management functions.

- Identify the basic characteristics of managerial work.
- List the four basic skills of an effective manager.
- State the differences among the four viewpoints of management.

CHAPTER OUTLINE

Preview Case Procter & Gamble Company

What Is Management?
Characteristics of successfully managed companies
Levels and types of managers

Approaches to Understanding Management
Managerial-functions approach
Managerial-roles approach

In Practice: Behind the Wheels of General Motors with Roger Smith

Characteristics of Managerial Work
Principal duties of first-line managers
Principal duties of middle managers
Changes in work characteristics for first-line and middle managers
Principal duties of top managers

Skills of Effective Managers
Technical skills
Human-relations skills
Conceptual skills
Communication skills
Relative importance of managerial skills

Viewpoints of Management
Traditional viewpoint

*International Focus
    Traveling Overseas: Picking Your
    Fellow Passengers*
Behavioral viewpoint
Systems viewpoint
Contingency viewpoint

Management as a Dynamic Process

*Management Incidents and Cases
    Mary Kay Cosmetics*

PREVIEW CASE

PROCTER & GAMBLE COMPANY

On a crisp morning in November 1837, James Gamble began his daily rounds. He pushed his cart through the streets of Cincinnati, knocking on doors, collecting meat scraps and wood ashes for his new business. Late in October, he and his brother-in-law, William Procter, combined their small soap- and candle-making businesses into one, forming a partnership called Procter and Gamble & Co. (P&G). At considerable sacrifice, even to the point of selling Procter's wagons and horses, they pooled their resources and opened a small shop, with Gamble in charge of production and Procter keeping the books.

In the beginning they spent much of their time boiling fats in a huge kettle behind the shop and delivering their goods by wheelbarrow. But even with these primitive techniques, the partners quickly developed a reputation for quality products and honest business dealings. Both were devout Protestants with strong religious and moral convictions. These qualities formed the basis of a strict ethical code that guided their company for generations.

From this small shop in Cincinnati has grown the P&G of today, with more than 50 plants throughout the United States and major operations in 24 foreign countries. From an initial investment of $7192.24, the company's annual sales have grown to more than $13 billion. Procter & Gamble sells roughly one-half of the laundry detergent, one-third of the bar soap and toothpaste,

and two-thirds of the disposable diapers sold in the United States. These products carry major brand names such as Pampers, Folgers, Crest, Duncan Hines, and Tide.

What is the secret behind this great success? Perhaps we can look to the founders themselves for the answer. From the very beginning, Procter & Gamble stubbornly refused to compromise on the quality of their products. At a time when technology was primitive and consistency was difficult, people knew they could depend on P&G's soaps, candles, and oils. The founders also emphasized development of new products and improvement of old ones; they used knowledge learned on one product to help them produce and improve the next one. Procter & Gamble were excellent strategists, carefully planning moves into

Source: Courtesy of the Procter & Gamble Company.

new and innovative product areas. They excelled at playing the price game with their competitors and found ways to produce high-quality goods for reasonable prices. As the company grew, they managed this growth by staying with a familiar area of consumer goods, which provided demand stability even in times of economic downturns.

As descendents took over the management from Procter & Gamble, the company's goals remained the same. Today's managers foster innovation by encouraging development of new products to compete directly with existing products of the company: Gleem competes with Crest, Zest competes with Safeguard, and so on through the product lines. The company often leads the way with technological breakthroughs and new ideas. When attempting to enter the quality tissue market with a new product, Certain, the company tried it first in test markets in Iowa, Nebraska, and Wisconsin before being satisfied with its quality and marketability. Two other brands, Banner and Summit, compete in the generic and private label tissue market against Charmin. However, not all products have been successful. The generic versions of nearly everything that P&G makes have cut into its profit margin. The biggest setback was Rely, a super-absorbent tampon. Procter & Gamble voluntarily suspended this product from the market in September 1980 to remove it and the company from controversy surrounding toxic-shock syndrome, a sometimes fatal illness. Procter & Gamble took a loss of $75 million on this product. As the company goes into new market areas with more aggressive advertising during the 1980s, the guiding principles of planning and innovation continue to direct its growth.[1]

During the last 50 years, every developed country has become a society of organizations. Ours is no exception. At various times in our lives, each of us will become a member of an organization—school, college, church, fraternity or sorority, sports team, armed forces, homeowners' association, or a business. These organizations differ from one another in numerous ways. Some, like the armed forces or large corporations, spend millions of dollars recruiting members and developing highly sophisticated control methods to ensure that members conform to the organization's rules and regulations. Others, like a neighborhood homeowners' association and the Parent–Teachers Association, spend relatively little money attracting members and impose few controls on their members' behavior. Each of us could write an autobiography as a series of encounters with organizations. Consider, for example, your life and the organizations you have encountered or will encounter from birth to death.

You probably were born in a hospital.

Your birth was registered by a city or county bureau of records.

You were educated in a school system and assigned to a variety of teachers.

When old enough, you were licensed to drive by a state agency.

You are loaned money for a car or house by a financial institution.

If you travel abroad, you are required to carry a passport issued by an agency of the U.S. government.

Your marriage is registered by the bureau of records.

Home furnishings and food are purchased from businesses whose owners you do not know.

By the time you are 30 years old, you will have moved at least twice, relying on a moving company to transport your belongings.

Quite likely, you or someone you know will be granted a divorce by state courts, with the aid of a law firm.

At your death, you and your survivors will be ministered to by representatives of at least three organizations: a law firm, the church, and the undertaker![2]

This book is about how organizations are managed and how managers set and achieve their goals. *Managers* give direction to the organizations they manage. They have to think through an organization's goals, set objectives, and organize resources to achieve results. In performing these functions, managers everywhere face the same types of problems. They have to organize work in ways that increase efficiency and effectiveness, lead employees toward productivity and achievement, and be responsible for the social impact of the organization on society. The primary purposes of this book are to help you understand how managers accomplish these tasks and to make you aware of the skills you need to be an effective manager. We did not try to include every problem managers might face—just those with which all managers can be expected to deal—regardless of their backgrounds and goals and the size of organization.

WHAT IS MANAGEMENT?

Management is the art of getting things done through other people. Managers achieve an organization's objectives by arranging for others to do things, not by performing all the tasks themselves. In fact, most employees do nonmanagerial work. Receptionists, file clerks, secretaries, security guards, janitorial staffs, and maintenance people are all nonmanagers.

Characteristics of Successfully Managed Companies

Good management is essential to the success of a company. In an attempt to find out what managers of successful companies do, Tom Peters and Bob Waterman, management consultants, studied 43 well-run companies, including International Business Machines (IBM), Procter & Gamble (P&G), Minnesota Mining and Manufacturing (3M), Texas Instruments (TI), and Dana, among others.[3] The study identified eight common characteristics, or principles, of these successfully managed companies.

1. *A bias toward action.* Managers avoid long, complicated business plans, preferring to *do it, fix it, try it.* Goals are few and well-defined. Problems are handled quickly by either an individual troubleshooter or a temporary task force. Ideas are solicited regularly, tested quickly, and either implemented or rejected. At P&G new product ideas must be condensed to a one-page memo.

2. *Simple form and lean staff.* Although all 43 companies studied are big—the smallest, McDonald's, has annual sales in excess of $1.9 billion—they are structured into smaller segments. Hewlett-Packard, a firm with more than 57,000 employees, is divided into small entrepreneurial units no larger than 1200 employees each. Within the units, key activities are assigned to small, manageable groups. These groups are kept small to avoid slow decision making, excessive rules and regulations, and breakdowns in communication.

3. *Continued contact with customers.* Personal contact with customers and customer-satisfaction surveys guide managers' decisions. Senior executives and others regularly visit customers. Customers can provide new product ideas as well as steady sales. Ensuring satisfaction with sales and service requires prompt delivery and complaint processing. Caterpillar Tractor Company's motto "24-hour parts delivery anywhere in the world" and IBM's "processing of customer complaints within 24 hours of receipt" are ways these two companies strive to serve their customers.

4. *Productivity improvement through people.* To increase productivity, employees jointly set goals with managers and are given autonomy to reach them. At TI, shop-floor teams set goals that are reasonable and attainable, but stretch people. Almost all the companies in the study use recognition programs such as awarding badges, pins, medals, and bonuses.

5. *Operational autonomy to encourage entrepreneurship.* Managers are allowed to be entrepreneurs. Within broad guidelines, plant managers at Dana are free to make purchasing decisions and to start productivity programs on their own. IBM's fellows program is intended to permit proven senior managers to explore their ideas with a minimum of red tape.

6. *Stress on one key business value.* Managers set one priority and try to do that one thing well; for example, customer service at IBM, productivity improvement at Dana, new product development at 3M, and product quality at P&G. The company does not allow conflicting values to weaken its primary emphasis. As employees who are steeped in these corporate values are promoted, they become role models for newcomers and the process continues.

7. *Emphasis on doing what they know best.* A successful company defines its strength—marketing, customer contact, new-product innovation, low-

cost manufacturing—then builds on it. At Johnson & Johnson, a retired manager stated: "Never acquire any business you don't know how to run." That is, don't move into businesses that look attractive but require corporate skills the company does not have.

8. *Simultaneous loose–tight controls.* If a few variables are tightly controlled (for example, costs and revenues), management may allow leeway in day-to-day operations. Minnesota Mining and Manufacturing uses return on sales and number of employees as yardsticks for control. Yet it gives managers a lot of freedom within those limitations.

By sticking to these eight basic principles, the successful companies studied have achieved better than average growth. Their managers are able to change direction—and to change quickly. They aim their sights externally at their customers and their competitors, as well as on their own financial reports.

Achieving excellence in management requires time and effort, repetition, simplification, and the use of tools such as plant visits, effective communication, and focused systems and procedures. Ignoring the eight basic principles may mean that a company will lose vitality, stop growing, and lose out competitively.

Levels and Types of Managers

Different levels and types of managers are typically found in different organizations. Harry Cunningham is the president of Kmart; he manages a corporation that has thousands of employees and operates more than 3000 Kmart stores. Don Bolger manages a local Dairy Queen, which has only five employees. Both are managers but their jobs are not the same. Thus managers can be classified by their level in an organization and by their responsibilities. Figure 1.1 shows the basic levels of managers.

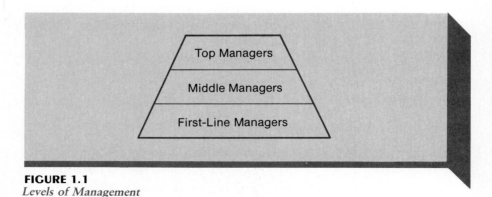

FIGURE 1.1
Levels of Management

First-Line Managers — Formak

Directly responsible for the actual production of goods and services, **first-line managers** have various titles: section chief, lead person, supervisor. The employees who report to them do the production work of the organization. For example, first-line managers in a steel plant supervise employees who make steel, operate and maintain machines, and write shipping orders. This level of management is the link between higher-level managers and nonmanagers. However, they spend little time with middle and top managers and people from other organizations; most of their time is spent with workers. First-line managers often lead hectic, interrupted work lives, spending most of their time communicating and solving problems in their own work areas. They work on the "firing line," where the action is.

Middle Managers — give orders to formans — to get the Job done

As an organization grows and becomes more complex, so do its problems. Attention must be focused on coordinating the activities of people, determining which products or services should be provided, and deciding how to market these products or services to customers. These problems are dealt with by **middle managers,** who receive the broad, overall strategies and policies from top managers and translate them into specific objectives and programs that can be implemented by first-line managers. Therefore middle managers spend about 80 percent of their time talking on the phone, in committee meetings, and preparing reports.

Top Managers   Design Goals for Company Goals

Managers who are responsible for the overall operations of an organization are **top managers.** Typical titles of top managers are *chief executive officer, president, chairman,* and *executive vice-president.* Top managers establish objectives, policies, and strategies—and represent their organizations in community affairs, business deals, and government negotiations. They spend most of their time with other top managers in the company, people outside the company, and, to a lesser extent, middle managers and other subordinates. Lee Iacocca, chairman of Chrysler Corporation, spends approximately 25 percent of his time dealing with governmental agencies and Congress on behalf of Chrysler's attempt to tell its story with respect to energy conservation, health, safety, capitalism, and tax reform.[4]

Functional and General Managers

Clearly distinguishing among the three levels of managers can help you understand the jobs different managers perform. However, in large organizations distinctions among managers are also based on the scope of activities managed. **Functional managers** are responsible for specialized areas of operation, such as accounting, personnel, payroll, finance, marketing, and production. Functional managers supervise people who specialize and have skills in one particular area. A typical functional manager is the head of a payroll department, who does not determine the salaries of managers and employees but is responsible for making sure that payroll checks are issued on time and in the correct amounts.

General managers are responsible for the overall operations of a company, a division, or a plant. General managers hold functional managers accountable for their specialized areas. Richard Grogan is a general manager; he runs Trans-National Truck, a division of Schneider Transport. Grogan is responsible for directing the personnel and operations of the division in its attempt to capture a larger share of the trucking business in the rapidly growing southwest.

SUMMARY

The word *manager* is a broad one. It includes the managers of small businesses as well as chief executive officers of multinational corporations; plant managers as well as first-line production supervisors; and generalists as well as specialists. The typical categories of managers are referred to throughout this book as we explain what managers do and how they do it.

APPROACHES TO UNDERSTANDING MANAGEMENT

Now that you have learned something about the basic things that successfully managed companies do and the types of managers that organizations employ, we turn to consideration of two approaches used for understanding what managers do and how they do it. The *managerial-functions* approach focuses on *what* managers do. The *managerial-roles* approach focuses on *how* they perform their jobs. An understanding of both approaches is necessary for you to fully appreciate the function and scope of management.

MANAGERIAL-FUNCTIONS APPROACH

Successful management involves active participation by managers in the four basic managerial functions: planning, organizing, leading, and controlling (as shown in Fig. 1.2). These functions are interrelated and most managers use combinations of them simultaneously to solve problems facing their companies.

PLANNING

The *planning* function is the process of making decisions about the future. Planning is needed to help an organization define its objectives and establish procedures for reaching them. Procter & Gamble, IBM, McDonald's, Boeing, Coca-Cola, and Burger King, among others, use plans for three reasons: (1) plans enable managers to identify and commit the firm's resources to achieve-

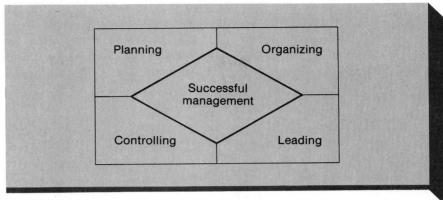

FIGURE 1.2
Basic Managerial Functions

ment of particular objectives, such as profits, market share, and social responsibility; (2) plans enable managers to decide which activities are consistent with stated objectives, and (3) plans enable managers to measure progress toward the objectives, so that corrective action can be taken if progress is unsatisfactory.

Organizing

Once managers have prepared plans and established objectives, they must design and develop a structure that will allow them to carry out their plans and meet their objectives successfully. *Organizing* is the process of creating such a structure. It involves setting up appropriate departments, job descriptions, rules, regulations, and procedures. Organizing is also a way for managers to coordinate human and material resources effectively. Much of an organization's success depends on managers' ability to get resources and utilize them efficiently. The National Aeronautics and Space Administration (NASA) must use a different kind of organizational structure than the one designed by managers at Levi Strauss & Company. NASA brings together scientists, engineers, propulsion experts, computer programmers, guidance specialists, and other professionals to design and conduct the space program. At Levi Strauss, producing blue jeans requires an efficient assembly line and workers who do repetitive tasks. The professionals at NASA are organized to achieve the goals of the program, which does not require them to work on assembly lines; likewise, the goals of Levi Strauss do not require an assembly-line worker to write a computer program. Thus staffing of an organization proceeds directly from objectives, plans, organizational structure, and the types of skills needed.

Leading

After plans have been made, a structure created, and appropriate personnel hired, someone must lead the organization. Some managers call this process *directing* or *influencing*. Whatever the name, **leading** refers to getting others to perform tasks that will help the organization achieve its objectives. Leading does not simply start after completion of the planning and organizing functions; in fact, leadership is often crucial to their success. Keys to effective leadership are proper communication and motivation.

Controlling

The process by which a person, group, or organization consciously influences what others do is called **controlling.** As you read the eight characteristics of successfully managed companies, did you notice that the last one referred to controlling? Through the control function, managers can

1. establish standards of performance;
2. measure current performance against these standards; and
3. take action to correct any deviations.

Just as the thermostat in a home sends signals to the cooling or heating system that the temperature is either too hot or too cold, so do control systems signal managers that action needs to be taken. Leading involves motivating others, whereas controlling involves directing their behaviors.

Summary

We presented the four basic managerial functions without discussing their interrelationships. As you use this book, you will find frequent references to these interrelationships, which illustrate how managers actually do their jobs.

Managerial-Roles Approach

The managerial-roles approach focuses on how managers actually perform the four basic functions.[5] A **role** is an organized set of behaviors. Henry Mintzberg studied a variety of managerial jobs to arrive at 10 roles most often played by managers. Each of these roles can be placed in one of three categories: interpersonal, informational, and decisional (as shown in Fig. 1.3).

Before discussing these roles, we should make four points: (1) every manager's job consists of some combination of roles; (2) the roles played by managers often influence the characteristics of managerial work (discussed in the next section); (3) the roles are described separately for your understanding (in practice, they are highly integrated); and (4) the relative importance of these roles can vary considerably by managerial level and function.

Interpersonal roles

Interpersonal roles arise directly from a manager's formal authority and involve interpersonal relationships. The **figurehead role** reflects the manager's responsibility for representing the organization at ceremonial and symbolic functions. It is the most basic and simple of all managerial roles. The president who greets a touring dignitary, the mayor who gives a key to the city to a

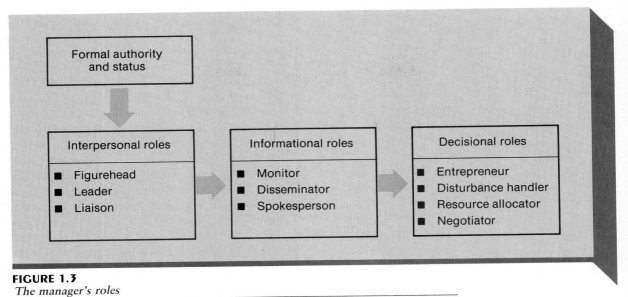

FIGURE 1.3
The manager's roles

Reprinted by permission of the *Harvard Business Review*. Exhibit from "The Manager's Job: Folklore and Fact" by Henry Mintzberg (July–August 1975). Copyright © 1975 by the President and Fellows of Harvard College; all rights reserved.

local hero, the supervisor who attends the wedding of the machine operator, the sales manager who takes an important customer to lunch—all are performing ceremonial duties important to the organization's image and success. While these duties may not appear to be important, they are expected of managers; they symbolize management's concern about employees, customers, and the community.

The ***leadership role*** involves responsibility for directing and coordinating the activities of subordinates to accomplish organizational objectives. Some aspects of the leadership role have to do with staffing: hiring, promoting, firing. Others have to do with motivating subordinates to ensure that the needs of the organization are met by the employees. Still other aspects of the leadership role have to do with controlling the activities of subordinates and probing for problems that need managerial attention.

The ***liaison role*** refers to dealing with people other than subordinates or supervisors, such as clients, government officials, members of boards of directors, and suppliers. The liaison role enables the manager to gain support for the organization from those outside the organization who can affect its success.

Informational roles

Effective managers build networks of contacts for sharing information. Because of these contacts, managers emerge as the nerve center of their organizations. Many of the contacts established while performing interpersonal roles give managers access to large amounts of information. Three roles—monitor, disseminator, and spokesperson—describe the informational aspects of managerial work.

The *monitor role* is the process of receiving and screening information. Just as a radar unit scans the environment, managers scan their environments for information that may affect their organization's performance. Since a good part of the information received by managers is oral (from gossip and hearsay, as well as formal meetings), they must be able to make decisions about the value of the information and whether to use it.

The *disseminator role* is the sharing and distribution of information to subordinates and others in the organization. Sometimes special information is passed along to certain subordinates as *privileged* information; privileged because these subordinates would not otherwise have access to it and because it should go no further. Passing information on to subordinates is often difficult and time-consuming. Thus a manager must decide which and how much information will be useful to subordinates.

Finally, in the role of *company spokesperson,* managers transmit information to others, especially those outside the organization, as the official position of the company. But the role of spokesperson is not confined to external relations. In November 1983, Lee Iacocca explained Chrysler's financial position, union negotiations, and the energy crisis while informing stockholders, and employees, and the general public that the corporation had just turned a profit and repaid its government loan.

Decisional roles

Managers need information in order to make intelligent decisions about committing their organizations to new courses of action. Decisional roles are perhaps the most important of the three categories of roles, since managers play a key part in the decision-making system of an organization.

The *entrepreneurial role* involves the design and initiation of planned change. Managers play this role when they seek to improve an organization's position by initiating new projects, launching a survey, or testing a new market. When Harry Cunningham became general vice-president of S. S. Kresge Company in 1957, he devised a new direction for the company: discounting. Before the first Kmart store opened, he committed the company to $80 million in leases and merchandise for the original 33 stores. He became the nation's premier discounter, changing the direction of Kresge and the meaning of discount stores in the United States. As an entrepreneur, Cunningham was a designer and initiator of change.

The *disturbance-handler role* is played when managers deal with involuntary situations and changes that are sometimes beyond their immediate control, such as strikes by labor, bankruptcy of major suppliers, or breaking of contracts by customers. Disturbances may arise because poor managers ignore situations until crises occur. However, even good managers cannot possibly anticipate all the consequences of their decisions or control the actions of others that affect their company.

The *resource-allocator role* involves making choices among competing demands for money, equipment, personnel, and access to a manager's time. What proportion of the budget should we earmark for advertising and what proportion for improving an existing product line? Should we add a second shift or should we pay overtime to handle new orders? Managers must continually make such choices in the allocation of resources, but especially when performing the planning function.

Closely linked to the resource-allocator role is the *negotiator role.* This is the process of meeting and discussing differences with individuals or groups for the purpose of reaching an agreement. Negotiations are an integral part of a manager's job. They are particularly difficult when a manager must deal with others (such as unions or political-action groups) who do not share the manager's objectives.

SUMMARY

We discussed the 10 managerial roles separately, but they are not independent and their relative importance can vary. Although they form a whole, the type of organization, the management level, and the effect on a person's career may cause certain roles to be more important than others—and their relative importance to a manager may change from time to time. As chief executive officer at General Motors, Roger Smith has multiple roles. These roles are identified in brackets in the description of his activities since joining GM.

IN PRACTICE
Behind the Wheels of General Motors with Roger Smith

In 1980, the year before Roger Smith became the 10th Chief Executive Officer of General Motors, GM was in the red for the first time in more than 50 years. During 1981, Smith's in-house cost-cutting measures, including inefficient plants and the sale of the company's New York City office building, resulted in a profit of $33.4 million. In 1982, he consolidated and modernized GM plants, got wage concessions from the union, and saw GM's profits reach $926 million [leadership role]. In 1983, GM sold a record number of cars (4.1 million) and recorded record profits of $3.8 billion. In 1984, profits were slightly over $4.7 billion.

Smith began his GM career in the finance department at GM. "Being part of the finance staff," he says, "you're a little bit back from all the gung-ho spirit you normally get from other divisions, and you develop a more pragmatic attitude. Believe me, I've had my share of pet projects that just didn't fly. I've always felt that GM had not, in the past, quit early enough on some projects. One of my major roles is to manage change. Strategic planning is worthless without strategic management."

(continued)

Traditionally, the word *change* has not been a commonly used term at GM. However, the radical reorganization of GM in late 1984 has changed this, Smith simplified GM's five separate car divisions (Cadillac, Buick, Oldsmobile, Pontiac, and Chevrolet) into just two groups—one responsible for development and production of small cars, the other focused on the larger models. Smith also turned foreign rivals into partners when GM moved into joint ventures with Suzuki, Isuzu, and Toyota [entrepreneurial role].

In 1985, Smith announced that a new car, the Saturn, will be made and sold by a new subsidiary. The goal of this new corporation is to produce the Saturn, a car that could get 45 miles per gallon, by the late 1980's [figurehead role]. Creating the Saturn Corporation was an innovative step for GM. Not only will the car be built by a completely new organization, the first such addition since GM purchased Chevrolet in 1918, but they will be built under a new labor contract and sold by a new network of dealers. "We hope this car will be less labor intensive, less material intensive, less everything intensive than everything we have done before," Smith says [resource-allocator role].

Under Smith's leadership, GM has made some other business acquisitions. In 1984, GM bought EDS (Electronic Data Systems), an information processing company that devised governmental and industrial computer programs. EDS's annual growth rate has been about 20%. Some computer industry analysts say that after the eventual shakedown in computers, only a half dozen big international players will survive, including IBM, AT&T, and either ITT or GM—EDS. GM also has joined with a Japanese firm to produce robots.

Smith's management style has broken with GM's tradition. He has streamlined GM's penchant for paper pushing and has opted for a hands-on, more participative management style. This means that managers have more authority to make decisions. Smith describes the job assignment that had the greatest impact on his career:

> It was a worldwide operation and entailed everything from the production of a million valve lifters a day to marketing locomotives selling at half a million dollars a crack.
>
> Since our automotive side was making good money, we never got into too much trouble or got much attention from others in the company. It was running my own thing—a pretty nice deal, being left alone.[6]

CHARACTERISTICS OF MANAGERIAL WORK

Among the thousands of books and articles written about managers, relatively few examine what managers actually do. From these limited studies we get the impression that managers spend most of their time reading reports and attending meetings in air-conditioned offices, rushing to the airport to catch a plane, entertaining important customers, and solving complicated problems.

This impression is somewhat accurate for top managers—as far as it goes—but what about first-line and middle managers? The American Telephone and Telegraph Company (AT&T) studied the behaviors of its 170,000 first-line and 60,000 middle managers.[7] The following description of duties—and changes in these duties—for first-line and middle managers is based largely on the findings of this study. Although the Bell System is enormous, with assets of $114 billion, many of its characteristics can be found in other organizations.

Principal Duties of First-Line Managers

Newly appointed first-line managers generally have much to learn—and much to unlearn. If they had been production workers, they must learn to let others do the work that they had been doing until recently; to put aside thoughts about how much better and faster they could do it themselves; and to derive satisfaction from the accomplishments of others, rather than from their own output. They must learn to plan and schedule work formerly laid out for them and not wait for their bosses to tell them what to do. In doing so, they must also learn how the work of their groups fits into that of the total organization and how to share staff services with others in the organization.

The first-line manager may also be a recent college graduate who is responsible for the work of both blue-collar workers and professionals. For this reason and because products and processes have become more complex, the first-line manager has less hands-on skills in performing a particular job than in the past, but administrative skills are more important. Effective first-line managers have good interpersonal skills: communicating, coaching, counseling, and providing feedback on performance to subordinates.

Table 1.1 illustrates the 14 principal duties that first-line managers perform. Looking at the rank order of importance and the percent of time spent on each duty, we note that these managers perform the four basic managerial functions (planning, organizing, leading, and directing). How well they perform these functions depends on how well they play informational and decisional roles. Solving problems and communicating up, down, and across departmental lines are important activities for these managers.

Principal Duties of Middle Managers

Many middle managers started their careers as first-line managers or production workers. Normally, middle managers spend several years as first-line managers in order to develop and hone technical skills and knowledge. Most would agree that the change from first-line to middle management represents a difficult, sometimes traumatic, transition. Although middle managers perform many of the same principal duties of first-line managers, as shown in Table 1.2, middle managers must identify more closely with company, as opposed to departmental objectives. Middle managers are more involved in setting company objectives and take on increased responsibility for achieving them. The time frame is different, also. Instead of thinking in terms of days or weeks, middle managers think in terms of months. While these managers

TABLE 1.1 ■ PRINCIPAL DUTIES OF FIRST-LINE MANAGERS

RANK ORDER	DUTY	PERCENT OF MANAGER'S TIME	FREQUENCY OF PERFORMANCE
1	Controlling (work activities)	15	Every day
2	Solving problems	12	Every day
3	Planning (work activities)	11	Every day
4	Communicating informally and orally	11	Every day
5	Communicating with superiors	11	Every day
6	Providing performance feedback to subordinates	10	Every day
7	Coaching subordinates	10	Every day
8	Writing letters and memos	6	Every day
9	Creating and maintaining a motivating atmosphere	5	Every day
10	Managing time	3	Every day
11	Attending meetings	3	Twice monthly
12	Reading and other self-development activities	1	Weekly
13	Career counseling with a subordinate	1	Bi-monthly
14	Representing the company	1	Monthly

Source: Adapted from *Performance Based Supervisory Development* by Charles McDonald, © 1982, HRD Press, Amherst, MA 01002. Reprinted by permission of the publisher. All rights reserved.

TABLE 1.2 ■ PRINCIPAL DUTIES OF MIDDLE MANAGERS

RANK ORDER	DUTY	PERCENT OF MANAGER'S TIME	FREQUENCY OF PERFORMANCE
1	Controlling	21	Every day
2	Developing subordinates	14	Every day
3	Planning	14	Every day
4	Managing time	10	Every day
5	Attending meetings	8	Every day
6	Making decisions	5	Every day
7	Reading and other self-development activities	5	Every day
8	Providing performance feedback to subordinates	4	Every day
9	Writing letters and memos	4	Every day
10	Creating a motivating atmosphere	3	Every day
11	Communicating upward	3	Every day
12	Performing community-relations activities	3	Bi-monthly
13	Communicating downward	3	Every day
14	Communicating with peers	3	Every day

Source: Adapted from *Performance Based Supervisory Development* by Charles McDonald, © 1982, HRD Press, Amherst, MA 01002. Reprinted by permission of the publisher. All rights reserved.

perform all four basic managerial functions, they spend more time leading than do first-line managers. This emphasis is indicated by the relative importance of developing subordinates, deciding how to allocate time, and attending meetings.

The major roles that middle managers play are interpersonal and informational. The problems faced by these managers are *people-centered,* as opposed to *technical.* Delegation of authority to implement decisions made by top managers and coordination with other managers are crucial activities.

Changes in Work Characteristics for First-Line and Middle Managers

With the strong emphasis on ways to increase productivity, first-line and middle managers of the 1980s can be expected to play more roles at various times in many different circumstances. At times they must be leaders, entrepreneurs, and decision makers. At other times they must be planners and resource allocators. This increased flexibility is critically important, for example, as the Bell System competes in the rapidly changing business world and adapts to the breakup of AT&T. Each operating company is faced with the multiple challenges of keeping pace with changes in consumer needs and desires, upgrading equipment to be more energy efficient, and, at the same time, reorganizing personnel and procedures.

First-line managers

Such demands affect the first-line manager's job in four ways. First, these managers will assume greater responsibility for the work of their departments, with staff specialists (quality control, personnel, industrial engineering) providing guidance and support. Second, their jobs will be more precisely defined than in the past, when many of these jobs were poorly defined and ambiguous. Third, workers they supervise will be less satisfied with authoritative management, will want more gratifying jobs, and will seek the chance to participate in decisions that affect their work. Fourth, the work itself is changing. The design and manufacture of products are being modified to meet new energy-efficiency standards and new safety and health requirements. The increased use of robots will displace people in performing certain routinized jobs, while creating new jobs with higher skill and knowledge requirements. More and more employees will deal with words and symbols rather than materials and products. First-line managers must adapt to these changes in the nature of work as much as, if not more than, the employees they supervise.

Middle managers

Middle managers are faced with a different set of challenges. First, these managers are more remote from the technical aspects of production work. Because they often lack hands-on knowledge, the need to delegate effectively is essential. Second, these managers must develop new skills and knowledge in order to cope with a new set of demands from top management. These skills involve the ability to negotiate with first-line managers and gain acceptance of top management's goals; compromise and consensus to achieve support are becoming more and more important. Attendance at meetings with other middle and top managers demands greater communications skills, especially oral. Third, these managers must be increasingly concerned with developing subordinates and providing them with lines of information and visibility to other middle and top managers.

Principal Duties of Top Managers

The pressures and demands on the time and attention of top managers can be intense. Tightly scheduled workdays, heavy travel requirements and work weeks of 60 hours or longer are not uncommon for a top manager. During a typical day, a top manager disposes of 36 pieces of mail, handles five telephone calls, and attends eight meetings. A true break is a luxury. Coffee is taken during meetings, and lunchtime is often devoted to meetings with other managers, business associates, community representatives, or government officials. When free time does occur, eager subordinates press to see the manager.

Four out of five week nights are spent working for the company; one night is spent working late at the office and another entertaining business associates; on the other working nights, the typical top manager goes home, not to relax but to use it for a branch office. Even recreational activities and social events are often arranged for business purposes. Thus top managers seldom stop thinking about the job and playing the roles it demands. Such an approach to time management succeeds in getting the work done, but it creates stresses on most families.

SKILLS OF EFFECTIVE MANAGERS

Effective managers need to use four basic types of skills: *technical, human-relations, conceptual,* and *communication skills.*[8] The relative degree and mixture of the skills needed by a particular manager depends on the level of management occupied, types of responsibilities assigned, and the particular role of the manager in the organization. The mix of skills needed by the manager of a local 7-Eleven store is likely to be quite different from that needed by a regional vice-president of Southland Corporation, which operates all 7-Eleven stores. The store manager is likely to need relatively high technical and human-relations skills, whereas the regional vice-president needs high conceptual, human-relations, and communication skills.

Skill refers to an ability that is not necessarily inborn, can be developed, and is related to performance. The separation of managerial skills into four distinct categories is useful only for discussion purposes. In practice, these skills are closely related and it may be difficult to tell where one begins and another ends.

Technical Skills

Technical skills involve the ability to apply specific methods, procedures, and techniques in a specialized field. We can easily visualize the technical skills of design engineers, market researchers, accountants, musicians, and computer programmers. Such technical skills are concrete and are often emphasized in educational courses and on-the-job training programs in accounting, statistics, engineering, mathematics, finance, and medicine. Although managers will use technical skills to varying degrees, their main concerns will be identifying, developing, and improving the technical skills needed by others throughout the organization.

Human-Relations Skills — give Extra Attention

Human-relations skills include the ability to lead, motivate, manage conflict, and work with others. Whereas technical skills emphasize working with things (techniques or physical objects), human-relations skills focus on working with people. In the long-run, organizations have only one true resource: people. Thus human-relations skills are a vital part of the job of all managers, regardless of level (from supervisor to vice-president) or function (production, marketing, finance).

Conceptual Skills

Conceptual skills involve the ability to (1) see the organization as a whole and recognize its relationship to the larger business world; (2) understand how the parts and functions of the organization depend on each other and how changes in one part can affect the others; and (3) know how to diagnose and assess different types of management problems. The development of conceptual skills requires thinking in terms of (1) relative emphasis and priorities among conflicting objectives and criteria; (2) relative tendencies and probabilities (rather than certainties); and (3) rough correlations and patterns among elements (rather than clear-cut, cause-and-effect relationships).

Communication Skills — Extra Attention

Communication skills reflect a manager's ability to send and receive information, thoughts, feelings, and attitudes. As found by AT&T in their study of first-line and middle managers, a large portion of a manager's time is spent communicating. In addition, the 10 managerial roles are based on the assumption that managers possess basic written, oral, and nonverbal (facial expressions, body posture) communication skills.

Recruiters look for people who can communicate effectively. They often comment that professional programs in universities spend too much time developing technical skills and not enough time developing communication skills.

Relative Importance of Managerial Skills

The relative importance of these four types of skills at each level of management is shown in Fig. 1.4. Note that communication skills are basic to the other three and are important at all management levels.[9] Communication skills are necessary for the effective display of human-relations, technical, and conceptual skills to others. Even a manager's best ideas and intentions will have little impact on an organization if they cannot be effectively communicated to others.

The need for the other three types of skills varies widely among the three management levels. Technical skills are most important to first-line managers and decrease in importance as a manager moves up in the organization. The supervisor of an assembly line for Xerox Corporation's memory typewriters, for example, is likely to need more technical skills than the company president

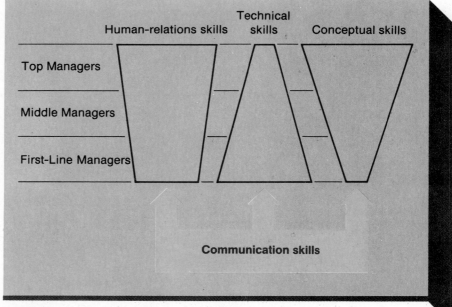

FIGURE 1.4
Four Basic Managerial Skills

because the problems brought to the supervisor are primarily technical. Human-relations skills are important at every level in the organization. They are somewhat more important for middle managers and more important yet for top managers, whose days are spent mostly in communicating with others and in dealing with problems brought to them by others.

The higher that managers are in an organization, the more they are involved in complex decisions. Top managers need substantial conceptual ability to recognize the important factors in a situation and how they interrelate. Without this ability, managers cannot make decisions that will further the interests of the entire organization.

VIEWPOINTS OF MANAGEMENT

Obviously, no single book about management can teach you enough to become an effective manager. Learning how to be an effective manager requires not only knowledge and personal ability but also actual experience. When people join organizations, their first task usually is to learn to be effective subordinates. To become managers, most people have to prove themselves as subordinates. Those who move into management positions will also have an acquired understanding of how organizations are run and how managers make decisions. In coming to this understanding, they will discover that there is more than one way to manage. In fact, there are four different generally recognized viewpoints of management: traditional, systems, behavioral, and contingency.

TRAdiTiONAl VIEWpOINT

The *traditional viewpoint* is based on a body of knowledge and skills that managers have used historically in dealing with management issues and problems. It emphasizes order, stability, and formal management procedures for carrying out the planning, organizing, leading, and controlling functions. The treatment of management processes by early writers tended to focus on finding a *best* way to manage that applies to all situations, thereby establishing universal principles.

Traditionalists often write about the planning and organizing functions as though people, especially nonmanagers, are primarily interested in money or job security. Traditionalists give the impression that management is much more rational and orderly than it actually is. However, the traditional viewpoint is useful because it emphasizes *what* managers should do. Other viewpoints are needed to illustrate more fully *how* managers perform their jobs. Knowledge of the four basic managerial functions needs to be supplemented with additional concepts and situational refinements to be of practical use to most managers.

INTERNATIONAL FOCUS

Traveling Overseas: Picking Your Fellow Passengers

Executives in U.S. corporations are confronting an inescapable reality: In spite of formidable trade barriers raised over the years, the business community is becoming increasingly internationalized. For those U.S. corporations moving into the international arena, the implications for the managerial team are significant. Some of the more successful international firms are characterized by an organizational culture that spreads functions across national borders, decentralizes decisions, focuses on strategies not products, and emphasizes timely action. As Franco Debenedetti, Managing Director of Olivetti, and other CEOs of international firms have suggested, managers should possess the following skills and characteristics.

CULTURAL FLEXIBILITY

The Center for Creative Leadership's work on successful executives indicates the importance of being able to talk and work with a variety of groups. In the case of international management, that ability needs to be extended across national or cultural lines. Management in an international area requires more than the ability to influence groups such as customers, the officials of the union representing workers, and the board of directors. It now takes understanding and appreciating the difference in, say, a prospective Norwegian client's needs from those of a Spanish customer. This requires an ability to empathize with prospective partners or customers, taking a step above one's own national perspective, and developing a healthy curiosity and respect for other cultures.

THEORETICIAN-EMPIRICIST

When Debenedetti reflects on his most successful managers, it is clear that the key decisions to be made are not day-to-day, operational issues. His executive team requires broad strategists whose thinking goes beyond the existing prod-

Source: Excerpted from "Traveling Overseas: Picking Your Fellow Passengers," by David L. DeVries. *Issues and Observations,* Greensboro, NC: Center for Creative Leadership,© November 1984 p. 6.

Behavioral Viewpoint

The *behavioral viewpoint* draws on a body of knowledge about how people behave and why they act the way they do. The importance of this viewpoint becomes apparent when we realize that it is only people that have goals and act. Organizational accomplishments result from decisions made by people and by people working together.

Knowledge of behavioral concepts enables managers to be aware of how their behavior affects those around them. One of the keys to improving

uct lines of the corporation. These managers are market or technology focused, not product driven. This means thinking in terms of customer problems, not company solutions. They also show almost an obsession with collecting up-to-date information on how their strategies are working in each of the wide variety of markets they are serving.

INTERPRETING CORPORATE STRATEGY

Key managers in successful international corporations spend an unusual amount of their time in face-to-face discussions with their staff about strategy. These executives must be willing and able to explain where the corporation is going and what that means for each of its divisions. They must also be detectives, probing local management for data and trends that should affect overall corporate strategy. International corporations that do not listen carefully to local management lose money. Not only should corporate strategy be communicated, basic values need to be stated. That we pride ourselves on our technological advances, for example, is a message as important for an international firm to communicate as its sales objectives.

TIMELY ACTION

Managers with an ability to take timely action appear to be in great demand in successful international companies. As one CEO said, ". . . it is better to be quick and approximate than slow and precise." Managers must be willing to take the heat from top management when they, or their staff, short circuit established channels. In an international corporation the communication channels can be longer with more frequent interruptions. It is easy to track decision times in months, not days or weeks, in large international companies.

productivity is motivating people. Adopting the latest production methods, technology, and computer system does not guarantee good job performance. Success depends on motivated employees who are committed to the organization's objectives. How managers communicate, motivate, and resolve conflicts can either foster the cooperation necessary for or set up road blocks to increased productivity.

In this book we apply behavioral concepts from several disciplines—anthropology, economics, political science, psychology, and sociology—to enhance your understanding of management, people, and organizations. From anthropology, managers learn of the wide-ranging differences among societies and how organizations, even though different, can operate effectively. From psychology, managers learn to understand and deal with differences among individuals, as well as to understand better their own goals, needs, and motives. From sociology, managers learn the importance of values and the various ways of relating to those whose values differ from their own. From political science, managers learn about the sources and uses of power.

Systems Viewpoint

Drawing on work from many fields, systems theorists analyze an organization in terms of systems—inputs, processes, and outputs—with a view toward improving operations. The *systems viewpoint* is a way of observing, thinking about, and solving problems. Unlike the traditional and behavioral viewpoints, it is not based on a coherent body of knowledge.[10]

Every person, group, or organization can be viewed as a subsystem of a larger system and as interdependent with other subsystems. For example, subsystems of a company include the planning, organizing, leading, and controlling functions. However, the company itself can be viewed as a subsystem of its parent corporation; it in turn is a subsystem of the nation's economic subsystem, which is part of the world's economic system. Such relationships are illustrated in Fig. 1.5, in which subsystems are called *levels*. Note that each lower level represents a successively simpler part of an overall system.

The levels studied depend on the problem to be solved. For example, the president and chief executive officer of American Airlines, Robert L. Crandell, is studying innovative ways to increase employee productivity. To do that, he created task forces to study the U.S. economy, to work with the unions representing pilots, flight attendants, and ground personnel, and to determine customer satisfaction. In essence, he's studying the problem by looking at the effects on American Airlines of different levels of a system.

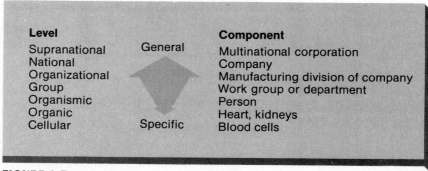

Level		Component
Supranational	General	Multinational corporation
National		Company
Organizational		Manufacturing division of company
Group		Work group or department
Organismic		Person
Organic		Heart, kidneys
Cellular	Specific	Blood cells

FIGURE 1.5
Levels in World Economic Systems

Source: Adapted from Robert Kreitner: *Management,* Second Edition, p. 54. Copyright © by Houghton Mifflin Company. Used by permission.

The systems viewpoint is useful because it keeps us from assuming simple cause-and-effect relationships. It also cautions us against a false sense of certainty about the definition of a problem and having the ultimate answer to it. Although the systems viewpoint constantly directs our attention to complex relationships, it does not provide us with concrete answers for dealing with them. Managers may experience various feelings—joy, frustration, achievement, ambiguity—in their efforts to understand the relationships among and to direct the key subsystems in their organization. However, the struggle is worthwhile if the end result is more effective management.

CONTINGENCY VIEWPOINT

The *contingency viewpoint* recognizes that there is no *best* way of managing for all situations; that it is possible to use the other three viewpoints independently or in combination in order to deal with different situations that confront managers.[11] However, this viewpoint does not mean that managers are free to manage according to their personal biases and whims. Given certain situations, managers need to determine which approaches and practices are likely to be more effective than others. In other words, the contingency viewpoint requires the development of conceptual skills: managers must diagnose and understand a situation—and which approach is likely to be most successful—before proposing a solution.

Thus the contingency viewpoint holds that the effectiveness of different managerial styles, guidelines, or techniques, will vary according to the situation. In applying it, managers use the concepts developed by traditionalists, behavioralists, and systems analysts but go beyond them to identify an approach appropriate to the situation. This blending process is illustrated in Fig. 1.6. Neither the contingency viewpoint nor the state of management knowledge has been developed sufficiently to offer detailed prescriptions for the best way to manage in all situations. Rather, the essence of the contingency viewpoint is that management practices generally should be consistent with the requirements of the *external environment,* the *tasks* to be performed, and the characteristics of the *people* who will perform the tasks.[12] These are called *contingency variables.*

Use of contingency variables

The relative importance of each contingency variable will depend on the type of managerial problem being considered. For example, in designing an organizational structure, a manager should place considerable emphasis on the nature of the external environment and the information processing requirements involved. The structure of the U.S. Internal Revenue Service (IRS) is vastly different from that of American Airlines. The IRS has a fairly stable set of customers, most of whom must file their tax returns on or before April 15 each year; it hires many part-time people during the peak tax season to process returns and answer questions and then lays them off after the peak

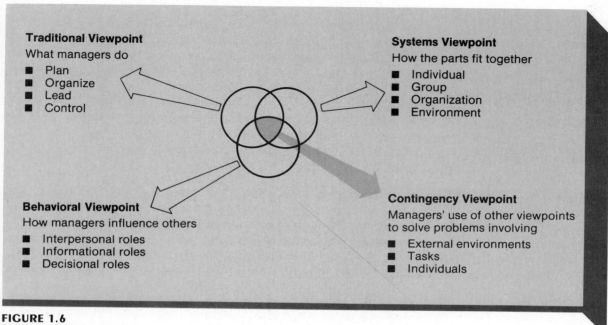

FIGURE 1.6
Viewpoints of Management

has passed. American Airlines, though, has many competitors and a constantly changing set of passengers whose demands for information (ticket cost, flight number, arrival and departure times) must be processed immediately; its continuous information-processing requirements call for more reliance on full-time personnel.

The tasks performed by employees might range from highly routine to highly nonroutine. A routine task is one performed repeatedly in a well-defined manner, such as keyboarding tax-return information into the IRS computers. Nonroutine tasks, on the other hand, are those in which there is a lot of variety and more than one way of getting the job done. At American Airlines the customer service representative may have to check numerous flight schedules, connections, and comparative costs to find the best answer for a customer.

People, the third contingency variable, have varying degrees of tolerance for repetition or uncertainty in their work. Their motivations, abilities, and personalities may make them effective in one type of position but ineffective in another. The person keyboarding information for IRS should be able to tolerate a high degree of repetition and not be easily bored. The American Airlines customer representative should be flexible and at ease with the uncertainty of having to answer many different kinds of requests and solve many different kinds of problems.

One of management's objectives in addressing contingency variables is to create a good match among the external environment, tasks, and people. For example, McDonald's, Burger King, and Roy Rogers restaurants operate in an environment that appeals to similar customers: those who want fast service, consistent quality, and low prices. The employees perform tasks that are relatively routine and most want only part-time work. The chance to earn money in a clean and comfortable environment is important to them. Under these conditions, the traditional use of rules and regulations is likely to be highly successful.

SUMMARY

In summary, the contingency viewpoint focuses on (1) the idea that, although there is no *best* way, not all ways of managing are equally effective; (2) diagnosis of each situation and the approaches that could be used; and (3) selection of the approach and methods that are likely to be most effective. The contingency viewpoint will be applied to a variety of managerial issues, topics, and problems throughout the rest of this book.

MANAGEMENT AS A DYNAMIC PROCESS

The process of organizing, obtaining resources, and accomplishing objectives through people—that is, managing—is dynamic rather than static, as shown in Fig. 1.7. Managerial thought evolves when new theories are presented or new management practices are tried. If the theories seem to have merit or the practices appear to succeed, their use becomes more widespread until (over a period of time) they become accepted ways of managing. The recent emergence of Japanese management methods is an example of the evolution in management thought. These methods are being used as models for improving efficiency and quality control by more and more companies. This is happening because the methods have been tried and proved in one cultural setting (and therefore could be successful in others) and because managers are faced with urgent problems caused by a series of internal and external forces.

The four basic managerial functions must address the internal (to the organization) forces at work in decision making. The most powerful are the changing nature of work and demands by employees for greater participation in decisions that affect their work. In performing the planning function, managers must consider these forces; in performing the organizing, leading, and controlling functions, managers must adapt to them successfully. The results from each function affect the others and thus decision making is a constant process of planning, trial, evaluation, and adjustment.

A series of major external forces in recent years has had tremendous impact on managerial decision making: high rates of inflation (an environ-

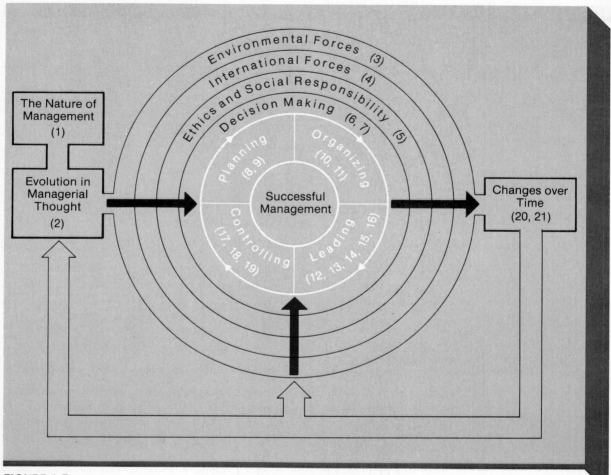

FIGURE 1.7
Management as a Dynamic Process

Note: The numbers in parentheses identify
the chapters in which each topic is presented.

mental force); the explosion in computer technology, fueled by development and production of the silicon chip (an environmental force); skyrocketing oil prices and limits on production (an international force); serious foreign-import competition in terms of quality, price, and market share (an international force); and public policy expressed in laws and regulations aimed at improvement of the physical environment and the health and safety of consumers and workers (ethical and social forces). Managers of companies that are affected by such forces face immediate challenges to the ways they have thought, planned, and acted in the past. If decision making is not adjusted to these realities, companies will not be able to compete successfully and will decline. Perhaps the best example of an industry's response to these external forces is that of the automakers. The managers of these companies had to rethink their objectives and ways of doing business; restructuring of their decision-making processes was as broad, in some cases, as the restructuring of their production methods and facilities; every level and most functions of these organizations had to be changed in some way; and these changes, in turn, affected their suppliers and the suppliers' decision-making processes.

Thus change is a constant and is the dynamic in management. The success of managers and their companies depends largely on how well change is accommodated.

CHAPTER SUMMARY

Societies need organizations because people working together can accomplish things that individuals cannot. Dealing with and working within organizations will occupy a great deal of your time and attention throughout your lifetime.

Organizational objectives are established and achieved by people. Managers perform specific functions and play a variety of roles in pursuing organizational objectives. There are three basic levels of managers—top, middle, first-line—and each level performs different kinds of jobs. Managers perform planning, organizing, leading, and controlling functions. They use technical, conceptual, human-relations, and communication skills; the amount and type of skill needed varies, depending on the level of management and the role of the manager at any given time. The major roles that managers play are interpersonal, informational, and decisional.

There are four viewpoints of management. The traditional viewpoint emphasizes the orderly application of tested management principles. The behavioral viewpoint emphasizes people and how to manage them successfully. The systems viewpoint emphasizes the relationships among tasks in the organization and how the organization responds to its environment. The contingency viewpoint emphasizes that there is no best way to manage and that the managerial approach used must fit the circumstances.

Management is a dynamic process. Internal and external forces cause the need for change. How well managers and their decision-making processes respond determines whether a company grows and prospers or declines.

MANAGER'S VOCABULARY

behavioral viewpoint
communication skills
contingency variables
company spokesperson
conceptual skills
contingency viewpoint
controlling
disseminator role
disturbance-handler role
entrepreneurial role
figurehead role
first-line managers
functional managers
general managers
human-relations skills
leadership role
leading
liaison role
management
managers
middle managers
monitor role
negotiator role
organizing
planning
resource-allocator role
role
skill
systems viewpoint

technical skills
top managers
traditional viewpoint

REVIEW QUESTIONS

1. What is management?
2. What are the eight characteristics of successfully managed companies?
3. What are the four basic managerial functions?
4. What are the three major roles that managers play?
5. What are the four skills of effective managers?

DISCUSSION QUESTIONS

1. What are the major differences between the work of first-line and middle managers?
2. Give examples of the contingency approach as it applies to your study habits.
3. Contrast and compare the differences among the traditional, behavioral, systems, and contingency viewpoints of management.
4. What roles do managers play in doing their jobs?
5. Using the eight characteristics of successfully managed companies, evaluate Procter & Gamble. Why do you think this company was singled out to illustrate management principles?

MANAGEMENT INCIDENTS AND CASES

MARY KAY COSMETICS

It may not seem to be the best time for someone to start a business, but for Mary Kay Ash, bored with retirement, it was the right answer. Since its founding in 1963, Mary Kay Cosmetics, Inc., has grown from a local Dallas, Texas, firm with a nine-member sales force into an international organization that sold more than $323 million worth of cosmetics in 1983, with a sales force of approximately 194,000 independent beauty consultants.

Mary Kay didn't just start a company in one day. She first thought about it quite a while and wrote down all her ideas about running a company that dealt with direct sales. She had plenty of ideas, too, because she

had spent 25 years working in direct sales with Stanley Home Products and the World Gift Company. At World Gift she began in sales and moved up to national training director in a relatively short time. Her suggestions often were passed off by the men she worked for as simply her "thinking like a woman again." By taking all these ideas and finding answers for all the problems she had encountered, Mary Kay came up with a marketing plan for what she believed could become a successful company.

In the early days of the company, she had final approval over all decisions. She hired experts to guide her in making business and production decisions, areas she professed little knowledge of. She also installed the personnel policies that are still in effect.

Mary Kay is now chairman of the board and makes personal appearances at all company-sponsored events. She is also available to talk with her salespeople (the directors and consultants) when they call. She relates well to people and believes that it is important to the company, as well as to herself, to stay in touch with directors. Thus she spends a lot of time traveling throughout the country, attending meetings and training sessions. Her day ends at six or seven o'clock in the

Mary Kay Ash is an example of a manager concerned with issues of environment, planning, and control, who was not afraid to make her slightly offbeat organizational vision a reality.

Source: Photo courtesy of Mary Kay Cosmetics, Inc.

evening, when she leaves her office with that day's mail, ready to start the process all over again early the next morning.[13]

Questions

1. Describe Mary Kay Ash's work activities.

2. What managerial roles does she play?

3. What management functions does she use to manage the company?

REFERENCES

1. D. Darlin and B. Abrams, "Procter & Gamble Co. Starts to Reformulate Tried-and-True Ways," *Wall Street Journal,* March 20, 1983, p. 1ff; S. Oscar, *Eyes on Tomorrow—The Evolution of Procter & Gamble.* New York: J. G. Ferguson, 1981.

2. Adapted from H. Aldrich, *Organization and Environment.* Englewood Cliffs, N.J.: Prentice-Hall, 1979, p. 3.

3. Adapted from T. Peters and R. Waterman, *In Search of Excellence.* New York: Harper & Row, 1982; T. Peters, "Putting Excellence into Management," *Business Week,* July 21, 1980, pp. 196–201.

4. Speech in Dallas, Texas, November 3, 1983.

5. Most of the materials in this section are from H. Mintzberg, "The Manager's Job, Folklore and Fact," *Harvard Business Review,* 1975, **53**:49–61. *Also see* J. Kotter, "What Effective General Managers Do," *Harvard Business Review,* 1982, **60**:56–67; R. Stewart, "A Model for Understanding Managerial Jobs and Behavior," *Academy of Management Review,* 1982, 7:7–14; J. Paolillo, "Manager's Self-Assessments on Managerial Roles: The Influence of Hierarchical Level," *Journal of Management,* 1981, 7:43–52; F. Luthans, S. Rosen-krantz, and H. Hennessey, "What Do Successful Managers Really Do? An Observation Study of Managerial Activities," *Journal of Applied Behavioral Science,* 1985, **21**(3):255–269.

6. Abstracted from A. Fisher, "GM's Unlikely Revolutionist," *Fortune,* March 19, 1984, pp. 106–112; D. Kubit, "Roger Smith—GM's Big Surprise," *Nation's Business,* February 1985, pp. 32–36.

7. C. MacDonald, *Performance Based Supervisory Development.* Amherst, Mass.: Human Resource Development, 1983.

8. R. Katz, "Skills of an Effective Administrator," *Harvard Business Review,* 1974, **52**:90–101.

9. P. Drucker, *Management: Tasks, Responsibilities and Practices.* New York: Harper & Row, 1974.

10. D. Katz and R. Kahn, *The Social Psychology of Organizations,* rev. ed. New York: John Wiley & Sons, 1978; W. Richard Scott, *Organizations: Rational Natural and Open Systems.* Englewood Cliffs, N.J.: Prentice-Hall, 1981.

11. D. Hellriegel, J. Slocum, and R. Woodman, *Organizational Behavior,* 4th ed. St. Paul, Minn.: West, 1986.

12. For a review of the literature, see H. Tosi and J. Slocum, "Contingency Theory: Some Suggested Directions," *Journal of Management,* 1984, **10**:9–26; D. Miller, "Toward a New Contingency Approach: The Search for Organizational Gestalts," *Journal of Management Studies,* 1981, **18**:1–26; A. Van de Ven and R. Drazin, "The Concept of Fit in Contingency Theory." In *Research in Organizational Behavior,* vol. 7. L. Cummings and B. Staw (Eds.). Greenwich, Conn.: JAI Press, 1985, 333–365.

13. Prepared by J. Crawford, Cox School of Business, Southern Methodist University, Dallas, 1983. Used by permission of Mr. Gerald Allen, Mary Kay Cosmetics, Dallas, Texas.

Evolution of Managerial Thought

LEARNING OBJECTIVES

After studying this chapter, you should be able to:

- Describe the four major viewpoints of management and how they evolved.

- Identify how principles from the four viewpoints of management can be used by today's managers.

- List the differences among the four viewpoints of management.

- Discuss the contributions and limitations of each viewpoint of management.

- Discuss how the contingency viewpoint of management attempts to blend the contributions of the other three viewpoints to solve contemporary management problems.

CHAPTER OUTLINE

PREVIEW CASE

Coca-Cola Company

When the Coca-Cola Company was formed in 1892, the drink had already been sold at drugstore soda fountains (originally as a headache remedy) for six years. Asa G. Candler, first president of the new company, planned to continue selling the drink only at soda fountains. Benjamin Thomas, a southern lawyer who served as chief clerk in the offices of the Assistant Army Quartermaster during the Spanish–American War, had noticed the brisk sales of bottled carbonated drinks to American soldiers stationed in Cuba. Thomas presented his idea of selling bottled Coca-Cola, but Candler was not interested. Candler sold the exclusive rights to distribute bottled Coca-Cola in the United States to Thomas and his partner, Joseph Whitehead, for one dollar in 1899.

Thomas and Whitehead realized that they personally could not establish bottling plants throughout the entire country. They subcontracted the exclusive right to bottle Coca-Cola to franchise managers in different regions.

As sales skyrocketed, Candler began to realize the value of the franchising system and started repurchasing the bottling rights. With the repurchase of these rights from Thomas and Whitehead, Candler no longer had a firm grasp on the details of the company's organizational requirements. Additional management personnel were needed in the areas of marketing, production, finance, accounting, and purchasing. As the organization grew, Candler had to delegate authority and responsibility to others in the organization. The use of rules and regulations provided the means for the company to grow.

In 1919, the Candler interests sold the Coca-Cola Company to Atlanta banker Ernest Woodruff and an investor group he had organized. In the mid-1920s the company moved into the international market, exporting syrup concentrate to be processed overseas. Today, the company issues all franchises and the business has grown to the point where sales exceed $6 billion annually, with operations in more than 155 countries.

When Thomas and Whitehead initiated the franchise system, they probably had no idea of what a clever organizational scheme they had de-

Source: Photo courtesy of the Coca-Cola Company.

vised. *The Coca-Cola Company (franchiser) licenses others (franchisees) to sell its products.* Usually each franchisee pays an initial fee and annual fees for the right to use the trade name and to obtain managerial and financial help. Most importantly, franchisees are guaranteed a standardized product from the company. A major advantage for the franchiser is that a franchise can be withdrawn if performance slips or the company's rules and regulations are not followed.

The Coca-Cola Company currently divides the world into four operating regions, with an executive vice-president in charge of each. One region covers the United States; another, Latin America; a third, Europe and Africa; and the fourth, Canada and the Pacific. In the United States, 16 syrup-distribution outlets are geographically organized to serve the 500 bottling plants.

The structure of the company has changed from a functional form to a product form. Different product lines are profit centers, responsible for manufacturing, marketing, and distributing their own products. With the approval of top management, managers of these product lines can purchase other firms that fit the company's business strategy. To coordinate these diverse product lines, planning is now highly formalized. Planning departments in each product line assist both top management of the product line and the company's managers at headquarters. Policies and procedures are established by management at headquarters in order to maintain common practices among the various product-line groups.

Growth has presented a variety of management problems. In 1985, Coca-Cola changed its formula and started selling the "New Coca-Cola" in an attempt to capture a larger market share. Another problem is allocation of resources among multiple-product lines (Columbia Pictures Industries, Inc., Minute Maid, Snow-Crop) that serve a wide diversity of customers in different countries. Doing business in the multinational market requires decisions and strategies much different from those made when the company was operating only in the United States. For example, when the company gave an Israeli firm a franchise to bottle Coca-Cola in Israel, the company's products were boycotted in Arab countries. To complicate the problem, the company at that time also owned Aqua Chem, which had a huge stake in Saudi Arabia's plans to spend several billion dollars desalting seawater over the next few years. The company resolved the problem by selling Aqua Chem to Tenco in 1982. India posed a different problem: The Indian government insisted that multinational companies transfer some knowledge and ownership to Indian firms. The Coca-Cola Company refused to reveal its secret formula to any firm, and this decision meant losses in the potentially lucrative Indian market.[1]

T his Preview Case illustrates some of Coca-Cola's management problems over time. Many of today's successful companies have encountered and solved similar problems of planning, coordination, and decision making. In this chapter, we will examine some of the ways in which management thought and practice have evolved. As with other types of knowledge, there has been an explosion of ideas and thoughts about management in recent years. Nevertheless, the same basic management problem exists today as it did in ancient times: What is the best way to manage an organization?

To help you understand current management thought, a look at the evolution of management is important. We must know where we have been before we can determine where we are or where we want to go. The manager who has that perspective and is up-to-date on existing theories and practices

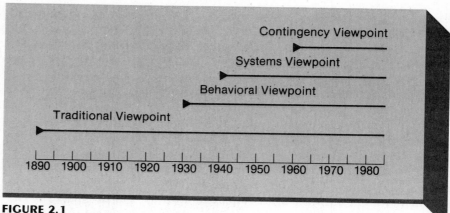

FIGURE 2.1
History of Managerial Thought

can form a sound personal concept of management. However, managers too often retain management principles and practices that are out of step with current organizational and managerial realities.

This chapter presents the four well-established viewpoints of management that were highlighted in Chapter 1: the traditional (sometimes called the classical), the behavioral, the systems, and the contingency viewpoints. Each viewpoint is based on different assumptions about the behavior of people in organizations, the key objectives of an organization, the types of problems emphasized, and the solutions used. Figure 2.1 shows when each viewpoint gained acceptance and began to be widely used. The time lines indicate that all still influence the thinking of managers. The diversity of thought represented by these viewpoints can be confusing, and a major purpose of this chapter is to indicate not only how each has contributed to modern management practices, but also why each can be used effectively in various circumstances.

TRADITIONAL VIEWPOINT OF MANAGEMENT

The oldest and perhaps most widely accepted viewpoint of management among practitioners is the **traditional** (or classical) **viewpoint.** Since the beginning of recorded history, groups of people have been organized and managed; even today in the rural villages of Indonesia, recognized leaders perform the four basic functions of management. The traditional viewpoint focuses on *managers* and how they should plan, organize, lead, and control the activities of employees in order to accomplish organizational objectives. There are three main branches of the traditional viewpoint: bureaucratic management, scientific management, and administrative management.

BUREAUCRATIC MANAGEMENT

The term *bureaucratic management* refers to a system of management that relies on rules and regulations, hierarchy, division of labor, and procedures. Max Weber, a German social historian, is the individual most closely associated with the bureaucratic model. Writing in the early 1900s, he was one of the first to deal systematically with problems of organization. He discussed not only the structure of complex organizations, but also the broad economic and social issues facing society. Thus his ideas on bureaucracy represent only a part of his total contribution to our knowledge.[2]

Characteristics

Seven characteristics are usually associated with a bureaucratic organization: a formal system of rules and regulations, impersonality, division of labor, hierarchical structure, lifelong career commitment, a detailed authority structure, and rationality. Together they represent a formal, somewhat rigid method of managing.

Rules and regulations. A formal system of *rules and regulations* controls the decision-making behavior of all employees and specifies how they must act on the job. Bureaucracies are based on the idea that rules and regulations help to provide the order needed to reach organizational goals. Adherence to these rules and regulations ensures uniformity of procedures and operations, regardless of an individual manager or employee's personal desires. Rules and regulations also provide a means by which top management can direct and coordinate the efforts of middle managers and, through them, the efforts of first-line managers and employees. Managers may come and go, but rules and regulations ensure organizational stability.

Impersonality. Reliance on rules and regulations leads to *impersonality*. Impersonality means that all employees are subject to the same rules and regulations and are saved from the personal whims of managers. Although the term often has negative connotations, Weber believed that impersonality guaranteed job security for employees: Superiors evaluate subordinates objectively on performance and expertise rather than subjectively on personal or emotional considerations. In other words, impersonality was designed to preserve objectivity and minimize the individuality of the bureaucrat.

Division of labor. Managers and employees perform officially prescribed and assigned duties that are based on specialization and expertise. *Division of labor* is the actual dividing of a task into more specialized and simpler parts. This enables the organization to utilize personnel efficiently: managers can be assigned to particular areas in which they are expert; other employees can be assigned simpler tasks, which are not only easier to do but are also more repetitive than complex tasks.

At the Dallas Marriott Hotel, for example, the convention sales manager is an expert on hosting conventions—and he is in charge of only that part of the hotel's operations (Fig. 2.2). Thus, when faced with a problem involving a convention, the general manager knows to whom to go for answers. Another consequence of specialization is that new employees are able to learn simple tasks and necessary skills quickly. Replacement of personnel for many assembly-line tasks is easy. For example, an employee turnover rate as high as 90 percent per year on the packaging line of a Frito-Lay plant does not present a problem when an unskilled person can be trained for the work in half an hour.

Hierarchical structure.   Most organizations have a pyramid-shaped *hierarchical structure,* as illustrated in Fig. 2.3. Jobs are ranked vertically in the

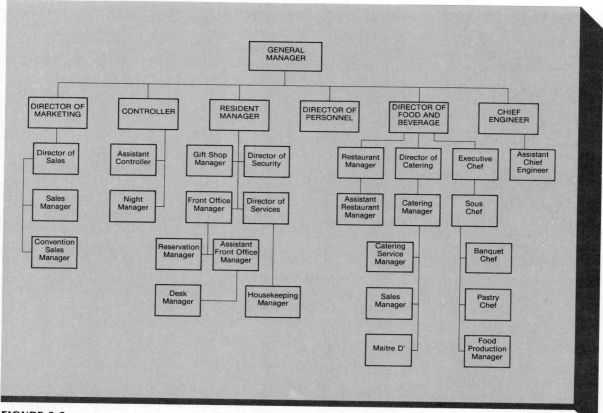

FIGURE 2.2
Dallas Marriott Hotel Quorum Center

Source: Denise Robinson, Director of Human Resources, Dallas Marriott Hotel, June 1985.

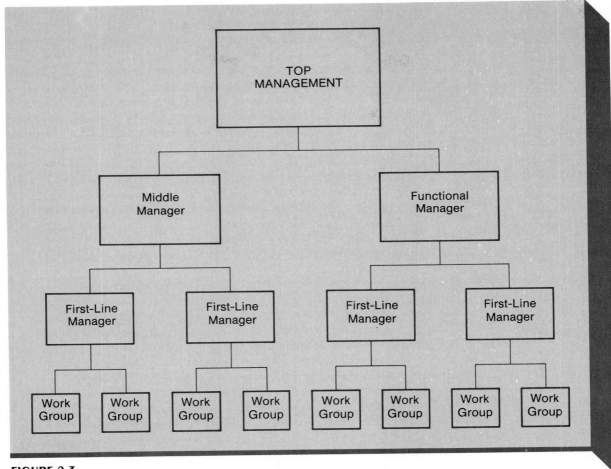

FIGURE 2.3
Hierarchical Organization Structure

organization by the amount of authority (the right to make a decision) given to each job. Typically, power and authority increase with level in the hierarchy. Each lower-level position is under the control and direction of a higher-level position.

According to Weber, a well-defined hierarchy controls the behavior of employees. Referring again to Fig. 2.2, we note the vertical relationships between successive levels at the Marriott Hotel are clearly defined. For example, the night manager is responsible and accountable to the controller for activities of the hotel between 11:00 P.M. and 7:00 A.M. The controller, in turn, reports to the general manager. Through this structure, all activities can be directed and coordinated to achieve the hotel's goals.

Lifelong career commitment.   According to the bureaucratic model, employment is a *lifelong career commitment.* This means that an employee and the company view themselves as committed to each other over the working life of the employee. In essence, an employee's technical qualifications alone are sufficient for continued employment; job security is guaranteed as long as the person is qualified. Entrance requirements, such as level of education or past experience, are used to ensure technical qualification rather than reliance on patronage for initial employment. Job security, tenure, incremental salary levels, and pensions are used to ensure the satisfactory performance of assigned duties.

Promotion is granted when an employee demonstrates the technical competence required to handle the demands of the next higher job. The assumption is that organizational level corresponds closely with expertise. Technical qualifications can often be determined by written and oral examination results, amount of formal education, and previous work experience. For example, promotion through government civil service ranks is determined by technical qualifications and seniority.

Authority structure.   A system created by the use of rules, regulations, impersonality, division of labor, and hierarchical structure is tied together by an *authority structure*—the right to make decisions of varying importance at different levels of an organization. Weber identified three types of authority structures. The first type, *traditional authority,* is based on tradition or custom. The divine right of kings and the authority of tribal witch doctors are examples of traditional authority, which occurs rarely in modern organizations.

The second type, *charismatic authority,* occurs when subordinates comply voluntarily with a leader and suspend their own judgment because of the extraordinary personal capacities, strengths, or powers perceived in the leader. Social, political, and religious movements are often headed by charismatic leaders (Jesus, Joan of Arc, Gandhi, Hitler, Martin Luther King). Charismatic authority is not often found in the business world.

The third type, *rational-legal authority,* is based on impersonal laws, rules, and regulations that apply to all employees. A superior is obeyed because of that person's position in the organization's hierarchy. This authority depends on acceptance of the rules and regulations by members of the organization. A manager's behavior is consistent with these rules and regulations.

Rationality.   Bringing order to a system of activities involves *rationality.* Thus an organization should be run logically and "scientifically"; all decisions should lead directly to achieving the organization's objectives. When activities are goal-directed, financial and human resources can be used more effectively. General organizational objectives can be broken down into more specific objectives for each part of an organization. At Motorola, for example, the corporate objectives are to serve the needs of the community by providing products and services of superior quality at a fair price to customers, while earning profits large enough to maintain the growth of the firm. One departmental objective, that of the research and development (R&D) department, is to pursue new technology and transform technological breakthroughs into high-quality products and services. If all of the company's departments reach their objectives, the overall corporate objectives are reached.

Ranking of bureaucratic orientation

The seven characteristics of bureacracy can be used to place organizations along a continuum from low to high bureaucratic orientation. As indicated in Fig. 2.4, organizations may not fall at either extreme of this continuum. Rather, their ranking depends on the degree to which they exhibit various bureaucratic characteristics.

One of the problems encountered in transforming these seven characteristics into an overall rating is that of measurement. For example, one organization may be highly bureaucratic in its division of labor and low in its structure, whereas in another organization the levels of bureaucracy for these characteristics may be reversed. Are these two organizations equally bureaucratic? In general, government agencies, such as the U.S. Postal Service, and some companies rank high in bureaucratic characteristics and can be placed near the highly bureaucratic end of the continuum. On the other hand, companies such as Hewlett-Packard and Tandem Computers, among others, rank low in these characteristics. They can be placed at or near the other end of the continuum.

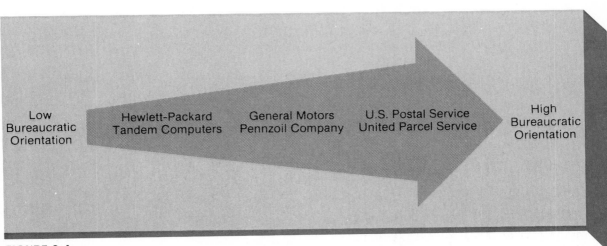

FIGURE 2.4
Bureaucratic Orientation

However, ranking organizations is more complex than this. The degrees of bureaucracy in an organization's divisions and departments can vary considerably. For example, General Motors and Pennzoil are near the middle of the continuum (Fig. 2.4). But their research and development departments are likely to be less bureaucratic than the organization as a whole. Similarly, General Motors' production departments are concerned with producing standardized goods (such as automobiles, Delco batteries, and trucks) and are likely to be more bureaucratic. Thus only in the broadest sense can an organization be placed on this continuum; a diagram such as Fig. 2.4 is best suited for making *general comparisons* of the bureaucratic orientation of organizations. It masks important variables and relationships among characteristics and specific operating methods. A more accurate view of the bureaucratic orientation of a company requires examination of these factors in more detail. United Parcel Service (UPS) is a living example of Weber's bureaucracy. Rational-legal authority is the basis for the company's bureaucratic design. Bureaucratic structure is an important reason for UPS's excellent record of performance and growth.

IN PRACTICE
United Parcel Service

United Parcel Service specializes in the delivery of small packages. It can deliver a package anywhere in the United States for $2–$3. The company sees itself in price competition with the U.S. Postal Service, Federal Express, and Purolator Courier. Unlike the Postal Service, UPS pays taxes on real estate, income, and fuel, and cannot subsidize packages with revenue from first-class letters—and still makes an excellent profit.

Why has UPS been so successful? There are several reasons, but two important ones are automation and bureaucracy. Automation is visible in the 100 mechanized hubs that can sort 40,000 packages per hour; one center can sort 60,000 packages per hour. United Parcel Service handles 6 million packages a day and yet is so efficient that it can send a truck to pick up packages from a home or business, deliver packages door-to-door, and still make money.

Many efficiencies are realized through utilization of the bureaucratic model of organization. The company is bound up in rules and regulations. There are safety rules for drivers, loaders, clerks, and managers. Strict dress and appearance codes are enforced—no beards, hair cannot touch the collar, no sideburns, mustaches must be trimmed evenly and cannot go below the corner of the mouth, and so on. Rules specify the cleanliness of buildings and property. For example, all UPS delivery trucks must be washed inside and out at the end of every day. Each manager is given bound copies of policy books and is expected to use them regularly.

Jobs are broken down into a clearly defined division of labor. Employees at UPS plants perform the specialized duties of drivers, loaders, clerks, washers, sorters, and property maintenance. The hierarchy of authority is clearly defined and has eight levels, extending from a washer at the local UPS plant up to the company president.

Technical qualification is UPS's criterion for hiring and promotion. The UPS policy book says, "A leader does not have to remind others of authority by use of a title. Knowledge, performance, and capacity should be adequate evidence of position and leadership." Favoritism is forbidden. Each person sets performance goals and has an equal opportunity to succeed. Promotions and salary increments are based on objective performance criteria, not on a person's background or position in the organization.

Finally, UPS thrives on written records. Daily worksheets that specify performance goals and work output are kept on every employee and department. Operating costs and production runs are recorded and compared to those of competitors. Daily employee quotas and achievements are accumulated on a weekly and monthly basis. Computer systems have been installed to facilitate the record-keeping process.[3]

ANTICIPATED BENEFIT OF BUREAUCRACY

The anticipated benefit of bureaucratic management is efficiency, as shown in Table 2.1.[4] A bureaucracy functions best when large amounts of routine work are to be done. Lower-level employees handle the bulk of the work by simply following rules and regulations. It is only the exceptional case, one to which the rules do not apply, that must be called to the attention of a manager. The manager or, if necessary, a higher-level manager, can then decide whether to change the rules, make an exception to the rules, or ignore the case. Lower-level managers and employees are not expected to use discretion and can be evaluated on the basis of how well they conform to the rules.

TABLE 2.1 ■ ANTICIPATED BENEFIT AND UNANTICIPATED EFFECTS OF BUREAUCRACY

CHARACTERISTIC	ANTICIPATED BENEFIT	UNANTICIPATED EFFECT
Rules and regulations Impersonality Lifelong career commitment Division of labor Hierarchical structure Authority structure Rationality	Efficiency	Rigid rules and red tape Protection of authority Slow decision making Incompatibility with technology Incompatibility with values

Possible ɴᴇɢᴀᴛɪᴠᴇ ᴇϝϝᴇᴄᴛꜱ oϝ bᴜʀᴇᴀᴜᴄʀᴀᴄʏ

The same characteristics that make bureaucratic management a potentially efficient way to run an organization can lead to inefficiencies. Table 2.1 shows five often unanticipated negative effects of bureaucracy.

Rigid rules and red tape.   Robert McLaughlin was a mail sorter in Des Moines, Iowa, for 11 years. His supervisor docked him $400 in wages because he did not follow a rule. The Postal Service's manual, *Operations Methods Improvement,* tells sorters how to sit on their stools and sort letters; the right way to hold a letter is at a 45-degree angle. McLaughlin held his letters at a 90-degree angle. The program manual contains a drawing showing the right and wrong ways. According to his supervisor, McLaughlin violated the rule and therefore was fined.[5]

Rigid adherence to rules and regulations for their own sake is a major complaint of employees in many organizations; little individual freedom and creativity are permitted. For most people bureaucracy means routinization, task specification, and red tape. An ever-increasing number of rules and regulations, procedures, and programs to control individual employee behavior usually accompanies a bureaucracy. This can lead to low motivation, entrenched "career" employees, high turnover among the ablest employees, and shoddy work. When confronted with bureaucratic delays and incompetence, it is easy for us to feel that "The Bureaucrat's Prayer" has been answered.

The Bureaucrat's Prayer

Oh, Thou, who seest all things below
Grant that thy servants may go slow;
That we may study to comply
With regulations til we die.

Teach us, O Lord, to reverence
Committees more than common-sense;
Impress our minds to make no plan
And pass the baby when we can.

And when the Temper seems to give
Us feelings of initiative,
Or when, alone, we go too far,
Recall us with a circular.

'Mid fire and tumult, war and storms,
Sustain us, Blessed Lord, with forms,
Thus may thy servants ever be
A flock of perfect sheep for Thee.

ANONYMOUS

Protection of authority.   A study of the Tennessee Valley Authority (TVA) revealed that a central problem was the need for delegation of power and decision making to lower-level managers. This need emerged from the increasing complexities of managing the numerous projects undertaken by the TVA. However, when given this opportunity, some lower-level managers chose to neglect the organization's goals in favor of more limited personal goals: goals that would maximize their own self-interest and prestige within the organization. These managers became "empire builders," valuing their increased power, status, and pay. They brought in unneeded subordinates, added more space and physical facilities, and used certain projects to inflate their personal importance to the organization. All of this suggests that bureaucracies may encourage managers to perform at minimum productivity while protecting and expanding their authority. Reaching the organization's objectives may become secondary to their self-interests.

Slow decision making. Large, complex organizations are highly dependent on timely decisions. Delays in reaching a decision may cause delays in handling a customer's complaint, resolving an employee grievance, or solving a production problem—any of which could lead to more serious situations. In a highly bureaucratic organization, adherence to rules, regulations, and procedures may come to be regarded as more important than high-quality, timely decisions. In such cases, rules and regulations take on a life of their own. Formalism and ritualism delay decisions until all the red tape has been cleared, the petty insistence on the privileges of power and status has been played out, and the possibility of an error in judgment has been minimized.

Incompatibility with technology. Differences in technology makes the universal application of bureaucratic management principles difficult. For example, in automobile assembly plants, each work station along the assembly line contributes its own small part of the total car. The work is routine and repetitive and can be covered easily by rules and regulations. However, people working on the space shuttle for NASA face unique problems each time there is a launch. These unique problems require a constant search for solutions. Multiple specialists are brought together to solve problems as they arise. Rules and regulations have much less meaning where the nature of the problem itself changes.[6]

Incompatibility with values. Professional values (such as advancing scientific knowledge, serving professional organizations, and finding innovative solutions to problems) may be incompatible with the bureaucratic values of efficiency, order, and stability. Since more and more professionals are being hired by bureaucratic organizations and are assuming more important decision-making positions in them, this criticism is highly relevant. For example, to the bureaucrat, authority is related to hierarchical position; to the professional, authority is derived from personal competence or technical expertise. Work routine and standard operating procedures are of prime importance to the bureaucrat; in contrast, the professional stresses the uniqueness of prob-

INTERNATIONAL FOCUS

BUREAUCRATIZATION OF THE ROMAN ARMY

During the Republican era, Rome's military objectives were the defense of Rome and the expansion of Roman influence in the Mediterranean basin. The environment in which the army operated at this time was unstable, with powerful and civilized foes in North Africa and the Balkans. The variety of disciplined, clever, and unpredictable foes presented the Roman army with problems that were neither standard nor well-understood. That is, in its battles anything could happen—and it did—and the legions had to be ready for it.

The Roman army developed an organizational structure to match its environmental and technological requirements. Each legion was made up of about 4200 men, and was organized according to functional specialties and individual skills. There were light infantry, who could be used as scouts, pickets, or even dismounted cavalry; heavy assault troops, the hastati; the pride of the army, the principes; and the reserves, staffed by aging veterans.

The authority structure of the Republican legion had a lean and flat configuration. There were only three hierarchical levels: the consul on top; under him six tribunes; and on the battle line the centurions. As with every army from the beginning of time, there were also sergeants. This structure allowed power to be decentralized effectively.

Finally, and perhaps most importantly, the Army of the Republic was a citizen army, made up of landowners. They were called up in a yearly levy, at which time they democratically elected their most important military leaders.

THE CHANGE TO BUREAUCRACY

The legions of the Republic may have been too successful. Their conquests were partly to blame for the bureaucratization of the army. Because of expansion, war had become big business with multinational flavoring. Protracted campaigns a long way from home became common. The environment was

Source: Excerpted from M. J. Gent, "Theory X in Antiquity, or the Bureaucratization of the Roman Army," *Business Horizons*, January–February 1984, pp. 53–55. Copyright 1984 by the Foundation for the School of Business at Indiana University. Adapted with permission.

lems and their solution and advocates change through research and development.[7]

CURRENT VIEW OF BUREAUCRATIC MANAGEMENT

Although bureaucratic management principles are not used by all organizations, those managers who do use them recognize bureaucracy's limitations. In the early days of NASA, James Webb, its former administrator, used a bureaucratic structure to establish the overall objectives of the space program. Each of NASA's centers, such as the Johnson Space Center in Texas or the Kennedy Space Center in Florida, in turn, had certain objectives to achieve.

more stable. It consisted of clearly identified frontier areas to be pacified and maintained.

Under these conditions, the legions adopted a more routine work-flow technology. The army was now trying to turn out a uniform product on a grand scale. It felt that it knew exactly what had to be done to handle its *raw material:* It had to oppose forces made up of rag-tag hordes of undisciplined, uncivilized barbarians. In this new army, functional specialties were soon done away with. Equipment, training, and tactical maneuvers were standardized. All infantry legionnaires now possessed the same few low-level skills which were, however, highly developed.

At the dawn of the Empire, the army had grown from an average strength of 8 legions to 28 legions. Each legion was also enlarged by about 1000 troops. The authority structure was made taller, from three hierarchical levels to five. The elected consul gave way to a person appointed by the emperor. The second-in-command was an aristocratic tribune. The other tribunes were young politicians going through the motions of military service as a step in their careers. They were assigned staff jobs—the army's first purely bureaucratic job. A new, critical office was established: camp prefect. This was usually occupied by an older man, a veteran who had risen through the centurial (fighting) ranks. Centurions were no longer elected, but appointed by the emperor. Those of the first company had higher rank. In fact the principal centurion of the first company was considered a member of *upper management.*

Decision making in the Imperial Army was highly centralized and standardized. Apart from the invasion of Britain, the whole first century A.D. was dedicated to the dull, unimaginative task of consolidating frontiers. Generals and their commanders had few patent strategies and tactical options to choose from. This state of affairs was the dream come true of Weberian bureaucratic efficiency.

These objectives had to be coordinated if NASA were going to reach its overall objectives. During launch, computers and other on-line electronic systems rather than rules and regulations were relied upon to complete the launch and make in-flight corrections.[8] Similarly, many universities use bureaucratic principles when registering students for classes. These principles enable universities to enroll a large number of students in a very efficient fashion. However, most faculty members do not follow set rules and regulations when teaching. Therefore the use of these principles varies according to the situation. For processing large amounts of information for which the *best* way has been found, the bureaucratic model works very well.

Scientific Management

By the end of the nineteenth century, manufacturing firms were becoming larger and more complex. Managers were no longer directly involved with production; they spent more of their time on administrative problems—planning, scheduling, and staffing. Managers also had difficulty in keeping up with changes in technical methods of production; they no longer had a basis for judging a fair day's work on the part of employees. To overcome these problems, Frederick W. Taylor introduced *scientific management,* which focused on the shop level and worker–machine relationships in manufacturing plants. It emphasized a philosophy that management should be based on proven fact, not guesswork or hearsay.[9] Taylor advocated techniques, such as time-and-motion studies, standardized tools, individual incentives, and functional foremanship, to arrive at the *best* way for an employee to do a job.

The changing technology created a need for specialists who understood production operations and could solve the common problems that threatened operating efficiency. Taylor, a mechanical engineer, focused on the human aspect of the new machine-oriented production system. In order to expand productivity, ways had to be found to increase the efficiency of workers. The goal was to define precisely all aspects of the worker–machine relationship.

Taylor believed there was a best way to perform any given task. Like Weber, Taylor believed that an organization should be governed by definite, predictable methods, logically determined and written into rules. Efficiency could be increased by having workers perform repetitive tasks that did not require problem-solving activities; furthermore, performance should be described in quantitative terms (such as number of units produced per shift).

Time-and-motion studies

The nature of a task was to be determined by a *time-and-motion study.* It involved identification and measurement of all movements made by a worker when performing a task. The results were analyzed in order to eliminate movements that slow down production. Productivity was measured in terms of both time and costs.

An objective of the time-and-motion study was to make a job highly routine and efficient. Eliminating wasted effort and detailing a specific sequence of activities would minimize the amount of time, money, and effort needed to produce a product. However, a standard method and time for task accomplishment could not be stated unless other factors, such as machine speeds, machine feeds, and supplies of raw materials, were standardized as well. Thus Taylor undertook analyses of work flows, supervisory techniques, worker fatigue, and inventory storage.

Functional foremanship

Taylor's idea of functional foremanship was based on his principle of specialization. To Taylor, who viewed expertise as the only source of authority,

Frederick W. Taylor began his career as a pattern maker and machinist in late-nineteenth-century Philadelphia. Later, as engineer and inventor, he developed the "Taylor system" of scientific management.

the gap between managerial expertise and authority was a problem. Since a single foreman could not be expected to be an expert in all of the tasks supervised, the foreman's particular area of specialization was the same as the foreman's area of authority. *Functional foremanship* refers to multiple foremen for each worker. Workers would have eight foremen: one each for planning, production scheduling, time-and-motion studies, and discipline, as well as four on the shop floor to deal with such matters as machinery maintenance, machine speeds, and feeds of materials into the machine.

Individual incentives

Taylor believed that workers' underlying motivation was money. Scientific management was based on the assumption that workers would be rational, follow management's orders, and respond to incentives in order to earn more money. He assumed, too, that management would be receptive to the use of incentives because increases in productivity would more than compensate for higher labor costs.

An individual piecework system was recommended as the primary pay system. If workers met a quota, they were paid a standard wage rate. Workers who produced more than their quotas were paid a higher rate for all pieces produced, not merely those exceeding the standard. Clearly, employees would work harder if they could earn more money. For example, each worker who produced 100 automobile tires was paid $100; each worker who produced 110 tires would be paid $120. The 100 tires was the standard for which the company paid $1.00 per tire. By producing 10 tires more than the standard, a worker was paid the adjusted rate for all 110 tires. Under this rate system, workers were encouraged to surpass previous performance standards and earn even more money. Taylor believed that because companies benefited from increased productivity (in sales and profits) there would always be work.

Current view of scientific management

Companies such as Burger King, Corning Glass, B. F. Goodrich, U.S. Steel, and General Motors have used Taylor's principles to make finished products better and faster than Taylor could ever have dreamed. Scientific management methods have been applied to a variety of problems. For example, the emphasis that Taylor placed on the selection of workers made many companies realize that, without proper ability and training, employees cannot be expected to do their jobs properly. The importance of Taylor's work caused managers to seek the *best* way to do things in a given situation. But Taylor did not simply take one answer and apply it to every situation; he scientifically studied each situation to find its unique characteristics before he recommended a solution.

Unfortunately, the proponents of scientific management misread the human side of the problem. When Taylor formulated his theory, he believed that workers were motivated primarily by a desire to earn money to satisfy their economic and physical needs. He overlooked the social needs of workers and, to many workers, job satisfaction means as much as or more than money. Workers have gone on strike to protest poor working conditions, the speedup of an assembly line, or harassment by management. Managers today cannot assume that workers are interested only in higher wages or that dividing jobs into their simplest tasks ensures a quality product, high morale, and organizational effectiveness.

IN PRACTICE
BURGER KING

Burger King's executives like to say that theirs is a company run by 50,000 teenagers. But those kids are getting more expensive every day and, to control labor costs, Burger King has refined the making of hamburgers by applying scientific management principles. In the fast-food industry, an increase in production means extra sales. According to one manager, "Nobody cares how many hamburgers we can make between 11:00 P.M. and 6:00 A.M. What counts is production at peak times."

In order to increase productivity at peak times, every employee movement has been measured and adjusted by the use of time-and-motion studies. For example, at drive-in windows, just moving the bell hose—which triggers a loud ring when cars drive over it—has made a big difference. Through time-and-motion studies, it was discovered that order-takers needed 11 seconds to react to the ring. The hose was moved back 10 feet, so that the order-taker could be waiting to check off what the customer wanted by the time a car had stopped at the order machine. This change permitted Burger King to save 30 seconds per customer, or to handle an extra 30 orders an hour at the drive-in window.

To serve those extra orders, Burger King had to increase its production inside. Computerized french-fry machines were installed and television terminals were placed in the kitchen to enable the chef to read incoming orders off the screen. Time-and-motion engineers even have visions of machines that will mix, pour, and cap soft drinks automatically.

Managers and employees who suggest ways to improve productivity get cash awards. All employees are constantly encouraged to fine-tune what goes on within the restaurant in order to bring Burger King neck-and-neck with its archrival, McDonald's. As one Burger King executive said, "The new attention to productivity amounts to nothing more than getting back to the basics."[10]

Administrative Management

Administrative management focuses on the performance of managers in the basic functions of planning, organizing, leading, and controlling. This model of management evolved during the early 1900s and is most closely identified with Henri Fayol, a French industrialist, whose most famous work on management was not translated into English until 1949. Fayol believed that his success as a manager was due not to his personal qualities but to the methods he used. He believed that managers would be successful if they understood and applied the basic functions and principles of management.[11]

This model focuses on the formal aspects of organizational structure and minimizes the human factor. It holds that management's main tasks are to (1) discover a set of functions that, if performed, will enable an organization to reach its goals; and (2) group tasks to maximize productivity and efficiency and minimize cost.

MANAGEMENT FUNCTIONS

We defined and gave examples of the basic **management functions**—planning, organizing, leading, and controlling—in Chapter 1. We do not examine them further here because each function is discussed fully and separately in later parts of this book.

MANAGEMENT PRINCIPLES

Fayol developed 14 management principles and believed that managers could become more effective through formal training in them. These principles are:

1. *Division of labor.* The more people specialize, the more efficiently they can perform their work.

2. *Authority.* Managers have the right to give orders so that they can get things done.

3. *Discipline.* Members of an organization need to respect the rules and agreements that govern the organization.

4. *Unity of command.* Each employee must receive his or her instructions about a particular operation from only one person. Fayol believed that if an employee were responsible to more than one boss, conflicting instructions and confusion would result.

5. *Unity of direction.* The efforts of employees should be coordinated and directed by only one manager in order to avoid different policies and procedures.

6. *Subordination of individual interest to the common good.* The interests of employees should not take precedence over the interests of the organization as a whole.

7. *Remuneration.* Compensation for work done should be fair to both the employee and employer.

8. *Centralization.* Decreasing the role of subordinates in decision making is centralization; increasing their role is decentralization. Fayol believed that managers should retain final responsibility but that they also need to give their subordinates enough authority to do their jobs properly. The problem is to find the proper amount of centralization in each case.

Henri Fayol, turn-of-the-century industrialist and pioneer of administrative management techniques.

9. *Scalar chain*. The line of authority in an organization—often represented by the neat boxes and lines of the organization chart—runs in order by rank from top management to the lowest level of the company.

10. *Order*. Materials and people should be in the right place at the right time. In particular, people should be in the jobs or positions best suited for them.

11. *Equity*. Managers should be both friendly and fair to their subordinates.

12. *Stability and tenure of staff*. A high employee turnover rate is not good for the efficient functioning of an organization.

13. *Initiative*. Subordinates should be given the freedom to formulate and carry out their plans.

14. *Esprit de corps*. Promoting team spirit will give the organization a sense of unity.

Current view of Fayol's principles

Many of Fayol's principles are still used in organizations. (In Chapters 6 and 10 you will see why many of these principles are important in the everyday running of a company.) You should remember that a principle is seldom applied in exactly the same way. Situations change and so, too, must the application of a principle. In large companies too much specialization leads to the blurring of lines of authority. At one steel plant, for example, the maintenance superintendent took orders from the plant manager, chief engineer, and production manager. In this case, we have a violation of Fayol's principle of the unity of command: The maintenance superintendent was reporting to more than one person.

General Characteristics of the Traditional Viewpoint

The bureaucratic, scientific, and administrative-management models are still used and referred to by management practitioners and writers. Therefore it is useful to pinpoint the similarities and differences. The similarities are summarized in Table 2.2.

All three models emphasize the formal aspects of organization. Traditionalists were concerned with the formal relations among departments, tasks, and structural elements of organizations. Seat-of-the-pants management practices were replaced with theoretical and scientific concepts. Division of labor, hierarchical arrangements of positions, and rules and regulations were the chief ingredients in these models. Decisions were made to maximize economic rewards. Even today, time-and-motion studies prescribe the appropriate movements for performing a task most efficiently.

Although it was surely recognized that people had feelings and were influenced by their friends in the organization, the overriding focus was on job performance. For example, Taylor was concerned with eliminating the

TABLE 2.2 ■ SIMILARITIES AMONG TRADITIONAL-VIEWPOINT MODELS

I. STRUCTURE
1. focus on
   a) division of labor
   b) hierarchical and functional processes
   c) structure
   d) span of control
2. assumptions are implicit
3. emphasize principles

II. PEOPLE
1. machines
2. economic or job security motives only
3. must adjust to job
4. can be hired and fired as need arises

III. LEADERSHIP
1. single leader
2. chosen on merit
3. chosen by superiors
4. relies on authority in position
5. leader's task to achieve organizational (rather than subordinates') goals
6. unitary goal

IV. DECISION MAKING
1. consciously rational
2. efficiency sole value criterion
3. maximizing decisions

bad feelings between workers and management. His incentive system was intended to provide workers with a monetary reward for their work. Similarly, the bureaucratic model gave attention to job security, career progression, and protection of the worker from management's arbitrary whims. However, none of these models dealt much with informal or social relationships and the psychological aspects of work. Rather, they all assumed that a sound job description along with well-written rules and regulations would ensure efficient performance—the primary standard against which employee performance was to be judged.

All three models highlight the role of the manager.[12] The bureaucratic model suggests that a strong relationship exists between expertise and organizational level. A superior is to be obeyed by subordinates because of his or her higher position and presumed greater expertise. Emphasis on structure in the administrative-management model and strict division of labor in the scientific management model are based on similar reasoning.

An important difference among the three models is the part of the organization emphasized. Taylor studied production workers and how their productivity could be improved through time-and-motion studies. Fayol developed principles for managers to follow. He believed that structure was needed to make sure that all important functions are performed; if people were to work together, it was necessary to define clearly what they were trying to accomplish and to make sure that everybody saw how their work related to achievement of the organization's objectives. Weber's bureaucratic model was designed to be a rational blueprint of how an organization should work overall, with emphasis on rules and regulations. The clear delineation of authority and responsibility would make it easy to evaluate manager and employee performance and to distribute rewards fairly.

BEHAVIORAL VIEWPOINT OF MANAGEMENT

In the 1920s and 1930s managers began to see that the traditional viewpoint was shortsighted and incomplete because it largely ignored the feelings of employees—the **human-relations** aspect of management. Managers still encountered difficulties with workers because they did not always follow what management thought was rational behavior. Moreover, workers were not performing up to their physical capabilities as Taylor had predicted they would. Effective managers did not consistently follow Fayol's principles. The *behavioral viewpoint* of management focuses on helping managers deal more effectively with the *people side* of their organizations. It emphasizes not what managers do, but how they do it. The behavioral viewpoint emerged, in part, from the work of Elton Mayo and his associates at the Hawthorne plant of the Western Electric Company from 1927 to 1932.[13]

The Hawthorne Experiments

Mayo was called in by Western Electric when researchers who had been experimenting with work-area lighting reported some puzzling results. They had divided employees into a test group that was subjected to deliberate changes in lighting and a control group for whom lighting remained constant throughout the experiment. When lighting conditions for the test group were improved, productivity increased, just as expected. But the researchers were mystified by a similar jump in productivity when lighting was reduced to the point of twilight. To compound the mystery, the control group's output kept rising with each change in the test group's lighting conditions, even though the control group experienced no such changes.

In a new experiment, Mayo and his Harvard co-worker, Fritz Roethlisberger, placed two groups of six women in separate rooms. The researchers changed conditions in one room and left them unchanged in the other. The changes included shortening coffee breaks, allowing the group to choose its own rest periods, and letting the group have a say in other suggested changes.

Once again, output of the workers in both the test and control groups increased. The researchers felt they could rule out financial incentives as a cause, since the payment schedule for the control group was not changed. Mayo concluded that a complex emotional chain reaction was behind the productivity increases. Because the employees in the test and control groups had been singled out for special attention, they developed a group pride that

Mayo (top) and Roethlisberger's Hawthorne Experiments tested the effects of changes in employee working conditions and benefits on productivity.

motivated them to improve their work performance. The sympathetic supervision they received further reinforced their motivation.

The result of these experiments gave Mayo his first important discovery: When special attention is given to workers by management, productivity is likely to change regardless of actual changes in working conditions. This phenomenon became known as the ***Hawthorne effect.***

However, one question remained unanswered: *Why* should special attention and the formation of group bonds result in such strong reactions? To find the answer, Mayo interviewed workers. This led to his most significant finding: Informal work groups—the social environment of employees—greatly influence productivity. Many of the employees found their lives inside and outside the factory dull and meaningless. But their workplace friends, chosen in part because of mutual antagonism toward "the bosses," provided some meaning to their working lives. For this reason, group pressure, rather than management demands, had the strongest influence on employee productivity.

In order to maximize output, Mayo concluded, management must recognize employee needs for recognition and social satisfaction; the informal work group could become a positive, productive force if management provided employees with a sense of dignity and a sense of being appreciated. To Mayo, then, the concept of *social Man* included workers who were motivated by social needs, wanted on-the-job relationships, and were more responsive to work-group pressures than to management-motivated incentives and bonus systems.

Mary Parker Follett theorized that employee productivity was directly affected by human relations between management and employees, and among peer group members.

Source: Joan C. Tonn and the Urwick Management Centre.

Follett's Contribution

Following the same lines of thought as Mayo and Roethlisberger, Mary Parker Follett advocated a philosophy that if managers treated workers more humanely, productivity would increase.[14] She felt that managers had to recognize that each person was a collection of emotions, beliefs, and feelings. She proposed several guidelines for establishing the proper climate for relations between workers and managers. First, results can be achieved most easily when workers and managers communicate effectively and directly; speaking directly with workers, at their skill and motivation levels, is the best way to solve problems. Second, managers should plan for coordination of employee efforts and involve workers in this planning process; managers cannot assume that because they tell workers to do something it will get done. Third, authority should not be based solely on formal position in the hierarchy but on a manager's greater knowledge and expertise.

Summary of Assumptions

In summary, the basic assumptions of the behavioral viewpoint of management are:[15]

1. Workers basically are motivated by *social needs* and obtain a sense of identity through association with others.

2. Workers are more responsive to the social forces of the *peer group* than to the incentives and controls of management.

3. Workers are responsive to management *to the extent* that a supervisor can meet a subordinate's social and personal needs.

IN PRACTICE
Hewlett-Packard Company

From two men with one good product in 1939, the Hewlett-Packard (H-P) Company has grown into a multinational corporation with 57,000 employees, 4,000 high-technology products, and over $3 billion in annual sales without losing its friendly atmosphere. The friendship begun by Bill Hewlett and Dave Packard has evolved into a participative management philosophy known as the *H-P way*. This philosophy stresses individual freedom and initiative to get the job done. It fosters a feeling of personal responsibility in employees for the company's success. People like working for Hewlett-Packard. They have a higher degree of job identification and loyalty than most firms can claim.

"Everybody is equally important in the company," Packard, chairman of the board, asserts. He describes his management philosophy as management by objective, but admits it is more than that.

"You establish some objectives for people, provide some incentive, and try not to direct the detailed way in which they do their work. People will accomplish more if given an opportunity to use their talents and abilities in the way they work best. You've got to avoid having too rigid an organization."

Shirtsleeve informality goes all the way up to the executive offices. Doors are always open and the offices are unpretentious. "We find better uses for our profits than plushing up executive offices," Packard says.

One manager at Hewlett-Packard described his style as "management by walking around." Managers mingle with their employees to get to know them on a personal basis and to keep lines of communication open. They provide direction to employees in the form of well-defined and negotiated goals, shared data, and the support of necessary resources. Employees are encouraged to make suggestions, to be innovative. Everyone is on salary and flexible time schedules with no time clock to punch, another indication of the trust Hewlett-Packard has in them.

"Everybody we hire, we hire forever," is a maxim of the H-P way. The company hires young people right out of school. Employees are trained in personnel development programs designed to maintain H-P culture and values. Another way it preserves its culture and values is to promote from within.

"We feel the company is better off if, when we hire somebody, they have some assurance of staying with the company," Packard says. "This is particularly true of technical and management people. We have always operated our research and development program on the basis of maintaining a given level of activities and utilizing people in the most productive way possible—not hiring a lot of people for a new project and then letting them go."

The H-P spirit is one of the company's real strengths, according to Dave Packard. "It's the key to productivity and to leadership. It's the key to continuing progress and success in our company."[16]

Current Thought

The behavioral view of management highlights the importance of a manager's leadership style and group dynamics. It stresses the human and social needs of the employee, and the influence of an organization's social environment on the quality and quantity of the work produced.

However, actual results often run counter to what Mayo had expected. Improving working conditions and the human-relations skills of managers do not always result in higher productivity. Economic aspects of work are still important, as predicted by Taylor. Although employees enjoy co-workers who are friendly, low salaries can still lead to absenteeism and turnover. The structure of the organization and the assignment of an employee to routine and boring tasks are not likely to contribute to a worker's motivation, regardless of the social environment. Thus human behavior on the job is more complex than originally thought by Mayo. Building on the work of Mayo and his colleagues, later behavioral scientists created theories that would more accurately explain the behavior of people at work. (See Part V.)

SYSTEMS VIEWPOINT OF MANAGEMENT

During World War II, the British developed a team of mathematicians, physicists, and other professionals to solve wartime problems. This team of professionals formed the first operations research (OR) group and were able to analyze complex problems, such as convoy makeup and submarine locations. The team was able to achieve significant technological and tactical breakthroughs because of their ability to handle complex systems problems that could not be handled by intuition or experience. Systems analysis was developed further during the war and applied to military logistical problems and war-materiel production. It later became an accepted tool in the Department of Defense (DoD), the space program, and throughout private industry.

The *systems viewpoint* of management focuses on the development of models of systems to solve problems.[17] The models show, in symbolic terms, how all relevant factors of a problem are interrelated. With the aid of the computer, mathematical models have been constructed to simulate and solve many possible situations facing today's managers in the areas of marketing, production, finance, and personnel management. Development of the computer greatly increased management's ability to perform and analyze complex quantitative studies of business problems; the large number of computations necessary in many types of these analyses cannot be handled easily without computers.

Use of Quantitative Techniques

Quantitative techniques are well-established problem-solving tools in most large organizations. Two primary situational factors are present when managers use quantitative models to help them solve problems. First, the number of variables is extremely large. For example, imagine employees of the Federal Reserve Board trying to simulate the effects of an inflation rate of 10 percent per year on the U.S. economy, with all its variables, over the next five years without the aid of a computer. It would not be possible. Moreover, by changing the values of variables and analyzing different assumptions with the computer, a range of anticipated effects can be determined. Second, quantitative techniques permit managers to trace the economic implications of making a particular decision. These techniques are best suited for analyzing explicit (countable or quantifiable) variables, such as sales, payroll expenses, number of units processed, employee turnover, and profits. For example, when David Garrett, president of Delta Airlines, wanted to learn how a new employee contract would affect Delta's monthly payroll for its 36,000 employees, the task was relatively simple. The new figures were entered into the computer and a projected payroll was obtained. Besides payroll activities, Delta's management uses quantitative techniques for aircraft scheduling, capital budgeting, spare parts control, manpower planning, and aircraft maintenance scheduling.[18]

The range of quantitative decision-making tools useful to management is becoming broader. Present-day management uses inventory-decision models, statistical decision theory, linear programming, and many other similar tools. Chapters 7 and 19 discuss how systems analysis and quantitative techniques can be applied to the solution of management problems. In the largest companies, groups of managers called management scientists tackle a broad range of important business problems using sophisticated mathematical models.

IN PRACTICE
Tandem
Computers

At Tandem Computers, James Treybig, the founder of this fast-growing, $100 million-a-year company, has found creative ways to use the computer. Tandem is a people-oriented company that is noted for its Friday afternoon beer parties, employee stock options, flexible working hours, company swimming pool, and a mandatory sabbatical leave policy for all employees. However, Tandem's informal style is possible only because of the firm's system of computer controls. Eight separate computer systems check production, cost, quality, and management reporting. With the computers keeping track of company performance in key areas, managers are free to concentrate on people. This has produced highly visible results: The company has no trouble attracting good people in a highly competitive area and enjoys an extraordinarily low turnover rate of 8 percent in an industry where high turnover is the norm.[19]

Current Thought

Systems analysis and quantitative techniques have been used primarily in operations management and the technical planning and decision-making areas of management. They have not yet reached the stage where they can be used effectively to deal with the human side of the organization. At present, variables related to behavioral considerations and human values cannot be built into a mathematical model. Since these subjective variables must be considered by a manager before making a decision, managerial judgment remains important in arriving at a final decision.

CONTINGENCY VIEWPOINT OF MANAGEMENT

The traditional, behavioral, and systems viewpoints represent different approaches to management, but all three highlight the essential functions of a manager. In Chapter 1, we said that the *contingency viewpoint* of management tries to integrate various contributions from the other three views. The theme of the contingency approach is: *It all depends*. That is, in real life, the success of any technique or solution often depends on the situation.

The contingency viewpoint was developed by managers and consultants who had tried to apply the concepts of traditional, behavioral, and systems thought to numerous problems. They often found that a method that worked well in one situation was ineffective in another and sought explanations for such inconsistencies. The answer for these people was simple and logical: Results differ because the situation differs; thus the application of various management tools and techniques must be appropriate to the situation. According to the contingency viewpoint, the job of the manager is first to diagnose a situation and then identify the technique or principle that will best contribute to the solution of the problem in terms of the organization's structure, resources, and goals.

IN PRACTICE
Westinghouse Electric Corporation

At Westinghouse Electric Corporation, top management in Pittsburgh was ready for new ideas that would improve the firm's performance. The 1970s had seen Westinghouse's management involved in a highly publicized bribery case, a string of unprofitable acquisitions, and a major financial loss on the sale of its consumer appliances business. Additionally, Westinghouse was facing stiff competition from the Japanese.

A traditionalist might argue that productivity could be increased if a new work simplification program were installed. This new program would enable Westinghouse to do more with fewer people, less money, and less time, and in less space. A behavioral scientist might argue that if Westinghouse adopted a more participative management style to replace its old chain-of-command approach to solving problems, productivity through teamwork would improve. A management scientist might argue that if Westinghouse had better computer facilities, software, and management information systems to forecast production and delivery schedules, productivity would improve. The manager holding the contingency viewpoint would ask: "Which method will work best at Westinghouse in the 1980s?" Since most of the workers are skilled and training opportunities are available, work simplication might not be the best solution. If financial resources had not been drained by bad management practices during the 1970s, new computers and software could have been purchased.

The solution for Westinghouse was to adopt the recommendations of the behavioral scientist. Participative management was introduced at Westinghouse in 1980. Douglas Danforth, vice-chairman, is a hands-on manager who instinctively puts his arm around a worker or pats the employee on the back to reward high performance. To reinforce Danforth's philosophy, selected employees were trained to be team leaders for participative councils. Committees made up of employees from all levels, not just management, were formed to solve problems. It took time for managers and workers to see improvement in profits and not all managers and workers enthusiastically adopted the system. But Westinghouse has experienced a decline in the number of grievances filed, lower absenteeism rates, and higher productivity.[20]

Current Thought

Although it is not still fully developed, the contingency viewpoint is helpful to managers because it emphasizes a situational approach.[21] Critics argue that it is really nothing new but merely a meshing of techniques from the other viewpoints of management. The contingency viewpoint does draw heavily from the other viewpoints. However, it offers the *flexibility* of applying principles and tools from those viewpoints selectively and where most appropriate. The absolute principles advocated by traditional, behavioral, and systems theorists should be used only after the realities of a situation have been properly diagnosed. Such a diagnosis involves the nature of a situation and the means by which you, as a manager, can influence it.

CHAPTER SUMMARY

Three well-established viewpoints of management—traditional, behavioral, and systems—have contributed to our understanding of organizations and how to run them. Each viewpoint offers a different set of solutions to managerial problems. The traditional viewpoint attempts to solve management problems by the application of logic and well-designed organizational structures. Weber's bureaucratic model dealt with how managers can structure specialized jobs for subordinates to ensure predictable results. Rules and regulations prescribe behavior on the job. Taylor attempted to arrive at the *best* way to do a job. Once the best method had been determined and taught to all workers, a standard production time could be used for motivational purposes. This scientific approach to management led to development of the time-and-motion study and the piece-rate system of pay. Fayol emphasized the four distinct functions a manager should perform: planning, organizing, leading, and controlling. He developed a set of principles to help managers perform these functions.

The behavioral viewpoint started with the human-relations movement in the Hawthorne plant of the Western Electric Company. Whereas the traditional viewpoint focuses primarily on rational decision making by a manager, the behavioral viewpoint of management gives major consideration to the feelings of the worker and the work group. The finding of the Hawthorne experiment was that social and human factors could be more important than physical factors in influencing productivity.

The systems viewpoint stresses the application of systems analysis and mathematical models to management decision making. With the development of the computer, many more variables could be analyzed quantitatively, giving managers a better and more complete understanding of the situations and options with which they have to deal.

A fourth viewpoint of management, the contingency viewpoint, is not so well established. It offers managers the flexibility to draw on the approaches and techniques of the other three, depending on the diagnosis of the situation or problem faced. The contingency viewpoint requires managers to be aware of the complexity of a situation before choosing a solution. Since there is no *best* theory of management, managers holding the contingency viewpoint will find many theories, principles, and techniques useful to them in diagnosing and solving problems.

MANAGER'S VOCABULARY

administrative management
authority structure
behavioral viewpoint
bureaucratic management
contingency viewpoint
division of labor
functional foremanship
Hawthorne effect
Hawthorne experiments
hierarchical structure
human relations
impersonality
lifelong career commitment
management functions

rationality
rules and regulations
scientific management
systems viewpoint
time-and-motion study
traditional viewpoint

REVIEW QUESTIONS

1. Describe the characteristics of Weber's bureaucratic model.

2. What are the three important aspects of Taylor's theory of scientific management?

3. State Fayol's 14 managerial principles and give examples of each.

4. What are the three basic assumptions of the behavioral viewpoint?

5. What types of problems does the systems viewpoint examine?

6. What are the key features of the contingency viewpoint?

DISCUSSION QUESTIONS

1. Why is it important for you to understand the evolution of management thought?

2. Compare and contrast the assumptions of the bureaucratic and human-relations approaches to management.

3. What are the similarities and differences among the three management approaches in the traditional viewpoint? What names do you associate with each?

4. How did Westinghouse Electric Corporation use the three basic assumptions of the human-relations approach to solve their problems?

5. How does Hewlett-Packard use bureaucratic methods to increase productivity and effectiveness?

MANAGEMENT INCIDENTS AND CASES

Austin Industries

An analysis of the accident records at Austin Industries revealed that one type of job was responsible for the majority of lost-time accident cases. It was a punch press operation involving a 30-second cycle:

1. Left hand picks up 4-inch square, 1-inch thick piece of metal.

2. Left hand places metal on drill press.

3. Right hand presses button activating press.

4. Hydraulic press punches 1-inch hole through center of metal.

5. Right hand removes metal and places it in box to right of press.

Employees were paid on a piece-rate basis. George Huber, an industrial engineer, believed that they were tempted to work too fast and in their haste often failed to remove the left hand before activating the machine with the right hand. The result was severed or badly mashed fingers. In order to eliminate such accidents, Huber installed a safety device requiring each punch-press operator to attach a strap to both wrists in such a way that movement of the right hand to activate the press pulled the left hand free of the punch area.

Immediately after installation of this safety device, such accidents were eliminated completely. However, after several months, the same type of accident began to occur again. An investigation revealed that employees involved in such accidents did not have the safety device attached to their wrists at the time of the accident. Apparently, employees were avoiding use of the attachment when they thought they could do so without detection. They were unlikely to admit it, but Huber suspected that they believed the safety device caused them to be less productive, thereby affecting their piece-rate compensation.

Questions
1. Using Taylor's concepts, explain what happened.

2. If you were George Huber, what would you do?

REFERENCES

1. Adapted from M. Hooper, *The Coca-Cola Company* (unpublished manuscript), Edwin L. Cox School of Business, Southern Methodist University, Dallas, 1980; correspondence from Philip F. Mooney, Manager, Archives Department, The Coca-Cola Company, November 12, 1984.

2. R. Daft, *Organizations: Theory and Design.* St. Paul, Minn.: West, 1983, pp. 129–149; M. Weber, *The Theory of Social and Economic Organization.* Trans. by A. Henderson and T. Parsons. New York: Free Press, 1947.

3. Adapted from R. Daft, *Organizations: Theory and Design.* St. Paul, Minn.: West, 1983, pp. 126–127.

4. M. Crozier, *The Bureaucratic Phenomenon.* Chicago, Ill.: University of Chicago Press, 1964; J. Cheng and Wm. McKelvey, "Toward an Integration of Organization of Research and Practice: A Contingency Study of Bureaucratic Control and Performance in Scientific Settings," *Administrative Science Quarterly,* 1983, **28:**85–100; R. Weiss, "Weber on Bureaucracy: Management Consultant or Political Theorist?" *Academy of Management Review,* 1983, 2:242–248.

5. *Dallas Morning News,* December 12, 1980, p. 18A.

6. D. Gerwin, "Relationships between Structure and Technology." In *Handbook of Organizational Design,* Vol. 2. P. Nystrom and Wm. Starbuck (Eds.). New York: Oxford University Press, 1981, pp. 3–38.

7. P. Birnbaum, "Integration and Specialization in Academic Research," *Academy of Management Journal,* 1981, **24:**487–503.

8. J. Webb, *Space-Age Management.* New York: McGraw-Hill, 1969.

9. F. Taylor, *Scientific Management.* New York: Harper & Row, 1947; E. Locke, "The Ideas of Frederick Taylor: An Evaluation," *Academy of Management Review,* 1982, 7:14–24.

10. E. Meadows, "How Three Companies Increased Their Productivity," *Fortune,* March 10, 1980, pp. 93–101.

11. N. Mouzelis, *Organization and Bureaucracy: An Analysis of Modern Theories.* Chicago, Ill.: Aldine, 1968, pp. 79–96.

12. H. Koontz, "The Management Theory Jungle Revisited," *Academy of Management Review 5,* 1980, 175–188.

13. E. Mayo, *The Social Problems of an Industrial Civilization.* Boston, Mass.: Harvard University, Graduate School of Business, 1945; R. Greenwood, A. Bolton, and R. Greenwood, "Hawthorne A Half Century Later: Relay Assembly Participants Remember," *Journal of Management,* 1983, **9:**217–231.

14. L. Parker, "Control in Organizational Life: The Contribution of Mary Parker Follett," *Academy of Management Review,* 1984, 9:736–745.

15. G. Homan, *The Human Group.* New York: Harcourt, Brace and World, 1950, pp. 48–81.

16. "David Packard of Hewlett-Packard—A Faithful Employer," *Nation's Business,* 1974 (January), pp. 37–42: R. Von Werssowetz and M. Beer, *Human Resources at Hewlett-Packard,* Cambridge, Mass.: Harvard Business School, Case No. 9-482-125, 1982; and A. Clegg, *Comparison of Management Styles, Organizational Culture and Strategies at Hewlett-Packard and Texas Instruments Incorporated* (unpublished paper), Cox School of Business, Southern Methodist University, Dallas, 1984.

17. E. E. Adam Jr., "Toward a Typology of Production and Operation Management Systems," *Academy of Management Review,* 1983, 8:365–375.

18. J. Guyan, " 'Family Feeling' at Delta Creates Loyal Workers, Enmity of Unions," *Wall Street Journal,* July 7, 1980, p. 13ff.

19. T. Deal and A. Kennedy, *Corporation Cultures: The Rites and Rituals of Corporate Life.* Reading, Mass.: Addison-Wesley, 1982.

20. J. Main, "Westinghouse's Cultural Revolution," *Fortune,* 1981 (June 15), pp. 74–93; S. Anreder, "Switch at Westinghouse: Its Efforts to Turn Its Business Around Are Paying Off," *Barrons,* 1981 (September 21), pp. 49–50; "Operation Turnaround," *Businessweek,* December 5, 1983, p. 124ff.

21. D. Miller, "Toward a New Contingency Approach: The Search for Organizational Gestalts," *Journal of Management Studies,* 1981, **18:**1–27; H. Tosi and J. Slocum, "Contingency Theory: Some Suggested Directions," *Journal of Management,* 1984, **10:**9–26; A. Van de Ven and R. Drazin, "The Concept of Fit in Contingency Theory." In *Research in Organizational Behavior.* L. Cummings and B. Staw (Eds.). Greenwich, Conn.: JAI Press, pp. 333–365.

PART II

ENVIRONMENTAL FORCES

ENVIRONMENTAL FORCES ACTING ON ORGANIZATIONS

CHAPTER 3

LEARNING OBJECTIVES

After studying this chapter, you should be able to:

- Describe the seven megatrends that are affecting many organizations and their management.

- Explain the five competitive forces facing most business organizations.

- Describe six political strategies used by managers to limit control of a business by external groups.

- Indicate how differences in cultural values influence the decisions and behaviors of managers.

CHAPTER OUTLINE

Preview Case American Telephone and Telegraph

Environmental Turbulence
Megatrends
Task environments

Competitive Forces
Rivalry among competitors

In Practice: The Airline Industry
Threat of new entrants
Threat of substitute products or services

In Practice: Greyhound Bus Lines
Bargaining power of customers

International Focus
Global Competition: A Buyer's Market
Bargaining power of suppliers

In Practice: A Large Midwest Company

Political Forces
Sources of political forces
Political strategies

In Practice: Bargaining with the Federal Government

Cultural Forces
Importance of values
Work-related value framework
Implications of work-related value differences

Management Incidents and Cases
Southern Realty Investors, Inc.

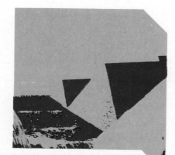

PREVIEW CASE

American Telephone and Telegraph

Charles L. Brown, chairman of the board of American Telephone and Telegraph (AT&T), provides the following perspective on the increased environmental complexity and change facing AT&T and firms in other major industries.[1]

At a time when some of America's major industries are undergoing radical changes, it may seem presumptuous to suggest that change in one particular industry is more extensive than in any other. Nevertheless, I believe that to be true of telecommunications.

Two overriding forces are driving change in telecommunications. One is political. The political process shapes public policy. Through this process a new national telecommunications policy has evolved. It is primarily a product of federal regulatory and judicial decisions. Stated simply, this new policy tells us that hereafter competition, not government, will be the *principal* regulator of the telecommunications industry.

The second force driving change in telecommunications is technology. It was basic advances in science and data processing technologies that set in motion the reexamination of past regulatory policies that has led to the changes taking place in the 1980s.

First, how did we get from there to here? Starting in the late 1960s, the Federal Communications Commission (FCC) began making a series of *ad hoc* decisions aimed at introducing competition in selected parts of the telecommunications market.

The first major step was the FCC's Computer Inquiry Two decision, adopted in its final form in October, 1981. This decision distinguished between basic local and long distance services on the one hand, and enhanced services and customer-premises equipment on the other—the former to remain regulated, the latter to be detariffed. For the Bell System to operate on a detariffed basis (that is, to market and price enhanced services and new customer-premises equipment without having to file regulatory tariffs beforehand), it was necessary to establish a fully separate subsidiary. And so American Bell was born.

The second major development was the Con-

Source: Courtesy of AT&T.

sent Decree agreement reached between AT&T and the U.S. Justice Department in January 1982. The Consent Decree required us to divest the Bell operating companies that provided local telephone services in various states. In December 1982 we filed a reorganization plan, subject to court review, with a target date for divestiture of January 1, 1984. On that date, the 22 wholly owned Bell operating companies, having been grouped into seven regional companies, were divested. Remaining part of AT&T are Bell Laboratories, the Western Electric Company, American Bell (our interexchange long distance operations), and AT&T International.

These twists and turns in the development of a new policy and structure frequently tend to overshadow the primary cause for our changes—technology. Until recently, telecommunications and data processing were separate technologies. We now have technology that makes it possible to manage information when you want it, where you want it, and in the form you want it.

From the customer's point of view, the bottom line of these technological advances is an array of innovative communications terminals and systems that is increasingly making the *information age* far more than a catch phrase of futurologists.

Finally, a few words about the Bell System's new international role. There is a lively appreciation throughout the world of the need to establish a solid communications infrastructure. In 1980, we consolidated our international subsidiaries into a single organization, AT&T International. Our share of the total market outside the United States is relatively small at the moment. But we expect to change that. AT&T International is rapidly developing professional in-country sales forces in a number of key markets. We are internationalizing our designs and products, and we have undertaken a substantial research and development program to market a line of products that will sell well anywhere in the world.

All in all, then, while we may look back with some nostalgia on the days when ours was a relatively stable and certain industry, we believe we have good reason to look ahead with optimism and more than a little sense of adventure. Ours is a grand past, and we expect no less of our future.

The interplay between environmental influences and organizations is well illustrated in the AT&T case. These environmental influences include new electronic technologies, new firms exploiting these technologies to compete directly with AT&T, and new rules of the game from the government. The decisions by the Federal Communications Commission eliminated AT&T's monopoly over long distance telecommunications and encouraged competition in producing and selling telephones, reduction of rates for services, and the like.

The AT&T case captures the main thrust of this chapter. We present the broad outlines of environmental forces and competitive trends facing managers in the United States. We then review the effects of political factors on the management of organizations. We conclude with some comments on cultural concepts and how they can influence the role of organizations in society, as well as their internal patterns of management.

ENVIRONMENTAL TURBULENCE

In his book *Managing in Turbulent Times,* Peter Drucker concluded that "Some time during the 1970s, the longest period of continuity in economic history came to an end. At some time during the last ten years, we moved into turbulence."[2]

A ***turbulent environment*** is one that is complex, changing, and unpredictable. It is extremely challenging for managers and organizations to cope with this type of environment.[3] Of course, the relative importance of turbulence will vary by size and complexity of organization. Small firms and those operating in relatively simple industries (such as fast foods, packaging, and printing) are less likely to be affected than large firms and those operating in complex industries (such as aerospace, chemicals, and medicine). In addition, turbulent environments do not have an impact on all employees, divisions, and departments of the same organization with equal force or in the same form. For example, the turbulence being experienced by AT&T appears to have had much greater impact on top management and the marketing and research and development divisions than on other areas of the firm, such as the residential installation division or compilers of the white- and yellow-page telephone directories. In general the basic sources of turbulence for many organizations and individuals have been identified as ***megatrends*** by John Naisbitt in his book of the same name.[4]

Megatrends

Megatrends are the broad patterns of change that are redefining society in the United States and other advanced industrial countries. They were identified by synthesizing a large amount of detailed information into a set of general directions in which advanced industrial societies seem to be moving and that will have major effects on their citizens and businesses. The term comes from the use of *mega* (meaning *great*) with the word *trend* (meaning *direction*). Figure 3.1 shows seven of Naisbitt's megatrends, the implications of which are central to our purpose and will be developed throughout the rest of this book. Thus our objective here is only to define and describe them briefly.

Naisbitt claims that advanced industrial societies are shifting to information societies. In industrial societies, capital (money) has been the strategic resource. In the future, the strategic resource will be information. Computer technology is to the information age what mechanization was to the industrial age. The revolution in information technology was seen as the primary force causing the many changes by AT&T. The movement from *forced technology* to *high tech/high touch technology* is based on the idea that, whenever new technology is introduced into a society, there must be a counterbalancing human response—that is, high touch—or the technology is rejected. Thus there is a growing need for balance between our physical and spiritual (cultural values and attitudes) realities.

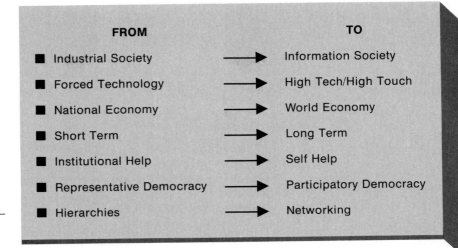

FIGURE 3.1

Seven Megatrends

Source: J. Naisbitt, *Megatrends*. New York: Wagner Books, 1982.

Forced technology is illustrated by the regimentation and conformity required of workers as a result of the widespread use of mass production (assembly-line) technology. Within the office environment, forced technology is suggested by clerical personnel sitting in large rooms at desks, neatly arranged in rows, performing routine tasks with typewriters or computer terminals. These uses of technology are seen as forcing so much regimentation of behavior on workers that many become dissatisfied and alienated from their work. The movement toward high tech/high touch attempts to provide people with more control over technology and to provide them with the opportunity to work in small groups. This helps to meet human needs for some degree of control and social contact.

The movement from a national economy to a world economy—no longer dominated by the United States—is a key megatrend. More and more U.S. industries face global interdependencies and global competition. This suggests the need to shift from *short-term* to *long-term* considerations in strategic planning. Managers increasingly need to think about key issues with time horizons of 5–10 years, not just the implications of key issues for the coming year's profit and loss statement.

The movement from institutional help to self-help reflects the idea that Americans are reclaiming their traditional sense of self-reliance after four decades of increasing reliance on large scale, impersonal governmental institutions to meet various needs. Consistent with the self-help trend is the trend from representative democracy to participatory democracy. The guiding principle in participatory democracy is that people must be part of the process of arriving at decisions that affect their lives. Citizens, workers, and consumers are demanding and getting a greater voice in the decision-making processes of government, business, and the marketplace. The shifts to self-help and participatory democracy are closely associated with the movement from hierarchies to networking. Rigid hierarchies may increasingly be replaced or modified by various types of networking arrangements. Networking places increased emphasis on peer relationships rather than superior–subordinate relationships to solve problems.

Task Environments

The *task environment* includes all those forces external to the organization that directly influence the firm's survival, growth, and success.[5] These forces are likely to be exerted by customers, suppliers, competitors, political groups, and government regulatory agencies, among others.

As mentioned in Chapter 1, the task environment is an important contingency that needs to be evaluated by managers in considering a wide variety of problems.[6] Such problems involve decisions about what plans to develop, how to structure the organization, and what types of control techniques to use. However, the task environment is set within the general environment that affects all firms.[7] For example, the economic systems in the United States and Canada are relatively free and based on market competition, in contrast to the economic system in Russia. For an individual organization, the basic economic and cultural systems of a society are a *given* and are viewed as part of the general environment.

Figure 3.2 illustrates the types of environmental forces that have an impact on business organizations. The task environment always includes the competitive forces shown. However, the political and cultural forces shown will not always be classified as part of the task environment of an organization. For example, unions are shown as a political force; for Ford, General Motors, and Chrysler, the United Auto Workers union is part of their task environment because it has a *direct* impact on them. However, IBM and Hewlett-Packard are nonunion firms; unions are not part of their task environments but may have *indirect* effects on them as part of the general environment. For example, indirect effects could result from successful union efforts to gain passage of legislation that affects all workers, union and nonunion alike.

COMPETITIVE FORCES

At least five forces in the environment directly affect the degree of competition in an industry and the businesses that operate within it: competitors, potential entrants, substitute products or services, customers, and suppliers. The long-term profit potential for the firms in an industry is strongly influenced by the combined strength of these forces. One expert notes that "The forces range

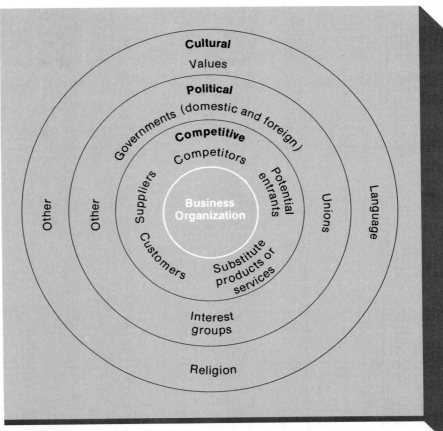

FIGURE 3.2
Environmental Forces and Business Organizations

from intense in industries like tires, paper, and steel—where no firm earns spectacular returns—to relatively mild in industries like oil-field equipment and services, cosmetics, and toiletries—where high returns are quite common.[8]

Managers must diagnose each of these competitive forces and their combined strength before making decisions about future courses of action for their companies. To not do so would ignore the forces that generally have the most direct impact on a company's success or failure.

Rivalry among Competitors

The single most important day-to-day environmental force for a firm is likely to be rivalry with its competitors. Bruce D. Henderson, founder and chairman of the Boston Consulting Group, comments:

> For virtually all competitors their critical environment constraint is their interface with other competitors. Therefore, any change in the environment that affects any competitor will have consequences that require some degree of adaptation. This requires continual change and adaptation by all competitors merely to maintain relative position.[9]

Rivalry among competitors involves the use of tactics such as price competition, advertising promotions, greater customer service or warranties, and improvements in product or service quality. Competitors use these tactics to try to improve their relative position in an industry or to respond to the actions of others. Since firms in an industry are often interdependent, price cuts by one firm often invite countermoves by other firms. All may be worse off if price cuts by one firm are countered by price cuts of others, resulting in lower profits or even losses. In contrast, advertising rivalry may increase demand for a product and an industry as a whole—leaving all of the firms better off. With deregulation of the airline industry in 1978, price rivalry became a common competitive tactic.

IN PRACTICE
The Airline Industry

The deregulation of price and other competitive factors in the airline and other regulated industries began slowly in 1974. In 1978, Congress passed the Airline Deregulation Act. With deregulation, 14 new nonunion airlines (such as Air West, Muse Air, and People Express) emerged. These new airlines, with lower labor, maintenance, and capital costs, immediately began to compete by cutting prices. The 11 established trunk airlines (including American, Delta, Eastern, and United) often found it necessary to react with their own price cuts on a route-by-route basis to avoid losing significant numbers of customers. Price cutting and other forms of competitive rivalry (such as frequent-flyer awards) were related to the bankruptcy and reorganization of Braniff and Continental. They also spurred severe cost cutting—especially through pay and benefit cuts and other union-contract concessions—by Eastern, PanAm, Republic, TWA, United, and Western. The pressure on managers to improve the productivity of the 11 established airlines was enormous. For example, during 1982, labor costs as a percent of total costs varied from 34% for Western and 37% for Eastern to 19% for Muse and 27% for Southwest.[10] Total costs for Eastern and Western exceeded their revenues. Thus, one way of reducing losses and restoring profits is to reduce the relative share of revenues used to pay the costs of labor. The competitive rivalry created so much disruption that some executives have called for certain forms of reregulation in the transportation, communications, and banking industries to restore stability.[11]

The ultimate rationale for deregulation is that—in the long run—customers are better served with lower prices and better quality, and resources are more efficiently used. For example, based on inflation-adjusted 1976 dollars, the lowest round-trip airfare between New York and Los Angeles was $312 in 1976 versus $195 in 1984 and 1985.[12]

The deregulation of recent years does not necessarily mean a total hands-off policy by the government. For instance, the Airline Deregulation Act requires air service to be provided to 555 communities that were eligible for service before 1978. Airlines are paid a government subsidy if they have to serve small, money-losing communities.[13]

THREAT OF NEW ENTRANTS

The threat of new entrants depends on the relative ease or difficulty that new firms would face in starting up to compete with established firms in an industry. High economies of scale, well-developed product differentiation, high capital requirements, and restrictive government regulation are four common barriers to entry.

The term *economies of scale* refers to the decrease in per-unit costs as the volume of goods and services produced by a firm increases during a given period of time. The potential for economies of scale in the airline industry is substantial. An example is air-passenger and air-cargo services. All the available space in a Boeing 747 cannot be filled with passengers. The bottom portion of the plane contains an enormous amount of empty space, even if all the passengers were to bring extra baggage. Most of the costs associated with flying a United Airlines 747 from New York to Los Angeles are the same whether this space is filled with revenue generating cargo or is left empty. United, by competing in both the passenger and freight businesses, takes advantage of the economies of scale offered by the 747.

Product differentiation is the creation of something that is unique in terms of quality, price, design, brand image, or customer service. A new McDonald's restaurant has an immediate identity: compare it to the situation facing someone attempting to open an unheard of fast food outlet in direct competition with McDonald's. Ronald McDonald is second only to Santa Claus as the most recognized person in the world.

Capital requirements are the dollars needed to meet initial equipment, supplies, advertising, research and development, and other start-up costs. The capital requirements for a new steel mill are in the hundreds of millions of dollars, whereas those for an exercise studio (with no special equipment) might be $20,000 or less. A barrier to entry is *government regulation,* if it bars or severely restricts potential new entrants from entering an industry. Even today, airline competition is somewhat restricted by the need to receive approval from the Federal Aeronautics Administration (FAA) to land at an airport.

THREAT OF SUBSTITUTE PRODUCTS OR SERVICES

The threat of substitute products or services is the possibility that customers will have their needs met in alternative ways. The introduction of television into the home had a devastating impact on movie theaters during the 1950s and 1960s. The rapid development of cable networks (Home Box Office, MTV) in the 1980s is seen as a threat to ABC, CBS, and NBC. Deregulation and the speed of technological change are probably the major sources of this type of threat at the present time. Deregulation in the airline and bus industries led to fare price cutting and created new, intense competition for Greyhound Bus Lines.

IN PRACTICE
Greyhound
Bus Lines

During 1983, Greyhound Bus Lines faced the loss of customers because of relatively low airfares offered by People Express, Southwest, and New York Air, among others, and the entry of new bus companies into the industry as a result of deregulation. In order to hold the line on costs and respond to these competitive threats, Greyhound's management accepted a nasty strike in 1983 by the Amalgamated Transit Union. Management refused to meet demands for increased pay and benefits because it believed that the company's ability to compete with discount airlines and nonunion bus lines would suffer. The union finally accepted a settlement that involved a 7.8% wage cut, a freeze on cost-of-living adjustments through May 1986, employee contributions to the pension fund equal to 4% of gross wages, and other concessions. The president of one union local commented: "It's better to eat a little crow than get replaced."[14]

IMPACT OF TECHNOLOGY

The tools, techniques, and procedures used to transform resources into goods or services are, collectively, called *technology*. A technology usually has two components: (1) *hardware*, or physical objects; and (2) *software*, consisting of the information base and instructions for the hardware.[15] For example, in the computer industry computer hardware includes data-input devices (such as a keyboard), semiconductors, transistors, electrical connections, tape drives, data-output devices (such as printers and video screens), and metal frames; computer software includes coded commands, instructions, and other informational elements required to enable the hardware to process data in the form needed.

The shift from an industrial society to an information society has been made possible by the explosion in computer technology. It has also increased threats of substitute products or services in many industries. The banking industry accelerated the pace of substitution with automatic teller machines, home banking, electronic fund transfers, and instant electronic cash management systems.[16] These changes reduced significantly the number of tellers needed in a typical bank.

The threat of substitution can be a powerful stimulus to innovate by firms with an established product or service. The manufacturers of photoflash bulbs are said to have delayed for 20 years the widespread adoption of the electronic flash for amateur use. They achieved this by continually producing lower cost and more convenient flashbulb systems.[17]

Between 1975 and 1984, 100 new firms dedicated to pioneering new products from biotechnology were formed with initial investments totalling $2.5 billion.[18] Biotechnology, which usually involves various gene manipulations, has the potential for offering new solutions to unresolved problems in areas as diverse as birth defects, crop yields, and consumer products. For example, the aspartame sweetener, a product of biotechnology, is used extensively in sugar-free drinks and was readily accepted as a substitute for other artificial sweeteners in 1983 because it did not leave an aftertaste.

The threat of substitute products or services is generally of much greater importance to managers today than 20 years ago because technology is changing so fast. At the same time it spurs innovation and improvement in many industries.

Bargaining Power of Customers

Customers for goods or services have a natural desire to try to force down prices, obtain higher quality or more services (while holding price constant), and increase competition among sellers by playing these firms off against each other. The bargaining power of customers is likely to be relatively great if the following characteristics are present.

- The customer purchases large volumes relative to the supplier's total sales. Sears and Kmart have clout with some producers because of their large volume purchases.
- The product or service represents a significant cost to the customer. Customers are generally more motivated to search for ways of cutting those costs that are a significant part of their total costs. Prior to full deregulation of AT&T in 1984, MCI Communications Corporation effectively attracted firms and individuals with substantial long-distance telephone expenses. MCI offered discounts of as much as 20% below AT&T's Wide Area Telephone Communications Services (WATS).[19] Deregulation and new technology have substantially increased the power of large customers in bargaining with AT&T over the long-distance rates it charges.

INTERNATIONAL FOCUS

Global Competition: A Buyer's Market

American high-tech companies looking to expand their operations overseas are hot commodities both to industrialized and to third-world nations. By attracting foreign investment, many countries hope not only to employ and train their workers in fast-growing high-tech fields but also to enter lucrative markets now controlled by the United States and Japan. With these objectives, industrial development agencies (IDAs) around the globe are luring potential developers with such incentives as tax holidays, free-trade zones, free land, and outright grants of cash.

The most generous packages are now being offered by European, southeast Asian, and Caribbean nations. While Common Market countries are competing for companies that want to take advantage of the burgeoning European market for such products as semiconductors and personal computers, southeast Asian and Caribbean countries are pursuing firms interested primarily in cheap labor.

"It's a buyer's market out there," says Té Revesz, an analyst with Business International, a New York based consulting firm that specializes in multinational corporations. "No matter what area of the world a company wants to locate in, it should have no problem finding a country that will go out of its way to be accommodating."

ATLANTIC CROSSING

Since World War II, Far Eastern competition has ravaged the shipbuilding, steel, and textile industries upon which most European nations have traditionally built their economies. With its current priorities, however, "the European

Source: Frank J. Catalano, "Global Competition: A Buyer's Market," *High Technology,* Vol. 5, No. 1. Copyright January 1985, p. 38. Reprinted with permission, High Technology Publishing Corporation, 38 Commercial Wharf, Boston, MA 02110.

■ Customers pose a realistic threat of *backward integration* into a supplier industry. General Motors and Ford have used the threat of self-manufacture or the acquisition of supplying companies as a bargaining lever to get lower prices from suppliers. Southland Corporation, operator of more than 7000 7-11 stores and the largest independent seller of gasoline, purchased Cities Service Refining Company to make sure that its stores had an adequate supply of gasoline at the lowest price possible.

Bargaining Power of Suppliers

The bargaining power of suppliers depends on how much they can raise prices and/or reduce the quality of goods and services provided to customers. Of course, not all suppliers or customers will have equal power.[20] Powerful

Economic Community [the Common Market] is trying to skip an entire generation of product development and move directly from heavy industry into high tech," says L. Clinton Hoch, a site selection consultant with Fantas (Millbury, N.J.). Europe hopes to replace old markets with new ones as well as to revive some dying industries with new processes such as computer-aided design and manufacturing (CAD/CAM).

Toward achieving those ends, the Common Market has set up the European Strategic Program for Research in Information Technologies (ESPRIT). Among the areas ESPRIT has targeted for further development are microelectronics, software, advanced information processing, office automation, and computer integrated manufacturing. While government-sponsored research will be crucial to the development of these fields, so will foreign investment. "Common Market countries realize they have a lot to catch up on and that they can't do it alone," says Hoch. "They're hoping that technology from U.S. and Japanese companies locating within their borders will eventually be transferred to home-owned firms."

As countries attract foreign investors and position themselves for shares of future world markets, they are also providing jobs for their workers. In France, where unemployment has stood at about 9 percent since 1980, U.S. companies are creating more than 6000 new jobs a year, according to the French IDA. The British IDA estimates that U.S. investments accounted for more than 11,000 new jobs last year in Great Britain, where the unemployment rate is around 11 percent.

suppliers may be able to squeeze higher prices out of business customers or consumers. The general characteristics that make customers powerful are similar to those that make suppliers powerful. Let us consider three additional characteristics that tend to increase the bargaining power of suppliers.

- There is only one, or just a few, firms in the supplier industry (a monopoly or oligopoly), and it is more concentrated than the group of customers it sells to.

- The suppliers do not find any single customer group to be especially important to their own long-term welfare. In contrast, when suppliers' welfare is tied to a particular customer group, they are more likely to support it through reasonable pricing and other forms of assistance, such as research and development and political lobbying. For example, the suppliers who sold a significant portion of their products to Chrysler made pricing and financing concessions to help Chrysler survive during its 1980–1983 crisis period.

■ Suppliers pose a realistic threat of *forward integration* into customer groups such as manufacturers, wholesalers, or retailers. In 1983, Kuwait Oil Company began a major program of acquiring chains of retail gasoline stations in Western Europe, one of the major markets for oil from Kuwait.

**IN PRACTICE
A Large Midwest
Company**

A telecommunications manager with a large midwest company shares his displeasure with AT&T in the 1970s, prior to deregulation: "They had taken the posture of a monopoly (single supplier), although some employees tried to work their way out of that. But generally, it was so ingrained for them to think 'We're the best. You have to come to us,' that it made their priorities different. We had to keep calling for repairs on the same circuits. They weren't being fixed."

As a result of deregulation and major advances in information technology, this midwest company was able to install a $150,000, 24-channel, dual-tower microwave system with 16 voice channels, 2 data channels, and 6 reserve channels. The telecommunications manager comments, "My real payback came in about two and a half years. But, you take over the responsibilities that Bell had—or that somebody had—to keep the network running smoothly."[21]

POLITICAL FORCES

For some organizations, such as telephone companies and airlines, political forces are a central part of their task environments. Changes in political forces on organizations have been especially significant over the past 20 years and are likely to continue to be in the future. Managers must diagnose these forces and find effective ways to deal with them.

Sources of Political Forces

Conflict and disagreement over goals and values in a society are often expressed through political and legal forces. For example, the general goals and values associated with individual freedoms, freedom of the press, private-property rights, and free enterprise are widely accepted in the United States. However, many regulatory agencies and interest groups operate—often in conflict with each other—to define and influence the day-to-day interpretation of these general goals and values.

Political and legal forces operate on a business through its **political system.** This political system extends beyond governmental institutions to include the whole complex of groups, institutions, and individuals possessing power to influence or control a firm's decisions, survival, or growth. For a business firm, the important components in the political environment include trade associations, major customers, government agencies, labor unions, stockholders, consumer groups, environmental groups, minority groups, and foreign governments, among others.[22] These components can both influence and be influenced by managers.

Political Strategies

Managers use *political strategies* in dealing with important and powerful components in their companies' general and task environments.[23] Figure 3.3

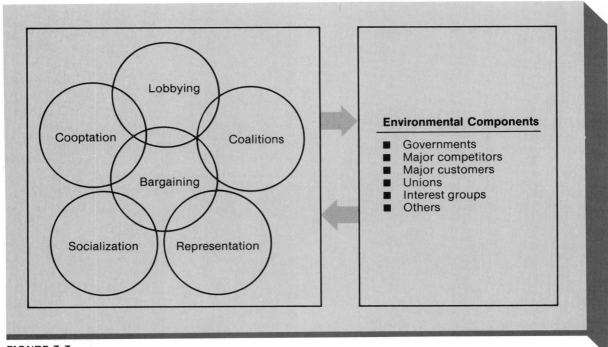

FIGURE 3.3
Organizational Political Strategies

identifies six of the major political strategies that managers use to influence and respond to environmental components: bargaining, cooptation, lobbying, coalitions, representation, and socialization. These strategies are not mutually exclusive; they usually are used in some combination; and each strategy often contains elements of others. The bargaining strategy probably is the most important political strategy. The other five strategies almost always contain some degree of bargaining. Accordingly, bargaining is shown in the center of Figure 3.3 and overlaps with the other five political strategies.

Bargaining strategy

The negotiation of an agreement between two or more organizations or individuals about the exchange of goods, services, or expected behaviors involves *bargaining*. Bargaining means that each party decides what it must do to satisfy the other(s) and normally occurs as result of disagreements. It can take place only when the parties believe that some form of agreement is both possible and beneficial to them. As illustrated in the In-Practice case, business firms (or representatives of business, such as the Chamber of Commerce) often bargain with governmental agencies.

IN PRACTICE
Bargaining with the Federal Government

One hundred sixteen federal government agencies now regulate business, of which 20 sprang up during the 1970s. They include the Environmental Protection Agency (EPA), the Consumer Product Safety Commission (CPSC), the Occupational Safety and Health Administration (OSHA), and the Department of Energy (DOE). The total number of employees in the 10 most important federal regulatory agencies increased from 17,200 in 1970 to 31,600 in 1980 and then declined by about 6.9% to 29,750 employees in 1984. While deregulation has reduced the need for managers of once regulated industries (banking, securities, airlines, telecommunications, trucking, railroads) to bargain with employees of governmental regulatory agencies, it certainly hasn't been eliminated. Recently some industries have even engaged in bargaining with regulatory agencies for the continuation of federal regulation. For instance, Whirlpool Corporation is fighting the Energy Secretary's efforts to let individual states, rather than the federal government, set mandatory efficiency standards for appliances. Whirlpool management maintains that uniform federal regulations would be less costly than a hodgepodge of state regulations.[24]

Cooptation strategy

The strategy of *cooptation* is used when an organization wants to influence certain powerful environmental components and formally brings their representatives into its managerial decision-making process.[25] The intent is to create a favorable impression, gain valuable knowledge and experience, expand networks, and obtain fair (if not preferential) treatment for the company. Thus cooptation also is one way for an organization to adapt to its environment. Individuals or groups that were previously outside the organization are now in a position to influence its stability, growth, and chances of survival.

Paradoxically, the process of cooptation can affect an organization's autonomy. The coopted individuals can influence and shape the organization's future course of action, which may reduce its freedom and flexibility (at least in the short run). For example, bankers are often given positions on the boards of directors of corporations after loaning them significant amounts of money. The bankers gain a voice and possibly even a veto in decisions concerning additional borrowing or other long-term obligations.

In recent years, Chrysler, Eastern Airlines, and a few other firms have placed union presidents on their corporate boards. This act is usually a concession to obtain more favorable provisions in existing union contracts or to reduce union wage and benefit demands during negotiation of a new contract.

Lobbying Strategy

The attempt to influence decisions of an administrative or legislative branch of government through persuasion and the provision of information is called *lobbying.* Congress and regulatory agencies, such as the Securities and Exchange Commission (SEC), the Federal Communications Commission (FCC), and the Interstate Commerce Commission (ICC), are the targets of continual lobbying efforts by organizations affected by their decisions. Business organizations whose stability, growth, and survival are influenced by the decisions of these groups typically use high-ranking officials in their organizations as lobbyists.

For example, every major airline and the three leading broadcast networks (ABC, CBS, and NBC) are represented by corporate vice-presidents in Washington, D.C. Only the largest corporations, such as the major airlines, broadcast networks, AT&T, and General Motors, can afford to lobby on behalf of their own interests. Therefore the most common form of lobbying is carried out by trade associations representing the interests of a group of individuals and organizations.[26] Approximately 4,000 national lobbying organizations are represented in Washington, D.C. An additional 75,000 state and local associations and organizations occasionally lobby Washington decisionmakers. Two of the largest associations representing business interests are the National Chamber of Commerce, with about 36,000 business and organizational members, and the National Association of Manufacturers, with about 16,000 member corporations.[27]

Lobbyists represent interest groups that attempt to direct policy and decision making. Large lobbying organizations influence political processes and popular opinion regarding national causes.

Source: Dennis Brock/Black Star.

Coalition strategy

A *coalition* is the combination of two or more organizations formed to obtain common goals and increase their influence over their environment.[28] Economic self-interest typically is the main reason that coalitions are formed, especially when they are created to influence government actions. Three broad categories of economic issues motivate the formation of coalitions: government policy (control of raw materials and taxes), foreign relations (control of foreign sales and investment in overseas plants), and labor relations (multiemployer bargaining associations, such as those commonly found in the construction industry).

Some of the uses for a coalition strategy are to

■ oppose or support legislation, the nomination of heads of regulatory agencies, and the regulations issued by such agencies;

■ promote particular products or services, such as oranges or railroads;

- construct facilities beyond the resources of any one firm, such as electric generating plants;
- represent the interests of particular groups, such as women, the elderly, minorities, and particular industries; or
- secure higher prices for goods or services for groups such as the Organization of Petroleum Exporting Countries (OPEC).

A coalition, like cooptation, both broadens and limits the power of management. It is broadening when it makes possible the attainment of objectives that would otherwise be unattainable by an individual firm. It is limiting when it requires a commitment to making certain joint decisions in the future. For example, members of the OPEC coalition bargain to reach some degree of agreement about the range of prices to be charged for different grades of oil and the amount of oil each country will supply to the market.

REPRESENTATION STRATEGY

Organizations sometimes encourage or require their members to form or join other groups or organizations. The primary purpose of this political strategy is to gain *representation* in order to serve the interests of the representative's organization or group. This is often a subtle and indirect strategy. School administrators, for example, often receive paid time off and the use of school resources to participate in voluntary community associations that might support the school system. Some of these organizations include the Chamber of Commerce, Elks, Kiwanis, Moose, Rotary, and United Way. Another form of representation, usually based on some legal requirement, involves the selection of representatives by specified groups to give them a voice in the organization's decisions.

Corporate boards of directors are legally required to represent the interests of stockholders. This is supposed to be done by having the boards review (or initiate) and approve all major policies and decisions. Recent disclosures about corporate price fixing, bribing, and polluting make it appear that the boards of some major corporations have not been overly conscientious in carrying out their responsibilities. Suggestions for correcting this situation include the following.[29]

- Clearly separate the board from operating management.
- Employ a full-time chairperson for the board.
- Have the chief operating executive report to the whole board, not just to the board chairperson.
- Pay active board members for their time and efforts.
- Require boards to take initiative and not just react to proposals or other matters brought to their attention by management.

Whether such proposals will result in better representation of stockholders remains to be seen.[30] However, the domination of boards of directors by members of management appears to be on the way out. Insider-dominated boards have been criticized by shareholders and regulators for representing the interests of management more than the interests of the stockholders. Changes in the membership of boards of directors will result directly from pressures and demands by a corporation's environmental components.[31]

Socialization strategy

Socialization is the attempt to indoctrinate people in beliefs or values consistent with those of an organization or the broader society. It is assumed that people who accept and support these basic values are less likely to be sympathetic toward positions that threaten the organization or the political system in which it operates.

The so-called American business creed stresses the idea that a decentralized, privately owned, free, and competitive system in which the price mechanism is the major regulatory or control system is desirable and should be continued; that governmental actions interfering with or threatening this system should be opposed and stopped. During the 1980 and 1984 presidential campaigns, Ronald Reagan frequently expressed his belief in this creed.

Organizational socialization refers to the formal or informal attempts to *mold* employees into having certain desired attitudes and ways of dealing with others and their jobs. Of course, socialization attempts by top management can be offset or reinforced by the expectations and pressures exerted by an employee's fellow workers or others. As described in Chapter 2, Hewlett-Packard and its H-P Way has a well-developed strategy of organizational socialization. This includes a set of videotapes shown to all new employees explaining the importance and expectation of becoming part of the H-P Way.

CULTURAL FORCES

Underlying and complementary to the competitive and political forces within a particular nation are various cultural forces. However, these cultural forces are often not as visible as competitive and political forces.

For our purposes, *culture* is defined as the *shared* characteristics and values that distinguish the members of one group of people from those of another.[32] A culture thus encompasses a group of people who share a common language, religion, level of technological development, and set of values.[33] We focus on *patterns of values* that are generally characteristic of certain nations. A *value* is a basic concept that has considerable importance and meaning to individuals and a society, and is relatively stable over time.[34] A *value system* is the sum of a person or group's values that normally fits into a pattern of relative importance and meaning. A value system usually consists of value concepts that are compatible and supportive of one another.

Importance of Values

Managers need to appreciate the significance of values and value systems, both their own and those of others. They are significant because they determine in large part how a manager

- views other people and groups, thus influencing interpersonal relationships;
- perceives situations and problems;
- goes about solving problems;
- determines what is and is not ethical behavior;
- leads and controls employees; and
- structures organizational tasks.[35]

Let us now consider four values that have considerable significance for managers within their own and in other countries.

Work-Related Value Framework

This value framework was developed by Geert Hofstede.[36] It is outlined here and expanded upon in Chapter 4. Hofstede's framework is based on a major research project undertaken while serving as a behavioral scientist at IBM. The project and related research involved 116,000 completed questionnaires concerning work-related value patterns of industrial employees in 50 countries and three regions at two different times. Important differences among the countries studied can be explained by four value dimensions: power distance, uncertainty avoidance, individualism (versus collectivism), and masculinity (versus femininity).[37] The following discussion of each dimension includes study results for four nations: Canada, France, Mexico, and the United States. In the study, rank 1 is the lowest and rank 50 is the highest.

Power-distance dimension

Power distance is the extent to which the people in a nation generally accept the unequal distribution of power among individuals and institutions. The less powerful as well as more powerful would need to support this unequal distribution for a nation to be characterized as high on the power-distance dimension. At the societal level, power distance relates to the fundamental issue of perceptions of human inequality and the translation of individual differences in strengths and talents into social differences in power and wealth.

Results for the four selected nations showed:

Nation	Rank
Canada	15
France	38
Mexico	46
United States	16

Relative to those from the 50 nations studied, Canadian and U.S. subjects scored on the low-to-moderate end of the power-distance dimension. One conclusion to be drawn is managers operating in these countries should be aware of the general belief in equal rights (including equal opportunity) and should not set themselves apart too much from subordinates by giving the appearance of being superior or unique.

Uncertainty-avoidance dimension

Uncertainty avoidance is the extent to which a people feels threatened by ambiguous and risky situations and tries to avoid or reduce these situations. At the societal level, uncertainty avoidance relates to fundamental concerns about life and death, the unavoidable uncertainty of the future, and the ways in which societies try to enable members to cope with uncertainty. Results for the four selected nations showed:

Nation	Rank
Canada	12
France	41
Mexico	33
United States	11

Canadian and U.S. subjects scored on the low end of the uncertainty-avoidance dimension. This suggests that Canadian and U.S. managers share a relatively high acceptance and tolerance of risk compared to those in many other nations, including France and Mexico. Canadian and U.S. managers are more likely to be receptive to changes in rules, open competition, and trying out new ideas.

Individualism dimension

Individualism refers to the extent to which society expects people to take care of themselves and their immediate family and that people believe they are masters of their own destiny. The opposite of individualism is *collectivism,* a tight social framework in which group members (relatives, clans, organizations) focus on the common welfare and feel an absolute loyalty to each other. At the societal level, the degree of individualism relates to the basic issues of individual rights, opportunities, and responsibilities versus social and political control of the individual. Results for the four selected nations showed:

Nation	Rank
Canada	46
France	40
Mexico	20
United States	50

The Canadian and U.S. subjects scored on the high end of the individualism dimension. This distribution fits the frequent characterization of these two countries as being more *I* societies than *we* societies. A strong sense of individualism is also necessary for the support and maintenance of a free and competitive (market-based) economic system. Individual merit and incentive pay systems are consistent with high individualism. Group-incentive pay and seniority systems are more likely to be found in high collectivism countries.

Masculinity dimension

Masculinity refers to the relative importance of assertiveness and acquisition of money and things, as well as the degree of *not* caring for the quality of life or other people. The opposite end of the masculinity dimension is *femininity.* At the societal level, the masculinity dimension addresses the degree of the division of a society by sex, and what represents appropriate roles for men and women. Results for the four selected nations showed:

Nation	Rank
Canada	28
France	17
Mexico	45
United States	36

The United States—and even more so the Mexican subjects—leaned toward the high masculinity end of this value dimension. However, the scores for Canada and the United States are probably lower than they would have been 30 years ago and are likely to drop even further in the future. This is because of the recent significant pressures to change and actual changes in such stereotypes as "men should behave assertively and women should be nurturing" or "sex roles in society should be clearly differentiated."

Implications of Work-Related Value Differences

The four work-related value dimensions—power distance, uncertainty avoidance, individualism, and masculinity—in combination provide one way of

One work-related value dimension—that of mascu-linity versus femininity—is changing rapidly as atti-tudes become less stereo-typical and as societal roles become less sexist.

Source: Owen Franken/Stock, Boston.

understanding and predicting the expectations of groups of employees in various nations. For example, individually based reward and incentive systems are often received with a positive response in Canada and the United States (high individualism) but negatively perceived in Japan (high collectivism). Let us consider another example. The management literature of Canada and the United States (low to moderate on power distance) often supports participative management, but the initiative for encouraging greater participation is sup-posed to come from management, not the workers. In contrast, France—with its relatively high power distance score—has little concern about the North American style of participative management. But the French do seem to have great concern with who has power and what they do with it.[38] Additional implications of this value framework and cultural forces will be woven into the next and later chapters.

CHAPTER SUMMARY

The chapter reinforced the argument for the develop-ment of managerial conceptual skills presented in Chap-ter 1; skills needed to perform effectively the liaison, monitor, and disturbance-handler roles. The *liaison role* involves the manager in dealings with people outside the organization in order to gather information from environmental components that can influence the or-ganization's success. This chapter stressed the need for identifying environmental trends and value systems, ex-amined some of the major environmental forces at work, and indicated how to assess such information. In the *monitor role*, managers scan the environment for information that may affect their organizations' performance. The chapter scans, as would a manager, some of the broad themes and characteristics of organizational environments that are likely to influence managerial decision making and practices at home and abroad. The *disturbance-handler* role requires managers to respond to situations beyond their immediate control. Disturbances may arise because managers ignore environmental forces until a crisis develops. Thus, our discussion of political strategies suggests useful means for anticipating, avoiding, reducing, or responding to environmental disturbances. These political strategies include bargaining, cooptation, lobbying, coalitions, representation, and socialization.

This chapter also provided basic information concerning three key environmental forces—competitive, political, and cultural—that need to be anticipated and addressed in the decision-making process.

The United States, Canada, and the other industrialized nations have literally become part of a worldwide economy that affects virtually every consumer, employee, and manager. The increasingly turbulent and worldwide economy, especially for the industrialized nations, can be characterized by seven megatrends: (1) industrial society to information society; (2) forced technology to high tech/high touch; (3) national economy to world economy; (4) short-term thinking to long-term thinking; (5) institutional help to self-help; (6) representative democracy to participatory democracy; and (7) primary reliance on hierarchies to primary reliance on networking. These megatrends impact five forces in the environment that directly affect the degree of competition in an industry and the businesses that operate in it. Each of these competitive forces—competitors, potential entrants, substitute products or services, customers, and suppliers—was examined.

MANAGER'S VOCABULARY

bargaining
capital requirements
coalition
collectivism
cooptation
culture
economies of scale

femininity
government regulation
individualism
lobbying
masculinity
megatrends
organizational socialization
political strategies
political system
power distance
product differentiation
representation
socialization
task environment
technology
turbulent environment
uncertainty avoidance
value
value system

REVIEW QUESTIONS

1. What megatrends are operating to fundamentally change advanced industrial societies?

2. What are the five basic competitive forces that need to be continuously monitored by managers of businesses?

3. Which political strategies can be used by managers in dealing with environmental forces?

4. What are the four value dimensions of the work-related value framework and how can they be used to characterize cultural differences and similarities?

DISCUSSION QUESTIONS

1. Should efforts to deregulate markets by government be increased or decreased? Explain.

2. How would you describe yourself in relation to the four value dimensions presented in the chapter?

3. Do you think that business groups—such as the Business Roundtable, the U.S. Chamber of Commerce, and the National Association of Manufacturers—should be allowed to lobby for their interests before Congress or administrative agencies? Explain.

4. What problems do you think women and minority college graduates will have in their first supervisory roles? Use the value framework presented to develop your assessment.

5. Do you think increases in the competitive forces on firms, especially over the past five years, are desirable? Explain.

MANAGEMENT INCIDENTS AND CASES—

Southern Realty Investors, Inc.

In the late 1940s a northern industrialist came to the shores of southeast Florida and recognized what he believed to be an area for future growth and investment in real estate. Subsequently, he formed Southern Realty Investors, Inc. (SRI). From wealth accumulated in his worldwide business interests, he purchased $700 million worth of Florida property. Through this massive land investment strategy, Southern Realty Investors, Inc., became the largest single property owner in the state.

Conflicts over growth

As the years passed the reputation of Florida as a retirement area flourished and the population of the state grew astronomically, especially along the Atlantic coast. The obvious result of the land rush was soaring property values. Such rapid growth caused a backlash against feared overbuilding by developers. In 1973, the residents of San Remo, gem of the gold coast, enacted a *growth cap* ordinance, which severely restricted the rights of property owners in the use of their land. As adopted, this law uses municipal zoning regulations to reduce the density (number of dwelling units per acre) allowed in the development of land. Fully implemented, the regulations would allow the city of San Remo to reach a maximum population of 105,000 persons.

The initiative for the growth cap grew out of a severe water shortage three years before, when water had to be rationed, that caused severe economic and personal hardships throughout the southern part of the state. Fears that such a catastrophe could happen more easily with uncontrolled growth led citizens groups to circulate petitions that forced the issue of the growth cap—first with the city council and ultimately on the ballot.

Opponents of the move to limit growth included land developers (including the most vocal opponent, Southern Realty Investors, Inc.), the Chamber of Commerce (representing local businesses), the building and construction trades, and other related groups. Their arguments were centered on the proposition that growth in a desirable region such as San Remo is inevitable. Orderly growth is desirable but an outright limit on growth within the city itself would have the effect of "building a wall" around San Remo. This in turn would force the overflow population into the surrounding county and result in exactly the kind of undesirable overcrowded sprawl the antigrowth forces sought to prevent. Southern Realty Investors pointed out in a well-financed publicity campaign that such actions by the community would result in economic and social strangulation.

Strategies and tactics used by SRI

Southern Realty Investors' land developments, in the opinion of most unbiased observers, are noted for low density and high property values. An outstanding example exists within the city limits of San Remo itself. The San Remo Yacht and Country Club features very low-density, single-family housing. The most prestigious section of town, it is the home of most of the community's social, political, and business leaders.

The company's officers acted as informal speakers for the progrowth, anticap forces. They were aided in their opposition by Jim Donner, a local attorney, an eloquent speaker and former minority leader in the Florida House of Representatives.

Current and former members of the city council received complimentary memberships in San Remo's internationally known resort. Some also were owners in SRI. In addition, the company's community activities and involvement in local affairs were well known, with the company supporting financially and in other ways several community charities and projects of various local organizations.

The situation in San Remo came to a dramatic head the night of the city council debate over putting the growth-cap question to a vote of the people. On one side with SRI was an impressive array of business, political, and legal talent. Arrayed against these forces was a coalition of the Audubon Society, local environmentalists and ecology buffs, citizens fearful of the disadvantages of higher density, and a large number of interested citizens and citizen groups.

Southern Realty Investors was careful, in the heated debate, to align itself not only with the interests of big business, but also to show that the small, individual landowner could be hurt most by adoption of the growth cap. The company spokesperson pointed out that if the cap were adopted the city would, in effect, be able to destroy the small investor's land value by refusing to permit the land to be used to its fullest extent.

Emotional arguments intimated that these landowners would not be permitted even to build a home for themselves on their small lots (if the 40,000-unit limit had already been reached). Supporters of the growth cap replied that this was sheer emotional fantasy, a smokescreen to hide profiteering by large landowners and developers; that their proposal would achieve the 40,000-unit ceiling through remedial zoning, so that at least one dwelling unit would be permitted on each standard building lot within the city, as then defined.

Polarization of the community

In that council meeting, and in the weeks before the referendum, the community became polarized, with each side accusing the other of political subterfuge; charges and countercharges went far beyond the actual issues under consideration. Southern Realty Investors spent thousands of dollars in an expensive publicity campaign, while citizen donations financed a strong (although more limited) procap effort. San Remo became the rallying point for environmentalists from across the country, who made personal appearances and gained much publicity for the "brave efforts of the citizens' groups." San Remo was billed nationwide as the test case, the forerunner for other efforts to restrict local growth.

The outcome

In the election the growth cap proposal was victorious, with 60 percent of the vote. The city council began actions to implement the cap, and SRI filed suit in Federal District Court to overturn the cap as unconstitutional, claiming it deprived the company and other individuals of their right to dispose of their land as they see fit.[39]

Questions

1. What value concepts seemed to be given high priority by the growth advocates and the nongrowth proponents?

2. What were the political strategies and tactics used by the managers of Southern Realty Investors? Do you think they used the best political strategies and tactics available, given the circumstances?

3. Do you feel that the passage of the growth-cap referendum excessively violates the rights of owners to the use of their property? Explain.

4. If Southern Realty Investors is not successful in its suit to overturn the law as unconstitutional, what should the managers of this firm do next?

REFERENCES

1. Adapted and modified from C. L. Brown, "Recasting the Bell System," *Columbia Journal of World Business,* Spring, 1983, pp. 5–7. *Also see* "Did It Make Sense to Break Up AT&T?" *Business Week,* December 3, 1984, pp. 86–100.

2. From P. F. Drucker, *Managing in Turbulent Times.* New York: Harper & Row, 1980, pp. 3, 153, 154.

3. J. E. McCann and J. Selsky, "Hyperturbulence and the Emergence of Type 5 Environments," *Academy of Management Review,* 1984, **9**:460–470; M. Magnet, "It's Shape Up or Shake Out in a Shook-Up World," *Fortune,* June 10, 1985, pp. 166–172.

4. J. Naisbitt, *Megatrends.* New York: Warner Books, 1982.

5. R. Duncan, "What Is the Right Organization Structure?" *Organizational Dynamics,* 1979, **7**:59–80.

6. W. R. Boulton, W. M. Lindsay, S. G. Franklin, and L. W. Rue, "Strategic Planning: Determining the Impact of Environmental Characteristics and Uncertainty," *Academy of Management Journal,* 1982, **25**:500–509; R. C. Schwab, G. R. Ungson, and W. B. Brown, "Redefining the Boundary Spanning Environment Relationship," *Journal of Management,* 1985, **11**:75–86; L. Fahey and V. K. Narayanan, *Environmental Analysis.* St. Paul, Minn.: West, 1986.

7. L. J. Bourgeois III, "Strategy and Environment: A Conceptual Integration," *Academy of Management Review,* 1980, **5**:25–39.

8. M. E. Porter, *Competitive Strategy: Techniques for Analyzing Industries and Competitors.* New York:

Free Press, 1980, p. 4. *Also see* M. E. Porter, *Competitive Advantage: Creating and Sustaining Superior Performance.* New York: Free Press, 1985.

9. B. D. Henderson, "The Anatomy of Competition," *Journal of Marketing,* Spring, 1983, pp. 7–11.

10. "Airlines In Turmoil," *Business Week,* October 10, 1983, pp. 98–101.

11. S. J. Tolchin and M. Tolchin, *Dismantling America: The Rush to Deregulate.* Boston: Houghton Mifflin, 1983.

12. "Deregulating America," *Business Week,* November 28, 1983, pp. 80–98.

13. C. F. Hitchcock, "A Flak Jacket for Deregulated Skies," *Wall Street Journal,* October 25, 1983, p. 15; K. Labich, "Fare Wars: Have the Big Airlines Learned to Win?" *Fortune,* October 29, 1984, pp. 24–28.

14. "If Anyone Won the Strike, Greyhound Did," *Business Week,* December 19, 1983, pp. 39–40.

15. E. M. Rogers, *Diffusion of Innovations,* 3rd ed. New York: Free Press, 1982, p. 12.

16. G. L. Parsons, "Information Technology: A New Competitive Weapon," *Sloan Management Review,* Fall 1983, pp. 3–13; J. F. Magee, "What Information Technology Has in Store for Managers," *Sloan Management Review,* Winter 1985, pp. 45–49.

17. L. Stiele, "Managers' Misconceptions about Technology," *Harvard Business Review,* November–December, 1983, pp. 133–140.

18. "Biotech Comes of Age," *Business Week,* January 23, 1984, pp. 84–94.

19. F. Allen and J. A. White, "MCI to Cut Its Long Distance Phone Rates To Keep Pace With AT&T's Proposed Cuts," *Wall Street Journal,* October 6, 1983, p. 14.

20. D. Ulrich and J. B. Barney, "Perspectives in Organizations: Resource Dependence, Efficiency, and Population," *Academy of Management Review,* 1984, 9:471–481.

21. "Dialing Dilemmas: How Telecom Managers Are Learning to Cope with the AT&T Divestiture," *Datamation,* January, 1984, pp. 118–124.

22. T. M. Jones, "An Integrating Framework for Research in Business and Society: A Step Toward the Elusive Paradigm? *Academy of Management Review,* 1983, 8:559–564.

23. A. K. Gupta and L. J. Lad, "Industry Self-Regulation: An Economic, Organizational, and Political Analysis," *Academy of Management Review,* 1983, 8:416–425; T. K. McCraw, "Business and Government: The Origins of the Adversary Relationship," *California Management Review,* Winter, 1984, pp. 33–52; G. A. Danke, "Regulation and the Sociopathic Firm," *Academy of Management Review,* 1985, 10:15–20.

24. J. S. Lublin and C. Conte, "Federal Deregulation Runs into a Backlash, Even from Business," *Wall Street Journal,* December 14, 1983, pp. 1, 8; R. A. Leone, "Examining Deregulation," *Harvard Business Review,* July–August, 1984, pp. 56–58.

25. P. Selznick, *TVA and the Grass Roots.* New York: Harper Torchbook, 1966, pp. 13–16.

26. J. C. Alpin and W. H. Hegarty, "Political Influence: Strategies Employed by Organizations to Impact Legislation in Business and Economic Matters," *Academy of Management Journal,* 1980, 23:438–450; B. D. Baysinger, G. D. Keim, and C. P. Zeithaml, "An Empirical Evaluation of the Potential for Including Shareholders in Corporate Constituency Programs," *Academy of Management Review,* 1985, 28:180–200.

27. O. Hall, *Cooperative Lobbying—The Power of Pressure.* Tucson: University of Arizona Press, 1969.

28. S. B. Bacharach and E. J. Lawler, *Power and Politics in Organizations.* San Francisco: Jossey-Bass, 1980.

29. C. Brown, *Putting the Corporate Board to Work.* New York: Macmillan, 1976; W. R. Boulton, "The Evolving Board: A Look at the Board's Changing Roles and Information Needs," *Academy of Management Review,* 1978, 3:827–836; "A Landmark Ruling That Puts Board Members in Peril," *Business Week,* March 18, 1985, pp. 56–57; M. C. Knapp, "The Increasing Risks and Responsibilities of the Bank Director's Role," *Business Horizons,* March–April, 1985, pp. 7–21.

30. A. E. Schwartz, "Shareholder Democracy: A Reality or Chimera?" *California Management Review,* Spring, 1983, pp. 53–67.

31. S. C. Vance, *Corporate Leadership: Boards, Directors and Strategy.* New York: McGraw-Hill, 1983.

32. G. Hofstede, "The Cultural Relativity of the Quality of Life Concept," *Academy of Management Review,* 1984, 9:389–398.

33. S. Ronen and O. Shenkar, "Clustering Countries on Attitudinal Dimensions: A Review and Synthesis," *Academy of Management Review,* July 1985, 10(1):435–454.

34. G. England, "Organizational Goals and Expected Behavior of American Managers," *Academy of Management Journal,* 1967, 10:107–117.

35. G. England, O. Dhingra, and N. Agarwal, "The Manager and the Man: A Cross-Cultural Study of Personal Values," *Organization and Administrative Sciences,* 1974, 5:1–97; C. S. McCoy, *Management of Values: The Ethical Difference in Corporate Policy and Performance.* Marshfield, Mass.: Pitman, 1985.

36. G. Hofstede, *Culture's Consequences: International Differences in Work-Related Values.* Beverly Hills, Calif., and London: Sage, 1980.

37. G. Hofstede, "National Cultures in Four Dimensions: A Research-Based Theory of Cultural Dimensions among Nations," *International Studies of Management and Organization,* 1983, 13:1–2, 46–74.

38. G. Hofstede, "Motivation, Leadership, and Organization: Do American Theories Apply Abroad?" *Organizational Dynamics,* Summer, 1980, pp. 42–63.

39. Adapted from the case developed by P. Preston (University of Texas at San Antonio) and T. Zimmer (Clemson University). Used with permission.

INTERNATIONAL FORCES ACTING ON ORGANIZATIONS

LEARNING OBJECTIVES

After studying this chapter, you should be able to:

- Explain six possible degrees of involvement and complexity for a firm engaged in international business.

- Contrast firms with international divisions from those that operate as multinational corporations.

- Identify the major international competitive trends facing many firms and industries throughout the world and especially in the United States.

- List the competitive objectives to be achieved by establishing production plants in host countries.

- Describe the four major factors that influence the degree of political risk associated with investments in host countries.

- Indicate how the political systems of countries, including their laws and regulations, influence market forces in international business.

- Explain how differences in cultural forces influence the general characteristics of American versus Japanese organizations.

CHAPTER OUTLINE

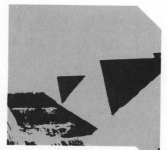

PREVIEW CASE

GE's Jones Comments on International Business

Among chief executive officers, few are admired as much as Reginald H. Jones, former chairman of General Electric Company—a huge multinational corporation. Shortly after his retirement, *Dun's Business Month* requested that he share his informed thoughts "on who is to blame and what can be done" about the alleged loss of competitiveness of American industry. Some of his perspectives are shared here.[1]

Government and business bear responsibility for the loss of competitiveness of U.S. industry in world markets, according to Jones. He believes that both government officials and business leaders have concentrated too single-mindedly on domestic matters and ignored the international arena. "We have not thought through what our policies are, and we take action on many domestic matters without any regard for the impact on international trade—whereas the governments of our international competitors don't make a move unless they are fairly certain that it won't have substantial deleterious effects on their trade competitiveness," he says.

In particular, Jones believes the government should attack nontariff barriers. (A *tariff* is a tax imposed by government on imported or, in some countries, exported goods. A nontariff barrier, for example, would be a government rule on the number of items of a particular product that can be imported.) "We are correct to continue our em-

phasis on free trade," he says. "But we have got to insist that it be free and fair trade—and there are too many instances in which there is discrimination against us through a host of nontariff barriers. We must knock these nontariff barriers out."

Jones thinks that the U.S. tax system also puts companies at a disadvantage when competing abroad. "In the European Economic Community, every major competitor has a value-added tax system that refunds taxes paid on products that are exported. Yet when we ship into that nation, we are met at the border with the requirement that we pay the VAT. We paid income taxes in the U.S. and with the VAT we get, in effect, a double whammy," he notes. (A *value added tax* (VAT) is similar to a sales tax, but applied on all intermediate transactions—such as manufacturer to

Courtesy of General Electric Company.

wholesaler to retailer—not just on sales to the final consumer.)[2]

Jones believes that, in an era of global competition, U.S. antitrust policies are outmoded. "We must alter our approach to recognize that competition is international," he maintains. "Can you conceive of any other government attempting to break up one of its most successful high-tech companies, such as an IBM? We used to argue about the need to break up General Motors, and yet today GM is fighting for its life. Why? International competition." Jones blames management itself for underestimating its foreign competitors, being too short-term oriented, and for getting sloppy about cost containment during the late 1970s. "We are much more humble today than we were. What has happened in Detroit has had a tremendous impact on American industry. There have been great object lessons taught to us in steel, autos, television, and many other industries that cannot be ignored."

Jones also believes that business schools must prepare managers better to meet international competition. American management has been sensitized to the need for a participative approach that involves the worker in trying to find answers to problems. Business-school curriculums are increasingly emphasizing organizational behavior, employee–management relationships, and the manager's production responsibilities. But, Jones says, "we have a way to go."

While the job of rebuilding America's competitive strength is huge, Jones is optimistic. He concludes: "I am pleased that in industry after industry now I see cost-containment activities that will stand us in good stead for years to come. Managements today are more concerned with productivity. We have many areas of high technology where the U.S. is either in the lead or is pushing very hard for leadership. I am very encouraged by these developments."

Jones's comments suggest some of the changing and complex international forces currently facing many industries and businesses. The international competitive and political forces encountered by the managers of U.S. business firms are especially evident.

The general purpose of this chapter is to examine the types of internationally related competitive, political, and cultural forces that must be understood and diagnosed for effective management—especially as inputs to the planning process. Figure 4.1 is an adaptation of Fig. 3.2. It suggests the potential diversity and complexity of a multinational corporation's external environment: Competitive, political, and cultural forces need to be dealt with within and among regions of the world, as well as countries within regions.

INTERNATIONAL INVOLVEMENT AND COMPLEXITY

The relative importance of international competitive, political, and cultural forces varies widely among industries and firms because of their different levels of direct international involvement. Figure 4.2 shows graphically the relative degree of complexity (vertical axis) facing management as a result of

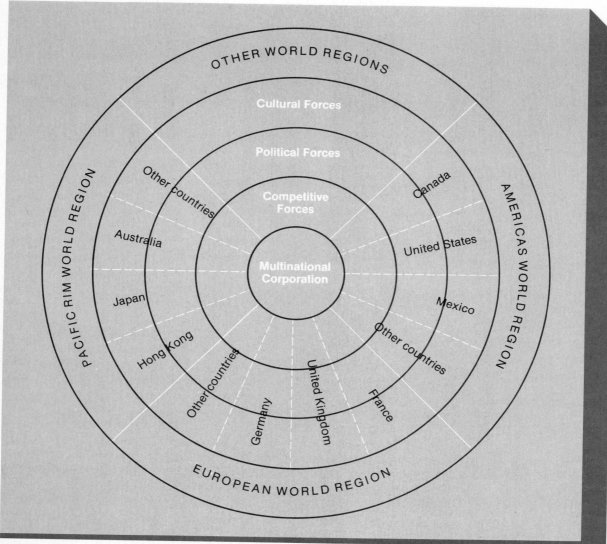

FIGURE 4.1

Environmental Forces and Multinational Corporations

each level of involvement (horizontal axis). It also shows how a firm's involvement might progress over time from the use of commission agents to that of a full-fledged multinational corporation. The pattern followed by a particular firm is likely to be strongly influenced by the types of competitive forces it faces, as well as the goals and strategy decided upon by the key decisionmakers in the firm.

Initial Stages of Involvement

In the initial stage of international involvement, a firm may seek out (as a result of an inquiry from outside the firm or a perceived opportunity to sell its products abroad) a **commission agent.** A commission agent is a middle person (or firm) who represents firms in foreign transactions. The agent normally receives some percentage of the value of the transactions (a commission) as compensation. As the firm's exports increase, management may hire an export manager to take over the tasks and services offered by the commission agent. An **export manager** is an employee of the firm and actively searches out foreign markets for the firm's product.[3] The export manager typically has a small staff, possibly only a secretary, and travels abroad extensively.

As export activities and sales continue to expand, the export manager's role may evolve into a full-fledged export department. An **export department** often (1) represents the interests of foreign customers to other departments and top management within the firm; (2) meets the increasing needs for

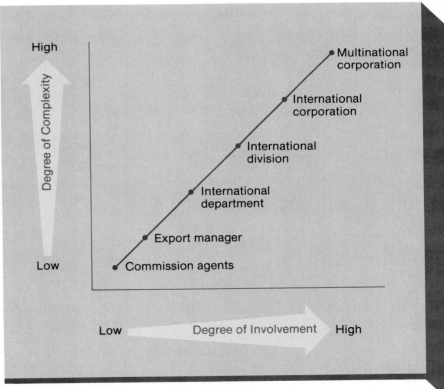

FIGURE 4.2
Degrees of Involvement and Complexity in International Business

services by foreign customers; (3) makes special arrangements for customs clearance and international shippings; (4) facilitates trade financing; and (5) arranges for the collection of accounts receivable from these customers.[4] An export department may also establish branches abroad to handle sales and promotional tasks.

International Division

The next level of commitment to doing business internationally occurs with the creation of an international division within the company. An *international division* continues to handle marketing- and financing-related tasks abroad, but adds manufacturing operations in one or more foreign countries. These manufacturing operations may range from assembly plants to full-scale manufacturing plants; no longer is all of the manufacturing done by domestic plants. Domestic operations may become even more separated from international operations. Within large international divisions, each country or world region might be further broken out as a separate subsidiary. For example, subsidiaries could be created for an Americas world region (Canada, Mexico, United States, Central and South America), a European world region (France, Germany, the United Kingdom, or other countries), and for a Pacific Rim world region (Australia, Japan, Hong Kong, or other countries)—depending on the size of markets and scope of manufacturing served by the international division.

International Corporations

Many large firms in the United States, Canada, and other countries operate with one international division. However, separate international divisions for each major product group may be established in corporations that have diverse product lines. These firms are called *international corporations.* An international corporation is one with significant business interests that cut across national boundaries, often focusing on the import or export of goods or services, with one or more production and marketing subsidiaries operating in other countries.

Multinational Corporations

Some major firms in the United States, Canada, Europe, Japan, and other countries operate as *multinational corporations*—the last major threshold in the degree of involvement and complexity associated with international business. A multinational corporation is one in which (1) all key managers try to take a worldwide view in assessing problems and opportunities; (2) there are one or more subsidiaries operating in at least several countries; and (3) there is a willingness by top management to consider a variety of locations in the world to make sales, obtain resources, and produce goods. There are two major categories of industries in which multinationals compete: multidomestic and global.[5] In a *multidomestic industry,* a company pursues separate strategies in each of its foreign markets and views competitive challenges independently from market to market. Each overseas subsidiary is somewhat independent. The multinational headquarters coordinates financial controls and marketing (including product-name) policies worldwide and may centralize some R&D and production. But strategy and operations are decentralized. Each subsidiary is a profit center and is expected to contribute earnings and growth in line with its market opportunity.[6] A number of successful U.S. companies are in multidomestic industries, including Procter & Gamble in household products, Honeywell in controls, Alcoa in aluminum, and General Foods in product-labeled foods.

A *global industry,* in contrast, pits one multinational's entire worldwide product and market positions against another's. Subsidiaries in various countries are highly interdependent in terms of strategy and operations. A subsidiary in one country may specialize in manufacturing only part of its product line, exchanging products with other subsidiaries in the system. However, profit targets vary, depending on the impact of a subsidiary's operations on the cost position or effectiveness of the worldwide system—or on the subsidiary's position relative to a key global competitor.

A global business competes worldwide against a small number of other multinationals in the world market. Major decisions are made by top management. However, various aspects of plant operations may be either decentralized or centralized, depending on the situation. The company seeks to respond to particular local market needs, while avoiding a lessening of efficiency in the global system.[7]

An increasing number of U.S. multinationals are in global industries. Among them, along with their principal competitors, are: Caterpillar and Komatsu in large construction equipment; Timex, Seiko, and Citizen in watches; and General Electric, Siemens, and Mitsubishi in heavy electrical equipment. The Caterpillar Tractor Company is one multinational corporation that has had to cope with a variety of domestic and international environmental forces.

IN PRACTICE
CATERPILLAR
TRACTOR COMPANY

Caterpillar Tractor Company (Cat) turned the manufacture and sale of large-scale construction equipment into a global business and achieved world leadership in that business. In recent years, it has faced a strong Japanese competitor, Komatsu, and other forces.[8]

Navy Seabees who left their Caterpillar equipment in other countries following World War II planted the seeds of globalization. The company

(continued)

established independent dealerships to service these fleets. The dealerships provided a highly profitable flow of revenue from spare parts, which paid for stocking new units. Caterpillar dealerships quickly became self-sustaining and to this day are larger and better financed than most of their competitors. As of 1984, the company had 213 dealerships around the world. This global distribution system is one of Cat's two major barriers against competition.

The company used its worldwide production scale to create its other barrier. Two-thirds of the total product cost of construction equipment is in heavy components: engines, axles, transmissions, and hydraulics. Manufacturing of this equipment requires heavy investment in plant and equipment and is highly sensitive to economies of scale. Caterpillar turned its network of dealerships in different countries into a cost advantage. This was accomplished by designing product lines that use identical components and by investing heavily in a few large-scale, state-of-the-art component manufacturing facilities to fill worldwide demand. (*State of the art* means that the process and/or product is among the most advanced and sophisticated in its field.)

The company supplemented its centralized production plants in the United States with assembly plants in each of its major markets (Europe, Japan, Brazil, Australia, and so on). These plants permitted Cat to add local product features and avoid high transportation costs. Most important, Cat became a direct participant in local economies. The company achieved lower costs without sacrificing local product flexibility and became a friend rather than a threat to local governments. No single world model was forced on the customer, yet no competitor could match Caterpillar's low production and distribution costs. However, with the substantial dropoff in sales and profits in 1982–1984, Caterpillar management started a major cost-cutting program. They set up plans to cut costs by 22% by 1986. This involved shutting down six plants. Also, their U.S. work force alone was cut from 60,000 in 1979 to 44,000 in 1984.

Caterpillar maintained its position against Komatsu and gained a greater share of the world market through 1981. The two companies increasingly dominate the market relative to their competitors, who compete only on a domestic or world-region basis.

Even with its well-thought-out strategies, Caterpillar has faced severe price competition, especially from the Japanese. In response, Cat management has cut prices. Much of the intense price competition has been a direct result of the increasing value of the U.S. dollar relative to other currencies. This makes it easier for Komatsu to compete on price in the United States and more difficult for Caterpillar to compete on price throughout the world. Stephen Zelnak Jr., president of Martin Marietta Corporation's construction aggregate division comments, "We told Caterpillar people (that) if they didn't get more competitive on price, we wouldn't be buying their machines in the same large proportion as we have in the past." Although Mr. Zelnak still believes that Caterpillar's large dealer network offers the best products, parts, and service, he adds: "If the Japanese reliability is reasonably good and the price is 15% to 25% less, then I can't ignore them."[9] In late 1984, Komatsu announced a plan to open its first assembly plant in the United States in 1985 or 1986, probably in the southeast. Komatsu's U.S. sales increased from about $130 million in 1983 to $300 million in 1984.

Again, the Caterpillar Tractor Company illustrates the intricate competitive and political issues facing one globally oriented multinational corporation. Let's now consider some general international competitive forces that have struck many firms, especially those headquartered in the United States.

COMPETITIVE FORCES

International Competitive Trends

The ratio of imports to exports (measured in dollars) gives a sense of the growing relative importance of international business and world economic interdependency. This ratio was about 6 percent for the United States in 1973. Today, it has risen to over 18 percent and is expected to continue to rise.[10] Many other countries, including Canada, Japan, Germany, and France, have much higher ratios.

The United States, Canada, and other countries are tied to world competition. The United States exports about 20 percent of its industrial production. The yield from two out of five acres of farm production, such as corn and wheat, is sold abroad. One out of six jobs in U.S. manufacturing comes from exports. About one-third of U.S. corporate profits comes from international trade and foreign investment. About 70 percent of U.S. manufactured goods must directly compete with goods manufactured abroad. More than half the nation's supplies of 24 important raw materials—from petroleum to cobalt—comes from foreign sources.[11]

In recent years, the number of U.S. industries facing intense foreign competition in their home markets has grown. Textiles and apparel were the first. These industries lobbied for governmental protection in the 1950s, when imports took only a small share of the market. They have now been joined by the steel, auto, footwear, and electronics industries, to name only a few, in seeking import protection from the government. The United States historically has had a commitment to an open international trading system. This commitment is now threatened by domestic political pressures to safeguard U.S. markets.[12]

Objectives for Establishing Production Plants in Host Countries

A number of multinational corporations based in the United States and other countries have established production plants in various parts of the world. Companies have a variety of objectives, mostly competitive, for establishing production plants outside their home country in a foreign, or *host*, country. Five of these competitive objectives are identified and discussed in the following paragraphs.[13]

In the past 20 years, American trade has become increasingly threatened by foreign competition, particularly in manufacturing industries. Early development of robots like these, which handle welding and the more dangerous tasks of manufacturing, gave the Japanese a cutting edge that has had a particularly strong impact on North American and European economies.

Source: Andrew Sacks/Black Star

To protect and maintain a market position abroad

Some firms have been forced to establish production facilities in foreign markets that once were served through exports, but later threatened with high tariffs or quotas. The three-year voluntary restraint on passenger car exports from Japan to the United States was renewed with some modification for 1984: The limit was increased by 170,000 to a total of 1,850,000 passenger cars.[14] These quotas motivated Nissan to open its first U.S. manufacturing plant with 3.4 million square feet of space in Smyrna, Tennessee, in 1983. The joint venture between Toyota and General Motors to make subcompacts at a mothballed GM plant in Fremont, California, was also motivated by quotas and international competition.[15] Toyota invested $150 million in the idle plant, which could provide as many as 3000 jobs at the plant and another 9000 jobs in related industries.[16] The plant opened in early 1985.

To eliminate or reduce high transportation costs

Transportation costs are particularly important if the per-unit transportation cost relative to the per-unit selling price is high, such as with Caterpillar. For example, the cost of shipping bottled or canned Coca-Cola from the

United States to Great Britain and other countries would exceed the cost of production. Consequently, the company has production plants throughout the world.

To beat competitors to a larger share of an expanding foreign market

A firm can meet a growing demand for its product quickly, and at the same time, create good relations with the host country's customers and government. Moreover, the first firm in may receive reduced taxes for several years, free land, low-interest loans, and a guarantee of minimum labor conflict as additional incentives from the country for the firm to locate there. The political leadership of a country may justify these incentives as a low price for stimulating its economic development and standard of living.

To achieve the economic benefits of vertical integration

A company in the oil exploration and drilling business may integrate *downstream* by acquiring or building an oil refinery or distribution system in a foreign country that has a market for refined products. Kuwait Oil Company, as mentioned earlier, has purchased chains of gasoline stations in Western Europe, which is a major market for Kuwait's crude oil. Conversely, a company that has strong distribution channels (such as gas stations) in a country but which needs a steady source of supply of gasoline at predictable prices may integrate *upstream* by starting or purchasing an oil-exploration and drilling company.

To keep customers by locating plants near them

This objective is closely related to the first objective. The U.S. government has put pressure on Nissan and Toyota, among other firms, to open plants in the United States rather than only to import parts for assembly. If the U.S. government imposed extremely heavy import taxes on Japanese-made cars, the prices of these cars probably would increase substantially. This could place the Japanese companies at a competitive disadvantage with U.S. automakers. In addition, some customers may decide not to purchase imported products if they feel that industries and jobs in their own country are being threatened by unfair competition from foreign firms.

Information Technology

A competitive force of growing importance for many nations and firms is the new forms of information technology. Nations have begun to see information as a new resource and information technology as a way to apply information to solve political, economic, and social problems. A report to the President of France on computerization argues that if France does not "respond effectively to the serious new challenges she faces, her internal tensions will deprive her of the ability to control her fate." Many Third-World leaders believe that the political and economic fortunes of their countries rest on the application of computer-communication technology.

Electronic technologies—communications and computers—provide industrializing nations with an opportunity to be competitive on a more secure if not equal footing. Brazil, for example, no longer accepts the traditional framework of international cooperation between countries of different levels of technological development. Its industrialization policy calls for the absorption of technology, not merely its transfer.[17]

IN PRACTICE
A Consumer Products Company

A regional vice-president for Europe, Africa, and the Middle East of a $1.2 billion division of a consumer-products company noted: "Until three years ago, my six European affiliates were very much self-contained operations. Today, however, I see these companies as an integrated set of manufacturing resources that supply different markets with products made wherever my cost advantage is greatest. Specialization and automation are key to lowering my manufacturing costs in each country. Some countries now have to concentrate on a limited number of components and/or products. Rarely can one country, or even one plant, manufacture a complete product. The plants in one country now must supply others located elsewhere."

This executive acknowledged, however, that the division's earlier management information system was designed for a time in which each regional office acted separately. The system was not coordinated across national boundaries. There was no central coordination of data for manufacturing operations, and the transfer of production information between plants was a slow, mostly manual, process. Thus it was difficult for managers in one country to find out what was going on elsewhere.[18]

POLITICAL FORCES

Political forces acting on a firm that engages in international business can be viewed as risks. The types and degrees of such risks must be diagnosed and addressed by the firm's managers.

Political Risks

An issue of increasing concern to all multinational corporations is the *political risk* associated with their present or proposed investments in host countries. Political risk is the probability that political events and actions—especially through current or possibly new governmental policies and laws—will negatively affect the long-term profitability of an investment.[19] One aerospace executive expressed his perceptions of increasing political risks for managers, both in the United States and abroad, in these pessimistic words: "Restrictions on the activities of multinational companies are being proposed and will, to a serious degree, be adopted in almost every country. These take the form of increased taxation, restrictions on the transfer of technology, antitrust regulations, restrictions on foreign ownership, restrictions on repatriation of capital and earnings, restrictions on imports and exports (both tariff and nontariff barriers), and restrictions on the employment of expatriate personnel, to mention some important ones."

Risk Factors

Various techniques have been developed for assessing political risks. These techniques may involve the assessment of several hundred political, economic, and sociocultural variables in a particular country. These variables can generally be classified under four major factors (as shown in Fig. 4.3): domestic

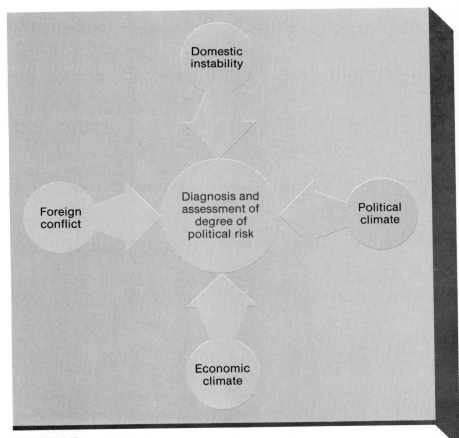

FIGURE 4.3
Factors Influencing the Degree of Political Risk for Investments

instability, foreign conflict, political climate, and economic climate, which can be defined as follows:[20]

Domestic instability refers to subversion, rebellion, and turmoil within a nation. Variables in this category are riots, purges, assassinations, guerrilla wars, and government crises.

Foreign conflict refers to the hostility that a nation shows toward other nations. This could range from the expulsion of diplomats to outright war.

Political climate refers to whether a government is likely to swing too far left or too far right politically. Typical variables in this category are size of the communist party, the number of socialist seats in the legislature, the role of the military in the political process, and the amount of control exercised by extreme right-wing groups.

Economic climate refers to market and financial controls associated with investments. Included in this category are a government's policies regarding regulatory and economic controls (including wage and price controls), as well as the government's ability to manage its own economic affairs (inflation and debt level controls).

The political issues that create conflicts for multinational corporations are both wide-ranging and numerous. For example, a study by Gladwin and Walter of five multinationals—Dow Chemical Company, Gulf Oil Company, International Telephone & Telegraph (ITT), Hoffman-LaRoche Company, and Rio Tinto-Zinc Company (RTZ)—identified 650 internationally and politically related conflicts with which their managements had to cope between 1969 and 1978.[21] Gulf experienced 100 of these conflicts, several of which are sufficient to provide a sense of the range of internationally related issues faced by multinationals. The brief description of each incident presents the opponents, issue, location, and year of resolution for Gulf.

**IN PRACTICE
Gulf Oil
Company**

Gulf versus Weathermen Underground: Bombing of the upper floors of Gulf's international headquarters in Pittsburgh caused $350,000 damage. It was followed the next day by a bomb threat because of "crimes" by Gulf, including financing of the Portuguese in the war in Angola (United States, 1974).

Gulf versus American Jewish Congress: A shareholder resolution called for disclosure of Gulf's practices in regard to the Arab boycott of Israel. Gulf negotiated an agreement with the AJC to provide such information, removing the need for a shareholder vote on the issue (United States, 1977).

Gulf versus Church Women United, and others: A shareholder resolution asked Gulf to establish a policy that would prohibit "contributions or grants to any political party or for any purpose that could be reasonably construed to be political to the Republic of Korea." The resolution was withdrawn when Gulf agreed to adopt such a policy (United States, 1978).

Gulf versus Bolivian Government: The Bolivian government demanded that Gulf disclose details of bribes allegedly paid in the 1960s to Bolivian officials or face cutoff of remaining payments from nationalization of Gulf's operations in 1969. After Gulf revealed $460,000 in such payments, the Bolivian government rejected the charges that its late President Barrientos received any money, jailed Gulf's representative in the country, called for an Organization of American States (OAS) condemnation of Gulf's "sordid activities," and convicted Gulf's chairman in absentia (Bolivia, 1975).

Gulf versus Westinghouse Electric Corporation: A damage suit was brought by Westinghouse against Gulf, RTZ, and 27 other uranium producers charging price fixing and market allocation by the international uranium cartel. Gulf countersued in 1978, charging Westinghouse with seeking to monopolize the uranium, nuclear fuel, and power reactor businesses. Gulf's chairman also charged Westinghouse with trying to hide its "greed or managerial mistakes" in the nuclear power business by raising a "uranium cartel smokescreen" (United States, 1977).[22]

A recent study of 72 countries ranked 63 percent of them in the high-political-risk category, based on a five-year forecast. High risk was defined as a probability of 25 percent or more that turmoil will affect international business during the forecast period. Among the countries included as high in political risk are Argentina, Bolivia, Iran, Israel, Pakistan, South Africa, and Zambia. Some of the low-risk countries include Austria, Ireland, Japan, Singapore, Sweden, the United States, and the Federal Republic of Germany (West Germany).[23]

Influencing Competitive Forces

In the Preview Case to this chapter, Reginald Jones commented that "[U.S.] Government and business bear responsibility for the loss of competitiveness of U.S. industry in world markets. We have not thought what our policies are, and we take action on many domestic matters without any regard for the impact on international trade." However, the U.S. government did attempt to influence international market forces and assist U.S. industry in meeting increasing international competition by enactment of the Export Trading Company Act in August 1982.

Export Trading Company Act of 1982[24]

The Export Trading Company Act of 1982 was passed after three years of debate and lobbying. The Act deals with two institutional barriers to developing export markets: (1) commercial banks had been prohibited from

INTERNATIONAL FOCUS

REUTERS—FROM PIGEONS TO SATELLITES

Without a doubt, the most well-known of all news and financial information services is Reuters. From its origins as the world's first financial communications company in 1850 (carrier pigeons took closing stock prices from Brussels to Aachen), Reuters has developed and expanded to become one of the world's largest (and probably most comprehensive) financial information networks.

Services are delivered with maximum speed and efficiency through sophisticated communication systems, which Reuters has developed and in some cases pioneered. The company's global communications constitute one of the most extensive private networks in the world.

As well as its general news services, Reuters provides in-depth financial and economic news. One of the most popular innovations in this area was the introduction of the Monitor system in 1973, which is updated continuously by dealers simply typing in new rates. The beauty of the system is that contributors are also subscribers. Initially, the service provided only foreign-exchange and money-market rates but, over the years, Reuters has added Euro-bonds, equities, and commodities rates, plus a mixed bag of information useful to the international shipping and oil markets.

The Reuters Monitor Dealing Service was introduced in 1981 and enables dealers to contact each other worldwide and conclude trades on a strictly confidential basis. It takes only a few seconds and is much faster than conventional telex or telephone. It is currently available for foreign-exchange and bullion deals. The company is also branching out into new product areas, including graphics, historical data, data-manipulation systems, and the Reuters Position Keeping service, which eradicates the need for hand-written dealing tickets so that dealers can keep track of their position. The company envisages substantial growth in these areas in the future. Competition comes from both the media news and financial information services, although no other single

Source: "From Pigeons to Satellites," *The Banker,* October 1984, p. 73.

developing close relations with their manufacturing clients; and (2) antitrust laws had been enforced without any consideration of their impact on international competitiveness.

One of the Act's major provisions permits commercial banks, with the approval of the Federal Reserve Board, to own equity in export trading companies through bank holding companies and similar means. This allows for a much closer link between banking services and trading activities. The Act also permits export trading companies to receive prior and specific exemption from antitrust litigation. This exemption applies to their exportation of competing lines of goods or services, as well as to joint exportation efforts with competing firms. Even if these firms were later found in violation of antitrust laws, the financial penalty is limited to a single-damage amount

company competes with Reuters in both markets. The main rivals in media news are the Associated Press and United Press International, and on the financial side, Dow Jones, ADP Comtrend, Commodity News Service, Quotron, Telekurs and Quick.

Telerate (or AP Dow Jones/Telerate outside North America) offers extensive financial information—U.S. credit markets, world currency markets, commodities and a broad mix of news services. Geographically, although Telerate covers 30 countries, it still tends to be heavily biased towards the United States. One area where Telerate has the edge over Reuters, however, is in U.S. government securities, without doubt the most important of the world's bond markets. The inclusion of such prices by Cantor Fitzgerald (one of the five principal brokers) has been a major driving force behind Telerate's growth in recent years.

ADP Comtrend, another market leader in the dissemination of electronic price and information services with special emphasis on commodities, has recently launched its TrendSetter system. The most significant design feature of the system is that by incorporating a continuous flow of price data on a powerful personal computer, there is now no need for expensive interfaces with other systems. ADP Comtrend hopes that TrendSetter will bridge the gap that exists between the personal computer and management's need to control real-time market data in tabular and graphic displays. Interfaces with a host computer and with ADP data bases are also possible.

Future methods of data transfer are likely to become less reliant upon telephone line networks especially as satellites become more easily available. At the moment, satellite technology is really used only in the U.S. due to regulatory restraints elsewhere, but it is hoped that this situation will ease in Europe.

rather than the customary and punitive triple damages. If they are found not guilty, they can automatically recover actual legal expenses.

The tone of the Act is to encourage the Federal Reserve Board to promote support of export trading companies. These trading companies are permitted to deal in imports and become involved in financing manufacturing activities at home and abroad. Congress would like to see American export trading companies develop the way Japanese general trading companies grew: as large multinational trading and investment firms. Export trading companies are encouraged to handle multiproduct lines. By taking title to the goods and services of their suppliers, export trading companies reduce the uncertainties and risks associated with foreign trade. This is especially important for small to medium-sized manufacturing firms. Like their Japanese competitors, American export trading companies are expected to serve as the entrepreneurial organizers of foreign trade.

In 1982, GE established an export trading firm to provide an entrepreneurial focus for its overseas trading activities and to expand its foreign trade beyond GE products and GE-related companies. Through 1984, about 90 percent of GE Trading's exports were the company's own products. But GE plans to grow into new areas and expects its trading company to become profitable in 1985. Sears, Roebuck and Company also formed its own export trading company to turn its worldwide purchasing networks into sales networks for handling American goods and services. Through 1984, its trading company was not profitable. By the end of 1984, the U.S. Department of Commerce (DoC) had issued certificates to 45 firms to operate as export trading companies.

Changing the Behavior of Managers

In 1975 and 1976, it was disclosed that some of the largest U.S. multinational corporations had paid millions of dollars in bribes to foreign politicians and government officials. One of the U.S. corporations receiving front-page attention for bribing foreign officials was Lockheed Aircraft Corporation. The resulting furor and conflicting positions taken suggest extreme differences in beliefs about what constitutes appropriate behavior by key decisionmakers who are involved in international business.

These differences resulted in much controversy and many conflicting pressures over the desirability and form of legislation to control the actions of multinational and international corporations concerning the payment of bribes and influence peddling abroad. This controversy was settled, at least temporarily, with the passage of the Foreign Corrupt Practices Act of 1977. The investigations of Lockheed and several other multinationals influenced the provisions written into the Act.

IN PRACTICE
Lockheed
Aircraft
Corporation

In September 1975, Daniel Haughton, then president of Lockheed Aircraft Corporation, in testimony before the Senate Foreign Affairs Subcommittee on Multinational Corporations, stated that his company paid more than $202 million in agents' commissions between 1970–1975. At least $22 million of these "commissions" were earmarked for bribes to foreign officials.

Commenting on the payments, Haughton stated, "Lockheed does not defend or condone the practice of payments to foreign officials. We only say that the practice exists, and that in many countries it appeared, as a matter of business judgment, necessary in order to compete against both U.S. and foreign competitors."

On October 21, 1975, Lockheed admitted in the Washington Federal District Court to making "under-the-table payments" to promote sales in 15 foreign countries including at least one major nation in Western Europe.

On February 4, 1976, Senator Frank Church, chairman of the Senate Subcommittee on Multinational Corporations, released 146 pages of Lockheed internal documents. There was a strong feeling among some Lockheed executives that the company was "being made to pay for the sins of all the multinationals." One member of the Board stated that Lockheed was being treated unfairly because "foreign payoffs are too common and old" a practice to get very excited about. Many of Lockheed's 58,000 employees became angry over what they felt was unfair treatment of their company for what was considered to be common practice for many major corporations.

On February 13, 1976, Haughton, now Lockheed's board chairman, and A. Carl Kotchian, board vice-chairman, resigned at a special meeting of the Lockheed board of directors. The two men, however, were retained as consultants and advisors for ten years at a "fair and generous amount although less than they were drawing."

On March 3, 1976, Lockheed announced that the firm's future international activities would be directed from the home office. According to a Lockheed spokesperson, "Lockheed International reported to the corporate organization, but it was a separate company. Now the international operations will come under the newly established vice-president for international marketing and will become a part of the corporate organization instead of being a separate company."[25]

Foreign Corrupt Practices Act of 1977

On December 20, 1977, President Carter signed into law the Foreign Corrupt Practices Act. This act makes it a crime for American corporations to offer or provide payments to officials of foreign governments for the purpose of obtaining or retaining business. The act established specific record-keeping requirements for publicly held corporations to make it difficult for managers to conceal political payments prohibited by the Act.[26] Violators of this law, both corporations and managers, face stiff penalties. A company may be fined up to $1 million. Any of its managers who directly participated in violations of the Act or had reason to know of such violations face up to five years in prison and/or $10,000 in fines.

The Act prohibits corporations from paying the fines imposed on their directors, managers, employees, or agents. The Act does not prohibit *grease* payments to employees of foreign governments whose duties are primarily ministerial or clerical. These generally are small payments—almost gratuities—that are used to get lower-level government employees to expedite required paperwork or forms. These payments are sometimes required to persuade such employees to perform their normal duties.[27]

Continuing controversy. Since its enactment, the Foreign Corrupt Practices Act has been subjected to much critical analysis.[28] Many practical arguments have been made in favor of its repeal. An Export Disincentives Task Force was created by President Carter in 1978 to recommend ways of improving U.S. exports. The task force claimed that economic losses resulted from the reduced ability of American corporations to do business abroad. It further claimed that political losses came from the creation of a holier-than-thou image in relation to other countries. Congress is now considering changes in the Act, some of which are likely to be enacted.

A Louis Harris survey of high-level executives of 1200 large U.S. corporations suggests attitudes that favor certain changes in the law:

- 68 percent of the executives favor reducing the detailed record-keeping requirements on all international business transactions.

- 65 percent of the executives favor allowing payments to foreign officials when they speed or unblock routine government actions (grease payments, which are not prohibited by the law).

- 64 percent of the executives favor making the law more specific as to who in a foreign country can legally receive grease payments.

- 46 percent of the executives favor and 44 percent oppose eliminating the criminal penalties for violating the accounting sections of the law.

- 42 percent of the executives favor and 46 percent oppose easing U.S. executives' accountability when they delegate to an agent the authority to make payments.

Multiple Political Strategies

All of the political strategies identified in Chapter 3 for coping with powerful environmental components are used by firms operating in other countries. As you may recall, these political strategies include bargaining, lobbying, coalitions, representation, socialization, and cooptation.[29] The discussions and negotiations leading to the passage of the Foreign Corrupt Practices Act of 1977 were accompanied by extensive use of the bargaining and lobbying strategies by many corporations. This legislation and the controversy surrounding it are examples of how businesses must deal with conflicting pressures from domestic and foreign political environments. More recently, many U.S. industries and firms have been lobbying for higher tariffs and quotas on imports from foreign competitors. For example, in 1984, U.S. Steel filed unfair trade complaints with the Department of Commerce and the (U.S.) International Trade Commission against steelmakers in Spain, South Africa, Argentina, Finland, and Austria. U.S. Steel claimed that these steelmakers were *dumping* steel in the United States at 10–95 percent below fair market cost. U.S. Steel wanted the federal government to impose duties on the products to offset these lower prices. The entire steel industry lobbied Congress and the administration in 1984 to pass legislation imposing a five-year, 15-percent quota of the domestic steel market on foreign producers. Foreign steel accounted for about 21 percent of the U.S. market in 1983.[30] In early 1985, the administration imposed some quotas—but not all that the industry had asked for—on foreign steel.

CULTURAL FORCES

Underlying the day-to-day competitive and political forces to be found within and among nations in international business are various cultural forces. Cultures differ in many respects. Four of these differences that have direct implications for international business are: view of change, time orientation, language, and value systems.[31]

View of Change

Cultures may differ substantially in their view toward change. Non–Western cultures often see change as something that occurs naturally. It is part of the evolution of human beings and the universe as defined by a Supreme Being. There tends to be a passive or reactive view of social change in such societies. In contrast, Western cultures tend to take a more proactive view of change. The assumption is that change can be shaped and controlled by people to achieve goals. Western managers who are assigned to non–Western countries by their multinationals often run into difficulty when trying to introduce innovations in the work place because of the passive or reactive view of change.

Time Orientation

Western cultures—especially in the United States and Canada—perceive time as an extremely scarce resource. This is illustrated by phrases like *time is money* and *time is the enemy*. The popularity of several books written about time management represents an almost frantic concern with how managers use their time. The need to establish time deadlines for work to be done and to stick to them is a basic assumption in Western-style management. In contrast, Eastern cultures view time in a more relaxed fashion, seeing it as an unlimited and unending resource. For a Hindu, time does not begin at birth or end at death. Belief in reincarnation gives life a nontemporal dimension and hence time is perceived as an inexhaustible resource. This attitude toward time makes people in Eastern cultures quite casual about keeping appointments and meeting deadlines—an indifference that makes many Americans who deal with them anxious and frustrated.

Language Differences

Language serves to bind as well as to separate cultures. Fluency in another language can give an international manager a real competitive edge in understanding and gaining the acceptance of people from the host culture. The ability to speak a language correctly is not enough. A manager also needs the competency to recognize the nuances of nonverbal gestures, idiomatic phrases and sayings, especially when negotiating.[32] The story is told of some U.S.

executives who were trying to bargain with some Japanese executives. The American head negotiator made a proposal. The head Japanese negotiator was silent. This meant he was considering the offer. But the American took this to mean that the offer wasn't good enough. So the American raised the offer! Again, the Japanese considered in silence, and again the discomfort of the silence led the American negotiator to raise the offer! Finally, the American reached his limit, and an agreement was struck. The Japanese head negotiator had obtained several concessions simply because the American negotiator had misread the meaning of silence to the Japanese.

Value Systems

In Chapter 3, we discussed how value systems can differ among individuals and countries. We used four value dimensions (power distance, uncertainty avoidance, individualism, and masculinity) to illustrate their effect on management. Given the continuing interest in and concern over the competitive challenge by Japanese firms and competitive barriers to Japanese markets,[33] let us compare Japan and the United States in terms of those four value dimensions as well as others introduced in this section.[34] The management implications of these comparisons will then be developed.

U.S. and Japanese Societies

Of the 50 countries studied, Japan, with a rank of 21, had a somewhat higher power-distance ranking than the United States, with a rank of 16. In contrast, Japan had a very high uncertainty-avoidance ranking of 46, whereas the United States had a relatively low ranking of 11. Japan and the United States also differed substantially in terms of individualism. The United States had the highest individualism score, whereas Japan scored more toward collectivism. Japan had the highest masculinity score; the United States had a score on the masculinity end of the masculinity–femininity continuum, but not nearly as high as that of Japan. Overall, differences in human-resource management in Japan relative to that in the United States tend to be reasonably consistent with these differences in values.[35] An especially important value difference relates to individualism versus collectivism.

Relative to that of the United States, the societal value system in Japan is less diverse. Severe conflicts caused by underlying differences in values occur less often in Japan than in the United States. The overriding common value in Japanese society has been identified as collectivism.[36] In contrast, the concept of individualism is highly valued by Americans.

Collectivism means that people identify strongly with and are known by the groups to which they belong, from the family all the way to the total society. It emphasizes group goals and a dependency on others. The individual is governed by the norms (rules) of each group. Groups are not thought of as being made up of individual people. Rather, the group exists first and absorbs the person into it. The Japanese form of collectivism leads to group cohesion.

The short-term sacrifice or denial of the individual's wants for the benefit of the group is likely to exist. Japan's high levels of achievement are group-oriented. In contrast, achievement in the United States is relatively individualistic.[37]

James Hodgson, a former U.S. ambassador to Japan, explains the basic differences between U.S. and Japanese societies as follows:

> American society is first and foremost underpinned by that venerable Judeo-Christian objective of individual justice. The Japanese, however, spurn individual justice as a priority goal. Instead they seek something in many ways the opposite; they seek **group harmony.** We American justice-seekers speak proudly of our **rights.** The harmony-minded Japanese stress not rights but **relations.** They reject our emphasis on individual rights as being divisive and disruptive.
>
> The distinction that emerges from all this may be capsulized simply. In American life the individual strives to **stand out.** The Japanese citizen, however, seeks to **fit in.** And fit in he does—into his family, his schools, his company, his union, his nation. Japan is a nation where the parts fit.
>
> We Americans make our national policy decisions and settle our many differences largely through adversary proceedings—we compete, we sue, and we vote. In Japan "adversarism" is **out.** Consensus is **in,** and it has been for centuries. The Japanese do not consider 51 percent a "majority," at least not a workable majority.[38]

U.S. and Japanese organizations

The fundamental differences in broader societal values are evident in some of the differences between U.S. and Japanese organizations. Does this mean that U.S. managers cannot transfer to their organization any of the ideas that have worked so well in Japanese management? Not at all. In fact some of these management processes and practices have been successfully adapted to U.S. operations.[39]

In identifying differences between U.S. and Japanese organizations and management practices, you need to recognize that we are painting a broad picture. The differences among U.S. firms and managers are much greater than the differences you are likely to find among Japanese firms and their managers. This is because the values and philosophies of managers in the United States are more diverse than those in Japan.

Table 4.1 compares and summarizes nine basic characteristics of U.S. and Japanese organizations; characteristics that are strongly influenced by the contrasting values of the two nations. The theme of individualism in the United States versus collectivism in Japan is apparent in the nine dimensions in Table 4.1. For many Japanese, the company is not only a place of work, but also a sharing and caring group. It is a place where someone is treated like a member of a family. Japanese employees are often proud of their company's success and frequently identify themselves with their company: an employee becomes Mr. Yamada of Sony, Mr. Tanaka of Toyota, Ms. Ogawa of Honda, and so on.[40]

TABLE 4.1 ■ CHARACTERISTICS OF MANY U.S. AND JAPANESE ORGANIZATIONS

DIMENSION	MANY (NOT ALL) U.S. ORGANIZATIONS	MANY (NOT ALL) JAPANESE ORGANIZATIONS
Employment	On average, short term, but varies widely; unstable and uncertain	Long term (lifetime in larger organizations); relatively secure and stable
Attitude toward work	Individual responsibilities	Collective responsibilities, group loyalty, duty-oriented
Decision making	Individual-oriented; relative top–down emphasis	Consensus and group oriented; bottom–up emphasis
Relationship with employees	Depersonalized; emphasis on formal contracts; employee resents organizational intrusion into personal affairs	Personalized; employee treated as a family member; paternalism, lifelong employment; employee expects organization to show concern for personal affairs
Evaluation and promotion	Rapid	Slow
Salary	Merit pay based on individual contribution	Heavy emphasis on seniority early in career; subtle shifts to merit pay later in career
Controls	Formal rules and regulations	Informal rules and regulations
Competition	Relatively free and open among individuals	Very low among individuals within groups; very high among groups, such as with other organizations
Careers	Specialized career paths	Nonspecialized career paths

Source: Adapted from W. G. Ouchi and A. M. Jaeger, "Type Z Organization: Stability in the Midst of Mobility." *Academy of Management Review,* 1978, 3:305–314. Used with permission.

The Nenko system

The characteristics of Japanese organizations fit into a general pattern known as the ***Nenko system,*** which provides the basis for the form of management commonly used in large-scale Japanese organizations. Its characteristics are summarized in Table 4.1. The Nenko system is a natural outgrowth of the broader Japanese culture and economy.[41] It cannot be transferred on a one-to-one basis to organizations in other cultural and economic environments, such as the United States with its relatively high emphasis on individualism.[42]

Employment security. The Nenko system stresses lifelong employment with a particular firm. After completing his or her formal education, the individual joins an organization and is expected to remain with it until retirement. This normally occurs at about 55 years of age. Of course, the obligation is mutual. The employer is not supposed to fire or lay off an employee, except in extreme circumstances.

In recent years, there has been some loosening of this pattern of mutual lifelong commitment. Some employers have successfully raided (hired away from) other firms to obtain highly skilled employees. Large employers also use a higher percentage of temporary employees, especially women and retired employees, who can be laid off.

Emphasis on seniority. The amount of compensation and opportunities for promotion are heavily based on *seniority,* that is, the length of an employee's service. Many employees believe that competence (in a job) increases automatically with seniority. Many managers are compensated almost entirely on the basis of seniority. After a manager has reached about 45 years of age, more weight is given to performance than seniority in salary increases.

The possible implications of these contrasts were noted by Morita Akio, president of the Sony Corporation, who observed:

> Fortunately Japan has a lifetime employment system, which encourages the long-range view even among lower and middle management levels. For example, a member of our company may be stationed in some far-off land, struggling to learn in a country with entirely different customs and characteristics. But he realizes that with the knowledge he has gained in five years or so, he might become chief of the department in our head office that deals with this area, and that in ten years he may become director in charge of our international operations, and later have the chance of becoming a top executive of our company. He, therefore, is keenly interested in how strong the company will be in five or ten years from now, at the same time that he gives his attention to the business at hand. He is thus not only working constantly to achieve today's objectives but also paying close attention to what should be accumulated over the years ahead.[43]

Group loyalty. There is an intense sense of group loyalty and shared obligations under the Nenko system. People tend to think of themselves in terms of the groups to which they belong. This results in a strong feeling of duty and loyalty to the group. Performance standards for determining promotability (for people who meet the seniority test) give heavy weight to criteria such as flexibility, group support, and company loyalty. Japanese managers see their companies and their employees as an extension of their families. Long-term commitments by managers and employees to their organizations also encourage the long-term training and development of employees.

Group decision making. Extensive use is made of group practices that lead to group consensus. This consensus is aimed at *defining the questions* needing attention rather than at deciding what should be done. This process of group decision making is much more time consuming than letting one person make a decision and tell the group. However, implementation tends to be quicker. People are more familiar with the reasons for doing something and the merits of doing it.

In Japanese organizations ideas often flow up from the bottom, rather than just down from the top. Anyone with a stake in a major problem or decision is consulted. A consensus is almost always reached by those involved before a decision is implemented. This occurs even though the seniority system is strong. This means that younger employees are not cut out of the decision-making process simply because they don't have as much seniority as older workers.

Notable exceptions.   There are notable exceptions to the Nenko system in Japanese society. Highly capable and assertive individuals *do* leave their firms and start businesses of their own or join smaller organizations. Firms started by individualistic entrepreneurs include Honda Motor, Sony, and Matsushita, among others. Moreover, the numerous small-scale Japanese enterprises (300 or fewer employees) cannot afford to and do not offer fringe benefits as extensive as those of the giants. They also offer less job security because these firms are less secure in their markets. There is also some evidence that the younger generation of Japanese is not quite as devoted to long hours of hard work. As *Fortune* magazine suggests: "They're not trying to reform the world. Their greatest expression of rebellion is a simple and apparently healthy determination to get a little fun out of life."[44]

Theory Z

In 1981, William Ouchi put in book form his observations of some U.S. firms that seem to represent a mixture of the characteristics of many U.S. and Japanese firms. Table 4.2 highlights these characteristics, for which Ouchi coined the term *Theory Z* to describe such an approach to management.[45]

TABLE 4.2 ■ THEORY-Z CHARACTERISTICS

- Commitment to long-term employment
- Emphasis on collective decision making
- Expectation of individual responsibility
- Relatively slow evaluation and promotion
- Trust as a cornerstone in all relationships among managerial and nonmanagerial personnel
- Creation of a sense of intimacy, involvement, cooperation, and closeness within the organization—like a family
- Maintenance of flat hierarchies (few levels) and emphasis on work groups to get jobs done
- Use of implicit, informal controls with formalized measures of performance

Source: Adapted from W. Ouchi, *Theory Z: How American Business Can Meet the Japanese Challenge.* Reading, Mass.: Addison-Wesley, 1981.

Theory Z is a theory of how employees *should* be managed to maintain or improve the productivity and effectiveness of organizations, especially of large industrial organizations operating within industrial societies.[46] Hewlett-Packard—described in Chapter 2 as an example of a firm with the behavioral viewpoint of management—is considered by Ouchi to be a Theory-Z organization. The preamble to the statement of corporate objectives for Hewlett-Packard—written by David Packard, chairman of the board, and William Hewlett, then president and chief executive officer and now vice-chairman of the board—provides additional insight into how the firm applies Theory-Z principles.

IN PRACTICE
THEORY Z AT HEWLETT-PACKARD

The achievements of an organization are the result of the combined efforts of each individual in the organization working toward common objectives. These objectives should be realistic, should be clearly understood by everyone in the organization, and should reflect the organization's basic character and personality. If the organization is to fulfill its objectives, it should strive to meet certain other fundamental requirements:

FIRST, the most capable people available should be selected for each assignment within the organization. Moreover, these people should have the opportunity—through continuing programs of training and education—to upgrade their skills and capabilities. This is especially important in a technical business where the rate of progress is rapid. Techniques that are good today will be outdated in the future, and people throughout the organization should continually be looking for new and better ways to do their work.

SECOND, enthusiasm should exist at all levels. People in important management positions should not only be enthusiastic themselves, they should be selected for their ability to engender enthusiasm among their associates. There can be no place, especially among the people charged with management responsibility, for half-hearted interest or half-hearted effort.

THIRD, even though an organization is made up of people fully meeting the first two requirements, all levels should work in unison toward common objectives and avoid working at cross purposes if the ultimate in efficiency and achievement is to be obtained.

It has been our policy at Hewlett-Packard not to have a tight military-type organization, but rather, to have overall objectives which are clearly stated and agreed to, and to give people the freedom to work toward those goals in ways they determine best for their own areas of responsibility.

Our Hewlett-Packard objectives were initially published in 1957. Since then they have been modified from time to time, reflecting the changing nature of our business and social environment. This booklet represents the latest updating of our objectives. We hope you find them informative and useful.

/s/ *David Packard*
    Chairman of the Board

/s/ *William Hewlett*
    President and Chief Executive Officer[47]

Do not assume that a Theory-Z firm like Hewlett-Packard won't exercise top–down decision-making authority. For example, on July 16, 1984, H-P announced a sweeping structural reorganization designed to accelerate its transition from a company run by engineers for engineers to one with the marketing clout needed to reach a wider audience and compete with an increasingly aggressive IBM. H-P's overhaul unifies the previously fragmented marketing efforts of its two biggest product lines: computers and instruments. Its new structure, engineered by President and Chief Executive Officer John A. Young, regroups H-P's dozens of product divisions into sectors that are focused on markets rather than on product lines. Two major sectors will now sell computers; one will concentrate on business customers, while the second will market computers and instruments to scientific and manufacturing customers. H-P is merging its two biggest product lines because industrial customers increasingly are buying computers linked with instruments for testing and process control.[48]

CHAPTER SUMMARY

When an industry or business enters the international arena, it is exposed to new and complex competitive, political, and cultural forces. The degree of complexity increases with the degree of involvement, which can range from a firm's use of a commission agent to becoming a multinational corporation.

International competition is intense, particularly in the steel, auto, electronics, and textile and apparel industries. A major competitive strategy is to build and operate production plants in host countries in order to maintain market positions, minimize transportation costs, beat competitors to a new or an expanding market, benefit from vertical integration, and keep customers. Other strategies involve appeals to governments for protection and incentives.

This chapter focused on topics that relate primarily to the *liaison* and *monitor* managerial roles. Liaison must be established and maintained with domestic and foreign governments, as well as customers at home and abroad. Because of significant political and cultural differences, liaison in international business operations is much more difficult. For example, the explanation of Japanese values and patterns of management should increase your sensitivity in relating to people in countries with different value systems.

In playing the monitor role, managers involved in international business must be aware of developments in other countries and know what to look for when doing business abroad. For example, the entire discussion of political system influences should increase your awareness of the monitoring skills needed in international business.

MANAGER'S VOCABULARY

commission agent
domestic instability
economic climate
export department
export manager
foreign conflict
global industry
international corporation
international division
multidomestic industry
multinational corporation
Nenko system
political climate
political risk
tariff
Theory Z
value added tax

REVIEW QUESTIONS

1. What are the six possible levels of involvement and complexity in international business for a firm?

2. What international competitive trends face many industries and firms?

3. What competitive objectives might be achieved by establishing production plants in host countries?

4. What are the four major factors that determine the degree of political risk associated with investments in host countries?

5. What are some ways by which the political system can influence market forces in international business?

6. What characteristics differentiate many Japanese organizations and management from many U.S. organizations and their management?

DISCUSSION QUESTIONS

1. Should managers in another country try to adopt more of the characteristics identified for Japanese organizations in Table 4.1? Explain.

2. Should the Foreign Corrupt Practices Act of 1977 be eliminated or changed? Explain.

3. Would you like to work under the Nenko system? Explain.

4. Was Lockheed Aircraft Corporation wrong in giving bribes to secure orders from other countries? Explain.

5. What do you see as the major political risks for a foreign multinational firm considering the establishment of a subsidiary in a host country?

MANAGEMENT INCIDENTS AND CASES

All Shave in Saudi Arabia

Mike Lacey lay on his bed and watched as the fan went around. He felt whipped and didn't really know what to do next. All week he had been trying to influence Mustafa Almin and he had had no more effect than the fan was having on the heat of Riyadh.

Three years ago the All Shave Company, of which Mike was Middle Eastern Manager, had been very successful exporting razors and blades to Saudi Arabia. Then, in the face of possible import restrictions, the company had turned over its business to a new company financed by the Almin family. The family was an impressive collection of leading Saudi industrialists who had built a fortune on the production of steel products like picks and shovels and were then interested in expanding to new fields. All Shave received a minority interest in the new business in return for its trade name and technical aid.

The contract with the Almin family had also specified that they would "actively promote All Shave products." Mike thought that it was clearly understood that this meant continuing the aggressive promotion which had been used in Saudi to build the company's sales in the sixties from nothing to a high level. Under Almin management, however, All Shave sales had dropped steadily. It was soon evident that the Almins were not pushing sales, and in visits and correspondence, the company applied increasing pressure for more activity.

When nothing happened, Mike finally decided he would go to Saudi and stay until he could find a way to get the Almins moving. That was over six weeks ago. He had spent the first month in the field. He found All Shave products were being sold from Almin warehouses with virtually no sales effort and that promotion was limited to a few newspaper advertisements and a scattering of posters distributed by the company's regular salesmen. No additional salesmen had been added for All Shave accounts. The selling activity fell far short of All Shave's former program and that of its leading competitor. Mike then worked up a detailed program designed to re-establish All Shave's market position.

For the past week he had been trying to convince Mustafa Almin, the sixty year old head of the family, that the program should be adopted. But he had argued in vain. Mike had pointed to the low sales volume and to the Almins' limited program which he asserted did not meet the agreement. He had supported his proposals in the greatest detail, arguing particularly that All Shave's previous success and the present results achieved by their competition proved that strong promotion was worthwhile.

Mustafa Almin had expressed appreciation for Mike's interest and efforts but had agreed to nothing. He explained that a sales drop was inevitable with the change to the Saudi manufacturer. Though sales were lower, the company was making a reasonable profit. He said that to fulfill the contract terms he had undertaken newspaper advertising even though he did not believe in it and its blatant character reflected on the prestige of the Almin family name.

He believed that a good product was its own best advertisement and on that basis the Almin family had built a great business. He also observed that the closest competitor sold a higher quality blade than All Shave and it was quite probable that this, rather than the promotion, accounted for their success. In any case, several British concerns in related fields did very little advertising and, since they had been in India for many years, Mr. Almin felt their approach to the market was probably sounder.

Mike found it hard to meet these arguments. He was sure he was right and equally sure that Mr. Almin was a very competent businessman, who should be able to see the logic of his proposal. He had great respect and liking for Mr. Almin, and he believed that once he grasped the value of promotion, he would do great things for All Shave in Saudi Arabia.

But how could he convince him?

Mustafa Almin settled himself to relax before the evening meal and reflected for a moment on the events of the past week. He had spent a great deal of time with the boy from the United States. He was a good boy, full of energy and ideas. He wished he could do something to help him. He drove so hard, and for what? This whole arrangement with the All Shave Company had turned out rather differently from what the Almins had expected. The product was good and, left to themselves, his family could develop it into a good business, as they had with the rest of their operations.

But, they were not left to themselves. Instead, there had been constant pushing and arguing. These people from the United States never seemed to be satisfied with anything. Now they sent out this young man who scarcely knew Saudi to tell the Almins how to run their business. It was not pleasant at all. He hoped the young man would give up soon.[49]

Questions

1. What should Mike Lacey do?
2. What should the All Shave Company do?
3. What alternative strategies might All Shave have used in doing business in Saudi Arabia?

REFERENCES

1. Adapted with permission from "How to Hone the U.S. Competitive Edge," *Dun's Business Month,* July 1983, pp. 38–42. *Also see* Committee for Economic Development, *Strategy for U.S. Industrial Competitiveness.* New York: Committee for Economic Development, 1984; F. C. Carlucci, "Global Economic Order—Facing the Challenge," *Sloan Management Review,* Spring 1985, pp. 65–68; B. R. Scott and G. C. Lodge (Eds.), *U.S. Competitiveness in the World Economy.* Boston: Harvard Business School Press, 1985.

2. D. P. Rutenberg, *Multinational Management.* Boston: Little, Brown, 1982, p. 89.

3. A. Phatak, *International Dimensions of Management.* Boston: Kent, 1983, pp. 9–12; M. Leontiades, *Multinational Business Strategy: Techniques and Guidelines for Management.* Lexington, Mass.: Lexington Books, 1984.

4. Y. Tsurumi, *Multinational Management: Business Strategy and Government Policy,* 2nd ed. Cambridge, Mass.: Ballinger, 1984, pp. 234–240.

5. T. Hout, M. E. Porter, and E. Rudden, "How Global Companies Compete," *Harvard Business Review,* September–October 1982, pp. 98–108; "Drastic New Strategies to Keep U.S. Multinationals Competitive," *Business Week,* October 8, 1984, pp. 168–172.

6. G. H. Garnier, "Context and Decision Making Autonomy in the Foreign Affiliates of U.S. Multinational Corporations," *Academy of Management Journal,* 1982, **25**:893–908. *Also see* K. J. Hladik, *International Joint Ventures: An Economic Analysis of U.S.–Foreign Business Partnerships.* Lexington, Mass.: D. C. Heath, 1985.

7. T. Levitt, "The Globalization of Markets," *Harvard Business Review,* May–June 1983, pp. 92–102.

8. Adapted from T. Hout, M. E. Porter, and E. Rudden, "Global Companies"; "A Shaken Caterpillar Retools to Take on a More Competitive World," *Business Week,* November 5, 1984, pp. 91–94; "Komatsu Digs Deeper into the U.S.," *Business Week,* October 1, 1984, p. 53; R. Neal, "See the Nice, Gray Cat," *Forbes,* May 6, 1985, p. 31.

9. H. S. Byrne, "Caterpillar, Facing Japanese Competition in Earth-Movers, Tries to Regain Footing," *Wall Street Journal,* December 9, 1983, pp. 52–53.

10. Tsurumi, *Multinational Management . . . ,* p. 1; President's Commission on Industrial Competitive-

ness, *Global Competition: The New Reality,* Vol. II. U.S. Government Printing Office, Washington, D.C., 1985.

11. G. C. Lodge and W. R. Plass, "U.S. Trade Policy Needs One Voice," *Harvard Business Review,* May–June 1983, pp. 75–83.

12. L. Tyson and J. Zysman, "American Industry in International Competition: Government Policies and Corporate Strategies," *California Management Review,* Spring 1983, pp. 27–52; R. McKenna, M. Borrus, and S. Cohen, "Industrial Policy and International Competition in High Technology," *California Management Review,* Winter 1984, pp. 15–32.

13. Phatak, *International Dimensions . . . ,* pp. 14–16. *Also see* J. Garland and R. Farmer, *International Dimensions of Business Policy and Management.* Boston: Kent, 1986; J. D. Daniels and L. H. Radebaugh, *International Business: Environment and Operations,* 4th ed. Reading, Mass.: Addison-Wesley, 1986.

14. A. Nag, "Japan's Biggest Auto Makers Get Stronger as U.S. Export Rules Penalize Small Rivals," *Wall Street Journal,* January 18, 1984, p. 1.

15. D. Jedlicka, "Nissan Running Plant with a Japanese Flair," *Houston Chronicle,* December 24, 1983, Section 3, p. 2.

16. "Despite Uproar, FTC Approves Joint Venture by GM, Toyota," *Houston Chronicle,* December 23, 1983, Section 3, pp. 1–2.

17. H. S. Dardick, "The Emerging World Information Business," *Columbia Journal of World Business,* Spring 1983, pp. 69–76; J. D. Frame, *International Business and Global Technology.* Lexington, Mass.: Lexington Books, 1983; J. I. Cash Jr. and B. R. Konsynski, "IS Redraws Competitive Boundaries," *Harvard Business Review,* March–April 1985, pp. 134–142; R. Sarathy, "High-Technology Exports from Newly Industrializing Countries: The Brazilian Commuter Aircraft Industry," *California Management Review,* Winter 1985, pp. 60–84.

18. Adapted from M. D. Buss, "Management International Information Systems," *Harvard Business Review,* September–October 1982, pp. 153–162.

19. M. Fitzpatrick, "The Definition and Assessment of Political Risk in International Business: A Review of the Literature," *Academy of Management Review,* 1983, 8:249–254; T. W. Shreeve, "Be Prepared for Political Changes Abroad," *Harvard Business Review,* July–August 1984, pp. 111–118.

20. D. Haendel, *Foreign Investments and the Management of Political Risk.* Boulder, Colo.: Westview Press, 1979.

21. T. N. Gladwin and I. Walter, *Multinational Under Fire: Lessons in the Management of Conflict.* New York: Wiley-Interscience, 1980. *Also see* O. Williams, "Who Cast the First Stone," *Harvard Business Review,* September–October 1984, pp. 151–160.

22. Adapted from Gladwin and Walter, *Multinational Under Fire . . . ,* pp. 12–26.

23. W. D. Coplin and M. K. O'Leary, "Political Forecast for International Business," *Planning Review,* May 1983, pp. 14–21; "Political Risk Assessment: A Brief Review of the State of the Art," *New International Realities,* August 1983, pp. 15–24.

24. Y. Tsurumi, "Export Trading Company Act of the U.S.: The Beginning of a New Industrial Policy," *Pacific Basin Quarterly,* Fall 1982, pp. 3–5; J. G. Kaikati, "The Export Trading Co. Act: A Viable International Marketing Tool," *California Management Review,* Fall 1984, pp. 59–70. J. W. Dizard, "Sears' Humbled Trading Empire," *Fortune,* June 25, 1984, pp. 71–76.

25. Adapted and used with permission from "Lockheed Aircraft Corporation." In R. Hay, and E. Gray (Eds.), *Business Society: Cases and Text.* Cincinnati: South-Western, 1981, pp. 134–137.

26. M. Pastin and M. Hooker, "Ethics and the Foreign Corrupt Practices Act," *Business Horizons,* November/December 1980, pp. 43–47; G. C. Greanias and D. Windsor, *The Foreign Corrupt Practices Act: Anatomy of a Statute.* Lexington, Mass.: Lexington Books, 1982.

27. H. Baruch, "The Foreign Corrupt Practices Act," *Harvard Business Review,* January–February 1979, pp. 32–50; H. Tong and P. Willing, "What American Managers Should Know and Do About International Bribery," *Baylor Business Studies,* January 1983, pp. 7–19.

28. "The Antibribery Act Splits Executives," *Business Week,* September 19, 1983, p. 16.

29. J. L. Graham and R. A. Herberger, Jr. "Negotiators Abroad—Don't Shoot from the Hip," *Harvard Business Review,* July–August 1983, pp. 160–168; R. L. Tung, "How to Negotiate with the Japanese," *California Management Review,* Summer 1984, pp. 62–77; S. A. Lenway, *The Politics of U.S. International Trade: Protection, Expansion, and Escape.* Marshfield, Mass.: Pitman, 1985.

30. S. Carey, "U.S. Steel Plans to Cite 5 Nations in Trade Actions," *Wall Street Journal,* February 9, 1984, p. 2; "The Worldwide Steel Industry: Reshaping to Survive," *Business Week,* August 20, 1984, pp. 150–154.

31. N. Adler, "Cross-Cultural Management: Issues To Be Faced," *International Studies of Management and Organization,* No. 1–2, 1983, pp. 7–45; J. F. Hartley, "Ideology and Organizational Behavior," *International Studies of Management and Organization,* No. 3, 1983, pp. 7–34.

32. R. Tung, *Business Negotiations with the Japanese.* Lexington, Mass.: Lexington Books, 1983; R. L. Tung, *Expatriate Assignment: Lessons From Japanese Multinationals.* Lexington, Mass.: Lexington Books, 1984; R. Vernon, R. Wells, and L. T. Wells Jr., *Manager in the International Economy,* 5th ed. Englewood Cliffs, N.J.: Prentice-Hall, 1986; S. Ronen, *Comparative and Multinational Management.* New York: John Wiley & Sons, 1986.

33. C. Johnson, "The Internationalization of the Japanese Economy," *California Management Review,* Spring 1983, pp. 5–26; J. P. Alston, "Japan as Number One?: Social Problems of the Next Decades," *Futures,* 1983, **15**:342–356.

34. G. Hofstede, "National Cultures in Four Dimensions: A Research-Based Theory of Cultural Differences among Nations," *International Studies of Management and Organizations,* No. 1–2, 1983, pp. 46–74; Y. Lee and L. Larwood, "The Socialization of Expatriate Managers in Multinational Firms," *Academy of Management Journal,* 1982, **26**:657–665; N. Adler, *International Dimensions of Organizational Behavior and Cross-Cultural Management.* Boston: Kent, 1986.

35. R. Ballon, "Non-Western Work Organization," *Asia Pacific Journal of Management,* September 1983, pp. 1–14; A. Howard, K. Shudo, and M. Umeshima, "Motivation and Values among Japanese and American Managers," *Personnel Psychology,* 1983, **36**:883–898; E. Novis, "Using an American Perspective in Understanding Another Culture: Toward a Hierarchy of Needs for the People's Republic of China," *Journal of Applied Behavioral Science,* 1983, **19**:249–264.

36. S. Uemura, *Japanese Organizations and Environmental Changes.* The Research Institute, Momoyama Gakuin University, 1979; D. W. Plath (Ed.), *Work and Lifecourse in Japan.* Albany, New York: State University of New York Press, 1983.

37. A. Bird, "A Comparison of Japanese and Western Management," *Management Japan,* Autumn 1982, pp. 21–24; J. Smith, "The Japan Syndrome: Demystifying Japanese Management," *Management Decision,* 1983, **21**:25–33; K. Uchihashi, "Japanese Technological Development: Imaginative Teamwork Plus Fierce Competition," *Wheel Extended,* 1984, **14**(1):70–77; I. Nonaka and J. K. Johansson, "Japanese Management: What about the 'Hard' Skills," *Academy of Management Review,* 1985, **10**:181–191.

38. J. Hodgson, *The Wondrous World of Japan.* Washington, D.C., American Enterprise Institute, 1978, p. 3.

39. S. Marshland and M. Beer, "The Evolution of Japanese Management: Lessons for U.S. Managers," *Organizational Dynamics,* Winter 1983, pp. 49–67; Y. Zussman, "Learning from the Japanese: Management in a Resource-Scarce World," *Organizational Dynamics,* Winter 1983, pp. 68–80; C. Y. Yana, "Demystifying Japanese Management Practices," *Harvard Business Review,* November–December 1984, pp. 172–176, 180–182.

40. T. Ozawa, "Japanese World of Work: An Interpretive Survey," *MSU Business Topics,* Spring 1980, pp. 45–55.

41. T. Oh, "Japanese Management—A Critical Review," *Academy of Management Review,* 1975, **1**:13–25; H. Kinoshita, "Matsushita's Basic Business Principles," *Management Japan,* Spring 1983, pp. 26–32; S. Takamiya, "Development of Japanese Management after World War II," *Management Japan,* Spring 1983, pp. 10–18.

42. M. Matsushita, "The Matsushita Management Philosophy in the United States," *Management Japan,* Spring 1982, pp. 10–13; J. Keys and T. Miller,

"The Japanese Management Theory Jungle," *Academy of Management Review,* 1984, 9:342–353.

43. F. Gibney, *Japan: The Fragile Super Power.* Tokyo: Tuttle, 1975, p. 206.

44. "Japan Takes a Swing at Leisure," *Fortune,* May 14, 1984, pp. 170–177. *Also see* S. P. Sethi, N. Namiki, C. L. Swanson, *The False Promise of the Japanese Miracle: Illusions and Realities of the Japanese Management System.* Boston: Pitman, 1984; F. Luthans, H. S. McCaul, and N. G. Dodd, "Organizational Commitment: A Comparison of American, Japanese, and Korean Employees," *Academy of Management Journal,* 1985, 28:213–219.

45. W. Ouchi, *Theory Z: How American Business Can Meet the Japanese Challenge.* Reading, Mass.: Addison-Wesley, 1981. *Also see* W. Ouchi, *The M-Form Society: How American Teamwork Can Recapture the Competitive Edge.* Reading, Mass.: Addison-Wesley, 1984; C. W. Joiner Jr., "Making the

'Z' Concept Work," *Sloan Management Review,* Spring 1985, pp. 57–63.

46. J. Sullivan, "A Critique of Theory Z," *Academy of Management Review,* 1983, 8:132–142; S. Durlabhji, "Japanese-Style American Management: Primary Relations and Social Organization," *Human Relations,* 1983, 36:827–840.

47. W. Ouchi, *Theory Z . . . ,* pp. 225–226.

48. "Why Hewlett-Packard Overhauled Its Management," *Business Week,* July 30, 1984, pp. 111–112; B. Uttal, "Mettle-Test Time for John Young," *Fortune,* June 29, 1985, pp. 242–248.

49. This case was prepared by Professors Ellen Cook and Phillip Hunsaker along with Mohammed Ali Alireza, all of the University of San Diego, as a basis for class discussion rather than to illustrate either effective or ineffective handling of an administrative situation. Copyright © by Ellen Cook, Phillip Hunsaker, and Mohammed Ali Alireza.

Ethics and Social Responsibility in Management

LEARNING OBJECTIVES

After studying this chapter, you should be able to:

- Explain three ethical approaches to decision making and behaviors of managers and firms.

- List the standards advocated by the utilitarian ethical approach.

- List six rights advocated by the moral-rights ethical approach.

- List five principles advocated by the justice ethical approach.

- Identify the strengths and weaknesses of the utilitarian, moral-rights, and justice ethical approaches.

- Describe the traditional, stakeholder, and affirmative social responsibility concepts.

- State the differences among the three social responsibility concepts in terms of the utilitarian, moral-rights, and justice ethical approaches.

- Identify the obligations of managers and business firms under each of the social responsibility concepts.

CHAPTER OUTLINE

PREVIEW CASE

Sun Ship

After operating its shipbuilding subsidiary for 64 years in Chester, Pennsylvania, an industrial city some 15 miles south of Philadelphia, the Sun Company announced in January 1981 that Sun Ship planned to get out of the business of making ships. Over a period of 18 months, the company said, it would work off a backlog of orders for hulls in various stages of completion and reduce its work force from 4200 to 1100. The smaller group would be retained for a modest ship-repair and industrial metal-fabricating operation. Early in 1982, the assets of Sun Ship would be sold to Pennsylvania Shipbuilding Company, a newly organized affiliate of Levingston Industries of Orange, Texas.

The company offered employees facing dismissal generous early retirement or severance pay benefits, provided career counseling and job-placement assistance, and arranged for educational help and retraining programs. Sun also negotiated an agreement with the City of Chester and adjacent Eddystone Township (where part of the shipyard was located) to make certain *payments in lieu of taxes* during a phasedown period of several years following the announcement. This would compensate the municipalities for the loss of anticipated revenues. The company further agreed not to ask for a reduction of property taxes on facilities and equipment no longer in productive use. It also made substantial up-front contributions to local charitable and service organizations, such as the Chamber of Commerce and the United Way. This would make up for an expected loss of income by those groups during a three-year transition period.

Sun Ship provided support to a newly formed community economic development organization, the Riverfront Development Corporation (RDC). The RDC was established by the corporate and financial community as a private, nonprofit organization to find a means of reviving the area's economy. Sun made an initial grant of $360,000. The company also offered a challenge grant of up to $1,000,000 to match contributions from other industries and foundations for the purpose of establishing a capital fund to stimulate development of new businesses. In addition, Sun assigned two of its executives to work full time with RDC on financial and marketing problems.

In all, the company spent, or planned to spend, tens of millions of dollars toward repairing the damage done to employees and the community by closing its shipbuilding operation.[1]

Source: © 1978 Joel Gordon.

Did Sun Ship's management act in an ethical and socially responsible manner? Various standards and principles can be applied when we judge the ethics and social responsibility of a firm's actions.[2] Many of us might feel that Sun Ship represents an ideal model—one worthy of being followed by other companies facing decisions to cut back, close down, or relocate plants. However, critics of Sun Ship management view the cutback decision and subsequent actions as a mixed record. The critics agree that Sun Ship behaved ethically and responsibly in taking into account the impact of the decision on the employees and community. But, they maintain that the company should have notified those involved long before it did, while there was still time for the employees and community to do something about the decision.[3] If labor costs and productivity were the key issues in the decision to cut back—as the company claimed—the critics assert that management had an ethical and social obligation to give timely notice. This notice should have spelled out the company's intention to discontinue the shipbuilding operation unless the workers were willing to make concessions regarding work practices, pay scales, and absenteeism.

The Preview Case presents an example of an ethical approach to managerial decision making. Varying reactions to this approach show that conflicting views are often held by different interest groups in judging whether management has acted in a socially responsible manner. This chapter focuses on: (1) three ethical approaches to decision making and behaviors of managers and firms; (2) the ethical dimensions of virtually every significant decision and act of management; and (3) the conflicting forces on managers resulting from diverse social-responsibility concepts.

ETHICS AND LEGALITY

Concept of Ethics

Webster's defines *ethics* as a set of moral principles or values that govern the actions of an individual or group. Ethics may also be thought of as the process of clarifying what constitutes human welfare and the kinds of decisions and behaviors necessary to promote it.[4] Values are fundamental to ethics. Some values are likely to be widely shared, while others are not. The process of "clarifying what constitutes human welfare" is dynamic and is strongly influenced by fundamental values and changes in them over time.

Even if there is full agreement on what constitutes human welfare, debate is likely to focus on the kinds of decisions and behaviors necessary to advance it.[5] In other words, people and groups often differ on the *means* used to achieve shared values. For example, some share the value that a government and its people have ethical and social responsibilities to assist the poor and less fortunate in a society. However, some argue that it is unethical and socially irresponsible to tax heavily those who have achieved high incomes to support the poor. They argue that many of these people earned their high incomes through hard work, investing in college educations, and taking risks and that a substantial portion of their incomes should not be taken from them and given to others.

Ethical/Legal Framework

The idea of operating *according to the law* is often an inadequate basis for managerial decisions and behaviors. The Preview Case represented a complex situation for Sun Ship management. Their decisions and behaviors may not have been totally ethical and socially responsible. But, none of their critics accused them of being totally irresponsible or unethical, either—and virtually no groups claimed that management did anything illegal.

The easiest type of situation for managers to deal with involves decisions that are clearly ethical and legal; that is, societal values and standards of behavior have been written into clearly understood and accepted laws. Under the old legal concept of *caveat emptor*—let the buyer beware—firms frequently defended all of their actions as being legal. During the 1950s and 1960s, the public increasingly questioned this view. Shifting attitudes and values concerning *appropriate* behavior by business firms led to a flood of consumer legislation in the United States during the late 1960s and 1970s. This legislation substantially diminished the concept of caveat emptor. For example, during the 1960s, it was common for banks, loan companies, and other lenders to express interest rates in ways that did not convey the true and effective annual rates of interest charged on consumer loans. A substantial segment of the public came to view this as unethical and socially irresponsible behavior. Today federal law requires a clear statement of the effective annual rate of interest on all loan agreements.

Perceived Trends in Ethical Behavior

Recent surveys conducted by the Gallup organization for *The Wall Street Journal* suggest that the general public and business executives in the United States think that there is an increasing tendency for people to engage in unethical and illegal behaviors. According to the surveys, 65% of Americans think that the overall level of ethics in our society has declined in the past decade. Only 9% think that it has risen. When asked what unethical business practices, if any, have become more common in recent years, a financial-service manager states: "Bribes, falsifying documents, improper financial statements, bid rigging, price collusion. . . ."[6] Another executive adds: "Individual ethics in business practices have fallen due to increased pressure to show profit or gain quarter by quarter."[7]

Executives reported considerable pressures and temptations to act unethically or illegally. Nearly 40 percent stated that their superiors, at some point, had asked them to do something they considered to be unethical. One in ten said that a superior had asked him or her to commit an act the executive thought was illegal. Forty-seven percent said that they had dismissed at least one subordinate for unethical behavior.[8] A majority of the general public has adopted a cynical view of the ethics practiced by business executives.[9] Only 18 percent of the public rated the honesty and ethical standards of business executives as very high or high.

Possible reasons for these beliefs about the current state of ethics in business include: (1) the increased necessity for managers to make decisions in a complex and ambiguous environment characterized by changing and diverse value systems; (2) the increased tendency for business managers to have their decisions and actions publicly judged by groups with diverse values, interests, and approaches; and (3) the growth in the size and scope of major firms and their activities.

THREE ETHICAL APPROACHES FOR MANAGEMENT

Cavanagh, Moberg, and Velasquez have outlined three ethical approaches commonly used for making personal and managerial decisions and guiding behaviors.[10] In brief, they are:

1. *Utilitarian approach.* It judges the effects of decisions and behaviors on those who are directly involved and in terms of providing the greatest good for the greatest number of people.

2. *Moral-rights approach.* It judges the consistency of decisions and behaviors with maintenance of certain fundamental personal and group liberties and privileges.

3. *Justice approach.* It judges the consistency of decisions and behaviors with maintenance of equity, fairness, and impartiality in the distribution of benefits (rewards) and costs among individuals and groups.

Each approach provides a different, but partially related, set of principles or standards for deciding or judging the *right or wrong* and *good or bad* of managerial decisions. There are other important ethical approaches and systems for decision making and behavior, but they are beyond the scope of this book.

As suggested in Fig. 5.1, each of the three ethical approaches can reinforce decision making or pull such decision making in somewhat different directions. All of these approaches can operate in any complex decision-making process, such as the Sun Ship case. The ideal state is where all three approaches come together in decision making. In Fig. 5.1, this is represented by the area

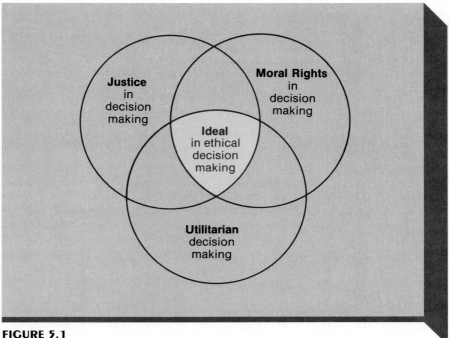

FIGURE 5.1
Decision Making and Ethical Approaches

where the three circles overlap. This figure also suggests the *ideal* is more likely to be the exception than the rule in the majority of managerial decisions.

Utilitarian Approach

The **utilitarian approach** involves judgment of behaviors and decisions by their effects on others. Utilitarian decisions and behaviors are generally intended to create the greatest good for the greatest number.[11] One guiding standard for managers is to estimate the effect of *each alternative* being considered on those who would be affected and to select the one benefiting the greatest number of people.

The utilitarian approach focuses on *actions* and does not address the *motives* for such actions. When choosing the alternative that would produce the most net good, the manager accepts the fact that this alternative may produce some harm to others. So long as potentially positive results outweigh potentially negative results for an alternative—in comparison to those of other alternatives—the decision is accepted as both good and ethical. That some may be injured while others are helped is accepted as part of reality.

Merit pay—where employees can receive substantially different rates of pay—is justified ethically under the utilitarian approach. Those who perform best should get the highest raises. The free-market-based economic system—in which the competitive actions of one firm may create financial losses or bankruptcy of other firms—is also ethical under the utilitarian approach. The premise is that consumers receive the lowest prices and the best quality, relative to those available under alternative economic systems, and thus the greatest good is provided to the greatest number. Bankruptcy and loss of jobs resulting from market competition are viewed as necessary consequences of a free market economy.

From the perspective of the business firm and the manager, the utilitarian approach prescribes ethical standards for guiding decisions in the areas of organizational goals, efficiency, and conflict of interest.[12]

- *Organizational goals.* Goals should aim at satisfying those in the organization's task environment (customers, suppliers, lenders, employees, stockholders).[13] To do the greatest good for the greatest number in a competitive market system, managers are generally told to focus on maximizing profits; that this will ultimately result in the highest quality and lowest prices for consumers.

- *Efficiency.* Employees should attempt to attain organizational goals as efficiently as possible. This is to be achieved by consuming as few inputs (labor, land, capital, management) as possible and by minimizing external costs (air and water pollution, use of nonrenewable resources).

- *Conflict of interest.* Employees should use every effective means to achieve organizational goals. They should not interfere with achieving these goals and not let personal interests conflict significantly with organizational goals. A purchasing agent with a significant financial interest in one of the firm's suppliers is one example of a conflict of interest.

Two branches

The utilitarian approach contains two major branches: act and rule utilitarianism. *Act utilitarianism* results in decisions and behaviors that are based primarily on the outcomes or consequences of providing the most good for the greatest number (the end justifies the means). *Rule utilitarianism* results in decisions and behaviors that are based primarily on meeting predefined standards or rules. Conflict-of-interest rules in a firm's policies-and-procedures manual are an example of rule utilitarianism. Rule utilitarianism advocates the greatest good for the greatest number but does so on the basis of established rules rather than outcomes or consequences. It is often difficult for a manager to anticipate all the consequences of decisions and behaviors under act utilitarianism. However, it is usually fairly easy for a manager to assess whether a rule has been followed under rule utilitarianism.[14] A manager's ethical stance on *act* versus *rule* utilitarianism can lead to substantially different decisions and behaviors.

IN PRACTICE
Rollfast Bicycle Company

Rollfast Bicycle Company has been barred from entering the market in a large Asian country by collusive efforts of local bicycle manufacturers. Rollfast could expect to net $5 million per year from sales if it could penetrate the market. Last week a businessman from the country contacted the management of Rollfast and stated that for a price of $500,000 he could smooth the way for the company to sell in his country.

If you were responsible for making this decision, what are the chances that you would pay the price? Why would you take the action selected?[15]

Application of the utilitarian approach

Before reading further, you should respond to both of the questions posed in the Rollfast situation, jotting your responses on a sheet of paper. To respond to the first question (the likelihood of paying the price), you should use a 0–10-point scale: let 0 represent *definitely would not* and 10 represent *definitely would*. Select the point that represents your opinion and then respond to the second question (why you would take the action) by explaining your choice.

This ethical dilemma was presented to a sample of middle managers. The 105 usable responses are summarized in Table 5.1. The open-ended responses were classified as rule or act utilitarianism, as shown in the first column. The second column indicates the six major categories of justification. The third

TABLE 5.1 ■ SURVEY RESULTS—ROLLFAST BICYCLE COMPANY

ETHICAL APPROACH	CATEGORY OF JUSTIFICATION	MEAN SCORE	NUMBER OF RESPONSES
Rule utilitarianism	Against company policy	0.44	9
Rule utilitarianism	Illegal under Foreign Corrupt Practices Act	0.44	17
Rule utilitarianism	Bribe unethical	2.00	25
Act utilitarianism	No one hurt	5.75	4
Act utilitarianism	An accepted practice in other countries	6.92	24
Act utilitarianism	Not unethical; just the price of doing business	7.67	15
	Other responses		11
	Total		105

Source: Adapted from D. J. Fritzsche and H. Becker, "Linking Management Behaviors to Ethical Philosophy—An Empirical Investigation," *Academy of Management Journal*, 1984, 27:170.

column shows the mean score on the scale for those managers giving a particular rationale. The last column shows the number of managers indicating a particular rationale. Since the mean for the scale is 5.00, there was a better than 50 percent chance that 43 of the 105 managers who responded would elect to pay the bribe. Moreover, the ethical justification for paying the bribe was expressed consistently in the form of act utilitarianism, that is, ends justifying the means. Virtually the opposite results were found in the responses from the managers who selected very low probabilities of paying the bribe. They consistently identified a form of rule utilitarianism as the basis for their unwillingness to pay.

Effects of changes in values and attitudes

The utilitarian approach is most consistent with values and attitudes associated with the traditional work ethic and highly successful managers: desirability of profit maximization, individualism, rewards based on abilities and achievements, sacrifice and hard work, assertiveness and aggressiveness, competition, conflict, and acceptance of uncertainty and risk.[16] In the past 20 years, these values and attitudes—traditionally justified by some form of *act* and/or *rule* utilitarianism—have been increasingly challenged and tempered by the **moral-rights** and **justice approaches.**

Moral-Rights Approach

The moral-rights ethical approach involves behaviors and decisions that are consistent with maintaining certain fundamental liberties and privileges for all individuals and groups. These rights and privileges (life, freedom, health, privacy, property) are presented in documents such as the first 10 Amendments to the Constitution of the United States (known as the Bill of Rights) and the UN Declaration of Human Rights.[17]

Preservation of six moral rights are especially important in managerial decisions and behaviors.[18] They are identified and explained briefly.

Life and safety

Employees, customers, and the general public have the right *not* to have their lives and safety unknowingly and unnecessarily endangered. The U.S. Occupational Safety and Health Act of 1970 was justified in part on the basis of this moral right.

Truthfulness

Employees, customers, and the general public have the right *not* to be intentionally deceived on matters about which they have a right to know. The Truth-in-Lending Act of 1969 was justified by some on the basis of this moral right. The law requires creditors to disclose basic information about the costs and terms of credit to borrowers in consumer transactions.

Privacy

Citizens have the right to limit and control access to and use of information concerning their private lives by government agencies, employers, and others. The U.S. Privacy Act of 1974 was justified by some on the basis of this moral right. It places constraints on how certain kinds of information collected by the federal government can be used and limits those to whom the information may be released. This Act allows individuals to: (1) find out what information about them is collected, recorded, used, and maintained by the federal government; (2) review such records and have them corrected if there are inaccuracies; (3) prevent certain uses of such records by the federal government; and (4) bring suit for damages against those who intentionally violate the person's rights, as specified in the act.

Freedom of conscience

Employees and others have the right to refrain from carrying out any orders that violate their moral or religious beliefs. An Oregon court ruled in favor of a woman who had been fired for serving as a juror. Her boss had ordered her not to serve, knowing that she could get out of jury duty because of her young children.[19] The woman felt she had a moral obligation as a citizen to accept jury duty, if selected.

Free speech

Employees and others have the right to criticize conscientiously and truthfully the ethics or legality of actions by employers. Of course, this is true only so long as the criticisms do not violate the rights of others within or outside the organization. In 1981, the state of Michigan passed a Whistleblowers' Protection Act. This Act was stimulated by the actions of a Michigan chemical company that had sold contaminated animal feed (a fire retardant had been mixed in by mistake), including the issuance of a gag order forbidding its employees to report inside information to government investigators. Virtually all federal legislation enacted in the 1970s concerning mine and other occupational safety, pollution, and health safety contains provisions designed to protect employees who report violations of laws by their employers.[20]

Private property

People have a right to private property. This right enables people to acquire, own, use, and dispose of shelter and have life's basic necessities. John Locke, a seventeenth-century British philosopher, believed that man by nature has rights to life, political equality, and property. The state should not interfere with these rights but, owing to man's partial and biased nature, the state needs to protect them.[21] Locke's view of private property influenced Thomas Jefferson and other founding fathers of the United States: "The great and chief end . . . of men uniting into commonwealths, and putting themselves under government, is the preservation of their property: to which in the state of Nature there are many things wanting."[22] The legal and value systems of the United States, Canada, Great Britain, West Germany, and other free societies uphold the basic concept of private property. However, the concept of private property is only one among several rights or principles. During the past 25 years these other rights and the ethical principles of the justice approach have served as a justification for an outpouring of laws and court rulings that serve to limit, define, and redirect the freedoms and rights pertaining to the use of private property.

IN PRACTICE
Jane Smith

Jane Smith recently accepted a job with a young, vigorous microcomputer manufacturer. Microcomputer manufacturers are engaged in intense competition to become the first on the market with a software package that utilizes the English language. Thus the software could be easily used by the average customer. Smith's former employer is rumored to be the leader in this software development. When Smith was hired, she was led to believe that her selection was based on her management potential. The morning beginning her third week on the new job, Smith received the following memo from the company president: "Please meet me tomorrow morning at my office at 8:15 for the purpose of discussing the developments your former employer has made in microcomputer software."

If you were Smith, what are the chances that you would provide your new employer with the software information? Why would you take the action selected?

Application of ethical approaches

Again, you should respond to both questions for the Jane Smith situation. Remember, in responding to the first question, assume a 0–10-point scale: 0 represents *definitely would not* and 10 represents *definitely would*.

Table 5.2 shows the 108 usable responses to this ethical problem from the same sample of middle managers reported on in Table 5.1. As before, six major categories of responses (along with others) were obtained. The rule utilitarianism and moral-rights responses suggest that Smith should refuse to reveal the information. This is indicated by the low mean scores on the 10-point scale for the first three response categories. The act utilitarian responses indicated either some hedging ("provide some but not all information") or a clear tendency to give the information.

Justice Approach

The justice ethical approach guides decisions and behaviors on the basis of maintaining and being consistent with fairness, equity, and impartiality. The

TABLE 5.2 ■ SURVEY RESULTS—JANE SMITH

ETHICAL APPROACH	CATEGORY OF JUSTIFICATION	MEAN SCORE	NUMBER OF RESPONSES
Rule utilitarianism	Unethical for Smith to provide; unethical for employer to ask	0.80	15
Moral rights	Unethical for employer to mislead Smith when she was hired	1.86	22
Rule utilitarianism	Need to protect Smith's reputation	1.50	8
Act utilitarianism	Provide some but not all information	4.64	14
Rule utilitarianism	Decision based on whether security agreement in force	5.75	16
Act utilitarianism	Loyalty to new employer necessary to keep job	7.44	25
	Other responses		8
	Total		108

Source: Adapted from D. J. Fritzsche and H. Becker, "Linking Management Behaviors to Ethical Philosophy—An Empirical Investigation," *Academy of Management Journal,* 1984, 27:171.

ideas of fairness, equity and impartiality are rooted in the *liberty principle* and the *difference principle.*

Liberty principle

The liberty principle states that each person has a right to the most extensive basic liberty compatible with a similar liberty for others. Belief in the liberty principle is deeply ingrained in most Western societies. In the United States it is illustrated by the idea that everyone 18 years old or older has the right to vote in political elections regardless of education, income, gender, or race.

Difference principle

The difference principle states that social and economic inequalities are to be addressed so that the greatest benefits accrue to the most disadvantaged and that positions and offices are open to all under conditions that lead to fairness.[23] The difference principle suggests that actions which are to the disadvantage of the least well off are not ethical. This principle and its application is controversial in the United States, as in the case of affirmative-action programs, which are justified in part by the difference principle.

The utilitarian approach permits some individuals to become worse off so long as a greater number of others become better off. The Reagan administration's policy of letting unemployment rates increase substantially—even though the burden of unemployment may fall disproportionately on the poor, minorities, or the uneducated—would not create an ethical concern for utilitarians. This is because the greatest good for the greatest number would be served by a lower rate of inflation. However, it would be an ethical concern under the justice approach, which has a *tendency to equality* so that—over time—those who are worse off should benefit more than those who are better off.[24]

Three *implementing* principles are especially important parts of the justice approach: the distributive-justice principle, the fairness principle, and the natural-duty principle.

Distributive-justice principle

The **distributive-justice principle** means that different treatment of individuals should not be based on arbitrarily defined characteristics. For example, Title VII of the 1964 U.S. Civil Rights Act forbids employers from considering personal characteristics such as race, sex, religion, or national origin in decisions to recruit, hire, promote, or fire employees.

This principle prescribes that: (1) people who are similar in *relevant* respects should be treated similarly; and (2) people who differ in *relevant* respects should be treated differently in proportion to the differences between them. On this basis, the U.S. Equal Pay Act of 1963 holds that it is illegal to pay a different wage to women than is paid to men when the jobs in question

The distributive-justice principle of management ensures that treatment of employees is not based on arbitrary characteristics. For example, younger employees should have no advantages over older workers.

Source: Hazel Hankin/Stock, Boston.

require equal skill, effort, responsibility, and working conditions. The Act does allow differences in wages if the differences are due to the following relevant factors: a seniority system; a merit system; a system that measures earnings by quantity or quality of production; or a differential based on any (relevant) factors other than sex.[25]

Fairness principle

The *fairness principle* holds that employees are required to do their part, as defined by the rules of the organization, when two conditions are met: "first, the institution [organization] is just [or fair] . . . ; and second, one has voluntarily accepted the benefits of the arrangement or taken advantages of the opportunities it offers to further one's interests."[26] A just (fair) organization is one that satisfies the two principles of justice: the liberty principle and the difference principle. The main idea is that employees may be expected to engage in cooperative activities according to *rules,* even though this restricts their individual liberty. For example, rules limiting the liberty (freedom) of employees to be absent or late to work would be defined as fair because cooperation is needed for mutual gain. Excessive and random absenteeism and tardiness by some can negatively affect fellow workers and the organization as a whole.

Thus both a firm and its employees have obligations (responsibilities) under the fairness principle. These mutual obligations should satisfy the following criteria.

- They should be a result of voluntary acts. Employees cannot be forced to work for a particular firm and employers cannot arbitrarily be forced to hire a particular person.

- They should be spelled out in clearly stated rules. These rules should specify what both the employees and the organization are required to do.

- They are owed between individuals who are cooperating for mutual benefit. The employees and managers share a common interest in the survival of the organization.[27]

Some aspects of the fairness principle are illustrated by a State of New York Court of Appeals ruling late in 1982. The court decided that Wallace L. Weiner was entitled to sue McGraw-Hill for unjust dismissal. Weiner was fired after eight years of doing promotional work for McGraw-Hill. His claim was that the company handbook on personnel policies protected him against dismissal for other than "just and sufficient cause." The court ruled that the handbook provision constituted a contract between the employer and employee and that Weiner had a right to have his case tried in court.[28] Note that it did not rule on the merits of Weiner's case. In terms of the fairness principle, the court implied that the handbook on personnel policies (rules) represented the various mutual obligations between McGraw-Hill and its employees.

Natural-duty principle

The *natural-duty principle* refers to a variety of universal obligations, including (1) the duty of helping others when they are in need or jeopardy, provided that one can do so without excessive risk or loss to oneself; (2) the duty not to harm or injure another; (3) the duty not to cause unnecessary suffering; and (4) the duty to support and to comply with *just institutions*.

With respect to the last point, judges tend to frown on employee firings that they think may jeopardize the purpose and ideals of the legal system. This is consistent with the view by judges that the legal system attempts to be a just institution. For example, the first U.S. court decision in favor of a dismissed member of the International Brotherhood of Teamsters came in 1959. The court supported the union member's claim that he was fired for refusing to lie in court about certain activities of the union and a trucking firm.[29]

Concluding note

This discussion of the justice approach has only highlighted some of its major guidelines and principles for ethical behavior and decision making. In addition, we have not examined the numerous problems of interpretation and assessment that can enter into the decision-making process when managers attempt to apply the justice, utilitarian, and moral-rights ethical approaches.

IN PRACTICE
Master Millers Company

Master Millers Company has developed a special milling process that yields a wheat flour which, in turn, produces a lighter and more uniformly textured loaf of bread than conventionally milled wheat flour. Unfortunately, the process gives off more dust than the existing emissions control equipment can handle and still maintain emissions within legal limits. Owing to lack of availability, the company is unable to install new emissions control equipment for at least two years. However, if it waited for this equipment before introducing the new process, competitors would likely beat it to the market.

The general manager wants to use the new process during the third shift, which runs from 10 P.M. to 6 A.M. By using the process at that time, the new flour could be introduced and the excess pollution would not be detected because of its release in the dark. By the time demand becomes great enough to utilize a second shift, new emissions control equipment should be available.

If you were responsible, what are the chances you would approve the general manager's request? Why would you take the action selected?

Application of ethical approaches

Again, use a 0–10-point scale and answer the two questions posed. Table 5.3 shows the 103 usable responses from the same sample of middle managers reported on in Tables 5.1 and 5.2. Six major response categories (and other responses) were identified. The first three categories—represented by rule

TABLE 5.3 ▪ SURVEY RESULTS—MASTER MILLERS COMPANY

ETHICAL APPROACH	CATEGORY OF JUSTIFICATION	MEAN SCORE	NUMBER OF RESPONSES
Rule utilitarianism	Would be illegal	1.20	25
Justice	Concern for the environment and life	1.50	16
Act utilitarianism	Risk of getting caught; resulting negative consequences too great	1.53	15
Act utilitarianism	Not their fault; equipment would be installed if available	5.63	8
Act utilitarianism	The pollution would not really hurt the environment	6.72	18
Act utilitarianism	Large potential gain with low risk	6.80	5
	Other responses		16
	Total		103

Source: Adapted from D. J. Fritzsche and H. Becker, "Linking Management Behaviors to Ethical Philosophy—An Empirical Investigation," *Academy of Management Journal*, 1984, 27:172.

utilitarianism, justice, and act utilitarianism approaches—suggest a low probability of approving the general manager's request. About 55 percent of the responses fall into one of these categories. The other three response categories—suggesting a better than 50 percent chance of approving the request—represent a form of act utilitarianism.

Difficulties in Making Ethical Decisions

Two conclusions worth noting emerge from the responses to the three surveys of middle managers. First, rule or act utilitarianism dominated as the ethical approach underlying the middle managers' rationale or justification. The highest probabilities for taking a potentially *unethical* course of action consistently came from managers who justified their selection on the basis of act utilitarianism (the ends justify the means). Second, the justice approach to ethics showed up only once in the justifications, as did the moral-rights approach. Many of the conflicts between managers and consumer groups, employee groups, government agencies, and others may be a result of the tendency for managers to use act or rule utilitarianism as their ethical guide. In contrast, nonmanagement groups may have a greater tendency to use the justice or moral-rights ethical approaches in justifying their positions.

Managers who attempt to reach the *ideal* in making ethical decisions face many difficulties. It is very hard to meet fully the guidelines and principles of all three ethical approaches.[30] Thus the ideal is far more likely to be the exception than the rule. However, these ethical approaches—when used in combination to guide and assess possible decisions and behaviors—increase the probability that a manager will make decisions and engage in behaviors that are ethical and will be so judged. Decisions and behaviors cannot always be described as absolutely ethical or absolutely unethical; many can be seen in relative terms as more or less ethical than others. This is especially true for those managerial decisions that are complex, involve many groups and individuals, are controversial, and by their very nature involve risk taking.

Strengths and Weaknesses of Ethical Approaches

Each of the three ethical approaches—utilitarian, moral rights, and justice—has strengths and weaknesses in guiding managerial decisions and behaviors; they are summarized in Table 5.4 on p. 152. The utilitarian approach encourages the greatest good for the greatest number. This could be achieved ethically at the expense of some people and groups, especially those with little power. Utilitarian views are most compatiable with goals of efficiency, productivity, and profit maximization. There should be little question as to why it is overwhelmingly valued as a desirable ethical approach by many managers of business firms. In contrast, the moral-rights and justice approaches place greater emphasis on the personal rights of individuals and the need to distribute benefits and burdens among individuals fairly. If the moral-rights and justice approaches were used exclusively as ethical guides by managers, we would be more likely to see reductions in innovation, technological change, risk taking, and efficiency. Many struggles among groups concerning the meaning and implemnetation of the social responsibility concept for business firms reflect the potential conflicts between these three ethical approaches. One writer pessimistically asserts for the United States:

> Culturally we are suffering from the ravages of a *metaphysical* cancer—a psychological rejection mechanism that questions the possibility of anyone's being able to know right and wrong in absolute terms. This in turn destroys a culture's ability to develop a consensus on matters of right and wrong, which results in ethical schizophrenia—many ethical faces. This is the sickness that gives rise to the sharp differences which often arise between people—corporate executives and government regulators, agency heads and environmentalists, and so forth.[31]

SOCIAL RESPONSIBILITY, BUSINESS FIRMS, AND MANAGERS

We hold a more positive view of ethics and social responsibilities in the United States, in general, and in business practices, in particular. There is no single, agreed-upon concept of social responsibility for business firms and managers.

TABLE 5.4 ▪ STRENGTHS AND WEAKNESSES OF THREE ETHICAL APPROACHES TO MANAGERIAL DECISIONS AND BEHAVIORS

ETHICAL APPROACH	STRENGTH AS AN ETHICAL GUIDE	WEAKNESS AS AN ETHICAL GUIDE
Utilitarian The greatest good for the greatest number	1. Encourages efficiency and productivity 2. Consistent with profit maximization; is easiest for business managers to understand 3. Encourages looking beyond the individual to assess impact of decisions on all who might be affected	1. Virtually impossible to quantify all important variables 2. Can result in biased allocations of resources, particularly when some who are affected lack representation or *voice* 3. Can result in ignoring *rights* of some who are affected to achieve utilitarian outcomes
Moral Rights Individual's personal rights not to be violated	1. Protects the individual from injury; consistent with freedom and privacy 2. Consistent with accepted standards of social behavior independent of outcomes	1. Can imply individualistic selfish behavior that, if misinterpreted, may result in anarchy 2. Establishes personal liberties that may create obstacles to productivity and efficiency
Justice Fair distribution of benefits and burdens	1. Attempts to allocate resources and costs fairly 2. Is the *democratic* principle 3. Protects the interests of those affected who may be underrepresented or lack power	1. Can encourage a sense of entitlement that reduces risk, innovation, and productivity 2. Can result in reducing rights of some to accommodate rules of justice

Source: Adapted from M. Velasquez, D. V. Moberg, and G. F. Cavanagh, "Organizational Statesmanship and Dirty Politics: Ethical Guidelines for the Organizational Politician," *Organizational Dynamics,* Autumn 1983, p. 72. Adapted by permission of the publisher. Copyright © by the Periodicals Division, American Management Associations, New York. All rights reserved.

Given the diversity of values and ethical approaches operating in the United States and other societies, the lack of agreement over what social responsibility means is not surprising. Three of the more common concepts of social responsibility can be identified as the traditional, stakeholder, and affirmative. Each of these involves a different *relative* emphasis on the utilitarian, moral-rights, and justice ethical approaches, as shown in Fig. 5.2. We suggest, for example, that the traditional social-responsibility concept is guided primarily by the utilitarian ethical approach. On the other hand, the affirmative social-responsibility concept draws heavily on the justice and moral-rights ethical approaches *relative* to the utilitarian approach. Finally, Fig. 5.2 indicates that the degree and scope of a firm's obligations are relatively narrow and focused under the traditional social-responsibility concept; broaden under the stakeholder concept; and are quite broad under the affirmative concept.

Traditional Social Responsibility

The ***traditional social-responsibility*** concept holds that managers of business firms should serve the interests of stockholders. Their overriding obligation is to maximize stockholders' profits and long-term interests. Milton Friedman, economist and winner of the Nobel Prize, is probably the best known advocate

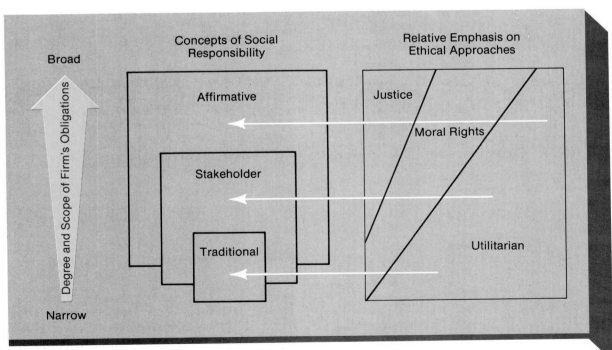

FIGURE 5.2
Social-Responsibility Concepts and Ethical Approaches

of the traditional social-responsibility concept.[32] Friedman holds that the use of resources in ways that do not clearly maximize stockholder interests amounts to spending the owners' money without their consent. Managers' actions are limited by the economic needs of their companies. Profit is still the bottom line for all firms. No executive can or should reduce the firm's profitability by involvement in social issues. Government, rather than business, is the institution best suited for solving social problems. Friedman states that "There is one and only one social responsibility of business—to use its resources and engage in activities designed to increase its profits so long as it stays within the rules of the game, which is to say, engages in open and free competition without deception or fraud."[33] The potential implications of using the traditional social-responsibility concept are illustrated in the decision facing West Manufacturing Company.

IN PRACTICE
West Manufacturing Company

West Manufacturing Company is faced with more demand for its product than it can meet. West's management does not care to encourage competition and would prefer to meet the demand itself, if possible. Unfortunately, their plants are already operating 24 hours per day, seven days a week. There is simply no further capacity. Management decides to relocate and build a new plant in order to consolidate and expand. Four years will be required to complete the new plant.

In the meantime, West discovers that an existing, abandoned plant can be acquired and refitted in six months for temporary use. This plant would not be efficient and would be only marginally profitable at best. However, it would help West to protect its market share, discourage new competitors, and help meet escalating demand until the new plant is ready for full operation.

Using the abandoned plant would create several problems for the small community in which West is presently located: it does not have the housing, school system, recreational services, roads, and other facilities needed to serve the plant and the expected influx of new employees and their families. The temporary plant would employ 1200 persons, which would mean the addition of 2500 to 3000 persons to the community. And, this plant would be closed again, as soon as the new plant is ready to go and the company relocates.

Management is pondering this decision and also trying to decide how much information about their long-term plans to share with the community. The managers feel that community knowledge about temporary expansion and ultimate relocation would result in controversy and certain costs to the company. The community is likely to oppose the relocation and unlikely to improve schools, recreational facilities, roads, and other facilities to permit temporary use of the abandoned plant, even with substantial financial contributions by the company. Local banks and other businesses would also be less than enthusiastic about financing building projects, home mortgages, or consumer loans of any description under these circumstances.[34]

Should the West management tell the community leaders anything? Under the traditional social-responsibility concept, the answer to that question is easy: Tell them nothing. Management is under no obligation to tell anyone about its deliberations and decisions. There is nothing illegal about West using the plant as a stop-gap, short-term measure and later relocating. Moreover, it represents the best alternative to maximize the long-term interests of the stockholders.

Stakeholder Social Responsibility

The *stakeholder social-responsibility* concept holds that managers of business firms have obligations to identifiable groups that are affected by or can affect the achievement of an organization's objectives.[35] They are called *stakeholders* and generally include groups in the firm's environment that have potential or real power to influence the firm's decisions and actions. Stakeholders usually include stockholders, important customers, competitors, government agencies, unions, employees, debt holders (banks, pension funds), trade associations, important suppliers, protest groups (typically targeted at the firm), and public interest groups (typically targeted at the firm's industry).

Under the stakeholder concept, the management of West Manufacturing has a social responsibility to inform the community of their short-term need to use the abandoned plant *and* their long-term goal of relocating. In addition, the company should work with the community and spend corporate resources to reduce both the short-term and long-term adverse impacts on the community.

The stakeholder social-responsibility concept is further illustrated by Johnson & Johnson's Credo, which is reprinted in Table 5.5. This statement also represents the ethical principles intended to guide the behaviors and decisions of their managers and employees.

The vast majority of business managers who claim to accept the stakeholder concept would probably endorse Peter Drucker's interpretation of a firm's obligations.[36] Specifically, he comments that

> The first "social responsibility" of business is then to make enough profit to cover the costs of the future. If this "social responsibility" is not met, no other "social responsibility" can be met. Decaying businesses in a decaying economy are unlikely to be good neighbors, good employers or "socially responsible" in any way. When the demand for capital grows rapidly, surplus business revenues available for non-economic purposes, especially for "philanthropy," cannot possibly go up. They are almost certain to shrink.[37]

This interpretation of the stakeholder concept makes capital formation a priority obligation for managers. Capital is seen as *essential* to creating tomorrow's jobs.

TABLE 5.5 ■ JOHNSON & JOHNSON CREDO

We believe our first responsibility is to the doctors, nurses, and patients, to mothers and all others who use our products and services. In meeting their needs everything we do must be of high quality. We must constantly strive to reduce our costs in order to maintain reasonable prices. Customers' orders must be serviced promptly and accurately. Our suppliers and distributors must have an opportunity to make a fair profit.

We are responsible to our employees, the men and women who work with us throughout the world. Everyone must be considered as an individual. We must respect their dignity and recognize their merit. They must have a sense of security in their jobs. Compensation must be fair and adequate, and working conditions clean, orderly and safe. Employees must feel free to make suggestions and complaints. There must be equal opportunity for employment, development and advancement for those qualified. We must provide competent management, and their actions must be just and ethical.

We are responsible to the communities in which we live and work and to the world community as well. We must be good citizens—support good works and charities and bear our fair share of taxes. We must encourage civic improvements and better health and education. We must maintain in good order the property we are privileged to use, protecting the environment and natural resources.

Our final responsibility is to our stockholders. Business must make a sound profit. We must experiment with new ideas. Research must be carried on, innovative programs developed and mistakes paid for. New equipment must be purchased, new facilities provided and new products launched. Reserves must be created to provide for adverse times. When we operate according to these principles, the stockholders should realize a fair return.

Source: R. N. Nelson, Commentary on "Business Ethics: On Getting to the Heart of the Matter," *Business and Professional Ethics Journal*, Fall 1981, p. 75.

Justification for the stakeholder concept

Three major justifications are commonly advanced for the stakeholder social-responsibility concept: (1) enlightened self-interest; (2) sound investment; and (3) avoiding interference.[38] The *enlightened–self-interest* view suggests that social responsibility can be extended to justify numerous managerial decisions and actions in the social arena. This includes the general idea that a better society creates a better environment for business.[39] The *sound-investment* view asserts that the stock market responds to the demonstration of social responsibility by the large corporation. Socially responsible firms are claimed to have stocks selling at higher prices than less socially responsible firms. This, in turn, influences the cost (interest rate) of capital and the firm's earnings. As might be expected, this is a highly controversial view.[40] Finally, the *avoiding-interference* view relates to preventing political actions and control by potentially powerful stakeholders such as government agencies and pressure groups. In effect, self-regulation by an industry as a whole or by the management of individual firms is often prescribed with this justification.[41] Johnson & Johnson's handling of the Tylenol scare in 1982 represents a good example of an application of the stakeholder social-responsibility concept.

IN PRACTICE
Johnson & Johnson

In October 1982, Johnson & Johnson, a leading manufacturer of health-care products, faced a crisis of unprecedented proportions. Seven persons had died in the Chicago area after taking capsules of Extra-Strength Tylenol. The capsules taken by the victims had contained lethal amounts of cyanide. Tylenol was the company's most important product, accounting for about 7 percent of its 1981 sales of $5.4 billion and 17 percent of its $467.6 million net earnings. Thus the crisis represented a serious threat to the future profitability of the brand and the company. In fact, many believed that the incident would cause lasting damage to the Tylenol brand name.

Johnson & Johnson's response to the bad news was swift and direct. Within hours of learning of the Chicago deaths, the company announced a recall of all 93,400 bottles of Extra-Strength Tylenol in the implicated batch. This decision was made quickly, even though tests on samples of the same batch did not reveal any contamination. This meant that the poisoning may not have occurred in manufacture. By noon the same day, the firm sent nearly half a million Mailgrams to physicians, hospitals, and wholesalers, alerting them to the danger. A press-relations staff member and several scientific and security people were flown to Chicago by corporate jet to assist in the investigation. A laboratory was set up outside Chicago and staffed with 30 chemists to help the authorities analyze samples of Extra-Strength Tylenol. Johnson & Johnson placed an additional 500 salespersons from two of its pharmaceutical divisions on call to help recall the Tylenol shipments. Late that evening the company offered a $100,000 reward to anyone who could give information leading to the arrest and conviction of the person or persons responsible for the murders. All advertising and promotion of Tylenol was suspended. One of the company's two plants manufacturing Tylenol capsules was idled.

The recall was expanded the following day to include a batch of 171,000 bottles that had been manufactured in another plant. The death of the latest victim had been traced to a capsule from that batch. But, the worst was yet to come. An apparently unrelated case of strychnine-contaminated Tylenol almost killed a man in Oroville, California. This prompted the company to extend the recall to *all* Tylenol capsules, both regular and extra-strength. Production of the capsules was temporarily halted. On October 5, 1982, within a week of the first Tylenol deaths, the company was beginning to pull back the product with a view to destroying the entire stock. Some 31 million bottles with an estimated retail value of $100 million were involved. The after-tax impact was expected to be approximately $50 million. The decision to recall all Tylenol capsules was considered by the company for four days. It was no doubt hastened by the California incident.

The company stated that its first reaction was to protect the public and inform them about rapidly unfolding developments. The recalls seem to have been decided on almost as a matter of course. In fact, James E. Burke, the chairman of Johnson & Johnson wanted to announce a total recall of all Extra-Strength Tylenol from the very beginning. Surprisingly, the Federal Bureau of Investigation (FBI) and the Food and Drug Administration (FDA) advised him against a premature recall. Their view was based on the grounds that such an

(continued)

action might "cause more public anxiety than it would relieve." Early during the crisis Burke said, "It's important that we demonstrate that we've taken every single step possible to protect the public, and that there's simply nothing else we can do."[42]

As a result of these and other actions by Johnson & Johnson, the following comments from the *Washington Post* were typical of media reaction: "Johnson & Johnson has effectively demonstrated how a major business ought to handle a disaster. From the day the deaths were linked to the poisoned Tylenol . . . Johnson & Johnson has succeeded in portraying itself to the public as a company willing to do what's right regardless of the cost."[43] The Johnson & Johnson Credo presented in Table 5.5 appeared to serve as a very real guide to management in their handling of the Tylenol incident. *Business Week* recently stated: "While many high-minded statements of corporate purpose are written and forgotten, J&J's is not."[44]

The 1982 Tylenol poisonings could have been a financial disaster for Johnson & Johnson, but the company's quick action and cooperation with investigators won favorable response from the public, the media, and competitors.

Source: Darlene Bordwell, Boston.

Affirmative Social Responsibility

The *affirmative social-responsibility* concept holds that managers of business firms are obligated to: (1) anticipate changes in their environment; (2) blend the firm's own goals with those of groups in the environment; and (3) take concrete steps to promote mutual interests between the firm and its various stakeholders, including the general public. This concept includes most of the obligations under the stakeholder concept *and* the above obligations. These obligations suggest the need, at least, for ongoing communication among managers of firms, stakeholders, and the general public. Thus business firms might anticipate and avoid problems, not simply react to them as a result of pressures.[45]

William C. Norris, the founder and chairman of Control Data Corporation, is one of a handful of business executives in the United States who advocate the affirmative social-responsibility concept. Norris comments:

> One key change is for business to take the initiative and provide the leadership in planning, managing, and implementing programs designed to meet society's needs and turn them into business opportunities. Along the way, business must cooperate with government, labor unions, universities, organized religion, and other influential segments of society. Where the resources of a single company are insufficient, as will often be the case, two or more companies should work together on joint projects or ventures. In any event, there should be an appropriate sharing of costs between business and government.
>
> It was our growing conviction that business could and should assume a leadership role that prompted Control Data to adopt such a strategy in the late 1960s. We have pursued it vigorously and with sound results ever since. In general, the reaction of the business community has been to view us as both unrealistic and idealistic and to assume that our "grand social experiment" will ultimately prove unsuccessful at the expense of our stockholders. At the same time, many persons in government and other sectors have welcomed the possibility of business as an ally while timidly withholding their full support, ostensibly awaiting more evidence of the strategy's effectiveness.[46]

INTERNATIONAL FOCUS

Stakeholder Social Responsibility at British Petroleum Company

British Petroleum (BP) companies, including Standard Oil of Ohio (SOHIO), operate in 70 countries and in a variety of activities. The BP group provides, on average, employment for some 132,000 people.

The health and safety of our employees and customers, as well as of any members of the public who might be affected by our activities, is a matter of

(continued)

primary concern. Health and safety considerations therefore feature prominently at each stage of the planning, development and operation of every BP project, and in the production, handling and ultimate use of every BP product.

Environmental conservation remains a cornerstone of BP's operating policy and we continue to develop the scientific and technical expertise needed to meet the increasingly varied requirements of the company's individual businesses. Research into the prevention of air and water pollution, and into ecology generally, much of it using mathematical modelling, featured prominently in the year's programme.

BP companies are an integral part of the communities in which they operate. We believe that we can contribute most effectively to these communities by conducting our business efficiently, successfully and profitably, thereby creating wealth and enhancing the business's value over the longer term. But if we are to operate effectively, a favourable climate of external opinion is of great importance.

We therefore give high priority to explaining to all sections of the community what we are doing and why we are doing it. Regular contact is maintained with politicians, civil servants, special interest groups, international organisations such as the EEC and UN, as well as with the media and business and local community leaders.

As an international group, we feel it is desirable that each national operating company should develop its own community support programme to suit local circumstances and conventions.

In the UK, group companies made donations totalling £1,343,000 to well over 500 charities. The principal beneficiaries were charities connected with medical research, disabled people, community health and welfare, conservation and youth activities.

Our other support for the community in the UK is mainly concerned with education, job creation, inner-city revival, and sponsorship of the arts, and of leisure and sport for young people. Some 400 schools, for example, entered the "Buildarobot" competition, part of BP's "Challenge to Youth" scheme. In the world of music, we support three national youth orchestras, children's concerts given by the London Mozart Players and scholarships at the Guildhall School of Music.

Community projects included support for eight enterprise agencies dedicated to creating jobs in inner-city areas, the management of several projects to convert disused factories into new business premises and the secondment of 15 BP staff for various periods to help with the establishment of businesses, particularly in inner-city areas.

Our education liaison programme, which includes links with some 200 UK schools, aims to improve the understanding of the role and contribution of industry and to promote greater economic and technical literacy amongst young people. Products from our range of specially produced teaching materials are supplied to over 40 countries around the world.

Source: "Stakeholder Social Responsibility at British Petroleum," *The British Petroleum Company Annual Report and Accounts,* London: 1983, pp. 26–27.

Obligations and the affirmative concept

The affirmative social-responsibility concept is the most difficult, complex, and expensive one to implement by managers. This is apparent from Table 5.6, which shows five example categories of obligations and corresponding examples of managerial obligations (expected concrete behaviors). Some of these obligations are also compatible with the stakeholder concept.

Social audit and report

A *social audit* and report are assumed to be an important obligation under the affirmative social-responsibility concept. This is typically viewed as an optional activity under the stakeholder concept. A social audit is a study and assessment of the social performance of a business, in contrast to a financial audit. The social audit focuses on actual behaviors, not on intentions. Table

TABLE 5.6 ■ EXAMPLES OF MANAGERIAL OBLIGATIONS UNDER THE AFFIRMATIVE SOCIAL-RESPONSIBILITY CONCEPT

EXAMPLES OF OBLIGATION CATEGORIES	EXAMPLES OF MANAGERIAL OBLIGATIONS
Search for legitimacy Ethical norms	Considers and accepts broader—extra-legal and extra-market—criteria for measuring firm's performance and social role. Takes definite stand on issues of public concern; advocates ethical norms for all in the firm, industry, and business in general. These ethical norms will be advocated even if they seem detrimental to the immediate economic interest of the firm or are contrary to prevailing ethical norms.
Operating strategy	Maintains and improves current standards of physical and social environment; compensates victims of pollution and other corporate-related activities even in the absence of clearly established legal grounds; evaluates possible negative effects of the firm's planned actions on other stakeholders, including the public, and attempts to eliminate or substantially reduce negative effects prior to implementation.
Response to social pressures	Accepts responsibility for solving current problems; willingly discusses activities with outside groups; makes information freely available to the public; accepts formal and informal inputs from outside groups in decision making. Is willing to be publicly evaluated for its various activities.
Legislative and political activities	Shows willingness to work with outside groups for good environmental laws; does not pursue special interest laws; promotes honesty and openness in government and in the firm's own lobbying activities.

Source: Adapted from S. P. Sethi, "A Conceptual Framework for Environmental Analysis of Social Issues and Evaluation of Business Response Patterns," *Academy of Management Review,* 1979, 8:63–74.

5.7 presents a model for corporate social auditing and reporting. This model and the American Institute of Certified Public Accountants recommend the use of objective narrative statements where quantitative measurements are unavailable. Thus the social audit aims at providing a reasonable profile of a corporation's performance in important environmental, cultural, and economic sectors without having to put a dollar sign on everything. While measurement problems still are great and the process is not totally accurate, a basic profile of social activities and achievement can be developed.

Some major business firms report on their social responsibility programs and activities as part of their corporate annual reports. These reports are distributed to stockholders and many other groups. Robert A. Anderson, chairman of the Atlantic Richfield Company (ARCO), is another of the handful of business executives promoting the affirmative social-responsibility con-

TABLE 5.7 ■ A MODEL FOR SOCIAL AUDITING AND REPORTING BY BUSINESS FIRMS

PART	CONTENTS
1. A list of social expectations and the corporation's response	A summary of what is expected for each program area (consumer affairs, employee relations, physical environment, corporations' local community development). A statement of the corporation's reasoning as to why it has undertaken certain activities and not undertaken others.
2. A statement of the corporation's social objectives and the priorities attached to specific activities	For each program area, the corporation's report on what it will try to accomplish and what priority it places on the programs and activities it will undertake.
3. A description of the corporation's objectives in each program area of the activities it will conduct	For each priority activity and program, the corporation's statement of a specific objective (in quantitative terms when possible), describing how it is striving to reach that objective (making available 10 qualified staff employees for a total of 400 hours of community service).
4. A statement indicating the resources committed to achieving objectives	A summary report, by program area and activity, of the costs—direct and indirect—assumed by the corporation.
5. A statement of the accomplishments and/or progress made in achieving each objective	A summary describing the extent to which each objective has been achieved. When feasible the description should be in quantitative terms. Objective, narrative statements should be used when quantification is not possible.

Source: Adapted from J. J. Carson and G. A. Steiner, *Measuring Business Social Performance: The Corporate Social Audit*. New York: Committee for Economic Development, 1974, p. 61. Used with permission.

cept. A recent ARCO annual report contained a separate section entitled "corporate responsibility." The company has demonstrated its commitment to the affirmative social-responsibility concept in a number of ways.

IN PRACTICE
Atlantic
Richfield
Company

The Atlantic Richfield Company joined with the U.S. Conference of Mayors in sponsoring a two-day meeting in Philadelphia to explore ways that cities and corporations, like ARCO, might work together to help ease the nation's urban problems. A follow-up conference in Houston examined successful public and private approaches to urban problems in the southwest.

The Atlantic Richfield Foundation also earmarked a major portion of its $32.5 million budget to programs designed to meet social needs in the cities. For example, a Foundation grant helped the Los Angeles Urban League Data Processing Skills Center retrain the unemployed in marketable computer skills. RAYS, a program to upgrade the job skills of Hispanics in east Los Angeles, and Central Park Five Council, a network of five major community groups serving a low-income Los Angeles neighborhood, also received Foundation assistance.

A $300,000 grant went to the Inner Cities Venture Fund of the National Trust for Historic Preservation to help renew inner-city housing in Los Angeles, Philadelphia, Chicago, Houston, Denver, and Louisville—six cities where ARCO has significant operations. The Atlantic Richfield Chemical Company continued its efforts to help revitalize Philadelphia's inner city. The chemical company arranged to invest $100,000 in the stock of the Philadelphia Small Business Investment Corporation, which provides capital to small, job-generating businesses.

Volunteerism is an increasingly important aspect of ARCO's community efforts. Foundation and company programs encouraged employees to contribute time and money to nonprofit organizations, and the Foundation matched employee and retiree contributions to qualified organizations on a two-to-one basis, disbursing $4.3 million—a 35-percent increase over the previous year. Employees and retirees can also request Foundation grants for organizations to which they volunteer their time. The Foundation also matches employee contributions to the United Way.[47]

CHAPTER SUMMARY

The overriding goal of this chapter was to make you aware of the increasing importance of ethical and social-responsibility issues facing managers. We demonstrated how three ethical approaches—utilitarian, moral rights, and justice—can be compatible with or different from the legal view when applied to managerial decisions and behaviors.

The results of opinion surveys indicate that managers and the general public are becoming more aware

of the importance of ethical approaches and social-responsibility concepts in managerial roles and functions. While this awareness is increasing, there is no corresponding increase in agreement over a *right* ethical approach or a *right* social-responsibility concept for business firms and managers. Just the opposite seems to be the case; there appears to be considerable diversity and disagreement within management as a group and among various stakeholders and the general public as to the proper ethical approaches or concepts of social responsibility.

Three concepts of social responsibility—traditional, stakeholder, and affirmative—were presented, along with implications of each. The relative emphasis on the three ethical approaches for each of the social-responsibility concepts was also developed.

The ethical approaches and social-responsibility concepts bear most heavily on managers' performance of the interpersonal *leadership* role and the four decisional roles: *entrepreneur, disturbance handler, resource allocator,* and *negotiator.*

MANAGER'S VOCABULARY

act utilitarianism
affirmative social responsibility
difference principle
distributive-justice principle
ethics
fairness principle
justice approach
liberty principle
moral-rights approach
natural-duty principle
rule utilitarianism
social audit
stakeholder
stakeholder social responsibility
traditional social responsibility
utilitarian approach

REVIEW QUESTIONS

1. What does it mean to judge a decision on the basis of an ethical versus a legal perspective?

2. What are three common ethical approaches to decision making and behaviors?

3. What are the differences between rule and act utilitarianism?

4. What do the liberty and difference principles prescribe, as part of the justice ethical approach?

5. What are three concepts of social responsibility?

6. What are the obligations of managers and firms under the affirmative social-responsibility concept?

DISCUSSION QUESTIONS

1. Should managers use the justice ethical approach for guiding their decisions and behaviors? Explain.

2. Do you favor more strongly the utilitarian or moral-rights ethical approach as a guide for managerial decisions and behaviors? Explain.

3. Assume that you have 100 points to allocate among the utilitarian, moral-rights, and justice approaches to convey the relative emphasis managers should place on each of them. How would you allocate the 100 points? Explain.

4. Which of the social-responsibility concepts do you favor for use by firms and managers? Justify your choice.

5. Do you think that the ethics of managers in general are likely to improve or worsen in the future? Explain.

MANAGEMENT INCIDENTS AND CASES

SUE JONES

Sue Jones, a senior editor at J&P Publishing Company, has just received a manuscript from one of her most successful authors. It provides the most authoritative account yet published of the history of the development of the atomic bomb. However, the final chapter contains a detailed description of how the bomb is made. Jones has tried to convince the author to omit the last chapter stating that such information should not be made readily available to the mass market in paperback form. The author believes that the chapter is critical to the success of the book and thus will not agree to its deletion.[48]

Questions
1. If you were Jones, what are the chances you would publish the book? Use a 0–10-point scale; 0 represents *definitely would not* and 10 represents *definitely would.*

2. Why would you take the action selected?

JACK WARD

Jack Ward is working in product development for an autoparts contractor. Ward's firm received a large contract last summer to manufacture transaxles to be used in a new line of front-wheel–drive cars that a major auto manufacturer plans to introduce in the near future. The contract is very important to Ward's firm, which has recently fallen on hard times. Just prior to obtaining the contract, half of the firm's employees, including Ward, had been scheduled for an indefinite layoff.

Final testing of the assemblies ended last Friday and the first shipments are scheduled for three weeks from today. As Ward began examining the test reports, he discovered that the transaxle tended to fail when loaded at more than 20% over rated capacity and subjected to strong torsion forces. Such a condition could occur with a heavily loaded car braking hard for a curve while going down a mountain road. The results would be disastrous. The manufacturer's specifications call for the transaxle to carry 30% of its rated capacity without failing. Ward showed the results to his supervisor and the company president, who indicated that they were both aware of the report. Given the low likelihood of occurrence and the fact that there was no time to redesign the assembly, they decided to ignore the report. If they did not deliver the assemblies on time, they would lose the contract. John must now decide whether to show the test results to the auto manufacturer.[49]

Questions

1. If you were Ward, what are the chances that you would notify the auto manufacturer? Use a 0–10-point scale; 0 represents *definitely would not* and 10 represents *definitely would*.

2. Why would you take the action selected?

REFERENCES

1. Adapted from J. P. Kavanagh, "The Sinking of Sun Ship: A Case Study in Managerial Ethics," *Business & Professional Ethics Journal,* Summer, 1982, pp. 1–13.

2. J. P. Kavanagh, "Ethical Issues in Plant Relocation," *Business & Professional Ethics Journal,* Winter 1982, pp. 21–33. *Also see:* A. B. Carroll, "When Business Closes Down: Social Responsibilities and Management Actions," *California Management Review,* Winter, 1984, pp. 125–140.

3. Kavanagh, "The Sinking of Sun Ship . . . ," p. 4.

4. C. Powers and D. Vogel, *Ethics in the Education of Business Managers.* Hastings-on-Hudson, New York: Institute of Society, Ethics and the Life Sciences, 1980; J. R. Glenn, *Ethics in Decision Making.* New York: John Wiley & Sons, 1986.

5. V. E. Henderson, "The Ethical Side of Enterprise," *Sloan Management Review,* Spring 1982, pp. 37–47; R. Fisher, "He Who Pays the Piper," *Harvard Business Review,* March–April 1985, pp. 150–159.

6. R. Rickleffs, "Executives and General Public Say Ethical Behavior Is Declining in U.S.," *Wall Street Journal,* October 31, 1983, p. 25. *Also see:* W. M. Hoffman and J. M. Moore, *Business Ethics: Readings and Cases in Corporate Morality.* New York: McGraw-Hill, 1984.

7. Rickleffs, "Executives and General Public . . . ," p. 25.

8. R. Rickleffs, "Public Gives Executives Low Marks for Honesty and Ethical Standards," *Wall Street Journal,* November 2, 1983, p. 27. *Also see:* S. Flax, "How to Snoop on Your Competitors," *Fortune,* May 14, 1984, pp. 29–33.

9. R. Rickleffs, "Executives Apply Stiffer Standards than Public to Ethical Dilemma," *Wall Street Journal,* November 3, 1983, p. 27.

10. Portions of this section are adapted from G. F. Cavanagh, D. J. Moberg, and M. Velasquez, "The Ethics of Organizational Behavior," *Academy of Management Review,* 1981, 6:363–374. *Also see* W. A. French and J. Granrose, *Practical Business Ethics.* Columbus, Ohio: Merrill, 1986.

11. J. S. Mill, *Utilitarianism.* Indianapolis: Bobbs-Merrill, 1957 (1863).

12. R. C. Chewning, *Business Ethics in a Changing Culture.* Richmond, Va.: Robert F. Dame, Inc., 1983; O. E. Williamson, *The Economic Institutions of Capitalism.* New York: Free Press, 1986.

13. D. S. Sherwin, "The Ethical Roots of the Business System," *Harvard Business Review,* November–December 1983, pp. 183–192; B. Z. Posner and W. H. Schmidt, "Values and the American Manager: An Update," *California Management Review,* Spring 1984, pp. 202–216.

14. V. Barry, *Moral Issues in Business.* Belmont, Calif.: Wadsworth, 1979.

15. This and the next two In Practices were adapted from D. J. Fritzsche and H. Becker, "Linking Man-

agement Behavior to Ethical Philosophy: An Empirical Investigation," *Academy of Management Journal,* 1984, **27:**166–175.

16. R. C. Chewning, "Can Free Enterprise Survive Ethical Schizophrenia?" *Business Horizons,* March/April 1984, pp. 5–11; G. England, O. Dhingra, and N. Agarwal, "The Manager and the Man: A Cross-Cultural Study of Personal Values," *Organization and Administrative Sciences,* 1974, **5:**1–97.

17. M. Velasquez, D. V. Moberg, and G. F. Cavanagh, "Organizational Statesmanship and Dirty Politics: Ethical Guidelines for the Organizational Politician," *Organizational Dynamics,* Autumn 1983, pp. 65–80.

18. G. F. Cavanagh, *American Business Values,* 2nd ed. Englewood Cliffs, N.J.: Prentice-Hall, 1984, p. 143; S. B. Foote, "Corporate Responsibility in a Changing Legal Environment," *California Management Review,* Spring 1984, pp. 217–228.

19. D. W. Ewing, "Your Right to Fire," *Harvard Business Review,* March–April 1983, pp. 32–34, 38, 41–42; D. W. Ewing, "How to Negotiate with Employee Objectors," *Harvard Business Review,* January–February 1983, pp. 103–110.

20. D. W. Ewing, "Due Process: Will Business Default?" *Harvard Business Review,* November–December 1982, pp. 114–128; F. Elliston, *Whistleblowing: Managing Dissent in the Workplace.* New York: Praeger, 1985.

21. J. D. Aram, *Managing Business and Public Policy: Concepts, Issues, and Cases.* Boston: Pitman, 1983, p. 21.

22. J. Locke, *Concerning Civil Government.* London: J. M. Dent and Sons, 1924, p. 180. *Also see* I. Maitland, "The Limits of Business Self-Regulation," *California Management Review,* Spring 1985, pp. 132–147.

23. J. Rawls, *A Theory of Justice.* Cambridge, Mass.: Harvard University Press, 1971, pp. 60, 302.

24. G. R. Laczniak, "Framework for Analyzing Marketing Ethics," *Journal of Macromarketing,* Spring 1983, pp. 7–18.

25. R. S. Schuler, *Personnel and Human Resource Management,* 2nd ed. St. Paul, Minn.: West Publishing, 1984, pp. 306–307.

26. Rawls, *A Theory of Justice,* pp. 111–112.

27. T. W. Dunfee, "Employee Ethical Attitudes and Business Firm Productivity," *Wharton Annual—1984,* 1983, pp. 8, 75–86.

28. Ewing, "Your Right to Fire," p. 38.

29. Ewing, "Your Right to Fire," p. 34.

30. G. T. Wilson, "Solving Ethical Problems and Saving Your Career," *Business Horizons,* November/December 1983, pp. 16–20; R. Jackall, "Moral Mazes: Bureaucracy and Managerial Work," *Harvard Business Review,* September–October 1983, pp. 118–130.

31. Chewning, "Can Free Enterprise Survive . . . ?" pp. 5–11. *Also see:* T. Donaldson, *Corporations and Morality.* Englewood Cliffs, N.J.: Prentice-Hall, 1982.

32. M. Friedman, "A Friedman Doctrine: The Social Responsibility of Business Is to Increase Its Profits," *New York Times Magazine,* September 13, 1970, pp. 32, 33, 122, 124, 126.

33. Friedman, "A Friedman Doctrine . . . ," p. 126.

34. Adapted from D. R. Dalton and R. A. Cosier, "The Four Faces of Social Responsibility," *Business Horizons,* May/June 1982, pp. 19–27. Copyright © 1982 by the Foundation for the School of Business at Indiana University. Reprinted by permission.

35. R. E. Freeman and D. L. Reed, "Stockholders and Stakeholders: A New Perspective on Corporate Governance," *California Management Review,* Spring 1983, pp. 88–106; J. A. Sonnenfeld, *Corporate Views of the Public Interest.* Boston: Auburn House, 1981; R. Ford and F. McLaughlin, "Perceptions of Socially Responsible Activities and Attitudes: A Comparison of Business School Deans and Corporate Chief Executives," *Academy of Management Journal,* 1984, **27:**666–674.

36. P. F. Drucker, "The New Meaning of Corporate Social Responsibility," *California Management Review,* Winter 1984, pp. 53–63. *Also see:* D. R. Cressey and C. A. Moore, "Managerial Values and Corporate Codes of Ethics," *California Management Review,* Summer 1983, pp. 53–77.

37. Drucker, "The New Meaning . . . ," p. 62.

38. H. Mintzberg, "The Case for Corporate Social Responsibility," *Journal of Business Strategy,* Fall

1983, pp. 3–15. *Also see:* M. Sashkin, "Participative Management Is an Ethical Imperative," *Organizational Dynamics,* Spring 1984, pp. 4–22.

39. K. Davis and W. C. Frederick, *Business and Society: Management, Public Policy, and Ethics.* New York: McGraw-Hill, 1984; A. F. Buono and L. Nichols, *Corporate Policy, Values, and Social Responsiveness.* New York: Praeger,1985; R. Buchholz, *Business Environment and Public Policy,* 2nd ed. Englewood Cliffs, N.J.: Prentice-Hall, 1986.

40. P. L. Cochran and R. A. Wood, "Corporate Social Responsibility and Financial Performance," *Academy of Management Journal,* 1984, 27:42–56.

41. D. A. Garvin, "Can Industry Self-Regulation Work?" *California Management Review,* Summer 1983, pp. 37–52.

42. Adapted from Davis and Frederick, *Business and Society . . . ,* pp. 549–560.

43. Johnson & Johnson, *The Tylenol Comeback.* Company publication, 1983, p. 8.

44. "Changing a Corporate Culture: Can Johnson & Johnson Go from Band-Aids to High Tech?" *Business Week,* May 14, 1984, p. 132.

45. J. F. Post and J. F. Mahon, "Articulated Turbulence: The Effect of Regulatory Agencies on Corporate Responses to Social Change," *Academy of Management Review,* 1980, 5:399–407; J. J. Chrisman and A. B. Carroll, "Corporate Responsibility—Reconciling Economic and Social Goals," *Sloan Management Review,* Winter 1984, pp. 59–65; P. T. Jones, "Sanctions, Incentives and Corporate Behavior," *California Management Review,* Spring 1985, pp. 119–131.

46. W. C. Norris, *New Frontiers for Business Leadership,* Minneapolis: Dorn Books, 1983, pp. 49–50.

47. Adapted from *Atlantic Richfield 1982 Annual Report.* Los Angeles: Shareholder Relations Department, Atlantic Richfield, 1983, p. 30.

48. Adapted from Fritzsche and Becker, "Linking Management Behavior to Ethical Philosophy . . . ," pp. 1, 172.

49. Adapted from Fritzsche and Becker, p. 173.

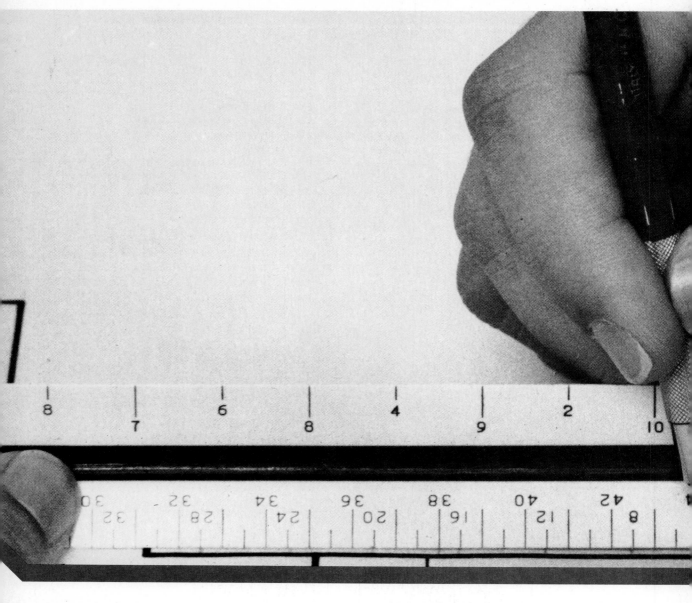

PART III

DECISION MAKING AND PLANNING

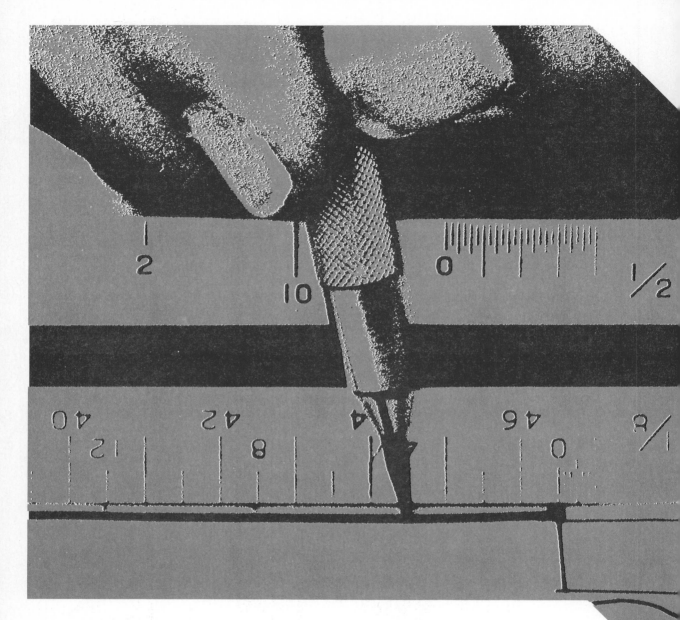

Fundamentals of Managerial Decision Making

LEARNING OBJECTIVES

After studying this chapter, you should be able to:

- Identify various combinations of problem/solution decision situations.

- Describe the differences between routine, adaptive, and innovative decisions.

- Explain the impact of certainty, risk, and uncertainty in managerial decision making.

- State the nature of objectives and their role in decision making.

- Apply the steps of the rational decision model.

- Explain the bounded rationality decision model.

- Describe the political decision model.

CHAPTER OUTLINE

PREVIEW CASE

Pearle Vision Centers

As part of an aggressive growth strategy several years ago, the Searle Optical Group, which operates Pearle Vision Centers, secured $600,000 for incremental advertising to supplement its budget of $12,000,000. Since a complete schedule for the year's media plan had already been developed, the additional dollars could be used in any number of ways. Most company executives, including James Rothe, then senior vice-president of marketing, felt that television was the most effective medium for Pearle Vision Centers advertising. Given that decision, the immediate problem was to identify alternative ways of spending the $600,000. The general objectives were to increase public awareness, improve the company's image, and increase traffic and sales at the more than 700 Pearle Vision Centers throughout the country. The basic alternatives identified with the assistance of an ad agency included: (1) buying an additional three weeks of network TV time to supplement the planned 26 weeks targeted at reaching 7.8 million households; (2) increasing the advertising levels in the top 25 TV markets (New York City, Dallas, Los Angeles, San Francisco, and so on) for a month; (3) buying 14 weeks of ads on a spot schedule; or (4) sponsoring one of the early-morning shows: "Today" (NBC), "Good Morning America" (ABC) or "Morning" (CBS).

The decision to purchase sponsorship of one of the early-morning weekday shows was made by Rothe. He felt that this alternative provided the best exposure and format for Pearle's advertising. In addition, he felt that the existing network and spot schedules were adequate. Thus he was seeking alternative exposure options. The "Good Morning America" show had slightly higher total Nielson ratings than the "Today" show, and substantially more than "Morning." The ratings of "Good Morning America" indicated that it was viewed by a somewhat more affluent and well-educated audience. Also, more business travelers watched that show than the others. These data led Rothe to select "Good Morning America." Negotiations with ABC's executives enabled Pearle Vision Centers to secure more than 30 weeks of coverage on the show at the rate of two 30-second commercials per week. An announcement of the "Good Morning America" advertising was sent to each Pearle Vision Center to inform the managers of the additonal promotional support for their stores.[1]

Source: Darlene Bordwell, Boston.

This Preview Case illustrates some of the fundamentals of decision making by managers on a daily basis: defining problems, gathering information about the problems, identifying and assessing possible alternative solutions, and making judgments (choices) about what to do. These fundamentals and others are developed throughout the chapter.

Consistent with the situation facing Jim Rothe at Pearle Vision Centers, the primary objective of this chapter is to explain a variety of ideas that can be helpful in diagnosing different types of decision-making situations, selecting among alternative ways for making decisions, and understanding the basic forces that can influence decision making.

PRECONDITIONS FOR DECISION MAKING

As suggested in Fig. 6.1, four preconditions must exist for meaningful decision making to occur; that is, it is likely to take place only if the answer to the following four questions is *yes*.[2]

1. *Is there a gap (or difference) between the present situation and some desired objective?* At first this gap may be only some vague sense of dissatisfaction. Let us assume that you have been out of college for four years and have received pay raises averaging 8 percent per year. Considering your job responsibilities and your relative performance, you feel a sense of dissatisfaction.

2. *Is the decisionmaker aware of the significance of the gap?* Over time, you realize that you should be earning about 20 percent more than you are. This feeling increased when you contacted a professional employment agency about another job and learned more about salaries in other companies.

3. *Is the decisionmaker motivated to act on the gap?* After discussing your dissatisfaction with your manager, you learn that the company is in such a weak financial position that pay raises for the coming year will be very small: The maximum raise will be 8 percent. According to your manager, many others in the organization are in your same situation. You decide to go to an employment agency to find out about job alternatives. The employment agency indicates that the only jobs available at an acceptable salary would require you to relocate 600 miles from home. This creates a lot of stress. All of your friends and family are located in the city where you work. Because you want very much to maintain close personal and family ties, you never explore these other jobs. Thus the decision-making process is ended without a full exploration of alternative possibilities.

4. *Does the decisionmaker have the resources (ability, money, will) to act on the gap?* Since you decided not to relocate, you think about opening up a McDonald's outlet. Unless you could raise $500,000 or more, there'd be no point in thinking further about this alternative possibility.

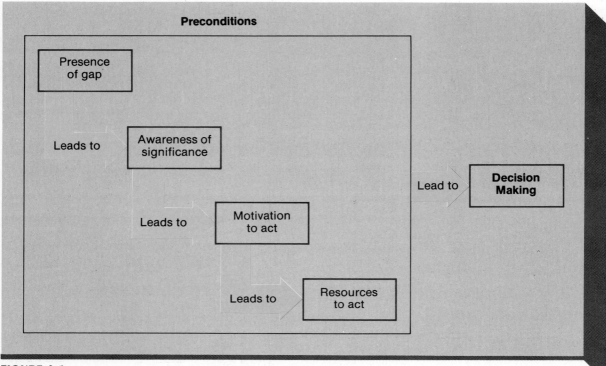

FIGURE 6.1
Preconditions for Decision Making

Most managers are faced with having to assess these four preconditions for a variety of decision situations that confront them daily. These assessments take place so fast in the minds of managers that they may not be consciously aware of making them.

CONTEXT FOR MANAGERIAL DECISION MAKING

PROBLEM—SOLUTION DECISION SITUATIONS

Figure 6.2 provides a basic framework for understanding the wide variety of problem—solution situations experienced by managers. We have broadly classified managerial decisions as routine, adaptive, and innovative. The type of problem and possible alternative solutions in the decision situation are keys to each classification.[3]

The vertical axis in Fig. 6.2 indicates that managers deal with organizational problems ranging from known and well-defined problems to ambiguous and undefined problems. A bank teller with a cash drawer out of balance at the end of the day is an example of a known and well-defined problem. In contrast, considerable ambiguity and differences of opinion are involved in determining why women are not moving faster into top management positions. At one extreme, many women—and a few men—maintain that women are the victims of blatant sexism. At the other extreme, many men—and a few women—believe that women are unsuitable for the highest managerial jobs. In between, a large group of men and women see discrimination as the major problem, but can't define precisely what they mean by the term.[4]

The horizontal axis in Fig. 6.2 indicates the general types of alternative solutions that are available to managers for dealing with problems, ranging

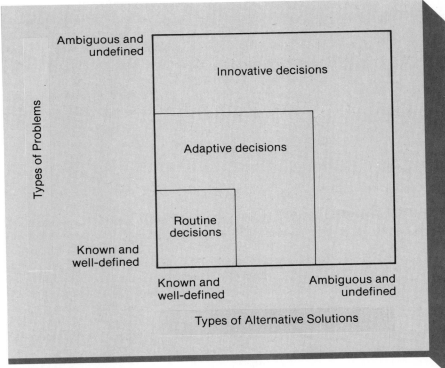

FIGURE 6.2
Matrix of Problem–Solution Decision Situations

Source: Adapted from W. R. Boulton, *Business Policy: The Art of Strategic Management.* New York: Macmillan, 1984, p. 187.

from known and well-defined alternatives to ambiguous and undefined alternatives.

Routine decisions

Managers make *routine decisions* in response to relatively well-defined and known problems. Available alternative solutions are often found in established rules, standard operating procedures, and, increasingly, in computer programs. Cleaning buildings, processing payroll vouchers, preparing customers' orders, and making travel arrangements are only a few examples of duties that require only routine decisions.

Adaptive decisions

Managers also make *adaptive decisions* from choices that involve a combination of (1) the diagnosis of problems by managers through systematic analysis; and (2) the development of modified alternative solutions from those readily available. Adaptive decisions often involve building upon and making changes in past decisions and practices, rather than abruptly departing from the past. In the Preview Case, Jim Rothe of Pearle Vision Centers made an adaptive decision when he decided to go with "Good Morning America" for the $600,000 in supplemental advertising. Japanese radio manufacturers made significant in-roads into the U.S. market with the application of adaptive decisions—in terms of both problem definition and alternative solutions. In contrast, U.S. manufacturers apparently assumed that they faced relatively routine decisions in order to survive in this market.

IN PRACTICE
Japanese Radio Manufacturers

Many financially oriented, diversified U.S. electrical manufacturers (for example, General Electric and RCA) simply treated radios as a product line. They were convinced that every product line has its natural cycle of growth, stability, and decline in sales. The radio was treated as a product that had passed its peak. Thus the radio business was a prime candidate for financial *milking,* or the harvesting of profits for use elsewhere in the company.

However, Japanese radio manufacturers made entirely different decisions. They didn't treat radios as merely a product line: The business they were in was radios. They focused on the business line of goods into which radios fell and did not blindly accept the assumption that radios were in a mature (no-growth) stage. Instead, they created a demand for audio entertainment based on consumers' basic listening desires. They studied the times, places, and occasions of consumer behavior in listening to broadcasts and recorded music. The resulting success of composite products, such as radio cassettes and Sony's Walkman, is history. The fact that consumers in the United States and other countries throughout the world are buying these products in such numbers is proof that user demand was there all the time.[5]

A crucial lesson is that managers play an important role in making judgments about the types of problems and possible alternative solutions available to them. Managers all too often may have a tendency to focus on routine decisions, when adaptive, even innovative, decisions care called for by the nature of the problem. Thus a manager's ability to diagnose a problem and see its potential solution in new ways is crucial.

INNOVATIVE DECISIONS

Managers who make *innovative decisions* are involved in a combination of (1) the discovery, identification, and diagnosis of ambiguous and undefined problems; and (2) the development of unique, novel, and creative possible alternative solutions. Innovative decisions represent a break with the past. They also require that managers look at both problem definition and possible alternative solutions in new ways, as illustrated in the problem facing Recreational Equipment Company.

IN PRACTICE
RECREATIONAL
EQUIPMENT
COMPANY

A business professor was supervising teams of college students in a special-projects, small-business course. The student teams were assigned to local companies that needed financial counseling. One of the firms sold water-recreation equipment. Since sales were highly seasonal, the owner asked the students to develop a forecasting technique that could accurately predict fluctuations in sales. When the team was reviewing available techniques, one of the members brought up an interesting point. He wondered, "Why focus on better sales-forecasting techniques?" He argued that the owner should try to reduce the highly seasonal sales (a controllable action) rather than attempt to predict the seasonal pattern (an uncontrollable event). After much analysis the team recommended that the firm sell winter-recreation equipment in order to smooth out the highly fluctuating levels of sales. The firm implemented the recommendation and the seasonal sales fluctuations were eliminated.[6]

By emphasizing the need for more accurate techniques for estimating sales, the company's owner had defined the problem narrowly, focusing on uncontrollable events. He should have also looked at the situation more broadly and assessed what might be done, if anything, about sales fluctuations.

Most innovative decisions have the following characteristics.

- They usually represent a series of mini-decisions made over a period of months, or possibly even over several years.

- They sometimes represent an individual event but, more often, many people are involved in various ways and at various times.

- They normally do not unfold in a logical, orderly sequence. Solutions may be decided upon before problems are fully understood and action on earlier problems may affect current decisions.

- Innovative decision making by managers takes place in the midst of a lot of other managerial activities. The numerous interruptions and juggling of managerial life have strong effects on decision-making activities.[7]

McCall, Kaplan, and Gerlach further suggest that:

Solving important problems will never be the logical, orderly process that most of us strive for, no matter how orderly the plan. Defining problems will remain an evolutionary process affected by points of view, vested interests, and the bits and pieces of information available at any given time. Pressures will ebb and flow, shifting attention from one problem to another, changing definitions involving and excluding various individuals. Sometimes the real problem won't materialize until well into the decision-making process; or maybe not until after some action has been taken. People will take hip shots when they should have been more thoughtful; relatively simple problems will at times end up in convoluted decision-making cycles. Finding truth will remain problematic.[8]

Conditions Affecting Decision Making

Managers have to make decisions on the basis of the amount and accuracy of information available to them. Their decisions involve *future* actions and results, which cannot be foreseen, and therefore involve risk. Routine decisions are most often made under conditions that approximate certainty and low levels of risk. Adaptive decisions are usually accompanied by moderate levels of uncertainty and risk. Finally, innovative decisions generally involve high levels of uncertainty and risk.

States of nature

We use the term ***states of nature*** to identify those factors that managers cannot control but which can influence the outcomes (results) of their decisions.[9] These factors can range from megatrends to entrance of new competitors to alternative solutions for a specific problem. Managers must attempt to not only identify these factors but also to estimate their potential impact on managerial decisions. Because these factors will come into play in the future, they can be extremely difficult to anticipate, much less predict. More often than not, managers have to make judgment decisions based on the information available to them. The amount and accuracy of information, including forecasts, and managers' diagnostic skills are vital parts of dealing with states of nature in decision making.

For illustrative purposes, we can group states of nature under three conditions that affect decision making: certainty, risk, and uncertainty. These conditions are shown as a continuum in Fig. 6.3. When managers can identify states of nature and their potential impacts with great confidence, we say that decisions are made under the ***condition of certainty.*** As the amount of information about states of nature decreases, managers have to estimate the probability of their occurrence (based on either objective or subjective probabilities); we call this the *condition of risk* in decision making. At the other extreme, managers may have virtually no information about states of nature and no way to assign even subjective probabilities to the likelihood of their occurrence; we call this the *condition of uncertainty.*

CONDITION OF CERTAINTY

Decision situations under certainty are those in which managers are fully informed about a problem, the possible alternative solutions, and the outcomes (results) of those solutions; that is, managers can control (or at least anticipate) events and be sure of the outcomes. Once managers have identified alternative solutions and the expected outcomes for each, the decision is

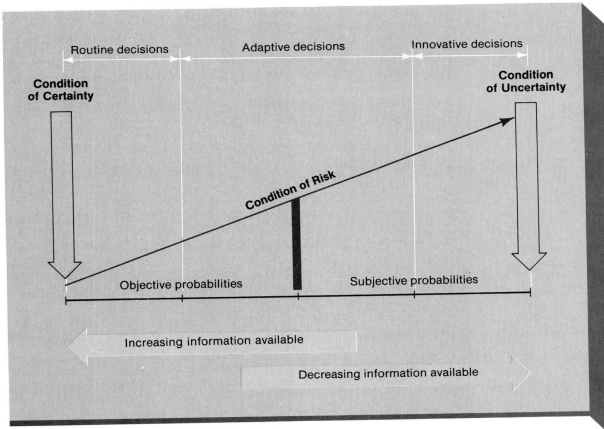

FIGURE 6.3
Continuum of Conditions Affecting Decision Making

relatively easy. The managers simply choose the alternative solution with the best outcome or *payoff*. For example, all other things being equal, a purchasing manager is expected to purchase a standard grade of paper from the supplier who offers the lowest price.

However, in actual practice, the decision process is not so simple. There usually are many possible alternative solutions to a problem and it would be extremely time-consuming and expensive to calculate expected outcomes for all of them. And, for top and middle managers, decision making under conditions of certainty occurs infrequently.

Some decisions, especially those made by first-line managers, closely approximate the condition of certainty. For example, a manager may decide to

INTERNATIONAL FOCUS

Risk Analysts: Commonsense and Skepticism

The world is full of political risk analysts, each offering—for a suitably large fee—his own exclusive insight into the future.

Not surprisingly, America is the country where the analysts flourish and where they are held in highest regard. It was there that the Association of Political Risk Analysts (APRA) was founded after the U.S. oil companies and other multinationals woke up one day to find that an Ayatollah had replaced a friendly Shah.

Some analysts believe they can translate political trends into mathematical formulae, and so arrive at a risk score for a country. They will try to construct the political equivalent of an economic model, feeding in such variables as the calory per capita intake of the populace (hunger breeds revolution). Others, less ambitious, merely collate reports with the aid of local panellists—politicians, academics, and the like—and do something to remedy the often woeful ignorance that educated businessmen display of areas such as Central America.

For the most part, export credit insurers will have little to do with professional analysts. Underwriting political risk remains a largely instinctive business; it is more a matter of balancing a portfolio—making a book—and reflecting on past experience before setting a premium that the market will bear.

That is not to say that underwriters, whether in the private market or in official agencies, ignore the obvious sources of information. These include IMF, World Bank of OECD reports, embassy despatches, bank economists' country profiles, the daily newspaper, and even on occasion the prognostications of the CIA.

Much political analysis is essentially economic analysis. The point at which a country's debt service ratio becomes unsupportable, its dependence on world commodity prices, its balance of payments trend, rate of inflation, money

Source: Excerpted from *The Banker*, April 1984, p. 40.

have some employees who are doing routine tasks work overtime. The cost of the overtime can be determined with certainty; the manager can expect with certainty the production of at least a minimal number of additional units. Thus the cost of the extra units can be figured with virtual certainty before the overtime is ordered.

Condition of risk

Managers can estimate the level of *risk* involved in decisions when they can define the nature of the problem, the probability of the occurrence of relevant states of nature, the possible alternative solutions, and the probability of each solution leading to the desired outcome. *Probability* refers to the

supply—all these may be more important than, say, the internal struggles of its military regime. Again, a dramatic *coup d'etat* in Bolivia may have less important economic repercussions than the peaceful election of a Socialist government in France.

Judgments are still qualitative rather than quantitative, although economic modelling is increasingly being used—by the Export Credits Guarantee Department, for example—to test qualitative assessments. The ECGD is developing a 'Z-score' technique, familiar to business schools as a tool for predicting corporate failure, as a way of anticipating by about a year the moment that a country is likely to seek rescheduling of its foreign debt.

Its Z-score equation contains 14 factors, a series of economic indicators each with its own weighting, added together to give a country rating. The system is used to cross-check the department's traditional assessment procedure for setting country limits and dividing markets into its four categories of risk. (Neither the limit nor the grade of a country is disclosed.)

For the broker and underwriter in the private market, political risk analysis is perhaps less important still. He is concerned not so much with the country as with the track record of the exporter.

'Everyone thinks it's frightfully glamourous,' says a Lloyd's underwriter. 'But to some extent, the more boring we are, the more successful we are. Fundamentally it's commonsense, with a certain degree of scepticism, that makes an underwriter. It's no good having grand ideas.'

In some ways political risk analysis is just a new name for an old game. Armen Kouyoumdjian, secretary of the European branch of APRA, said: 'People have been doing it since before Christ: diplomats and businessmen, anyway, have been doing it for donkey's years.'

percentage of time that a specific outcome would occur if a particular decision were made a large number of times.[10] The most commonly used example of probability is that of tossing a coin: With enough tosses of a coin, heads will show up 50 percent of the time.

The amount and quality of information available about relevant states of nature can vary widely. The interpretation of this information and estimates of risk by managers can vary even more. The type, amount, and reliability of information determine whether managers can use one or the other of two types of probability estimation: *objective probability* and *subjective probability.* (See Fig. 6.3.)

Objective probability.   This method is used in decision situations in which managers can determine—on the basis of facts and figures—the likelihood that each state of nature will occur. Managers cannot be certain about *which* events will occur or *when* certain events might occur. However, by examining past records, they can determine the likelihood of occurrence for each decision outcome for a given event. For example, life insurance companies cannot determine the year in which each of their policyholders will die. However, these companies do establish objective probabilities of how many of their policyholders, in various age categories, will die in a particular year. These objective probabilities are based on the expectation that past experience will be repeated in the future.

Changes in states of nature can make past records and practices inapplicable. Iran and Iraq began to attack ships carrying oil in the Persian Gulf in 1984. Prior to the attacks, maritime-insurance premiums were quite stable and were based on extensive historical records of losses resulting from accidents (ships running aground or into each other), bad weather, and the like. Shortly after the attacks on the first five ships, the companies insuring ships that use the Gulf substantially increased their premiums on the basis of little more than educated guesses as to future losses from such attacks. Over a six-month period, the premium for a typical large oil tanker making a one-week trip in the Persian Gulf to and from an Iranian oil terminal rose from $500,000 to more than $4 million.[11] The insurance companies could no longer use objective probabilities to assess the risk of loss they might have to absorb. A crucial state of nature had changed for the insurance companies.

Subjective probability.   This method is used in decision situations in which managers must rely on their own subjective judgments and beliefs to determine the likelihood of occurrence for possible states of nature. Probabilities are assigned subjectively and may vary from one manager to another, depending on the manager's intuition, previous experience with similar decision situations, expert opinions, personality traits (such as risk taking versus risk avoidance), and other factors.

The use of subjective probabilities can be illustrated by the case of a theater owner who is thinking about changing the price of popcorn. What effect would a 10-percent price increase have on the average amount of popcorn sold per theater customer? The owner might estimate that there is a 30-percent chance of sales dropping off by 5 percent, a 10-percent chance of sales dropping by 10 percent, and a 50-percent chance that sales will stay the same. He does not know and must decide whether to risk the price increase. A more complex example of the use of subjective probabilities is that of forecasting international business risks in various countries.

IN PRACTICE
Risk Index for International Business

Frast and Sullivan, a risk-analysis consulting firm, annually develop risk forecasts for 81 countries over an 18-month period. Their forecasts cover five major categories of risk.

1. *Most likely regime:* This states the subjective probability of which government is most likely to be in power 18 months from now and of the current government being in power at that time. The latest risk index was developed in early 1984. Note that a 60% probability was assigned to the reelection of Ronald Reagan as President of the United States.

2. *Probability of turmoil:* This presents the subjective probability of international business loss from political upheaval, including riots, demonstrations, terrorism, civil war, and international war, over the next 18 months.

3. *Financial risk:* This is the subjective probability that a country will reschedule debt payments, undertake major devaluations of its currency, restrict currency outflows, and delay payments to creditors over the next 18 months. The consulting firm translates its subjective probability ratings (0–100) for each financial risk factor into an overall rating scheme of A+ through D−. A rating of A+ is given for least financial risk and that of D− for the most financial risk. A country could receive one of 12 ratings for financial risk: A+, A, A−, B+, B, B−, C+, C, C−, D+, D, or D−.

4. *Investment risk:* This reports the subjective probability that firms will experience losses as a result of direct capital investments in plant, equipment, and other assets within a particular country over the next 18 months. As with financial risk, an A+ through D− rating scale is used.

5. *Export risk:* This presents the subjective probability that firms will experience losses as a result of tariff and nontariff barriers to exporting their goods to a country as well as the difficulties exporters might face in trying to collect on their goods sold over the next 18 months. Again, an A+ through D− rating scale is used.

Table 6.1 shows the 1984 risk indices for nine of these 81 countries.[12]

TABLE 6.1 ■ 1984 RISK INDICES FOR INTERNATIONAL BUSINESS IN NINE COUNTRIES (18-MONTH FORECAST)

COUNTRY	MOST LIKELY REGIME	PROBABILITY OF TURMOIL	FINANCIAL RISK	INVESTMENT RISK	EXPORTING RISK
Argentina	Alfonsin, 60%	Moderate 26%	D+	C	D
Canada	Conservatives, 50%	Low 6%	B+	A−	A
France	Center Socialist, 50%	Low 17%	B−	C+	C+
Japan	Traditional LDP, 65%	Low 10%	B+	A−	B
Mexico	De la Madrid, Technicians, 65%	Moderate 30%	C−	C+	D+
Nigeria	Pragmatic Military, 55%	High 30%	D+	D+	D−
United Kingdom	Thatcher Hard-Liners, 85%	Low 15%	A+	A+	A
United States	Reagan, 60%	Low 8%	A+	A+	A
West Germany	Kohl, 75%	Low 7%	A+	A+	A+

Source: W. D. Coplin and M. K. O'Leary, the 1984 Risk Index For International Business, *Planning Review*, May 1984, 37-38. Published by Robert J. Alio & Associates, Inc., for the North American Society for Corporate Planning.

Condition of UNCERTAINTY

This condition involves decision situations in which managers cannot assign even subjective probabilities to the occurrence of possible states of nature; that is, managers have little or no information, insight, or intuitive judgment to use as a basis for assigning probabilities. In fact, managers may not even be able to define the nature of a problem or alternative solutions to it. In the extreme case, managers will not be able to identify the relevant states of nature.[13]

Dealing with varying degrees of uncertainty is central to the jobs of top managers and various professional groups in organizations, such as research and development engineers, market researchers, and planning staffs.[14] Firms launching projects or programs involving significantly different products or services for new types of markets that require the use of novel technologies do so under the conditions of uncertainty. This is generally true even if the firms engage in considerable research and planning prior to committing resources to the production of substantially new products or services. Let us consider the case of the Concorde.

IN PRACTICE
The Concorde

The decision by the French and British governments to collaborate on constructing a supersonic (1350-mph) passenger plane was a major decision made under the condition of uncertainty. When the plan for constructing the Concorde was announced in 1962, the estimated developmental costs were $150 million. When its started flying in 1976, the developmental costs had spiraled to more than $2 billion. The first group of 16 Concordes is also the last. The Concorde costs about twice as much as a Boeing 747 to operate and burns about three times as much fuel per passenger mile; it is five to 17 times as polluting, depending on the specific pollutant, of the atmosphere. Moreover, the noise levels and possible harm to the ozone layer are potentially severe problems.[15] In short, many of the present-day concerns about the Concorde could not even be identified in 1962 or, if they could, were not thought to be relevant problems at that time or for the future.

British Airways and Air France are the only airlines flying the Concorde; each has seven of these planes. Air France is flying only four of its seven Concordes, and only between Paris and New York. However, British Airways has turned the Concorde white elephant into a profitable operation by developing the Concorde business around superluxury package charters for the well-to-do.[16] This market niche was developed by British Airways management in 1983, after some seven years of operation and millions of dollars in operating losses for the Concorde. The two governments do not expect to ever recover their $2 billion in developmental costs.

Development of the Concorde clearly required a whole stream of innovative decisions to be made under the condition of uncertainty. Because hindsight is often 20/20, we should not criticize too harshly those who made the decisions to proceed with the development of the Concorde in the early 1960s. After all, under the condition of uncertainty, we cannot—by definition—predict future outcomes. "The impossibility of total prediction is clearly illustrated by the principle that if we had tomorrow's newspaper today, a good deal of it [events] would not happen."]¹⁷ There are certain irreducible uncertainties for managers and all of us in our day-to-day lives.[18]

OBJECTIVES AND DECISION MAKING

Objectives and the setting of objectives are important in helping people and organizations to create some sense of order, direction, and meaning in their environments. This is an especially important part of the decision-making processes used by managers.

This section is limited to a presentation of several introductory ideas about the importance, types, and role of objectives. We consider them in more detail in Chapters 7–9.

Nature of Objectives

Objectives are results to be attained. Objectives generally suggest a *direction* for actions and decisions, as well as a specified *quality* or *quantity* of the results desired. In the Preview Case, Jim Rothe of Searle set forth general objectives to "increase awareness, improve image, and increase traffic and sales at the more than 700 Pearle Vision Centers throughout the country." These general objectives did not state specific quantities, but they did indicate a direction and sense of quality desired in the use of $600,000 in supplemental advertising funds. Objectives also may be termed goals, ends, missions, purposes, standards, deadlines, targets, and quotas.[19] Regardless of the label, *objectives* specify a state of affairs that someone thinks is desirable for an organization or themselves. The objectives chosen do not always prove to be effective for the organization's long-run survival and growth. For example, Henry Ford's objective of producing only black Model-T Fords was ultimately detrimental to the company's success.

The types and levels of organizational objectives represent a continuous decision problem for all managers. A for-profit firm's general objectives of survival, growth, and profitability often remain stable. Its subobjectives, such as types of goods marketed and services provided, usually shift significantly over time. An example of changes in subobjectives is Kresge's marketing change in the mid-1960s to capture a new type of customer, the discount shopper. These changes in subobjectives were accompanied by a change in name—from Kresge to Kmart. In 1984, management broadened the subobjectives and introduced financial services into some Kmart stores.

Reasons for setting objectives

There are many possible reasons for setting objectives, depending on whether your point of reference is the organization as a whole, a specific department or division within an organization, management as a group, or individual employees. Four basic reasons for setting organizational objectives are identified in Fig. 6.4.

Objectives help to channel decisions and *direct the efforts* of an organization. They provide a set of stated expectations that all members of the organization can understand and try to achieve.

IN PRACTICE
IBM's Business Objectives

IBM's strategy is aimed at taking full advantage of the promising potential we see for the information industry in the 1980s and beyond. At the core of that strategy are three primary business objectives:

We are firmly committed to profitable growth. We are expanding our traditional business and investing in a variety of new entrepreneurial opportunities with high, long-term potential.

We intend to be the product leaders, to stay in the forefront of the industry in technology, reliability, quality, and value across our entire product line.

We are concentrating on efficiency in every aspect of our work. We want to be not only the low-cost producer of the highest quality products in the industry, but also the low-cost developer, seller and servicer.

Our progress toward meeting our business goals [objectives], detailed in this annual report, demonstrates that IBM is well prepared to meet the competitive tests of our changing industry—that our strategy for the '80s is working.

IBM employees in every area of the business have responded with significant contributions to our ambitious goals. They continue to be IBM's greatest asset. Their dedicated efforts have always been the key to our success.

January 25, 1983, by order of the Board of Directors

/s/ *John R. Opel*   /s/ *Frank T. Cary*
President and CEO   Chairman of the Board[20]

Objectives are an important *aid in planning.* After diagnosing problems and the environment, managers generally need to establish objectives as a basis for their planning efforts. Objectives also often *help to motivate* people and stimulate better performance. Objective setting, if done properly, has been found to raise productivity and improve the quality of work of managers and nonmanagers alike.[21]

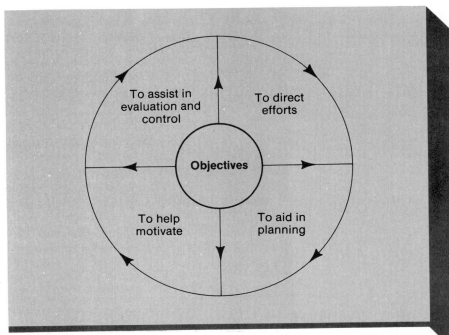

FIGURE 6.4
Reasons for Setting Organizational Objectives

Finally, objectives assist in the *evaluation and control* of individual and organizational performance. Or, according to an old saying, "If you don't know where you're going, you'll never know when you get there." The controlling aspect of setting objectives is not limited to use by superiors with subordinates. For example, you are using this book as part of a course and may have set an objective of achieving a grade of "B." When the results of the first exam are returned, let's assume your grade is a "D." This *feedback* might serve as a powerful incentive for assessing why you received a "D" grade and what you need to do to avoid this result on the next exam. In sum, you have engaged in a self-controlling set of activities aimed at achieving your objective.

Objectives can be stated in closed or open form. **Closed objectives** specify in quantifiable terms what is to be achieved (including how much), for whom, and within what time period. Closed objectives become inoperative when met. A simple closed objective is "to reduce my weight by 20 pounds within three months." It states what in quantitative terms (20 pounds of weight) and for whom (me), and specifies a measurable time period (three months). **Open objectives** provide broad direction and channeling for managerial decision making. An example of open organizational objectives are those of IBM, which were presented in the preceding In Practice. These objectives provide a general sense of direction and guidance in day-to-day efforts and decision making throughout the company.

Hierarchy of Objectives

Within organizations, efforts are usually made to link objectives between organizational levels and across interdependent departments. This is no easy task and is the source of many conflicts in organizations.

A **hierarchy of objectives** represents the formal linking of objectives of lower-level departments or individuals with those of higher-level departments or individuals. Successful use of the hierarchy-of-objectives approach requires that lower-level objectives must be achieved to enable the achievement of higher-level objectives.

Figure 6.5 provides a simple illustration of a hierarchy of objectives for an organization with five levels. It shows that, for each succeeding, lower level in the hierarchy, objectives tend to become increasingly detailed, narrower in scope, and easier to measure. The directional arrows between levels indicate that the *setting* of objectives need not and should not always flow from the highest level to each lower level. The setting of objectives often involves the flow of decisions between levels as well as across departments or divisions at any given level.

Figure 6.5 is a simple model because it does *not* show several aspects of setting objectives. It does not show all the performance objectives to be found at each level in an organization. Nor does it show the interaction between interdependent departments at a given level, such as between the production and marketing departments. In addition, the hierarchy of objectives shown in Fig. 6.5 does not reflect the potential influence of various stakeholders in the setting of objectives.

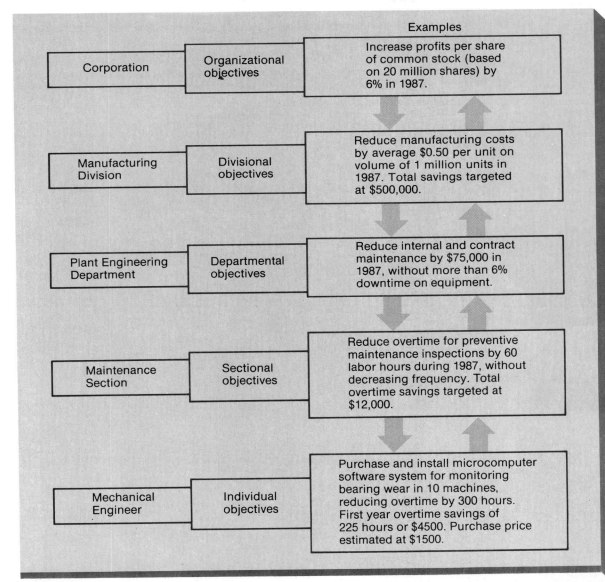

FIGURE 6.5
Simple Model of a Hierarchy of Objectives

Objective Setting and Stakeholders

Objectives are not set by managers in a vacuum: A variety of forces, often expressed through stakeholders, impact on an organization and its managers in the setting of objectives. The examples of stakeholders presented in Fig. 6.6 tend to fall into two major classes: internal and external. Both play a role in the demands, constraints, and choices faced by managers in the setting of objectives.[22]

Internal stakeholders generally are groups (coalitions) of full-time employees or volunteers who attempt to exercise power within the organization to further their own interests (objectives). Different groups of internal stakeholders do not always agree on the same objectives or the means for achieving

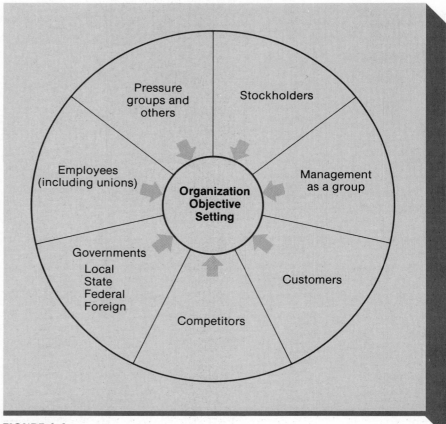

FIGURE 6.6
Organization Objective Setting: Internal and External Stakeholders

the objectives of their departments, divisions, or the organization as a whole. For example, when Ford, General Motors, and other firms announced the bonuses distributed to their managers in 1984, it was reported that Ford chairman Philip Caldwell received total compensation of $7,292,000.[23] Union workers in the auto firms responded with howls of outrage and the general reaction of "We'll get ours in the next round of negotiations." *External stakeholders* generally are groups (coalitions) in the environment with potential or real power to influence the organization.[24]

Expectations of powerful stakeholders create **demands** for setting certain objectives that must be achieved by an organization.[25] For example, governmental legislation, governmental agency interpretation and implementation of the legislation, and court rulings have resulted in the setting of objectives for hiring and promoting minorities and females by some companies. **Constraints** limit the types of objectives that may be pursued: Objectives are expected to be legal and ethical. For example, a manager facing declining sales could not legally establish objectives for the production and marketing of heroin. **Choices** are objectives over which managers have discretion; that is, objectives that managers can, but don't have to, choose. For example, the top managers of Kresge didn't have to choose the objective of meeting discount shopper needs and changing their name to Kmart. But they did and it turned out to be an important choice by top management.

The relative degrees of choice that managers have in setting organizational objectives varies greatly. Figure 6.7 shows the general relationship between the degree of managerial choice and the amount of power exercised by external stakeholders. The vertical axis shows the relative managerial choice from low discretion to high discretion. The horizontal axis shows the range of external-stakeholder power from low constraints and demands to high constraints and demands. The diagonal line suggests that managers can be primarily *proactive* in setting organizational objectives where their discretion is relatively high and external-stakeholder constraints and demands are relatively low. This is the situation at IBM. At the other extreme, managers tend to be *reactive* when they have relatively low discretion to set objectives in the face of relatively high constraints and demands imposed by powerful stakeholders. Some utility companies that generate electricity from nuclear energy seem to have fallen into this situation. Many firms that operate in highly competitive markets can be characterized as having a proactive–reactive balance in the discretion available to managers in setting objectives relative to the power of external stakeholders in dictating objectives. The J. C. Penney Company is an example of proactive–reactive balance. It is reactive to the actions of competitors and the changing patterns of consumer tastes. On the other hand, Penney's has been very proactive in selecting the market niches in which it wants to compete and in leading the way in certain market niches.

The important role of stakeholders in the processes of setting organizational objectives, in particular, and making managerial decisions, in general,

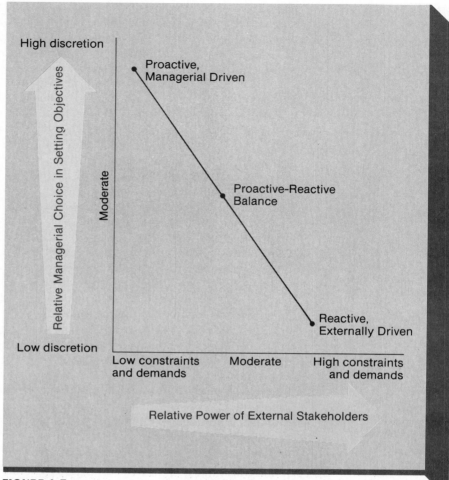

FIGURE 6.7
*Stakeholders' Power and Managerial Choice in Setting
Organizational Objectives*

has been summed up this way:

> The societal outputs desired from the organization can only be anticipated by those sectors of society who come into contact with it—shareholders, customers, suppliers, lenders, the community, government and regulatory agencies and employees—in short, the organization's stakeholders. Stakeholders are thus the claimants of organizational effectiveness—it is they who are the judges of organizational effectiveness. Thus, in order to be effective, an organization has first to determine who its stakeholders are, and then to determine the outputs desired by its stakeholders. This process soon highlights the problem of conflicting demands made by the different stakeholder groups.[26]

MODELS OF MANAGERIAL DECISION MAKING

In this last section of the chapter we present three models of managerial decision making: rational, bounded rationality, and political. These models bring together a number of the ideas already presented.

Rational Decision-Making Model

The *rational decision-making model* includes a variety of prescriptions to be followed by managers for increasing the likelihood that they will make logical, intelligent, and well-founded decisions. We describe briefly some of these prescriptions for three expressions of rationality: that of the decisionmaker, the decision, and the decision process.

Rationality of decisionmaker

It is easy, but incorrect, to suggest that individual rationality or irrationality depends on the extent to which a rational decision process is used. A decisionmaker who defies laws of reason and logic is usually considered irrational by other groups or individuals, regardless of the process. Generally, we find it easier to make judgments of irrationality about means than about objectives. For example, a residential building contractor interested in minimizing construction costs probably would consider it irrational for carpenters to use only hand hammers when faster and low-cost power hammers are available.

The significance of individual values and objectives in assessing rationality or irrationality cannot be overstated. For example, people who oppose draft registration may view it as an irrational decision that will increase the chance of war. On the other hand, proponents of registration may claim that it is a rational step, that it improves the country's ability to respond to threats to its security, and that it serves as a deterrent to potential enemies. Thus differences in values and objectives can cause one person to view a decision as rational, while another calls the same decision irrational.

Rationality of decision

A *rational decision* permits maximum achievement of objectives within the limitations of the environment in which it is made. This definition assumes that an objective is known, but it does not address the rationality of that objective. Our position is that the rationality of objectives (what we want to achieve) must be considered along with the rationality of means (how we are going to achieve the objectives). For example, many public utilities have as an objective the reduction in cost of generating electricity, which is a rational objective. One of the means for achieving this objective is to minimize the cost of fuel that goes into generating each kilowatt hour of electricity. Some power plants are designed so that they can shift from one type of fuel to another, depending on relative fuel costs per kilowatt hour of power generated from natural gas, oil, or coal. If the per-unit cost of using natural gas skyrockets relative to that of oil or coal (everything else equal), a rational decision would be to shift to oil or coal.

RATIONALITY OF DECISION PROCESS

We often emphasize the rationality of the process used by managers and others in arriving at decisions. The rational decision model prescribes certain basic steps for arriving at decisions. As shown in Fig. 6.8, a rational decision process begins with problem identification and assessment and moves through a series of steps to follow-up and control.

Problem awareness and diagnosis.   Problem awareness and diagnosis relate directly to the idea that, if managers are unaware of problems and their possible causes, no decision making will take place.[27] Problem awareness and diagnosis involve three interrelated conceptual skills: noticing, interpreting, and incorporation. ***Noticing*** means that managers distinguish among a number of forces in their environment and decide what is relevant to a problem. ***Interpretation*** means that managers assess the forces they have noticed and decide what they think is causing the problem. Finally, ***incorporation*** means that managers remember their interpretations and relate them to the current or desired state of the organization or department and to future problems.[28] If noticing, interpreting, and incorporating in the diagnosis of a problem are in error, the only way of selecting a good alternative solution is at random.

Set objectives.   Once problems are defined, managers can often set objectives that, if reached, would eliminate the problem. For example, management might conclude that it has a problem of excessive manufacturing costs. The hierarchy of objectives—as in Fig. 6.5, from the manufacturing-division level to the mechanical-engineer level—could be used to convert this problem into a series of objectives. The objectives would spell out the results desired: what is to be achieved and by what date. The objective of the plant engineering department shown in Fig. 6.5—that is, to reduce internal and contract maintenance by $75,000 in 1987, without more than 6 percent downtime on equipment—is the type of objective that could be set to reduce production costs.

In an uncertain decision situation, the setting of objectives could be the major decision problem, requiring identification of *alternative objectives,* comparison and evaluation of the alternatives, and choice among them. You might have an overall objective of pursuing a career in business but might be uncertain right now about the specific path to follow. Should you set an objective of becoming an accountant, a wholesale sales representative, or one of several hundred other identifiable careers in business? Regardless of your answer, you will find it necessary to consider alternative path objectives.

Search for possible alternative solutions.   Managers must look for possible alternative solutions to help achieve a desired objective.[29] This might mean seeking information both inside and outside the organization, engaging in creative thinking, consulting experts, undertaking research, and similar actions. When a manager cannot identify any feasible alternative solutions for reaching the objective, the manager may have to change the objective. The popularity of books such as *In Search of Excellence: Lessons from America's Best-Run Companies* (with sales of more than one million copies) shows that

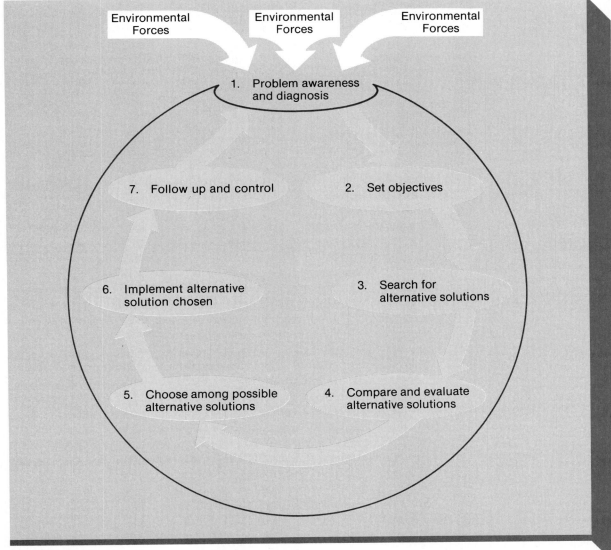

FIGURE 6.8
Prescribed Steps in the Rational Decision-Making Process

managers and others want to see if the lessons from well-managed companies can provide alternative solutions for helping them to meet their objectives.

Compare and evaluate possible alternative solutions.   Once the possible alternative solutions have been identified, they must be compared and evaluated. This step in rational decision making zeros in on expected results, including the relative costs of each of the alternative solutions.[30]

Choose among possible alternative solutions.   Decision making is popularly associated with a final choice. The final choice, however, is really only one step in the rational decision-making process.[31] Many managers complain that when recent college graduates are given a project they tend to present and discuss only one possible solution. Without an explicit comparison and evaluation of several possible alternative solutions, a manager must accept or reject the choice being presented. The rationality and limitations of a preferred choice become easier to understand and appreciate if all the steps of the rational decision-making process are followed.

Choosing among possible alternative solutions might appear to be straightforward. Unfortunately, choosing among proposed alternative solutions may be difficult when the decision problem is complex, ambiguous, and involves high degrees of risk or uncertainty.[32]

Implement alternative solution selected.   In one sense, the action step of decision making begins with the implementation of the alternative solution chosen. A *good* decision is not necessarily a *successful* one. A technically outstanding decision may not be accepted by those who have the power to implement it. Thus the technically best decision made at one management level may be turned into a bad decision by those at another level. If the selected alternative solution cannot be implemented, an effort should be made to identify new possible alternative solutions.

Follow-up and control.   Implementing the selected alternative solution will not automatically lead to the desired objective. Managers must follow up during implementation to make sure that the program or project is accomplishing the results needed and to take corrective action if it isn't.

Since many factors affecting the decision process change continually, the follow-up and control phase also may indicate a need to redefine the problem or revise the objectives. The feedback from this phase could indicate that the entire decision-making process should be started over.

Some final comments on the rational decision-making model

The process of rational decision making outlined in Fig. 6.8 probably is most useful for adaptive decisions. They involve risk characterized by objective probabilities or possibly some degree of subjective probabilities. Routine and recurring decisions do not require use of all of the steps shown in Fig. 6.8. If, for example, a particular type of decision problem tends to recur often, a manager would not need to search repeatedly for possible alternative solutions. Most likely the solution, in the form of a routine policy or procedure, would be available.

The decision-making process presented in Fig. 6.8 might best be thought of as an *ideal* model for nudging all of us closer to rationality in making decisions. This ideal process is probably only approximated by managers and organizations. When dealing with some types of decision problems, managers do not even make an effort to approximate the prescribed ideal of a rational decision process.[33] The following two decision models are based on observations of managerial decision-making in practice. They suggest why the ideal may be the exception rather than the rule, especially at middle- and top-management levels.[34]

Bounded Rationality Decision-Making Model

The *bounded rationality decision-making model* reflects the tendency of managers to (1) set less than the highest objectives (satisfice); (2) engage in a limited search for possible alternative solutions; and (3) have inadequate information and control of the factors influencing the outcomes of their decisions.[35] The bounded rationality decision-making model provides a general description of day-to-day decision processes used by many managers.

This model is useful because it emphasizes the limitations of the decision-maker's rationality and it partially explains the differences in decisions arrived at by managers, even when they appear to have the same information. Let us consider the three elements of the bounded rationality decision-making model: satisficing, limited search, and inadequate information and control.

Satisficing

When managers do not set the highest objectives, they settle for acceptable objectives that might be easier to obtain, less controversial, or otherwise safer. This is called *satisficing.* For example, one objective of a business might be to maximize profits. Profit levels are often expressed as desired objectives, such as a 15-percent rate of return on investment or a 10-percent increase in profits over the previous year. These objectives may not be the maximum that can be attained. They may represent little more than subjective judgments of top management about reasonable objectives; objectives that are challenging, but not too difficult to achieve.

The bounded-rationality decision model was first introduced by Herbert Simon in the mid-1950s. The creation of this model was a significant factor in the decision by the Swedish Academy of Sciences to award him the 1978 Nobel Prize in economics for his "pioneering research into the decision-making process within economic organizations." In an interview almost 35 years after introducing the bounded rationality decision-making model, Simon described satisficing in these words for a management audience:

> Satisficing is intended to be used in contrast to the classical economist's idea that in making decisions in business or anywhere in real life, you somehow pick, or somebody gives you, a set of alternatives from which you select the best one—maximize. The satisficing idea is that first of all, you don't have the alternatives, you've got to go out and scratch for them—and that you have mighty shaky ways of evaluating them when you do find them. So you look for alternatives until you get one from which, in terms of your experience and in terms of what you have reason to expect, you will get a reasonable result.
>
> But satisficing doesn't necessarily mean that managers have to be satisfied with what alternative pops up first in their minds or in their computers and let it go at that. The level of satisficing can be raised—by personal determination, setting higher individual or organizational standards, and by use of an increasing range of sophisticated management science and computer-based decision-making and problem-solving techniques.
>
> As time goes on, you obtain more information about what's feasible and what you can aim at. Not only do you get more information, but in many, if not most, companies there are procedures for setting targets, including procedures for trying to raise individuals' aspiration levels [objectives]. This is a major responsibility of top management.[36]

Limited search for alternative solutions

Managers usually make a limited search of the possible alternative solutions to reach desired objectives. Managers consider such alternatives only until one is found that appears adequate as a means for obtaining the desired objective. For example, in choosing the best job, college graduates cannot evaluate every possible job in the world for which they might be qualified. They might die of old age before obtaining all the information needed for a decision.

Even the rational decision-making model recognizes that identifying and assessing proposed alternative solutions costs time, energy, and money. The key difference under the bounded rationality decision-making model is that managers stop searching for alternative solutions as soon as they hit upon one that seems acceptable for reaching their objectives.

Inadequate information and control

Bounded rationality holds that managers frequently have inadequate information about decision problems and that some factors outside managers' control will influence the actual results of their decisions. Management might make a decision to purchase a number of automatic stamping machines to make disc brakes for automobiles. With the resulting reduction in labor costs, the machines could pay for themselves within two years. But, management did not anticipate resistance by union members and the decline in automobile sales. Consequently, the automatic machines are not used effectively, as planned, and the payback period extends from the expected two years to five years.

Managers searching for alternative solutions to a problem are confined by restrictions on time, money, and energy. Results are often achieved through limited discussion and expedient decision making by small groups.

Source: Christopher Morrow/ Stock, Boston.

Political Decision-Making Model

The *political decision-making model* refers to those decision processes that are a direct result of the vested interests (objectives) of internal and external stakeholders who have power. Before describing the political decision-making model, we need to define power. *Power* is the ability to influence or control departmental, divisional, or organizational decisions and outcomes.[37] To have power is to be able to influence or control the definition of problems, the choice of objectives, the choice of alternative solutions to be considered, selection of the alternative to be implemented, and, ultimately, the actions and success of the organization.

Problem definitions and objectives

The political decison-making model describes internal and external stakeholders as those who try to define problems for their own advantage and to meet their own objectives. For example, the Surgeon General's Office of the United States and the American Cancer Society have defined cigarette smoking as a major health problem. However, the U.S. tobacco industry has consistently argued that tobacco products do not represent a significant health problem and have lobbied against restrictive legislation and regulations. The definition of problems often become subject to negotiation between stakeholders. While cigarettes have not been taken off the market, an agreement was reached some years ago for tobacco companies to put health-warning statements on each cigarette package and to discontinue advertising cigarettes on television.

The political decision-making model clearly assumes and recognizes the likelihood of conflicting objectives among internal stakeholders, among external stakeholders, and between internal and external stakeholders. Often, no clear winner emerges from such conflicts.

Decision process and decision

Conflicts in setting objectives will be strongly influenced by the relative power of the stakeholders. If power is concentrated in one stakeholder, the organization's major objectives are likely to be a reflection of that stakeholder's interests. In contrast, if there is a balance of power among several stakeholders, decision making that involves extensive negotiation and compromise is to be expected. The decision process in this model is often disorderly and characterized by the push and pull of those stakeholders with power and conflicting objectives.[38] When power is balanced, the decision process may lead to compromise—as with most union–management bargaining—or end in a stalemate—as has been common in relations between the United States and Russia.

Information and search for alternative solutions

We can assume that at least some of the objectives pushed by stakeholders represent a *win–lose* situation: My gain is your loss and your gain is my loss. Accordingly, stakeholders often distort and selectively withhold information to further their own interests. The amount and diversity of information entering into the decision process is often limited to that which serves the current interests of the stakeholders. This can severely limit management's ability to make innovative decisions which, by definition, require creating, gathering, and analyzing *all* relevant information, as well as fully exploring the possible alternative solutions.[39] Stakeholders, especially those *within* an organization, often see and use information as one of their major sources of power. The rational decision-making model calls for managers to present openly all relevant information. Managers operating under the political decision-making model would view such free disclosure of information as naïve and only leading to further problems. In addition, relevant information is often (1) fragmented and based on informal (person-to-person) communications; (2) qualitative rather than quantitative (such as, "Those computer printouts don't really matter around here."); and (3) defined by what the powerful stakeholders think (such as, "What does the boss think?").[40]

IN PRACTICE
TEXAS INSTRUMENT'S HYBRID COMPUTER

Texas Instruments, Inc. (TI), is touted as a company that has good management practices. This high-technology (consumer electronics) company has developed and implemented many innovative management systems, consistent with its objective of manufacturing and marketing a continuous stream of new products. Their *Product–Customer–Center* concept and *Objectives, Strategies, and Tactics* system were implemented to ensure that profit awareness and responsibility are created at the lowest levels of management. New product development is guided by long-term organizational objectives and strategies.

These management systems helped TI to achieve phenomenal growth for a number of years.[41] It is now a giant company with annual sales of more than $5 billion and a worldwide work force of 81,000 people. The political story behind its bungled attempt at entering the personal computer market with its Model 99/4 is therefore all the more intriguing.[42] The company invested $20 million over a three-year period in developing a home computer for which it could not find a market. The Model 99/4 was conceived as a sophisticated video game in the consumer-products division. After many months of development, and the involvement of a number of people in one product-customer center, it was upgraded to a primitive home computer and transferred to another center. Before the final product was developed, the project was transferred to a third center and reworked as a more powerful personal computer. The design changes imposed by three different product-customer centers resulted in a hybrid product, one that was too costly for the mass market, and too limited for the sophisticated user.

Internal competition among divisions (a carefully fostered cultural characteristic at TI) encouraged a *not-invented-here* syndrome. Program managers tend to ignore projects not initiated by their divisions. The product-customer center structure that served as the framework for task assignment, performance evaluation, and reward system encouraged managerial commitment to a narrow set of subsystem (P-CC) objectives. This structure obstructed and even distorted information flows in product development activities for the personal computer, eventually leading to product failure and lost growth opportunities.[43]

CHAPTER SUMMARY

This chapter focused on the fundamentals of managerial decision making. These fundamentals come into play whether managers are dealing with the managerial functions of planning, organizing, leading, or controlling.

Managers face a wide range of decision problems. We developed this idea by identifying various combinations of types of problems—ranging from known and well-defined problems to ambiguous and undefined problems—and types of possible alternative solutions—again, ranging from known and well-defined to ambiguous and undefined. Based on combinations of these problem–solution types, we identified three major

classes of managerial decisions: routine, adaptive, and innovative. Each of these classes of managerial decisions involve the identification and assessment of states of nature and tend to be made under three decision-making conditions: (1) routine decisions under certainty or under risk involving objective probabilities; (2) adaptive decisions under risk with low-to-moderate degrees of objective or subjective probability; and (3) innovative decisions under risk with a high degree of subjective probability or under uncertainty.

We discussed the nature and setting of objectives, as well as their important role in guiding the efforts of companies, divisions, departments, managers, and employees.

We brought all of these together in the three models of managerial decision making. The rational decision-making model focuses on the steps and practices prescribed for making decision processes and decisions by managers more rational—the ideal. In contrast, the bounded rationality decision-making model and the political decision-making model represent the observed decision processes and decisions of managers and organizations—the practical. All three of these models are useful. The rational decision-making model is instructive in helping managers to be more systematic and objective in their decision making. The bounded rationality decision-making model keeps us humble by pointing out the limits and problems we face in the impossible quest for pure rationality. Finally, the political decision-making model emphasizes the role that power and diverse stakeholders' interests play in some decision-making situations. In particular, innovative decisions tend to be limited by political decision-making processes in terms of problem identification, setting of objectives, generation of possible alternative solutions, and even the choice of the alternative solution to be implemented.

MANAGER'S VOCABULARY

adaptive decisions
bounded rationality decision-making model
choices
closed objectives
condition of certainty
condition of risk
condition of uncertainty
constraints
demands
external stakeholders
hierarchy of objectives
incorporation
innovative decisions
internal stakeholders
interpretation
noticing
objective probability
objectives
open objectives

political decision-making model
power
probability
rational decision
rational decision-making model
routine decisions
satisficing
states of nature
subjective probability

REVIEW QUESTIONS

1. What are the basic types of problem–solution decision situations that may be experienced by managers?

2. What are the characteristics of routine, adaptive, and innovative decisions?

3. What is meant by *states of nature* in managerial decision making?

4. What is the nature and role of objectives in managerial decision making?

5. What are the main characteristics of the three models of managerial decision making (rational, bounded rationality, and political)?

DISCUSSION QUESTIONS

1. What is the difference between the rationality of the decision itself and the rationality of the decision-making process? Try to identify a personal example of a situation in which the decision seemed rational, but the decision-making process did not.

2. Why can an organization sometimes expect managers, who are limited by the concept of bounded rationality, to make reasonably *rational* decisions?

3. What might a hierarchy of objectives look like for yourself? Begin with the taking of this course as the lowest subobjective.

4. What are some personal examples of decision problems you have encountered that involved conditions of certainty, risk, and uncertainty? Explain.

5. How can the characteristics of the decisionmaker influence the decision-making process? Give one example of how your nature seems to influence your decision making.

MANAGEMENT INCIDENTS AND CASES——

FACIT AB COMPANY

Facit AB Company grew large and profitable while making and selling business machines and office furnishings. Although Facit made many products, its top managers believed that their key product line was mechanical calculators. They saw products such as typewriters, desks, and computers as peripheral. In fact, the top managers declined to authorize the production of computers and electronic calculators designed by one of the company's subsidiaries. Facit concentrated on improving the quality and lowering the costs of mechanical calculators, which facilitated their production and sale. Technological change was seen as slow, incremental, and controllable. In the mid-1960s, Facit borrowed large sums of money and built new plants that enabled it to make better mechanical calculators at lower costs than any other company in the world. Between 1962 and 1970, employment rose 70 percent and sales and profits more than doubled. By 1970, Facit employed 14,000 people who worked in factories in 20 cities in 5 countries, or in sales offices in 15 countries.

Electronics engineers were located only in a small, jointly owned subsidiary. The engineers within Facit itself concentrated on technologies clearly relevant to mechanical calculators. Facit understood these technologies well. Top, middle, and lower-level managers agreed on how a mechanical-calculator factory should look and operate, what mechanical-calculator customers wanted, what was the key to success, and what was unimportant or silly. Procedures were pared to essentials, bottlenecks were eliminated, and no resources were wasted gathering irrelevant information or analyzing tangential issues. Costs were low, service fast, glitches rare, understanding high, and expertise great.

One loyal customer finally canceled a large order for voting machines after Facit had failed repeatedly to produce machines of adequate quality. Some lower-level managers and engineers were acutely aware of the electronic revolution in the world at large. However, this awareness did not penetrate to top management. The advent of electronic calculators took Facit's top managers by surprise. Relying on the company's information-gathering procedures, the top managers surmised that Facit's mechanical-calculator customers would switch to electronics very slowly because they liked mechanical calculators. Facit had no system for gathering information from people who were buying electronic calculators.

Actual demand for mechanical calculators dropped fast. Facit went through two years of loss, turmoil, and contraction. The top managers' contraction strategy aimed at preserving the mechanical-calculator factories by closing the typewriter and office-furnishings factories. With bankruptcy looming, the board of directors sold Facit to a larger firm.

Facit's top managers had viewed their company as a harmonious system that evolved slowly by conforming to plans. They believed that their industry was focusing on price competition instead of technologically stable products. For many years, their central challenge had been competitive threat. They did interpret electronic calculators as a new aspect of competitive threat. This marginal revision left the central challenge basically the same, so it could be met through the familiar planned evolution. Two years of plant closings, managerial transfers, and financial losses convinced the top managers that planned evolution no longer met the challenge of competitive threat. They thought that the company was designed to change slowly and could not change quickly. They didn't think that a harmonious system for producing mechanical calculators could ever be able to produce electronic calculators. The top managers perceived the competitive threat as an unmeetable challenge. After Facit was sold, the new top managers did not even see the competitive threat.

The new top managers discovered that demand for typewriters was at least three times and demand for office furnishings at least twice the company's production capacities. Sales personnel had been turning down orders because the company could not fill them. Indeed, Facit faced weak competition in the sale of typewriters and office furnishings. Moreover, its subsidiary had designed electronic calculators and computers. The company turned around in less than a year, including the addition of electronic products.[44]

Questions

1. What difficulties in problem identification are illustrated by this case, especially in terms of noticing, interpretation, and incorporation?

2. How did problem identification and diagnosis influence the choice of objectives by the old management versus the new management?

3. What aspects of the political decision-making model are illustrated in the case?

REFERENCES

1. J. Rothe (president of Texas State Optical Group, then senior vice-president, Searle Optical Group), 1984.

2. K. MacCrimman and R. Taylor, "Decision Making and Problem Solving," *Handbook of Industrial and Organizational Psychology.* M. Dunnette (Ed.). Chicago: Rand McNally, 1976, pp. 1397–1453.

3. C. E. Watson, "Managerial Mind Sets and the Structural Side of Managing," *Business Horizons,* November–December 1983, pp. 21–27.

4. S. Fraker, "Why Women Aren't Getting to The Top," *Fortune,* April 16, 1984, pp. 40–45; "Women at Work: They've Reshaped the Economy—and Now Their Wages Will Rise," *Business Week,* January 28, 1985, pp. 80–85; P. Dubono, "Attitudes Toward Women Executives: A Longitudinal Approach," *Academy of Management Journal,* 1985, **28:**235–239.

5. Adapted from K. Ohmae, *The Mind of the Strategist: The Art of Japanese Business.* New York: McGraw-Hill, 1982, pp. 150–155.

6. Adapted from H. J. Brightman, *Problem Solving: A Logical and Creative Approach.* Atlanta, Ga.: Business Publishing Division, Georgia State University, 1980, pp. 168–170.

7. M. W. McCall Jr., R. E. Kaplan, and M. L. Gerlach, *Caught in the Act: Decision Makers at Work,* Technical Report No. 20. Greensboro, NC: Center for Creative Leadership, August 1982. *Also see:* M. W. McCall Jr. and R. E. Kaplan, *Whatever It Takes: Decision Makers at Work.* Englewood Cliffs, N.J.: Prentice-Hall, 1985; M. Murray, *Decisions: A Comparative Critique.* Marshfield, Mass.: Pitman, 1985.

8. McCall, et al., "Caught in the Act . . . ," p. 64.

9. A. Oxenfeldt, *Cost-Benefit Analysis for Executive Decision Making.* New York: AMACOM, 1979, p. 39. *Also see:* R. N. Taylor, *Behavioral Decision Making.* Glenview, Ill.: Scott, Foresman, 1984.

10. D. W. Miller and M. K. Starr, *The Structure of Human Decisions.* Englewood Cliffs, N.J.: Prentice-Hall, 1967, p. 75.

11. L. Thorson, "Tanker Insurance Rates Soar after Iraq's Latest Attack Claims," Bryan-College Station *Eagle,* May 26, 1984, p. 13. *Also see* K. R. MacCrimmon and D. A. Wehring, *Taking Risks: The Management of Uncertainty.* New York: Free Press, 1986.

12. Adapted from W. D. Coplin and M. K. O'Leary, "The 1984 Risk Index for International Business," *Planning Review,* May 1984, pp. 34–40.

13. J. G. March, "Theories of Choice and Making Decisions," *Society,* November–December 1982, pp. 29–39; J. G. March and R. Weissinger, *Ambiguity and Command: Organizational Perspectives on Military Decision Making.* Marshfield, Mass.: Pitman, 1986.

14. D. B. Hertz and H. Thomas, *Risk Analysis and Its Applications.* New York: John Wiley, 1983.

15. N. Taylor, "The Concorde Going Nowhere Fast," *MBA,* Fall 1976, pp. 55–56.

16. "Concorde Is Now Solid Moneymaker for British Airline," *Houston Chronicle,* March 25, 1984, Section 4, p. 5. *Also see* J. P. Newport Jr., "A Call to Revive the U.S. SST," *Fortune,* May 13, 1985, p. 77.

17. K. E. Boulding, "Irreducible Uncertainties," *Society,* November–December 1982, p. 17.

18. J. R. Harrison and J. G. March, "Decision Making and Postdecision Surprises," *Administrative Science Quarterly,* 1984, **29:**26–42; B. Goitein, "The Danger of Disappearing Postdecision Surprise: Comment on Harrison and March, 'Decision Making and Postdecision Surprises,'" *Administrative Science Quarterly,* 1984, **29:**410–413: R. F. Harley, *Management Mistakes,* 2nd ed., New York, John Wiley & Sons, 1986.

19. M. D. Richards, *Setting Strategic Goals and Objectives.* St. Paul, Minn.: West, 1986.

20. *IBM Annual Report 1982.* Armonk, New York: International Business Machines Corporation, 1983. *Also see* "IBM: More Worlds to Conquer," *Business Week,* February 18, 1985, pp. 84–87ff.

21. E. A. Locke and G. P. Latham, *Goal Setting: A Motivational Technique that Works.* Englewood Cliffs, N.J.: Prentice-Hall, 1984; H. Weirich, *Man-*

agement Excellence. New York: McGraw-Hill, 1985.

22. R. Stewart, *Choices for the Manager.* Englewood Cliffs, N.J.: Prentice-Hall, 1982.

23. "Executive Pay: The Top Earners," *Business Week,* May 7, 1984, pp. 88–116.

24. H. Mintzberg, "Power and Organization Life Cycles," *Academy of Management Review,* 1984, 9:207–224.

25. R. Mason and I. Mitroff, *Challenging Strategic Planning Assumptions.* New York: John Wiley, 1981; I. I. Mitroff, *Stakeholders of The Organizational Mind.* San Francisco: Jossey-Bass, 1983.

26. A. L. Mendelow, "Setting Corporate Goals and Measuring Organizational Effectiveness—A Practical Approach," *Long Range Planning,* February 1983, pp. 70–71.

27. H. J. Brightman, *Problem Solving: A Logical and Creative Approach.* Atlanta, Ga.: Business Publishing Division, Georgia State University, 1980, pp. 161–192; W. F. Roth, *Problem Solving for Managers.* New York: Praeger, 1985.

28. S. Kiesler and L. Sproull, "Managerial Response to Changing Environments: Perspectives on Problem Sensing from Social Cognition," *Administrative Science Quarterly,* 1982, 27:548–570.

29. D. N. Dickson (Ed.), *Using Logical Techniques for Making Better Decisions.* New York: John Wiley, 1983.

30. E. F. Harrison, *The Managerial Decision-Making Process,* 2nd ed., Boston: Houghton Mifflin, 1981.

31. J. March and H. Simon, *Organizations.* New York: John Wiley, 1958.

32. M. Homes, *Executive Decision Making.* Homewood, Ill.: Richard D. Irwin, 1962, pp. 89–93; D. J. Isenberg, "How Senior Managers Think," *Harvard Business Review,* November–December 1984, pp. 81–90.

33. B. M. Bass, *Organizational Decision Making.* Homewood, Ill.: Richard D. Irwin, 1983.

34. Suresh Srivastva and Associates, *The Executive Mind: New Insights On Managerial Thought and Action.* San Francisco: Jossey-Bass, 1983.

35. H. Simon, *Reason in Human Affairs.* Stanford University Press, 1983; C. R. Schwenk, "The Use of

Participant Recollection in the Modeling of Organizational Decision Processes." Unpublished manuscript, 1984; P. C. Nutt, "Types of Organizational Decision Processes," *Administrative Science Quarterly,* 1984, 29:414–450.

36. J. M. Roach, "Simon Says: Decision Making Is a 'Satisficing' Experience," *Management Review,* January, 1979 (New York: AMACOM, a division of American Management Associations, 1979), pp. 8–9.

37. H. Mintzberg, *Power in and Around the Organization.* Englewood Cliffs, N.J.: Prentice-Hall, 1983.

38. J. Pfeffer, *Power In Organizations.* Boston: Pitman, 1981; C. Eden, S. Jones, and D. Sims, *Messing About in Problems: An Informal Structured Approach to Their Identification and Management.* New York: Pergamon Press, 1983; W. B. Stevenson, J. L. Pearce, and L. W. Porter, "The Concept of 'Coalition' in Organization Theory and Research," *Academy of Management Review,* 1985, 10:256–268.

39. M. L. Fennell, "Synergy, Influence, and Information in the Adoption of Administrative Innovations," *Academy of Management Journal,* 1984, 27:113–129.

40. J. L. Bower, "Managing for Efficiency, Managing for Equity," *Harvard Business Review,* July–August, 1983, pp. 83–90.

41. M. Jelinek, *Institutionalizing Innovation: A Study of Organizational Learning.* New York: Praeger, 1979.

42. B. Uttal, "TI's Home Computer Can't Get in the Door," *Fortune,* June 16, 1980, pp. 39–40.

43. P. Shrivastava and I. Mitroff, "Sources of Irrationality in Organizational Actions." Unpublished manuscript, 1984.

44. W. H. Starbuck and B. L. T. Hedberg, "Saving an Organization from a Stagnating Environment," in H. B. Thorelli (Ed.), *Strategy + Structure = Performance.* Bloomington, Ind.: Indiana University Press, 1977, pp. 249–258. *Also see:* P. C. Nystrom and W. H. Starbuck, "To Avoid Organizational Crises, Unlearn," *Organizational Dynamics,* Spring 1984, pp. 53–65.

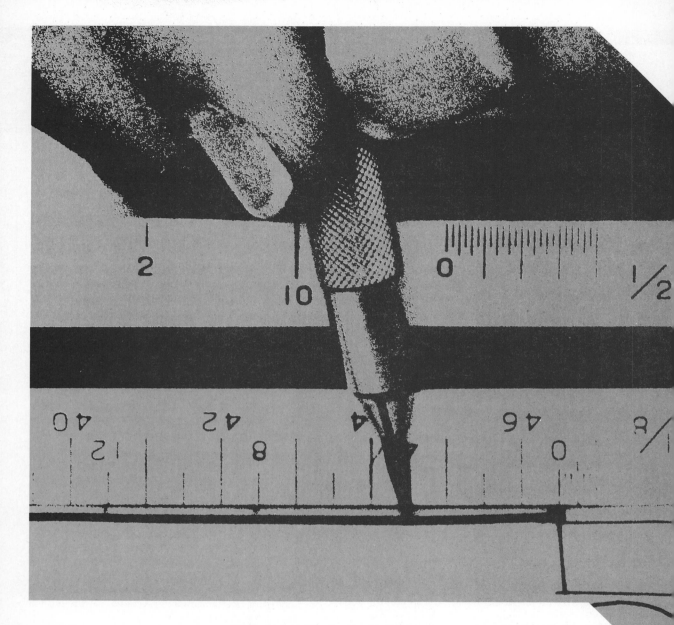

Aids for Managerial
Decision Making

LEARNING OBJECTIVES

After studying this chapter, you should be able to:

■ State the uses and limitations of normative decision models.

■ Describe two aids for making routine decisions: rules and standard operating procedures and the linear-programming model.

■ Describe and apply three aids for making adaptive decisions: break-even model, pay-off-matrix model, and decision-tree model.

■ Describe and apply one aid for making innovative decisions: Osborn's applied-imagination model.

■ Apply several decision-making aids.

CHAPTER OUTLINE

PREVIEW CASE

WHAT'S RATIONAL?

Suppose you were lucky enough to be offered these alternatives:

1. Accept the payment of a tax-free gift of $1 million.

2. Toss a fair coin. If heads comes up, you get nothing; if tails comes up, you get a tax-free gift of $3 million.

Which would you choose? Would it be the certain $1 million, or the 50–50 chance of $3 million or nothing?

When confronted with this choice, most people say they would choose the certain $1 million, even though the gamble has what is called an expected value of $1.5 million. (The term *expected value* is the product of the hoped-for gain and the probability of winning it: $3,000,000 \times 0.50$, in this case.) Said another way, the average winnings in this case, if you gamble repeatedly, are half again as large as your winnings if you take the certain $1 million.

Indeed, even when the possible winnings on the gamble increase to $5 million if tails comes up, many people will still prefer the certain $1 million!

This is especially perplexing when we read some of the articles about the application of decision theory to business decisions. Many writers assume, without apparent question, that a manager will of course want to choose that alternative which maximizes the expected, or average, return.

There is little or no recognition of the fact that *rational* people, whether they are managers or bartenders, sometimes prefer an alternative other than the one with the highest expected value.[1]

© 1984 Dave Schaefer/The Picture Cube.

Τhis Preview Case illustrates one of the common limitations to many of the quantitative decision-making aids presented in this and other chapters. Namely, a *rational* course of action arrived at through the step-by-step procedures required by quantitative decision-making aids may not be seen as rational by the decisionmaker. Several factors account for this seeming inconsistency. First, most quantitative decision-making aids consider only the conscious and intellectual side of individuals' stated preferences for risk taking and uncertainty. However, the courses of action that individuals actually select may be heavily influenced by emotional and subconscious reactions to states of nature involving risk and uncertainty. Second, many quantitative decision-making aids simply don't take into account critical factors that have a bearing on some decisions, such as political forces both within and outside the organization.

While recognizing the limitations of decision-making aids in some situations, numerous aids have been developed over the past 40 years that are quite helpful in specific types of decision situations.[2] The purpose of this chapter is to discuss a few of the decision-making aids particularly appropriate for each of the basic types of decisions introduced in the previous chapter—routine decisions, adaptive decisions, and innovative decisions. Normative decision-making aids that are limited primarily to particular managerial processes or functions—such as planning or operations management—are presented in later chapters.

NORMATIVE DECISION-MAKING MODELS

Normative decision-making models provide various step-by-step procedures that prescribe how managers should go about making decisions to define or reach their objectives.[3] The prescribed steps in the rational decision-making process presented previously in Fig. 6.8 is a general type of normative decision-making model. As you will recall, this process includes seven steps: (1) problem awareness and diagnosis; (2) set objectives; (3) search for alternative solutions; (4) compare and evaluate alternative solutions; (5) choose among possible alternative solutions; (6) implement the alternative solution selected; and (7) follow up and control. Each of the normative models presented in this and other chapters considers some of these steps as they apply to specific decision problems. The variety and potential complexity of normative decision-making models is so great that entire courses and curriculums have been developed to understand and apply them.

RANGE OF ASSUMPTIONS

The normative decision-making models identified as aids for making routine and adaptive decisions generally contain the following assumptions:

- The objectives are known and agreed on.
- The nature of the problem can be roughly defined and agreed on.
- Some information about the decision problem can be provided.
- The state of nature in the decision problem can range from certainty to uncertainty.[4]

The aid presented for making innovative decisions does not make all of these assumptions. The Osborn applied-imagination model is often most useful with decision situations where the objectives are not yet known and agreed on and/or the nature of the problem is not yet defined and agreed on.

POTENTIAL BENEFITS

Normative decision-making models do not provide specific answers to management problems. They aid managers by providing step-by-step procedures for reaching a decision and clarifying the risks or uncertainties facing managers. By improving the decision-making process, managers may derive the following potential benefits from normative models.[5]

- A manager's hunches are more likely to focus on the crucial elements of a decision problem.

- Hidden assumptions and their logical implications are more likely to be brought out into the open and made clear. This is because normative decision models require the specific identification of assumptions and the assessment of different alternatives.

- The reasoning underlying a recommendation may be communicated to others more effectively. If all assumptions, alternatives, and probabilities are laid out in the open, the reasons for the final recommendation should be easier to follow.

- A manager's judgment can be improved and the area in which judgment has to be exercised might be reduced. This is because there usually is a greater emphasis on defining the true nature of the problem, collecting relevant information, and quantifying where possible.

RELATIONSHIP TO PROBLEM—SOLUTION DECISION SITUATIONS

Figure 6.2 presented a matrix of problem—solution decision situations. It was used to describe three general classifications of managerial decisions: routine, adaptive, and innovative. Figure 7.1 shows this same matrix, on which we have plotted the six decision-making aids presented in this chapter. Each plot indicates the general types of decision situations in which each of the decision-making aids may be used to greatest benefit. With the exception of the Osborn model, the assumption is that the types of problems facing the manager are reasonably known and well-defined.

As suggested in Fig. 7.1, rules and standard operating procedures, as well as the linear-programming model, are often useful aids for many routine decisions. The break-even, payoff-matrix, and decision-tree models are often most useful in making many adaptive decisions. However, these aids can also be used by a manager in making routine decisions. Osborn's applied-imagination model technically can be utilized as an aid in making routine and adaptive decisions. However, its greatest usefulness is as an aid for making innovative decisions.

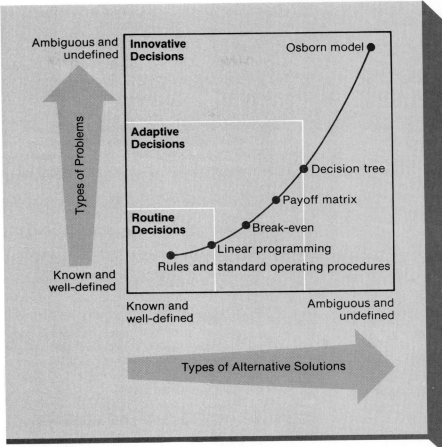

FIGURE 7.1
Selected Decision Aids in Relation to Problem–Solution Decision Situations

AIDS FOR MAKING ROUTINE DECISIONS

Routine decisions are based on choices available to managers when a problem is known and relatively well-defined. Computers increasingly are being programmed to process and even make routine decisions.[6] Rules and standard operating procedures are general aids for making routine decisions over a wide range of structured problems. The linear-programming model is a more specialized aid for structured but complex decision problems.

Rules and Standard Operating Procedures

Rules and standard operating procedures are fundamental and central to bureaucratic management. A *rule* specifies a course of action that must be followed. Rules are used to establish uniformity in the process by which routine decisions are made and actions are taken by managers in dealing with routine problems. A *standard operating procedure* is a series of rules that must be followed in a particular sequence when dealing with certain routine decision problems. In other words, standard operating procedures (SOPs) prescribe a step-by-step process for handling certain problems in an organization.[7] Rules and SOPs place the greatest limitations and controls on managers. These spell out how managers should make certain decisions and what they should decide.

Organizational rules and SOPs touch employees in their daily work lives, even to death. This is illustrated by the rules and SOPs to be followed in the event of death of an employee or student at Texas A&M University.

IN PRACTICE
Death of University Employees or Students

EMPLOYEES

Any employee of the University who first becomes aware of the death of a present or former employee of the University is requested to check by phone with the University Police Office to insure that that office is aware of the person's death. The University Police Office remains open on a twenty-four hour basis and may be notified at any time.

The University Police will call and notify the following offices of the person's death as soon as the offices are open for business:

1. Office of the President
2. Office of the appropriate Vice President
3. Vice President for Student Services
4. Appropriate Dean or Director
5. University Information Office

If the University Police should receive the first notification of the death after offices are closed but prior to 11:00 p.m., that office will notify the Assistant to the President and the appropriate Dean or Director at once and notify the other offices early the following morning. Similar arrangements will apply on holidays and Sundays.

In each case, the appropriate Dean or Director is responsible for notifying Department Heads and Supervisors in the area of responsibility where the deceased worked, and extend such expressions of sympathy as are deemed to be appropriate.

Where flowers or letters of sympathy on behalf of the University are in order, the Assistant to the President will see that appropriate measures are taken.

Where University insurance or other benefits resulting from University employment are involved, the appropriate Dean or Director will see that the beneficiaries are properly notified and assist them in coordinating with the appropriate Personnel Office benefits representative.

Where it is considered appropriate for a resolution to be adopted by the University, the resolution should be prepared by the Department Head and submitted as an Agenda Item for the Board of Regents.

STUDENTS

Any employee or student of the University who first becomes aware of the death of a student of the University is requested to report such knowledge to the University Police Department, providing the significant and important details available at the time.

Upon receipt of the information, the University Police Department will notify immediately the Office of the Vice President for Student Services. (If the information is received after business hours, the Vice President for Student Services will be called at his or her home. If he or she cannot be reached, the call will be made to the homes of the Associate Vice President or the Assistant Vice President, in that order.)

The Office of the Vice President for Student Services will notify the Office of the President, and also set in motion the Silver Taps ceremony. In addition, the Vice President for Student Services will notify other concerned and appropriate persons.

This statement appears in the *Policy and Procedures Manual, Texas A&M University.* It has a classification number (12.8) and an issue date (January 14, 1980). This manual provides administrators with policies, rules, and SOPs for handling the stream of routine decisions made daily throughout the University. For example, this manual outlines rules and SOPs in such routine decision areas as retention and disposition of public records, safeguarding classified information, carpeting and draping of University offices, rental of off-campus space, student records, outside employment and consulting, sexual harassment, affirmative action, travel regulations, standards of conduct of state officers and employees, construction procedures for managing contracts of $100,000 or less, procurement of classroom furniture, permission to pay for monthly employees, refuse collection and landfill operations, and so on.

Texas A&M University is not unique in having rules and SOPs to guide and direct managers in dealing with routine decision problems.

Linear-Programming Model

The *linear-programming model* is most useful to a manager in making routine decisions that involve relatively structured but very complex problems. In general, this model is a decision aid for use with quantifiable objectives and helps the manager to determine the best allocation of physical and capital resources across activities.[8] Several conditions must be met before this model can be used.[9]

- The variables in the decision problem must be quantifiable: dollars, pounds, hours, gallons, or other continuous units of measurement. A continuous unit of measurement permits exact comparisons between different amounts of the unit; that is, 10 gallons of gasoline is exactly 10 times one gallon of gasoline or six hours is exactly one-half of 12 hours.

- The relationships among the variables must be linear. In other words, a change in one variable should lead to a directly proportional change in another variable. For example, the number of a particular item sold increases by 2 percent for every 1 percent decrease in its sales price.

- The relationships among the variables can be expressed as mathematical equations.

- These equations are developed with constraints that describe the restrictions that the decision variables must satisfy. One constraint might simply be that no employee should work more than 40 hours per week.

- The variables and relationships among the variables are assumed to be known and controllable by the decisionmaker.

- There is a single quantifiable objective to be maximized (profits) or a single quantifiable objective to be minimized (costs).

Where hundreds of variables and equations are involved, as in the operation of an oil refinery, the linear-programming model becomes quite complex, requiring the use of a computer. This model is used extensively in the solution of decision problems such as the routing and scheduling of school buses, scheduling the manufacture of products and allocation of machinery, and making overtime assignments in ways that avoid accusations of race or sex discrimination in the allocations. The detailed procedures for constructing a linear-programming model are beyond the scope of this book. If you are interested in further information about linear programming, see the excellent presentation by Dinkel and Kochenberger.[10]

In a relatively short period of time, the computer has become an invaluable tool for management decision making.

Photo courtesy of Wang.

IN PRACTICE
The Textile Mill in India

Many of the textile firms in India use manual operations-planning methods. Such routine planning involves the allocation of looms to the various styles produced. Most firms plan for only one to two months at a time. Traditional decision-making methods generally result in a suboptimal product mix and a suboptimal decision on the quantities of yarn to be processed into different fabrics (for example, dyed cloth and printed cloth). In addition, the economics of important options—buying yarns for certain styles, selling yarn spun in the mill, and so on—cannot be effectively evaluated.

In one textile mill, management replaced the previously used decision-making methods with a linear-programming model. When they used the model, the managers learned several things. They confirmed that both fixed and variable costs (costs that vary with the level of production) had increased sharply in recent years. They found that, now, total revenue generated per shift did not even meet fixed costs, regardless of the production level. Their analysis showed that the product mix should be improved and that fixed labor costs should be spread over a seven-day week. The linear-programming model helped them to evaluate the use of additional shifts in certain work areas, to evaluate the effects of purchasing new equipment, and to identify bottlenecks in the production process. It also enabled the managers to decide to eliminate some product styles and increase the prices of others. Financial performance improved considerably after introduction of the linear-programming model in this textile mill.[11]

AIDS FOR MAKING ADAPTIVE DECISIONS

Adaptive decisions are based on choices that involve some combination of: (1) the modification of readily available alternative solutions; and (2) the diagnosis of problems by the use of systematic analysis. Three aids for decision making—break-even model, payoff-matrix model, and decision-tree model—are particularly useful in helping managers to diagnose systematically problems that may require adaptive decisions to solve.

Break-Even Model

The *break-even model* can be useful in projecting profits, controlling expenses, and determining prices. It shows the basic relationships among the number of units produced (output), the dollars of sales revenue, and the levels of costs and profits for a firm or a product line. The model can be developed from historical data or estimates; one based on historical data, for example, might be used to make year-by-year comparisons for a product line. The model also can be used to identify any changes in the relationship between the number of units produced and costs per unit.

Variables and relationships
The major variables in the break-even model include the following:

- *Fixed costs:* those costs that remain constant regardless of the number of units produced. Within a given year, the following types of costs might remain fixed: insurance premiums, real-estate premiums, real-estate taxes, administrative and supervisory costs, and mortgage payments on the physical plant.

- *Variable costs:* those costs that tend to vary with changes in the number of units produced. They do not necessarily vary proportionally for each additional unit of output. Variable costs might include those for direct labor, electricity, raw materials, packaging, and transportation.

- *Total costs:* the sum of the fixed and variable costs.

- *Total revenue:* the total dollars received from sales.

- *Profit:* the excess of total dollar sales over total dollar costs.

- *Loss:* the excess of total dollar costs over total dollar sales.

- *Break-even point:* the point at which total costs equal total sales. It may be expressed in terms of total dollar revenues or total units produced.

Figure 7.2 illustrates the relationships among the variables in a break-even model. The vertical axis represents sales or costs in dollars and the horizontal axis represents units produced (output). We plot total costs (fixed plus variable costs) and total revenues for various production levels to show profit, loss, and the break-even point.

LIMITATIONS

Although the break-even model is a useful aid for decision making, it has several limitations. The assumption that expected profits depend only on various levels of units sold may be misleading. Profits are also influenced by such factors as changes in the price or quality of competing products, changes in production processes (such as a more sophisticated copying machine), or

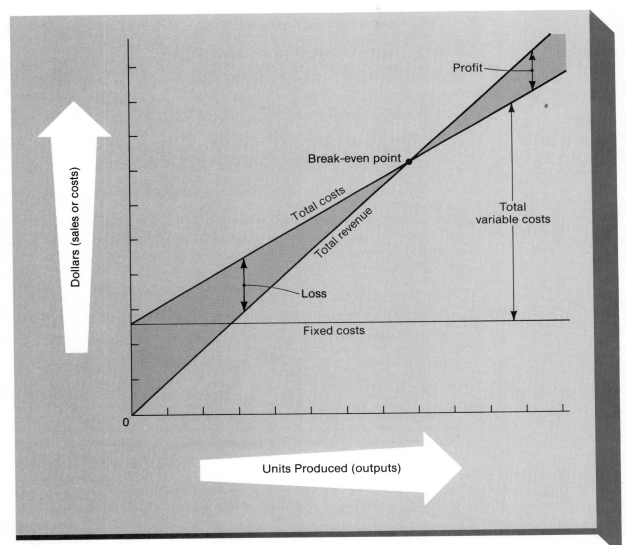

FIGURE 7.2
Illustrative Break-Even Model

IN PRACTICE
Copy Mart

The break-even model often is a useful starting point for making some types of investment decisions. One of the authors of this book was trying to determine whether to open a copying service near a college campus. Bits and pieces of information about actual and estimated costs included: (1) the operating losses to be expected with different levels of sales; (2) the break-even point; and (3) the operating profits to be expected with different levels of sales. The required capital investment was only $3000, so he decided to exclude the capital investment from the break-even model. The data used to develop the monthly break-even model are shown in Table 7.1. Fixed costs were defined as rent, manager's salary and fringe benefits, part-time help, advertising, and lease of the copying machine. Variable costs included the paper, toner (ink), developing fluid, and extra help when production exceeded 40,000 copies per month.

Figure 7.3 is a graph of the break-even model for the copy service, which shows several important things. First, Copy Mart must sell about 90,000 copies

TABLE 7.1 ■ DATA FOR MONTHLY BREAK-EVEN MODEL FOR COPY MART

FIXED COSTS	MONTHLY BASIS
Rent (includes heat and electricity)	$ 300
Manager's salary and fringe benefits	1200
Part-time help: (20 hrs/month × $4.00/hr)	80
Advertising	220
Lease of copying machine	1200
Total fixed costs	$3000

CONSTANT VARIABLE COSTS	PER COPY
Paper	$0.004
Toner (ink) and developing fluid	0.002
Total constant variable costs	$0.006

OTHER VARIABLE COSTS	PER COPY
Part-time help (needed after 40,000 copies have been produced in a month)	$0.01

REVENUE	PER COPY
Estimated revenue (actual prices range from $0.05 to $0.02 per copy, depending on the number of copies of a single sheet)	$0.045

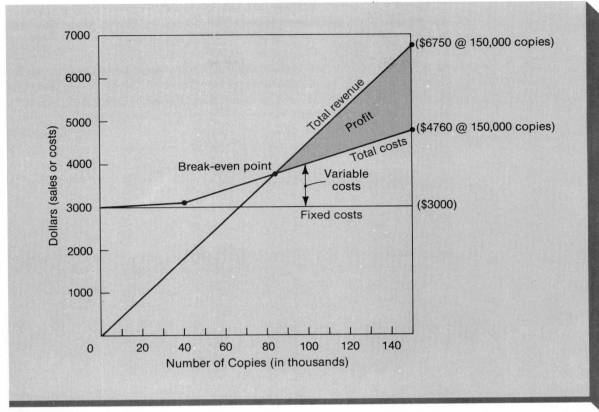

FIGURE 7.3
Monthly Break-Even Model for Copy Mart

per month to break even. Second, fixed costs (estimated at $3000 per month) are high but variable costs (estimated at up to $1760 for 150,000 copies) are relatively low. Third, the estimated maximum production capacity with one machine is 150,000 copies per month. After the break-even point, profits are expected to rise sharply for each additional copy sold. Charging different prices, leasing the copying machine on different payment plans, or leasing a different make of machine all would lead to different break-even points.

Since fixed costs are, by definition, relatively stable, the success of Copy Mart would depend on generating a high sales volume. The owner expected to stimulate demand by placing ads in community and student newspapers, giving introductory discounts on prices, and guaranteeing satisfaction. What actually happened? The estimated break-even model for Copy Mart did, indeed, closely approximate what actually happened.

improved marketing effectiveness (such as a new television commercial that really *"sells"*). An increase or a decline in general business activity may shift the relationships among the variables. For example, a surge in general business activity might rapidly drive up the cost of raw materials, whereas a substantial drop in business activity might result in sharply reduced raw material prices.

A manager can partially overcome these limitations by developing several break-even models. Each model constructed should be based on different assumptions and estimates. However, a manager still may need to consider factors other than those used with a break-even model. Some of these will be presented in the explanations of the payoff matrix and decision tree.

Payoff-Matrix Model

The *payoff-matrix model* is a useful decision aid for helping managers to evaluate alternatives.[12] A basic assumption in the model is that the manager is able to identify desired objectives *and* specify alternatives (strategies). The payoff-matrix model can be applied to a host of decision problems, such as whether to make long-distance phone calls person-to-person or station-to-station, whether to increase or decrease the price of a product, or whether to rent or buy an office building.

Variables and relationships

The payoff-matrix model is a two-dimensional list of figures or symbols arranged in rows and columns that identifies the possible states of nature, probabilities, and outcomes (payoffs) associated with each strategy (alternative). A payoff matrix is shown in Table 7.2. The basic variables in the payoff-matrix model are:

- *Strategies (S).* These are the alternatives that have been identified and might be followed. They are shown in Table 7.2 as $S_1, S_2, S_3, \ldots, S_n$. In the Copy Mart In Practice, charging different prices for xerox copies would represent alternative strategies.

- *States of nature (N).* These are anticipated, possible future conditions that are relevant to the decision. They are shown as $N_1, N_2, N_3, \ldots, N_m$ in Table 7.2. As related to the Copy Mart In Practice, they could be different levels of expected market demand for copies.

- *Probability (P).* This represents the likelihood that each state of nature will occur. The sum of the probabilities must equal 1.0. We always assume that at least one of the states of nature will occur. A matrix with four states of nature could have probabilities of 0.1, 0.2, 0.2, and 0.5 (equals 1.0). Probabilities are shown in Table 7.2 as $P_1, P_2, P_3, \ldots, P_m$. This payoff matrix indicates that the decision is to be made under the condition of risk. For the condition of certainty, the payoff matrix would show only one state of nature. For the condition of uncertainty, the payoff matrix would not show any probabilities for the states of nature.

TABLE 7.2 ■ BASIC PAYOFF MATRIX

STRATEGY (ALTERNATIVES)	POSSIBLE STATE OF NATURE				
	N_1	N_2	N_3	$\cdots$	N_m
	Probability that each state of nature will occur				
	P_1	P_2	P_3	$\cdots$	P_m
	Outcome of Strategy				
S_1	O_{11}	O_{12}	O_{13}	$\cdots$	O_{1m}
S_2	O_{21}	O_{22}	O_{23}	$\cdots$	O_{2m}
S_3	O_{31}	O_{32}	O_{33}	$\cdots$	O_{3m}
.	.	.	.		.
.	.	.	.		.
.	.	.	.		.
S_n	O_{n1}	O_{n2}	O_{n3}	$\cdots$	O_{nm}

■ *Outcome (O).* This expresses the payoff that can be expected for each possible combination of strategy and state of nature. An outcome could be a profit or loss. For example, O_{11} in Table 7.2 shows the outcome *if* the first state of nature (N_1) occurs and *if* the first strategy (S_1) is chosen. Each such outcome is labeled a ***conditional value.*** That is, its value is based upon a particular state of nature and a specified strategy.

Expected values

The payoff matrix is most useful when either objective or subjective probabilities can be assigned to states of nature. To work toward a decision when the matrix consists of two or more states of nature, we must calculate the ***expected value*** for each strategy. An expected value is the weighted-average outcome for each strategy; that is, it is the sum of the conditional values after each has been multiplied by its probability of occurrence. For example, the expected values for the payoff matrix in Table 7.2 can be presented as follows (where EV = expected value).

$$EV_1 = P_1O_{11} + P_2O_{12} + P_3O_{13} + \cdots + P_mO_{1m}$$

$$EV_2 = P_1O_{21} + P_2O_{22} + P_3O_{23} + \cdots + P_mO_{2m}$$

$$EV_3 = P_1O_{31} + P_2O_{32} + P_3O_{33} + \cdots + P_mO_{3m}$$

$$EV_n = P_1O_{n1} + P_2O_{n2} + P_3O_{n3} + \cdots + P_mO_{nm}$$

IN PRACTICE
Stadium-Expansion Decision

The president of a university is trying to decide how many seats to add to the football stadium. The information available and assumptions are as follows:

1. Most of the games during the past two years have been sold out.

2. If more seats had been available, additional tickets could have been sold.

3. The president and administrative staff believe that the football team will be good, if not excellent, during the next three years. The squad has many first-team sophomores and juniors—and an excellent crop of freshmen should be ready to play.

4. A modular seating system has been decided on because of its low cost, excellent quality, and ease of installation. The modular system under consideration comes in units of 4000 seats.

5. Moderate increases (4 percent per year) are anticipated in the current student population of 30,000 and the local town population of 100,000. The town is located 30 miles from a major metropolitan area.

The president and the staff have decided to consider four strategies. They have also developed subjective probabilities for four levels of demand for additional seats (states of nature). It has been determined that the cost of each module of 4000 new seats will be $30 per seat per year during the period chosen to pay for the construction costs. The maximum potential revenue per season will be $80 per seat.

CONDITIONAL VALUES

The conditional values for the first year can be determined for each strategy and state-of-nature combination by using the following equation:

$$CV = (R \times Q_D) - (C \times Q_C),$$

where CV = conditional value, R = revenue per seat, Q_D = quantity of seats demanded, C = total costs per seat, and Q_C = quantity of seats constructed. Thus, if 4000 seats were demanded (Q_D) and 4000 seats were constructed (Q_C), the equation can be applied as follows:

$$CV = (\$80 \times 4000) - (\$30 \times 4000)$$
$$= \$320,000 - \$120,000$$
$$= \$200,000 \text{ (profit)}.$$

On the other hand, if 16,000 seats were constructed (Q_C) and only 4000 seats were demanded (Q_D), there would be a loss of $160,000. For this situation, the equation is applied as follows:

$$CV = (\$80 \times 4000) - (\$30 \times 16,000)$$
$$= \$320,000 - \$480,000$$
$$= \$160,000 \text{ (loss)}.$$

TABLE 7.3 ■ CONDITIONAL VALUES FOR STADIUM EXPANSION DECISION (IN $000)

SEATS CONSTRUCTED (STRATEGIES)	SEAT DEMAND (STATES OF NATURE)			
	4000	*8000*	*12,000*	*16,000*
4,000	$200	$200	$200	$200
8,000	80	400	400	400
12,000	− 40	280	600	600
16,000	− 160	160	480	800

Conditional values show what would happen *if* each demand and seat expansion combination were to occur. Referring to the conditional values given in Table 7.3, we note that there is *no* consideration of the probabilities associated with the states of nature (different possible demands).

CALCULATING EXPECTED VALUE

The president and the staff have assigned the following subjective probabilities of demand to the four strategies being evaluated.

Seats Sold Out	Probability of Only This Level of Demand
4,000	0.50
8,000	0.30
12,000	0.15
16,000	0.05
	1.00

Thus they believe that there is a 50-percent probability that all 4000 seats will be sold out, but only a 5-percent probability that all 16,000 will be sold out. From the information in Table 7.3 and these probabilities, we can develop an expected-value matrix.

Our first step is to multiply each conditional value by the probability of occurrence assigned to each state of nature. For example, the *expected value* for constructing 4000 stadium seats and having a demand of 4000 seats is

(continued)

determined as follows:

$$EV = CV_{4000} \times P_{4000}$$
$$= \$200,000 \times 0.50$$
$$= \$100,000.$$

We then determine the *total* expected value for constructing 4000 seats by adding the expected values for each of the probabilities of seat demands. The total expected value for each combination is shown in Table 7.4. For example, the total expected value for constructing 8000 seats is $240,000. Given the information and assumptions in this problem, we find that the optimum solution would be to construct 8000 seats.

TABLE 7.4 ■ EXPECTED VALUES FOR STADIUM-EXPANSION DECISION (IN $000)

STRATEGY (SEATS CONSTRUCTED)	SEAT DEMAND				TOTAL EXPECTED VALUE
	4000	8000	12,000	16,000	
	Probability of Demand				
	0.50	*0.30*	*0.15*	*0.05*	
4,000	$100	$ 60	$ 30	$ 10	$200
8,000	40	120	60	20	240
12,000	− 20	84	90	30	184
16,000	− 80	48	72	40	120

DECISION-TREE Model

Many people claim that "decision-tree analysis is the most widely used form of decision analysis. Managers have used it in making business decisions in uncertain [and risky] conditions since the late 1950s."[13]

The *decision-tree model* identifies the relationships among future decision strategies, states of nature, and present decision strategies. It is very effective in probing judgments when more than one person is involved in making the decision, which is a common situation in many organizations.

If a *sequence* of decisions must be considered in an analysis of a decision problem, the decision-tree model is usually more useful than the payoff-matrix model. The decision tree permits managers to break a problem into a sequence of logically ordered smaller problems. The solutions to the smaller problems can then be combined to provide a solution to the larger problem.

This aid for decision making is appropriate for complex problems that have significant financial implications, such as problems in marketing, pricing, plant expansion, introducing new products, or buying another firm. In short, the decision tree is an effective tool for assessing choices, risks, objectives, and monetary gains.[14]

Variables and relationships

Thousands of calculations and branches can be involved in the use of a decision tree. The critical elements in its construction are the assumptions and probabilities from which the payoffs are estimated. The key variables in a decision tree are:

■ The *skeleton* of the decision tree. This represents pictorially the possible *courses of action,* the *outcome* from each course of action, and the *states of nature* identified.

■ The *probabilities* of the various outcomes.

■ The *conditional payoffs* (or costs) associated with the outcomes.

■ The *expected values* associated with the payoffs or costs.

The skeleton of the tree is made up of nodes (usually represented by circles, squares, and rectangles) and lines that connect the nodes. The nodes may represent (1) a course of action to be taken; (2) an outcome from an action that is taken; or even (3) the probabilities of the various states of nature. Each outcome is linked to a subsequent action. This process permits a decisionmaker to consider and follow to its conclusion every reasonable alternative course of action. The skeleton, variables, and relationships between the variables in a decision-tree model are illustrated in Fig. 7.4.

The In Practice about an oil-drilling decision provides a simplified example of the decision-tree model, including a graphic illustration of the skeleton, variables, and relationships among the variables.[15] It demonstrates the impact of individual differences in payoffs and the probabilities of obtaining the payoffs.

IN PRACTICE
Oil-Drilling
Decision

A decision-making group consisting of three individuals—Mr. Smith, Mr. Jones, and Ms. Williams—is involved in a joint venture in speculative oil drilling. The three decisionmakers must choose between two drilling sites. They can't afford to drill on more than one site at a time. Each person has read the geological reports and has prepared a decision tree summarizing his or her thinking about where to drill.

Figure 7.4 shows the decision trees prepared by Smith, Jones, and Williams. It shows the three possible outcomes from drilling a well at each site: a

(continued)

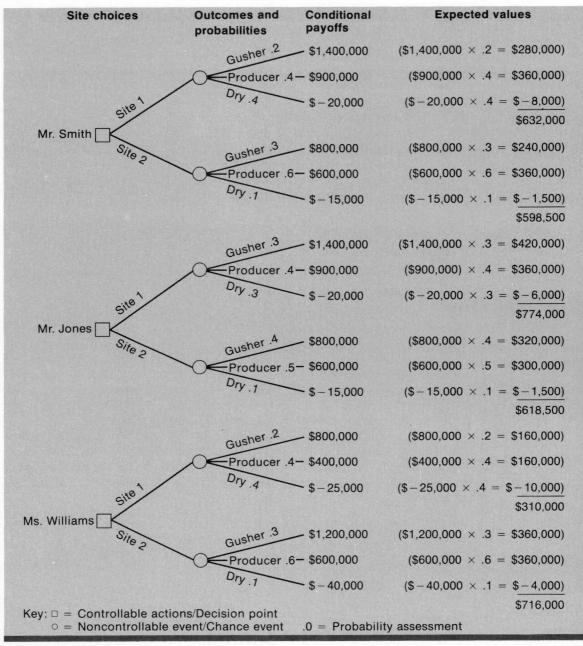

Site choices	Outcomes and probabilities	Conditional payoffs	Expected values

Mr. Smith

Site 1
- Gusher .2 — $1,400,000 — ($1,400,000 × .2 = $280,000)
- Producer .4 — $900,000 — ($900,000 × .4 = $360,000)
- Dry .4 — $−20,000 — ($−20,000 × .4 = $−8,000)

$632,000

Site 2
- Gusher .3 — $800,000 — ($800,000 × .3 = $240,000)
- Producer .6 — $600,000 — ($600,000 × .6 = $360,000)
- Dry .1 — $−15,000 — ($−15,000 × .1 = $−1,500)

$598,500

Mr. Jones

Site 1
- Gusher .3 — $1,400,000 — ($1,400,000 × .3 = $420,000)
- Producer .4 — $900,000 — ($900,000) × .4 = $360,000)
- Dry .3 — $−20,000 — ($−20,000 × .3 = $−6,000)

$774,000

Site 2
- Gusher .4 — $800,000 — ($800,000 × .4 = $320,000)
- Producer .5 — $600,000 — ($600,000 × .5 = $300,000)
- Dry .1 — $−15,000 — ($−15,000 × .1 = $−1,500)

$618,500

Ms. Williams

Site 1
- Gusher .2 — $800,000 — ($800,000 × .2 = $160,000)
- Producer .4 — $400,000 — ($400,000 × .4 = $160,000)
- Dry .4 — $−25,000 — ($−25,000 × .4 = $−10,000)

$310,000

Site 2
- Gusher .3 — $1,200,000 — ($1,200,000 × .3 = $360,000)
- Producer .6 — $600,000 — ($600,000 × .6 = $360,000)
- Dry .1 — $−40,000 — ($−40,000 × .1 = $−4,000)

$716,000

Key: □ = Controllable actions/Decision point
   ○ = Noncontrollable event/Chance event   .0 = Probability assessment

FIGURE 7.4
Decision Trees for Oil-Drilling Investors

Source: Reprinted by permission from *Business* magazine, "Decision Science Concepts—Foundation for the Future," by Marvin Berhold and John Coffman, January–February 1979. Copyright © 1979 by the College of Business Administration, Georgia State University, Atlanta.

gusher, a producer, or a dry well. Figure 7.4 shows considerable variation in the three people's thinking about the sites. For example, Smith thinks that there is a 20-percent chance of having a gusher at Site 1. If a gusher occurs (conditional value), he thinks that the payoff will be substantial: a whopping $1.4 million. Williams also thinks that there is a 20-percent chance of a gusher at Site 1, but she is not nearly as optimistic as Smith over the conditional value from a gusher. Williams thinks that the maximum return from a gusher at Site 1 is $800,000.

The decision-tree model, like the payoff-matrix model, requires that conditional payoffs be adjusted by their probability of occurrence. The expected values are calculated in the right-hand column of Fig. 7.4. Based on these expected values, Williams has a very strong preference for Site 2 ($716,000 expected value) over Site 1 ($310,000 expected value). By contrast, Smith has a positive, but not overwhelming, preference for Site 1; his expected values are $632,000 for Site 1 and $598,500 for Site 2. Jones has a definite preference for Site 1, with an expected value of $774,000, over Site 2, with an expected value of $618,500.

These conflicting opinions could be resolved in several ways in order to reach a group decision. One obvious way would be for Smith, Jones, and Williams to state how they used and evaluated the available information. This could result in changed opinions and revised decision trees. They might want to collect additional information by having more tests and experiments made. A geologist might be hired to provide more geological information. Since Smith and Jones favor Site 1 and Williams would strongly oppose this site, Williams might drop out so another investor could be found. If all else fails, the investors could decide to part ways or to seek different sites.

AIDS FOR MAKING INNOVATIVE DECISIONS

Five decision-making aids have been highlighted so far. With the exception of the model based on rules and standard operating procedures, they involve substantial managerial judgments. The objective(s) to be attained, the definition of the problem(s), the making of assumptions, and the assignment of probabilities all require judgment decisions—initial decisions in the process that are not directly aided by the models.

In this section we present one model that does provide a process for helping managers to identify objectives, problems, and alternatives.

INTERNATIONAL FOCUS

The Case for Japanese Creativity

"What sort of philosophy has made possible Japan's rapid technological development?" is a question I am frequently asked when I lecture Western audiences. Since the assumption of some guiding set of principles is part of the Western cultural bias, I begin by answering simply. "Our philosophy consists in having no philosophy." But as this answer tends to leave my listeners more confused than before, I go on to outline four basic factors that I believe underlie our success.

The first of these is quite simply the vitality and resilience of the Japanese people. The second factor that works to our advantage is our aptitude for absorbing information. Japan's educational system fosters the capacity to digest vast quantities of knowledge in a very short time. Even more important, perhaps, is the ability of the Japanese to suppress their individual egos, making them open to receive others' ideas and know-how. This principle is basic to the teaching of Japan's traditional arts, where the disciple must practice self-negation in order to absorb the method of his master.

The third point to consider is the fact that Japan was originally forced to run to catch up with the industrial West. As any skier knows, it is much easier to follow in the tracks of an experienced skier than to blaze a trail in fresh snow. There is a huge difference between making a discovery and duplicating one. The United States paved the way for Japan's progress with the development of the transistor in 1947. Japan wasted no time following in the tracks American researchers had laid.

This leads us to the final factor, namely, the maturing of modern technology. Where modern technology is concerned, some scholars have called the transistor the key technological discovery of the 20th century. The transistor led to the birth of the integrated circuit, and this, in concert with modern information theory and digital signal processing, forms the core of today's advanced electronics. Having lived through all these developments, I am keenly aware of how the technology has matured.

The pitfalls inherent in mature technology are what slowed the United States down. They also explain how, in the space of 35 years, the Japanese, with their talent for absorbing and applying information, were able to catch up and join the front-runners.

Does Japan have what it takes to pull ahead of the pack? Some experts say there is an essential ingredient lacking. In Japan today, there is talk of "developing creativity" in order to forge ahead, with brand-new technologies, Western-style. The assumption, of course, is that the Japanese are not fundamentally creative.

Foreign commentators have long held that Japan's technological development is a result of imitation, not creative thinking. But this notion is based on an exceedingly narrow definition of creativity.

Source: Excerpted from "The Case for Japanese Creativity," by Makoto Kikuchi, Director of the Sony Corporation Research Center, in *IHJ Bulletin: A Quarterly Publication of the International House of Japan*, Summer 1984, vol. 4, no. 3, pp. 1–2.

Osborn's Applied Imagination Model

Osborn's applied imagination model prescribes a process for addressing unstructured problems, the solution of which usually requires innovative decision making. This model builds upon cooperation and the minimization of criticism among participants. It is intended for use with groups of decisionmakers, such as a manager and subordinates or a management team.

The five decision-making aids discussed previously tend to focus on *reasoning* and *vertical thinking* abilities. Reasoning is the ability to analyze and to judge. Reasoning is often enhanced by vertical thinking, which is characterized by careful, logical, and step-by-step analysis. These decision aids build from one bit of information to another to reach the correct answer. In contrast, Osborn's applied imagination model is intended to stimulate *creativity* and *lateral thinking.* Creativity is the ability to visualize, to foresee, and to generate ideas. Creativity is often enhanced through lateral thinking, which expands the mind by encouraging exploration and fostering curiosity; that is, it encourages the identification and consideration of new problems and the creation of new solutions.[16]

Osborn's applied imagination model is a creative problem-solving process that is comprised of three major functions:

- *Fact-finding,* which refers to problem-definition and preparation. Problem definition calls for picking out and specifying the problem. Preparation calls for gathering and analyzing the pertinent data.

- *Idea-finding,* which refers to idea production and idea development. Idea production calls for thinking up tentative ideas as possible leads. Idea development calls for selecting the most likely of the resultant ideas, adding others, and reassessing all of these by such means as modification and combination.

- *Solution-finding,* which refers to evaluation and adoption. Evaluation calls for verifying the tentative solutions by tests and otherwise. Adoption calls for deciding on, and implementing, the final solution.[17]

Fact-finding phase

Although the Osborn model provides some hints for improving fact-finding, they are not nearly as well developed as his procedures for idea-finding.[18] One way to improve fact-finding is to begin with a wide view of a problem area and then use a narrow focus to define the subproblems. One caution should be stated here: Sufficient time must be allowed for accurate and adequate problem definition.

Idea-finding phase

The model maintains that a person can deliberately increase the generation of good ideas by following two principles:

■ *Defer judgment.* You can think up almost twice as many good ideas in the same length of time if you defer judgment until after you have created an adequate checklist of possible leads to a solution.

■ *Quantity breeds quality.* The more ideas you think up, the more likely you are to arrive at the potentially best leads to a solution.[19]

IN PRACTICE
GE's GENERAL
ENGINEERING LAb

The General Engineering Laboratory received a request from an operating department to suggest a device by which a lamp could be turned on when you walked into a room, "so you would not have to fumble trying to find the lamp switch and knock the lamp down and fall over a chair and break your leg." The brainstormers met a couple of times over a two-week period to further define the types of technical and related problems that would probably have to be dealt with to address the general problem presented to them. At the end of this time, they made a proposal to the operating departments that for a certain figure and in a certain length of time, they would think up a device to meet the specifications.

In the given period and within the budget, the brainstorm group came up with what has since been marketed under the trade name of *Touchtron*. You simply touch the side of the lamp and the lamp turns on. You touch it again and the lamp turns off. General Electric executive C. Frank Hix, Jr., commented: "It is hard to go anywhere in a General Electric lab today without finding this time-taking type of problem approach being used by our engineering staffs."[20]

Idea-spurring questions. To help activate idea production, Osborn developed 75 questions for use in **brainstorming** a problem. Brainstorming is a method designed to encourage and support the free flow of ideas within a group, while suspending all critical judgments. Many of the idea-spurring questions are designed to encourage freewheeling thinking. The group leader is required to use some judgment about which of the questions are most likely to generate ideas for the problem at hand and is not expected to use all 75 of them in a session. The following are a few of the types of questions that could be used in a brainstorming session.[21]

How can this issue, idea, or thing be put to other use?

How can it be adapted?

How can it be modified?

How can it be reduced?

How can it be substituted for something else, or can something else be substituted for part of it?

How could its elements be rearranged?

How could it be reversed?

How could it be combined with other things?

Brainstorming session. In a group session, questions such as the preceding would be explored through brainstorming. Consistent with the two principles of idea-finding, a brainstorming session should adhere to the following four rules.[22]

■ *Criticism is ruled out.* Critical judgment of ideas must be withheld until later.

■ *Freewheeling is welcomed.* The wilder the idea, the better; it is easier to tame down than to think up.

■ *Quantity is wanted.* The greater the number of ideas, the more the likelihood of useful ideas.

■ *Combination and improvement are sought.* In addition to contributing ideas of their own, participants should suggest how ideas of others can be turned into better ideas, or how two or more ideas can be joined into still another idea.

These rules are intended to separate judgment and creative imagination. The two are incompatible and relate to different steps in the decision-making process. The leader of one brainstorming group communicated this idea by stating: "If you try to get hot and cold water out of the same faucet at the same time, you will get only lukewarm water. And if you try to criticize and create at the same time, you can't turn on either *cold* enough or *hot* enough ideas. So let's stick solely to *ideas*—let's cut out *all* criticism *during* this session."[23]

The ideal number of participants in a brainstorming session is 5–12. The brainstorming phase should normally run not less than 20 minutes or longer than an hour. Of course, brainstorming could consist of several idea-generating sessions. For example, a different session could be used for each of the questions identified previously. Guidelines for leading a brainstorming session are outlined in Table 7.5.

Solution-finding phase

The solution-finding phase reverts to the more common decision-making processes that require judgment, analysis, and criticism. A variety of decision-making techniques and procedures—such as those presented earlier in the chapter—can be used. To get this phase underway, the group leader could ask the participants to identify from one to five of the most important ideas generated. This could be asked in terms of the overall brainstorming process

TABLE 7.5 ■ GUIDELINES FOR LEADING A BRAINSTORMING SESSION

BASIC LEADERSHIP ROLE

1. Make a brief statement of the four basic rules.
2. State the time duration for the brainstorming session.
3. Read the problem and/or related question to be discussed and ask, "What are your ideas?"
4. When an idea is given, you should summarize it, using the same words as the speaker to the extent possible, so that it can be recorded by an individual or an audio tape machine. Follow your summary with the single word "next."
5. There is little else you should say. Whenever the leader participates as a brainstormer, the productivity of the group is usually reduced.

HANDLING PROBLEMS

1. When someone talks too long, wait until he or she takes a breath (everyone must stop to inhale sometime). Break into the monologue, summarize what was said for the recorder, point to another participant and say "next." Caution the next contributor to keep his or her statement brief.
2. When someone becomes judgmental or starts to argue, stop him or her; say, for example, "That will cost you one coffee or coke for each member of the group." One such fine usually takes care of the argumentation problem.
3. When the discussion stops, relax and let the silence continue. Say absolutely nothing. No group of five or 10 persons can look at each other for more than three minutes without feeling compelled to say something. This pause should be broken by the group and *not* the leader. It is natural and to be expected that in the average 50-minute brainstorming session periods of silence will develop after somewhere between 20 and 40 minutes. This period of silence is called the "mental pause" because it is a change in thinking. All the usual ideas are exhausted; the participants are now forced to rely on their creativity to produce new concepts.
4. When someone states a problem rather than a solution, repeat the problem; raise your hand with your five fingers extended, and say, "Let's have five solutions to the problem." You may get only one or you may get ten, but you're back in the business of constructive thinking.

Source: Adapted from A. F. Osborn, *Applied Imagination: Principles and Procedures of Creative Problem-Solving,* 3rd rev. ed. New York: Charles Scribner's Sons, 1963, pp. 166–196.

or in terms of each of the questions considered. These ideas might be jotted down on a piece of paper by each participant and evaluated on a five-point scale, such as giving five points to an extremely important idea to one point for a possibly important idea. The results of this preliminary evaluation indicate what actions or ideas should be investigated further.

The Osborn applied imagination model has been used by many firms, such as General Motors, IBM, and U.S. Steel. It has also been used by nonbusiness organizations including the Air Force, Army, and U.S. Civil Service.[24]

A basic assumption of the Osborn applied imagination model is that most people and groups have the potential for greater creativity and innovation in decision making. However, for a variety of reasons, creativity and innovation become blocked. The Osborn model is designed to help reduce these blockages and to prescribe step-by-step procedures for stimulating creative and innovative ideas. There is no guarantee of innovative outcomes from the use of this or other models intended to stimulate creativity. Rather, the appropriate and sincere use of this or other models will normally increase creativity and innovation in managerial decision making.[25]

CHAPTER SUMMARY

This chapter has focused on developing your skills in making the decisions required of the entrepreneur and the resources-allocating manager. The decision-making models that stress reasoning and vertical thinking provide methods for rationally assessing new projects or proposals and allocating resources (money, equipment, personnel) to obtain the best payoffs. In addition, the Osborn model for stimulating creativity and innovation should assist you in thinking and acting more like an entrepreneur.

Each of these models involves one or more of the steps that comprise the rational decision-making process: (1) problem awareness and diagnosis; (2) setting objectives; (3) searching for alternative solutions; (4) comparing and evaluating alternative solutions; (5) choosing among possible alternative solutions; (6) implementing alternative solutions selected; and (7) follow up and control. Rules and standard operating procedures and the linear-programming model were identified as two aids especially useful for making routine decisions. Rules and SOPs tend to focus on steps 6 and 7 of the rational decision-making process, whereas the linear-programming model focuses on steps 4, 5, and 6 and can be applied to relatively structured but complex problems.

Adaptive decision making can be aided by the break-even, payoff-matrix, and decision-tree models. These models tend to address steps 3, 4, and 5 of the rational decision-making process.

Finally, innovative decisions may be aided by the Osborn applied imagination model. Its greatest contribution is in steps 1, 2, 3, and 4 of the rational decision-making process when used to cope with unstructured problems. This aid for making innovative decisions attempts to stimulate creativity and lateral thinking.

All of the models presented in this chapter prescribe ways for approaching various types of problems that confront top, middle, or first-line managers. These problems can affect virtually any department of an organization: accounting, data processing, finance, marketing, personnel, production, and others.

MANAGER'S VOCABULARY

brainstorming
break-even model
break-even point
conditional value
creativity
decision-tree model
expected value
fact-finding
fixed costs
idea-finding
lateral thinking
linear-programming model
loss
normative decision-making model
Osborn's applied imagination model
outcome
payoff-matrix model
probability
profit
reasoning
rule
solution-finding
standard operating procedure
states of nature

strategies
total costs
total revenue
variable costs
vertical thinking

REVIEW QUESTIONS

1. What are the uses and limitations of normative decision-making models?

2. What are the differences between rules and standard operating procedures and the linear-programming model?

3. When can a decision-tree model be used more effectively than the payoff-matrix model?

4. What are the main characteristics of Osborn's applied imagination model?

5. What aids for decision making may be especially useful for routine decisions, adaptive decisions, and innovative decisions?

DISCUSSION QUESTIONS

1. Why should you, as a future manager, be interested in models of decision making?

2. How might differences in individual opinions influence the use of the decision-tree model?

3. What are the similarities between the break-even, payoff-matrix, and decision-tree models?

4. Why might some managers hesitate to use decision-making aids like Osborn's applied imagination model?

5. Do you think too much effort goes into developing vertical thinking skills versus lateral thinking skills? Explain.

MANAGEMENT INCIDENTS AND CASES

Pittsburgh Steel Works

As manager of the Allegheny plant of Pittsburgh Steel Works, you have been approached by a representative of Ace Drug Company. He has offered to immunize your employees against a new strain of the American flu at a cost of $5 per employee. The flu has reached epidemic proportions on the West Coast. According to the U.S. Public Health Service, there is a 10-percent chance that this type of flu will reach epidemic proportions in the East, a 10-percent chance that it will reach semiepidemic proportions, and an 80-percent chance that it will strike one person in 1000. You estimate that, if an epidemic occurs, half your employees will contract the flu. If a semiepidemic occurs, 25 percent will be stricken. You have 2000 employees and, since the flu lasts three days, you estimate that each employee stricken will miss three days of work (excluding weekends). The average employee-day lost costs $30.

Questions

1. Develop a payoff matrix based on the information available.

2. Should you have your employees vaccinated?

EMPEROR PRODUCTS CORPORATION

The president and staff of Emperor Products Corporation, a medium-sized electronics-component manufacturer, are trying to decide whether to increase the current output of one of Emperor's products by installing an additional semiautomatic machine or by putting its employees on overtime.

Initial decision

After much discussion, they agree that there is a 0.60 subjective probability that sales would increase by 20 percent and a 0.40 subjective probability that sales would decrease by as much as 5 percent. After developing figures on the dollar consequences for the next year only, they reached the following conclusions.

1. Strategies: overtime versus one new unit of equipment.

2. States of nature: sales rise (0.60 probability) versus sales drop (0.40 probability).

3. Net cash flow: net-cash-flow implications shown in the tabulation.

State of Nature	Strategy	
	New equipment	Overtime
20% sales rise	+$460,000	+$440,000
5% sales drop	+$340,000	+$380,000

They construct a simple decision tree to take into account the probabilities of the two events. Their decision tree suggests that the expected payout will be $416,000 for the overtime alternative and $412,000 for the new-equipment alternative. At this point, the *best* decision appears to be the overtime alternative.

Construct this decision tree and show the calculations that serve as the basis for this initial decision.

Further consideration

The executives decided to further evaluate their apparently best alternative (strategy) by extending the decision-tree model another year. After extensive discussion, they concluded that the longer-term prospects for the product in question are excellent. Accordingly, they worked out the following probabilities:

1. If sales decreased by 5 percent the first year, there is a 0.80 subjective probability that they will increase by 20 percent and a 0.20 probability that sales will increase by only 10 percent in the second year.

2. If sales rise by 20 percent in the first year, they expect a 0.50 probability that second-year sales will increase 20 percent and a 0.50 probability that sales will increase by 10 percent.

Questions

1. Using this additional information, develop a two-year decision model.

2. Which alternative now appears to be the best?

REFERENCES

1. Adapted from R. O. Swalm, "Utility Theory—Insights into Risk Taking." In D. N. Dickson (Ed.), *Using Logical Techniques for Making Better Decisions.* New York: John Wiley & Sons, 1983, pp. 73–94. *Also see* M. Magnet, "How Top Managers Make a Company's Toughest Decision," *Fortune,* March 18, 1985, pp. 52–59.

2. H. A. Linstone, *Multiple Perspectives for Decision Making: Bridging the Gap Between Analysis and Action.* New York: Elsevier Science Publishing, 1984; D. J. Clough, *Decisions in Public and Private Sectors: Theories, Practices and Processes.* Englewood Cliffs, N.J.: Prentice-Hall, 1984; L. M. Austin and J. R. Burns, *Management Science: An Aid for Managerial Decision Making.* New York, Macmillan, 1985.

3. S. Kossauf, *Normative Decision Making.* Englewood Cliffs, N.J.: Prentice-Hall, 1970.

4. P. Nutt, "Models for Decision Making in Organizations and Some Contextual Variables Which Stipulate Optimal Use," *Academy of Management Review,* 1976, **2**:69–80; P. C. Nutt, "Types of Organizational Decision Processes," *Administrative Science Quarterly,* 1984, **29**:414–450.

5. D. N. Dickson (Ed.), *Using Logical Techniques for Making Better Decisions.* New York: John Wiley & Sons, 1983; D. W. Bunn, *Applied Decision Analysis.* New York: McGraw-Hill, 1984.

6. J. C. Papageorgiou, "Decision Making in the Year 2000," *Interfaces,* 1983, **13**:77–86.

7. H. Simon, *Administrative Behavior,* 3rd ed. New York: Macmillan, 1976.

8. D. S. Hirshfeld, "From the Shadows," *Interfaces,* 1983, **13**:72–76.

9. J. J. Dinkel and G. A. Kochenberger, *Using Management Science: A Workbook.* Houston: Dame Publications, 1980. *Also see:* D. G. Luenberger, *Linear and Nonlinear Programming,* 2nd ed. Reading, Mass.: Addison-Wesley, 1984; S. M. Lee, L. J. Moore, and B. W. Taylor III, *Management Science,* 2nd ed. Dubuque, Iowa: Wm. C. Brown, 1986.

10. Dinkel and Kochenberger, *Using Management Science. . . ,* pp. 77–96.

11. Adapted from S. C. Bhantnagar, "Implementing Linear Programming in a Textile Unit: Some Problems and a Solution," *Interfaces,* 1981, **11**:87–91.

12. R. Schlaifer, *Analysis of Decisions under Uncertainty.* New York: McGraw-Hill, 1969.

13. J. W. Ulvila and R. V. Brown, "Decision Analysis Comes of Age," *Harvard Business Review,* September–October 1982, p. 131.

14. A. Oxenfeldt, D. Miller, and R. Dickinson, *A Basic Approach to Executive Decision Making.* New York: AMACOM, 1978.

15. This application is drawn from M. Berhold and J. Coffman, "Decision Science Concepts—Foundations for the Future," *Business,* 1979, **29**:9–16. *Also see:* C. T. L. Janssen and T. E. Daniel, "A Decision Theory Example in Football," *Decision Sciences,* 1984, **15**:253–259.

16. A. F. Osborn, *Applied Imagination: Principles and Procedures of Creative Problem-Solving,* 3rd rev. ed. New York: Charles Scribner's Sons, 1963; E. De Bono, *Lateral Thinking.* New York: Harper &

Row, 1970; W. R. Smilor (Ed.), *Corporate Creativity: Robust Companies and the Enterpreneurial Spirit.* New York: Praeger, 1984; P. F. Drucker, *Innovation and Entrepreneurship: Practices and Principles.* New York: Harper & Row, 1985.

17. Osborn, *Applied Imagination . . . ,* p. 86.

18. A. B. Van Gundy Jr., *Techniques of Structured Problem Solving.* New York: Van Nostrand Reinhold, 1981, pp. 92–101. *Also see* G. Pinchot III, *Intrapreneuring.* New York: Harper & Row, 1985.

19. Van Gundy, p. 124.

20. Van Gundy, pp. 93–95.

21. Van Gundy, pp. 229–290.

22. Van Gundy, p. 156.

23. Van Gundy, p. 156.

24. C. Gregory, *The Management of Intelligence: Scientific Problem Solving and Creativity.* New York: McGraw-Hill, 1967.

25. D. A. Whetten and K. S. Cameron, *Developing Management Skills.* Glenview, Ill.: Scott, Foresman, 1984; M. Sinetar, "Entrepreneurs, Chaos, and Creativity—Can Creative People Really Survive Large Company Structure?" *Sloan Management Review,* Winter 1985, pp. 57–62.

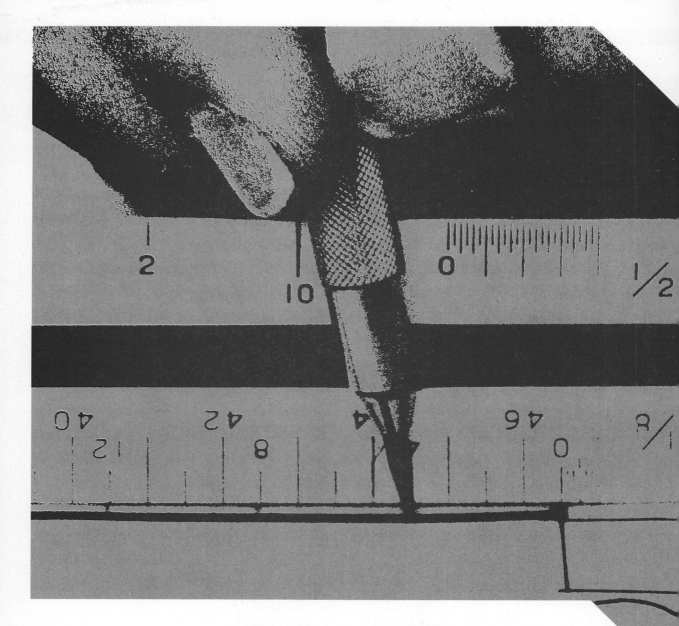

Strategic Planning

CHAPTER 8

LEARNING OBJECTIVES

After studying this chapter, you should be able to:

- Define strategic planning, tactical planning, and strategies.

- Describe when planning is likely to be effective or ineffective.

- Identify the sequence of steps and the activities involved in the strategic planning process.

- Evaluate environmental threats and opportunities in relation to organization strengths and weaknesses.

- Describe six investment strategies and the conditions under which they are most likely to be effective.

CHAPTER OUTLINE

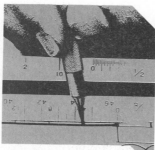

PREVIEW CASE

Chrysler—A Commentary by Lee A. Iacocca

When I [Lee A. Iacocca, chairman of Chrysler Corporation] came to Chrysler in 1979, the Michigan State Fairgrounds were jammed with thousands of unsold, unwanted, rusting Chryslers, Dodges, and Plymouths. Foreign operations were leeching the lifeblood out of the company. And worst of all, cars were coming off the assembly line with loose doors, chipped paint, and crooked moldings.

The Chrysler experience highlighted some painful realities!

■ The quality of our products had declined.

■ Work practices had shortchanged productivity.

■ Foreign countries that the United States had defeated in war and rebuilt in peace were beating this country in its own markets.

Chrysler took some strategic steps to turn the situation around.

First, the company reduced salary expenses dramatically, cutting literally half the work force from about 160,000 to about 80,000. And those 80,000 are now producing a broader range of cars and trucks than they ever did before. That is the simple definition of productivity: more product, more volume, half the people. Part of the medicine was administered to the white-collar work force; it was cut in half, from 40,000 to 21,000 people. Union and nonunion workers made wage and benefit sacrifices, saving $1.2 billion.

Courtesy of Chrysler Corporation.

"We have one and only one ambition. To be the best. What else is there."

Lee A. Iacocca

Second, the company reduced fixed costs by about $2 billion on an annual basis. Chrysler closed or consolidated 20 obsolete and outmoded plants. More important, the company modernized the remaining 40 plants to make them among the most efficient and productive in the industry. Chrysler cut its break-even point to *half* the level of 1980. It used to be 2.4 million units; now it's under 1.2 million.

Third, Chrysler simplified operations by reducing the number of different parts in its manufacturing system by one-third—from 75,000 to 40,000 items. And in the process, the company shook $1 billion out of inventory.

Fourth, Chrysler launched an all-out, deadly serious program to improve the quality of both its finished products and the components that go into them. The company worked meticulously both internally and with its suppliers, using the latest methods of preventive surveillance and statistical controls.

Fifth, Chrysler restructured its balance sheet. The company retired its U.S. bank debt by converting $1.3 billion of debt into preferred stock and acquired some financial breathing room. The company also changed some preferred stock into common stock, which further strengthened Chrysler's capital base.

Sixth, and ultimately most important, management ensured that Chrysler will be a potent force in the years to come by embarking on a five-year, multibillion dollar product program—the most ambitious in its entire history.

The results of these striking and strategic steps are a matter of public record. Chrysler is now different than it was only a few years ago: half the size, but twice the company. Management is fully prepared to do whatever is necessary to keep Chrysler on the leading edge of innovative design, production, and marketing. One pillar of the foundation upon which the new Chrysler is built is the best automotive quality in the industry—and the company stands behind it with more than slogans and claims.

Over the past few years, Chrysler has developed an intensive program to upgrade quality in order to reduce maintenance and warranty costs, to cut the number of defects in all automobiles, and to deliver to customers the kinds of cars that will compete against the best in the world.

The future for Chrysler looks bright. The company has come a long way from where it was a few years ago when it set out to prove, against all odds, that Chrysler was worth saving. The company got its financial house in order, got costs in line, cut the break-even point down to size, and developed an exciting array of new products. Chrysler put a strong dealer organization and some tough, experienced people in Detroit in place. Chrysler is eager to compete and is planning to outrun the best of them in the next few years.[1]

The Chrysler case provides a feel for the nature of strategies and strategic planning in action. Some people now speak of the *New* Chrysler Corporation and the *rebirth* of a company to underline the dramatic shift in basic objectives and strategic actions.[2] The shifts between 1979 and the present have been felt at all levels of the organization, right down to the assembly worker who bolts fenders to the cars. The Preview Case suggests how market competition and declining profits can motivate top managers to reevaluate and change a firm. The Chrysler situation is somewhat unusual in that a new management team introduced the new strategic planning and courses of action. Of the 400 top managers at Chrysler in 1978, about 80 percent were replaced by 1983. About half of the new managers were not from Chrysler and the other half were promoted from lower levels at Chrysler.[3] Harold Sperlich, the president of and third in line at Chrysler, comments on what he found when he joined the firm in 1977.

> What I found was a company that was in a mess. Products were not strong, quality was not good, and costs were out of line. People in the place were unfocused, unmotivated, and poorly managed. Management was primarily short-term profit-oriented.
>
> The piece I was involved in, when I came into the company, was the product area. What we started back then—this was before the company actually went into the problem period I'm talking about—was a process to rebuild a fundamental product posture that was quite different from what Chrysler had previously been involved in. It was predicated on converting the fleet to predominantly front-wheel drive, top-quality products that would be best in class and in the market, which is really the deepest part of what a company is all about.
>
> The company must first make a commitment to the market—that is, we will serve in certain areas of excellence—and the degree to which the market responds to our efforts will depend on how well we do that. That commitment had to be made to the market by launching product programs that would be superb automobiles and trucks.[4]

The Chrysler experience clearly suggests that top managers are intimately involved in the strategic planning process. The effectiveness of this process can have dramatic impacts on the organization. These impacts can range from growth to stagnation to failure. Chrysler seems to have experienced both extremes.

The overall objective of this chapter is to introduce some basic ideas about and procedures to be used in planning—especially strategic planning—that can result in effective strategic courses of action. The first part of this chapter presents some basic information about the nature, role, and scope of planning. The second part of the chapter discusses the basic issues and steps in the strategic planning process.

BASICS OF PLANNING

We defined *planning* in general terms in Chapter 1 as the formal process of making decisions that are intended to affect the future. We now define planning more completely as the formal process of making decisions to (1) choose overall organizational objectives for both the short run and the long run; (2) choose divisional, departmental, and even individual objectives based on these overall organizational objectives; and (3) choose the strategies (courses of action) that can achieve the objectives. For example, one of the first short-term organizational objectives for Chrysler in 1979 was to reduce substantially its break-even point by cutting overhead (fixed costs). Two of the major

*Creation of an organiza-
tional plan involves input
from all levels and long
hours of interaction and
discussion.*

Source: Christopher Morrow/
Stock, Boston.

strategies chosen to achieve this objective were reducing the work force from 200,000 to 101,000 employees and closing 20 of its 60 manufacturing plants.

Planning is often considered *the* most basic management function. The steps followed in formal planning are consistent with those in the rational decision-making model. (See Chapter 6, especially Fig. 6.8 for a review of these steps.) If *rational plans* are created, it logically follows that *rational methods* of organizing, controlling, and leading should be designed to help implement the plans.[5]

Throughout most of this chapter we discuss planning from the perspective of the rational decision-making model. However, we do selectively weave into the discussion some perspectives from the bounded rationality and political decision-making models. (Both of these models were also discussed in Chapter 6.)

Although the distinctions are not always clear, there are two basic types of planning: **strategic planning** and **tactical planning.**

Figure 8.1 shows their general relationship in an overview of the business planning process. Strategic planning creates key objectives and strategies. Tactical planning translates general company or major business-unit strategies and objectives into detailed implementation strategies. Implementation strategies are expressed in the form of detailed budgets, departmental action plans, proposed changes in organization structure, control techniques, and the like.

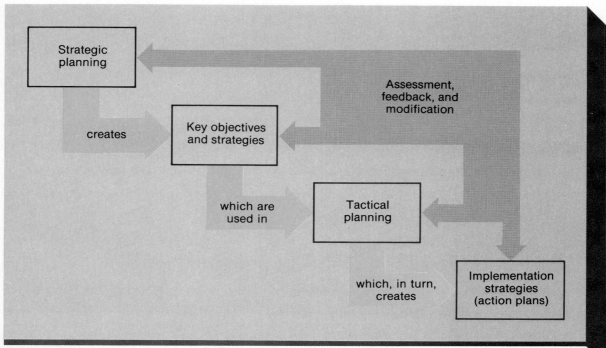

FIGURE 8.1
Overview of the Business Planning Process

Focus of Strategic Planning

Strategic planning is the process of making choices about an organization's mission, objectives, strategies, policies, and major resource allocations.[6] A *mission* is the business (or businesses) that a company is currently in and desires to be in for some time into the future. When Lee Iacocca became the chairman and chief executive officer of Chrysler Corporation in 1979, he and the other top managers faced a basic choice as to the future mission of Chrysler. Many were suggesting that Chrysler should get out of the automobile business as soon as possible and reorganize through bankruptcy proceedings. Iacocca and the other top executives reaffirmed the company's mission to remain as a full-line manufacturer of passenger cars. This decision led to the need for making a variety of other decisions. For example, top management made a strategic decision to seek federal legislation that would allow the federal government to guarantee the loans that banks and others made to Chrysler. After much controversy, the Chrysler Corporation Loan Guarantee Act of 1979 was passed. This Act provided loan guarantees of up to $1.5 billion for loans made prior to December 31, 1983. These loans were to be repaid by the end of 1990.[7] In 1984, Chrysler paid off all the loans that had been guaranteed by the Loan Guarantee Board created by the Act.

Decisions concerning major resource allocations can be illustrated by the five-year, $9.5 billion plan for new products and the modernization of Chrysler's auto plants in 1984.[8] One of the stated objectives of Chrysler's new product plan is "to use a single platform—drivetrain, floorpan, and suspension parts—to create a variety of vehicles including high-margin [profit] convertibles and jazzy vans."[9]

Typical issues considered in strategic planning are shown in Table 8.1. As you read down the list, the issues and questions move from a focus on

TABLE 8.1 ■ TYPICAL ISSUES AND QUESTIONS CONSIDERED IN STRATEGIC PLANNING

1. RECORD CURRENT STRATEGY:

- What is the current strategy?
- What kind of business does management want to operate?
- What kind of business does management feel it ought to operate?

2. IDENTIFY PROBLEMS WITH THE CURRENT STRATEGY:

- Are trends discernible in the environment that may become threats and/or missed opportunities if the current strategy is continued?
- Is the company having difficulty implementing the current strategy?
- Is the attempt to carry out the current strategy disclosing significant weaknesses and/or unutilized strengths in the company?

3. DISCOVER THE CORE OF THE STRATEGY PROBLEM:

- Does the current strategy require greater competence and/or resources than the company possesses?
- Does it lack sufficient competitive advantage?
- Will it fail to exploit opportunities and/or meet threats in the environment, now or in the future?

4. FORMULATE ALTERNATIVE NEW STRATEGIES:

- What possible alternatives exist for solving the strategy problem?
- To what extent do the company's competence and resources limit the number of alternatives that should be considered?
- To what extent do management's preferences limit the alternatives?

5. EVALUATE ALTERNATIVE NEW STRATEGIES:

- Which alternative *best* solves the strategy problem?
- Which alternative offers the *best* match with the company's competence and resources?
- Which alternative offers the *greatest* competitive advantage?

6. CHOOSE A NEW STRATEGY:

- What is the *relative significance* of each of the preceding considerations?
- What should the new strategy be?

Source: Adapted from Frank F. Gilmore, "Formulating Strategy in Smaller Companies," *Harvard Business Review*, 1971, p. 80. Copyright © 1971 by the President and Fellows of Harvard College. All rights reserved.

current strategy, its problems, and missed opportunities to possible new strategies to the selection of a specific strategy. In sum, strategic planning often includes the following activities and issues.

- Diagnosing the external environment(s) and stakeholders that impact the organization.
- Defining the basic nature and mission of the organization.
- Formulating the organization's basic and important objectives, including the customers to be served, the products and/or services to be marketed, and the geographical areas in which the firm intends to compete.[10]
- Identifying, evaluating, and selecting the fundamental strategies (i.e., courses of action) for the organization.

Focus of Tactical Planning

Tactical planning is the process of developing detailed and short-term decisions concerning what is to be done, who is to do it, and how it is to be done. Managers of departments at the lower levels of an organization are most involved in tactical planning.

Thus tactical planning often includes the following activities and issues.

- Developing the annual budgets for each department, division, and project.
- Deciding on the detailed means for implementing the objectives and strategies developed in strategic plans.
- Formulating courses of action for improving and coordinating current operations.

One reason for making tactical plans is to enable a department to anticipate the actions of other departments or outside suppliers with which it is interdependent. For example, Ford Motor Company develops monthly and quarterly plans with tire companies for the delivery of certain quantities and types of tires to its various production plants.

Linking Strategic and Tactical Planning

Table 8.2 summarizes the different focuses of tactical and strategic planning. Despite these differences, strategic and tactical planning are linked in a well-designed planning system.

**IN PRACTICE
A Major Chemical
Company**

The vice president for planning of a major chemical company explains his company's views on the linkages between strategic and tactical planning.

We have a very close link between the long-term plan and tactical plans. In fact, the first phases of the tactical plans are coordinated in the corporate planning department. During this process, we set the detailed objectives and guidelines for next year's tactical plans and ensure that they are in line with our long-term strategic objectives. It also helps us to discuss allocation of resources before all the details of the budget are prepared. Only after the framework for the tactical plans with regard to manpower, volume, and financial objectives has been established is it turned over to the controller's section for the preparation of the final budget, which goes down to the cost-center level.

We find that this top-down approach is much more efficient than the traditional bottom-up budgeting done in many companies. Under the latter system, everyone first prepares a whole shopping list of items that add up to more than the total the company can afford. In the end, all the numbers have to be either pared down or changed completely to conform to strategic objectives. Under our system, allocation of resources takes place first, and we tell the operating divisions that these are the parameters within which they can work. Based on this, they must then set their own priorities.[11]

Purposes of Strategic and Tactical Planning

Organizations can survive only if they are able to manage change while maintaining a degree of stability to avoid a sense of confusion and lack of direction. Organizations that efficiently manage both change and stability will progress and grow. As the rate of change and complexity of the business world increase, new and better ways must be found to understand, anticipate, and respond to changes. Planning is a key management process for helping organizations to maintain stability and, at the same time, to change.

We already know that one of the important activities in managerial decision making is the establishment of organizational, divisional, departmental, and individual objectives (the hierarchy of objectives presented in Chapter 6

TABLE 8.2 ■ FOCUSES OF TACTICAL AND STRATEGIC PLANNING

DIMENSION	TACTICAL PLANNING	STRATEGIC PLANNING
Types of decisions	Routine and adaptive	Adaptive and innovative
Condition of decision making	Certainty and risk (objective probabilities)	Risk (subjective probabilities) and uncertainty
Where plans are developed	First-level to middle management	Middle to top management
Time horizon	Short term (usually two years or less)	Long term (usually three years or more)
Intended purpose	*Means* of implementing strategic plan	Assuring long-term survival and growth

and shown graphically in Fig. 6.5). This activity is part of the planning process and involves both strategic and tactical planning. Let us now look at this in a different way—at the organizational level of the hierarchy—in terms of the purposes of the planning process: to help achieve intermediate and ultimate organizational objectives.

Figure 8.2 suggests that the three primary objectives of planning are to (1) identify opportunities that will occur in the future; (2) anticipate and avoid future problems; and (3) develop courses of action. If these planning objectives can be achieved, the organization has a better chance to achieve its intermediate objectives; that is, to adapt and innovate in order to create desirable change, improve the effectiveness of employees and managers, and maintain its stability. Managers seek all these outcomes because they should, in turn, lead to the achievement of ultimate organizational objectives; that is, to long-term growth, profitability, and survival of the organization. Figure 8.2 also shows the focuses of strategic and tactical planning in relation to these sets of objectives. Note that both strategic and tactical planning are very much concerned with developing courses of action, improving the effectiveness of employees and managers, and ensuring profits.

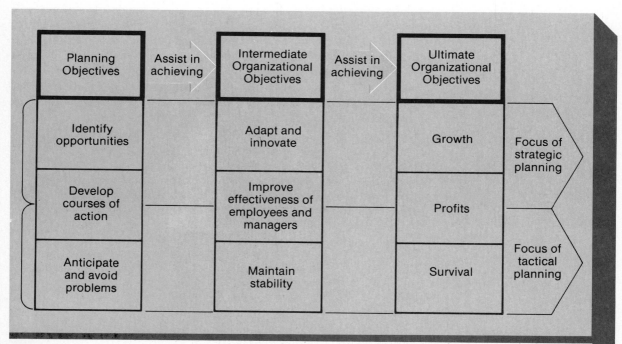

FIGURE 8.2
Purposes of Strategic and Tactical Planning

STRATEGIES

Strategies are the major courses of action that are chosen to help achieve important organizational objectives.[12] Organizations may set important objectives with respect to their major stakeholders—stockholders, employees, customers, suppliers, lenders, government. For example, an objective for stockholders could be to minimize the fluctuations in the price of stock as much as possible. A strategy of maintaining a steady dividend payout from year to year, as at AT&T, is one type of action for achieving this objective.

When taken together, the major courses of action represent the overall organizational strategy.[13] A strategy or set of strategies is an output from strategic planning. The concepts of strategy and strategic planning are relatively straightforward in firms such as McDonald's, Maytag, or Mary Kay Cosmetics that operate in one or two lines of products or services. For firms operating in multiple markets with numerous products or services, these concepts are much more complicated.[14] General Electric, for example, has many companies and divisions within seven major sectors:

1. Power systems (turbines and generators, construction and engineering services, nuclear products and services, power delivery and transformers).

2. Natural resources (coking coal, steam coal, oil and natural gas).

3. Services and materials (plastics, GE Credit Corporation, GE Venture Capital).

4. Technical systems (aerospace, medical systems, industrial electronics).

5. Consumer products (major appliances, lighting products, room air conditioners, broadcasting and cablevision).

6. Aircraft engines (commercial and military jet engines); ship propulsion.

7. International (foreign multiindustry affiliates, export and licensing support, marketing support).[15]

In a large and complex organization like GE—$28 billion in sales and 330,000 employees in 1984—its companies and divisions are typically called strategic business units. A *strategic business unit* (SBU) is a division or company within an organization that serves a distinct product–market segment, has a well-defined set of customers, and/or includes a specific geographic area.[16] Strategic business units at GE include the Lighting Systems Products Division (product–market segment), Military and Small Commercial Engine Operations (set of customers), and Far East Area Division (geographical area).

IMPACT OF ORGANIZATIONAL DIVERSITY ON THE PLANNING PROCESS

When a company operates many different businesses, it is diversified. Diversification usually occurs in four stages: (1) a single business; (2) a dominant business; (3) related businesses; and (4) unrelated businesses.[17]

A *single-business firm* is one that provides a limited number of products or services to a particular part of an overall market. McDonald's is an example of a firm that is positioned in the fast-food segment of the restaurant industry.

A *dominant-business firm* is one that serves the various segments of a particular industry or market. For example, Standard Oil Company of Cali-

INTERNATIONAL FOCUS

Big Challenge Ahead for Chemical Firms

The major problem American chemical manufacturers face today is the strong dollar. The biggest challenge they will face tomorrow is competition from new manufacturers in the Middle East who have the advantage of the lowest-cost feedstock in the world.

So says Carl De Martino, and it is his job to know. He is a group vice president for Du Pont Co., the largest American chemical company and one of the world's giants. De Martino is responsible for all of Du Pont's international chemical and non-energy business.

Overseas operations are big business for Du Pont. Last year, the company's international chemical sales totaled $4.6 billion, even after a $200 million loss for currency exchanges. The sales included $2 billion from products manufactured in the United States, but sold overseas, and $2.6 billion from products made overseas.

The strong currency situation, combined with the relatively expensive oil, natural gas and petroleum-derived feedstocks American companies use to manufacture petrochemical products, means that some U.S.-made goods are priced too high to sell in the international markets.

"We estimate that the dollar is 45 percent overvalued," he said. "This puts us at a tremendous competitive disadvantage."

This problem will get worse in the next few years as the massive petrochemical complexes now under construction in Saudi Arabia and elsewhere start operations.

"The startup of those Middle East plants is going to very profoundly affect the petrochemical industry in this country," De Martino said.

He cited three advantages these plants will have over the domestic chemical producers.

First, they will be operating with raw materials that are essentially free, particularly the natural gas that until now has been flared off in the field. Second, the strong dollar makes goods priced in other currencies much less expensive. And finally, import tariffs and other trade barriers that foreign governments impose add to the price of American products.

Du Pont saw the current trends developing years ago and began making its plans accordingly. It got out of some businesses, increased its emphasis in other areas and added new product lines. In other words, the chemical giant has been repositioning itself to deal with the changing market.

Source: Excerpted from "Big Challenge Ahead for Chemical Firms," by Barbara Shook. *Houston Chronicle*, November 26, 1984, Section 2, p. 1.

fornia (SOCAL) engages in worldwide, integrated petroleum operations that include exploring for and developing crude-oil and natural-gas reserves; transporting crude oil, natural gas, and petroleum products by pipelines, oil tankers, and motor vehicles; operating large refinery complexes; and marketing a complete line of petroleum products (Chevron). In 1984, SOCAL acquired

"We have been getting into areas where Du Pont has something special to offer," De Martino explained. "We have been trying to get away from direct competition with the low-cost commodity chemical producers, and we are already well down that road."

Internationally, the best-selling products are specialty agrichemicals, materials used in the electronics industries and specialty fibers.

The fastest growing overseas markets for Du Pont are in the Pacific basin, primarily Japan, Taiwan, Korea and Singapore, but the company's traditional markets in Europe, Canada and Latin America are holding up well.

De Martino said that in spite of the enormous financial troubles many Latin American nations have incurred, sales for Du Pont are up 14 percent so far this year. "It is an enigma," he said. "But we have been there for a number of years, and we have people experienced at working in conditions with annual inflation rates of 200 or 300 percent." Different countries and regions have varying degrees of instability, both political and monetary, he pointed out. This is a situation that Du Pont recognizes, but it accepts the risks, within reason, as part of doing business.

"You can't stay out of every part of the world because there is a little risk," De Martino said.

One way Du Pont minimizes its risks is to employ as many local nationals as possible. Of the 35,000 people employed overseas, De Martino estimates that only about 1 percent are American citizens.

A lot of developing countries ask foreign companies such as Du Pont to bring in technology, to use certain local resources or to permit local investment in equipment and research and development.

Du Pont prefers to establish wholly owned subsidiaries in the countries where it has operations because this arrangement gives the company more control over the total business and technology. De Martino said that Du Pont will form joint ventures with local firms if necessary, but one thing it does not like to do is sell its technology.

The company spends a lot of money developing its processes and products, he explained. Those costs cannot be recovered if it has to sell the technology rather than manufacturing the products itself.

Gulf for approximately $13.2 billion. This acquisition was consistent with strengthening SOCAL's competitive position in the petroleum industry.

The third diversification stage is reached when a company becomes a *related-businesses firm.* In this stage, a firm diversifies into related products or services.[18] Two companies that appear to function in this stage are IBM and GE. For example, IBM provides numerous products and services, ranging from typewriters to personal computers to sophisticated computers, to businesses related to information processing.

An *unrelated-businesses firm* provides diverse products and services to many different markets and industries. These types of firms are often referred to as *conglomerates.* In these firms, the executives of each strategic business unit are responsible for the strategic planning of their division or company. Their strategic plans are submitted to corporate-headquarters executives for review, approval, or modification. The headquarters executives are heavily involved in determining which firms they might acquire, divest themselves of, and reduce, maintain, or increase through capital investment decisions. United Technologies is an example of such a firm. Its product lines are wide-ranging, including Pratt and Whitney jet engines, Carrier air conditioners, Otis elevators and escalators, Sikorsky helicopters, and Inmont inks (used in printing, publishing, and packaging), among others.

These stages of diversification and their relationship to the relative scope of strategic planning are plotted in Fig. 8.3. Firms such as United Technologies, Gulf & Western, and W. R. Grace Company that provide numerous products and services to unrelated markets must have a wide-ranging planning system. In contrast, firms like McDonald's, Maytag, and Mary Kay Cosmetics that are involved in single-product or service lines do not require nearly as elaborate a planning system (which is not to suggest that planning is a simple process in single-product–line firms).

Impact of Managers on the Planning Process

The need for managers to engage in planning can be summed up by the following notable quotes.

- Any organization that doesn't plan for its future isn't likely to have one.
- The most effective way to cope with change is to help create it.
- Planning without action is futile; action without planning is fatal.
- When you don't know where you're going, any road will get you there.

Top managers may spend a considerable amount of time on planning in order to define future directions for a company and to develop alternative strategies for different business conditions.[19] The importance that top managers place on planning determines in large part the importance that others in the organization give it and how they view the planning process. Middle

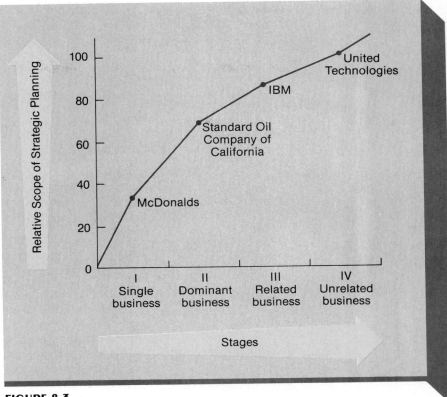

FIGURE 8.3
Stages in Organizational Diversity and Planning

managers often are involved in the preparation of strategic plans and in translating them into tactical plans in conjunction with first-line managers. Large companies generally have planning staffs that assist managers in identifying objectives, alternative courses of action, and probabilities of outcomes. Planning staffs can also be extremely useful in helping to achieve interdivisional and interdepartmental coordination and in helping the organization adapt and innovate to achieve desired change.[20]

The planning process can improve managerial effectiveness by changing the ways in which managers view their jobs. Table 8.3 lists several of these ways. In general, participation in planning broadens managers' outlooks and extends their time frames of reference.

However, managers can lose sight of the purposes of planning and the process can fail them. General Electric began to introduce a number of changes in its planning system in 1983. These changes emphasized the use of planning as a means of adapting to and creating change, as well as improving mana-

TABLE 8.3 ■ HOW PLANNING CAN IMPROVE MANAGERIAL EFFECTIVENESS

- Increases a manager's ability to be proactive in seeking out and creating new opportunities.
- Forces a manager to think analytically and evaluate alternatives, thus improving decisions.
- Establishes a framework for a manager's decision making that is consistent with top management's objectives.
- Modifies a manager's approach by broadening day-to-day decision making to include future-focused thinking and decisions.
- Helps a manager to react on a timely basis to uncontrollable events through the development of contingency plans.
- Provides a basis for a manager to measure organizational and individual performance, thus determining progress toward objectives.
- Increases a manager's sense of involvement and motivation.
- Improves communication between a manager and others in the organization.

Source: Adapted from D. B. German, "Techniques of Planning in Employee Relations," *Personnel Journal,* 1979, 58:761–770. Reprinted with permission of *Personnel Journal,* Costa Mesa, California. Copyright © November 1979; all rights reserved.

gerial effectiveness, and deemphasized the use of planning as a means of maintaining stability. The GE experience also suggests that tensions and conflicts often develop between the planning objectives concerned with adaptation and innovation versus the maintenance of stability.

IN PRACTICE
Changes in Planning at General Electric Company

Management planning at GE used to be dominated by a system of annual, highly formalized presentations based on what executives call *THE BOOKS.* (You can hear the capital letters as they say it.) Jack Welch, GE's chairman and chief executive officer, comments: "By the time [the problem] got to the top, it had become a solution, not a problem." This emphasis on planning, Welch feels, too often kept managers from doing their main job: running the business.

So Welch has scrapped the fixed sessions and instituted a system of operating (tactical) plans that may be changed without formal meetings if circumstances change. However, the company's well-established monthly financial reporting system remains unchanged, preventing any nasty fiscal surprises.

Another significant change flowed from this more flexible planning system. Welch well knows that, in big organizations, too many people are afraid to take chances and are afraid to speak up if they disagree with policy. "It's really the heart of the issue," says Welch. "Can we take the punitive aspects out of having our people tell us the truth? We have to get people to trust that they can take a swing and [for the right reasons] not succeed. In big corporations, the tendency is not to reward the good try."

Things move faster at GE today. At the major appliance group in Louisville, Roger Schipke, the vice-president in charge, wanted to turn the existing management system on its head. Ten vice-presidents quickly became four; 10,000 salaried people switched bosses.

"Under the old GE system," Schipke says, "we'd have done one-eighth [of the change] this year, another eighth next year and, if we had begun to build our confidence, maybe a quarter more the following year."[21]

When Planning Is Likely To Be Effective

Consistent with the contingency theme of this book, planning needs to fit the purposes and situations it is intended to serve.[22] Planning and plans are *means*, not *ends*.

Mitchell's planning law

A planning executive at Dow Chemical Company, J. Ernest Mitchell Jr., developed *Mitchell's planning law,* which states: "He who allows detailed trivia to smother clarity of purpose shall suffer the flames of hell."[23] The graphic form of this law is shown in Fig. 8.4. The numbers used on the vertical and horizontal scales are for illustrative purposes only. The arrow on this graph suggests that organizational effectiveness should increase quite rapidly as more effort is expended on planning, but only up to a critical point. Beyond that point, additional planning is likely to cause organizational effectiveness to drop rapidly and can even become counterproductive. When this critical point is reached, formal planning should stop.

Mitchell's planning law recognizes that some managers approach planning from one of two extremes. At one extreme is "extinction by instinct." This occurs when managers are so concerned with immediate problems and making quick decisions that they do not plan adequately for the future. Firms operating in a simple and stable environment may use this approach for years without loss in profitability, but firms operating in a complex and changing environment are likely to fail or stagnate with little or no strategic planning.[24]

The other extreme is "paralysis by analysis."[25] This occurs when managers try to plan for every detail and possibility. The planning process gets so bogged down that important decisions are not made when they are needed. Dow's philosophy is that planning systems must be designed for people, not for machines. Accordingly, Dow developed six essentials for good planning, which are summarized in Table 8.4. These six essentials are useful guidelines for any organization or manager. However, they cannot guarantee that the decisions made in the planning process will be effective.

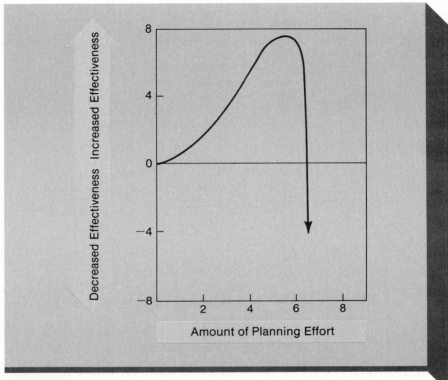

FIGURE 8.4
Mitchell's Planning Law

Source: "Planning: The Dow Chemical Company." Unpublished paper presented by J. E. Mitchell Jr., Director of Corporate Planning, Dow Chemical Company, at the *Business Week* Strategic Planning Conference, Los Angeles, California, March 6–7, 1979, p. 26. Used with permission.

Risk reduction and understanding

Planning is likely to be effective when it reduces risks and uncertainties *or* improves managerial understanding of the risks and uncertainties associated with their decisions. Planning cannot eliminate risks and uncertainties, or, as one planning manager noted: "No amount of sophistication is going to dismiss the fact that all our knowledge is about the past and all of our decisions are about the future."[26]

The capability for responding to risks and uncertainties can be improved through contingency planning. ***Contingency planning*** involves identifying alternative future possibilities and developing a plan of action for each of them. For example, a number of large companies have developed contingency plans for action in the event that the flow of foreign oil is sharply reduced.

Ability and outlook of key managers

Planning can help competent and knowledgeable managers to make better decisions. It cannot compensate for key managers who lack ability and skill. H. Edward Wrapp, who serves on a number of boards of directors, comments:

> My argument is that a good general manager has to know a lot about the industry in which he is operating, and particularly the markets and product capabilities. He has to develop sensitivities to the marketplace to help him make those very difficult, razor-edge decisions on product development, market strategy, and such. You don't just pick that up overnight. I think some of the disasters in marketing and product decisions have been made by people who just did not understand the subtle things that were important in their particular industry.[27]

Assumptions made by key managers about the future can also influence the effectiveness of a company's strategic planning.[28] Sometimes, the key managers of all the firms in a particular industry are so busy focusing on what each other is doing that they fail to consider and look for potentially important technological changes from outside their industry. Firms in the film and camera industry did not develop the instant, finished-print film. The Polaroid Corporation, which had not been involved with either film or cameras, invented and marketed such a system. Similarly, IBM, a firm which started out selling punchcard sorters, was the first to develop the electric typewriter. At that time Royal and Remington, two major old-line typewriter companies, were merely working on ways to improve the manual typewriter.[29] Ironically, IBM, the established leader in the computer industry, was very late in entering the personal computer market. Of course, since its entry in 1981, IBM has been a fierce and effective competitor. In fact, in 1984, some declared IBM the winner in the personal computer industry.[30]

TABLE 8.4 ■ DOW'S ESSENTIALS FOR GOOD PLANNING

- ■ Planning must have the unqualified and open support of top management.
- ■ Line management must be heavily involved and do a major part of the planning.
- ■ The professional planning staff must supply the consistent framework. In Dow, planning people must have extensive line experience before they are candidates for planning.
- ■ The planning process should be as nearly continuous as feasible . . . part of the corporate way of life.
- ■ Strategic planning, which introduces flexibility, must be used to balance the inflexibilities introduced by budgeting and operational planning.
- ■ If planning does not result in DECISIONS and ACTION, don't do it!

From J. Mitchell Jr., "Corporate Planning: The Dow Chemical Company." Unpublished paper presented at the *Business Week* Strategic Planning Conference, Los Angeles, California, March 6–7, 1979, pp. 23–24.

In sum, planning is more likely to be effective when:

- The costs versus the benefits of planning efforts are explicitly considered.
- The essentials of good planning, such as those in Table 8.4, are followed.
- Top management accepts the fact that planning can reduce risks and uncertainties or improve the understanding of risks and uncertainties, but cannot eliminate them.
- Key managers have the ability to plan, as well as to manage.

PROCESS FOR STRATEGIC PLANNING

Strategic planning is a process that includes a sequence of steps for developing strategic plans.[31] The basic steps and issues of strategic planning are highlighted in Fig. 8.5. The solid arrows indicate the *primary* sequence of planning steps; however, the sequence is *not* just one-way in practice. Obviously much interaction and revision occurs. For example, a proposed strategy might have to be abandoned if it cannot be implemented for some reason that was not apparent when the strategy was chosen.

Organization Definition ☐ *

Organization definition is determined by the answers to the following types of questions: (1) Who are we? (2) What do we want to become? (3) What are our organizational objectives? Political forces and stakeholders in ☐ play a key role in the current organization definition and possible changes in it. Their influence must not be underestimated.

External political forces

Stakeholders—both within an organization and outside it—have an interest in organization definition.[32] The organization definition of firms like AT&T and Bank of America is influenced by state and federal regulatory agencies. On the other hand, key managers do influence and negotiate with powerful stakeholders in the environment; the dashed arrow in Fig. 8.5 between ☐ and ☐ suggests this interplay between organization definition and environmental threats and opportunities. The American Telephone and Telegraph Company initially followed a strategy of lobbying in Washington, D.C., to have legislation passed prohibiting certain types of market competition. As you might recall from the Preview Case to Chapter 3, when this attempt failed AT&T

---

* Note that this boxed number corresponds to that of a step in the sequence for strategic planning in Fig. 8.5. These boxed numbers appear in the text, as appropriate, for reference purposes throughout the rest of this chapter.

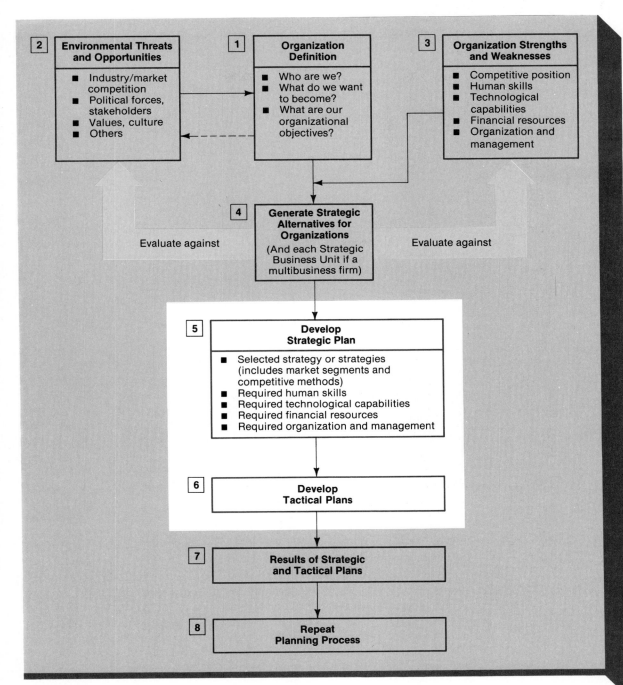

FIGURE 8.5
A Simplified Process for Strategic Planning

management went through the difficult experience of redefining what AT&T was to become and what some of its basic objectives would be. AT&T management then made significant organizational changes in marketing, products, and services as a result of this organization redefinition.

Internal political forces

The power of stakeholders also influences the answers to questions of organization definition. The W. T. Grant Company provides an example of internal power struggles interacting with market forces that eventually led to its bankruptcy.

IN PRACTICE
W. T. Grant
Company's
Bankruptcy

The W. T. Grant Company is a good example of a firm that was unclear about both its strategic and tactical plans. Its failure was due to high-level management power struggles and middle to lower-level management which could not develop or implement tactical plans. Grant's management could not make up its mind about what kind of firm it wanted. "There was a lot of dissension within the company whether we should go the Kmart route or go after the Ward and Penney position," says a former executive. "Ed Staley and Lou Lustenberger were at loggerheads over the issue, with the upshot being we took a position between the two that consequently stood for nothing."

From 1963 to 1973 Grant opened 612 stores and expanded 91 others, with the bulk of the increase starting in 1968 under the guidance of president Richard W. Mayer and chairman Edward Staley. "The expansion program placed a great strain on the physical and human capability of the company to cope with the program," says current chairman James G. Kendrick. "These were all large stores—6 million to 7 million square feet per year—and the expansion of our management and organization just did not match the expansion of our stores." Adds a former operations executive: "Our training program couldn't keep up with the explosion of stores, and it didn't take long for the mediocrity to begin to show."[33]

Organizational objectives

After the organization has been defined, *organizational objectives* can be developed.[34] These objectives normally specify the general directions and areas in which accomplishments are desired. Sometimes these broad statements of objectives present the general future conditions desired without reference to a definite time period. This is illustrated by the statement of corporate-wide objectives of Hewlett-Packard in Table 8.5. The profit objective of Hewlett-Packard states: "To achieve sufficient profit to finance our company growth

TABLE 8.5 ■ STATEMENTS OF ORGANIZATIONAL OBJECTIVES FOR TWO FIRMS

HEWLETT-PACKARD CORPORATION OBJECTIVES

- *Profit.* To achieve sufficient profit to finance our company growth and to provide the resources we need to achieve our other corporate objectives.

- *Customers.* To provide products and services of the greatest possible value to our customers, thereby gaining and holding their respect and loyalty.

- *Field of interest.* To enter new fields only when the ideas we have, together with our technical, manufacturing and marketing skills, assure that we can make a needed and profitable contribution to the field.

- *Growth.* To let our growth be limited only by our profits and our ability to develop and produce technical products that satisfy real customer needs.

- *People.* To help our own people share in the company's success, which they make possible: to provide job security based on their performance, to recognize their individual achievements, and to help them gain a sense of satisfaction and accomplishment from their work.

- *Management.* To foster initiative and creativity by allowing the individual great freedom of action in attaining well-defined objectives.

- *Citizenship.* To honor our obligations to society by being an economic, intellectual and social asset to each nation and each community in which we operate.

ROBERTSHAW CONTROLS COMPANY OBJECTIVES 198—

- Minimize historical trends in sales and profits.
  (Objective: 10 percent profit before tax is necessary to assure adequate stockholder return and reinvestment in corporate growth.)

- Increase Robertshaw's sales and profits in the international market.
  (Objective: 10 percent minimum annual profit growth assures compounding profitability and established positive trend line.)

- Increase utilization of stockholders' equity through return on assets and return on investment justification.
  (Objective: 10-15 percent annual sales growth is required to double the sales of the corporation every five to eight years.)

- Review all product lines and products that cannot justify continuance based on ROA.
  (Objective: Within the broad parameters of sensors and associated controls, Robertshaw can develop adequate diversification and maximize in-house abilities and expertise.)

- Establish corporate and divisional financial standards.
  (Objective: To evaluate and justify investments in new or old areas of opportunity to verify the potential for the corporation to achieve an industry position of no less than third.)

- Develop improved consumer awareness and recognition of Robertshaw.
  (Objective: The criteria for growth must include favorable corporate identity at the consumer and investor levels.)

Source: Adapted from Y. Shetty, "New Look at Corporate Goals." © 1979 by the Regents of the University of California. Reprinted from *California Management Review* 22(2):72 by permission of the Regents.

and to provide the resources we need to achieve our other corporate objectives." At other times, specific objectives and time periods are tied to key objectives. This is illustrated by the statement of objectives for the Robertshaw Controls Company, also shown in Table 8.5. Several specific profit-related objectives are stated, including the objective that "10 percent profit before tax is necessary to assure adequate stockholder return and reinvestment in corporate growth."

Environmental Threats and Opportunities ☑

In Chapters 3 and 4, we discussed a variety of environmental forces—threats and opportunities, both domestic and international—that are important to strategic and tactical planning. Let us now consider one segment of these forces—industry/market competition forces—and their importance in strategic planning. We use the microcomputer industry to illustrate the diagnosis of such forces and strategies for coping with them effectively.

Industry/market competition

Consistent with our presentation in Chapters 3 and 4, Michael Porter has suggested a framework for diagnosing the forces that drive the industry/market competition confronting a firm at any given time. This framework is shown in Fig. 8.6.[35] The five forces identified in this figure (and discussed initially in Chapter 3) impact on the overall profit potential, growth prospects, and even the likelihood of survival for a firm. The strategic planning process *must* include a careful diagnosis of each force. Each force includes a number of specific variables that can be diagnosed but consideration of all of them is beyond the scope of our discussion. Thus we simply define each force and highlight a couple of its variables. You might find it helpful to refer back to Chapter 3 for a more complete description of each force.

Rivalry among existing competitors. The intensity of rivalry among existing competitors varies with their perception of threats or opportunities, actions taken, and reactions to those actions. These actions and reactions often result from price increases or decreases, advertising battles, introduction of new products, and changes in customer service.[36] Two variables of this force are *number of competitors* and *rate of industry growth*.

Growth in the microcomputer industry has been explosive. The number of competitors grew from one firm in 1975 to 29 firms in 1977 and then to more than 200 firms in 1984. The competitive rivalry among these firms—in terms of price cutting and product changes—became especially intense starting in 1981, the year IBM entered the industry. Production capacity and sales in 1975 were only about 200 units per month. In 1984, the industry produced more than 500,000 microcomputers per month.[37]

This growth has been a two-edged sword for firms. Because of the low barriers to entry, technological breakthroughs, and the explosive growth of the market, many new competitors entered the industry. As a result, prices fell and competition intensified during this period; industry experts forecast a major reduction in the number of competitors.

Threat of new competitors. The entry of new competitors is often a response to the high profits earned by established firms and/or a high rate of industry growth. The threat of new competitors depends substantially on the barriers to entry and the reactions that new competitors expect from established competitors. *Barriers to entry* are those factors that make it relatively

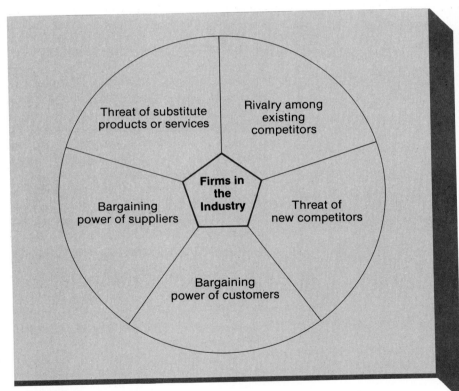

FIGURE 8.6
Primary Forces Driving Industry–Market Competition

Source: Adapted from Michael E. Porter, *Competitive Strategy: Techniques for Analyzing Industries and Competitors.* New York: Free Press, 1980, p. 4.

easy or difficult to enter the industry. Two important barriers include: *economies of scale* and *capital requirements.*

Economies of scale are the decreases in the per unit costs of a product (or service) as the volume increases.[38] Economies of scale were not much of a barrier to entry in the microcomputer industry in its early years. Apple Computer started as a garage operation in 1976; it shipped 150 microcomputers in its first year. IBM entered the industry with a production capacity of 20,000 units per month in 1981 and increased its capacity to some 100,000 units per month by 1984. IBM has followed a strategy of building highly automated and efficient plants to reduce the per-unit production costs of its personal computers. This raises barriers to entry for new competitors and is also making it more difficult for the smaller microcomputer manufacturers to make a profit or even survive.

Capital requirements refer to the amount of money needed by a firm in order to become a serious competitor. Capital requirements in the microcomputer industry started at almost nothing in 1975 and amount to tens of millions of dollars today. This large amount of capital is needed to achieve a competitive economy of scale in production and to launch a successful marketing program.[39]

Bargaining power of customers. The bargaining power of customers depends on their relative ability to play one firm off against another to force down prices, demand higher quality, or get more products (or services) for the same price. As indicated in Chapter 3, the bargaining power of customers is likely to be greater in the following situations.

- The customers are few in number and purchase large volumes relative to the total sales of the seller.
- The customers purchase products or services from the industry that are standard and undifferentiated.
- It is easy for customers to switch from one seller to another.[40]

The relative bargaining power of customers in the microcomputer industry was very low in 1975 but has increased substantially since that time. Microcomputer manufacturers are increasingly dealing with large-scale purchasers such as Computerland, government agencies, GM, Bank of America, and State Farm Insurance Company. In 1983, the president of Computerland stated: "Three years ago, we had to go to the manufacturers—now they come to us."[41] Standardization in products or services tends to increase customer power. The greatest push toward standardization occurred after the introduction of the IBM Personal Computer in November 1981. The term *IBM compatible,* used by both software and hardware manufacturers, testifies to this standardization trend. Standardization increases the ability of customers to switch from one manufacturer to another (for example, from Apple to IBM).

I believe that ideas derived from outside "hints" can be creative. One historian has suggested that the creativity of the Japanese lies in their ability to make the most of outside stimuli. I agree, and I believe this helps explain why the mature phase of electronics, which lends itself more to elaboration and refinement rather than brand-new concepts, has helped give Japan a competitive edge in technological development.

The following scenario has occurred more and more often of late. An American researcher presents some abstract concept for a new mechanism or process at a scientific symposium. Within six months or a year he finds a Japanese paper has been published analyzing each facet of his idea in detail using a working model, when neither the American nor his colleagues had made any progress with it.

Rather than saying the Japanese are good imitators, it might be more accurate to say that they excel at putting two and two together. Surely this is a form of creativity also. But perhaps it is collective, rather than individual creativity.

Although the Japanese lack a central, guiding philosophy, something at work in the society at large keeps moving us in the right direction. In the West, a handful of highly talented individuals shoulder the burden of progress. They find it hard to believe that Japan has advanced as a result of all its people pulling together. Instead they like to believe the MITI (Ministry of International Trade and Industry) bureaucrats have directed every move.

A journalist from a British financial magazine recently asked me, "Frankly now, how many times a year is the president of Sony called to MITI and told to conduct research on a certain subject with government funds?" I answered quite honestly that I had never heard of such a thing in my life. But my interviewer seemed unconvinced.

Of course, the Japanese are attracted to Western-style creativity. But creativity in science and technology is tied to much broader cultural values. In order to adopt Western-style creativity wholesale, we would first have to adopt Western-style individualism. And to do that, we might have to give up the very qualities that enabled us to overtake the United States in 64 kilobit RAM VLSIs, for example. As a side effect, our subways might become sinister places, unsafe at night. We might turn into a litigious society, resorting to legal confrontation to settle every minor dispute.

The Japanese should give serious thought to their goals, social as well as economic, and consider whether it is in their interests to abandon what has served them so well thus far. It may be that the world today could do with more, not less, of the kind of creativity that has made Japan the technological giant it is today.

Bargaining power of suppliers. The bargaining power of suppliers is said to increase when they can increase prices or reduce the quality of their products and services with minimal fear of customer reactions. The situations that tend to make suppliers more powerful are similar to those that make customers more powerful. Again, as indicated in Chapter 3, the bargaining power of suppliers is likely to be greater in the following situations.

- The suppliers are few in number and are more concentrated than the buyers in each industry they sell to.
- The suppliers do not have to worry about readily substitutable products or services for sale to their customers.
- The suppliers' products or services are differentiated.[42]

The relative bargaining power of suppliers to microcomputer manufacturers has increased, but not dramatically, between 1975 and 1985. A number of components make up a microcomputer, but the most important is the *microprocessor.* The microprocessor—sometimes known as the computer-on-a-chip—is the central processing unit (CPU), or the unit that processes and manipulates the data inputed into the microcomputer. It is a thin wafer of silicon on which thousands of integrated circuits have been inscribed. There are about two-dozen significant firms that supply critical microcomputer components. The major suppliers of microprocessors are Intel, Motorola, and Texas Instruments. The potential power of these suppliers seems to have been neutralized by the perceived and actual threat of Japanese suppliers.

Suppliers that have developed popular microprocessors, such as the Intel 8080 and the Intel 8086 (introduced in 1984), have been able to exert some power over buyers through price increases.[43] However, the high rate of technological change in microprocessors and the ability of others to match the competition has tended to limit the power of suppliers. Nonetheless, one of the reasons given for the purchase of some Intel stock by IBM was IBM's desire to limit the potential supplier power of Intel. (Intel is a major supplier to IBM and other microcomputer manufacturers.)

Threat of substitute products or services. The threat of substitute products or services reflects the ability and willingness of customers to change their purchasing patterns. Substitutes limit the amount that firms in a particular industry can charge for their products or services without risking a loss in sales. Natural gas, oil, and coal tend to be substitutes for each other among public utilities. Price increases in oil may be offset somewhat by shifts to natural gas or coal (assuming that the prices of natural gas and coal do not also increase).

There are currently no ready substitutes for microcomputers. However, microcomputers have quickly become substitutes for many products: calculators, electric typewriters, traditional word processors, and mid-size computers, among others.

The threats and opportunities identified through the diagnosis of these five industry/market forces (as well as the other types of forces discussed in Chapters 3 and 4) represent the external environment, which must be analyzed for an organization. The results of this external analysis must be assessed in relation to those of an internal analysis, which focuses on an organization's strengths and weaknesses.

ORGANIZATION STRENGTHS AND WEAKNESSES ③

The diagnosis of internal strengths and weaknesses seeks to identify an organization's capabilities and distinctive competencies relative to competitors or potential competitors.[44] This diagnosis focuses on the organization's relative competitive position, human skills, technological capabilities, financial resources, organization and management depth, and the values and background of key executives. The potential impact of the values and inclinations of key executives on strategic decisions shouldn't be underestimated. Consider this characterization of RCA during the 1972–1982 period:

> Few companies have been battered as badly by their own managements as RCA Corp. Under its last four chief executives, each of whom pursued a different strategy, the company has been diversified, divested, directed toward long-term goals, redirected toward short-term goals, nearly done in by a massive acquisition, diddled out of dollars by huge employment and disemployment contracts, and finally drawn back to its roots—all in the space of 10 years.[45]

The top management situation at RCA has turned around in recent years. At present, RCA appears to be focusing with reasonable success on three core businesses: entertainment, electronics, and communications.

Most managers find it easier to diagnose threats, opportunities, and strengths than weaknesses. Weaknesses are often interpreted as the fault of managers. Thus managers sometimes see statements of organizational weaknesses as personal threats to their position, influence, and self-esteem. However, the weaknesses are not self-correcting and are likely to become worse if they are not factored into the strategic planning process.

Table 8.6 shows a simplified framework for diagnosis that managers can use in assessing an organization's strengths and weaknesses. This framework is illustrative, not exhaustive, of the variables that would be evaluated in such an assessment. But, this framework applies to the entire organization (or strategic business unit). Many organizations require all managers to develop statements of opportunities, threats, strengths, and weaknesses for their divisions or departments. The specific issues raised and variables used by a plant manager will be different from those of the chief executive officer. The plant manager will probably focus on tactical types of opportunities, threats, strengths, and weaknesses. In contrast, the chief executive must assess the organization as a whole in strategic terms. After diagnosing a firm's opportunities, threats, strengths, and weaknesses, managers can turn to the generation of strategic alternatives for the organization and evaluate them against their diagnosis.

TABLE 8.6 ■ SIMPLIFIED FRAMEWORK FOR DIAGNOSIS OF ORGANIZATION STRENGTHS AND WEAKNESSES

Instructions: Evaluate each category item on the basis of the following scale.

A = Superior to or better than anyone else. Beyond present need (top 10%).
B = Better than average. Good performance. No problems.
C = Average. Acceptable. Equal to competition. Not good, not bad.
D = Problems here. Not as good as it should be. Deteriorating. Must be improved.
F = Real cause for concern. Situation bad. Crisis. Must take action to improve.

		SCALE				
CATEGORY	**ITEM**	*A*	*B*	*C*	*D*	*F*
Finance	Availability of loans	——	——	——	——	——
	Debt–equity ratio	——	——	——	——	——
	Inventory turnover	——	——	——	——	——
	Profit margin	——	——	——	——	——
	Etc.	——	——	——	——	——
Production	Labor productivity	——	——	——	——	——
	Plant/store location	——	——	——	——	——
	Degree of obsolescence	——	——	——	——	——
	Quality control	——	——	——	——	——
	Etc.	——	——	——	——	——
Organization and administration	Ratio staff to line managers	——	——	——	——	——
	Quality of staff	——	——	——	——	——
	Quality of middle managers	——	——	——	——	——
	Communications	——	——	——	——	——
	Etc.	——	——	——	——	——
Marketing	Share of market	——	——	——	——	——
	Product/service reputation	——	——	——	——	——
	Advertising efficiency/effectiveness	——	——	——	——	——
	Consumer complaints	——	——	——	——	——
	Etc.	——	——	——	——	——
Technology	Product/service	——	——	——	——	——
	Research and development capabilities	——	——	——	——	——
	Etc.	——	——	——	——	——

Source: Adapted from M. L. Kastens, *Long-Range Planning for Your Business,* pp. 52–53. Copyright © 1976 by AMACOM, a division of American Management Associations, New York. Adapted by permission of the publisher. All rights reserved.

Generate Strategic Alternatives   4

The generation and evaluation of strategic alternatives is considered here only from the point of view of a strategic business unit. A single-business firm like McDonald's would be considered as a strategic business unit. A company such as GE is made up of a number of related businesses and has many strategic business units.

Two general variables often recommended for diagnosis in assessing alternative strategies are the *product/service life cycle* and the relative *competitive position* of the strategic business unit. These two variables are often evaluated in combination to suggest what type of investment strategy is likely to be appropriate for each of the firm's line of products or services.

Product/service life cycle

The product/service life cycle refers to the market phases for many products and services. One version of this life cycle is shown in Fig. 8.7. The vertical axis indicates the degree to which the industrial or consumer market demand for the product or service is increasing, on a plateau, or decreasing. The horizontal axis indicates the span of time. For fads like the Michael Jackson Victory Tour in 1984 and space-war toys, the time period required to go through the five phases might be a year or less. For other products or services, the time period might be quite lengthy. Gasoline products for automobiles have been on the market for more than 70 years and just now appear to be in the advanced maturity phase.

Figure 8.7 indicates the life-cycle phases for a number of other products and services. Strategic planning for each product or service is influenced by the life-cycle phase: introduction, growth, maturity, decline, or termination. All products and services need not move through these stages, as if a biological time clock were in control. Management can influence the cycle by finding new uses and new customers for a product or service. Such interventions could shift a product or service that had been in decline into a new growth stage. Some years ago, Japanese manufacturers, unlike U.S. manufacturers, did not assume that motorcycles and radios were in the advanced maturity stage.[46]

The strategies and functional areas (marketing, production, R&D) emphasized are likely to change for different stages of the product/service life cycle. During the introduction and growth phases, the dominant concerns might be with product development (R&D) or finding new customers (marketing). During the maturity and decline stages, the dominant concerns might shift to reducing per-unit costs (production) through efficiency measures such as shutting down plants, cutting white-collar overhead costs, acquiring or selling out to competitors, and the like.

Relative competitive position

Competitive position refers to a comparative assessment of a strategic business unit with its competitors. This assessment may result in an overall rating such as strong, average, weak, or drop out. A *strong* rating would be viewed as an organization strength and a *weak* or *drop-out* rating would be viewed as an organization weakness in ③ (Fig. 8.5). These summary ratings are based on a diagnosis of factors such as the following.

- Share of market by strategic business unit.
- Technological position and capabilities.
- Managerial capabilities.
- Relative financial strength.
- Image and customer loyalty.[47]

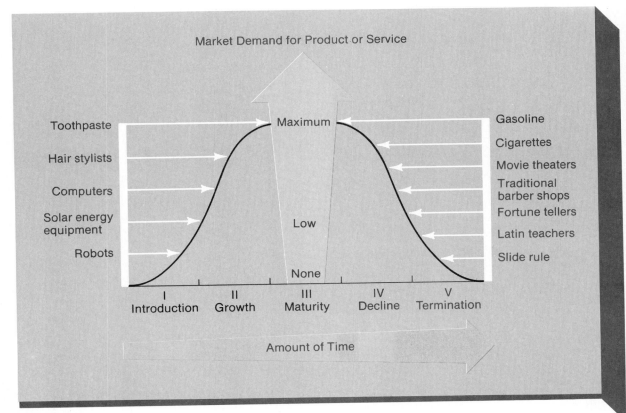

FIGURE 8.7
Product/Service Life Cycle

Source: Adapted from S. Michael, "Guidelines for Contingency Approach to Planning," *Long Range Planning*, 1979, **12**(6):63. Reprinted with permission from *Long Range Planning*. Copyright © 1979, Pergamon Press, Ltd.

INVESTMENT STRATEGIES

The product/service life cycle and relative competitive position of a strategic business unit jointly influence selection of an appropriate investment strategy. Figure 8.8 shows six basic investment strategies and the conditions under which each strategy should normally be followed for superior, overall, long-term performance of a strategic business unit.

The nature and level of investment serve to differentiate these six strategies as follows:

- **Share-increasing strategies** attempt to significantly and permanently increase the market share for an SBU. The level of investment is likely to be substantially greater than is typical for the industry. When IBM entered

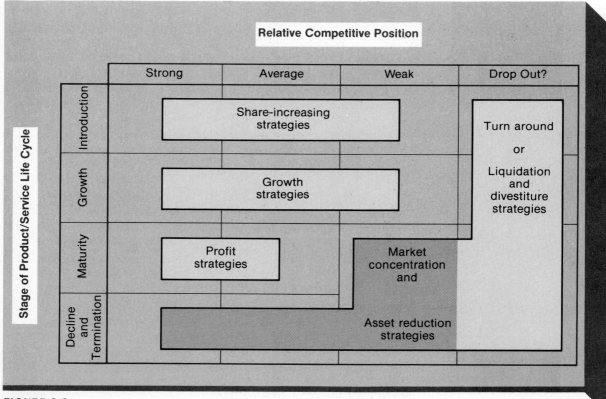

FIGURE 8.8

Basic Investment Strategies under Different Conditions

Source: Adapted from C. W. Hofer, "Conceptual Constructs for Formulating Corporate and Business Strategies." Dover, Mass.: Case Publishing, No. BP-0041, p. 32. Copyright 1977 by Charles W. Hofer. Used with permission.

the personal computer industry, it invested tens of millions of dollars more in production plants and marketing than had been typical of other entrants.

■ *Growth strategies* are designed to maintain the relative market share for an SBU in rapidly expanding markets. Investments above the industry average may not be needed. However, because of rapid market expansion, high investments in absolute terms may be needed. In 1984, Apple Computer opened a $20 million, highly automated and efficient plant to hold and increase its market share by being price competitive.

■ *Profit strategies* focus on the efficient utilization of an SBU's existing resources and skills. Investment is often intended to increase efficiency—rather than expand capacity—and to maintain existing resources. The SBU normally generates *excess* cash that can be allocated to other purposes, such as higher dividends, quicker payoff of debt, or new investments. U.S. Steel has shut down plants and constructed new, more efficient plants to increase its efficiency, maintain profits, and reduce the progressive loss in market share to foreign steel firms.

■ *Market-concentration and asset-reduction strategies* involve efforts to reduce or refocus the market segments served by an SBU and to reduce the amount of human, physical, and financial resources devoted to the SBU. These strategies may involve selling or shutting down some operations, laying off employees, pulling out of some geographic areas, and the like. The various acquisitions and disposal of parts of the acquisitions that have taken place between oil companies (such as Standard Oil of California's acquisition of Gulf in 1984) are examples of this strategy.

■ *Turnaround strategies* represent dramatic actions taken to reverse the declining state of a business. The key actions outlined in the Chrysler Corporation Preview Case represent a turnaround strategy. Turnaround strategies seem to be more common when new top management is brought into an organization and/or the ownership of the firm changes.

■ *Liquidation and divestiture strategies* are planned efforts to withdraw from the business by selling the SBU or shutting it down with the objective of generating as much cash as possible. ITT's sale of Continental Baking Company in 1984 is an example of this strategy.[48]

Strategic investment decisions such as these are made by top managers and boards of directors. Strategic alternatives also need to be generated and evaluated in major functional areas for each SBU. For example, during the introductory stage for soap and skin products, a common marketing strategy is to distribute free samples or offer generous coupon redemptions. Other functional areas requiring strategic investment planning include personnel, finance, production, physical distribution, and research and development.[49]

Develop Strategic Plan ⑤

After the investment strategies have been selected, it is necessary to develop a strategic plan for an SBU. This plan should specify the actions needed in order to achieve the SBU's objectives. Technological capabilities, financial and human resources, and organization and management capabilities are addressed in the development of a strategic plan.

The major functional areas of an organization almost always require some attention in both strategic and tactical plans. The five basic missions of Whirlpool's corporate research, with corresponding general objectives and type of planning involved, are:

- Current product R&D—extend and complement division engineering (tactical planning).
- Manufacturing systems R&D—apply new and improved technologies to manufacturing systems (tactical planning).
- New opportunities—identify and develop avenues for new growth opportunities (strategic planning).
- Technological research—seek, identify, and develop technologies to improve Whirlpool's competitive position (strategic planning).
- Continuing support—meet needs of the corporation for support and service (tactical and strategic planning).[50]

Develop Tactical Plans ⑥

The development of tactical plans should be guided by the strategic plans, as shown in Fig. 8.5. The intended purpose of tactical plans is to help implement strategic plans. Tactical plans are normally developed by first-line to upper middle managers.

American Orthodontics is a Sheboygan, Wisconsin, company in which strategic and tactical planning by managers at all levels helps to achieve organizational objectives. This firm produces consumable orthodontic products, had 185 employees in 1984, and sells its products worldwide.

**IN PRACTICE
American
Orthodontics**

Daniel Merkel, president of American Orthodontics, describes the planning function for his company in the following terms.

Both long-term (strategic) and short-term (tactical) planning play extremely significant roles in the success of our company. To take the same plan that worked yesterday and use it with any degree of success in today's market is impossible. Every two months, I meet with our entire management team specifically to address short-term planning. Some of the issues we discuss include the alignment of sales territories, production needs, pricing and other marketing strategies, and personnel requirements.

In our long-range planning, we address wider issues, such as present and future competition and tapping opportunities available to our company through penetration of new markets. These long-range plans are developed annually. We project detailed plans that cover the next three years. At the same time, we formulate less detailed plans that project six years into the future.

My role in the planning process is to focus on strategic issues. I address broad issues and then encourage individual managers to develop detailed action plans. In a typical planning session, ideas are discussed and progressively refined until they become more realistic. After the meeting, a formal plan is put in writing and distributed to all managers for future reference. The plan acts as a reference tool for all managers to ensure that their daily activities are compatible with the general plan. Our plans have compared very favorably with actual results because we are conservative in our forecasts. My philosophy is to set targets that are challenging but attainable.[51]

Results of Strategic and Tactical Plans ⑦

As with any management process or activity, the implementation of strategic and tactical plans must be monitored and assessed. If the results hinder or don't contribute to the achievement of objectives, either the objectives or the strategies should be changed. Earlier in the chapter, we noted that top executives at GE came to the conclusion that highly formalized planning was emphasized too much. Planning was approaching "paralysis by analysis." Accordingly, GE made some changes in its planning process.

Repeat Planning Process ⑧

The external environment and other forces affecting organizations change constantly. Sometimes these changes are gradual, predictable, and tactical in impact. At other times changes are abrupt, unpredictable, and strategic in impact.[52] Regardless of the severity and impact of these changes, planning should be viewed and undertaken as an ongoing management process.

CHAPTER SUMMARY

The planning purposes, issues, objectives, and processes that were presented in this chapter should assist in the development of your abilities to perform successfully the managerial roles of *entrepreneur* and *resource allocator*. It may be some time before you are in a position to actively participate in strategic planning, but you are likely to be involved soon with tactical planning. However, an appreciation of strategic planning should aid you in developing tactical plans.

The issues and activities of strategic planning change with the times and with key decisionmakers. Strategic planning requires that key managers make many important judgment decisions. Both of these factors should be evident from the examples of actual industry and company experiences cited. Planning is a form of decision making. The basic decision-making concepts and techniques used in planning were developed in Chapters 6 and 7. In this chapter we expanded the definition of planning that was given in Chapter 1 and described the planning process in terms of the focuses and purposes of strategic and tactical planning and their linkage. This included a statement of the primary objectives of planning: (1) identify opportunities; (2) anticipate and avoid problems; and (3) develop courses of action.

Organizational diversity and managers both have impacts on the planning process. The stage of diversity (single business, dominant business, related businesses, and unrelated businesses) determines the complexity of the planning process for a firm in terms of factors to be considered and the number of people in the organization that have to be involved. Managers, particularly top managers, can easily influence the attitudes of others in the organization concerning the value of planning. We also learned that planning can be effective under certain conditions, ineffective under others, and even counterproductive under others.

In the second part of the chapter we presented and reviewed the sequence of steps and the procedures of the process for strategic planning: (1) define the organization; (2) assess environmental threats and opportunities; (3) assess the organization's strengths and weaknesses; (4) generate strategic alternatives; (5) develop a strategic plan; (6) develop tactical plans; (7) analyze results; and (8) repeat the planning process. However, the actual process of strategic planning is not usually as systematic or as rational as this eight-step sequence. Managers may well jump back and forth between steps and even skip steps as they develop strategic plans for their organization. In addition, we need to reemphasize that the political-decision model—described in Chapter 7—may have a powerful influence in some organizations on how the planning process unfolds and which issues are considered.

MANAGER'S VOCABULARY

barriers to entry
capital requirements
competitive position
contingency planning
dominant-business firm
economies of scale
growth strategies
liquidation and divestiture strategies
market-concentration and asset-reduction strategies
microprocessor
Mitchell's planning law
organization definition
organizational objectives
planning
product/service life cycle
profit strategies
related-businesses firm
share-increasing strategies
single-business firm
strategic business unit (SBU)
strategic planning
strategies
tactical planning
turnaround strategies
unrelated-businesses firm

REVIEW QUESTIONS

1. What are planning, strategic planning, and tactical planning?
2. What are strategies?
3. When is planning likely to be effective?
4. What are the major steps in strategic planning?
5. Which types of environmental threats and opportunities should organizations monitor and diagnose?
6. How can top managers go about evaluating alternative investment strategies?

DISCUSSION QUESTIONS

1. Most of us have a strategy even if we are not consciously aware of it. What is your strategy for the next year? Two years? Four years?
2. When can planning serve to increase or reduce risk for an organization?

3. How have the primary forces driving industry/market competition affected companies in the airline industry?

4. Identify one firm with which you are familiar. Where does this firm seem to fall in the product/service life cycle?

5. What do you perceive as the organizational objectives of the high school you attended? What seemed to be its strategy?

MANAGEMENT INCIDENTS AND CASES ___

Apple Computer

The Macintosh, the new computer that Apple started shipping January 24, 1984, comes with a hefty claim from John Sculley, company president. The Mac, he says, is "meant to supplant the PC on the desks of corporate America, just as the PC supplanted our own Apples over the last 18 months." Brave words. The landscape is strewn with the likes of Xerox, RCA, and GE, to name a few, who thought they could muscle a piece of IBM's claimed turf. There's even a chunk of Apple littering the ground, the Lisa workstation, which was introduced with high hopes and great flair last January. So why does Sculley think that this time will be any different?

Two reasons have been offered. The first is that both Sculley and company cofounder Steve Jobs have taken leave of their senses and are engaging in corporate egomania on a grand scale. Don't laugh. Other companies have fallen victim to their own machismo. But that's not the case here.

The second reason, and one that makes more sense, is that Apple has no intention of competing with IBM. It has simply put out a smokescreen to satisfy Wall Street. If the analysts believe that Apple must compete with IBM, why not help that belief and, meanwhile, get on with other business?

For evidence, there is the Macintosh itself. It's a product whose design clearly indicates its true market. No less telling is Apple's approach to marketing the Mac. The ads and marketing approach point away from a direct confrontation with IBM. If Apple were really going to compete with IBM, it would be selling Macintoshes directly into the top 500 corporations market. Why? Because the purchase and use of personal computers at the corporate level has long since shifted from the days when individuals bought personal computers and lugged them to the office. Instead, corporations buy personal computers by the freight-car load. The purchase decision has shifted to corporate data processing and finance committees. Direct selling to national accounts (such as GM, Penney's, GTE) already makes up a quarter of all personal computer sales, according to Future Computing, a Texas consulting firm that tracks the personal computer industry. It's hard to see how Apple, without its own national account sales staff, will win the battle for the middle-management desks of corporate America.

Yet, listen to Sculley on the subject of national account selling: "We will be selling the Macintosh through our established dealer network. Some of them have national-account sales staffs, but we think that the machine will sell well enough out of the computer stores." Sculley knows better. Lisa, in large measure, failed to crack the corporate market. The average Apple customer who buys in a computer store couldn't get a company to let him or her buy a $10,000 machine for work.

Then there is the Macintosh itself. Its best features are for computer novices: MacPaint, a program that creates graphic designs of stunning complexity, and MacWrite, a word-processing program that goes to ingenious lengths to set up the screen to look like a typewriter. Both are controlled by the machine's "mouse," which moves the cursor without the user's touching the keyboard. Such simplicity is not aimed at big corporations. The average middle manager has little need for the graphics capability of MacPaint. Most managers have a hard enough time writing reports, without having to worry about designing them as well.

Then where will all those machines wind up? A hint: There is broad agreement that only one-third of all the desks in America ever likely to be equipped with computers are corporate desks. The rest belong to individual and small business users, the very people who were Apple's original customers and who still buy the overwhelming majority of the 100,000 Apples sold every month.

Could such be Apple's real intent? Yes, if you listen to the words behind the words. Sculley has labeled the Macintosh "Apple's machine for well into the 1990s, maybe into the next century." He has backed those words with a $20 million automated facility to produce a Macintosh every 27 seconds. That factory allows Apple to make a Mac that has less than one percent of its value in labor. Thus its economies of scale should continue to rise as sales increase but only if the Macintosh has an indefinite life. Such a level of commitment is not corporate machismo. It is an agenda for a decade or more to come, and it is an agenda essentially saying that there are two major personal computer markets: the corporate world served by IBM and the rest served by Apple.

So why is Apple making such a show of attacking IBM? Apple has many markets, of whom software writers, dealers and customers are only three. Steve Jobs says: "We have to persuade Wall Street and the media within 100 days of introduction that we have a viable product." Apple's stock has taken quite a beating since the IBM PC was introduced. Because Wall Street's perceptions, not reality, determine which stocks are added to portfolios, Sculley and Jobs have decided to at least appear to play to those perceptions. In other words, a simple exercise in propaganda, 1984 style.

There could well be another reason for Apple's smokescreen. Besides its traditional market, Apple seems to be aiming the Macintosh at engineers and designers who need a reasonable amount of processing power on their desk. Jobs brags that the Macintosh "has the capabilities at least of a PDP-11 or a small VAX," both made by the number-two computer maker, Digital Equipment Corporation. Could DEC be Apple's true target?[53]

Questions

1. Based on Fig. 8.6, how would you characterize the primary industry–market competitive forces facing Apple?

2. What appear to be Apple's organization strengths and weaknesses?

3. Where would you position Apple on Fig. 8.9?

4. Do you think Apple has selected an effective market strategy? Explain.

REFERENCES

1. Adapted and excerpted from L. A. Iacocca, "The Rescue and Resuscitation of Chrysler," *Journal of Business Strategy*, Summer 1983, pp. 67–69, by permission of the publisher. Copyright © 1983 by Warren, Gorham and Lamont, Inc., 210 South Street, Boston, Mass. All rights reserved. *Also see* L. Iacocca with W. Novak, *Iacocca: An Autobiography.* New York, Bantam Books, 1984.

2. W. W. Burke, "Conversation with H. K. Burke," *Organizational Dynamics*, Spring 1984, pp. 23–36. *Also see* B. Stavro, "Is There Life after Iacocca?" *Forbes*, April 8, 1985, pp. 75–78.

3. Burke, p. 26.

4. Burke, p. 25.

5. C. R. Anderson, *Management: Skills, Functions, and Organization Performance.* Dubuque, Iowa: William C. Brown, 1984, pp. 19–20; R. E. Miles and C. C. Snow, "Fit, Failure, and the Hall of Fame," *California Management Review*, Spring 1984, pp. 10–28; G. D. Smith and D. R. Arnold, *Business Strategy and Policy.* Boston: Houghton Mifflin, 1985.

6. J. H. Grant and W. R. King, *The Logic of Strategic Planning.* Boston: Little, Brown, 1982, p. 3. *Also see:* J. W. Fredrickson and T. R. Mitchell, "Strategic Decision Processes: Comprehensiveness and Performance in an Industry with an Unstable Environment," *Academy of Management Journal*, 1984, 27:399–423; W. D. Guth (Ed.), *Handbook of Business Strategy.* Boston: Warren, Gorham and Lamont, 1985.

7. E. R. Nordtvedt, "The New? Chrysler Corporation." Boston: Case distributed by HBS Case Services. Harvard Business School, 1981.

8. "Record $802 Million Earned by Chrysler," *Houston Chronicle*, July 20, 1984, Section 3, p. 5.

9. "Can Chrysler Keep Its Comeback Rolling?" *Business Week*, February 14, 1983, p. 133; S. Flax, "Can Chrysler Keep Rolling Along?" *Fortune*, January 7, 1985, pp. 34–39.

10. R. C. Shirley, "Limiting the Scope of Strategy: A Decision Based Approach," *Academy of Management Review*, 1982, 7:262–268.

11. Adapted from R. O'Connor, *Tracking the Strategic Plan*, p. 14. Copyright © 1983, The Conference Board, Inc., 845 Third Avenue, New York, NY 10022.

12. R. Amara and A. J. Lipinski, *Business Planning for an Uncertain Future: Scenarios and Strategies.* New York: Pergamon Press, 1983, p. 5.

13. J. Bracker, "The Historical Development of the Strategic Management Concept," *Academy of Management Review,* 1980, 5:219–224; E. E. Chaffee, "Three Models of Strategy," *Academy of Management Review,* 1985, 10:89–98.

14. D. C. Hambrick, "Taxonomic Approaches to Studying Strategy: Some Conceptual and Methodological Issues," *Journal of Management,* 1984, 10:27–41.

15. *General Electric 1982 Annual Report.* Fairfield, Conn.: General Electric Company, 1983.

16. W. F. Glueck and L. R. Jauch, *Business Policy and Strategic Management,* 4th ed. New York: McGraw-Hill, 1984, p. 5.

17. M. Leontiades, *Strategies for Diversification and Change.* Boston: Little, Brown, 1980; K. R. Harrigan, "Formulating Vertical Integration Strategies," *Academy of Management Review,* 1984, 9:638–652.

18. H. Banks, "General Electric—Going with the Winners," *Forbes,* March 26, 1984, pp. 97–106.

19. L. J. Bourgeois III, "Strategic Management and Determinism," *Academy of Management Review,* 1984, 9:586–596; H. E. Wrapp, "Good Managers Don't Make Policy Decisions," *Harvard Business Review,* July–August 1984, pp. 8–21.

20. W. B. Blass, "Ten Years of Business Planners," *Long Range Planning,* June 1983, pp. 21–24.

21. Adapted from H. Banks, "General Electric—Going with the Winners," *Forbes,* March 26, 1984, pp. 97–106; "The New Breed of Strategic Planner: Number Crunching Professionals Are Giving Way to Line Managers," *Business Week,* September 17, 1984, pp. 62–68.

22. R. K. Bresser and R. C. Bishop, "Dysfunctional Effects of Formal Planning: Two Theoretical Explanations," *Academy of Management Review,* 1983, 8:588–599; A. R. Oliver and J. R. Garber, "Implementing Strategic Planning: Ten Sure-Fire Ways To Do It Wrong," *Business Horizons,* March–April 1983, pp. 49–51.

23. J. Mitchell Jr., "Corporate Planning: The Dow Chemical Company." Unpublished paper presented at *Business Week* Strategic Planning Conference, Los Angeles, March 6–7, 1979, p. 26.

24. B. S. Chakravarthy, "Strategic Self-Renewal: A Planning Framework for Today," *Academy of Management Review,* 1984, 9:536–547; W. F. Glueck and L. R. Jauch, *Strategic Management and Business Policy,* 2nd ed. New York: McGraw-Hill, 1984.

25. G. Steiner, "Does Planning Pay Off?" *California Management Review,* 1962, 5:37–39; D. L. Bates and D. L. Eldridge, *Strategy and Policy,* 2nd ed. Dubuque, Iowa: Wm. C. Brown, 1986.

26. "Does G.E. Really Plan Better?" *MBA,* 1975, 9:42–45.

27. "Don't Blame the System, Blame the Managers," *Dun's Review,* September 1980, pp. 82–88.

28. A. K. Gupta, "Contingency Linkages between Strategy and General Manager Characteristics: A Conceptual Examination," *Academy of Management Review,* 1984, 9:399–412; D. C. Hambrick and P. A. Mason, "Upper Echelons: The Organization as a Reflection of Its Top Managers," *Academy of Management Review,* 1984, 9:193–206; A. D. Szilagyi and D. M. Schweiger, "Matching Managers to Strategies: A Review and Suggested Framework," *Academy of Management Review,* 1984, 9:626–637.

29. L. Sayles, "Technological Innovation and the Planning Process," *Organization Dynamics,* 1973, 2:68–80.

30. "Personal Computers: And the Winner Is IBM," *Business Week,* October 3, 1983, pp. 76–79ff.

31. G. Steiner, *Strategic Planning: What Every Manager Must Know.* New York: Free Press, 1979; R. Justis, R. Judd, and D. Stephens, *Strategic Management and Policy: Concepts and Cases.* Englewood Cliffs, N.J.: Prentice-Hall, 1985.

32. I. MacMillan, *Strategy Formulation: Political Concepts.* St. Paul, Minn.: West, 1979; H. V. Wortzel and L. H. Wortzel, *Strategic Management of Multinational Corporations.* New York: John Wiley & Sons, 1985; P. S. Ring and J. L. Perry, "Strategic Management in Public and Private Organizations: Implications of Distinctive Contexts and Constraints," *Academy of Management Review,* 1985, 10:276–286.

33. Adapted from B. Tregoe and J. Zimmerman, "Strategic Thinking: Key to Corporate Survival," *Management Review,* 1979, **68**(2):7–14.

34. A. L. Mendelow, "Setting Corporate Goals and Measuring Organizational Effectiveness—A Practical Approach," *Long Range Planning,* February 1983, pp. 70–76; M. Useem, *The Inner Circle: Large Corporations and the Rise of Business Political Activity in the U.S. and U.K.* New York: Oxford University Press, 1984.

35. M. E. Porter, *Competitive Strategy: Techniques for Analyzing Industries and Competitors.* New York: Free Press, 1980; M. E. Porter, *Competitive Advantage: Creating and Sustaining Superior Performance.* New York: Free Press, 1985. *Also see:* W. E. Rothschild, *How to Gain (and Maintain) the Competitive Edge in Business.* New York: McGraw-Hill, 1984; B. R. Scott and G. C. Lodge (Eds.), *U.S. Competitiveness in the World Economy.* Boston: Harvard Business School Press, 1985; J. A. Young, "Global Competition: The New Reality," *California Management Review,* Spring 1985, pp. 11–25.

36. Porter, pp. 17–23. *Also see:* R. B. Lamb (Ed.), *Competitive Strategic Management.* Englewood Cliffs, N.J.: Prentice-Hall, 1984.

37. J. P. McCray, *The Evolution of Competitive Forces in the Microcomputer Industry and a Comparative Analysis of the Competitive Strategies Employed by Five Dominant Firms within the Industry.* Unpublished dissertation, Texas A&M University, 1985. *Also see* R. McKenna, "Market Positioning in High Technology," *California Management Review,* Spring 1985, pp. 82–108.

38. Porter, *Competitive Strategy . . . ,* pp. 7–17.

39. McCray, *The Evolution of Competitive Forces . . . ,* pp. 35–45.

40. Porter, pp. 24–27.

41. McCray, pp. 68–79.

42. Porter, pp. 27–28; C. S. Galbraith and C. H. Stiles, "Merger Strategies as a Response to Bilateral Market Power," *Academy of Management Journal,* 1984, **27**:511–524.

43. M. Egan, "LAN Plan Told," *MIS Week,* August 22, 1984, **1**:8.

44. M. E. Porter, *Competitive Advantage: Creating and Sustaining Superior Performance.* New York: Free Press, 1985; E. C. Fingerhut and D. G. Hatano, "Principles of Strategic Planning Applied to International Operations," *Managerial Planning,* September–October 1983, pp. 4–14.

45. "RCA: Will It Ever Be a Top Performer?" *Business Week,* April 2, 1984, p. 52. *Also see:* W. H. Newman, J. R. Logan, and W. H. Hegarty, *Strategy, Policy, and Central Management,* 9th ed. Cincinnati: South-Western, 1985.

46. K. Ohmae, *The Mind of the Strategist: The Art of Japanese Business.* New York: McGraw-Hill, 1982. *Also see:* R. A. Burgelman, "Managing the Internal Corporate Venturing Process," *Sloan Management Review,* Winter 1984, pp. 33–48; K. Ohmae, *Triad Power: The Coming Shape of Global Competition.* New York: Free Press, 1985; R. Burgelman and L. R. Sayles, *Inside Corporate Innovation: Strategy, Structure and Managerial Skills.* New York: Free Press, 1986.

47. C. R. Farguhar and S. J. Shapiro, *Strategic Planning in Canada: The Use of Analytical Portfolio Models.* Ottawa, Ontario: Conference Board of Canada, 1983, pp. 33–38. *Also see:* G. S. Odiorne, *Strategic Management of Human Resources: A Portfolio Approach.* San Francisco: Jossey-Bass, 1984; J. C. Anderson, *Human Resource Management: A Strategic Planning Approach.* Marshfield, Mass.: Pitman, 1985.

48. C. W. Hofer, *Strategic Formulation: Analytical Concepts,* 2nd ed. St. Paul, Minn.: West, 1986. *Also see:* D. C. Hambrick, "High Profit Strategies in Mature Capital Goods Industries: A Contingency Approach," *Academy of Management Journal,* 1983, **26**:687–707; H. K. Christensen, A. C. Cooper, and C. A. De Kluyver, "The Dog Business: A Re-Examination," *Business Horizons,* November–December 1982, pp. 12–18; T. L. Wheelen and J. D. Hunger, *Strategic Management and Business Policy,* 2nd ed. Reading, Mass.: Addison-Wesley, 1986; K. Hatten and M. L. Hatten, *Business Policy: Text and Cases.* Englewood Cliffs, N.J.: Prentice-Hall, 1986; R. Pitts and C. C. Snow, *Strategies for Competitive Success.* New York: John Wiley & Sons, 1986.

49. M. A. Hitt, R. D. Ireland, K. A. Palia, "Industrial

Firms' Grand Strategy and Functional Importance: Moderating Effects of Technology and Uncertainty," *Academy of Management Journal,* 1982, **25**:265–298; J. W. Fredrickson, "The Comprehensiveness of Strategic Decision Process: Extension, Observations, and Future Directions," *Academy of Management Journal,* 1984, **27**:445–466; L. G. Hrebiniak and W. F. Joyce, *Implementing Strategy.* New York: Macmillan, 1984.

50. W. Cutler, "Formulating the Annual Research Program at Whirlpool," *Research Management,* 1979, **22**:23–26. *Also see* J. R. Galbraith, *Strategy Implementation: The Role of Structure and Process.* St. Paul, Minn.: West, 1986.

51. Adapted from "Presidential Forum," *Small Business Report,* August 1984, pp. 44–45.

52. C. Summer, *Strategic Behavior in Business and Government,* Boston: Little, Brown, 1980, p. 3. *Also see* K. R. Harrigan, *Strategic Flexibility: A Management Guide for Changing Times.* Lexington, Mass.: Lexington Books, 1985.

53. Adapted from S. Kindel, "Applesause," *Forbes,* February 13, 1984, pp. 39–41; A. M. Morrison, "Apple Bites Back," *Fortune,* February 20, 1984, pp. 86–91ff; "IBM and Apple Battle for the Business Market," *Dun's Business Monthly,* April 1984, p. 123.

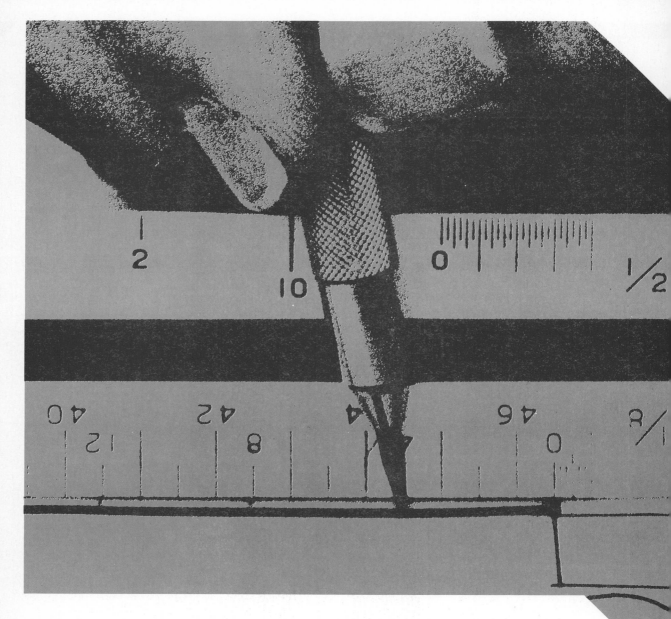

Planning Aids

LEARNING OBJECTIVES

After studying this chapter, you should be able to:

- Describe three forecasting techniques: scenarios, Delphi technique, and simulation models.

- Explain the dialectical inquiry method.

- Describe the conditions under which management by objectives (MBO) is most likely to be effective.

- Apply management by objectives as an aid to your personal planning and career development.

- List and describe the four major elements in the Program Evaluation and Review Technique (PERT).

CHAPTER OUTLINE

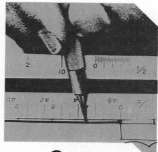

PREVIEW CASE

COMPUTER SOFTWARE FORECASTS

Computer software has become a big business in one of the fastest growing markets in the world. This young industry's outlook is fantastic, with 45% growth in 1984 pushing it to sales of $15 billion—$24.7 billion, perhaps, by 1987. Consumption of software, especially for microcomputers, is growing quickly because new computers and new kinds of users have huge appetites for new applications.

Two major trends are transforming the software market: standardization and user-friendliness. Application packages have been developed for standard software systems, such as the informal IBM Personal Computer standard. Other software systems are being written to run on a variety of different computer brands (Apple, IBM, TI).

The second big trend—and crying need—is the development of programs that are easy to learn and use. Robert Glidden, president of Perfect Software, Berkeley, California, says that the biggest problem now facing the software industry is "combining ease of learning and use with sophis-

ticated advanced features. Most programs are still far too hard to use for the functionality they provide. It is the job of the software companies to solve this. If we do not solve it in the next couple of years, it will slow down the growth of the [entire] microcomputer industry."

In the next 5–10 years, significant new developments in computer (especially, easy-to-use) software will create a true mass market for computers, spurring the growth of software and hardware alike. The emergence of integrated software systems, user interfaces with advanced graphics, natural-language programs, and other products based on artificial intelligence has the ball rolling. During the second half of the decade, the most successful software companies are likely to be those that create software that is easy to learn and use and can perform sophisticated, complex functions.[1]

Source: Darlene Bordwell, Boston.

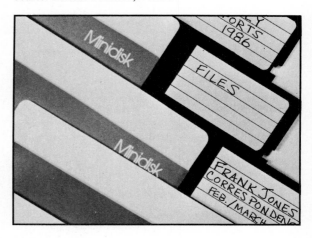

Are these forecasts and trends for the U.S. computer software industry valid? How heavily should a software company rely on these forecasts and trends in developing its strategic plan? Unfortunately, there are no simple answers to these questions. Forecasts—such as those for the computer software industry—are commonly made in most industries. Moreover, industry forecasts are typically used by firms in the development of their strategic and tactical plans.

As with all forecasts, an understanding of how they were developed and the assumptions upon which they are based is essential. The forecasts and trends identified for the U.S. computer software industry were published in *Electronics* magazine. The editors of this industry magazine prepare an annual world markets forecast of 12 electronics industries; they summarize their methodology as follows:

> The data presented in the forecast represents estimates by industry executives of industry-wide consumption at the factory level of the various kinds of equipment shipped by U.S. and foreign manufacturers. Simply put, consumption in the U.S. equals sales in the American market by U.S. companies, plus imports by foreign manufacturers; it does not include exports by U.S. producers.
>
> The survey was conducted in October and November [1983] through mailed questionnaires. Data received from industry sources was then reviewed and tabulated by the staff of *Electronics*. In some cases, follow-up calls were made to sources to get a better understanding of their responses.[2]

The forecasts and trends for the U.S. computer software industry essentially represent the judgments of industry executives. It is impossible to determine in advance if these are statements of common wisdom and foresight or statements of shared ignorance.

In this chapter we present four types of planning aids and techniques: forecasting, dialectical inquiry methods, management by objectives (MBO), and the program evaluation and review technique (PERT). Forecasting aids and the dialectical inquiry method are used primarily in strategic planning. Management by objectives and PERT, on the other hand, are of particular help in integrating and bridging strategic and tactical planning.

AIDS FOR STRATEGIC PLANNING

FORECASTING TECHNIQUES

Forecasting is the predicting, projecting, or estimating of future events or conditions in an organization's environment. Forecasting is an important part of any planning process because it is concerned with possible events or conditions that are outside the direct control of the firm. Firms like GE and Westinghouse develop forecasts for a variety of conditions: market, technological, values, political, and international, among others.

The basis of all forecasting is some form of extrapolation. *Extrapolation* is the projection of some tendency from the past or present into the future.[3] The simplest, and at times most misleading, form of extrapolation is the linear, or straight-line, projection of a past trend into the future. In the early 1960s, for example, several producers of baby foods assumed that birthrates of the recent past could simply be projected into the future. They ignored information about the increasing acceptance and effectiveness of birth control methods and that women's values, attitudes, and behaviors were changing.

Forecasting techniques are quite varied and can be extremely complex. We briefly review scenarios, the Delphi technique, and simulation models as examples of forecasting techniques that are commonly used in strategic planning.[4] The use of these techniques by managers represents an effort to obtain the best information possible for use in developing strategies and plans. As suggested in Fig. 9.1, scenarios, the Delphi technique, and simulation models overlap and support each other; they are not mutually exclusive.

SCENARIOS

A *scenario* is a written description of a possible future external environment that could face a firm or its strategic business units (in the case of a diversified firm). The word *scenario* became popular in 1967, with the publication of Kahn and Weiner's book, *The Year 2000*. Scenarios describe the expected interdependencies of critical issues, events, or other variables. *Multiple scenarios* are simply alternative sets of possibilities that could face a firm or its SBUs. Scenarios address two types of questions: (1) How might some potential (hypothetical) situation come about, step by step? (2) What alternatives exist at each step for preventing, diverting, or encouraging this pro-

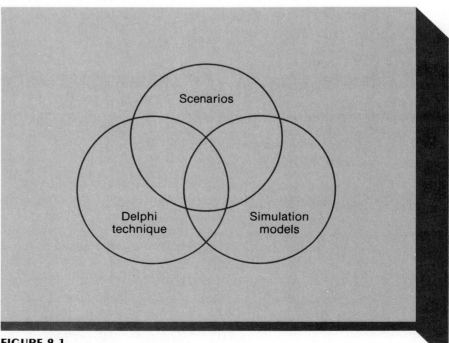

FIGURE 9.1
Overlaps in Forecasting Techniques

TABLE 9.1 ■ PURPOSES OF SCENARIOS

■ Provide a wide range of possibilities against which to evaluate strategies.

■ Provide a broader vision of alternative events.

■ Help identify events that warrant the development of contingency plans.

■ Expand the imagination and stimulate thinking about future environments.

■ Improve the ability to conceptualize and see broad patterns, generalizations, and interrelationships.

Source: Adapted from G. Steiner, *Strategic Planning: What Every Manager Must Know.* New York: Free Press, 1979, pp. 237–238.

cess?[5] Table 9.1 suggests that scenarios can serve a variety of purposes as an aid to planning.

There are several types of scenarios.[6] One common type is the normative-anticipatory scenario. The ***normative/anticipatory scenario*** describes the means that can be used to achieve certain desired objectives. The following is an illustrative scenario question: If the United States aims to lower its annual deficits to $50 billion by 1990, what measures (in what combinations and sequences) can and should be used by the federal government to reach this goal? Many of us frequently develop a normative/anticipatory scenario in our minds when we think about the future (what we want to achieve and how we might get there).

Scenarios are quite useful in forcing managers to evaluate proposals against future possibilities.[7] Dow Chemical Europe is one company that uses scenarios in its planning process.

**IN PRACTICE
Dow Chemical
Europe**

Frank Popoff, president of Dow Chemical Europe, explains how the company uses scenarios in its planning process.

Every industry must look ahead—one year, five years, ten years—and plan for the future political, social, and economic environment; the evolution of that particular industry; and how the industry must change to meet the problems and opportunities it judges it will face.

We have picked our niche as a balanced producer after wading through various strategies for change. Several principles have guided us.

In preparing for the future, we require a *concept* or a vision of what we will be. This guides the development and implementation of our strategy for change. Anything short of this makes us a potential victim of justifying our actions as we progress and of being a victim of change rather than managing it. In a time of change, it is all too tempting to "keep all options open" and have a smorgasbord of opportunities to develop. Instead, our core business

(continued)

should be joined by no more than a few well-defined new activities. These result from an intensive and rational study of priorities. To drift toward change without a concept and a clear set of objectives violates our most fundamental principle.

We require a *candid appraisal* of how well we fit our concept. If it can be served by our existing human, technological, and financial resources, then we are building on our strengths. If it cannot, then we must aggressively pursue those capabilities by whatever means are available to us.

Perhaps the means exist or are readily acquired to implement our concept; even so we must determine whether we are *suitably organized* to maximize our chances for success or whether a new format and plan are required.

It is prudent to prepare a *worst case* scenario. This assesses the risk and determines the amount of jeopardy to which our core business will be subjected. In so doing, we not only come to know our programs' sensitivities but also their relative importance.

It is mandatory to *share* our concept, excitement, and commitment for change with our entire organization. Failure to do so not only robs us of our maximum effort but often results in resistance to change and an adherence to familiar activities and the status quo.[8]

Delphi technique

The ***Delphi technique*** can be a useful aid in developing scenarios and evaluating the likelihood of their occurrence. It is a method for securing the consensus of experts regarding their predictions of the future or assessment of current needs.[9] This technique involves a step-by-step refinement of the experts' opinions to reach consensus. Because the technique relies on *opinions,* it obviously is not foolproof. However, the consensus arrived at achieves a higher degree of accuracy than a single expert opinion could be expected to give.[10]

The Delphi technique has gained considerable recognition as a forecasting technique for use in strategic planning. It was developed at the Rand Corporation in the early 1960s. Rand used it to obtain expert opinions about urgent national defense problems.

Basic steps.   The Delphi technique involves three basic steps.[11]

- A questionnaire is sent or given to a group of anonymous experts. It requests numerical estimates of specific technological or market possibilities—expected dates, volumes, developments—as well as the assignment of probabilities of occurrence for these possibilities.

- A summary of this first round is prepared. It may show the average, median, and quartile ranges of responses. This summary report is given to the experts. In the second round they are asked to revise their earlier estimates, if appropriate, or to justify their original opinions.

Another summary report is prepared from the second-round responses. This report often shows that a consensus is developing. The experts are then asked to indicate whether they support this emerging consensus and the explanations that accompany it. Minority opinions giving reasons for not joining the consensus are encouraged.

Three *rounds* with the experts are generally recommended. More rounds could be used but experts may begin dropping out after the third round because of other commitments. The number of participants has ranged from a few to 140 people; 15–20 experts are generally adequate.[12]

The heart of the technique is a series of questionnaires. The first questionnaire may include broadly worded questions. In later rounds, the questions become more specific because they are built on responses to the preceding questionnaires.

Delphi questionnaire.   Table 9.2 shows one type of Delphi questionnaire that has been developed for student and classroom use. The questionnaire is concerned with possible future developments in the typical American business firm within the next 20 years. You might want to take a few minutes now and answer the questions in Table 9.2

Sample applications.   In 1966, TRW, a major advanced-technology firm, began to use the Delphi technique for planning studies in such diverse fields as space, transportation, and housing. Goodyear Tire and Rubber Company uses the method in its planning of future tire research. In recent years, the Delphi technique has also been applied to help identify problems, set objectives and priorities, and identify solutions to problems in areas such as urban redevelopment, energy conservation, pollution control, and housing.

Simulation models

Managers use ***simulation models*** to forecast the effects of environmental changes and/or management decisions on an organization or any of its departments. The objective of simulation models is to reproduce or test a reality without actually experiencing the reality. Most simulation models are intended to let management ask numerous *what if* questions.[13] If inflation is 8 percent and management continues its past decisions and policies, *what* profits can be anticipated for next year? Or, *if* inflation is 12 percent and management opens two new plants, *what* profits can be expected next year? In order to answer such questions, analysts often have to develop mathematical equations so that step-by-step computations can be performed by computers.

Typical questions and variables.   A simulation model can help top managers to deal with three common questions: (1) What effects will a changed economy have on the organization, if the key decisions and policies of man-

TABLE 9.2 ■ DELPHI QUESTIONNAIRE REGARDING FUTURE DEVELOPMENTS IN AMERICAN BUSINESS FIRMS

Introduction

Each of the following 10 questions is concerned with future possible developments in the typical American business firm within the next 20 years or so.

Instructions

In addition to giving your answer to each question, you are also being asked to rank the questions from 1 to 10. "1" means you feel that you have the best chance of making an accurate projection for this question relative to the others. "10" means you regard that answer as least probable. Please rank all questions such that every number from 1 to 10 is used exactly once.

RANK (1–10)	QUESTIONS	(YEAR)*
_____	1. In your opinion, in what year will women serve as presidents of at least five of *Fortune Magazine's* 500 largest corporations?	_____
_____	2. In what year will most boards of directors of publicly held corporations contain members who represent primarily the consumer rather than the stockholders?	_____
_____	3. In your opinion, in what year will managers regularly be paid for working a 20-hour work week?	_____
_____	4. By what year will business have effectively reduced its pollution of the environment to a nondangerous level?	_____
_____	5. In what year will top management in half of the largest 100 manufacturing firms rely on computerized systems as their primary tool for planning?	_____
_____	6. By what year will the use of mind-stimulating drugs be employed by 10% of the chief executives as an aid in determining corporate policy alternatives?	_____
_____	7. In what year will energy prices make operations unfeasible for most American industrial corporations?	_____
_____	8. By what year will the M.B.A. degree be a minimum requirement for entry into the management training programs of most corporations?	_____
_____	9. In what year will prime interest rates make it totally prohibitive for corporations to expand their plant capacities?	_____
_____	10. In what year will most financial statements reflect a significant level of accounting for social costs and assets (e.g., pollution, welfare, and human resources)?	_____

* "Never" is also an acceptable answer.

Source: Dr. Harvey Nussbaum, School of Business Administration, Wayne State University, Detroit. Reprinted by permission.

agement are not changed? (2) What will be the effect on the firm when a particular decision or policy is altered in anticipation of or in response to certain changes in the economy (such as an increase in interest cost to 20 percent)? (3) Are there combinations of management decisions and policies that can enable the firm to take advantage of changes in the economy?

The types of environmental variables used in a simulation model could include inflation rate, short-term interest rate, tax rate, and unemployment levels. Some of the management decisions and policies included in a simulation model could affect prices charged, growth rate of products sold, dividend policy, operating cash, depreciation, and capacity expansion plans. The performance measures included in a simulation model could be an income statement, financial ratios (such as debt–equity ratio, return on equity, and earnings per share), and balance-sheet statements (assets and liabilities).

Sample applications.   Simulation models can be used for virtually any problem (profits, sales, earnings per share) or functional area (finance, marketing, personnel, production) in which there is a need for forecasting.[14] Let us consider two such applications.

The IBM World Trade Corporation, which is responsible for IBM's international business, makes considerable use of computerized simulation models. The elements of its simulation models include: (1) present operational activities; (2) forecasts about changes in costs, prices, investments, labor productivity, and so on; and (3) extrapolations from past performance. The effects of planning alternatives and assumptions are obtained by forecasting sales, comparative revenues, changes in income and expense accounts, and the like.[15]

Management and unions also utilize computer-based simulation models for the development of their collective-bargaining plans and for anticipating the long-term effects of each other's proposals. The vice-president of corporate planning at American Airlines stated: "When our pilot contract was under negotiation recently, the union requested a new limitation on the number of flight hours each pilot would fly per month. We were able to feed this limitation into our computers and relate it to production levels we had planned over the next five years. We were able to determine exactly what our crew costs over the five-year period would be with new flight hours and to compare them with present costs."[16]

Assessment of forecasting.   Because the future is rarely the same as the past, managers can mislead themselves if they base forecasting models entirely on historical relationships and data. This would be like steering a ship by watching its wake. A high degree of judgment and skill is needed to construct forecasting models.[17] A growing disenchantment with forecasting among managers is probably the result of unqualified faith in the ability of forecasters to forecast and in their results. Robert Lohr, a Bethlehem Steel executive, blames his firm's $768 million operating losses in 1982–83 partly on "the investments we made because we believed in the boom of 1981 that an economist promised us." A major metal-mining concern, AMAX, dug itself an $879 million hole over the past two years by heeding forecasts of continuing inflation. Those projections led the company to assume that prices for its copper, molybdenum, and other metals would keep rising. Instead, their market value has fallen 50% as of 1984.[18]

Even the most sophisticated forecasting and planning systems will not anticipate sudden changes and surprises. The so-called petroleum crisis of 1979–1980, for example, created problems for many major corporations that had modern forecasting and planning systems. Some of these firms simply weren't looking at this possibility. Others had forecasts of OPEC's actions but apparently felt that the probability was too low to justify planning for this possibility.

INTERNATIONAL FOCUS

FORECASTING AND DATA BASES

The manager of an international business requires various forecasts in order to make sound decisions. Forecasts for an international corporation, as for a domestic firm, are made at three levels: the economy, the industry, and the company. However, for an international business, identifying and forecasting the interdependence of different national economies is vital. The main difficulty a forecaster will encounter is the proper identification and incorporation of linkages among economies and industries.

Model building and forecasting efforts at the international level are relatively infrequent. Part of the problem appears to be the lack of adequate data. The international demographic, economic, and social indicators available for marketing research and sales forecasting are chronically inadequate. One authority asserts that

> They nevertheless form the statistical skeleton upon which nearly every international marketing research report is built, despite the fact that many of these indicators are fallible as regards international comparability and relevance to marketing to an extent that makes them not just irrelevant but positively misleading. They are data that are readily available: therefore they are used.

In evaluating international data bases, four questions should be asked:

1. Who collected the data? Would there be any reason for purposely misrepresenting the facts?

Excerpted and adapted from G. Rice and E. Essam, "Forecasting and Data Bases in International Business," *Management International Review*, 1984, **24**(4):59–71.

Tremendous progress has been made in the development of forecasting techniques over the past 25 years, but the future remains uncertain. In fact, over the past 25 years the increase in complexity and change in organizational environments may well have exceeded the improvements in forecasting aids and techniques.[19]

Dialectical Inquiry Method

Another aid for managers in making innovative strategic decisions was first proposed in 1969: the *dialectical inquiry method.*[20] There has been a growing interest in the potential usefulness of this method, especially during the past six years.

The dialectical inquiry method is a process for examining problems completely and systematically from two or more different and opposing points of

2. For what purpose were the data collected?
3. How were they collected?
4. Are the data internally consistent and logical in the light of known data sources or market factors?

For example, the World Bank's *World Tables* are a by-product of the World Bank's own statistical and analytical work with population and certain financial statistics obtained from other sources. United Nations' figures are gathered from statistical responses to questionnaires that are sent to more than 125 countries and areas. In the case of the International Monetary Fund's *International Financial Statistics,* the data are provided by national sources but are screened before being included in the statistics. If the compilers have any reason to believe that the data provided by a national government are doctored, they simply exclude them from the publication. Another advantage of *International Financial Statistics* is that the data are comparable and are provided monthly. Business International's *BI/DATA* is also a timely source because data are updated every six months. The time lag for publication of much international business data is at least two years (for example, some publications of the UN and the World Bank).

Only after evaluating the data base (in terms of coverage, availability, accuracy, and timeliness) should the forecaster begin the next step in selecting an appropriate forecasting method: the identification of the data patterns.

view.[21] It is especially useful with issues that require innovative solutions and have one or more of the following characteristics.[22]

- The problem may be known and well-defined but those charged with solving it cannot agree on a course of action.

- Managers cannot agree on a process for developing a course of action.

- Managers don't know or can't agree on a clear definition of the desired objectives, the factors under their control, or the factors beyond their control.

- Managers must deal with two or more stakeholders (stockholders, suppliers, customers, employees, governmental agencies) with a vested interest in the issue.[23]

- Managers face states of nature that involve a condition of high risk or uncertainty, as well as potential conflicting interests among stakeholders.[24]

The dialectical inquiry method consists of four phases: assumption-specification phase, dialectical phase, assumption-integration phase, and composite-strategy–creation phase. These phases and the elements within each phase are shown in Fig. 9.2. Generally, a group of 12–30 people will participate in the process.[25] Portions of each phase require all the participants to meet as a single group. However, most of the activities are undertaken by two-to-four working teams. Teams that are as different as possible from each other should be formed. These differences might reflect product lines, organization function, type of customers served, and so on.

Assumption-specification phase. The assumption-specification phase is intended to reveal the hidden or informal assumptions held by managers. For example, the managers of an electric utility who assume that their firm is a monopoly and in the business of providing electricity are likely to perceive problems and generate possible alternative solutions quite differently than do the managers of an electric utility who assume that their firm has many competitors and is in the energy business.

The following sequence of activities is prescribed to get managers to reveal and specify assumptions.

- State the existing or proposed strategy for dealing with a problem and/or the problems facing the organization.

- Identify any information that is believed to support the existing or proposed course of action and/or the definition of the problem(s).

- Identify the underlying assumptions upon which the existing or proposed strategy and data are based.

Assumptions are the conditions, events, or characteristics of problems and alternative solutions that we think might be true. When the weather reporter

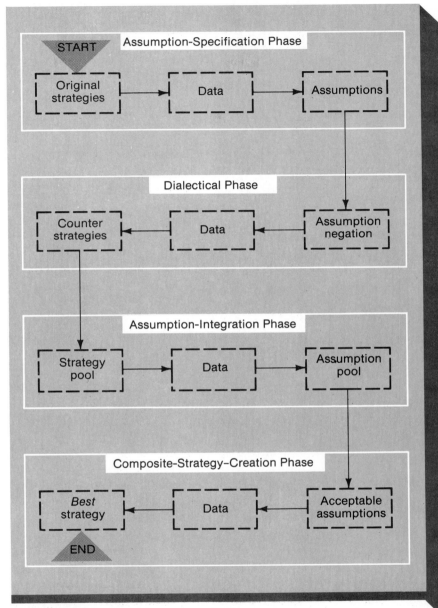

FIGURE 9.2
Dialectical Inquiry Method

Source: Adapted from I. I. Mitroff and J. R. Emshoff, "On Strategic Assumption-Making: A Dialectic Approach to Policy and Planning," *Academy of Management Review,* 1979, 4:5

predicts a clear or rainy day, there is an underlying assumption that the earth will continue in its pattern of rotation around the sun. A detailed list of assumptions that includes both probable and improbable conditions should be developed. This helps ensure that nothing is being left out. The assumption list should include, among other things, the objectives of the organization and the objectives of its stakeholders.[26]

Dialectical phase. The purpose of the dialectical phase is to identify new strategies or potential solutions. If needed, this phase can also be used to define the problem(s) differently. After problem identification, the following sequence of activities can be undertaken.

- Develop a list of assumptions that are the opposite of those upon which the original strategies were based. For example, those utility managers who assumed that they were operating in a monopoly would need to assume that their firm was operating in a highly competitive market. This activity is identified as *assumption negation.*

- Each assumption previously identified in the assumption specification phase is challenged with an opposite assumption. However, if the opposite assumption is implausible, it is dropped.

- This new list of opposite assumptions serves as a basis for searching for new data consistent with them. These assumptions could also serve as a basis for developing one or more entirely new strategies.

The dialectical phase ends when the managers conclude that no more plausible counterstrategies can be identified. Although not shown in Fig. 9.2, movement back and forth between some of the phases is likely, especially between the assumption-specification and dialectical phases.

Assumption-integration phase. The assumption-integration phase focuses on consolidating the diverse sets of assumptions generated in the first and second phases. There is no guarantee that a consolidated and acceptable set of assumptions will always emerge from this phase. If power is balanced among the participating stakeholders, the outcome could be a standoff. Or, the most powerful decisionmakers could impose their will. The following sequence of activities can eventually lead to an agreed-upon strategy.

- If various stakeholders are represented in the process, teams are formed representing the major stakeholder groups.

- Each stakeholder group ranks the assumptions associated with each possible strategy for two criteria: (1) the relative importance of each assumption to them; and (2) the relative certainty of each assumption.

- Each stakeholder group discusses in depth those assumptions that are considered to be very important but uncertain.

■ A representative of each stakeholder group presents its findings to the group as a whole.

■ Each group is asked to soften its assumptions to the extent possible in order to arrive at mutual conclusions.

Eventually, agreement on a set of assumptions or a set of compromise assumptions can be achieved. The greatest conflict is likely to be experienced in this phase of the process. It is also the most difficult phase because of the need to make decisions based on a new set of assumptions. Some of these assumptions are likely to be quite different from or extend the assumptions developed in the first phase.

Composite-strategy–creation phase. When an acceptable set of assumptions has been developed, the composite-strategy–creation phase proceeds in steps similar to those of the rational decision-making model. Decision-making aids such as the payoff-matrix model or decision-tree model can be quite useful in this phase of the process.

IN PRACTICE
New-Product Decision

Managers of a division of a large corporation were thinking about the release of a new product. Their focusing questions were twofold: Should the new product be released? If so, what should be the strategy for its release?

Eighteen key people, including the CEO and company vice-presidents, were assembled for a three-day planning session. During the first meeting, the group was polled about the major issues they felt should be resolved. Some 60 issues were mentioned; they were finally reduced to five key issues. Working teams were formed, based on individually preferred resolutions to those five issues.

The teams created their lists of stakeholders and rated their assumptions. Each team produced a graph to illustrate the degree of importance and degree of certainty of each assumption. Figure 9.3 is an example of their ratings. Then, meeting in a general session, the teams presented their results and debated their points of view. After intensive discussion, the group identified and assigned priorities to the remaining key issues. They are shown in the lower right-hand corner of Fig. 9.3 and include:

1. What should be the price of the product?

2. Should it be marketed directly or through dealers?

3. Will adequate funds for expansion be available from banks or through the issuance of new stock?

The issues shown in the upper left-hand corner of Fig. 9.3 (direct competition and supporting products) were not discussed because the group assigned a low degree of importance and a high degree of certainty to them.

(continued)

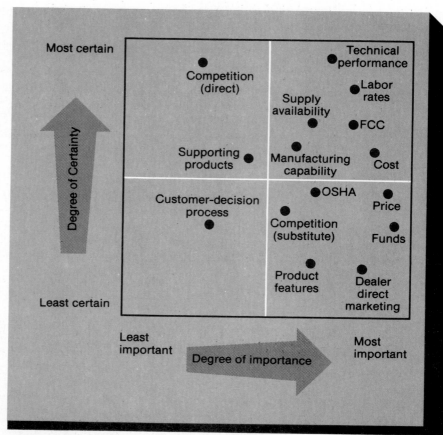

FIGURE 9.3
Assumption Plotting Graph

Source: Adapted from A. J. Rowe, R. O. Mason, and K. Dickel, *Strategic Management and Business Policy: A Methodological Approach*. Reading, Mass.: Addison-Wesley, 1982, p. 85. Adapted and used with permission.

Each of the teams investigated these issues over a nine-month period. The group discussed and debated the results in another planning session. The managers decided to release the new product, to market it directly, and to price it at $4000. Funds were obtained, production began, and, to date, no replacement technology has appeared on the horizon.

The critical issues were determined and evaluated through the dialectical inquiry method. Information requirements were identified and information relevant to the issues was collected and used. As a result, a strategy based on solid information rather than guesswork was formulated.[27]

Assessment of the dialectical inquiry method. There have been relatively few well-designed studies to date on the relative effectiveness of the dialectical inquiry method.[28] We suggest that its *automatic* use in many organizations is premature. The method is designed to increase conflict among managers and/or stakeholders and to sharpen alternative points of view. If the people involved have a history of intense political power struggles and high distrust of each other, the dialectical inquiry method may be a high-risk approach. Its use could deepen rather than resolve conflicts. Thus, like any planning aid or management approach, it should not be accepted unquestioningly for use in strategic-planning situations. The dialectical inquiry method is most likely to be effective in those situations that involve a high degree of uncertainty and basic agreement on the general objectives of the organization.[29]

AIDS FOR BRIDGING STRATEGIC AND TACTICAL PLANNING

MANAGEMENT by Objectives

Management by objectives (MBO) is a philosophy and system of management that serves as both a planning aid and a way of organizational life.[30] Management by objectives is one way for managers to integrate strategic and tactical planning in making day-to-day decisions.[31] It is a means for translating key corporate strategies into operational objectives and plans.

Philosophy and MANAGEMENT STYLE

The philosophy and management style of management by objectives are highlighted in Table 9.3. The table clearly indicates that MBO reflects a positive philosophy about people and a participative management style. In organizations where managers have a good grasp of its philosophy and style,

TABLE 9.3 ■ PHILOSOPHY AND MANAGEMENT STYLE OF MBO

- Mutual problem-solving between organizational levels in the establishment of objectives.
- Formation of trusting and open communication.
- Creation of win–win relationships.
- Rewards and promotions based on job-related performance and achievement.
- Minimal use of political games, fear, or force.
- Development of a positive, proactive, and challenging organizational culture.

MBO should lead to less paperwork and less concern about supervising nitty-gritty, day-to-day activities.

Sometimes, managers become fascinated with the procedures of MBO without adequately understanding or accepting MBO's philosophy. For example, managers in some companies have become so taken with the logical and rational flow of the MBO process that they continued to develop the process in greater detail. The results were paperwork monstrosities, leading to information overload and clogged decision-making channels.[32] These all-too-frequent and frustrating situations occur because the MBO process has been plugged into the decision-making system of the firm without adequate managerial diagnosis.

Basic MBO model

The basic management by objectives model is presented in Fig. 9.4. Seven interconnected, key steps comprise the MBO process.[33] Figure 9.4 also conveys the idea that the MBO philosophy and management style permeates all seven steps. Obviously, there is considerable interplay between the steps, as suggested by the arrows pointing upward in Fig. 9.4.*

Setting and linking objectives. The distinguishing feature of MBO is the establishment and linking of objectives for the organization as a whole, its departments, and as many individuals as possible.[34] The objective-setting stage (1–3) should provide clear answers to two basic questions: "Why are we here?" and "If this is why we are here, what should we accomplish?" The setting of objectives is likely to include managers at different levels as follows:

- Top managers set broad, organizational objectives that determine what the organization is and what it is trying to become.
- Top and middle managers develop more specific, strategic objectives. They are often quantitative and include time periods, such as an objective to increase profits by 20 percent within three years.
- Middle and first-line managers develop objectives for the various departments. For example, the production department may have an objective to reduce electrical consumption by 10 percent over the next 12 months.
- First-line managers and workers develop individual job objectives. For example, a machine operator may develop an objective to reduce waste and spoilage from 6 percent to 5 percent within the next six months.

Figure 9.5 shows the general relationship between strategic objectives for an organization (or an SBU) and selected functional departments such as marketing, production, and personnel (first two columns). The third column illustrates several types of departmental tactical objectives that are needed to

---

* Note that the boxed numbers in the text correspond to those of the steps in the MBO-process sequence shown in Fig. 9.4.

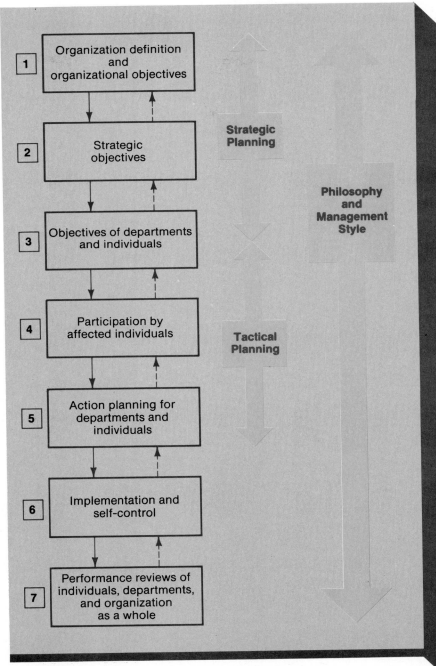

FIGURE 9.4
The Basic MBO Process

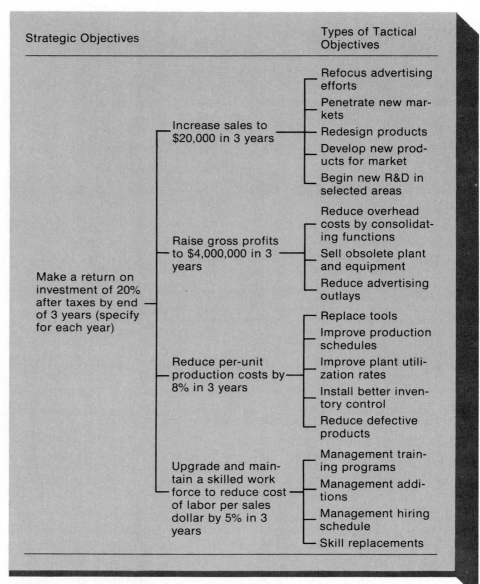

FIGURE 9.5
Linking Strategic and Tactical Objectives

Source: Adapted from G. A. Steiner, *Strategic Planning.* New York: Free Press, 1979, pp. 167–170.

help implement the strategic objectives. The basic idea presented in Fig. 9.5 is consistent with the hierarchy-of-objectives concept presented in Chapter 6.

Objectives ideally specify the quality and quantity of results expected within a defined period of time. They are set for the organization as a whole, each division or strategic business unit, each department, and each individual employee. Many organizations do not include objective setting for those individuals who perform highly routine and interdependent jobs. In routine jobs, such as assembly-line work, the employees may have little choice or control over how their work is performed or the pace at which they work. Their production is heavily influenced by the speed of the line and how well the assemblers in the earlier stages have done their jobs. In these situations, it is often more effective to set only team objectives.

Objectives are the standards for evaluating effectiveness. *Quantitative* objectives for a sales manager this year might be to (1) increase sales by 5 percent; (2) maintain private-label sales at 7 percent of total sales; and (3) keep expenses for advertising promotion at last year's level. The sales manager could also be accountable for *qualitative* objectives, such as (1) developing a sales-quota system for all salespeople; (2) preparing and recommending an incentive-compensation system for area managers; and (3) shifting the advertising emphasis from wholesalers to consumers.

Thus the process of setting objectives includes identifying specific areas of job or departmental responsibility and standards of performance.[35] Three things should be kept in mind:

1. Objectives should not be stated in such general terms that they have little personal significance for the manager or individual employee. A poor objective would be "Your job is to maximize the welfare of the firm and of society."

2. Objectives should not be stated in such detail that the manager or employee must concentrate on dozens of day-to-day objectives.

3. Consistent with the political decision-making model (Chapter 7), some decision areas may be so embedded in political power struggles and conflicts that efforts to set clear objectives for them may be futile. (In fact, such efforts could actually increase conflicts and power struggles.)

Intel Corporation is one comany that uses MBO successfully. In 1971, Intel invented the microprocessor, the specialized semiconductor chip that contains the "brain" of a computer. The company developed a leadership position in the industry because of its numerous innovative products. It currently has about 22,000 employees and sales of more than $1 billion annually.[36] In an interview with *Harvard Business Review* (HBR), Robert W. Noyce, co-chairman of Intel, commented on the company's commitment to MBO. Noyce's comments are of particular interest because he conveys a sense of Intel's (1) values and organization definition; (2) strategies and planning process; and (3) use of management by objectives as a planning aid and a management method for linking strategic and tactical planning.

IN PRACTICE
Intel Corporation

HBR: From its beginning, Intel has had a spectacular record. What's the secret of your success? Did you have a specific management philosophy from the start?

Noyce: No, you didn't have to then. In a small organization there's enough communication so that the objectives are very clearly defined to begin with. If you can't communicate with only 25 people, your communication skills are pretty awful. So our organization was very sharply focused. We knew what product we were going after; everybody understood that very well. That was almost enough of a statement of objectives to last through the first couple of years.

HBR: What is the management style now?

Noyce: Now we've run out of the collective experience of everyone. There's only one member of the board who has ever worked for a company larger than Intel—as Intel is today. And consequently, we feel that we're plowing new ground in terms of how we organize, how we do things, how we keep focus.

HBR: How do you keep focus?

Noyce: Well, the thing that we've been concentrating on recently is the culture. What makes Intel *Intel?* A lot of it is what has evolved because of the personalities of the people around. It is MBO practiced all the way through. I think there's a lot of lip service given to MBO, and it's not practiced. But here everybody writes down what they are going to do and reviews how they did it, how they did against those objectives, not to management, but to a peer group *and* management. So that's also a communication mechanism between various groups, various divisions, et cetera.

HBR: Do you have a formal way to do that, then?

Noyce: Yes, and it's pretty well built into the system. There is an openness, a willingness to discuss problems, identify them, which is not confrontational but rather, "Hey, I've got a problem. Here's how it's going." The executive staff, which basically consists of all the division managers, is truly an executive staff. They worry about the whole business, not just their own business, although they have the primary responsibility for their own business. There is very little in the way of staffers as such. Staff work is done by line management as a secondary assignment.

HBR: You don't have a separate planning function, then?

Noyce: No, strategic planning is imbedded in the organization. It is one of the primary functions of the line managers. They buy into the program; they carry it out. They're determining their own future, so I think the motivation for doing it well is high. Now that is not to say that we won't call on other resources. If we have a product area that we don't know much about, we certainly will call in a market research organization or whatever to give us more information to work on.

HBR: How do you keep making this a challenging place to work?

Noyce: I think it's because people have the control of their own destiny, and they get measured on it. They get their M&M candies for every job, as one of our business instructor's always said. It's now getting to be a real challenge. The question is whether we can do it right. A great deal of effort goes into thinking about how we plan it, how we operate it, and how we build incentives into it. Where are we going? Are we going where we want to go? How do we win at this game called business? And, as I say, I think that our team is made of high achievers who really want to do that. They still see plenty of challenges.

HBR: Is there a lot of internal competition?

Noyce: Well, there isn't the political infighting that you often see in companies. The direction is very carefully and definitely set, and everybody understands that. It's partly because of the way it's set—for both the MBO system and the strategic planning system. There just isn't room for politics in the organization. It is very quickly rooted out. Someone who's crawling over someone else's body just doesn't get very far.

HBR: How does it get weeded out, though?

Noyce: I think the information is open enough so that what the individual manager is doing is put under a microscope once every six months by all his peers. His peers know all those games, too, so politics just doesn't work. He doesn't get any support from his peers if he's doing that. It's an interactive company. Most of the divisions are heavily dependent on another organization that will let them get their job done.

HBR: It's a good idea to know where your strength lies. Would you say that's one of the key things?

Noyce: Yes, and certainly in strategic planning, the analysis of where our strengths and weaknesses lie is an essential part. We build on strengths and try to stay out of competition where we're weak. Our strength is clearly in the components manufacture, in the design capabilities there, so that's where we want to compete. That's where we want to do battle with our competition. We certainly don't want to compete with IBM, any more than we want to compete with

(continued)

General Motors. Just because we make an engine control, we don't want to make an automobile.

HBR: How would you say Intel differs from other companies in your industry?

Noyce: I used to characterize our business as compared to others in the industry as working on the edge of disaster. We are absolutely trying to do those things which nobody else could do from a technical point of view. We measure everything that we do so that when something goes wrong we have some idea of what it was that went wrong—a complex process. We've tried to extend that same philosophy to the running of the whole organization. You don't do something unless you know what you're doing. You don't change something unless you know that it's been done on a pilot basis, that it won't louse up something else.[37]

Organization definition and organizational objectives ①. As we discussed in Chapter 8, organization definition answers the following types of questions: (1) Who are we? (2) What do we want to become? (3) What are our basic objectives? Table 8.5 presented illustrations of statements of organizational objectives for two firms: Hewlett-Packard and Robertshaw Controls Company. Organizational objectives are often highly abstract and broad statements that change little, if at all, from one year to the next.

Strategic objectives ②. Strategic objectives typically are developed as part of strategic planning for the organization as a whole and for each strategic business unit. Strategic objectives are often more specific than organizational objectives. They also are more likely to be quantifiable and revised over time. (Refer back to Chapter 8, if necessary, for a more complete discussion of strategic objectives and strategies.)

Objectives of departments and individuals ③. There are four major reasons for setting departmental and individual objectives, whenever possible.

1. To force managers and others to recognize that there is *no single objective* for the organization, its departments, or its employees.
2. To force managers and others to recognize that objective setting *involves risk and uncertainty* in balancing and making tradeoffs among objectives.
3. To force managers and others to explicitly analyze and make decisions about relative *priorities*.
4. To force managers and others to explicitly analyze and make decisions about the *relationships among objectives* of the organization, objectives of the departments within the organization, and the objectives of the individuals within the departments.

Participation by affected individuals ☐4. Broad participation in the setting of objectives is generally recommended. When objectives are established and implemented only from the top down, MBO may be viewed by employees as a means of measurement and control and not as a planning and motivational system.[38] If MBO is used only to pressure people or departments into performing better, it might be expected to fail or to have limited success. However, there are situations in which some objectives have to be given from the top.[39] For example, the Environmental Protection Agency has forced companies to achieve certain environmental objectives within a specified period of time or pay stiff fines. As a consequence, department managers may be required by top management to set objectives relating to environmental hazards within their departments, even if they don't want to set such objectives and be held accountable for their achievements.

Ideally, the superior and subordinate attempt to reach a consensus on (1) the objectives the subordinate will attempt to achieve in a specific period of time; (2) the general means by which the subordinate will attempt to accomplish the objectives; and (3) how progress toward objectives will be measured and the specific dates for such measurements.[40] Even if agreement on these issues cannot be reached, the setting of objectives will normally lead to higher performance than if no objectives were set.[41]

Action planning for departments and individuals ☐5. After the objectives have been established, *action plans* should be developed for accomplishing the desired objectives. The vice-president of marketing whose objective is to increase sales volume by 10 percent within 12 months might develop the following action plan.

1. Release the new product that has been developed to supplement the product line by [date].
2. Evaluate the feasibility of a reduction in price to stimulate demand for products X and Y.
3. Increase the sales volume targets of sales personnel in Seattle, Boston, and Detroit by 10%.
4. Increase the on-time delivery for products X and Y by 5 percent.[42]

The extent to which an individual will be involved in developing an action plan varies. For example, developing a departmental action plan might involve group discussion by the departmental manager and employees.[43] On the other hand, an action plan to achieve an individual's objectives might be developed by the individual and submitted to his or her superior for comment.

Implementation and self-control ☐6. *Implementation* is the translation of objectives and action plans into day-to-day behaviors that lead to the attainment of stated objectives. This often means that managers must give greater freedom to subordinates in the choice of methods they use. Managers should be available to coach and counsel subordinates as needed. Their role is more to help subordinates reach objectives than to manage subordinates' hour-by-hour and day-to-day activities.

Self-control in this context means that employees will be given the opportunity and responsibility for controlling their own activities; that management trusts individuals to work effectively toward stated objectives. Individuals should feel free to discuss problems with their supervisors or others who can help them.

Performance reviews of departments and individuals ⑦. This last step in the sequence calls for systematic and scheduled reviews to measure and assess progress, identify and resolve problems, and revise, drop, or add objectives. If managers conduct these reviews properly, they can determine the significance of lessons from the immediate past and apply them in dealing with the future.[44]

Effective managers develop a method of translating corporate objectives to subordinates without dictating the subordinates' daily activities or stifling creativity.

Source: Stock, Boston.

The appraisal of a department or individual's achievements during a performance review ideally includes mutual problem-solving between the manager and subordinate. Obviously, this means that subordinates must participate in reviewing the performance of their department and/or their personal performance. The manager encourages subordinates to identify obstacles, problems, and ways to improve performance. Because objectives have previously been developed and agreed on (or, at least, accepted), the review process can focus on actual achievements. This method of evaluation is considerably different from that of evaluating personality traits or subjective characteristics such as *conscientious, enthusiastic,* and *creative.*[45]

Performance reviews provide feedback to an employee or a group of employees. This lets them know how well they are achieving the stated objectives. Knowledge of results is essential to improved performance; it aids in the development of new skills, behaviors, and attitudes. Management by objectives emphasizes that subordinates must review their own performance and participate in evaluating it if they are to operate under self-control.

Two objectives of a furniture salesperson may be a 10-percent sales increase and a 40-percent average mark-up on goods sold during the next year. With feedback regarding results in these areas, the salesperson will know how he or she is progressing toward achievement of these objectives. Unfortunately, the review process is not so simple. In the case of the salesperson, factors other than the salesperson's own behavior can influence actual results. These factors could include the state of the economy, store hours, advertising campaigns, and the availability of credit—all beyond the salesperson's control.

Significant parts of some managerial jobs may not lend themselves to the development of objective indicators of performance. Homer Wilson, vice-president of operations at Celanese Chemical Company, has said that one of his objectives is to build morale and develop people's careers. This type of objective must be evaluated on the basis of judgment. The manager must decide *whether* the objective was achieved before he or she can ask *why* it was—or wasn't.[46]

The MBO process does not call for managers to play a passive role in the performance-review step. However, it does require that managers shift from being judgmental and critical to being more helpful and willing to engage in mutual problem-solving. At times, we find that managers interpret this step and the whole MBO process as "soft." Quite to the contrary! People *are* demoted, dismissed, and otherwise held accountable under this system. The rationale and basis for such actions should be more apparent. Thus it should be easier for managers to make such decisions.[47] Moreover, the MBO process is intended to minimize the need for formal disciplinary action.[48]

We learned earlier about Intel's overall philosophy, MBO process, and planning in general. We now consider Intel's safeguards and other processes that attempt to minimize personal bias and distortion in making performance appraisals.

IN PRACTICE
Performance
Appraisal at
Intel

Andrew S. Grove, president of Intel, reports that three safeguards are used in its performance appraisal process.

Once an employee review is written up by a supervisor, the supervisor's manager oversees and approves the written evaluation. This manager is the second most qualified judge of the employee's performance—second, that is, to the employee's immediate supervisor. Being one level removed, they can put the employee's performance in broader perspective. They are in a position to compare it with the work of other people in the organization.

Our second check of the evaluation process stipulates that the personnel representative assigned to the employee's department approve the review. Although specialists from the personnel department probably can't judge the quality of highly technical endeavors, they are likely to catch signs of favoritism and prejudice. If they do, they should call it to the attention of the immediate supervisor's manager. For this to have real effect, we must give the personnel department enough clout to make their opinions and comments count.

The third check comes from setting up ranking sessions. In these sessions, supervisors meet with their peers and, together as a group, compare and rank all of their subordinates. Of course, no one supervisor can assess the work of all subordinates of his/her peers. But collectively, enough will be known about each employee to provide additional—and frequently conflicting—points of view to the assessment process. This process results in an outcome that is fairer for everybody.

Do such checks and balances weed out all bad evaluations? They do not. No system is foolproof, especially one that is necessarily laden with human judgment. Furthermore, such an evaluation process takes much more time and effort than simply listing a group of employees by date of hire and letting it go at that.[49]

Assessment of MBO

Research findings on the effectiveness of MBO are mixed. They are often difficult to interpret because neither the philosophy nor the steps outlined in Fig. 9.5 were fully implemented. In any event, two contrasting views of management by objectives can be presented.

- The MBO programs most likely to be successful include (1) emphasis on objective setting; (2) frequent interaction and feedback between subordinates and managers regarding progress toward objectives, stumbling blocks, or the need for revised objectives; and (3) opportunities for subordinates' participation in setting their objectives, even though the final objectives may reflect the needs of the entire organization.[50]

■ When MBO is used as a top-down club to control people, it is likely to be ineffective.[51] If the values of those in the organization are strongly antagonistic to its philosophy and system, then MBO is probably doomed to failure.

Critical factors in the implementation of MBO programs are the values, philosophy, and role of top management. Top managers cannot be passive: They must explain, coordinate, and guide the program. Some firms begin to manage by objectives only to discover unsound organization structures or poor administrative practices. When top management is committed to MBO, changes throughout the organization can be made more easily, with the support and cooperation of middle and first-line managers.

Management by objectives is not a cure-all for solving management problems but its potential benefits justify careful consideration by managers. The MBO process can effectively link different levels of an organization, as well as its tactical and strategic planning.

PROGRAM EVALUATION AND REVIEW TECHNIQUE

The *Program Evaluation and Review Technique* (PERT) is a technique for showing how a strategic objective can be achieved. It involves the use of a special type of flow diagram that shows the activities, events, and schedule required to reach an objective. It is normally used for projects that have not been done before and will probably not be done again in exactly the same manner. The types of projects that lend themselves to the use of PERT would be construction of the Golden Gate Bridge, the Empire State Building, Disney World and Epcot Center, and even a house. The purpose of PERT is to analyze and specify in detail what is to be done, when it is to be done, and the likelihood of achieving the objective on time. It consists of four major elements: a network; resource allocation; time and cost considerations; and the critical path.[52]

NETWORK

The *network* is the foundation of the PERT approach. A network is a diagram showing the sequence and relationships of activities and events for completing a project. *Events* are decisions or accomplishment of activities. *Activities* are the physical or mental efforts required to move from one event to another. Activities are identified, responsibility for them is determined, and the amount of time for accomplishment is stated. Relationships are indicated by the sequence of events and activities in the network. For example, in Fig. 9.6, *event* 3 cannot occur until *activities* A, B, and C have been accomplished. If these activities are the responsibility of different managers, these managers must coordinate their work.

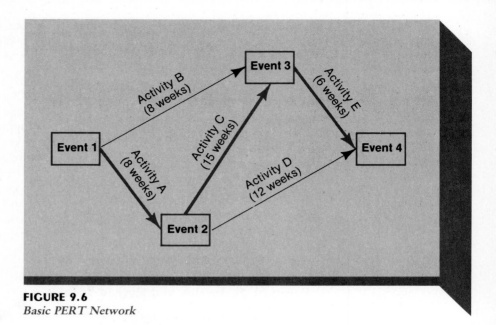

FIGURE 9.6
Basic PERT Network

RESOURCE ALLOCATION

In order to undertake the necessary activities, resources will be required. The availability of resources influences greatly the length of time between events and the costs associated with each activity. The types and amounts of labor, materials, equipment, and facilities needed to complete the activity must be estimated as accurately as possible. For example, in constructing a house, the first major activity is to excavate and pour footings. A contractor might estimate that one backhoe, one backhoe operator, and three laborers will be needed for four days (for a basic house without a basement). Other resources include sand for fill, wood for concrete forms, steel reinforcing rods, concrete, and the like.

COSTS AND TIME

The principal value of PERT is its ability to aid management in reducing costs and time requirements. Cost considerations are expressed in the form of estimated costs for each activity such as excavating and pouring footings in the construction of a house, against which actual costs can later be compared.

Time estimates for each activity are then made. For example, Fig. 9.6 shows that activity A, between events 1 and 2, should require eight weeks. Four time estimates are often developed for each activity.[53]

1. The ***most likely time*** is the estimated time required for an activity if normal problems and interruptions are considered. Figure 9.7 presents only the most likely times for each activity.

2. The ***optimistic time*** is the estimated time required for an activity if virtually no problems occur. In Fig. 9.7, we might estimate the optimistic time for activity C, between events 2 and 3, as 12 weeks, whereas the most likely time is shown as 15 weeks. The optimistic time is the minimum estimated time an activity will take. It is based on the assumption that everything will go right the first time.

3. The ***pessimistic time*** is the estimated time required for an activity if problems and interruptions of an unusual nature occur. In Fig. 9.7, we might estimate the pessimistic time for activity C as 18 weeks. The pessimistic time is the estimated maximum time an activity will take. It is based on the assumption that major problems will occur. However, even the pessimistic estimate of time does not normally include the rare possibility of catastrophic events: fires, tornadoes or hurricanes, floods, war, or riots.

4. The ***expected time*** represents some form of weighted average of the most likely, optimistic, and pessimistic time estimates.

Development of alternative time periods enables managers to anticipate and quickly react to problems or opportunities. If an activity is running behind schedule, a manager might find it advantageous to use overtime or hire additional people. Or, if an activity is ahead of schedule, the manager might speed up the delivery dates for supplies that are needed in later activities. These two types of responses are quite common uses of PERT on major construction projects.

Critical path

A ***path*** is the sequence of events and activities that should be followed over the course of a project. A complex project like the construction of Disney World or Epcot Center consists of thousands of activities and paths. Work is going on along each of the different paths separately and concurrently. The length of the entire project is determined by the *path with the longest elapsed time*. In order to shorten a project, managers must give the activities in the longest path the most attention.

The ***critical path*** is the longest time path through the network and determines the shortest possible completion time. Any delay of activities within the critical path will cause a delay in reaching the ultimate objective (occupying the building, opening Disney World, selling a new product). The critical path in Fig. 9.6 requires a total elapsed time of 29 weeks and can be found by adding the number of weeks scheduled for completion of the activities between events 1 and 2, events 2 and 3, and events 3 and 4.

IN PRACTICE
Constructing a House

The potential value of PERT and its key elements can be illustrated by its application to the construction of a modest single-story home with no basement. Table 9.4 shows the major activities, time estimates, the activity that must be completed immediately preceding the start of each subsequent activity, and the manpower needed for each activity. As you read down the list of major activities, it is apparent that they are presented roughly in the sequence required for completion. Each estimate of total time is based on the *expected work time* in days for completing each activity plus the *expected slack time* between the achievement of one event (site excavation and footings completed) and the start of the next activity (pour concrete foundations). For a general contractor that uses many subcontractors, it it almost impossible to schedule them so that they follow one another or work simultaneously on the house with precision. The total expected days do not include weekends and national holidays.

Nineteen categories of major job activities are identified in Table 9.4. Each of these categories could be broken into additional activities if a contractor wanted more detail.

A PERT diagram based on Table 9.4 is shown in Fig. 9.7 on p. 314. This network diagram contains (1) the major activities; designated as A, B, C, . . . , S; (2) the sequence of major job activities, and (3) the expected number of days between the beginning of a job activity and the start of the next. The circles designate events: Circle E1 represents the project beginning, circle E2 represents completion of the excavation and footings, and so on to circle E16, which represents project completion.

It is a relatively simple matter to find the critical path in Fig. 9.7. There are six paths in the construction of this house. To find the total completion time for each path, we simply add the days associated with job activity along the path, as follows:

$$A(6) + B(5) + E(1) + F(5) + H(13) + I(3) + J(1) + P(5) + Q(2) \quad = 41$$
$$A(6) + B(5) + E(1) + F(5) + H(13) + I(3) + K(10) + O(2) \quad\quad = 45$$
$$A(6) + B(5) + C(7) + G(3) + H(13) + I(3) + J(1) + P(5) + Q(2) \quad = 45$$
$$A(6) + B(5) + C(7) + G(3) + H(13) + I(3) + K(10) + O(2) \quad\quad = 49$$
$$A(6) + B(5) + C(7) + D(7) + L(3) + M(1) + R(5) + S(5) \quad\quad = 39$$
$$A(6) + B(5) + N(1) + R(5) + S(5) \quad\quad\quad\quad\quad\quad\quad\quad\quad = 22$$

The heavy arrows in color in Fig. 9.7 indicate the critical path. The critical path shows that 49 work days will be required to complete the house. Including weekends and holidays, this translates to about 10 weeks, or 2½ months. If the contractor wants to reduce construction time, efforts must be devoted to reducing the amount of time for those activities along the critical path. This is because the critical path is the *longest* time path.

TABLE 9.4 ■ ACTIVITIES AND TIMES FOR CONSTRUCTING A HOUSE

NAME OF JOB ACTIVITY	DESCRIPTION OF ACTIVITY	IMMEDIATE PRECEDING ACTIVITY	EXPECTED WORK TIME (DAYS)	EXPECTED SLACK TIME (DAYS)	TOTAL EXPECTED TIME (DAYS)	LABOR NEEDED
A	Excavate, pour footings	—	4	2	6	1 backhoe operator, 2 laborers
B	Pour concrete foundation	A	2	3	5	1 carpenter, 2 laborers
C	Erect frame and roof	B	4	3	7	5 carpenters, 5 laborers
D	Lay brickwork	C	6	1	7	3 masons, 2 laborers
E	Install drains	B	1	0	1	2 plumbers, 1 laborer
F	Install plumbing	E	3	2	5	2 plumbers, 1 laborer
G	Install wiring	C	2	1	3	3 electricians
H	Fasten plaster and plasterboard	F, G	10	3	13	2 laborers, 1 finisher
I	Lay finished flooring	H	3	0	3	2 carpenters
J	Install kitchen equipment	I	1	0	1	2 carpenters
K	Finish carpentry	I	7	3	10	2 carpenters
L	Finish roofing and flashing	D	2	1	3	4 roofers
M	Fasten gutters and downspouts	L	1	0	1	2 laborers
N	Lay storm drains	B	1	0	1	1 backhoe operator, 4 laborers
O	Sand and varnish floors	K	2	0	2	1 painter
P	Paint	J	3	2	5	2 painters
Q	Finish electrical work	P	2	0	2	2 electricians
R	Finish grading	M, N	2	3	5	3 laborers
S	Pour walks; landscape	R	5	0	5	1 landscape gardener, 2 laborers

Source: Adapted from J. D. Wiest and F. K. Levy, *A Management Guide to PERT/CPM*, 2nd ed. Englewood Cliffs, N.J.: Prentice-Hall, 1977, pp. 16–20. Adapted and used by permission of Prentice-Hall.

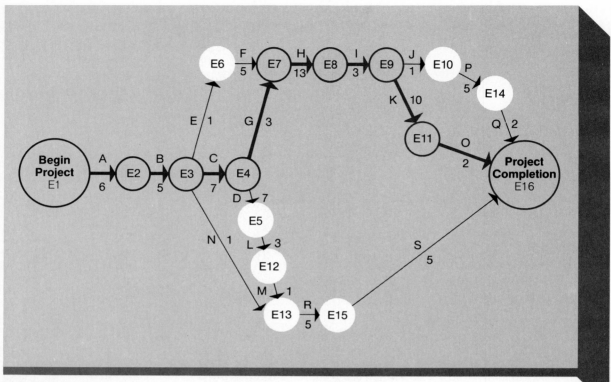

FIGURE 9.7
Simplified PERT Diagram for Constructing a House

NOTE: Heavy arrows in color indicate the critical path.

ASSESSMENT of PERT

The first major application of PERT occurred in 1958. It was used in the U.S. Navy's fleet ballistic missile program, more popularly known as the Polaris missile program, and was cited as a major reason for completion of this program two years ahead of the original schedule.

Some governmental agencies require companies with which they have contracts to use PERT or one of its variations. This technique has a wide range of action-planning applications, including those of filming a movie, building a plant, diversifying into a new business, or introducing a product.

After a project is underway, PERT becomes less of a planning aid and more of a control mechanism. Through a periodic reporting system, managers can monitor variances between actual and planned elapsed times and costs for each activity.

The application of PERT is most useful when projects are extremely complicated and require tight coordination among activities and events. The technique is an excellent method for reducing project time and cost requirements under the following conditions.[54]

- The project consists of a well-defined collection of job activities, which when all are completed marks the end of the project.

- The job activities may be started and stopped independently of each other. PERT is not good for continuous-flow processes such as oil refining, where jobs or operations necessarily follow each other in a strict time sequence.

- The job activities are ordered; that is, they must be performed in a technological sequence. Again, the foundation of a house must be constructed before the walls are erected.

CHAPTER SUMMARY

In this chapter, we presented only four of the many planning aids available to managers. We did this intentionally in order to convey a clear understanding of those that we believe are the most important and useful.

The discussion on forecasting was aimed at developing your abilities to perform the managerial role of *monitor*. This role focuses on scanning the environment for important signals and developments. The discussions on the dialectical inquiry method, management by objectives (MBO), and the program evaluation and review technique (PERT) should all serve to help develop your ability to perform the *entrepreneur* and *resource-allocator* managerial roles. The MBO presentation should also help you in performing the *leadership* managerial role.

The relationship of these planning aids to strategic and tactical planning is direct and clear. Through forecasting, we attempt to monitor the environment so that a sense of possible environmental futures can be developed. These possible environmental futures are a critical component in strategic planning. When we use the dialectical inquiry method, we increase the likelihood of a thorough analysis of strategic problems and development of innovative strategies. The dialectical inquiry method includes four phases: (1) assumption specification; (2) dialectical; (3) assumption integration; and (4) composite-strategy creation.

Management by objectives serves as a philosophy and method for linking strategic planning, tactical planning, and the day-to-day affairs of organizational life.

Seven interconnected, key steps comprise the MBO process: (1) organization definition and organizational objectives; (2) strategic objectives; (3) objectives of departments and individuals; (4) participation by affected individuals; (5) action planning for departments and individuals; (6) implementation and self-control; and (7) performance reviews of individuals, departments, and the organization as a whole. When the basic objectives and strategies have been developed for new or one-of-a-kind projects, PERT serves as a tactical planning aid to reduce time and costs for achieving them.

MANAGER'S VOCABULARY

action plan
activities
critical path
Delphi technique
dialectical inquiry method
events
expected time
extrapolation
forecasting
management by objectives (MBO)
most-likely time
multiple scenarios
network
normative/anticipatory scenario

optimistic time
path
pessimistic time
program evaluation review technique (PERT)
scenario
simulation models

REVIEW QUESTIONS

1. Define forecasting.
2. What are some ways of developing forecasts?
3. What is the dialectical inquiry method?
4. What is management by objectives?
5. What is the program evaluation and review technique?

DISCUSSION QUESTIONS

1. What are the similarities and differences between the Delphi technique and simulation models? Explain.
2. Use the management by objectives model to analyze the experiences you had in your last job. You should assess these experiences in terms of consistency with the basic MBO process in Fig. 9.5. Why might management not have used some or all of the steps in this process with you?
3. Use the program evaluation and review technique (PERT) to develop an action plan for the successful completion of your college education.
4. This chapter highlighted practices at Intel. What do you like and/or dislike about the Intel system of management as described? Explain.
5. Do you agree or disagree with the philosophy of MBO? Explain.

MANAGEMENT INCIDENTS AND CASES

Casual Togs

Casual Togs is a 20-year-old firm producing moderately priced women's apparel, headquartered in a midwestern city. About 80 percent of production is sold to large and middle-sized department stores in cities throughout the country. The remaining 20 percent is sold to small women's specialty shops. All clothes carry the firm's well-known brand label. Products are principally skirts and blouses, with some knitted dresses making up the balance.

The owner and principal stockholder, Cy Geldmark, is an entrepreneur. Geldmark served a long apprenticeship in the New York garment district and saved part of his meager wages until he could open his own firm, staffed primarily with relatives and friends. An innovator, Geldmark pioneered in the "mix and/or match" coordinate idea of fashion ensembles, whereby a customer of moderate means could build a complete wardrobe of work and casual clothes. Designers with trend-setting styles and above average quality (considering the semi-mass production methods employed) helped propel Casual Togs to a prominent position in the industry.

However, the mix-and-match coordinate idea was not patented and intense fashion competition has now developed from larger firms as well as from new, smaller companies with fresh fashion ideas. In Geldmark's words, price competition is "deadly." The company has rapidly expanded in the last five years, setting up production plants in eight southern states to capitalize on low wage rates in these areas.

All facilities in these states are leased. Notwithstanding the use of the latest in large-capacity cutters and high-speed sewing machines, production hinges on a great expenditure of careful, personal effort by the individual worker. Many quality checks are necessary before a garment is finished.

In an attempt to coordinate production and delivery, the company is constructing a new multimillion-dollar central distribution plant at the present home office location, where all administrative and some production functions are performed. All production runs will be shipped to this new facility; then they will be dispatched by a computer-programmed delivery–inventory scheduling method. This facility is planned to help cope with an increasingly serious problem of merchandise returned from customers who refuse acceptance because delivery is later than promised.

The industry is characterized by five distinct selling fashion "seasons"; consequently garments must be ordered, produced, and delivered within a relatively short time period. Based on pilot sales during the first two weeks of each season, forecasts are developed regarding the quantity and styles to be produced for the entire season. Once the bolts of cloth are cut into a particular season's patterns, there is no turning back. If pilot sales are not indicative of the rest of the season or if the sales forecast is in error, the company is saddled with stock that can be disposed of only through "off-price" outlets, usually at a loss.

In an effort to increase the accuracy of sales forecasting and to pinpoint specific reasons for late deliveries, Geldmark instituted a computer printout of each day's sales, as reported by telephone from field salesmen. This printout was, initially, distributed to the president, the vice-president of sales, the sales forecast manager, the treasurer, the production manager, and the eight regional sales managers. All of these people were located at the firm's headquarters offices. The printout was voluminous, often running one hundred or more pages.

Geldmark relied a great deal on his "feel of the situation" for making decisions. Although he made all final important operating and policy decisions, he said that all department heads should feel free to act as "you see fit"; he said that he would back any decision made without consultation with him. Despite Geldmark's exhortations that he need not be consulted, almost all vice-presidents and departmental managers conferred daily with him, usually regarding the progress of the then-current fashion season's products. During each fashion season many style modifications and quantity-level changes were made. With rare exceptions Geldmark made all important daily decisions in these matters.

These daily decision sessions were marked by emotional outbursts by various management personnel. The meetings were informal and nonscheduled and different groups would meet at different times with Geldmark. The groups were not formal or even based on functional problem lines. If one individual felt that a daily printout indicated change "X," regardless of whether or not it affected his department, he would go to the president asking that the change be effected. If another department manager or even a vice-president were present and disagreed, inevitably a shouting match developed in the president's office. Usually Geldmark remained impassive during these interchanges, giving his decision after all participants had finished.

Some management personnel said that Geldmark was "too lenient" and should curb these emotionally charged sessions because they were disruptive and led to erroneous decisions. These same critics pointed to Geldmark's reputation as an easy mark for suppliers; e.g., if a supplier had some previous tie from the old days or was remotely related to someone in Geldmark's family, he would be assured of at least some orders despite the fact that his prices were higher than those of competing suppliers.

Often the president's sister, Judy, who was vice-president in charge of administration, would wander into these daily decision sessions. She would often object to proposed changes on the grounds that they were "too damned expensive." She often countermanded a department manager's instructions and would hire and fire personnel without the manager's knowledge. Geldmark always backed Judy's decisions once they were made. Although the formal organizational chart depicted Judy and the treasurer as being on the same level, the treasurer, Stan Seeburg (Geldmark's nephew), was not allowed to approve any expenditure over $1000 without Judy's informal approval. But several sources reported that if Judy and her brother had an argument in private, Judy always deferred to her brother's decision.

For many years Geldmark's chief source of sales data and forecasts was Andy Johnson, sales forecast-budget manager. Johnson prepared daily, handwritten recaps from telephone reports in the earlier years and from the printout in more recent years. Using intuition and a very thorough knowledge of the garment industry, Johnson would prepare the season's forecasts and modify them as the actual sales starting coming in. He had rapport with Geldmark and was quite proud of the clearly evident esteem that the president had for him.

This rapport was important to Johnson for more than reasons of self-esteem. Johnson had been with the firm for 15 years but despite his knowledge had never been promoted. He resented this keenly. "At least," said Johnson once, "Cy listens to me more than these shirt-tail relatives." Johnson was one of the very few people who called the president by his first name in public.

In a recent change in office location, Johnson and his former co-worker, Sol Green, were moved from one large, shared office, which housed subordinates as well, to individual glass-partitioned offices. The subordinates were now located adjacent to Johnson's and Green's offices. After this move Green was promoted to manager of internal accounting and sales and was given control over all subordinates who previously had worked collectively for Johnson and Green.

Johnson was given one new man to help with sales forecasts and budgets. Johnson held a bachelor's degree in business. Smith, the new man, suggested several new methods of collating and analyzing the daily printout to Johnson, who abruptly rejected the ideas, saying, "Cy isn't used to getting data in that form; he would be confused by a change."

As the daily printouts began to be more detailed and more widely distributed, Johnson became more critical of them than usual. He said that they didn't "really" show what styles were leading and that there were many errors. Johnson quoted personal conversations with field salesmen to prove his points. When Smith cited several instances in which, on the recap, Johnson was combining several new styles in what had previously been one category, Johnson replied that he was using horse sense to report data in a way that Geldmark and others would best understand. Johnson was away from his desk for long periods of time, attending numerous management meetings that the president called. The pattern of these meetings was as before, or worse; there were loud, emotional arguments punctuated by fist-pounding and door-slamming.

The problem of returns was now most acute; on the average, 40 percent of all shipments were being returned. Although all management personnel agreed that the reason for returns was late delivery, there was no agreement as to what caused the late deliveries. Some managers argued that forecasting by styleline was inaccurate and resulted in poor production scheduling; others said that there was no coordination between the nine production centers and the shipping department which was located at the home office site. Still others said that shipping and/or production methods were not efficient. The production manager said that there was a disparity between the delivery dates given customers and those on the salesman's order, which served as the basis of a production run. The sales manager maintained that poor quality was the real reason for returns; customers did not want to become embroiled in arguments with home office personnel over quality questions and therefore they wrote "late delivery" on substandard merchandise because it was simpler.

In an effort to solve the dilemma, Geldmark hired an experienced market analyst who had a strong computer background, Stan Levin. Levin was given a private office and the authority to effect any changes he deemed necessary. Several events happened immediately: a sup-

plemental recap of the printout was published every day by Levin—in addition to Johnson's handwritten recap—and the printout format was changed. Green objected strongly to the new format, saying that it did not provide accounting with the categorizations necessary for their work. Johnson referred to Levin as "this egotistical, snot-nosed kid."

At the same time, several new designers were hired, salesmen's commissions schedules were changed, many regional vice-presidents were put on the road "temporarily," and Johnson, backed by Geldmark, cut all departments' budgets by 15 percent (the company was in the middle of a twelve-month budget period).

Approximately four weeks after all of these changes had occurred problems continued to arise. Returns had increased to an even higher level and many old customers had stopped ordering, saying that the poor quality and late deliveries made Casual Togs too undependable. Performance of the nine plant centers fell, on the average, 15 percent under previously established production goals. In addition, two of the new designers resigned. Johnson, Green, and Levin would not speak to each other. Johnson began distributing two daily sales recap reports to a select group of top managers and the computer services department complained directly to Geldmark that their new work load was too great because Levin now required them to produce a daily selling forecast, by week, month, and season.[55]

Questions

1. What are the primary reasons for this firm's problems?

2. Could any of the forecasting approaches discussed in this chapter be used by Casual Togs? How?

3. Could MBO help this firm? Explain.

4. Could PERT help this firm? Explain.

REFERENCES _____

1. Adapted from "U.S. Markets," *Electronics,* January 12, 1984, pp. 127–141. *Also see* "Superchips: The New Frontier," *Business Week,* June 10, 1985, pp. 82–85.

2. "U.S. Markets," p. 124.

3. D. Bell, *The Coming of Post Industrial Society: A Venture in Social Forecasting,* New York: Basic Books, 1973. *Also see* A. T. Sommers, *Keeping*

Track of the U.S. Economy. Lexington, Mass.: Lexington Books, 1985.

4. L. Fahey, W. R. King, and V. K. Narayanan, "Environmental Scanning and Forecasting in Strategic Planning—The State of the Art." In R. Hussey (Ed.), *The Truth about Corporate Planning: International Research into the Practice of Planning.* Elmsford, New York: Pergamon, 1983, pp. 495–509; A. Katz, "Evaluating the Environment: Economic and Technological Factors." In W. D. Guth (Ed.), *Handbook of Business Strategy.* Boston: Warren, Gorham and Lamont, 1985, pp. 2-1–2-18.

5. R. E. Linneman and H. E. Klein, "The Use of Multiple Scenarios by U.S. Industrial Companies: A Comparison Study, 1977–1981," *Long Range Planning,* December, 1983, pp. 94–101; R. E. Linneman and H. E. Klein, "Using Scenarios in Strategic Decision Making," *Business Horizons,* January–February, 1985, pp. 64–74.

6. H. Kahn and A. J. Wiener, *The Year 2000: A Framework for Speculation on the Next Thirty-Three Years.* New York: Macmillan, 1967.

7. C. Ducot and G. J. Lubben, "A Typology for Scenarios," *Futures,* 1980, **12**:51–57; P. C. Nutt, *Planning Methods.* New York: John Wiley & Sons, 1984.

8. Adapted from F. P. Popoff, "Planning the Multinational's Future," *Business Horizons,* March–April, 1984, pp. 64–68. Copyright © 1984 by the Foundation for the School of Business at Indiana University. Used with permission. *Also see* T. N. Gladwin, "Assessing the Multinational Environment for Corporate Opportunity." In W. D. Guth (Ed.), *Handbook of Business Strategy.* Boston: Warren, Gorham and Lamont, 1985, pp. 7-1–7-51.

9. K. Nair and R. K. Sarin, "Generating Future Scenarios—Their Use in Strategic Planning," *Long Range Planning,* June 1979, pp. 57–61.

10. A. Delbecq, A. Van de Ven, and A. Gustafson, *Group Techniques for Program Planning: A Guide to Nominal Group and Delphi Processes.* Glenview, Ill.: Scott, Foresman, 1975.

11. D. Roman, "Technological Forecasting in the Decision Process," *Academy of Management Journal,* 1970, **13**:127–138.

12. J. Pfeffer, *New Look at Education.* Princeton, N.J.: Western, 1969, p. 155.

13. R. Bunning, "The Delphi Technique: A Projection Tool for Serious Inquiry." In J. Jones and J. Pfeiffer (Eds.), *The 1979 Annual Handbook for Group Facilitators.* La Jolla, Calif: University Associates, 1979, pp. 174–181.

14. T. H. Naylor and H. Schauland, "Experience with Corporate Simulation Models—A Survey." In R. Hussey (Ed.), *The Truth about Corporate Planning: International Research into the Practice of Planning.* Elmsford, N.Y.: Pergamon, 1983, pp. 549–563.

15. H. J. Watson, "The Application of Simulation: A Survey of Industry Practice," *Interfaces,* 1983, **13**:47–52; R. J. Thierauf, R. C. Klekamp, and M. L. Rueve, *Management Science: A Model Formulation Approach with Computer Application.* Columbus, Ohio: Merrill, 1985; K. Olm, G. Eddy, and E. Krus, *Strategic Management Simulated.* Columbus, Ohio: Merrill, 1986.

16. H. Schollhammer, "Long-Range Planning in Multinational Firms," *Columbia Journal of World Business,* 1971, **6**:79–86.

17. G. Steiner (Ed.), *Managerial Long-Range Planning.* New York: McGraw-Hill, 1963, p. 60.

18. "The Forecasters Flunk," *Time,* August 27, 1984, pp. 42–44; L. H. Clark Jr. and A. L. Malabre Jr., "Business Forecasters Find Demand Is Weak in Their Own Business," *Wall Street Journal,* September 7, 1984, pp. 1, 18.

19. J. C. Chambers, S. K. Mullick, and D. D. Smith, "How to Choose the Right Forecasting Technique." In D. N. Dickson (Ed.), *Using Logical Techniques for Making Better Decisions.* New York: John Wiley & Sons, 1983, pp. 453–483.

20. T. H. Naylor, *Corporate Planning Models.* Reading, Mass.: Addison-Wesley, 1979; G. R. Warner, "Things to Come in Planning Technology," *Financial Executive,* May 1980, pp. 34–40; M. A. Moses, "Formal Corporate Strategic Planning Analysis Systems: A Computer-Based Approach." In W. D. Guth (Ed.), *Handbook of Business Strategy.* Boston: Warren, Gorham and Lamont, 1985, pp. 22-1–22-28.

21. R. O. Mason, "A Dialectical Approach to Strategic Planning," *Management Science,* 1969, **15**:B402–B414.

22. C. Schwenk and H. Thomas, "Formulating the Mess: The Role of Decision Aids in Problem Formulation," *Omega,* 1983, **11**:239–252. *Also see* H. I. Ansoff, "Strategic Response in a Turbulent Environment." In W. D. Guth (Ed.), *Handbook of Business Strategy.* Boston: Warren, Gorham and Lamont, 1985, pp. 4-1–4-17; D. Dery, *Problem Definition in Policy Analysis.* Lawrence: University of Kansas Press, 1984.

23. I. I. Mitroff and R. O. Mason, "Stakeholders of Executive Decision Making." In S. Srivastva and Associates (Eds.), *The Executive Mind.* San Francisco: Jossey-Bass, 1983, pp. 144–168.

24. A. Grandori, "A Prescriptive Contingency View of Organizational Decision Making," *Administrative Science Quarterly,* 1984, **29**:192–209.

25. I. I. Mitroff and J. R. Emshoff, "On Strategic Assumption-Making: A Dialectical Approach to Policy and Planning," *Academy of Management Review,* 1979, **4**:1–12.

26. I. I. Mitroff, *Stakeholders of the Organizational Mind.* San Francisco: Jossey-Bass, 1983.

27. Adapted from R. O. Mason, I. I. Mitroff, and V. P. Barabba, "Creating the Manager's Plan Book: A New Route to Effective Planning." In A. J. Rowe, R. O. Mason, and K. E. Dickel, *Strategic Management and Business Policy: A Methodological Approach.* Reading, Mass.: Addison-Wesley, 1982, pp. 82–86. Adapted and used with permission.

28. See the following as examples of assessments of this method: R. A. Cosier and J. C. Aplin, "A Critical View of Dialectical Inquiry as a Tool in Strategic Planning," *Strategic Management Journal,* 1980, **1**:343–356; R. A. Cosier, "Approaches for the Experimental Examination of the Dialectic," *Strategic Management Journal,* 1983, **4**:79–84; I. I. Mitroff and R. O. Mason, "The Metaphysics of Policy and Planning: A Reply to Cosier," *Academy of Management Review,* 1981, **6**:649–651; C. R. Schwenk and R. Cosier, "Effects of the Expert, Devil's Advocate, and Dialectical Inquiry Methods on Prediction Performance," *Organizational Behavior and Human Performance,* 1980, **26**:409–424.

29. P. C. Nutt, "Hybrid Planning Methods," *Academy of Management Review,* 1982, **7**:442–454.

30. G. Odiorne, *MBO II: A System for Managerial Leadership for the 80's.* Belmont, Calif.: Fearon Pitman, 1979.

31. W. Giegold, *Volume I: Strategic Planning and the MBO Process.* New York: McGraw-Hill, 1978.

32. J. Muczyk, "Dynamics and Hazards of MBO Application," *Personnel Administrator,* May 1979, pp. 51–62. *Also see* R. H. Kilmann, *Beyond the Quick Fix: Managing Five Tracks to Organizational Success.* San Francisco: Jossey-Bass, 1985.

33. W. Giegold, *Volume II: Objective Setting and the MBO Process.* New York: McGraw-Hill, 1978.

34. M. Richard, *Organizational Goal Structures.* St. Paul, Minn.: West, 1978.

35. For a more complete discussion of objective setting see: E. A. Locke and G. P. Latham, *Goal Setting: A Motivational Technique that Works!* Englewood Cliffs, N.J.: Prentice-Hall, 1984.

36. "The Fortune Directory of the Largest U.S. Industrial Corporations," *Fortune,* April 30, 1984, p. 286.

37. Reprinted by permission of the *Harvard Business Review.* Excerpts from "Creativity by the Numbers," an interview with Robert N. Noyce (May–June 1980). Copyright © 1980 by the President and Fellows of Harvard College; all rights reserved. *Also see* T. Wolfe, "The Tinkerings of Robert Noyce," *Esquire,* December 1983.

38. H. Levinson, "Management by Whose Objectives?" *Harvard Business Review,* July–August 1970, pp. 125–135.

39. H. Weihrich, "An Uneasy Look at the MBO Jungle: Toward a Contingency Approach to MBO," *Management International Review,* 1976, **16**:103–109.

40. D. Klinger, "Does Your MBO Program Include Clear Performance Contracts?" *Personnel Administrator,* May 1979, pp. 65–74; D. J. Fellner and B. Sulzer-Azaroff, "A Behavioral Analysis of Goal Setting," *Journal of Organizational Behavior Management,* 1984, **6**:33–51.

41. G. Shing-Yung Chang, "The Effects of Participative versus Assigned Goal Setting on Intrinsic Motivation," *Journal of Management,* 1983, **9**:55–64; M. Erez, "The Role of Goal Acceptance in Goal Setting

and Task Performance," *Academy of Management Review,* 1983, 8:454–463; G. P. Latham and T. P. Steele, "The Motivational Effects of Participation versus Goal Setting on Performance," *Academy of Management Journal,* 1983, 26:406–417.

42. A. Raia, *Managing by Objectives.* Glenview, Ill.: Scott, Foresman, 1974.

43. H. Weihrich, "TAMBO: Team Approach to MBO." *University of Michigan Business Review,* 1979, 31(3):12–17.

44. P. Mali, *Improving Total Productivity: MBO Strategies for Business, Government, and Not-for-Profit Organizations.* New York: John Wiley & Sons, 1978; M. K. McCuddy and M. H. Griggs, "Goal Setting and Feedback in the Management of a Professional Department: A Case Study," *Journal of Organizational Behavior Management,* 1984, 6:53–65.

45. W. Giegold, *Volume III: Performance Appraisal and the MBO Process.* New York: McGraw-Hill, 1978.

46. R. Babcock and P. Sorensen Jr., "An MBO Checklist: Are Conditions Right for Implementation?" *Management Review,* June 1979, pp. 59–62.

47. M. McConkie, "A Clarification of the Goal Setting and Appraisal Processes in MBO," *Academy of Management Review,* 1979, 4:29–40.

48. J. Quick, "Dyadic Goal Setting within Organizations: Role-Making and Motivational Considerations," *Academy of Management Review,* 179, 4:360–380.

49. Adapted from A. S. Grove, "Keeping Favoritism and Prejudice Out of Evaluations," *Wall Street Journal,* February 27, 1984, p. 22; A. S. Grove, *High Output Management.* New York: Random House, 1983.

50. J. Ivancevich, "Changes in Performance in a Management by Objectives Program," *Administrative Science Quarterly,* 1974, pp. 563–574; C. D. Pringle and J. G. Longenecker, "The Ethics of MBO," *Academy of Management Review,* 1982, 7:305–312.

51. S. Kerr, "Some Modifications in MBO as an OD Strategy," *Academy of Management Proceedings,* 1972.

52. *New Uses and Management Implications of PERT.* New York: Booz Allen and Hamilton, 1964. *Also see* J. Meredith and S. J. Mantel, *Project Management: A Managerial Approach,* 3rd ed. New York: John Wiley & Sons 1985; D. I. Cleland and W. R. King, *Systems Analysis and Project Management.* New York: McGraw-Hill, 1983.

53. R. W. Miller, "How To Plan and Control with PERT." In D. N. Dickson (Ed.), *Using Logical Techniques for Making Better Decisions.* New York: John Wiley & Sons, 1983, pp. 33–53.

54. J. D. Wiest and F. K. Levy, *A Management Guide to PERT/CPM,* 2nd ed. Englewood Cliffs, N.J.: Prentice-Hall, 1977, p. 3.

55. Developed by P. J. Wolff, Associate Professor, Dundalk Community College, Baltimore. Used with permission.

ORGANIZING

Basic Concepts of Organization Design

LEARNING OBJECTIVES

After studying this chapter, you should be able to:

- Discuss the key factors affecting the design of an organization.

- Identify four common ways managers group activities in organizations.

- List the advantages and disadvantages of these four ways.

- Describe the basic concepts of coordination and how they are used by managers.

- State the advantages and disadvantages of centralization versus decentralization.

- Identify the reasons why line and staff conflicts exist in organizations.

CHAPTER OUTLINE

PREVIEW CASE

Bausch & Lomb

In 1982, Bausch & Lomb's president, Dan Gill, stated that the Instrument's Division had one of the most exciting growth opportunities for the company since the division introduced the soft contact lens in 1971. In mid-1983, the Instruments Division reported huge losses in sales and profits. What happened?

The Instruments Division for Bausch and Lomb was an assortment of 30 different products that competed against Hewlett-Packard, Texas Instruments, IBM, and others. Top management at Bausch & Lomb hired Jim Edwards to turn the Instruments Division into a profitable one. Edwards announced a radical reorganization for the group. He divided manufacturing responsibility among three new divisions and created a fourth division to manage all sales and services. To carry out this new structure, he introduced the matrix management system he had used at IBM. Under this system, the head of a manufacturing division retained responsibility for the division's profits or losses, but had little direct control over the salesforce. The sales people reported to the head of marketing. Product managers with complete responsibility for a range of instruments acted as coordinators between separate manufacturing divisions and marketing.

On paper, the reorganization was appealing. It promised to bring Bausch & Lomb's formerly autonomous businesses into a manageable unit. This would have eliminated costly practices, such as overlapping research and development programs.

But the reorganization did not work out as planned and things fell apart. Salespersons who had been responsible for selling simple microscopes didn't have the knowledge to sell complex chemical analysis devices. The top managers of the three manufacturing divisions complained that they lost authority over the salesforce. As losses mounted, Edwards attempted to reduce costs. This was done by firing 10% of the salesforce, cutting R&D expenses, and delaying the introduction of new products. By mid-1983, the Instruments Division reported a 32% drop in income. The top management at Bausch & Lomb replaced Edwards. Dan Gill immediately did away with the matrix system and made all four instrument-division presidents report directly to him. He returned the sales and marketing responsibilities to each manufacturing division.[1]

Source: © 1974 Fundamental Photographs.

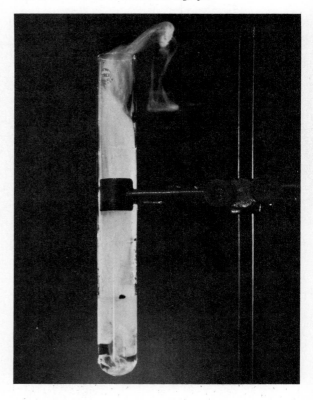

Edwards took over a division that was suffering from low motivation and morale, poor decision making, lack of coordination, and rising costs. When he examined these problems closely, he identified several factors. Motivation and morale were low because employees thought that they had little opportunity for responsibility, advancement, and recognition. Authority was not delegated sufficiently, which often resulted in late or inappropriate decisions. Adequate procedures for evaluating results did not exist. Methods for coordinating sales calls for the various product lines were lacking. Costs were rising because of duplication of activities. Some of the questions facing Edwards were:

1. Should the overall structure of the Instruments Division be centralized or decentralized?
2. Should divisions be established along product lines to secure the benefits of specialization?
3. What types of coordination mechanisms are there to choose from?

Edwards believed that the division's problems could be solved by a system that had worked well elsewhere. As Edwards found out, what he thought was a solution to the problem, wasn't. The questions that Edwards faced are the focus of this chapter; it provides some answers to these questions and presents alternatives that he could have chosen. The failure of this reorganization at Bausch & Lomb indicates that effective organizational restructuring must be based on a thorough understanding of the factors and people involved. In this chapter, we present the basic concepts of organizational structure. In Chapter 11, we will explore how environment, technology, and informational factors influence the design chosen by top managers.

ORGANIZING AND ORGANIZATIONAL STRUCTURE

In Chapter 1, we indicated that successful firms make sure that both resources and structure are appropriate to the tasks to be done. *Organizing* is the managerial function that is concerned with the arrangement of an organization's resources—people, materials, technology, and finances—in order to achieve organizational objectives. Organizing involves decisions about the division of work, the allocation of authority and responsibility, and the coordination of tasks. This function increases in importance as a firm grows because growth adds complexity. Whether growth means producing more of the same or entering new product or service lines, the number of functions, activities, and personnel increases. Consequently, top and middle managers become further removed from production work or the direct provision of services to customers. They are faced with the necessity of delegating more responsibility and authority. But, at the same time, they must retain a firm grasp on how well the organization is achieving its objectives. Thus the design of an *organizational structure* that addresses these problems is one of management's main concerns.

The organizational structure is the *formal* system of working relationships that both divides and integrates tasks. Its purpose is to enable the people in an organization to work together effectively by (1) allocating people and resources to tasks and providing the means for communication through job descriptions, organization charts, and lines of authority; (2) giving employees an understanding of what is expected of them through rules, regulations, operating procedures, and performance standards; and (3) assisting managers in making decisions and solving problems through procedures for collecting and evaluating information.

Elements of Organizational Structure

Five elements comprise an organization's structure.[2]

1. Specialization of activities
2. Standardization of activities
3. Coordination of activities
4. Centralization and decentralization of decision making
5. Size of the work unit

Specialization of activities refers to the identification and assignment of group and individual tasks throughout the organization. Middle managers often are given the responsibility for directing the work of several related groups of activities; functional and first-line managers usually are assigned one specific area of work, such as marketing, accounting, or quality control. Subordinates, individually or in work groups, are given specialized tasks to perform.

Standardization of activities refers to the procedures used by an organization to ensure predictable behaviors from its employees when doing their jobs. To standardize is to make uniform and consistent. Managers use written job descriptions, instructions, rules, and regulations to standardize the jobs of subordinates; application forms to standardize the selection of employees; and on-the-job training programs to develop special, standardized skills and to reinforce values that are important to the success of the organization.

Coordination of activities refers to the procedures that integrate the activities of employees within an organization. In bureaucratic organizations, rules and regulations may be sufficient to achieve coordination. In other types of organizations rules and regulations alone cannot achieve integration; knowledge of company-wide problems, willingness to share responsibility, and effective communication skills become the keys to achieving coordination.

Centralization and *decentralization* of decision making refers to the location of decision-making power. In a centralized organization, such as Tandy

Corporation, decisions are made by top managers and then communicated to lower-level managers. In a decentralized structure, such as Hewlett-Packard, some of the initial decision-making power is given to lower-level managers. Large business firms often use a combination of the two approaches, centralizing certain decision-making functions and decentralizing others.

Size of the work unit refers to the number of employees in a work group. The work group may be a division, department, task group, or some other subdivision of the organization. For our purposes, we use the term *department* for the work unit to identify a group of employees having a common task objective and set of activities. The number of employees in a department is dependent on the type of activity performed, the technology used, and the number of subordinates that a manager can effectively supervise.

The Organization Chart

One way of describing the relationship of these five elements for an organization is to show them on an *organization chart.* It is a diagram that indicates the location within the organization of decision-making positions, departments, and functions. Figure 10.1 is the organization chart for the Brooklyn Union Gas Company and illustrates what such charts normally show. Note that upper-level management positions are shown by position title and that the lines lead to departments (functions) for which each manager is responsible. The chart could be expanded to show the organizational structure in greater detail by including the titles of departmental managers and work groups of the departments according to the specific activities performed.

In general, the organization chart conveys five major points about an organization's structure.

1. *Activities of organization.* The chart as a whole indicates the range of activities in which the organization is involved.

2. *Subdivisions of organization.* Each box represents a subdivision of the organization responsible for a portion of the work.

3. *Type of work performed.* The label in each box indicates the department's area of responsibility.

4. *Levels of management.* The chart shows the management hierarchy; all persons who report to the same individual are on the same management level, or horizontal level on the chart.

5. *Lines of authority.* The lines that connect the boxes show the official lines of authority and channels of communication for the organization.

The advantages and disadvantages of an organization chart have been debated by managers for years.[3] One advantage is that the chart gives employees a picture of how the pieces of the entire organization fit together; how their specialized work relates to the whole. Managers, employees, and others also know who reports to whom. In addition, the chart pinpoints

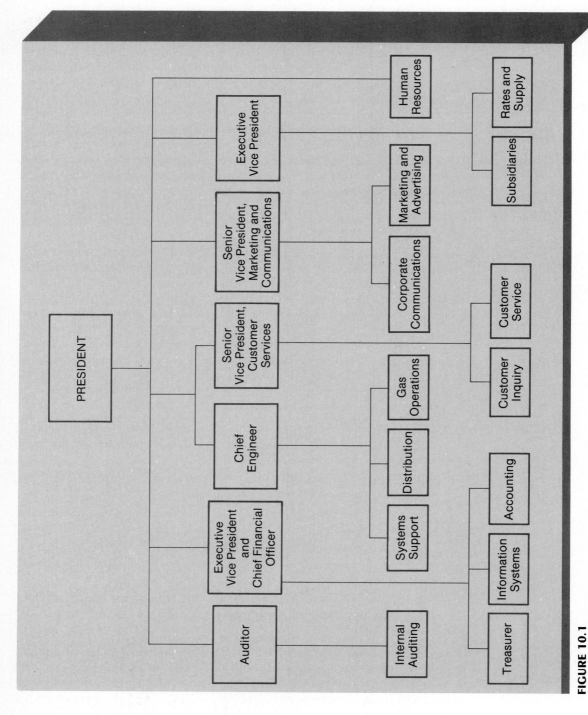

FIGURE 10.1
Organization Chart: Brooklyn Union Gas Company

Source: Harry Sutherland, Assistant Manager, Human Resources, Brooklyn Union Gas, Brooklyn, N.Y., 1985.

where an employee should go with a particular problem. Finally, the chart enables managers to see where potential gaps or duplication exists.

A major disadvantage of the organization chart is that it cannot show everything about an organization's structure—and it can become outdated very quickly. For example, it cannot show who has the greater degree of *informal* responsibility, authority, relationships, and channels of communication that have been established, without which an organization could not function. Finally, employees may infer status and power differences based on the distance their box is from the president's box. These disadvantages can be overcome if the charts are used only for their intended purpose: to reveal the basic, formal structure of the organization as a whole.

BASES OF DEPARTMENTALIZATION

A fundamental requirement in the design of an organization is that people be given levels of responsibility and authority that are consistent with the tasks to be performed. The total range of tasks to be performed by an organization have to be grouped and assigned to people in some systematic manner. Thus the question is: On what basis should the people in the organization be grouped? *Departmentalization* is the process of subdividing work and assigning it to departments within the company. This can be accomplished in four general ways: by function, place, product, and matrix; each has advantages for management.

Moreover, tasks and people can be grouped differently at various levels in the organization. Large organizations (IBM, GM, GE, Mellon Bank) often use several types of departmentalization. Such organizations have found that it is possible—and may even be necessary—to use several forms of departmentalization in order to deal with very complex situations, while maintaining the principle of division of work. Dividing the work is the essential first step but the problem of relating subordinates to supervisors, function to function, and manager remains.

The choice of how to group people and their activities depends on the factors that management believes are the most significant. However, we believe that the key to effective departmentalization is in grouping people and activities in a way that eases the flow of communication and information to get the job done.

DEPARTMENTALIZATION by FUNCTION

Functions are what an organization actually does (production, marketing, finance). *Functional departmentalization* groups members of an organization who have the expertise and draw on the same resources to perform a common

TABLE 10.1 ■ ADVANTAGES AND DISADVANTAGES OF FUNCTIONAL DEPARTMENTALIZATION

ADVANTAGES

1. Promotes skill specialization.
2. Reduces duplication of resources and coordination problems within functional area.
3. Enhances career development within department.
4. Superiors and subordinates share common expertise.
5. Promotes high-quality technical problem solving.

DISADVANTAGES

1. Emphasizes routine tasks.
2. Reduces communications between departments.
3. May create conflict over product priorities.
4. Can make scheduling difficult across departments.
5. Focuses on departmental as opposed to organizational issues.
6. Develops managers who are experts in narrow fields.

Source: Adapted from J. McCann and J. Galbraith, "Interdepartmental Relations." In *Handbook of Organizational Design,* vol. 2. P. Nystrom and W. Starbuck (Eds.). New York: Oxford University Press, 1981, p. 61.

set of activities. Functional grouping is a widely used and accepted managerial practice.[4]

The names of basic functions vary, depending on the nature of an organization. Hospitals do not have marketing departments but they do have radiology departments; churches do not have production departments but they do have education departments. Airlines (TWA, U.S. Air, Pan Am) use the terms *operations* (production), *traffic* and *finance*. Large department stores (Lazarus, May Company, J.C. Penney, Sears) use the terms *finance, general merchandising, publicity,* and *general superintendent;* for these businesses the traditional functions of production, selling, and finance are combined with other activities.

Advantages

The grouping of activities and employees by function has several advantages (Table 10.1), especially when an organization is small.[5] This method is particularly appropriate for a company that sells a narrow range of products or services almost exclusively within one market area. Activities are grouped in separate departments where specialists can work on problems common to only one set of activities. Methods of training, experience, and resources can be shared by everyone in the group. Job satisfaction is increased because people in the group share similar work interests. Employees have clearly defined career paths, which makes it easier for a company to hire and retain personnel.

Grouping by function is economical because it is a simple structure: there is only one sales function, one manufacturing facility, and one set of managers;

IN PRACTICE
STATE FARM
INSURANCE
COMPANY

State Farm Insurance Company is organized by function as shown in Fig. 10.2. Specialists in separate departments (actuarial, advertising, research) perform different functions, all of which contributes to the common service and its market. For example, all advertising for the company is handled by the advertising department at the home office. The advertising and other major functional decisions made in the home office are then communicated to the regional offices.

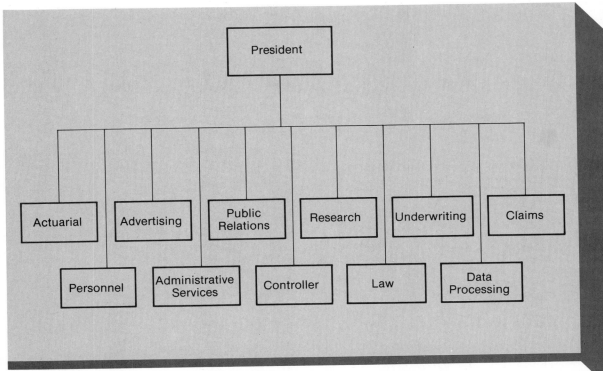

FIGURE 10.2
Departmentalization by Function: State Farm Insurance Company

Source: Adapted from the organization chart of the State Farm Insurance Company furnished by Richard Wagster, Division Manager, Dallas, 1985.

capital and administrative expenses can be held to a minimum. Decision making and strategic coordination are concentrated in the hands of top management, rather than being delegated to lower-level managers.

Disadvantages

Difficulties (Table 10.1) with functional departmentalization start to arise when an organization diversifies products, market, or services. Quick decisions are harder to get because functional managers have to report to headquarters. When friction develops, it can't be quickly resolved: A sales representative may lose a potentially good account by having to wait a long time for the production manager to make a product scheduling decision. It is often more difficult to determine accountability and levels of performance. Who is to blame for the loss in profits, production, sales, personnel? Coordination of departments may become a problem for top management; functional departmentalization tends to deemphasize the goals of the firm as a whole, allowing departments to concentrate on meeting their own budgets and schedules without regard for the entire organization. Finance people are finance experts and production people are production experts; experts often have difficulty seeing the point of view of others and the firm as a whole, thus complicating coordination among activities. In other words, people develop a loyalty to the department, creating walls between departments instead of identifying with their counterparts in other functional areas. Considerable effort is thus required by top management to ensure coordination.

Departmentalization by Place

Departmentalization on the basis of geographic area, or *place departmentalization,* is a rather common method of organization for firms that operate in many different locations. It is based on the assumption that efficiency will result from grouping all activities in a given territory and assigning overall responsibility for them to one manager. Place departmentalization is used by many major companies, which establish regional and district offices. Similarly, many federal agencies, such as the IRS, the Federal Reserve Board, the courts, and the Postal Service, use place departmentalization as the basis of organi-

**IN PRACTICE
Southland
Corporation**

Southland Corporation uses place departmentalization as the organizational structure for its 7000 7-Eleven stores. This structure, shown in Fig. 10.3, gives Southland the ability to respond easily to unique customer and marketplace characteristics in the various regions. It also has certain personnel-management implications. For example, in some regions the stores' employees are union members and in other regions they are not. Therefore different personnel procedures are used from region to region.

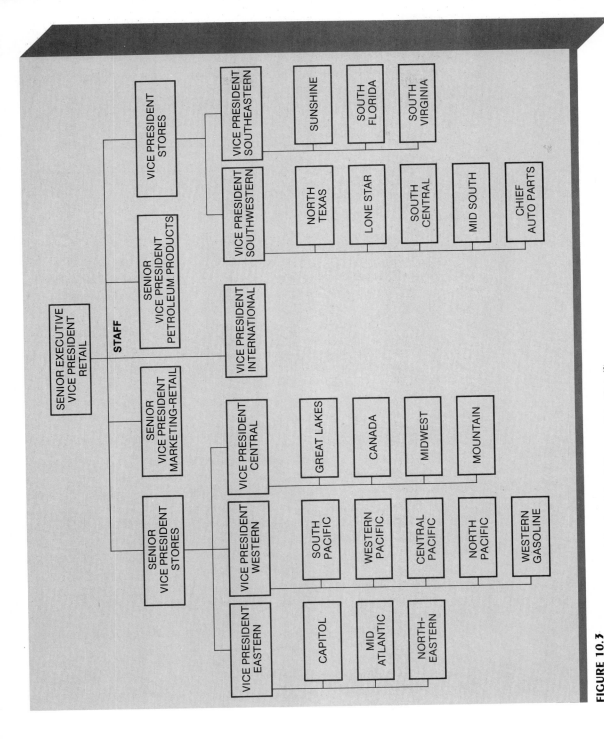

FIGURE 10.3

Departmentalization by Place: The Southland Corporation (Retail)

Source: Mark Rigg, Vice-President for Human Resources, The Southland Corporation, Dallas, 1985.

TABLE 10.2 ■ ADVANTAGES AND DISADVANTAGES OF PLACE DEPARTMENTALIZATION

ADVANTAGES

1. Equipment used for products all in one place.
2. Managers develop expertise in solving problems peculiar to one location.
3. Managers know customers' problems.
4. Suited for multinational organizations.

DISADVANTAGES

1. Duplication of all functions—accounting, purchasing, manufacturing—for each product line at all locations.
2. May cause conflicts between each location's objectives and corporate objectives.
3. May require extensive rules and regulations to coordinate and ensure uniformity of quality among locations.
4. Does not foster employees' knowledge of problems at other locations.

zation in providing nationwide services. Many multinational firms use this form of departmentalization because of cultural and legal differences in various countries.[6] Also, the lack of uniformity in market structure and differences in production methods make geographical considerations important for the multinational firm.

Advantages

The advantages of place departmentalization (Table 10.2) are primarily those of economy and efficiency. For the production function, this can mean location near raw materials or suppliers and/or in the primary market area for the finished products. Potential gains include lower costs for materials, lower freight rates, and (perhaps) lower labor costs. The marketing function can benefit from having salespeople spend more time selling and less time traveling. They can get to know the customer's needs and serve the customer better. Being closer to the customer may permit a salesperson to pinpoint the marketing strategy most likely to succeed in that area.

Disadvantages

Place departmentalization also has some disadvantages (Table 10.2). It clearly increases control problems for the central corporate staff and leads to duplication of activities that could be performed centrally under functional departmentalization. Regional and district managers usually want some control over their own purchasing, personnel, expensive computer equipment, and other internal activities. In order to ensure uniformity of services, extensive rules and regulations are used by the IRS, Southland (7-Eleven stores), Steak and Ale, Searle Optical, Zale Jewelry, and others to coordinate activities in their various districts.

Departmentalization by Product

An appropriate way to group activities when an organization produces two or more products that are different in technical makeup, production process, and market distribution is by *product departmentalization.*[7] This structure is being used more frequently, particularly by large multiproduct companies, such as PepsiCo, Procter & Gamble, General Foods Corporation, Mack Trucks, Johnson & Johnson, and others. These organizations started with a functional structure, but their growth and subsequent management problems made functional departmentalization unworkable and/or uneconomical.

Advantages
One of the advantages of product departmentalization (Table 10.3) is that all employees make specialized contributions to a particular product line. Costs, profits, problems, and successes can be pinpointed to specific products. This not only assists managers in assigning accountability, but also produces managers who are more likely to remain sensitive to product needs and changing consumer tastes.

TABLE 10.3 ■ ADVANTAGES AND DISADVANTAGES OF PRODUCT DEPARTMENTALIZATION

ADVANTAGES

1. Suited for fast changes in a product.
2. Allows for product visibility.
3. Fosters a concern for customers' wants and needs.
4. Clearly defines responsibilities.
5. Recognizes need for interdepartmental cooperation.
6. Develops managers who can think across functional lines.

DISADVANTAGES

1. May not use skills and resources effectively.
2. Does not foster coordination of activities across products.
3. Fosters politics in resource allocation.
4. Restricts problem solving to single product.
5. Limits career mobility for personnel outside their product line.

Source: Adapted from J. McCann and J. Galbraith, "Interdepartmental Relations." In *Handbook of Organizational Design*, vol. 2. P. Nystrom and W. Starbuck (Eds.). New York: Oxford University Press, 1981, p. 61.

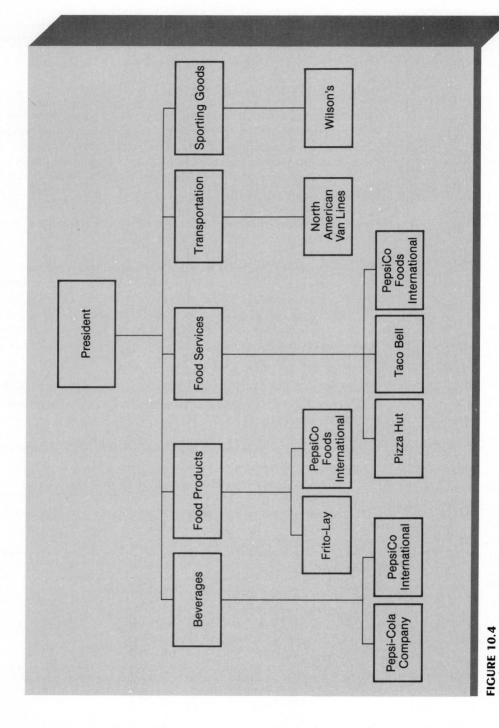

FIGURE 10.4
Product Departmentalization: PepsiCo, Inc.

Source: PepsiCo, Inc., *Annual Report*, 1984.

IN PRACTICE
PepsiCo, Inc.

PepsiCo, Inc., is engaged in five totally different areas of business, as shown in Fig. 10.4. Each of these product groups operates as an individual business. The president of PepsiCo believes that the strength of the company lies in its ability to combine the best efforts of entrepreneurial drive for success with strict central monitoring of planning, budgeting, and financial controls. So far as PepsiCo is concerned, the product form is ideal for rapid changes in the environment. In general, the greater the pressures for rapid responses to changes in the marketplace, the greater the advantage the product structure has over the functional form.

Disadvantages

The disadvantages (Table 10.3) of product grouping are similar to those encountered in place grouping. Both require a firm to have a proportionally larger number of managers; to direct individual product-line activities on one hand and to direct activities at multiple locations on the other. Most of the functional activities (marketing, finance, production) are duplicated for each product line, thus increasing the expense of doing business for the entire organization. While organization by product appears to enhance adaptability for each product line, extensive communication and coordinating mechanisms among the various product lines are required. Too frequently, top managers are drawn into day-to-day coordination, decision making, and problem solving. This is detrimental because it takes attention away from strategic issues.

Departmentalization by Matrix

Functional, place, and product departmentalization do not meet the needs of all organizations. In the functional structure, specialized skills may become very sophisticated, but coordination among professionals from highly specialized areas may be difficult to achieve. In the place structure, functions are duplicated at each location. In the product structure, functions are duplicated for each product line. The matrix structure attempts to combine the advantages of the functional and product designs while minimizing their disadvantages.

Matrix departmentalization is an organizational structure that uses multiple authority and support systems.[8] Every matrix contains three unique sets of relationships: (1) the top manager, who heads up and balances the dual lines of authority; (2) the matrix managers, who share subordinates; and (3) the subordinates who report to two different managers. One matrix manager is an expert in one of the specialized functional areas of the company (vertical line of authority). The other matrix manager is one who is expert in the team's assigned product (horizontal line of authority). These lines of authority are shown in Fig. 10.5.

Matrix structures were first developed in the aerospace industry.[9] The federal government wanted a single contact person in each company with whom it could work. To meet this need, Boeing, Lockheed, and McDonald-Douglas, among others, appointed a project manager. The project manager coordinates activities and shares authority with both functional and product managers. The matrix structure is now used in banking, management consulting firms, accounting firms, advertising agencies, and school systems. In some companies, such as Boeing, the matrix structure is found at all levels, while in others it is used only within certain departments or divisions.

Few organizations are able to make a sudden transition from a functional or product structure to a fully functioning matrix structure. As Jim Edwards found out at Bausch & Lomb, this design is not a cure-all for organizational problems. An effective matrix structure requires flexibility and cooperation from people at all levels of the organization. The complexity of the design requires open and direct communications. Special training in new job skills, such as conflict resolution or how to run an effective meeting, may be necessary for managers and subordinates when the matrix is introduced.

Advantages

The advantages (Table 10.4) of this form of departmentalization are that the matrix allows management to apply specialized skills to solve a problem

TABLE 10.4 ■ ADVANTAGES AND DISADVANTAGES OF MATRIX DEPARTMENTALIZATION

ADVANTAGES

1. Gives flexibility to managers in assigning people to projects.
2. Encourages interdisciplinary cooperation.
3. Develops project managers' human, conceptual, and administrative skills.
4. Involves and challenges people.
5. Makes specialized knowledge available to all projects.

DISADVANTAGES

1. Is costly to implement.
2. Requires good interpersonal skills.
3. May reward political skill as opposed to managerial skills.
4. Increases frustration levels for employees who now receive orders from two bosses.
5. May lead to more discussion than action.

Source: Adapted from J. McCann and J. Galbraith, "Interdepartmental Relations." In *Handbook of Organizational Design*, vol. 2. P. Nystrom and W. Starbuck (Eds.). New York: Oxford University Press, 1981, p. 61.

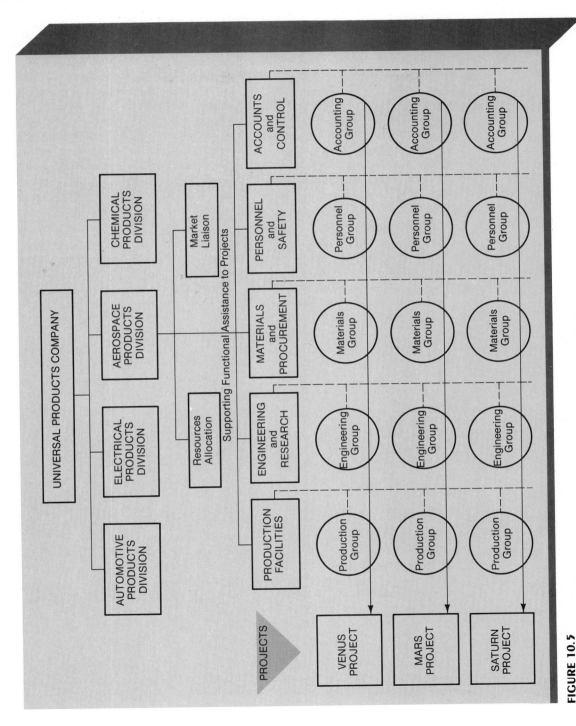

FIGURE 10.5

Matrix Departmentalization: Universal Products Company (Aerospace Division)

Source: John F. Mee, "Matrix Organizations," *Business Horizons*, Summer 1964, 7(2):70–72. Copyright © 1964 by the Foundation for the School of Business at Indiana University. Reprinted by permission.

with maximum efficiency. The problems of coordination, which we noted for both the functional and product designs, are minimized because most of the key personnel are assigned to the project. These people work as a team to solve all problems related to the project. In addition, the matrix structure gives management a great deal of cost-saving flexibility. People are assigned to the project only when they are needed for it and then are reassigned. The project manager can develop more fully and widely all three managerial roles—interpersonal, informational, and decisional—at lower levels in the organization. Finally, because of the diverse backgrounds represented on the project team (accounting, engineering, production, personnel, safety), the matrix design can encourage innovation, improve the quality of solutions, and make implementation of solutions easier.

Disadvantages

One disadvantage (Table 10.4) is that team members must possess good interpersonal skills to permit them to deal effectively with people from diverse backgrounds and departments. Also, employees accustomed to receiving orders from one supervisor now receive them from two. In addition, morale can be adversely affected by personnel shifts when a project is completed and a new one is started.

IN PRACTICE
A Business School

Most colleges of business have a functional structure. The chairperson of each department (marketing, finance, accounting, management) reports to the dean. As pointed out earlier, one problem with organizing by function is that coordination across departments can be poor. Students may feel that faculty members do not coordinate the amount of homework they assign, the content of their courses, and the scheduling of exams. In addition, faculty members are involved in various programs, which are analogous to product lines in companies.

The matrix form used by one business school is designed to capture the strengths of both the functional and product forms of departmentalization. Program directors serve as integrators. One director might be in charge of the MBA program, another in charge of the undergraduate program, and others in charge of the research function, and the executive education function, and so on. These directors have no direct authority over faculty members, but could secure the services of a particular faculty member for programs from the departmental chairperson. Once a faculty member accepts an assignment, he or she reports to both the program director and functional area chairperson as shown in Fig. 10.6. These people would coordinate the faculty member's activities. Some professors may work in more than one program, which is an example of shared resources.

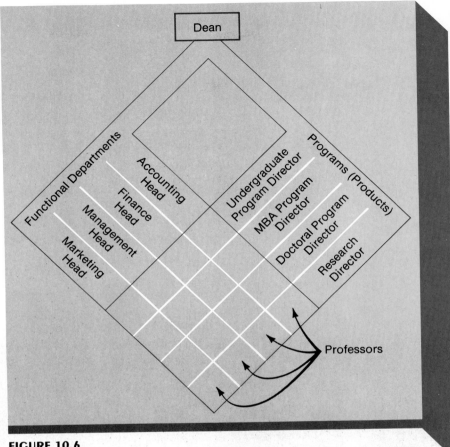

FIGURE 10.6
Matrix Departmentalization: A Business School

CONCEPTS OF COORDINATION

It is often said that good people can make any organizational structure effective. Although this may be an overstatement, people who can work together and cooperate to get things done are extremely valuable. Teamwork is especially relevant in sports. A team may spend hours practicing against a simulated opponent, but the actual game situation is one of ambiguity for both offensive and defensive players. However, during practice sessions, coaches develop players who can cooperate and work together most effectively. The players learn the parts they are to play in the cooperative effort and how each part relates to the others. Coordination is then required in the execution of their functions, particularly when players are called upon to innovate or adjust to the unexpected in a game situation.

Unity of Command

The *unity of command* principle states that a person should have only one boss. Every employee needs to know to whom he or she reports and, in the case of managers, who reports to them. Confusion over who makes decisions and who implements them should be minimized; uncertainty about whether to follow someone's directive can lead to serious productivity and morale problems. Matrix departmentalization clearly violates this principle.

The Scalar Principle

The *scalar principle* states that there should be a clear and unbroken chain of command linking every person in the organization with his or her superior. This principle is illustrated in Fig. 10.7 on pp. 346–347, which shows the structure of the Dallas police department. Suppose a sergeant in special operations wants to discuss a vehicle maintenance problem with the head mechanic in vehicle services. Adherence to the unity-of-command principle requires that the sergeant follow the chain of command through the head of special operations to the head of the patrol bureau. According to the scalar principle, the head of the patrol bureau would have to obtain permission from the head of the support services bureau who, in turn, would convey approval to the field support coordinator. Disapproval at any point in the chain would prevent the sergeant from talking to the head mechanic.

In general, the scalar principle requires that job-related communications between employees in different departments be approved by their respective superiors and that the superiors be kept informed of the outcome.[10] Obviously, strict adherence to this principle can waste time and money—and can be extremely frustrating. In fact, informal relationships across departmental lines spring up in most organizations (in violation of this principle) to facilitate communication and solve problems.

Span of Control

The *span of control* relates to the number of subordinates who report directly to a superior. The problem of span of control is as old as organizations.[11] It originates in the belief that a manager cannot effectively supervise a large number of people. This belief has been strengthened by the fact that military commanders find narrow spans of control to be most effective in combat situations. The traditional viewpoint of management holds that the number of subordinates reporting to any one manager should range between 4 and 12.

In actual experience, we find a variety of practices. A survey of 100 large companies by the American Management Association found that the number of executives reporting to the president varied from 1 to 24; only 26 presidents had 6 or fewer subordinates; the median number was 9. Comparable results have been found by other researchers. However, one consistent result is that in large organizations (those with at least $1 billion in annual sales), the span of control at the top tends to be no more than 12 and decreases as company size decreases.[12]

Factors affecting span of control

There is no correct number of subordinates that a manager can supervise effectively. Rather, several general factors affect a manager's span of control. According to the National Conference Board factors to be considered in determining the optimum span for a given situation are

1. the competence of the superior and subordinate;
2. the degree of interaction between departments being supervised;
3. the extent to which the supervisor must carry on nonmanagerial work;
4. the similarity or dissimilarity of activities being supervised;
5. the incidence of new problems in the supervisor's department;
6. the extent of standardized, objective rules and procedures within the organization; and
7. the degree of physical dispersion of activities.[13]

Guidelines for choosing a span of control

An appropriate span of control is difficult to establish. However, certain guidelines can help a manager to determine whether a span should be relatively narrow or broad.[14] These guidelines include factors relating to the manager, subordinates, and situation.

■ Factors relating to the manager. A broad span is appropriate when:
   1. the manager is well-trained and capable;
   2. the manager receives help in performing his or her supervisory duties;
   3. the manager has few nonsupervisory duties; and
   4. the manager prefers a *loose* rather than *tight* supervisory style.

■ Factors relating to subordinates. A broad span is appropriate when:
   1. subordinates are capable, well-trained, and committed to the manager's objectives;
   2. subordinates prefer to work without close supervision; and
   3. subordinates work in small groups whose objectives are the same as those of management.

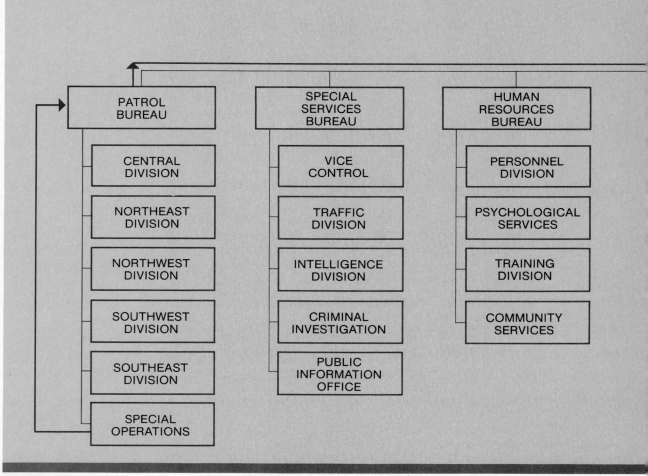

FIGURE 10.7
The Scalar Principle

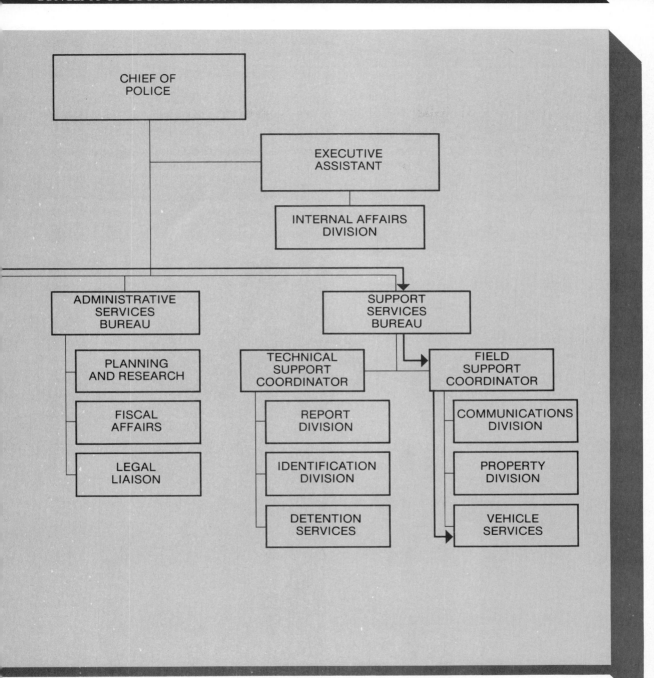

Source: Organization chart provided by the City of Dallas Police Department, 1985.

■ Factors relating to the situation. A broad span is appropriate when:

1. the work is relatively routine;
2. subordinates are performing similar work;
3. subordinates can work independently of each other; and
4. the work does not need a high degree of supervisory inspection.

In summary, some confusion has arisen about the ideal maximum number of subordinates that should report to a supervisor. There is, of course, no one such number. Rather, the maximum number of subordinates a manager can supervise effectively is a function of the three factors just discussed. Although there probably are limits for various situations, those numbers will vary in accordance with contingency factors and the importance given them by the manager and the organization.

Establishment of a supervisor's span of control includes consideration of a number of factors, such as the manager's training, the subordinates' need for supervision, and the type of work being performed by subordinates.

Source: John Lei/Stock, Boston.

AUTHORITY STRUCTURE

The authority structure of an organization makes possible the division of work and its coordination. The authority structure is the means by which activities can be assigned to managers. This structure establishes the basis for making various types of decisions. The higher a manager is in the structure, the greater the latitude for making decisions that commit the company's resources.

Authority

Authority is the right to make decisions and take actions. The traditional definition of authority is that it provides the direction and controls the flow of decisions through the unity of command from the top of an organization down.[15] Authority is exercised when a board of directors authorizes a bond issue in order to raise capital; when an executive approves a new advertising campaign; when a sales representative signs a contract with a client; when a manager promotes a production worker to foreman; and when a manager fires a subordinate. In short, authority is the cement of an organization's structure.

A different view of authority was held by Chester Barnard, president of New Jersey Bell Telephone Company from 1927–1948. He maintained that authority flows from the bottom up.[16] This view is known as the *acceptance theory of authority.* Barnard realized that not every decision made by someone's immediate supervisor could be analyzed, judged, and either accepted or rejected; rather, that most decisions or orders fall within a subordinate's *zone of indifference.* If a decision falls within that zone, the subordinate will comply without question; if it falls outside that zone, the subordinate will question whether to accept or reject it. The width of the indifference zone depends on the degree to which potential rewards exceed potential penalties. When a manager asks a secretary to take dictation, this request probably falls within the secretary's zone of indifference because it is a part of the job description. However, if a manager asks the secretary to dinner, this probably falls outside that zone, and the secretary may very well refuse.

If we merge the traditional definition of authority with that of Barnard, we can define authority as a superior's right to command the subordinate's acceptance of a superior's right to command.

Responsibility

Responsibility may be thought of as an owed obligation to perform assigned activities. This obligation is acquired when a person accepts the assignment. A manager has duties to carry out and is also responsible for the actions of subordinates. When Mark Rigg, Vice-President for Human Resources at Southland Corporation, gives David Blakke the authority to run training programs for new store managers, Blakke is responsible for conducting them. Responsibility demands that Blakke take his job seriously and that Rigg provide him with the tools (training rooms, manuals, visual aids, store managers' time) to accomplish the objectives of the program.

Accountability

Accountability requires that a person answer for the results achieved or not achieved in the performance of assigned duties. Each person in an organization is expected to demonstrate or report on the discharge of his or her responsibilities at some point in the work process. Such checks are needed to ensure that decisions are being made and activities are being performed properly. Since a superior cannot check everything a subordinate does, the manager establishes limits within which the work must be done and holds people answerable for their performance within these limits. Thus accountability always flows from the bottom up.

Accountability is the point at which authority and responsibility meet. In the Southland example, Rigg gave Blakke the authority consistent with the responsibility for conducting the training programs. Therefore he could properly hold Blakke accountable for the results. Managers do not have the right to hold a subordinate accountable when either authority or responsibility are lacking. When one or the other is inadequate, a person's accomplishments cannot be judged fairly.

Delegation

Delegation is the process of distributing and entrusting work to others. It involves assigning a person a duty to perform and giving that person adequate authority and responsibility to do the assigned work effectively. The process starts during the design of an organizational structure, when activities to be performed are divided up. It continues as new activities are added and in the everyday operations of the organization.

Delegation occurs when a company president assigns to an executive assistant the task of preparing a formal statement for presentation to a congressional committee; when the head of a computer department instructs a programmer to program and debug a new management reporting system; and when a production supervisor tells a mailroom clerk to get a package to the West Coast as quickly and cheaply as possible.

Authority is delegated when a superior gives decision-making powers to a subordinate. The process of delegation involves determining results expected, assigning tasks and the authority and responsibility to accomplish them, and accountability for accomplishment of the tasks. In practice, these fundamental aspects of the process are impossible to split. Louis Allen has listed six useful principles of delegation:

1. *Establish objectives and standards.* Subordinates should participate in developing the goals they are expected to meet. They should also agree to the standards that will measure their performance.

2. *Define responsibility and authority.* Subordinates should clearly understand the work and authority delegated to them and should recognize and accept their accountability for results.

3. *Motivate subordinates.* The challenge of the work itself will not always encourage subordinates to accept and perform delegated tasks. Managers can motivate subordinates by involving them in decision making, by keeping them informed and by helping them to improve their skills and abilities.

4. *Require completed work.* Subordinates should be required to carry work through to completion. The manager's job is to provide guidance, help, and information.

5. *Provide training.* Delegation can be only as effective as the ability of people to perform the work and make the decisions required. This calls for continuing appraisal of delegated responsibilities and training programs aimed at building on strengths and overcoming deficiencies.

6. *Establish adequate controls.* Timely, accurate reports should be provided so that subordinates can compare their own performance to agreed-on standards and correct their own deficiencies.[17]

Barriers to delegation

Managers often fail to delegate because of psychological and organizational barriers.[18] The greatest psychological barrier to delegation is fear; a manager is afraid that subordinates will not do the job properly and, as a result, the manager's performance will suffer. "I can do it better myself." "My subordinates are not capable." "It takes too much time to explain what I want done."—all are reasons why managers do not delegate. These reasons are justified only if subordinates are untrained or poorly motivated. However, the manager's responsibility is to take positive action to overcome such deficiencies. Managers may also be reluctant to delegate because they fear that subordinates may do the work their own way, do it too well, and outshine the managers.

Organizational barriers may block delegation. One barrier is the failure to define responsibility and authority. If a manager does not know what is expected or what to do, it is unlikely that he or she will be able to delegate decision making to others. If a manager does delegate under these conditions, it not only affects the manager but demoralizes subordinates because they feel that they are just spinning their wheels. Another barrier has to do with managers' reluctance to assume accountability for the work of subordinates. If there is not complete accountability, subordinates can pass the buck.

Overcoming barriers to delegation

The most basic requirement for effective delegation is the willingness by managers to give their subordinates real freedom to accomplish delegated tasks. Managers have to accept the fact that there are usually several ways of handling a problem and that their own way is not necessarily the one their subordinates would choose. In fact, subordinates may make errors in carrying out their tasks. They have to be allowed to develop their own solutions to problems and to learn from their mistakes. This is very difficult for many managers to accept but, unless they do, they cannot delegate effectively. They will be so busy with minor tasks or with checking on subordinates that their own important tasks will remain undone. Managers must keep in mind that the great advantages of delegation justify giving subordinates freedom of action, even at the risk of allowing mistakes to occur.

The barriers to effective delegation can also be overcome through improved communication and understanding between managers and subordinates. Managers who make it a point to learn the strengths, weaknesses, and preferences of their subordinates can more realistically decide which tasks can be delegated to whom. They will then have greater confidence in their delegation decisions. Subordinates who are encouraged by their managers to use their abilities and who feel that their managers will back them up will, in turn, become more eager to accept responsibility.

Decentralization

There is neither absolute centralization nor absolute decentralization. No one manager makes all the decisions; total delegation would eliminate the need for subordinate managers. In other words, there is a continuum of centralization and decentralization. An organization may be relatively centralized in some functions and relatively decentralized in others.

Decentralization refers to both a high degree of delegated authority and a basic management philosophy.[19] It requires a careful choice of decisions to delegate, selection and training of personnel to make the types of decisions delegated, and the formulation of adequate controls.

Westinghouse Electric Company is partially decentralized. With sales of over $10 billion, it is organized by both function and product, as shown in Fig. 10.8. Westinghouse's strategy is to expand into businesses that offer high growth and profitability and are closely related to its existing businesses. To achieve that strategy, it sold off its lamp, lighting fixture, and appliance business and bought businesses that make robots and power-generation equipment. Each of the company's major markets—nuclear energy and advanced technology, commercial and cable broadcasting—is evaluated in terms of two objectives: (1) base pricing, which measures the productive efficiency and rate of return on capital invested in each of the divisions; and (2) share-of-the-market standing, which indicates how well the division is competing in the marketplace as a seller.

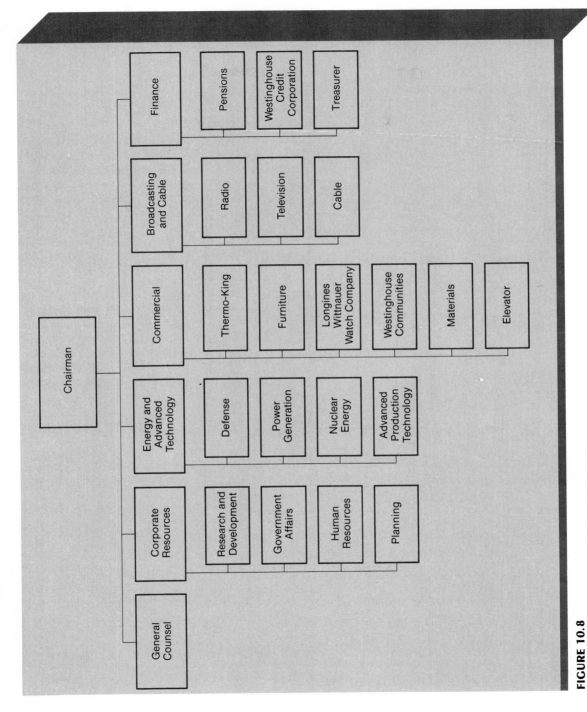

FIGURE 10.8
Table of Organization: Westinghouse Electric Company

Source: Adapted from Westinghouse management organization, July 1984.

Each of Westinghouse's divisions works to improve the productivity of its plants in different ways. Managers generally make most decisions without checking with corporate headquarters. For example, when television station WJZ in Baltimore decided to cooperate with local police in an anticrime project, the station manager committed the station on his own authority. Similarly, when Daniel Soraka developed Westinghouse's first robot, funds for that project were made available through his managers. Tactical, as opposed to strategic, decisions are made by managers closest to the scene of action.

Westinghouse operations are centralized in the areas of quality, personnel, and finance. For example, in 1982, Westinghouse began a company-wide program to use specialized techniques, such as quality circles, to improve product quality. These programs saved the company millions of dollars. In 1983, the company reached a three-year agreement with the labor unions that represent its 48,000 employees. Westinghouse must ensure standard policies and adherence to the labor contract at all locations.

Advantages of decentralization

When used successfully, decentralization has several advantages. First, it frees time for top managers to develop plans and strategies for the organization when they delegate tasks that require creativity and initiative, as well as routine tasks. Second, it develops managers' conceptual skills. One of the benefits of delegation, according to the president of GE, is that it prepares managers for positions that require greater judgment and acceptance of increased responsibility. Third, subordinates are often closer to the action than managers and can make a decision faster. Being closer to the action enables them to be aware of all the facts. Sometimes valuable time is lost when a subordinate must check everything with a manager. Fourth, it fosters a healthy achievement-oriented atmosphere among managers. GE's statement of corporate goals notes that decentralization fosters the development of all of an individual's talents.

Factors affecting decentralization

Six factors affect whether a manager chooses to decentralize and thus delegate decisions to subordinates.

Costliness of decisions. This is perhaps the most important factor in determining the extent of decentralization in an organization. As a general rule, the more costly the decisions to be made, the more likely it is that they will be made by top management. Decision costs may be in dollars or in such intangibles as the company's reputation, competitive position, or employee morale.

Uniformity of policy. Managers who value consistency favor centralization of authority. Managers may wish to assure customers that all will be treated alike with respect to quality, price, credit, delivery, and service. Uniform policies have definite advantages in the areas of cost accounting, production, and financial records because they enable managers to compare the relative efficiencies of various departments. The administration of a union–management labor agreement is aided by a uniform policy with respect to wages, promotions, vacations, fringe benefits, grievances, and similar matters.

Corporate culture.   Whether authority will be decentralized depends on the firm's *culture*. Marshall Field and Company and International Harvester Company have shown a marked tendency to keep authority centralized. Similarly, when Henry Ford Sr., the founder of the Ford Motor Company, ran the organization, it was highly centralized. Ford took pride in having no organizational titles for top management except those of president and general manager; he insisted, to the extent possible, on making all company decisions himself. Other companies, such as Sears, have a history of decentralization.

Availability of managers.   Too often there is a shortage of good managers. To have decentralization, many corporations ensure an adequate supply of trained managers by permitting managers to make mistakes that involve small costs. These firms believe that the best training in developing managerial potential is actual experience.

Control mechanisms.   Even the most avid proponents of decentralization (GM, du Pont, GE, Sears) believe that controls are needed to determine whether performance is meeting expectations. In the Marriott chain, each hotel collects certain key data: number of beds occupied, employee turnover, number of meals served, and average amount spent by a guest on food and beverages. Analysis of the data helps each manager to control important aspects of the operation and to evaluate the performance of the hotel against others in this chain.

Environmental influences.   External factors, such as national unions, federal and state regulatory agencies, and tax policies, also affect the degree of decentralization within a firm. Governmental policy on the employment of minorities, for example, makes it hard for a company to decentralize authority totally in making hiring decisions. If the federal government limits the number of hours worked and the minimum wages to be paid, a local manager cannot establish wages and hours that violate these laws.

The impact of national unions on long-term contracts exerts a centralizing influence on many organizations. When small local or regional unions represent employees in various departments, authority to negotiate the terms of labor contracts may be delegated by top management to departmental managers. But when national unions bargain on behalf of employees for an entire company—such as GM, B. F. Goodrich, and the National Football League, and many other large firms—management can no longer risk decentralization of labor negotiations.

INTERNATIONAL FOCUS

Nestlé

The former managing director of Nestlé, Pierre Liotard-Vogt, believes that Nestlé is truly a multinational company. The Swiss-based company was formed by a 1905 merger between an American-owned and German-owned company. More than 96 percent of sales are outside Switzerland, and about 40 percent of top management has had experience overseas. In 1984, Nestlé's sales from over 300 factories around the world exceeded $20 billion. Approximately 50 percent of those sales were from Europe, 17 percent in North America, and 13 percent in other industrialized countries. With such widespread operations, Nestlé maintains quite clear-cut policies on where decisions will be made and what role headquarters plays versus country managers.

A major responsibility of headquarters management is to make strategic decisions. In order to do this, top managers at headquarters handle all mergers and acquisition discussions as well as which new products the company will offer to the market. For example, when Nestlé acquired Libby, top management had to decide whether to continue having Libby's plant managers in the United Kingdom report to other Libby managers or to Nestlé's European managers. Since Nestlé was familiar with Libby's food products, top management made Libby's U.K. managers report to Nestlé's European managers. In another case, the acquisition of Stouffer Foods put Nestlé into hotel ownership and because Nestlé's top managers in Switzerland lacked hotel experience, they permitted many decisions to be made by Stouffer's management.

To maintain its profits and market share, Nestlé's relies heavily on the introduction of new products, as well as maintaining its profitable old ones. However, the introduction of new products overseas has not been without major problems. In 1980, the infant formula that Nestlé sold accounted for

Source: John Daniels, Ernest Ogram, and Lee Radebaugh, *International Business: Environments and Operations*, 3rd ed. Reading, Mass.: Addison-Wesley, 1982, pp. 462–464; Bill Beaver and Fred Silvester, "The Gall in Mother's Milk: The Infant Formula Controversy and the WHO Marketing Code." *Journal of Advertising*, 1982, 1(1):1–11.

LINE AND STAFF RELATIONSHIPS

In a typical business organization, **line functions** are concerned with the achievement of organizational objectives through delegation of authority, work assignments, and supervision of others in accordance with the scalar, or chain-of-command, principle. **Staff functions,** on the other hand, indirectly influence the work of others through the use of suggestions, recommendations, and advice. In general, line departments denote a *command* relationship within an organization; staff departments, an *advisory* relationship. In nonbusiness organizations, such as a hospital or university, this distinction between line

about 3 percent of its sales. The problem was that some people in the field of infant nutrition had stated that the decline in breast-feeding, particularly in poor urban areas of the world, was the result of effective advertising campaigns by Nestlé, Bordens, and others. According to some religious groups and doctors, breast-feeding was preferred to bottle-feeding. A coalition of activist groups banded together and produced a report entitled the "Baby Killer." These groups accused Nestlé of immoral and unethical promotion causing the deaths of thousands of babies. These groups then urged people in Third World countries to boycott the product. Many international groups, such as the World Health Organization, UNICEF, International Council of Infant Food Industries, appealed to the United Nations to produce an international Code of Ethics. After this Code was published, Nestlé and others stopped advertising its infant formula, although no evidence was ever presented by the activist groups which indicated that Nestlé's infant formula ever killed an infant. To prevent such recurrences, headquarters managers have reserved the right to make all decisions regarding new product introductions and advertising campaigns.

In spite of its centralized policies, Nestlé's local country managers still have some important decisions to make. For example, while product research is centralized, when a new product is introduced, headquarters managers will not force local managers to launch a promotional campaign to sell the product in a uniform way. If the product is introduced, local managers can change it so long as the changes are not in poor taste. Nestlé's best selling product, Nescafé instant coffee, is slightly different from country to country in terms of coffee blend and darkness of the roast.

and staff may be less clear. In a hospital, the physicians (technical staff) treat patients and the administrators concern themselves with hospital finance and maintenance. Similarly, in a university the faculty (professional staff) teach and do research, while the administrators (deans, vice-president) are involved in support and auxiliary functions.[20]

Staff departments provide services—planning, personnel, accounting, data processing—that cut across departmental lines. They also provide support services to line departments in work that requires specialized technical expertise and detailed attention. Staff people become experts in their given fields. Figure 10.9, which shows the organization chart of Standard Steel Company's

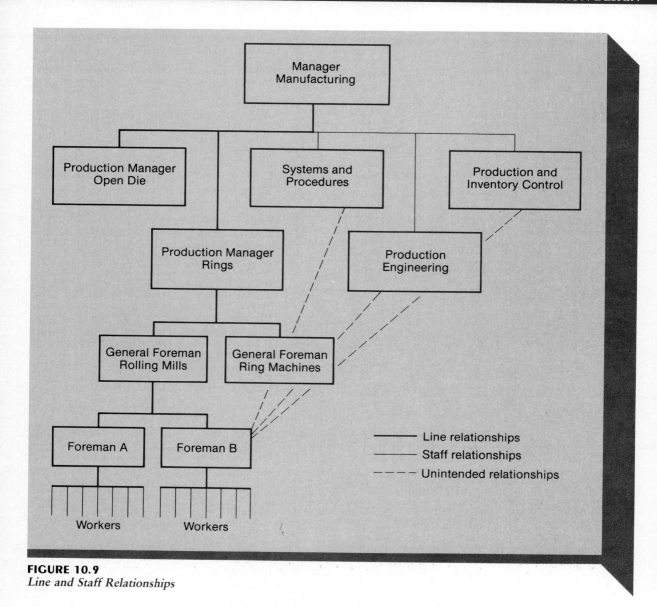

FIGURE 10.9
Line and Staff Relationships

production department, illustrates line–staff relationships for a department in a manufacturing firm.

In Standard Steel's manufacturing department, the staff performs three types of specialized assistance: systems and procedures, production engineering, and production and inventory control. Staff specialists also prepare and process data which line managers need for making decisions. For example, the production and inventory-control group customarily collects data on the cost of making a late delivery to an important customer, the number of jobs completed in each shop per day, and the level of inventory that should be stockpiled. These experts work closely with the systems and procedures personnel. When these experts have studied a problem, they submit their recommendations to the manager of manufacturing, who considers the recommendations and selects a course of action for implementation by the line managers.

Types of Staff Authority

When staff functions are separate from the line organization, as shown in Fig. 10.9, a decision must be made about the type of authority staff personnel should be given. Observation of actual staff departments suggests at least four types: advisory, compulsory advice, concurring authority, and command authority. Figure 10.10 portrays this authority continuum for staff departments.

Advisory

Many staff activities are purely advisory in nature. The manager is free to seek (or not to seek) the advice of staff specialists. The manager who is looking for a new electrical engineer may seek information from the personnel department about the average starting salary for graduates, the universities

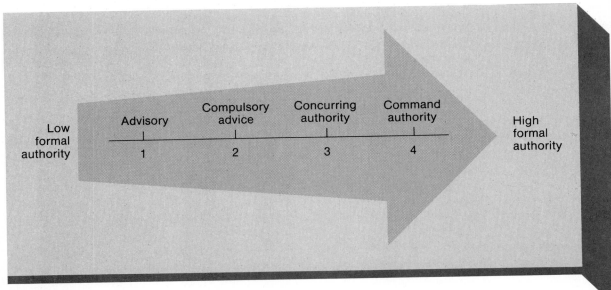

FIGURE 10.10
Continuum of Authority for Staff Departments

most likely to have qualified candidates, and the like. However, the department manager may accept or reject the information and recommendations, if any, given to him by the personnel department.

Compulsory advice

In the case of compulsory advice, a manager must at least listen to the appropriate staff department but need not follow its recommendation. Although this procedure does not limit the manager's decision-making discretion, it ensures that the manager makes use of the specialized talents of staff departments.

Concurring authority

Concurring authority requires that line and staff managers agree on a particular course of action. This procedure expands the staff manager's authority and restricts the line manager's decision-making discretion in those areas for which mutual agreement is required. Thus decisions involving the recruitment of a new electrical engineer are made jointly: the manager of the production department and the head of the personnel office must agree that certain academic criteria are valid, specific universities should be visited, the starting salary is consistent (internally) and competitive (externally), and so forth. When agreement cannot be reached, the issue is moved to the level of the organization where one manager has authority over both the line and staff departments involved.

Command authority

The strongest form of staff authority occurs when the line grants limited command authority to a staff department, permitting it to give orders and expecting that other departments will comply. If the personnel department has the authority to screen prospective candidates and reject those who do not meet established quality standards, the personnel department is exercising command authority in the area of hiring. In many organizations, personnel and industrial-relations departments exercise command authority over the use of psychological testing, hiring policies and procedures, employee counseling, and related employee activities and benefits.

Line and Staff Conflicts

Authority conflicts between line and staff departments can create a great deal of friction and many management problems in organizations. There are many reasons for these conflicts, but we will examine only some of the major ones.[21]

Personal characteristics

One factor that aggravates line–staff conflict is differences in personal characteristics. A group of line and staff managers was asked to rank personality traits on the basis of their importance to success. Traits included characteristics such as forcefulness, imagination, independence, cooperation, adaptability, and caution. The results indicated that staff managers felt they had to be more imaginative, cooperative, adaptable, and cautious but less forceful and independent to succeed in their jobs than did line managers.

Staff people are generally younger, better educated, more concerned with dress and appearance than are line people. They also have different recreational interests than line people and come from different backgrounds. Line managers are generally oriented toward advancement with the company; staff managers toward advancement in their profession. Line managers see their future in terms of loyalty to the organization; staff managers, to their profession. This difference in commitment and loyalty to the organization can lead to a conflict in interests. Thus staff research scientists may be most interested in making a contribution to their field with the development of a new product, whereas the line manager responsible for producing the new products is most interested in getting the product into consumers' hands and quickly recovering research and development costs.

Informal command authority

A second source of conflict is the fact that staff departments are usually located higher in the organization and are often called on by top management to analyze and make reports on operating divisions. Thus they acquire informal command authority, much to the dismay of line managers. These staff efforts are often perceived by line managers as attempts to check on and control the line departments. For example, refer back to Fig. 10.9 and consider the unintended relationships. The dashed lines represent informal functional authority acquired by staff people from the line foreman. Let us assume that the production engineer is asked to determine why foreman B's section is incurring unusually high costs. In a discussion with foreman B, the engineer encounters suspicion and a general lack of respect for his capabilities and work. The engineer completes his analysis and submits a report to the general foreman of rolling mills, the production manager—rings, and the manager of manufacturing. He explains his findings to the three line managers and goes on to relate the unproductive meeting with foreman B. He concludes by stating that he has little chance of influencing the foreman.

The managers know that costs in foreman B's section must be controlled. They arrange a meeting with the foreman to explain why costs must be reduced and why the procedures developed by the production engineer to cut costs must be implemented. After the meeting, the production engineer has a pleasant conversation with foreman B, who now seems very receptive to the engineer's ideas. Realizing that his superiors rely on the production engineer as an authority on engineering methods to control costs, the foreman no longer views the specialist as a nosy staff person, but as an individual with *authority* in this area. Eventually, the acceptance of staff recommendations and suggestions by first-line managers, as representative views of top and middle management, tends to create an authority link that is quite different from the prescribed formal arrangements. This is often more representative of the real working relationships of the group; the consequences are unintended but real.

Constructive resolution of conflict

Of course, conflict between line and staff managers is not inherently bad or adversely affects performance. In many cases, these differences have some merit and their resolution can lead to better decisions. In the situation involving the foreman and the production engineer, let us assume that the engineer's overriding concern with only an engineering solution to cost containment is too narrow a focus on the problem; that, in addition, there are personnel and materials-flow problems that the foreman has been reluctant to discuss. In this situation, a compromise solution is ultimately worked by incorporating the thinking of both the production engineer and foreman B. The engineer's work served as a catalyst to bring other problems into the open and spurred the foreman to express his ideas about solving them. What is important to the organization is that the disruptive effects of conflict be minimized and that conflicting viewpoints be reconciled constructively.

Location of Staff Departments

The location of staff departments in an organization's structure is usually determined by the differences between generalized and specialized functions. If the services of a staff department are used extensively throughout an organization, the department may need to be located relatively high up in the organization; general staff functions are usually centralized at the top of most large corporations. In the case of Westinghouse (Fig. 10.8), offices that handle corporate legal, government affairs, planning, human resources, and research and development comprise the general staff. These staff functions are usually managed by vice-presidents who are in policy-making positions rather than being in charge of operating divisions. At Westinghouse the vice-president in charge of human resources is responsible for developing company-wide personnel and industrial-relations policies. As part of their duties, the human-resources staff selects executive development programs appropriate to send managers to, develops brochures outlining the company's benefits and promotion policies for use by division personnel managers, and develops executive succession plans for the entire managerial staff.

If a staff group is assigned to provide needed services to a specific line function, the group should be located near that function. At Standard Steel, for example, the production and inventory-control manager reports to the firm's manufacturing manager because a major portion of that staff's work is oriented directly to manufacturing processes, as indicated in Fig. 10.9. Staff specialists often perform support functions (some of which would have to be performed by a line manager if there were no staff specialists) in a specific area; they usually report to the line manager of that department.

CHAPTER SUMMARY

A basic problem facing all managers is how to organize tasks and personnel to achieve organizational objectives most effectively. The basic process of grouping activities is departmentalization. There are four strategies for grouping activities: function, place, product, and matrix. Each has specific advantages and disadvantages and each presents problems for the manager in coordinating the activities of the various groups. The basic concepts of coordination are unity of command, the scalar principle, and span of control.

Unity of command means that each person has only one boss. The *scalar principle* refers to the chain of direct authority from superior to subordinate throughout an organization. *Span of control* addresses the problem of determining how many individuals should report to one manager; a number of contingency factors affect a manager's span of control.

The authority structure of an organization is the means by which the organization functions. *Authority* refers to a manager's right to make decisions and a subordinate's acceptance of this power. *Responsibility* is an owed obligation and goes hand in hand with authority. *Accountability* flows up from the bottom of the organization. Subordinates must answer to their superiors for results achieved (or not achieved) in doing their jobs. Whether authority is concentrated or dispersed throughout the organization depends on the degree of centralization or decentralization appropriate for the activities being performed. Decentralization represents a high degree of delegation of authority and reflects an underlying philosophy of an organization and its management.

Most large organizations utilize staff groups to provide generalized functions for the entire organization and specialized assistance to line departments. The authority granted to staff departments varies from purely advisory to actual decision making in specified areas. Authority conflicts between line and staff people present management problems that need to be resolved constructively.

MANAGER'S VOCABULARY

acceptance theory of authority
accountability
authority
centralization
coordination of activities
decentralization
delegation
departmentalization
functional departmentalization
line functions
matrix departmentalization
organization chart
organizational structure
organizing
place departmentalization
product departmentalization
responsibility
scalar principle
specialization of activities
size of the work unit
span of control
staff functions
standardization of activities
unity of command

REVIEW QUESTIONS

1. State the four bases of departmentalization and the advantages and disadvantages of each.

2. What is the principle of unity of command?

3. What is the principle of span of control? List the three important factors affecting a manager's span of control.

4. What are the differences among authority, accountability, and responsibility?

5. State the advantages and disadvantages of centralization and decentralization of authority.

6. What are some of the reasons for line and staff manager conflicts?

DISCUSSION QUESTIONS

1. If you were Jim Edwards at Bausch & Lomb, what alternative forms of departmentalization might you have chosen? Why?

2. How is your university or company organized? What are some of the limitations of this organizational structure?

3. Can an organization survive without staff people? If so, what might be some of the limitations of this organization?

4. Why is the span-of-control principle so important for managers?

5. Why do managers find it hard to delegate decision making to their subordinates?

MANAGEMENT INCIDENTS AND CASES

BEATRICE FOODS

Only a butter and egg company 90 years ago, Beatrice Foods of Chicago changed through the 1970s into a conglomerate including more than 400 business groups with annual sales of $9.19 billion. The food company had grown with an aggressive acquisition campaign during which it used its stock to buy small companies and expand their markets; then it left the new companies under the management of the original owners. By the 1980s, Beatrice Foods was producing 9000 products ranging from shower heads and steel tubing to tortillas and taffy bars. Some of its brand names were Samsonite luggage, Clark candy bars, La Choy Chinese Foods, Eckrich meats, and Meadow Gold dairy products, but many were smaller, lesser known firms. These companies evolved into a collection of small companies with no unified purpose or direction.

"People thought Beatrice was a well-run company, but nobody understood it," said an executive at a competitive firm. "You had to take it on faith."

Some of Beatrice's units, such as its Rosarita and Gebhardt Mexican food lines, competed against one another for supermarket shelf space. Managers of its three cheese companies didn't even talk to each other. "There were so many operating units—like islands, almost," said a retired dairy executive, "and each one was too small to compete with the Bordens or the Dart & Krafts or the Esmarks."

To capture more of the market, competitors such as Procter & Gamble and General Mills, were becoming more centralized and spending more on advertising and research and development. In contrast, Beatrice Foods groups were using some 140 different advertising companies, and spending only 2% of their earnings on promotion. A similar problem existed in the finance area. The corporate controller had a staff too small to monitor closely the financial information forwarded from over 400 companies to company headquarters. As a result, in May, 1982, Beatrice Foods posted its first quarterly earnings decline in 30 years.

Although the new CEO, James Dutt, had long been a believer in decentralization, he realized that many of the smaller companies had lost their momentum and direction after the original owners had retired. These companies needed increased staff support, particularly in marketing and financial control. Toward that end, Dutt centralized some advertising and purchasing, and reorganized Beatrice Foods into six operating groups. Some companies, such as Dannon Yogurt and Airstream Trailers, were sold. Rather than establishing a corporate marketing staff to aid businesses too small to have full-time marketing managers, the CEO created satellite marketing staffs for some products. Research and development was moved from the head office to the operating group. In addition to these changes, Dutt started a $10,000 bonus program to be awarded each year to the manager who launches the most successful new product. To improve communications between himself and the companies, Dutt has made videotapes explaining the new system to all managers. To further communications, he regularly schedules breakfast meetings with employees at all levels.[22]

Questions

1. What are some of the problems that Beatrice Foods was experiencing prior to James Dutt's presidency? How are these related to the structure of the firm?

2. Discuss the pros and cons of the new organizational structure implemented by Dutt.

3. What other forms of departmentalization could Dutt have chosen to reorganize Beatrice Foods? Why do you think he chose the one he did?

REFERENCES

1. S. Stratford, "Troubles at Bausch & Lomb," *Fortune,* January 23, 1983, pp. 104–105.

2. J. Stoner, *Management,* 2nd ed. Englewood Cliffs, N.J.: Prentice-Hall, 1982, pp. 260–264.

3. K. White, *Understanding the Company Organization Chart.* New York: American Management Association, 1963.

4. J. Child, *Organization: A Guide to Problems and Practice,* 2nd ed. London: Harper & Row, 1984, pp. 58–85; W. Astley and A. Van de Ven, "Central

Perspectives and Debates in Organization Theory," *Administrative Science Quarterly,* 1983, **28**:245–270.

5. J. McCann and J. Galbraith, "Interdepartmental Relations." In *Handbook of Organizational Design,* P. Nystrom and W. Starbuck (Eds.). New York: Oxford University Press, 1981, p. 61; R. Duncan, "What Is the Right Organization Structure?" *Organizational Dynamics,* Winter 1979, p. 64.

6. J. Daniels, E. Ogram, and L. Radebaugh, *International Business: Environments and Operations.* Reading, Mass.: Addison-Wesley, 1979.

7. H. Mintzberg, *Structure in Fives: Designing Effective Organizations.* Englewood Cliffs, N.J.: Prentice-Hall, 1983.

8. S. Davis and P. Lawrence, *Matrix.* Reading, Mass.: Addison-Wesley, 1977.

9. H. Koloday, "Managing in a Matrix," *Business Horizons,* March–April 1981, pp. 17–24.

10. H. Fayol, *General and Industrial Management.* C. Storrs (Trans.) London: Pitman, 1963, p. 34.

11. For an excellent overview, *see* D. Van Fleet, "Span of management research and issues," *Academy of Management Journal,* 1983, **26**:546–552.

12. H. Mintzberg, *The Structuring of Organizations.* Englewood Cliffs, N.J.: Prentice-Hall, 1979, pp. 134–147.

13. J. Stieglitz, "Optimizing the Span of Control," *Management Record,* 1962, **24**:25–29.

14. M. Keren and D. Levhari, "The Optimum Span of Control in a Pure Hierarchy," *Management Science,* 1979, **25**:1162–1172.

15. P. Blau, "The Hierarchy of Authority in Organizations," *American Journal of Sociology,* 1967, **68**:453–467.

16. C. Barnard, *The Functions of the Executive.* Cambridge, Mass.: President and Fellows of Harvard University, 1938.

17. L. Allen, *The Professional Manager's Guide.* Palo Alto, Calif.: Louis A. Allen & Associates, 1981, p. 120–122.

18. Mintzberg, *Structure in Fives . . . ,* pp. 95–120.

19. L. Jennergren, "Decentralization in Organizations." In *Handbook of Organizational Design.* P. Nystrom and W. Starbuck (Eds.). New York: Oxford University Press, 1981, pp. 39–59.

20. V. Nossiter, "A New Approach to Resolving the Line and Staff Dilemma. *Academy of Management Review,* 1979, **4**:103–107.

21. R. Griffin, *Management.* Boston, Mass.: Houghton Mifflin, 1984, pp. 293–296.

22. R. Griffin, *Management,* pp. 316–317; S. Shellenbarger, "Beatrice Foods Moves to Centralize Business to Reverse Its Decline," *Wall Street Journal,* September 27, 1983, p. 1ff.

Impact of Information Processing on Organization Design

CHAPTER 11

LEARNING OBJECTIVES

After studying this chapter, you should be able to:

- Discuss how different environments can influence the structure of an organization.

- Explain how technological interdependencies impact the design of an organization.

- State how environment and technology combine to determine the amount of information a firm must process.

- List two methods that firms can use to increase their *ability* to process information and two ways that firms can use to reduce their *need* to process information.

- State the differences between mechanistic and organic management systems.

CHAPTER OUTLINE

PREVIEW CASE

OVERHAUL AT GENERAL MOTORS CORPORATION

In 1921, Alfred Sloan faced a difficult problem. The fledgling General Motors Corporation could not match the Ford Motor Company in producing small, economical cars. Mr. Sloan, GM's chairman, decided to reorganize the company to produce a line of cars in several price areas, from economy models to luxury models. To do this, Sloan believed that each car line should be directed at a specific price and size segment of the auto market. Each line should be distinct, with no duplication or overlap between models.

For decades, GM adhered to these principles. But in the last decade, under intense pressure to improve fuel efficiency, GM has produced a series of look-alike cars that have confused both dealers and buyers. As each division tried to become a full-line auto company, the lines were blurred even further. Chevrolet, traditionally GM's premier small car division, began to sell cars as large as the biggest Buick while Cadillac, historically the company's large luxury car division, sold a subcompact.

The solution to the problem was to restructure the $75 billion company. Roger Smith, GM's chairman, announced in July, 1984, that GM would consolidate all its automotive engineering, manufacturing, and marketing operations into two large umbrella groups: one for large cars, to include the Oldsmobile, Buick, and Cadillac divisions; and one for small cars, meaning Chevrolet,

Pontiac, and GM of Canada. The new automotive structure was introduced in late 1984 and is shown in Fig. 11.1. Smith intends to restore some of the individuality of GM lines that Sloan insisted on years ago.

One of the primary objectives of GM's new organizing concept is to assign clear responsibility for the development of each product. Under the old structure, a car's design and engineering were scattered among numerous engineering activities. The Fisher Body and Assembly divisions had developed overlapping responsibilities in manufacturing. Under the reorganized structure, total responsibility for each car—design, development, production—will be assigned to one of the two new Groups. For example, an engineering department was once responsible only for a portion of a car: chassis, suspension, engine, or electronics.

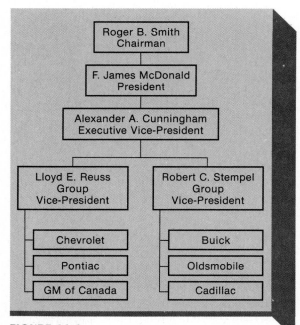

FIGURE 11.1
The New GM Automotive Structure

Source: General Motors Corporation
Public Affairs Newsletter, *GM*, February
1984, p. 2.

We don't buy just any seats. We design them.

GM begins with detailed studies of the human body. Biomedical research. The kind of comprehensive investigation of anatomy da Vinci undertook in the 1500s.

As a leader in the field of Human Factors Engineering, we design interiors scientifically to minimize the possible distractions from your driving.

It may take us two years and countless clay models to arrive at a more comfortable,

durable seat for new GM cars and trucks. But we think it's worth it.

And we believe old Leonardo would have thought so, too.

We believe in taking the extra time, giving the extra effort and paying attention to every detail. That's what it takes to provide the quality that leads more people to buy GM cars and trucks than any other kind. And why GM owners are the most loyal on the road.

That's the GM commitment to excellence.

Chevrolet • Pontiac • Oldsmobile • Buick • Cadillac • GMC Truck

Leonardo da Vinci gave us a great idea for bucket seats.

Let's get it together. Buckle up.

Nobody sweats the details like GM.

Source: Reprinted courtesy of General Motors Corporation.

Under the new organization, the engineering department will be responsible for all engineering work within its Group. Responsibility for car assembly has been placed within each Group because final assembly is critical to product quality control. Thus body design, manufacturing, and final assembly have been integrated to produce a higher-quality product. Elimination of the Fisher Body and Assembly divisions will give each Group vice-president control over the entire manufacturing process. The organization is intended to promote faster reactions to changes in the auto market. GM also believes that this reorganization will reduce costs by 25 percent.

While these dramatic changes were occurring in its automotive divisions, GM announced that it had agreed to buy Electronic Data Systems (EDS) for $2.5 billion. EDS, founded by entrepreneur H. Ross Perot, will provide the cornerstone of a GM information processing company. In acquiring EDS, GM must learn a new business. Unlike the auto business, where managers commonly think in terms of five-year design cycles, the computer software and services business moves much more rapidly. New products and services are introduced in 12–18 months. Perhaps just as challenging is the melding of two corporate cultures. Perot ran EDS as a paramilitary, macho company with great esprit de corps. Some people believe that Perot may have trouble fitting in with GM's conservative board. That deal came less than three months after GM purchased smaller companies engaged in artificial intelligence and a quality-control consulting group.

Smith stated that these acquisitions will advance GM's car-making methods, as well as provide new revenues. Company executives believe that EDS will provide the foundation for building a worldwide state-of-the-art voice-data and communication network. Smith believes that nonauto operations will contribute at least 10 percent of company sales by 1990 and 20 percent before the turn of the century. Smith's ultimate goal is to build a broader, more flexible company that can react quickly to changes in the marketplace.[1]

How do managers choose among different ways to organize? What are the best ways to achieve coordination among functions and departments? Should decision making be centralized or decentralized? When should task forces be used to work on a particular problem? These and other questions were partially answered in Chapter 10 and the GM Preview Case; they will be addressed further in this chapter.

Why is the design of an organization important? *Organization design* determines the structure and authority relationships of an organization.[2] The elements of an organization that can be designed were discussed in Chapter 10: division of activities and functions, or departmentalization; span of control; assignment of decision-making authority; and the location of line and staff personnel. In the process of designing an organization, managers invent, develop, and analyze alternative ways to combine these elements.

In approaching an organization design problem, managers have to answer three important questions:

1. How uncertain is the environment in which the organization operates?
2. How does technology affect the organization?
3. Who needs what kind of information to make a decision?

The first two questions have to do with two critical contingency variables that affect the design of an organization: environment and technology. These variables, in turn, affect the kinds and types of information that managers must process in making decisions. The purpose of this chapter is to present methods of designing an organization that gives adequate attention to these factors.

THE ENVIRONMENT AND ORGANIZATION DESIGN

In one sense, everything outside the organization can be considered as its external environment (Fig. 11.2). Many of the forces that shape the environment in which the organization operates were discussed in Chapters 3, 4, and 5. (See, also, Fig. 3.2.) We now want to stress the *degree of change* and *market segmentation* in the environment that influence an organization's structure, basis of departmentalization, coordination mechanisms, and control systems.[3] A firm that provides a product or service involving little technological innovation and relatively few competitors has a different set of problems from that of a firm providing a product or service in a market that is growing, changing, and competitive. The first environment is stable; the second, changing or uncertain. As we indicated in Chapter 3, the firm's competitive environment consists of its competitors, customers, suppliers, potential new entrants, and substitute products or services. Whether these are stable or changing has major implications for the internal structure of an organization, the type and amount of information needed in order to make decisions, and the management practices used in the organization. In general, most firms operate in both stable and changing environments; some departments may undergo little change, while others may change considerably. For example, at Xerox the production and marketing departments have changed substantially in order to respond to new technological advances and competitors. The

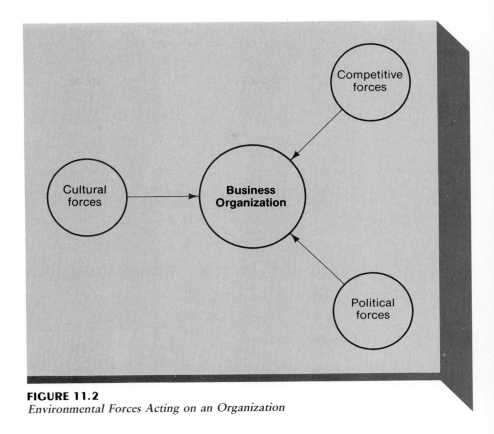

FIGURE 11.2
Environmental Forces Acting on an Organization

company's maintenance department, on the other hand, has experienced little change. Thus, as might be thought, at Xerox the departments affected most by changes in the environment have structures and coordination mechanisms that differ from those of the departments affected least.

Stable Environment

A *stable environment* is characterized by

■ products and services that have not changed much in recent years;

■ lack of technological innovation;

■ a fixed set of competitors, customers, and other stakeholders; and

■ consistent government policies of regulation and taxation.

Changes in a stable environment are relatively infrequent and, when they do occur, have a minimal impact on the internal operations of an organization. Top management can keep track of what is going on and make virtually all the necessary policy decisions. Companies in the brewing, coal-mining, glass container, paint, and food staples (flour, gelatin) industries operate in relatively stable environments. Although they may make slight changes in the product (such as the introduction of low-calorie, or lite, beer in the brewing industry), these changes can be incorporated easily into the existing technology of the firm.

Changes are likely to be in quantity (amount of beer or loaves of bread produced and sold). Such changes usually have little impact on organizational structure. The product itself is unlikely to change significantly; thus production managers are not faced with the need to change production processes. Firms in highly stable environments are likely to develop extensive distribution systems and invest heavily in capital equipment. These firms adapt to changes in demand by changing the size of the work force, not by changing the product or the method of production. For example, in the brewing industry, the production process requires a high capital investment and an extensive distribution system (beer distributors, trucks, warehouses). If there is a shift in demand, changes in the production system occur rather slowly, because the final product is still beer. If beer sales dropped off, Anheuser-Busch, Miller, or Coors, for example, would reduce the number of employees rather than seek new products (such as making wine or liquor). Changes in production methods and equipment would be too costly to permit profitable entry into related new product lines.

A stable environment provides a relatively high level of predictability. Firms operating in this environment are able to use common business indicators for planning and sales efforts.[4] The U.S. Department of Commerce prepares annual output projections for various industries based on changes occurring in the industry during the preceding 10 years. Firms operating in stable environments can use these indices for forecasting market changes and sales trends. Let us consider McDonald's as an example of a firm operating in a relatively stable environment.

IN PRACTICE
McDonald's

An analysis of McDonald's highlights business operations in a relatively stable environment. The typical franchise organization, such as McDonald's, Kentucky Fried Chicken, The International House of Pancakes, or Dunkin' Donuts, operates in a similar market environment. Competitors have similar promotional strategies and production technology. Technology tends to remain relatively constant, and the potential market is the same for all firms.

Ray Kroc, founder of McDonald's, opened his first restaurant in the Chicago area in April 1955. By 1985, the company operated more than 8000 restaurants, had sales in excess of $18.7 billion, and had sold more than 50 billion burgers. McDonald's had become the largest food-service organization in the world. McDonald's first menu focused on the hamburger, shake, and french fries. It has been expanded to include several sandwiches—the Big Mac®, The Quarter Pounder®, and Filet-O-Fish®—and several kinds of des-

McDonald's flourishes in a stable worldwide environment due to the efficiency of the organization's internal structure and the effectiveness of its management training.

Source: Arthur Tress/Magnum.

serts. A breakfast menu was introduced in 1976 and was an instant money-maker. What are some of the reasons for McDonald's success?

First, McDonald's franchisees and managers must attend an intensive 10-day training program at Hamburger University, the McDonald's International management training center in Elk Grove Village, Illinois. The curriculum includes work experience in a McDonald's restaurant and an intensive classroom program. Subjects taught by H.U. professors range from day-to-day management of a McDonald's restaurant to courses in business management, accounting, marketing, personnel management, and community relations. Trainees learn quickly that standards are important in maintaining the effectiveness of the company.

Second, the coordination mechanisms developed by McDonald's include not only a detailed organizational structure but also the continual provision of services (in terms of operations, public relations, advertising) to store managers by corporate staff. To ensure that the franchisees conform to McDonald's rules and regulations, the restaurants are visited regularly by area field consultants. McDonald's operating manual is a 385-page book covering the most minute details of operating an outlet.

Third, each McDonald's department has a specified job and extensive collaboration among headquarters departments and other organizational de-

(continued)

partments leads to similarity in design and control processes among the restaurants. For example, the design department at company headquarters works closely with each regional site and location department. This ensures that each restaurant meets the standards set by the organization and also blends to the extent possible with the general atmosphere and appearance of the community in which it is located.

Finally, the promotional strategy involves Ronald McDonald, who despite having become an international hero and celebrity, remains the same fun-loving clown that Kroc introduced to the world in 1963. A company survey indicated that 96 percent of all American children can identify Ronald McDonald, who is second in recognition only to Santa Claus. As Fred Turner, McDonald's Chief Executive Officer since 1973, says: "In an age when so many Americans are on the move, one of our main assets is our consistency and uniformity. It's very important that a man who's used to eating at a McDonald's in Hempstead, Long Island, knows he can get the same food and service when he walks into one in Albuquerque or Omaha."[5]

Changing Environment

A *changing environment* is characterized by

- products and services that change moderately or continually;
- major technological innovations that may make the old technology obsolete;
- ever-changing sets and/or actions of competitors, customers, or other stakeholders;
- unpredictable and changing governmental actions, reflecting political interaction between the public and various groups for consumer protection, product safety, pollution control, and civil rights; and
- rapid changes in the values and expectations of a large number of people.

Firms operating in this type of environment are likely to feel constant pressures to adapt their structures to changes in prices and customer demands. Products based on consumer preferences must be changed to meet new preferences and fads. Organizations in the telecommunications, computer, software, electronics, fashion, and pharmaceutical industries operate in changing environments.

Technological change

When technology is also changing, new ideas and concepts must be generated quickly. These new ideas can affect a product or the way in which it is manufactured. In the electronics industry, breakthroughs in integrated circuits and miniaturization significantly affected the nature of products. The introduction of electronic digital watches has had a tremendous impact on the market. For centuries, Swiss-made watches dominated the industry. The Swiss firms were independent and stressed the craftsmanship that went into each timepiece. When technology changed from hand-wound to electronic and digital watches, the Swiss were unable to meet the competition of these innovations. As a result, the entire Swiss industry suffered declining sales and revenue.

Similar changes have taken place in the personal computer, motorcycle, and microwave industries. Microwave ovens had been considered a luxury in most American households until 1984. But the microwave is becoming a mass-market appliance because of competition, which improved the technology and, at the same time, lowered prices. J. Hoyle Rymer, vice-president of Magic Chef, no longer sees the upscale suburban housewife as the primary market. The first microwave ovens made by Litton cost more than $750; now less costly ovens—some selling for as low as $150—are popular.[6] Sales are increasing by 33 percent per year and industrial analysts forecast that by the mid-1980s, industry sales will have grown from 6 million ovens in 1983 to more than 10 million ovens per year. The long-dominant U.S. and Japanese manufacturers, such as GE, Magic Chef, Litton, Nippon Electric, and Mitsubishi, are facing stiff competition from South Korean manufacturers. Some of the larger department stores, such as Kmart, J. C. Penney, and others, have signed agreements with South Korean manufacturers to provide microwave ovens for sale under the store's private label.

IN PRACTICE
IBM

In the fall of 1981, IBM finally announced a major reorganization. Typical of an essentially single-product-line firm, IBM had conducted its increasing volume of worldwide business using two different forms of organization. Operations in the United States were organized along product-group lines, such as data processing (main frame computers) and office equipment (typewriters and photocopiers). International operations were organized by place and coordinated through the IBM World Trade Corporation. National markets were grouped into world-region markets for the sale of both data-processing and office equipment.

The reorganization implemented in 1982 focused mainly on IBM's operations in the United States. The product form of organization was changed to the functional form, grouping functions such as sales, production, finance, and research and development. This reorganization was particularly needed in sales to eliminate a serious problem. Salespeople were scattered across product

(continued)

divisions and were all calling on the same customers, presenting them with different price quotes and financing agreements. The confusion and conflict among IBM sales representatives was one reason why IBM competitors, such as Digital Equipment and Data General, in the growing minicomputer market were able to take away some IBM business. Even in the main-frame computer markets, IBM has braced itself for fierce competition from three Japanese firms: Hitachi, NEC, and Fujitsu.

IBM made a strategic decision in the early 1980s to enter the personal computer and small photocopier markets in direct competition with Apple, Nixdorf, Radio Shack, Burroughs, and ITT. Thus it needed to reorganize itself to better serve the needs of its customers. Customers preferred dealing with one IBM salesperson who could handle all of the IBM product lines, rather than getting lost between the organizational cracks of IBM's internal bureaucracy.

While IBM was responding to changes in the market, it also faced new technological developments. With the spread of office automation and the development of *mechatronics,* the differences between the typewriter and word processor became blurred. Therefore IBM combined manufacturing and product development in order to keep abreast of the latest changes in the market. This move enabled IBM to take advantage of both stable and changing manufacturing and marketing trends.

In 1982, IBM made another strategic decision by creating a wholly owned subsidiary, the IBM Credit Corporation. The major function of this corporation is to remove financing problems from product and marketing managers. All leases and purchases of IBM equipment can be financed by the IBM Credit Corporation.[7]

Matching Structure to the Environment

Burns and Stalker found that firms operating effectively in stable environments choose organizational designs that are different from those of firms operating in changing environments. They labeled the two types of designs: mechanistic and organic.[8] The differences between these designs are highlighted in Table 11.1. The previous examples of Hewlett-Packard and McDonald's indicate how each of these firms is structured to compete successfully in its own environment. We can now classify Hewlett-Packard as an organic firm and McDonald's as a mechanistic firm.

A *mechanistic organization* is quite similar to the bureaucratic organization discussed in Chapter 2. In a mechanistic organization, the activities of the organization are broken down into separate, specialized tasks. Objectives and authority for each manager and subordinate are precisely defined. The line of authority is followed in making decisions.

The mechanistic design tends to be best suited for firms operating in stable environments, whereas the organic design tends to be best suited for firms operating in changing environments. In a stable environment, employees are likely to perform the same tasks over and over. Thus job specialization is appropriate. The objective of top management is to get employees to work as parts of a machine toward machine-like efficiency. When employees leave, others—like interchangeable parts—can be slipped into their places. Authority, responsibility, and accountability are arranged by levels. Decision making is centralized at the top; top managers decide what is important and how this information will be shared with others.

An *organic organization* is designed to foster teamwork. There is less emphasis on taking orders from a superior or giving orders to subordinates. Managers and subordinates are encouraged to communicate with anyone else in the organization who might help them solve a problem.

The organic design is better suited to a changing environment. Jobs must be constantly redefined to cope with the ever-changing needs of the organization. Employees must be skilled at solving a variety of problems. Decision

TABLE 11.1 ■ MECHANISTIC AND ORGANIC ORGANIZATIONS

MECHANISTIC	ORGANIC
■ Tasks are highly specialized.	■ Tasks tend to be interdependent.
■ Tasks tend to remain rigidly defined unless changed by top management.	■ Tasks are continually adjusted and redefined through interaction of employees.
■ Specific roles (rights, obligations, and technical methods) are prescribed for each employee.	■ Generalized roles (responsibility for task accomplishment beyond specific role definition) are accepted.
■ Structure of control, authority, and communication is hierarchical.	■ Structure of control, authority, and communication is a network.
■ Communication is primarily vertical, between superior and subordinate.	■ Communication is both vertical and horizontal, depending on where needed information resides.
■ Communications primarily take the form of instructions and decisions issued by superiors and of information and requests for decisions supplied by subordinates.	■ Communications primarily take the form of information and advice among all levels.

Source: Adapted from T. Burns and G. M. Stalker, *The Management of Innovation.* London: Tavistock, 1961, pp. 119–122.

making needs to be decentralized. Authority, responsibility, and accountability need to flow to the persons who have the greatest expertise to deal with problems. Managers and subordinates are encouraged to work together in teams and openly communicate with each other.

DiffERENTiATiON ANd iNTEGRATiON

The findings of Burns and Stalker were supported and extended by Lawrence and Lorsch.[9] They studied companies operating in stable and changing environments to see whether these firms were organized differently. They used the terms *differentiation* and *integration* to describe differences in organizations. Differentiation is a term used to represent the degree of difference that exists among the structures, tasks, and managerial orientation of various departments. Each department contains people whose attitudes and behaviors are appropriate for their specialized areas of expertise. For example, a production manager might think in terms of reducing costs, meeting daily production quotas, and following rules and regulations to ensure an efficient production process. In contrast, a marketing manager might think in terms of increasing volume, bending rules and regulations to satisfy an important customer, and introducing new products during the next three years. If managers and their departments markedly exhibit these differences, the organization can be classified as highly differentiated. A potential problem with a high degree of differentiation is that of bringing these people together to accomplish the organization's goals and objectives.

Integration refers to the degree to which the various departments work together as a team. Means of integration include rules and regulations, chain of command, task forces, and direct contact between managers.

Lawrence and Lorsch reasoned that firms facing different environments (stable versus changing) would exhibit varying amounts of differentiation and integration in attempting to compete successfully in the marketplace. They further reasoned that not all departments in an organization would be affected to the same extent.

They found that firms operating effectively in stable environments had fewer departments than those operating in changing environments. With respect to differences between departments, they observed that production departments for firms producing plastic products (changing environment) had long-established production processes and were organized along formal, mechanistic lines. On the other hand, the research and development departments of the same plastics firms were organized along organic lines. These departments faced the constant demand for development of new products and new ways to make plastic.

Lawrence and Lorsch also found that high-performance firms in both types of environments had higher degrees of integration than low-performance firms. Thus, the more that an organization can integrate its activities, the more effective it tends to be. The more effective firms used integrating tools such as task forces and integrators, whereas the less effective firms relied more on rules and regulations.

In summary, Lawrence and Lorsch support the importance of designing a structure to fit a firm's environment. They also emphasize the importance of integration within a firm but recognize that mechanistic organization in certain departments and organic organization in others does not necessarily reduce the effectiveness of the firm. If the production department faces a relatively stable environment and the marketing department faces a changing one, managers of these two departments are likely to choose different ways to divide up the work and coordinate subordinates in their department. The production manager will probably organize the department along mechanistic lines, while the marketing manager will choose a more organic structure.

TECHNOLOGY AND ORGANIZATION DESIGN

The technology that a firm uses to produce its products or provide its services represents the second major contingency variable that affects the design of an organization.[10] *Technology* is the process used to transform inputs (such as information, raw materials, and the like) into outputs (such as products or services). Most people associate the word technology only with assembly lines and production plants. However, technologies are also involved in teaching students, processing bank checks, entering a hospital, or going through the checkout counter at the grocery store. Thus technology can be analyzed in a variety of settings and its importance in the design of an organization cannot be overstated.[11]

Technology affects significantly the design of an organization because different types of technology generate various types of internal interdependence. That is, technology influences how departments or people interact to get a job accomplished. There are three types of technological interdependence: pooled, sequential, and reciprocal.[12] In *pooled interdependence,* little information flow is required between departments or people. Each department or person operates more or less independently of others. In *sequential interdependence* the flow of information and work between departments or people is serial. A supplies work to B, who in turn supplies work to C, and so on. In *reciprocal interdependence,* each department or person works with every other department or person. Work flows back and forth between departments until the task is accomplished. To understand more fully how these three types of interdependence can affect the organization design, we have chosen three sports—baseball, football, and basketball—to illustrate the concepts of pooled, sequential, and reciprocal interdependence.[13]

Pooled Interdependence: Baseball

In baseball, team-member contributions are relatively independent of each other. According to Pete Rose, "Baseball is a team game, but nine men who reach their individual goals make a nice team." When communication does occur, it is usually between no more than two or three players—for example, pitcher and catcher, baserunner, or infielder to infielder. Rarely are more than a few players directly involved in a given play.

The placement of the nine players in the field makes communication difficult. Players are spread over a wide playing area, especially in the outfield. This geographical distance combined with a relatively low need for communication between players, makes baseball an individual sport. The team's overall success is the sum of team members' individual performances. This is clearly seen when one team is at bat because players come to the plate one at a time. Of course, scoring typically requires a sequence of walks, hits, and sacrifices, but each player's contribution is basically independent of those of the others.

In baseball, coordination is achieved primarily by the structure of the game. There are few game plans to devise, with the possible exception of pitching rotation. Game decisions are made before the game starts (filling out the lineup card) and during it (making substitutions, positioning fielders, pinch hitting, stealing bases). The manager's job is to make decisions in a timely manner. Some of baseball's best managers have been described as superb tacticians.

Because baseball's basic unit is the individual, developmental efforts focus primarily on honing individual skills. Batting practice, running, and fielding practice focus primarily on improving the individual player. Clearly, certain team plays are important, such as double plays, pickoff attempts, sacrificing to advance a runner, relay throws, and so forth. But these team efforts rarely involve more than two or three players at a time and depend more on individual execution than on team play. Coordination between players requires that they follow certain rules and regulations. The rules and regulations relate to situations that are relatively stable, repetitive, and internally consistent. For example, the catcher is supposed to back up first base when the third baseman or shortstop throws to first. In fact, the first baseman counts on the catcher being there every time a ground ball is hit to either player when a runner is not in scoring position. Similarly, when a runner attempts to steal third base, the left fielder is supposed to back up third base in case the catcher's throw gets past the third baseman.

Implications for management

Companies that are organized like baseball teams include franchise operations (Burger King, Kentucky Fried Chicken, 7-Eleven Stores), bank holding companies, geographically organized firms (U.S. Postal Service, United Parcel

Service, North American Van Lines), and research laboratories (RAND, Bell Labs). For example, Southland Corporation's profits will increase in proportion to the profits of each of its 7-Eleven stores. However, each store manager is responsible for only his or her store. There is minimal communication among store managers. To assist managers in their operations and to ensure consistency, Southland Corporation suggests that these managers follow certain standard buying, hiring, advertising and other merchandising practices. Ray Kroc, founder of McDonald's and owner of the San Diego Padres baseball team until his death, stated that a well-run restaurant is like a winning baseball team: It makes the most of every member's talent and takes advantage of every opportunity to speed up service.

Sequential Interdependence: Football

Football resembles sequential interdependence in two ways. First, on offense, the line leads the backfield by providing the blocking necessary for running, passing, or kicking. This happens on every play. Second, the flow of plays usually required to score follows a set pattern. That is, the team is required to make ten yards in four attempts to move downfield. Every time it accomplishes that objective, it receives another four downs.

.The offensive players are not spread too far apart. This permits frequent communication between the players and allows the quarterback to change a play after he *reads* the defense. Further, most players on the field are involved in every play.

There is a continuous potential for change between offense and defense. Each team can turn the ball over to the other at any time as a result of a fumble, pass interception, or blocked kick. Apart from turnovers, the normal transition between these two teams is accomplished by specialists—kicking teams—who made the team solely on the basis of their play during these transitions (punts, kickoffs, and field goals).

The basic units in football are groups of players that perform offensive, defensive, and kicking functions. A team's overall performance is basically the sum of these groups' performances. Each group's challenge is to be as machinelike as possible. We can picture the football field as a factory, with the moving line of scrimmage representing the product flow through a factory. According to George Allen, former coach of the Washington Redskins:

> A football team is a lot like a machine. It's made up of parts. If one part doesn't work, one player pulling against you and not doing his job, the whole machine fails.

Coordination in football is achieved through planning. Of the three sports, football is the most strategy-intensive game. In the National Football League, each team plays only 16 regular-season games, compared to 82 in the National

Basketball Association and 162 in major league baseball. Therefore the average NFL game has five times more significance than the typical basketball game and ten times that of a regular-season baseball game. In the postseason playoffs, a football team is eliminated by a single loss. In contrast, each stage of the playoffs for baseball and basketball requires a series of games.

To achieve coordination within each squad—offense, defense, kicking—films of the upcoming opponent are run and rerun. This provides clues as to likely play sequences, formations, coverages, and so on. Each squad's own previous performance is also reviewed. A game plan is drawn up, and players are drilled in the strategy adopted to beat the opponent. Each player has a narrow job description that clearly outlines his responsibility and accountability. Football's combination of meticulous preparation, high information requirements, and specialized tasks helps to explain why there are more coaches per team in this sport than in either baseball or basketball.

The primary job of the coaching staff is to develop a strong esprit de corps and coordination within each squad. Players tend to identify more readily with their squad than with the team. Intersquad rivalry can prepare players physically and mentally for the next game. In the fall, newspaper sports pages are routinely filled with stories about fights breaking out between offensive and defensive squad members. These fights can help to maintain a squad's identity and feelings of unity.

Implications for management

Companies that use sequential interdependence range from automotive to large construction companies. The assembly line represents a carefully orchestrated set of predictable and sequential activities. Workers perform these activities time and time again. At Henry C. Beck Company, building a skyscraper follows certain steps. For example, after a site has been chosen, architects and engineers draft plans, after which ground is broken, a foundation is poured, steel girders are erected, plumbing and electrical work is started, siding is mounted, and the like. Unless the specified sequence of activities is followed, the building cannot be constructed.

Reciprocal Interdependence: Basketball

Basketball exhibits a high degree of reciprocal interdependence. This is demonstrated by the rapid movement of the ball among the players, up and down the court, and between the teams. The pace and style of the game are markedly different from baseball or football.

The players in basketball are tightly grouped in a small area. Every player is involved in (1) offense, defense, and transitions; (2) trying to score; and (3) handling the ball.

The team on offense may become the team on defense—and vice versa—instantaneously. The transition from offense to defense is not a separate part of the game involving specialized players but is a continuous part of the game's flow, involving all the players.

The basic unit in basketball is the team. With five players on the court, the team's performance is a function of player interaction. In addition, players sitting on the bench may be called on by the coach to play in combination with every other player on the team. This means that basketball is a team sport and cannot be thought of as an aggregate of different squads. The best basketball coaches teach players to forge themselves into a tightly knit unit.

The key coordinating mechanism in basketball is mutual adjustment by the players. Coordination by mutual adjustment may involve communication across hierarchical lines. The coach's tasks are to (1) develop the team's ability to adjust; and (2) intervene (call time outs, substitute players) on an exception basis. The game strategy of an effective basketball coach often resembles that of a counterpuncher in boxing. That is, when one coach changes strategy, the other coach must make successful adjustments to counter that strategy.

In basketball, interaction is more important than the sum of the individual player's actions. While a team of prima donnas can win it all in baseball, it is not likely to happen in basketball. Bill Bradley (former Princeton and New York Knickerbocker star) pointed out in 1977 after the talent-rich Philadelphia 76ers lost to the Portland Trail Blazers in the NBA finals: "Maybe someday a team will have so much individual firepower that on that alone it can win a championship. It hasn't happened yet." Julius Erving, Larry Bird, and Earvin "Magic" Johnson, among others, have stated that the basic skill in basketball is passing. Effective passing involves not only the person with the ball, but a continuous adjustment by others without the ball. An effective passing game lessens somewhat the need for outstanding shooters or rebounders because great passing teams usually get a high percentage of close-in shots, layups, and dunks.

To achieve tight interaction and integration among the players, the coach needs both interpersonal and technical skills. The coach must be aware of each player's unique personality and skills and be able to blend them into an effectively functioning unit. Successful coaches are good integrators.

Implications for management

Examples of firms that use reciprocal interdependence to reach their objectives include management-consulting firms, think-tank organizations, creative advertising firms, large accounting firms (Price Waterhouse, Coopers and Lybrand, Arthur Young), brokerage houses and state-of-the-art computer manufacturers. At McKinsey and Company, one of the world's largest management-consulting firms, a team is assigned to every project. Members of this team may be expected to know accounting procedures, how to perform financial analyses, conduct marketing research, reorganize a company, and similar operations. Members of a McKinsey team must exchange information frequently to coordinate their efforts in order to solve the client's problem.

TABLE 11.2 ■ SUMMARY OF STRUCTURE AND TECHNOLOGY RELATIONSHIPS

	TECHNOLOGICAL INTERDEPENDENCE		
STRUCTURAL DIMENSION	*Pooled*	*Sequential*	*Reciprocal*
Sport team	Baseball	Football	Basketball
Basic unit	Individual	Multiple groups	Teams
Development focus	Individual	Individual, group	Individual, team
Need for member coordination	Low	Moderate	High
Communication requirements among members	Low	Moderate	High
Integration achieved by	Standards, rules, and regulations	Planning of top management	Mutual adjustment of employees
Geographical dispersion of members	Wide	Somewhat clustered	Highly concentrated

Source: Adapted from R. Keidel, "Baseball, football, and basketball: Models for Business," *Organizational Dynamics,* 12 (Winter), 1984, pages 8, 13, and 17.

Summary of Technology and Structure Relationships

No company can easily be put into a single category of technological interdependence. A company or its various departments may reflect the different types of interdependence and illustrate how they can affect organization design. Table 11.2 summarizes technological interdependence relationships for the main dimensions of structural design. As companies mix different kinds of technologies, the job of the manager becomes more complex.

INFORMATION PROCESSING SYSTEMS AND ORGANIZATION DESIGN

The kinds of technology used, technological interdependence required, and the types of environmental forces confronted shape the information processing requirements for managers. The Preview Case about GM showed that changes in the marketplace played a major part in the decision to reorganize the company and buy EDS. The IBM In Practice related that company's problem with multiple salespersons calling on customers and giving them different prices, delivery dates, and so on. In both companies, important information was not being exchanged or processed. Managers need accurate and timely information if they are to guide their organizations successfully. Information enables the manager to anticipate and respond to market, technological, and resource changes in an effective manner. The more rapid the changes, the greater is the need for managers to process information.

Effects of Different Environments

As mentioned previously, companies competing in relatively stable environments often rely on rules, regulations, and planning to coordinate their operations. These integrative methods are effective as long as the environment remains stable. The information processing requirements for these firms are relatively modest. For example, firms selling ice cream or high school yearbooks can plan production schedules with relative assurance that sudden shifts in demand, resource supply, or technology will not disrupt their schedules. Information requirements consist mainly of data about past years' sales, costs, and production methods; these data are projected for the next planning period. Taylor Publishing Company publishes yearbooks for junior and senior high schools, junior colleges, and universities.[14] In 1984, the company sold yearbooks to more than 26,000 schools and colleges, a 35 percent share of this market. Because yearbooks are distributed during the spring months, February through May are peak production months. These production peaks are highly predictable, requiring overtime from all employees. Taylor also knows through records compiled by the Bureau of the Census that the number of children graduating from high school will decline from 2.7 million in 1984 to 2.2 million in 1991 and then rise again to 1984 levels by 1998.

Organizations operating in changing environments are typically unable to rely solely on past sales. Changes in demand, resources, supplies, and technology require adjustments during the production cycle. Managers need to receive accurate and timely information about these environmental changes in order to avoid on-the-spot plant adjustments that can disrupt production schedules. Coordination is more difficult because managers cannot preplan operations and devise rules and regulations to cover all situations. For example, Optigraphics is a company that produces 3-D buttons, stickers, and postcards. Each order requires a unique set of art and design work and machine time. Sometimes, the art and design work is farmed out to other companies to complete. Because these items appeal to fads, such as the Michael Jackson Victory Tour in 1984, the 1984 Olympics, or the 1984 Presidential race, customers constantly want their orders filled immediately. However, if art work is delayed, the entire production process is delayed. People and machines are idle and top managers must decide which order can be processed in place of the delayed one. The sales, production, purchasing, and marketing managers must get together to exchange ideas about what to do next.[15]

Although Parker Brothers' Monopoly remains a traditional board game, its production is subject to changes in competition due to a constant influx of new games into the market.

Source: David A. Krathwohl/ Stock, Boston.

Rapid environmental change can lead to information overload on managers. As a greater number of nonroutine events occur in the organization's environment, top managers are more drawn into the day-to-day operations of the business. Middle and first-line managers need to spend more time communicating with their superiors and other managers with whom they are interdependent. Some organizations such as NASA have been designed from the beginning to deal with high levels of information processing demands. Others face the problem only when their current design is incapable of dealing with changes in the environment. For these organizations, the problem becomes one of selecting an appropriate information processing strategy.

Information-Processing Strategies

The basic effect of rapid changes in an organization's environment is to create uncertainty. Uncertainty was discussed in the chapters on decision making (Chapters 6–8). From the standpoint of organization design, *uncertainty* refers to the difference between the amount of information required to perform a task and the amount of relevant information already possessed by the organization.[16] The effect of uncertainty is to limit managers' ability to plan for or make decisions in advance about the effects of change. Three factors contribute to this uncertainty: (1) the diversity of the organization's outputs; (2) the number of different technical specialists on a project; and (3) the level of difficulty in achieving objectives. The greater the diversity of products, the greater the number of different technical specialists, and the higher the performance objectives, the greater is the number of variables that must be considered in making decisions. Consequently, managers may not possess the information necessary to achieve organizational objectives. One of two general approaches can be used to solve this problem: (1) increase the organization's ability to process information; and (2) reduce the need to process information. These two general approaches and their strategies are shown in Table 11.3.

Increasing the Ability to Process Information

Managers can increase their organization's ability to process information by choosing to invest in *vertical information systems* or create *lateral relationships*.[17] Both of these strategies take the amount of information that needs to be processed as a given. They create processes whereby the organization can better manage the information. These strategies are especially useful when the people or departments involved are either sequentially or reciprocally interdependent.

TABLE 11.3 ■ INFORMATION PROCESSING STRATEGIES

GENERAL APPROACH	STRATEGY
Increasing the ability to process information	1. Investment in vertical information systems 2. Creation of lateral relations
Reducing the need to process information	1. Creation of slack resources 2. Creation of self-contained tasks or departments

Source: Adapted from J. Galbraith, *Designing Complex Organizations*. Reading, Mass.: Addison-Wesley, 1973, p. 15.

INTERNATIONAL FOCUS

EASTMAN KODAK

Eastman Kodak manufactures and markets photographic and chemical products worldwide. Worldwide sales were $10.6 billion in 1984. The imaging market, which generates about 80 percent of Kodak's revenues worldwide, includes film, paper, copiers, disc cameras, and related products. Many of these products are produced and then assembled in a variety of countries for sale worldwide. As one might expect, this creates tremendous difficulties in making sure that products and components are made in a coordinated fashion.

In the mid-70s, faced with the complexities of distance, governments, cultures, and competition, Kodak created an International Distribution Operations Committee to unite different business groups that had an effect on the movement of worldwide goods. The Committee was charged with locating where parts were in the shortest possible time to avoid delays in shipping these to customers. The departments that made recommendations to this Committee included Transportation, Product Handling, Estimating and Planning, Distribution systems, and International Order Services.

The International Order Service Department is critical because it essentially is the inventory management system used at Kodak. Any inventory management system is concerned with setting a reorder point that takes into account the lead time of shipment, the cost of carrying too many units in storage, and the cost of being out of items that should be carried in stock. Kodak found out that it needed to standardize the preparation of replacement orders from

Source: Abtracted from Eastman Kodak Company *1984 Annual Report;* John Daniels, Earnest Ogram, and Lee Radebaugh, *International Business: Environments and Operations,* 3rd ed. Reading, Mass.: Addison-Wesley, 1982, pp. 375–377.

Investment in vertical information systems.   This strategy enables managers to send information more efficiently up and down the chain of command. Methods used might range from the purchase of personal computers to hiring clerical assistants to organize and summarize information. Many new supermarkets have purchased new checkout machines that use optical scanners.[18] As the buyers' purchases pass over the eye of the scanner, cost, item type, and other data from the packages are read directly into a computer. Whenever the store manager wants to know the impact of a special coupon on the sales volume of a product, the results can be readily obtained from the computer. Ordering items from a warehouse can also be made more responsive to sudden shifts in customer preferences. These computer systems further enable the manager to determine the percentage of sales from each department (produce, meat, grocery, nonfoods). Finally, these systems reduce checkers' errors. Studies show that a tired checker can make errors averaging 1.5 percent on a checkout. Although the investment in these computer systems is expensive

its various plants. To do this, an international product numbering system was created so that each particular product, no matter where it was made or stored, could be counted. Whenever an order was placed from anywhere in the world, the order was immediately logged in the computer system. If the product was out of stock, a back-order notice was automatically sent to the buyer. A manufacturing plant was also notified to produce the product and ship the part to the buyer. If the product was available, the computer would tell the plant manager where to ship the part to the buyer.

Once the order was prepared for shipping, the Transportation Department was responsible for making sure that the goods got loaded on the right ship or plane and were delivered to the proper location. The Product Handling Department was responsible for seeing that the products were properly packed and marked for overseas shipment.

One of the keys to the whole operation's success was the Estimating and Planning Department. That department was responsible for merging the manufacturing, marketing, and distribution departments through a state-of-the-art computer system. Weekly reports were required to determine inventory levels of products worldwide and to match them with demand in different countries to see where products needed to be shipped to buyers that would minimize the shipping costs to Kodak.

(about $11,000 per checkout counter), the savings from reducing errors usually pay for the system in high-volume stores within a short time.

Examples of other businesses that have invested effectively in vertical information systems are Ticketron outlets, airline reservation systems, and off-track betting parlors. These systems allow rapid updating of constantly changing information that is needed by customers. In such firms, employees can obtain information quickly and serve customers without going through various levels of authority, and managers can obtain the information they need from the system.

Creation of lateral relations.   The second way to increase an organization's ability to process information is to increase coordination among functional departments. The purpose of this strategy is to push the level of decision making down to where the information exists rather than bringing the information up to top management. Whereas vertical information systems centralize decisions by bringing information to top managers, lateral relations decentralize decisions. There are two means of implementing this strategy.

The simplest form of lateral relations is to establish direct contact between two departments or people who share a common problem. The purpose is to facilitate joint decision making among them and to increase the number of managers who can deal with changes in the environment. This is illustrated in Fig. 11.3. If department A is about to fall behind in its production of parts that go to department D for further processing, the manager of A could contact D directly, instead of referring the problem up through E to G for a solution. If A and D can mutually agree on a solution, the number of problems flowing up the hierarchy is reduced. Top managers then have more free time to make decisions concerning problems that cannot be solved by direct contact between lower-level managers.

The second alternative is to create a new position to integrate information. The ***integrator role*** is designed to handle communication between two inter-dependent departments and bypass the formal lines of communication in the hierarchy. Product managers and expediters are examples of people who

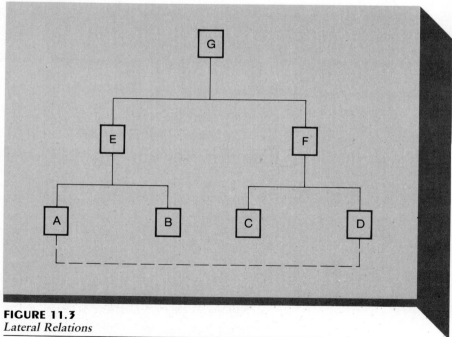

FIGURE 11.3
Lateral Relations

Source: J. Galbraith, *Organizational Design*. Reading, Mass.: Addison-Wesley, 1977, p. 113. Reprinted with permission.

facilitate communication between departments. Their job is to gather information from both departments and increase the flow of timely communication between them. In Chapter 10, we discussed the job of a project manager in matrix organizations. These people represent both the functional areas (marketing, accounting, finance) and product (at Boeing, a product manager is responsible for each model of plane: the 727, 737, and 757). In essence, project managers in a matrix organization perform integrating roles.

Reducing the need to process information

Managers can reduce the need to process information by reducing the number of exceptions that occur or reducing the number of factors to be considered when exceptions do occur. These two objectives can be achieved by strategies to create **slack resources** or **self-containment.**

Creation of slack resources.   This method involves stockpiling of materials, manpower, and other resources to enable an organization to respond to environmental changes. Other forms of slack resources include an organization's ability to lengthen production schedules and delivery times to buyers, increase lead times, and the like. When a firm intentionally overestimates the length of time needed to complete a project, it is creating slack in the schedule. This technique builds in additional time to allow the firm to deal with any unexpected difficulties that arise. The student who writes term papers in advance of their due date is creating slack in his or her schedule. This allows for editing, retyping, and completing assignments on time.

In a manufacturing firm, the effect of using slack resources is to reduce the interdependence between departments. If extra inventory is available to meet unexpected sales demand, less communication is needed among purchasing, production, and sales. However, if the purchasing manager keeps only a minimal amount of inventory on hand (no slack), the production and sales managers must coordinate their activities more closely to avoid running out of inventory.

Creating slack resources has some cost and customer-relations implications. In manufacturing businesses, increased lead time generates inventories that cost money. This money is tied up, when it could be used for other purposes. Extended planning, budgeting, and scheduling time horizons may lead to lower performance expectations in the firm. Finally, buyers may not be able or want to have their schedules extended because of their plans or commitments.

Creating self-contained tasks or departments.   The second method for reducing the need to process information requires that all activities for a given product or task be assigned to one group. This strategy involves choosing a product form of departmentalization instead of a functional form. As we discussed in Chapter 10, many firms pursue product forms of departmentalization because of problems with their functional organization. In a product firm (Procter & Gamble, Heinz, PepsiCo), each product group is provided with its own functional resources: accounting, marketing, manufacturing, personnel, finance. Reorganization around product enables an organization to achieve its desired level of flexibility and adaptability for each product line. This form of organization reduces the amount of information processed in two ways.

First, the product form reduces the number of different products and consumers for each group. That is, managers deal with a limited number of products and a common set of customers whose wants and desires are similar. For example, at PepsiCo, the Frito-Lay product managers focus only on snack foods, whereas, Wilson Sporting Goods product managers focus only on sporting goods. Therefore the managers of these product lines do not need to share information concerning manufacturing costs, delivery schedules, distribution channels, and the like because it is not relevant to the other managers.

Second, specialization across product lines is reduced. In a functional organization, the accountant must know something about each product; in the product structure, the accountant needs to know something about only one product line. Thus the amount of uncertainty is reduced because all information is now focused on a limited set of product problems.

In terms of information processing, managers of self-contained departments face less uncertainty than do other managers in an organization. They deal with a common set of buyers or manufacturers and do not have to coordinate their activities with others. In the Preview Case, we noted that GM created self-contained groups that now are responsible for styling, engineering, and manufacturing and have appropriate financial and personnel functions to make independent decisions. This reorganization reduced the need for managers from different groups to communicate with each other before making decisions.

Multinationals and Information Processing

The evolution of multinational companies over the past decade has been characterized by a growing conflict between the requirements for economic survival, adjustments to demands from host countries, and the integration needs of the company.[19] For some companies that have extensive manufacturing operations in several countries, one solution is to integrate the manufacturing process. Each plant produces only part of the product range, depending on the cost and availability of key resources in the production process (labor, energy, raw materials, and skills). This also achieves economies of scale. Texas Instruments' location of labor-intensive semiconductor finishing activities in southeast Asia or Ford and GM's European-wide manufacturing of autos illustrate this solution. The overriding reasons for this solution are to reduce costs and to capture large sales volumes. For example, Ford's manufacturing costs in Europe are estimated to be well below those of other companies manufacturing a comparable car.

Some companies, such as Westinghouse, ITT, and GTE, forgo the potential benefits of integration and give much more leeway to their subsidiaries. In this way, each subsidiary is free to pursue its own strategy to reach the corporation's goals. Where the host government plays an important role, such as in the nuclear engineering and electrical power industries, a national strategy seems more appropriate. Manufacturing is usually done entirely within the host country. In some industries, such as telecommunications and microelectronics, R&D activities are also carried out by employees working in the host country.

Each of these solutions has major implications for the information processing systems of a company. At Black and Decker decisions cannot be left to subsidiaries. They have to be reached by some group that collectively agrees on which plant will produce which products, how decisions will be made, and the like. Investment in vertical information systems were made by company managers because responsiveness to changes in the environment by the various plants is critical. Task forces that cut across formal structure are also used to bring about change.

IN PRACTICE
Black and Decker

Black and Decker, the power-tool maker that sells to do-it-yourselfers for household repairs, purchased GE's small-appliance business in 1984. Although Black and Decker has a 50 percent market share worldwide in power tools, competition is forcing changes in its manufacturing and marketing operations. The company plans to integrate its manufacturing and marketing operations for both power tools and small appliances on a worldwide basis.

Prior to 1984, Black and Decker had been organized along national lines: The Italian subsidiary made tools for Italians, the British subsidiary made tools for Britons, and so on. Black and Decker operated 25 plants in 13 countries on 6 continents. It was divided into three operating groups, each with its own corporate staff. Individual companies operated autonomously and communication among companies was practically nonexistent. Managers had complete control over their operations, under the assumption that they knew their respective countries and could best judge which products would succeed. Unfortunately, problems arose. For example, the dustbuster cordless vacuum cleaner had been a best seller since 1979 in the United States, but was not made available in Australia until 1983. At one point, Black and Decker's design centers produced designs for more than 250 different motor sizes, even though the company needed fewer than 10. Similarly, European managers refused to

(continued)

sell Black and Decker housewares, maintaining that these products were strictly for Americans.

Laurence Farley, chairman, realized that market distinctions were disappearing and implemented a worldwide strategy. The emergence of worldwide markets allows Black and Decker to standardize the manufacturing and distribution of its products. An automaker like Toyota, for example, produces cars with steering columns on the right or left side, depending on the destination of the car. That requires only minor modifications and most other features of the product are the same. Farley plans to do the same thing with small appliances. To implement this strategy, Black and Decker now requires that all its managers constantly communicate with each other. In 1984, Black and Decker introduced the Spacemaker series, which included a coffeemaker, electric knife, toaster oven, and can opener. These appliances are all designed to save space by being hung beneath kitchen cabinets. The series will be sold as a high-priced, color-coordinated group rather than as individual products. However, the individual products will be made in plants scattered around the world and shipped to each other for final assembly and distribution to stores. This new organization did not sit well with all managers. In the United Kingdom, where Black and Decker had an 80 percent share of the market, managers asked, "Why tamper with success?" Farley believed that even though Black and Decker had a large market share, the company was standing still. In order to emphasize his commitment to the new plan, he had to fire 25 European managers and drastically reduce the staffs of others.[20]

When a more national solution is pursued, there is little need to increase a firm's ability to process information among plants that operate in different countries; each plant operates independently. For example, at ITT, the interdependencies among product lines are minimal, allowing each product line to achieve a clear strategy for its business.

AN INTEGRATED FRAMEWORK FOR ORGANIZATION DESIGN

In Chapters 8, 10, and 11, we have presented many of the factors that managers must consider when designing an organization's structure.[21] The most important of these are *determinants* of organization design and are shown in Fig. 11.4. Thus the overall design of a structure depends on the situation, as determined by the interaction of environmental, technological interdependence, and information processing requirements.[22] Managers should consider carefully these determinants along with basic concepts when making organization-design decisions.

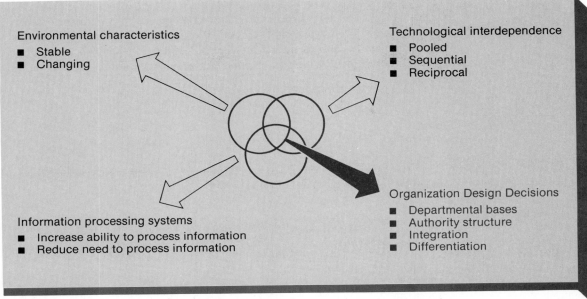

FIGURE 11.4
An Integrated Framework for Organization Design

If the environment is stable, information processing requirements for a firm are not great and a functional organizational structure is likely to be effective. Functional organizations achieve integration through the chain of command and by means of rules and regulations. Jobs are highly specialized within departments.

As the environment becomes less stable, information processing requirements for a firm increase, as do decision-making and integrating requirements. The use of teams, the integrator role, and, sometimes, a matrix form of departmentalization is more appropriate. These integrating mechanisms increase the ability of managers to process a great deal of information coming from an uncertain environment. The use of vertical information systems and the establishment of lateral relationships are important under these conditions. Members of functional and product departments are often reciprocally interdependent. Extensive communication is needed in order to achieve organizational objectives in an effective manner. The matrix organization is highly differentiated and achieves integration through organic as opposed to mechanistic means.

An alternative form of organization for a changing environment is the product form. This structure reduces managers' needs to process information across product lines. The establishment of self-contained tasks or departments means linkage by pooled interdependence. The product organization is typically less formalized, centralized, and standardized than a functional organization.

CHAPTER SUMMARY

This chapter presented an approach to organization-design decisions based on two contingency variables, environment and technology, which, in turn, influence the information processing requirements of an organization. These three factors are called the *determinants* of organization design.

Firms operating effectively in stable environments tend to have mechanistic systems. The more stable the environment, the more mechanistic is the design. Successful firms in changing environments tend to be both highly differentiated and highly integrated. The greater the rate of change, the more organic is the design.

The second contingency variable discussed was technology. Rather than focusing on specific technological advances, we approached the topic from the viewpoint of internal interdependence created by different technologies. The three forms of technological interdependence—pooled, sequential, and reciprocal—were illustrated by analogies to sports teams.

Both the environment and type of technological interdependence affect the general approach to information processing used and the strategy selected. We discussed two strategies for increasing an organization's ability to process information and two for reducing the need for information to be processed. Investment in vertical information systems and creation of lateral relations are strategies for increasing information-processing abilities. Reduction strategies include creation of slack resources and self-containment (product form of organization).

An integrated framework for organization design synthesizes the determinants and appropriate concepts of organization design. A design that fits the situation is the result.

MANAGER'S VOCABULARY

changing environment
differentiation
integration
integrator role
lateral relations
mechanistic organization
organic organization
organization design
pooled interdependence
reciprocal interdependence
self-containment
sequential interdependence
slack resources
stable environment
technology
uncertainty
vertical information systems

REVIEW QUESTIONS

1. What are the features of stable and changing environments?

2. What are the differences between a mechanistic and an organic organization?

3. Give examples of pooled, sequential, and reciprocal technological interdependence.

4. What are the ways that organizations can increase their ability to process information?

5. What are the ways that organizations can reduce their need to process information?

DISCUSSION QUESTIONS

1. Discuss some of the limitations involved in answering the question: "What is the best way to organize?"

2. What is the relationship between (a) differentiation and integration, and (b) environmental stability and change?

3. What managerial problems do the use of multiple forms of technological interdependence create?

4. Discuss the manner in which the environment and technology interact to influence selection of the most effective strategy for processing information.

5. This chapter discussed how the environment, technology, and information-processing needs can influence the structure of a firm. Examine your own university using these concepts.

MANAGEMENT INCIDENTS AND CASES

Environmental Control Systems (ECS)

Don Williams, president of ECS, continued to think about the Precision Dynamics contract. Precision Dynamics Corporation was a huge contractor involved in building ships and other large maritime projects for the commercial shipping industry. It looked fairly certain that Precision Dynamics was going to award an important subcontract to ECS. Environmental Control Systems would be responsible for developing and building the temperature-control systems for four new liquid natural gas tankers.

Naturally, Don was elated that Precision had been impressed with ECS's design proposals. Liquified natural gas (LNG) can be shipped only at extremely low temperatures. This had proved to be both difficult and dangerous. Previous designs had resulted in lost cargo and even the loss of ships. The freezing process sometimes caused tiny cracks to form in the ships' hulls. Because of the potential safety hazard, the Coast Guard had refused to certify some recently built tankers for LNG transport.

Based on an ingenious system that refrigerated the cargo tanks while forcing heated air between the tanks and the ship's hull, ECS's design promised to meet the needs of both shippers and the Coast Guard. This project represented quite a departure from ECS's usual business. Don was well aware that a successful design would really put his company on the map. It would also move it in a direction that fit his long-range strategic plans quite well. On the other hand, a major failure could bury his company forever.

Don was more concerned with the organizational problems than with the technical ones. The company had never attempted a job as large and complex as this one. It would put a tremendous strain on ECS in terms of time, manpower, and resources. The complex technology would require the close cooperation of all three operating divisions in both design and production. While the divisions shipped products to one another and occasionally borrowed ideas from each other, there were few mechanisms that would allow for coordinating complex and ongoing activities such as this. The contract was appealing, but it was also a gamble. Without close cooperation and coordination, it was sure to fail.

Environmental Control Systems had begun with Don's father. He was a machinist who used to assemble and ship ceiling fans from his garage as a part-time business. There had always been a small but steady demand for the fans. Don and his brothers and sisters had more or less grown up helping out with the business.

A few years after Don's graduation from college, his father suggested he take over the business and try to do something with it. All their orders had come from word-of-mouth or small ads in local bargain sheets. They had never tried to expand the market or reach more affluent buyers. Don decided to give it a try and placed ads in *The Ladies' Home Journal* and another women's magazine. Within months demand for the fans far exceeded the family's ability to meet it. Don hired three assemblers to work full time and started searching for a small manufacturing site.

Don expanded his advertising coverage and sales volume grew rapidly. Thanks to the rising costs of energy, consumers were anxious to lower energy costs and his advertising hit home. Within three years, Don's Sea Breeze Fan Company consisted of 20 production people, two foremen, and three salespersons who called on building contractors. Don and his foremen developed standardized procedures for the assemblers. He established quality standards with dependable suppliers and consistent procedures for moving new orders from sales through assembly to final shipping.

In his fourth year of operation, Don began manufacturing, not just assembling, his own fans. He did so primarily because he could not get his suppliers to provide the product he wanted. He had purchased the rights to a control mechanism that he believed would dramatically change the home-energy business. The mechanism consisted of an extremely sensitive heat sensor coupled with a microprocessor that could be programmed for both time and temperature. Since his regular suppliers could not produce electrical components compatible with the control device, Sea Breeze became an independent manufacturer of the new "smart" fans.

While the new product sold well at Kmart and other stores, Don was surprised at the number of inquiries the sales department received from other manufacturers. Some were interested in specially designed, controlled fan systems that would fit into their existing products. A number, however, were only concerned with the control device itself, not with the fan. In response to this new opportunity, Don set up a separate facility for manufacturing the control devices. He also established a small electronics engineering department to modify the control-fan systems according to customer requirements. As this engineering department developed increasingly sophisticated electronic knowhow, it became necessary for both the fan and control factories to constantly change their products and manufacturing processes in order to accommodate the new designs.

Within two years of introducing the "smart" fan, it was evident that something was seriously wrong at Sea Breeze Fan Company. Orders were up, yet profits were shrinking due to short production runs, constant changes in production designs, and increasing defect rates. Once-happy customers were complaining about critical orders arriving later than promised. Quality control was rejecting close to 9 percent of production for serious defects. Even the normally stable sales of regular ceiling fans were falling off due to the introduction of new models by competitors. Sea Breeze had not introduced a new model in over three years and was losing touch with consumer tastes.

Internally, tension was high and open conflict was frequent. One talented engineer had already quit the design group and a manager in the fan-production line was talking about leaving. Decisions were not being made in time to solve problems. Managers responsible for product designs or production runs were not getting the information or materials they needed to do their jobs.

During this period Don had the feeling he was working extremely hard and getting very little done. He constantly moved between the fan-production line, the control production line, and the design department. He never seemed to be at the right location when he had to be. He tried staying in his office and letting the problems come to him. He found, however, that by the time problems reached him the chance for him to make the best decision had already passed. He even had an elaborate on-line computer system installed that instantaneously relayed data from the production areas to his office. While this system allowed him to make some of the more routine decisions, he found that the most pressing issues, such as brainstorming a new design with an industrial customer or deciding on the advertising for a new consumer product, could not be programmed.

Exhausted and discouraged, Don finally realized he could no longer run the entire company by himself. He decided to formally divide the company into its logical divisions and appoint a general manager to head each one. Each division was made responsible for the design, production, and sale of its own products. Sea Breeze Fan Company became the Environmental Control Systems Corporation. The Sea Breeze Division was responsible for the production and marketing of a full line of ceiling, desk, and free-standing fans, including the "smart" fan. This was primarily a consumer-products division with a heavy marketing emphasis.

The Electronic Controls Division was responsible for the production and sale of the microprocessor control device. The product was now available in several designs, varying in application, cost, and technical sophistication. This division sold exclusively to industrial customers, including the Sea Breeze Division. Consistent quality, cost, and delivery were the major factors in this business.

The Special Systems Division was responsible for the design and production of specialized temperature-control and refrigeration systems for specific customers. These were generally industrial or scientific applications with unique and technologically difficult requirements. These customers were frequently more interested in the design of a successful prototype than in purchasing a large number of units. Production runs in this division were small. Technological competence was the primary factor in this business. Price was a relatively less important consideration.

The new organizational structure had taken some getting used to. At first, it was difficult for Don to avoid getting involved in the day-to-day details within each division. Within a year or so, however, he knew that the reorganization had been the right move. The Sea Breeze Division had successfully introduced two new models of fans. The Electronic Controls Division had cleared up its quality problems and was meeting cost and scheduling commitments. The Special Systems Division had added three new engineers and was fast gaining a reputation as an innovative problem-solver in the industry.

Each division was successfully adjusting to the demands of its particular business. In the process of making those adjustments, though, they had begun to operate as three independent companies. Electronic Controls, for example, billed Sea Breeze at the going market rate for its control mechanisms. Special Systems charged engineering and design costs to the manufacturing divisions as an outside consultant would do.

The division managers felt these "arm's length" arrangements were fair, and the company's smooth functioning gave Don little reason to argue. The Precision Dynamics contract, however, was an entirely new ball game. The project was far too big for any one division to handle and, in fact, no one division had the technical knowledge needed to do the whole job. The design required sophisticated engineering work from all three divisions. The technology had never been attempted before, and it was inevitable that at least some aspects of the plan would have to be modified or changed completely as the project progressed.

Don's first impulse was to accept the contract if it came through. After serious consideration, however, he had begun to think the job was simply beyond his company's capacity. The divisions had not worked closely together for several years now. Although ECS was not a large company, many of the newer engineers had not even met their counterparts in the other divisions. As far as Don knew, there were no really serious or ongoing conflicts between divisions. At the same time, there were no real communication links between them either. They had so successfully pursued their own separate businesses that at this point they really knew very little about each other's technologies, markets, or

problems. The more Don thought about it, the more he realized that without some system for integrating the intricate work of the three divisions, he would have to decline the Precision Dynamics contract.[23]

Questions

1. What type of interdependence currently exists between divisions? What type existed in the past? What will the interdependence be like if Don accepts the Precision Dynamics contract?

2. What integrating mechanisms have been used in the company to coordinate the flow of work and information? What environmental changes caused changes in integrating mechanisms?

3. Should Don refuse the new contract? Can the present organization successfully take on the contract? What alternatives are available to Don?

REFERENCES

1. These materials were adapted from the following sources: J. Holusha, "G.M.'s Overhaul: A Return to Basics," *New York Times*, January 15, 1984, p. F1; "G.M. Moves into a New Era," *Business Week*, July 16, 1984, pp. 48–54; D. Buss, "G.M. Is Mulling a Consolidation of Car Divisions," *Wall Street Journal*, January 3, 1984, p. 30; L. Cohen and C. McCoy, "Perot's Singular Style Raises Issue of How He'll Fit at G.M.," *Wall Street Journal*, July 2, 1984, p. 19; M. Brody, "Can GM Manage It All?" *Fortune*, July 8, 1985, pp. 22–28.

2. J. Galbraith, *Designing Complex Organizations*. Reading, Mass.: Addison-Wesley, 1973; L. Hrebiniak and Wm. Joyce, *Implementing Strategy*. New York: Macmillan, 1984.

3. P. Lawrence and J. Lorsch, *Organization and Environment*. Homewood, Ill.: Richard D. Irwin, 1967; P. Lawrence and D. Dyer, *Renewing American Industry*. New York: Free Press, 1983.

4. R. Duncan, "What Is the Right Organization Structure? Decision Tree Analysis Provides the Answer," *Organizational Dynamics*, Winter 1979, pp. 59–80; J. Pfeffer and G. Salancik, *The External Control of Organizations*. New York: Harper & Row, 1978; A. Van de Ven and R. Drazin, "The Concept of Fit in Contingency Theory." In L. Cummings

and B. Staw (Eds.), *Research in Organizational Behavior*, vol. 8, Greenwich, Conn.: JAI Press, 1985, pp. 333–366.

5. *Dallas Times Herald*, December 30, 1983; J. Clark, *Businesses Today: Success and Failures*. New York: Random House, 1979, pp. 32–43; R. Kroc, *Grinding It Out: The Making of McDonald's*. New York: Contemporary Books, 1977; M. Williams, "McDonald's Refuses to Plateau," *Fortune*, November 12, 1984, p. 34.

6. *Business Week*, July 16, 1984, pp. 30–31.

7. Y. Tourumi, *Multinational Management: Business Strategy and Government Policy*, 2nd ed. Cambridge, Mass.: Ballinger, 1984, pp. 231–233.

8. T. Burns and G. M. Stalker, *The Management of Innovation*. London: Tavistock, 1961.

9. P. Lawrence and J. Lorsch, *Organization and Environment*. Homewood, Ill.: Richard D. Irwin, 1967.

10. For a summary of this research, *see* J. Woodward, *Industrial Organization*. London: Oxford University Press, 1965; L. Fry and J. Slocum, "Technology, Structure and Workgroup Effectiveness: A Test of a Contingency Model," *Academy of Management Journal*, 1984, **27**:221–246; M. Hitt and R. Ireland, "Corporate Distinctive Competence and Performance: Effects of Perceived Environmental Uncertainty (PEU), Size and Technology," *Decision Sciences*, 1984, **15**:324–349.

11. D. Gerwin, "Relationships Between Structure and Technology." In P. Nystrom and Wm. Starbuck (Eds.), *Handbook of Organizational Design*. Clifton, N.J.: Oxford University Press, 1981, pp. 3–39; D. Comstock and W. Scott, "Technology and the Structure of Subunits," *Administrative Science Quarterly*, 1977, **22**:177–202.

12. J. Thompson, *Organizations in Action*. New York: McGraw-Hill, 1967.

13. This section draws from R. Keidel, "Baseball, Football and Basketball: Models for Business," *Organizational Dynamics*, Winter 1984, pp. 4–18.

14. P. Doyle, *Taylor Publishing Company Business Plan, 1984–1988*. Unpublished MBA Paper, Cox School of Business, Southern Methodist University, Dallas, 1984.

15. Information furnished by Ann Flavin, President, Optigraphics Corporation, July 1985.

16. J. Galbraith, *Organization Design*. Reading, Mass.: Addison-Wesley, 1977; D. Power, "The Impact of Information Management on the Organization: Two Scenarios," *MIS Quarterly*, 1983, 7(3):13–20; T. Mandeville, "The Spatial Effects of Information Technology," *Futures*, 1983, **15**:65–72.

17. This section draws from J. Galbraith, *Organization Design*, Chapters 6–10; J. Galbraith, "Designing the Innovating Organization," *Organizational Dynamics*, Winter 1982, pp. 5–25.

18. Information about supermarket computer systems furnished by James Dawson, Vice-President, Management Information Systems, Tom Thumb Page Supermarkets, July 1985.

19. For examples of how multinational companies structure themselves, *see* Y. Dores, "Strategic Management in Multinational Companies," *Sloan Management Review*, 1980, **21**(3):27–46; T. Herbert, "Strategy and Multinational Organization Structure: An Interorganizational Relationships Perspective," *Academy of Management Review*, 1984, **9**:259–271.

20. B. Saporito, "Black and Decker's Gamble on Globalization," *Fortune*, May 14, 1984, pp. 40–44. *Also see* Wm. Ouchi, *The M-Form Society: How American Teamwork Can Recapture the Competitive Edge*. Reading, Mass.: Addison-Wesley, 1984.

21. For excellent reviews, *see* M. McCaskey, "An Introduction to Organizational Design," *California Management Review*, 1974, **17**(2):130–137; M. Tushman and E. Romanelli, "Organizational Evolution: A Metamorphosis Model of Convergence and Reorientation." In L. Cummings and B. Staw (Eds.), *Research in Organizational Behavior*, vol. 8. Greenwich, Conn.: JAI Press, 1985, pp. 171–222, W. Randolph and G. Dess, "The Congruence Perspective of Organization Design: A Conceptual Model and Multivariate Research Approach," *Academy of Management Review*, 1984, **9**:114–127.

22. For some additional insights into this problem, *see* M. Maidique and R. Hayes, "The Art of High-Technology Management," *Sloan Management Review*, Winter 1984, pp. 17–31; J. Rockart, "The

Changing Role of the Information Systems Executive: A Critical Success Factors Perspective," *Sloan Management Review,* Fall 1982, pp. 3–13; M. Dollinger, "Environmental Boundary Spanning and Information Processing Effects on Organizational Performance," *Academy of Management Journal,* 1984, **27**:351–368; J. Fredrickson, "The Comprehensiveness of Strategic Decision Processes: Extension, Observations, Future Directions," *Academy of Management Journal,* 1984, **27**:445–466.

23. Case prepared by J. Kerr, Edwin L. Cox School of Business, Southern Methodist University, Dallas, 1985.

PART V

LEADING

Individual Motivation in Organizations

CHAPTER 12

405

PREVIEW CASE

McCormick & Company, Inc.

Before she began working at McCormick All Portions/Han-Dee Pak in Lewisville, Texas, Alice Lewis worked as a waitress and a spot welder. At 27, Lewis has had two husbands and at least four jobs, but for the past six months she has found a sort of contentment as a catsup packer at the McCormick plant.

She gets up at 5:00 A.M., feeds her two-year-old son, and drops him off at the sitter's house. She begins work at 6:30 A.M. Between then and 3:30 P.M., Lewis lifts an average of 280 fifteen-pound boxes of catsup destined for several fast-food restaurants. For this work, she receives $5.79 an hour.

Some days are bad. A machine may malfunction and cause the foil packets to leak, resulting in extra cleanup work for Lewis. Or there may be an increase in production. High production "does the manager good because he gets all this pat on the back about productivity, and it's you that's doing all the work," Lewis explained.

The machine on which Lewis normally works operates at approximately 76 strokes per minute. It pumps catsup into foil packets, heat-seals them, and spits them out onto a conveyor belt. Sometimes operators increase the rate to 86 strokes per minute. "One day I did 303,000 packets of catsup, and they went up and patted my operator. I said, 'Where the hell would that 303,000 be if it weren't for me?' "

"McCormick is a very people-oriented company," said plant manager Tarland Beauchamp. Each of the 80-odd Lewisville plant employees receives a turkey for the holidays, as well as a Christmas bonus that is usually equivalent to a week's salary or more.

"There's a lot of camaraderie here," said Beauchamp, who has a chemistry degree and used to work in edible oils (butter, margarine, and salad oil). He took a visitor on tour, tracing the route from tomato paste to catsup. Beauchamp's plant has nothing to do with the California tomatoes until they are already paste, which arrives in Lewisville in 542-pound steel drums.

The paste is pumped into stainless steel tanks the size of water heaters, where it is blended with water, vinegar, and spices. Next, the mixture is heated to 200° and transferred to a cooler, back into a homogenizer, into a cooler again, and then

Source: Darlene Bordwell, Boston.

from a holding tank into the hoses that run it through the machine that pumps catsup.

At some point in this process, the paste stops being paste and becomes catsup. If it contains 32.5 percent solids, it becomes "fancy" catsup. The catsup you get with your Big Mac® and fries costs you two or three cents.

During an average two-shift workday, employees at the Lewisville plant package 2.5–3 million units of catsup and related products. In addition to catsup, the plant packages taco sauce, salt, pepper, salad dressings, mustard, jams, and jellies.

Kay Farmer operates a jelly machine at the McCormick plant. She is 25 years old and has been married three times. Her son, James, was born when Farmer was 13 years old. Farmer can remember a lot of rough times she had between marriages. "I remember working for a boat company. I was making $1.80 an hour and I had three kids. I think, God, I can barely make it now; how'd I make it then?"

Farmer now makes $6.54 an hour. She dates Jeff Mercer, one of the lead people at the plant. Farmer's mother also works with her on the jelly machines. "Yeah, everybody's related around here," she explained.

Nan Ariola also works on a jelly machine at McCormick. On some days she does nothing but take cardboard trays off one machine and put them on a conveyor belt, where they will be filled with packets of jelly. She feels this job is harder than it looks. "You got to be able to think real quick, 'cause sometimes this little machine doesn't shoot the trays down quick enough. Then you scream."

Before working at McCormick, Ariola delivered telephone books and worked on cafeteria lines at a local middle school and a local nursing home. "Please don't ask us how we stay here this long, 'cause we don't know," she said, laughing. Kay Farmer says the good part is mostly due to the people she works with and not the job she does.[1]

W hat motivates these workers? What techniques should Beauchamp use to maintain their motivation to work? The Preview Case and these questions illustrate several points this chapter will cover in detail. First, managers are responsible for motivating people. They must provide good working conditions and must coordinate workers' efforts. Second, people have different wants and desires that influence their motivation to work. Third, job and organizational characteristics have an important impact on people's work motivation.

IMPORTANCE OF MOTIVATION

Since the mid-1940s, the increase in the U.S. productivity rate has dropped from about 3 percent per year to about 1.4 percent a year.[2] This downward trend has contributed to unemployment, decreased international competitiveness, and lower profits for many companies. A number of companies—General Foods, Honeywell, Kaiser Aluminum, Hughes Aircraft, and Burger King, among others—have instituted a wide variety of productivity improvement plans. Although the programs of these companies differ in content, they all have one key element: motivation of workers.

Motivation is anything that causes, channels, and sustains people's behavior. Managers in all types of organizations continually face motivational challenges because of the vast differences in and complexity of people's motivation to produce. Some people perform at high levels, require little direct supervision, and appear to enjoy what they are doing. Others perform at barely acceptable levels, need constant watching by their supervisor, and seem to live to celebrate TGIF (Thank God It's Friday).

For organizations to be effective, managers must come to grips with three motivational problems:

1. People have to be attracted to join an organization and remain with it.
2. People must perform acceptably the tasks for which they were hired.
3. People must go beyond routine work performance and be innovative on the job.[3]

Recruitment and Retention

In order to attract people to join the firm and remain with it, many companies provide pension plans, group-life and medical insurance policies, stock options, recreational programs for workers and their families, and various incentive programs. In addition, companies such as Motorola, Xerox, and Rolm rebate tuition for those who go back to school, and provide a network of schools and training centers where employees can learn everything from computer programming to international finance.

Job Performance

In an attempt to ensure that employees can perform the tasks for which they were hired, companies carefully screen applicants to determine whether they have the skills or can learn the skills needed for the job. Employee performance on the job is evaluated by a performance appraisal system by many, but not all companies. This system evaluates performance and indicates strengths, weaknesses, and skills in relation to the next higher-level job. At Holiday Inn, if a motel manager does not have the needed technical, administrative, or human-relations skills to be promoted, both the employee and the supervisor are responsible for helping the employee learn those skills. They may be gained through educational programs and on-the-job experience.

Innovation

Many companies are faced with the need for creative and innovative behavior. Foreign competition and high rates of technological and market change have substantially increased since 1980. To meet these challenges, Westinghouse

Quality circles are used in Japan as a means of improving product quality. The practice of employees and managers meeting on a regular basis to solve production problems has been adopted by many companies since the 1970s.

Source: Darlene Bordwell, Boston.

Electric Corporation's Public Systems Company formed more than 150 **quality circles** to find more innovative ways to do jobs.[4] Quality circles used by Japanese managers consist of workers and supervisors who meet on a regular basis to discuss product-quality improvement. The purpose of these circles is to find better ways of producing quality goods, not simply to serve as a sounding board for worker complaints. According to some members of Westinghouse's program, quality circles improve the worker–supervisor relationship by opening lines of communication. For Westinghouse, changes made by the circles resulted in more than $1 million savings in two years.

FACTORS AFFECTING MOTIVATION

Numerous factors that influence motivation have been identified. The three major factors are the individual, the job, and the organization, which are summarized in Table 12.1.[5]

Individual Characteristics

Needs, attitudes, values, and interests are the **individual characteristics** that people bring to their jobs. Obviously, these characteristics vary from person to person, and individuals' motivations therefore will differ. In the Preview

Case, Alice Lewis at McCormick & Company, Inc., was primarily interested in money, while Nan Ariola was interested in meeting her friends at work. In Chapter 4, we noted that people in other countries have needs and values that are different from those of many Americans.

Job Characteristics

Job characteristics are the dimensions of a job. The more important ones include the amount of skill variety, task identity, task significance, autonomy, and the extent to which the job gives an employee feedback about his or her performance. Many people would not like to do the jobs required at Mc-Cormick & Company, Inc., because they provide relatively low levels of variety, task identity, task significance, autonomy, and feedback. However, any job that is satisfying to a person, regardless of its characteristics, will be more motivating than a job which is not satisfying.

Organizational Characteristics

Supervisory practices, rules and regulations, and reward systems are *organizational characteristics.* These characteristics affect a person's desire to join and stay with an organization. They can arouse or stimulate particular needs, attitudes, and interests in the individual. For rewards to be motivating, they

TABLE 12.1 ■ FACTORS AFFECTING MOTIVATION IN ORGANIZATIONS

INDIVIDUAL CHARACTERISTIC	JOB CHARACTERISTIC	ORGANIZATIONAL CHARACTERISTIC
■ Needs security social self-esteem self-actualization	Skill variety	Immediate work setting peers supervisor
■ Attitudes toward self toward job toward aspects of work situation	Task identity	Organizational practices reward systems rules and regulations politics
■ Interest	Task Significance Autonomy Feedback	

Source: Adapted from L. Porter and R. Miles, "Motivation and Management." In J. McGuire (Ed.), *Contemporary Management: Issues and Viewpoints.* Englewood Cliffs, N.J.: Prentice-Hall, © 1974, p. 547. Reprinted by permission of Prentice-Hall, Inc.

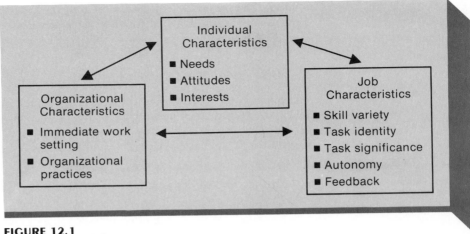

FIGURE 12.1
Interaction of Motivational Factors

must be administered fairly and based on performance. If rewards are based on seniority or nepotism, they are not likely to be motivating.

INTERACTION OF FACTORS

When we discuss motivation, we are talking about how the three major factors operate in combination to affect a person's motivation. These factors interact as illustrated in Fig. 12.1. Essentially these interactions involve (1) what the person *brings* to the work situation; (2) what the person *does* in the work situation; and (3) what *happens* to the person in the work situation. For example, in the Preview Case, the McCormick & Company, Inc., employees bring to the work situation certain expectations. How these expectations are met and linked to performance is influenced by the nature of their jobs and how they are dealt with by their supervisors and friends.

Managers must consider the interaction of all three characteristics—individual, job, and organizational—when attempting to motivate employees. In particular, managers need to understand that the use of certain types of rules and rewards can strengthen or weaken an employee's desire to perform effectively.

MOTIVATION: RECOGNIZING EMPLOYEE NEEDS

The motivational process begins with recognizing the **needs** that employees bring to the job. A need is a strong individual want or desire for something lacking in a person's life. For some, it is the desire to be well-liked, to achieve influence over others, or to find a secure job. Needs create tensions that are uncomfortable, and we look for ways to relieve these tensions. Ultimately, the goal is to reduce this tension by taking action to satisfy a need.

The Hierarchy-of-Needs Model

The most widely used model for the study of motivation in organizations is Maslow's *hierarchy-of-needs model.*[6] Maslow, a psychologist, proposed that people have a complex set of needs, which are arranged in a hierarchy of importance. Four basic assumptions underlly this hierarchy:

1. A satisfied need is not a motivator. When a need is satisfied, another need emerges to take its place, so people are always striving to satisfy some need.

2. The needs network for most people is very complex, with a number of needs affecting the behavior of a person at any one time.

3. Lower-level needs must be satisfied, in general, before higher-level needs are activated sufficiently to drive behavior.

4. There are many more ways to satisfy higher-level needs than there are to satisfy lower-level needs.

Maslow's model contains five need categories: physiological, security, affiliation, esteem, and self-actualization. They are arranged in the hierarchical order shown in Fig. 12.2.

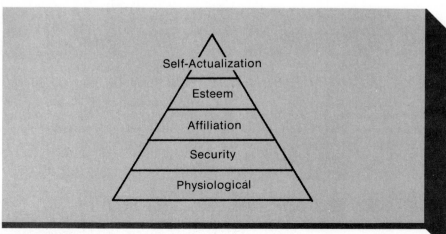

FIGURE 12.2
Maslow's Hierarchy of Needs

Physiological needs

Food, water, air, and shelter are *physiological needs.* They are basic human needs and occupy the lowest level in the hierarchy. Managers who attempt to motivate subordinates by addressing these needs assume that people work primarily for money; to achieve comfort, avoid fatigue, and the like. People satisfy physiological needs before turning to the higher-order needs. The primary motivation of a very hungry person is to obtain food. Many people, especially in Third World countries, are deprived of the means to satisfy basic physiological needs.

Security needs

The need for safety, stability, and the absence of pain, threat, or illness are *security needs.* Just as with physiological needs, when security needs are not satisfied, people become preoccupied with satisfying them. For many workers, security needs are expressed in the desire for a safe, stable job with medical, unemployment, and retirement benefits. Managers may attempt to satisfy these needs by emphasizing rules and regulations, job security, fringe benefits, and protection against automation. Subordinates who have strong security needs usually are not innovative. They try not to rock the boat and generally do as they are told, so long as their physiological and security needs are not threatened. For example, employees with high security needs may react violently against management's efforts to introduce new equipment or more efficient procedures by sabotaging or destroying equipment, engaging in wildcat strikes, or slowing production.

Affiliation needs

Friendship, love, and belonging are *affiliation needs.* This level in the hierarchy represents a clear-cut step above physiological and security needs. When affiliation needs are not met, the mental health of employees may be affected, resulting in frequent absenteeism, low productivity and job satisfaction, high stress levels, and even emotional breakdowns. Managers who recognize that subordinates are striving to satisfy affiliation needs are likely to act in a particularly supportive and permissive way. They emphasize acceptance by co-workers and participation in extracurricular activities, such as company-organized sports programs, picnics, and other social activities.

Esteem needs

Personal feelings of achievement or self-worth and recognition or respect from others are *esteem needs.* In satisfying these needs, people are concerned about opportunities for achievement, prestige, status, and promotion that will provide recognition of their capabilities, competence, and worth. Managers who focus on esteem needs to motivate employees tend to emphasize the difficulty of the work and skills required for success in contacts with employees. They publicly recognize and reward achievement. Lapel pins, articles in the company paper, published performance lists, bonuses, rewards for cost-saving suggestions, and the like may be used as a means of promoting employee pride. To the extent that this need is dominant, managers may promote both high satisfaction and performance through exciting and challenging work.

Self-actualization needs

Self-fulfillment and utilization of a person's total capabilities are **self-actualization needs.** A self-actualized person exhibits acceptance of self and others, initiative, problem-solving ability, spontaneity, and a desire for privacy. Managers who focus primarily on meeting these needs recognize that every job has features that allow innovation and challenge and helps employees to find them. Managers strive to involve employees in decision making, restructuring of jobs, or special assignments that use their special skills.

Using the Hierarchy-of-Needs Model

This model assumes that people are motivated to satisfy those needs that are important at any particular time in their lives. The strength of a specific need depends on its position in the needs hierarchy and the extent to which it and all lower-level needs have been satisfied. Maslow's theory predicts a dynamic, step-by-step, causal process of motivation in which behavior is governed by a continuously changing set of *important* needs. He did not claim that the hierarchy is a fixed, rigid order for all people. However, he did indicate clearly that physiological needs are the most basic and self-actualization needs are the least fulfilled.

Research supports the view that, unless basic needs are satisfied, people will not be concerned with higher-level needs. However, there is little evidence to support the view that the hierarchy exists as shown in Fig. 12.2 for any but the basic needs.[7] For example, studies do not indicate that social needs (aspects of Maslow's affiliation and esteem needs) have to be satisfied prior to self-actualization needs. Some people pay little attention to social needs so long as they are free to do what they do best, whether that be playing chess or lifting weights. Based on the research, then, it seems best for management purposes to assume a two-category hierarchy with physiological and security needs at the lower level and affiliation, esteem, and self-actualization needs at the upper level. Unless the lower-level needs are relatively well satisfied, the others will not influence behavior on the job. It also means that, when the lower-level needs of a person are threatened, they will become the most important. The existence of a two-category hierarchy means that if basic needs are satisfied, no single other need is likely to be the best or only one for motivating someone. In fact, more than one need may be important simultaneously. As a result, managers must continually adjust their ideas about what is motivating their subordinates or what is needed to motivate them. Identify the needs that motivate Kay Farmer in the Preview Case.

INTERNATIONAL FOCUS

The Chinese Needs Hierarchy

Trying to understand what motivates another person is never easy. But when that person is from another culture, the task becomes even more difficult. In recent years, many books have been written on how to motivate others from different cultures. These books have raised questions about the transferability of American norms and management practices to other cultures. This problem is clearly shown by examining the differences between the Chinese and American interpretation of Maslow's needs hierarchy.

Following liberation in 1949, the People's Republic of China put enormous energy into developing a new society. Most Chinese people involved in this movement speak well of those times. Although much suffering and deprivation occurred, the general thrust was forward and positive in tone. The Cultural Revolution in 1966, and for 10 years afterward produced a great upheaval. Structures and policies were dismantled. Intellectuals and those showing individualism in any way were verbally and physically attacked. Survival came to depend on unquestioning loyalty to Chairman Mao, and the good citizen's reward was to be cared for by the country in one way or another. Since 1976, people and policies have been freed considerably.

The following table lists the most apparent cultural assumptions underlying Chinese management concepts. An important communal thread in these assumptions ties together national loyalty, equity, avoidance of personal credit for accomplishment, communal property, and emphasis on group forces for

CULTURAL ASSUMPTIONS UNDERLYING CHINESE MANAGEMENT CONCEPTS

- The nation has priority over everything; loyalty to the country is of the utmost importance.
- Consideration for the family is very important.
- Personnel selection (leadership) is based upon exploits or ideological contribution.
- One should have great respect for age.
- Equity is more important than wealth.
- Saving and conserving (money, resources, etc.) is to be valued, as is high respect for traditional ways.
- It is considered unhealthy for individuals to stand out or take personal credit for their accomplishments.
- Every decision must take ideology into account.
- Communal property is more important than private possessions; collectivism is the best economic mechanism.
- Emphasis focuses upon group forces for motivational purposes.
- Emphasis focuses on central planning and the powerful state.

(continued)

motivation. The most basic assumption is that being a good member of society and putting group goals before individual needs should govern all practices. If you thank a Chinese person for their accomplishment, the reply is usually, "I am only doing my job." or "It is my duty."

With this brief perspective and cultural assumptions as background, we can formulate a hierarchy of needs for the People's Republic of China and compare it to the American version.

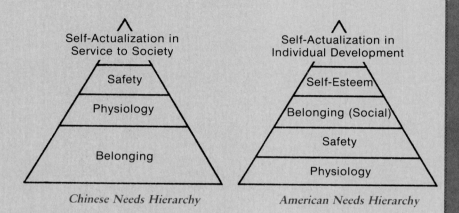

Chinese Needs Hierarchy   *American Needs Hierarchy*

Note that the needs are arranged differently in the two diagrams. The placement of belonging needs is radically different between Chinese and Americans. The Chinese stress loyalty and organizational and national unity; Americans stress the integrity of the individual and attainment of individuality. A Chinese work unit has many features of a company town, which most Americans dislike. Also note that self-actualization is needed for self-enhancement, whereas for the Chinese, self-actualization means the submersion of individual desires toward working for a better society.

Source: Adapted from Edwin Nevis, "Using an American Perspective in Understanding Another Culture: Toward a Hierarchy of Needs for the People's Republic of China," *Journal of Applied Behavioral Science*, 1983, 19(3):249–264.

MOTIVATION: ANALYZING THE JOB EXPERIENCE

Behavioral scientists have attempted to discover how particular jobs motivate people to perform. The appeal of scientific management to managers was the promise that it would lead to increased organizational efficiency (Chapter 2). Jobs designed according to the principles of scientific management tend to be highly specialized and standardized. Under such a system, mistakes are supposed to be minimized because each worker is doing one—and only one—

part of the job the best possible way. This would lead to high quality, because every worker could easily become an expert in a particular job. In addition, a supervisor need only to glance at workers to know whether they are performing. Assuming that workers are at their stations and doing a simple repetitive task, production should proceed according to management's plan.

The benefits of simple and highly specialized jobs seemed clear to managers. Since training workers costs little, they can be replaced without a great deal of expense. This increases management's control over the workers, since the threat of being fired can be very real to workers whose productivity is not up to standard. A solid case can be made for the economic advantages of having simple, repetitive, and relatively routine jobs.[8]

Despite its economic advantages, this approach creates a number of problems. Many people dislike such jobs intensely and find them to be boring and nonmotivating. In many cases, needs for self-actualization, esteem, and affiliation are not met. One of the first behavioral scientists to contribute to an understanding of the relationship between job characteristics and motivation was Frederick Herzberg.

Two-Factor Model

The first major study by Fred Herzberg and his associates examined the relationship between job satisfaction and productivity among a group of accountants and engineers.[9] In doing their research, they found that various employees named different job experiences that resulted in good and bad feelings about the job. If responsibility led to good feelings about the job, lack of responsibility was seldom given as a cause of bad feelings. If lack of job security caused dissatisfaction, it did not follow that high job security caused job satisfaction. Thus, there appeared to be two separate and distinct kinds of experiences: one set that satisfies and another that dissatisfies. Therefore the model based on this research has been labeled the *two-factor model.*

Motivator and Hygiene Factors

Herzberg's research led him to conclude that certain factors are associated with positive feelings about the job. He called them *motivator factors.* They include the work itself, recognition, responsibility, advancement, and growth and are *intrinsic* to the job. If these five factors are present, they build a high level of motivation and spur individuals to superior performance.

Herzberg further concluded that some job factors cause job dissatisfaction when they are not present. He called them *hygiene factors.* They include company policies, supervision, working conditions, co-workers, salary, and job security and are *extrinsic* to the job. When these factors are present, they do not necessarily lead to high performance and job satisfaction but are needed to maintain a reasonable level of satisfaction.

There is a major difference between motivator and hygiene factors. Motivator factors are *job centered* and focus primarily on the characteristics of

TABLE 12.2 ■ EXAMPLES OF MOTIVATOR AND HYGIENE FACTORS

MOTIVATOR FACTORS	HYGIENE FACTORS
■ Achievement	■ Company policy and administration
■ Recognition	■ Supervision
■ Work itself	■ Working conditions
■ Responsibility	■ Co-workers
■ Advancement and growth	■ Salary, status, and job security
Sources of Job Satisfaction	*Sources of Job Dissatisfaction*

the job. Is the job exciting, challenging, rewarding? Conversely, hygiene factors are associated with the *context* in which the work is performed. Is the cafeteria air-conditioned? Are rules and regulations fair? Does the firm have free parking spaces? Herzberg suggests that just because the cafeteria is air-conditioned and employees can park free does not necessarily mean that they will be more highly motivated to perform than if the cafeteria were not air-conditioned and they had to pay to park. Table 12.2 lists some motivator and hygiene factors. Go back to the Preview Case and pick out the motivator and hygiene factors.

Using the two-factor model

The managerial implications of the two-factor model are significant.[10] For many years, firms requiring workers to do routine assembly-line work have experienced problems of high turnover, absenteeism, grievances, low productivity and so on. These firms try to motivate people only through the use of hygiene factors, which can prevent job dissatisfaction but do not stimulate positive performance and attitudes. According to Herzberg and others, managers should direct their attention to motivator factors in order to remedy this situation.

The two-factor model has been criticized on a number of points, including its research methodology and lack of consideration of individuals' needs. However, many managers accept the two-factor model for four reasons. First, it is simple to understand and has a great deal of face validity. Managers can easily identify motivator and hygiene factors. Second, actions for improving performance are straightforward. Management must provide adequate hygiene factors so that the employee can concentrate on motivator-factor aspects of the work. Third, improved performance does not necessarily result from granting more-expensive fringe benefits or higher salaries. The two-factor model suggests that improvements in the quantity and quality of performance are possible without significant increases in labor costs. Fourth, many job-enrichment programs have been inspired by his work.

Job-Enrichment Model

The *job-enrichment model* extends the work of Herzberg by focusing on how specific job characteristics can be changed to affect motivation and job satisfaction. Although a number of different approaches to job-enrichment can be used, the common theme is that job enrichment enables workers to meet more of their higher-level needs. One of the most popular and extensively tested models is the job-enrichment model developed by J. Richard Hackman and Greg Oldham.[11]

Critical psychological states

As shown in Fig. 12.3, the job-enrichment model is based on the view that three *critical psychological states* lead to high work motivation and satisfaction. *Experienced meaningfulness* is the degree to which work is viewed as important, valuable, and worthwhile. If you believe that you are performing a trivial task—counting rubber bands being packed in a box or making change at a toll booth—your motivation to perform is not likely to be very high. This would be the case even when you have the sole responsibility for doing the task and receive feedback on how well or poorly you are doing it. *Experienced*

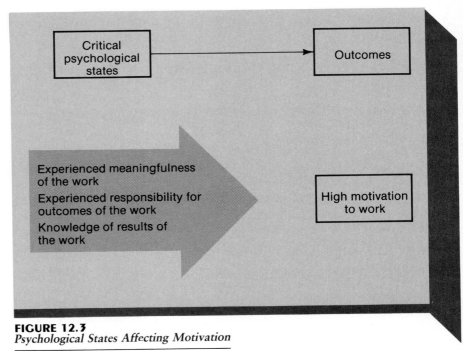

FIGURE 12.3
Psychological States Affecting Motivation

Source: J. R. Hackman and G. Oldham, *Work Redesign*. Reading, Mass.: Addison-Wesley, 1980, p. 73. Reprinted with permission.

responsibility is the extent to which a person feels personally responsible and accountable for the work being performed. If you view your work as dependent on rules and regulations, you have less reason to feel personally responsible for your actions. The opposite situation exists when you are accountable for your own behavior. ***Knowledge of results*** is the extent to which you receive feedback on how well or poorly you are doing your job. If your work is so arranged that you cannot see the results of your own efforts and know whether you performed poorly or well, you are not likely to have any feeling about how well you did. If any of the three psychological states is low, motivation is low.

We can illustrate these concepts by reference to the game of golf, which one of the authors likes to play. The game provides the player with immediate knowledge of results: The player hits the ball and sees where it goes. The total score on each hole indicates how well the golfer is playing against a standard (par). Personal responsibility for performance is high, although many times golfers make excuses for a poor performance. Experienced meaningfulness can also be high as wagers accumulate and a missed putt can be costly. So in golf, all three psychological states are present and motivation among regular players usually is high. Indeed, golfers exhibit motivated behavior rarely seen at work: getting up before dawn (for an early tee time), playing in rain and snow, feeling despair or joy (depending on how the round went), and even violence (breaking a club after a muffed shot).

TABLE 12.3 ■ KEY JOB CHARACTERISTICS FOR JOB ENRICHMENT

Skill Variety	The degree to which the job requires a variety of different activities in carrying out the work. It involves the use of a number of skills and talents.
Task Identity	The degree to which the job requires completing the whole job, an identifiable piece of work. That is, doing a job with a visible outcome from beginning to end.
Task Significance	The degree to which the job has a substantial impact on the lives or work of others in the company.
Autonomy	The degree to which the job provides substantial freedom, independence, and discretion to the individual in scheduling work and determining the procedures to be used in carrying out the task(s).
Feedback	The degree to which carrying out the work activities required by the job results in the individual's obtaining direct and clear information about the effectiveness of his or her performance.

Source: Adapted from J. R. Hackman and G. Oldham, *Work Redesign*. Reading, Mass.: Addison-Wesley, 1980, pp. 78–80. Reprinted with permission.

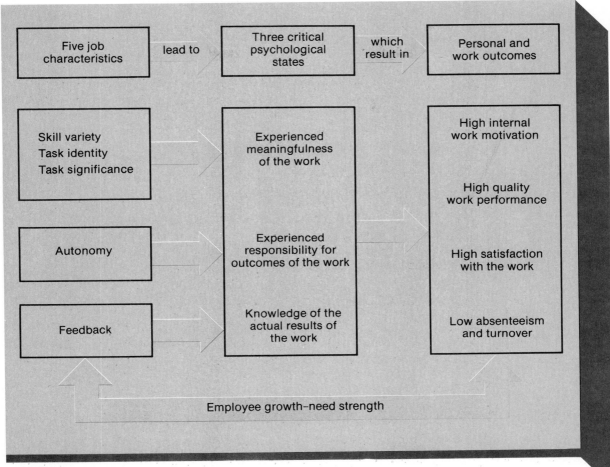

FIGURE 12.4
Hackman–Oldham's Job-Enrichment Model

Source: Adapted from J. R. Hackman and G. Oldham, *Work Redesign*. Reading, Mass.: Addison-Wesley, 1980, p. 83. Reprinted with permission.

INflUENCE of job chARACTERISTICS

Five key job characteristics influence the critical psychological states. Table 12.3 lists and describes these characteristics. As shown in Fig. 12.4, the first three job characteristics—*skill variety, task identity,* and *task significance*—all lead to experienced meaningfulness of work. When jobs do not have these characteristics, they may have little personal meaning. To offset such meaninglessness, workers sometimes play games in their mind. For example, parking lot attendants and traffic police occasionally admit to playing license-plate poker in their heads. A former newspaper carrier designed a game to keep himself motivated. He'd keep score on how many porches he hit with papers. He even created teams for the days of the week and created a series to determine which team won.

Autonomy fosters increased feelings of personal responsibility. When jobs provide substantial autonomy, performance will be viewed as highly dependent on employees' efforts and decisions, rather than on those of supervisors. As autonomy increases, employees tend to feel more personally responsible for their successes and failures on the job.

Knowledge of work results is determined by the amount of *feedback* that people receive. Ideally, feedback should be obtained from the task itself—such as when a golfer shoots par, or when a sales representative closes a deal with a customer—rather than from a supervisor. When this isn't possible—as in much staff work—the supervisor has a clear responsibility to give the employee adequate feedback.

Growth-need strength

Hackman and Oldham's model has one additional feature: *growth-need strength.* Each person responds to the same job in different ways because he or she brings to it different needs. As indicated in our discussion of needs, some people want only to satisfy their lower-level needs on the job; others want to satisfy their higher-level needs. Therefore, what may be a good job for one person may be a bad job for another. The job-enrichment model demonstrates this by showing that the relationships among job characteristics, performance and/or satisfaction are moderated by the strength of your need for growth. Growth-need strength reflects the desire for personal challenges, accomplishment, and learning on the job. Individuals with high needs for growth, creativity, and challenge are more likely to respond positively to jobs that provide more meaning, responsibility, and knowledge of results than if these needs were low. If an individual's growth needs are low, an enriched job may merely increase personal tension, stress, and job dissatisfaction. Let us look at how Sherwin-Williams Paint Company used the concepts of job enrichment to improve productivity.

IN PRACTICE
Sherwin-Williams
Paint Company

Sherwin-Williams instituted a job-enrichment program in its Richmond, Kentucky, plant in 1980. The goal of the plant manager was to operate a safe, clean, profitable, efficient plant producing the highest quality automobile refinishing paint in the world. The company thought that productivity could be greatly improved by enriching the workers' jobs. The manager said he believed people wanted to work in open and trusting ways and participate in business decisions as responsible employees.

To implement these ideas, employees were grouped into teams. Each member of the team was trained to perform all jobs assigned to the team. The teams have the autonomy to decide where members work, what work they do, and how to train others. For example, instead of doing just housekeeping chores, a worker does several different tasks related to the group's job. These tasks might include operating equipment, doing maintenance work, keeping quality control records, or restocking supplies.

The group is responsible for the results of its work. Raises are given to individual employees and are based on performance. Peers and the team leader evaluate each person's performance against standards set by the group and management. This occurs only after that person has mastered a set of skills. This establishes responsibility for performance and gives employees feedback on how well they are doing.

Employees are hired from applicants the company feels would enjoy working on challenging and significant tasks. They are encouraged to feel responsibility for the entire production process. They also are expected to acquire a working knowledge of customers' needs and the uses of Sherwin-Williams products. The technology requires careful production and quality control. Roughly $5 of the cost of producing a gallon of paint goes for raw materials. Since a typical batch is 4000 gallons, the cost of a single spoiled batch could come to $20,000—a good reason to have employees trained as skilled operators.

The plant itself is designed to foster job enrichment. It has an open work space that encourages workers to identify with the entire task and to share responsibility for all phases of production. This open space allows interaction between workers for both social and problem-solving chats.

Overall, the plant has been very successful. Absenteeism at the Richmond plant is 63 percent lower than at other Sherwin-Williams plants. There is very little turnover, and productivity is 30 percent higher than at the other plants. Cost per gallon of paint is 45 percent lower. The plant manager says that 75 percent of this reduction can be traced directly to the employees' superior performance.[12]

Using the job-enrichment model

During the past 10 years, job-enrichment programs have met with mixed success.[13] Many managers are skeptical about workers' ability to perform highly enriched jobs, while maintaining the same level of productivity. Managers point to the economic proof that scientific management and industrial engineering principles work. However, during the past two decades, behavioral scientists have challenged these principles and their results.

It is often difficult to assess the dollar value of results of job-enrichment programs. Managers ask, "What is the cost of a poor-quality decision? Of redundant inspections? Of absenteeism, turnover, or sabotage?" Unless measures are available to answer these questions, it is nearly impossible to determine whether job enrichment pays for organizations as anticipated.

Some union leaders and workers are not interested in enriching jobs. The worst possible circumstance for managers is to enrich jobs for employees who want only to satisfy their physiological and security needs at work. Clearly the enriched jobs would demand too much of those workers. Turnover, absenteeism, and shoddy workmanship would likely result. On the other hand, for workers capable of doing the work required on complex and challenging jobs—and who have a strong need for on-the-job personal growth—a job-enrichment program may well satisfy the needs of these individuals and the organization.

According to Hackman and Oldham, productivity can be improved if managers address either or both of the following problems.

1. Employees have low productivity because they are turned off by routine tasks.

2. There are redundant inspections that result in frustration and inefficient use of time.

When such problems are present, job enrichment is likely to improve employee attitudes and increase the quantity and quality of work.

MOTIVATION: EXPECTANCY AND REINFORCEMENT

Our discussion of motivation so far has focused on understanding the needs that employees might bring to the job and the effects of the job itself. The hierarchy-of-needs model states that an individual is motivated to satisfy needs. Depending on the individual's need state, certain types of behavior are more likely than others. The two-factor and job-enrichment models called our attention to the manner in which job characteristics can affect motivation. We now turn to two other motivation models—expectancy and reinforcement—that allow us to integrate elements of individual needs, job characteristics, and organizational characteristics into a more comprehensive view of motivating people on the job.

Expectancy Model

We can satisfy needs only by deciding what to do and then doing it. This often involves choosing among alternatives, which can require tradeoffs. For example, a manager has to decide whether a promotion and the increase in salary and status are worth uprooting the family; a production worker wonders whether accepting the foreman job would cut him off from his friends on the production line; and a college graduate considers whether to take the job at General Motors or IBM. The most widely accepted approach to explaining how people make such decisions is called *expectancy theory*. It says that people choose behaviors that they believe will lead to outcomes (pay, recognition from the boss, challenging assignments) that satisfy their goals.[14] The model based on this theory focuses on analyzing and predicting the courses of action that people will take when they must make decisions. Underlying assumptions of the model are that people will make rational decisions and that needs and past experiences influence the rational decision process.

Basic assumptions

The expectancy model rests on three basic assumptions:

1. *Behavior is determined by some combination of forces in the individual and work situation.* Maslow stated that people have different needs. How these needs will be fulfilled is influenced by the work situation.

2. *Individuals make conscious decisions about their own behavior in organizations.* People make decisions about whether to join the organization, come to work or call in sick, put in overtime, work for a promotion, and the like.

3. *Individuals choose among alternatives based on the expectation that a given behavior will lead to some desired outcome.* In essence, individuals tend to behave in ways that they believe will lead to desirable things (pay raises, promotions, job security) and avoid behaving in ways that they believe will lead to undesirable things (demotion, lay-off).[15]

Figure 12.5 presents the expectancy model graphically. It indicates that the amount of effort employees put into work activities is based on the perception that it will enable them to attain a desired performance level. This

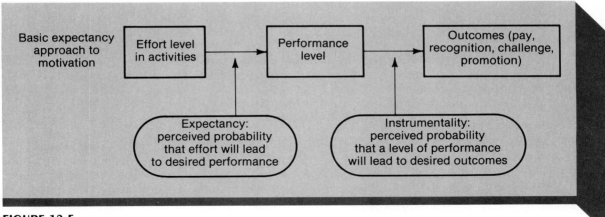

FIGURE 12.5
Basic Expectancy Approach to Motivation

is called *expectancy*. For example, if you attend class, study, and take notes, what is the probability that you will achieve the grade you desire in this class? If you believe that these activities will not lead to the desired grade, your expectancy would be zero. Therefore you would not study, attend class, or take notes as conscientiously as you would if you believe that these activities would lead to the desired grade.

The desired level of performance, in turn, is based on the perception that it will lead to desired outcomes. This is called ***instrumentality***. For example, if you achieve an A in this course, will that lead to things you desire, such as an improved grade-point average, opportunity for graduate school, or a chance of securing a better job?

Thus the motivational force to behave in a certain way is greatest when you believe that (1) a high level of performance is possible (expectancy); and (2) performance can lead to desirable outcomes (instrumentality). With this in mind, contrast the ways that two American Airlines employees approach their jobs.

IN PRACTICE
AMERICAN AIRLINES
RESERVATIONS
Office

Barbara Myers works for American Airlines and takes calls for reservations from 8:00 A.M. until 4:30 P.M. each day. By the end of the week, she has answered more than 1000 calls.

How does she feel about her job? She loves it. Barbara has been with the airline since her husband died nine years ago. Her day begins at 7:30 A.M. when she leaves her home for the short drive to the airport. As soon as she arrives at work, she gets ready to answer calls by putting on her headset and looking at the flight schedules.

Barbara's goal is to answer the phone before it rings three times. If all lines are busy, an automatic switching device diverts the call, the caller hears a recording, and is put on hold. The reservation agents try to avoid this because top management believes that customers get annoyed and sales are lost. Barbara's productivity rate is far above the minimum set by the company. After nine years on this job, she can carry on lively conversations with her co-workers and still answer the phones.

Barbara earns about $21,000 a year. She has made her job her life. "I would not recommend it to someone with a good education or who wants to move ahead," she says, "but for someone like me, it's great. You learn to take all calls in stride. I have made up my mind that I'll do this until I retire and I do not get bored."

Barbara cannot imagine any other way of spending a day. To her, going to the airport is as natural as eating and sleeping. It is, she says, "like anything else—you gotta eat, sleep, and work." Indeed, to her the airport is almost like home. "I was here in the ice storm, when most others stayed home," she said.

Barbara is proud of her record and is resentful of younger workers who are not willing to devote as much effort to the job as she does. "They want this job because they can fly to resort places with the company discount. I like this place, but it requires effort to do good work."

One co-worker that Barbara has little respect for is Sam Markham. He and Barbara work on the same shift. Most of Sam's time is spent answering calls like Barbara's. Sam is 21 years old and graduated from a local high school three years ago. He failed to find a job after graduation and took "what was available at the time."

Although he used to try hard, Sam has never mastered his job. He seems to lack an appealing telephone voice and the finger dexterity and hand speed required to do his job. His performance is constantly below standards.

How does Sam feel about his job? "I dread coming to work. The pay is too low, and the boredom is driving me crazy. Most of the other employees are older and have little interest in traveling and socializing. Did you ever hear of TGIF (Thank God It's Friday)? I cannot wait until my shift is over. My biggest fear is that I am trapped in this job and that I will never be able to get an office job."[16]

Applying the expectancy model to the job performances of Barbara Myers and Sam Markham, we can see why Sam has a low motivation to perform at the airline reservation office. To begin with, he does not believe that high performance can lead to anything he wants (instrumentality). According to Sam, the pay is low, the work is boring, and he does not have any interests in common with co-workers. Furthermore, Sam does not believe that he can perform at high levels (expectancy) because he lacks the skills and abilities (finger dexterity and hand speed) to achieve a high performance level. The situation for Barbara Myers is just the opposite. Barbara knows that she has the skills and abilities to do the job well and values the benefits the job brings her (friendly co-workers, good pay, interesting work). Barbara and Sam have developed very different expectations about the kinds of behavior that will lead to promotions, pay increases, job security, and job satisfaction.

Using the expectancy model

The expectancy model presents several specific steps that managers can take to motivate employees:

1. *Determine the rewards valued by each employee.* If rewards are to be motivators, they must be suitable for each employee. Managers can determine the rewards their subordinates want by observing their behaviors and by asking them.

2. *Determine the desired performance.* Managers must identify the level of performance wanted, so they can tell others what it takes to be rewarded.

It is often possible and desirable for managers and subordinates to discuss and try to reach mutual agreement on the types and levels of performance expected.

3. *Make performance levels attainable.* If people feel that the objectives management has set are unattainable, then their motivation will be low.

4. *Link rewards to performance.* To maintain or increase motivation, the rewards must be linked clearly to performance.

5. *Make sure that rewards are adequate.* Minor rewards will act as minor motivators.

The expectancy model is not without its limitations.[17] The major one has to do with complexity. Do people really consider how expectancies, instrumentalities, and outcomes interact every time they make decisions?[18] How do people decide that certain work outcomes are attainable, while others are not? Managers must recognize such limitations, but the model is invaluable in determining how to motivate employees. It requires the manager to concentrate on the needs that are causing certain behaviors and how people choose among alternatives.

Reinforcement Model

Throughout this chapter, we have implied the importance of rewards and punishments in motivating people. The primary managerial purpose of giving rewards is to influence the behavior of subordinates. The reinforcement model emphasizes the application of rewards and punishments. This approach to motivation has its foundations in the work of B. F. Skinner.[19] Stated very simply, the **reinforcement model** suggests that behavior is a function of its consequences (rewards or punishments), and behavior that gets rewarded is likely to be repeated. In other words, if you are rewarded (bonuses, pats on the back, privileges) for performing at a high level, you would continue to repeat your high level of performance; you know you will be rewarded. The basic reinforcement process is shown in Fig. 12.6. A person's response (behavior) to a stimulus (situation) results in specific consequences (rewards and punishments). If those consequences are unpleasant, individuals will tend to change their behavior in order to avoid them.

For example, if you come to class, take notes, study the text, take the examination, and receive a high grade, your behavior was rewarded. You will probably prepare for the next examination in the same way. On the other hand, if you did all those same things and did not receive a high grade, your behavior was not rewarded. According to the **law of effect,** only those behaviors that are positively rewarded are likely to be repeated. Thus you are less likely to study or take notes the same way, because that behavior led to a negative result (low grade); you will try a different approach to earning a positive reward.

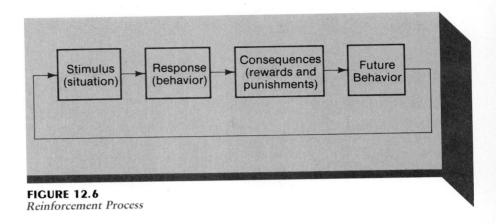

FIGURE 12.6
Reinforcement Process

Principles of behavior modification

There are three fundamental principles for modifying the behaviors of others.[20] These principles concern (1) measurable behavior; (2) types of reinforcement; and (3) schedules of reinforcement.

Measurable behavior. The focus is on *measurable* behavior (number of units produced, percentage of units found defective, number of meals served, number of students taught). The reinforcement model does not consider thoughts and feelings because these are difficult, if not impossible, to measure. This is one of the major differences between the reinforcement model and the hierarchy-of-needs, two-factor, and expectancy models. The latter models either directly or indirectly involve the concept of needs, whereas the reinforcement model does not. Only those behaviors that can be observed and measured are relevant to behavior-modification attempts.

Types of reinforcement. Two types of reinforcement strengthen or maintain behavior: positive reinforcement and avoidance (Table 12.4). *Positive reinforcement* is used to increase the likelihood that a desired behavior will be repeated. Reinforcers cause behaviors to be repeated. Therefore anything that serves to increase the likelihood of a *desired* behavior can be classified as a *positive* reinforcer. Some common positive reinforcers used by organizations include praise, promotion, and salary increases,[21] which most of us would regard as pleasant and desirable. However, most people have somewhat different opinions about what constitutes a reward and its importance. Thus managers find it difficult to develop a reward system that is appropriate for all or to tailor rewards to suit each employee.

Avoidance takes place when people learn to escape or avoid unpleasant consequences. Most students come to class on time in order to avoid a reprimand from the instructor. Similarly, most of us learn to drive carefully

TABLE 12.4 ■ REINFORCEMENT EFFECTS

REINFORCEMENT TYPE	STIMULUS	RESPONSE	CONSEQUENCE OR REWARD
Positive Application increases the likelihood that a desired behavior will be repeated.	Promotion will result from continued excellent performance.	Continued excellent performance	Promotion, salary increase, pat on the back
Avoidance Likelihood of desired behavior is increased by knowledge of consequence.	Reprimands will result from tardy behavior.	Punctuality	No reprimand
Punishment Application decreases the likelihood that an undesired behavior will be repeated.	Tardiness will not be tolerated.	Tardiness	Reprimand, demotion, fine
Extinction Removal of positive reinforcement to eliminate an undesired behavior.	(1) Prizes awarded for attracting new savings account customers.	High effort to attract new customers	Prizes
	(2) Prizes for attracting new savings account customer halted.	Reduction of effort to attract new customers	No prizes

Source: A. Szilagyi, *Management and Performance.* Glenview, Ill.: Scott, Foresman, 1984, p. 409.

through intersections to avoid traffic accidents. In both cases we are motivated to act in such a way that we avoid the unpleasant consequences that are likely to follow either tardiness or speeding through intersections.

Punishment and extinction are designed to reduce undesired behavior, rather than to reinforce desired behavior (Table 12.4). **Punishment** is the application of negative consequences after an undesired behavior has occurred. The purpose of punishment is to decrease the likelihood that the undesired behavior will be repeated. The employee who comes to work late, does not clean the work area, or turns out too many defective parts might be reprimanded by the manager. The disciplinary action might take the form of a day off without pay, a monetary fine, or a demotion if the behavior continues.

Extinction is actually the *absence* of reinforcement following an undesired behavior. In its simplest form, extinction involves the withholding of positive reinforcement. By simply ignoring the behavior, the behavior will eventually cease. In the classroom, the instructor who ignores disruptive students rather than giving them attention is trying to stop the undesired behavior (disruptions) through the use of extinction.

Schedules of reinforcement. There are many possible schedules of reinforcement. The four types most commonly used by managers are shown in Table 12.5. The *fixed interval schedule* provides reinforcement at fixed time intervals. Examples include the weekly, biweekly, or monthly paycheck. This type of reinforcement schedule provides the least incentive for individuals to perform well. Employees know that they will be paid for some minimal level of behavior during that time interval. Alice, Kay, and Nan at the McCormick & Company, Inc., plant in the Preview Case were on this reinforcement schedule.

A *variable interval schedule* uses time as the basis for reinforcement, but the time period between reinforcements varies. Most inspection crews work on this schedule. If employees do not know when their supervisor is going to drop in, they tend to maintain a reasonably high level of desired behavior.

A *fixed ratio schedule* reinforces employees after a fixed number of desired behaviors has occurred. Salespeople working on commissions and workers on piece-rate systems operate under this schedule. Motivation is usually high when employees approach the next reinforcement level.

TABLE 12.5 ■ SCHEDULES OF REINFORCEMENT

TYPE	DESCRIPTION	EXAMPLE
Fixed interval	Reinforcement given at a fixed time, regardless of behavior	Weekly, biweekly, or monthly paycheck
Variable interval	Reinforcement given at variable times, regardless of behavior	Praise, criticism
Fixed ratio	Reinforcement given after a fixed number of behaviors, regardless of time	Sales commissions, pay for piece-rate work
Variable Ratio	Reinforcement given after a variable number of behaviors, regardless of time	Promotions; Las Vegas slot machines

A *variable ratio schedule* involves varying the number of desired behaviors before reinforcement is provided. This is the most powerful type of reinforcement schedule in terms of maintaining desired behaviors. It is the most difficult for managers to use, with the exception of promoting employees. If employees were paid under this schedule, they would not know when to expect the reinforcement (paycheck); it would be difficult for them to pay bills on time or plan a trip because the paycheck would arrive at different times during the year. A manager who praises a salesperson after the third order, fifth order, tenth order, and seventeenth order is using a variable ratio schedule by varying the behaviors needed for reinforcement. (Gambling casinos use this reinforcement system to keep us playing the slot machines.)

After reading about the Henry Butts Oldsmobile dealership, you should be able to identify the three basic principles of the reinforcement model: measurable behaviors, types of reinforcement, and schedules of reinforcement.

IN PRACTICE
HENRY BUTTS Oldsmobile

Henry Butts Oldsmobile is the top-selling automobile dealership in the Dallas area and one of the top three Oldsmobile dealerships in the country. Sales manager Bob Short describes Butts's hiring policy and reward system in detail.

The dealership puts an inexperienced salesperson through a three- to seven-day training program that teaches basic product knowledge and selling techniques. Having completed this program, the new salesperson is placed on the sales floor with an experienced salesperson to learn the ropes observing and working there for approximately one week. The company rewards the experienced salesperson for aiding in the training process at the rate of $50 to $75 per day. This system not only rewards the mentor with money, but also with status. It also provides the new salesperson with immediate entrance and acceptance into the sales floor system.

Salespeople receive a straight commission on the percentage of gross profit for each sale. With a gross profit of $300 or less, the salespeople receive a 30 percent commission; over $300 they receive 33 percent. In addition to their commission, the salespeople also receive unit bonuses when they sell more than 11 cars per month. The unit bonus is determined by squaring the number of units sold. For example, salespeople who sell 12 cars receive 12 × 12, or $144; those who sell 20 cars receive 20 × 20, or $400.

The quantity of cars sold is important, but so is the gross profit obtained from each sale. Gaining that extra bit of gross profit usually requires extra effort on the salesperson's part. If no rewards were attached to the amount of extra effort required, the salesperson might be satisfied with a minimum deal. In addition to the higher commission received for every deal in excess of $300 gross profit, Henry D. Butts contributes $5 to a "December Fund" accrued for each salesperson. Last year, one salesperson was awarded $750 in December for selling 150 cars with gross profits in excess of $300 per deal.

Additional nonmonetary rewards are also used at Butts. Twice a year the company totals both the quantity and gross profit from deals for each salesperson. The top three are given their choice of any car on the lot to drive as their personal demo. The next 10 salespeople typically receive a lower-line car with few added options.

Mr. Short has three sales meetings per week, primarily to record and discuss the gross profits for the cars sold during the preceding two days. All the salespeople are listed vertically on a large board according to how well they did compared with others in last month's sales. A horizontal bar graph indicates how well they are doing in this month's sales. So three times a week, the salespeople can either pat themselves on the back because they are leading the pack or kick themselves because they are so far behind.

Butts Oldsmobile has a strict policy regarding dress code and attendance. A salesperson's appearance is of the utmost importance. This dealership is located in the North Dallas area—where customers are typically upper class and between the ages of 28 and 50—and the sales force must be dressed to please this clientele. If the salespeople are not dressed properly, they are fined and sent home for the day. The salespeople are required to attend and be on time for the three sales meetings each week, as well as for the floor shift to which they are assigned. If any of these rules are not followed, the offender is fined according to a schedule set by the management. The first offense requires a payment of $10; the second, $25; and the third, $50; there is no fourth opportunity—you're fired. The money obtained from these fines is used for parties for the sales force. A minimum monthly sales requirement is also established by the management: A person who sells less than 10 cars in two consecutive months is automatically fired.[22]

Using the reinforcement model

Hamner suggests six rules for use of the reinforcement model by managers.[23] These rules and comments on each one are given in Table 12.6. Encouraging results have been reported by a number of firms that use these rules, including Emery Air Freight, Michigan Bell, Standard Oil, GE, and Procter & Gamble. These firms report that positive reinforcement principles result in major gains in efficiency, cost savings, attendance, and productivity.

While the reinforcement model has many positive features, there are some problems with its use.[24] First, the model may oversimplify behavior because it does not recognize individual characteristics such as needs and values. Second, there may be too much emphasis on manipulation and control over others. Finally, with its heavy emphasis on external rewards, the model tends to ignore the fact that an increasing number of employees can be motivated by the job itself.

TABLE 12.6 ■ SIX RULES FOR USING REINFORCEMENT THEORY

RULE	COMMENT
■ Don't reward all individuals equally.	To be effective behavior reinforcers, rewards should be based on performance. Rewarding everyone equally in effect reinforces poor or average performance and ignores high performance.
■ Failure to respond can also modify behavior.	Managers influence their subordinates by what they do not do as well as by what they do. For example, failing to praise deserving subordinates may cause them to perform poorly the next time.
■ Tell individuals what they can do to receive reinforcement.	Setting performance standards lets individuals know what they should do to be rewarded; they can then adjust their work patterns to get these rewards.
■ Tell individuals what they are doing wrong.	If managers withhold rewards from subordinates without indicating why they are not being rewarded, the subordinates may be confused about what behaviors the manager finds undesirable. The subordinates may also feel that they are being manipulated.
■ Don't punish in front of others.	Reprimanding subordinates might sometimes be a useful way of eliminating an undesirable behavior. Public reprimand, however, humiliates subordinates and may cause all the members of the work group to resent the manager.
■ Be fair.	The consequences of a behavior should be appropriate for the behavior. Subordinates should be given the rewards they deserve. Failure to reward subordinates properly or overrewarding undeserving subordinates reduces the reinforcing effect of rewards.

Source: Adapted from W. Clay Hamner, "Reinforcement Theory and Contingency Management in Organizational Settings." In Henry L. Tosi and W. Clay Hamner (Eds.), *Organizational Behavior and Management: A Contingency Approach*, rev. ed., New York: Wiley, 1977, pp. 93–112.

CHAPTER SUMMARY

Motivation is an extremely important subject for managers. They must be able to motivate employees to achieve organizational objectives and personal goals. In Chapter 1, we indicated that managers play three roles: decisional, interpersonal, and informational. The manager whose goal is to increase the performance of subordinates will probably play all three roles. The *decisional role* is concerned with amount and kinds of rewards given to high- and low-performing subordinates. Subordinates may keep performing poorly regardless of the rewards unless the manager is able to communicate what is desired. Communication is part of the *informational role*. The manager, in addition to providing appropriate rewards and communicating adequately to subordinates, must have the ability to understand what individuals need from their jobs. These needs are uncovered through the *interpersonal role*.

We identified three characteristics that play an important role in understanding the motivation: individual, job, and organizational. The hierarchy-of-needs model shows how individual needs affect motivations. This model states that individuals are motivated to satisfy five needs: physiological, security, affiliation, esteem, and self-actualization. A satisfied need can no longer motivate the individual.

The two-factor model describes how job characteristics can affect motivation to perform and job satisfaction. This model identifies two classes of job characteristics—motivator and hygiene factors—that lead to different personal outcomes. In general, in order to increase employees' motivation to perform, managers should enrich workers' jobs. We examined the job-enrichment model in detail. This model emphasizes certain job characteristics that could lead to three critical psychological states: meaningfulness, responsibility, and knowledge of results. These states can affect job satisfaction and performance.

The expectancy model pulls together individual, job, and organizational factors. It shows how they interact to affect employees' motivation to perform a task. The expectancy model presents motivation, performance, and job satisfaction as dependent on the outcomes that employees want from their jobs. The effort put forth in various activities can lead to some desired performance level. This performance level, in turn, is instrumental in leading to the attainment of desired job outcomes.

The reinforcement model focuses on how job motivation can be maintained or increased. The assumption is that behavior resulting in pleasant or desirable consequences is likely to be repeated, whereas behavior resulting in unpleasant consequences is less likely to be repeated. Managers may use different techniques—positive reinforcement, avoidance, extinction, or punishment—to motivate others. These techniques may be put to use on any one of four schedules: fixed interval, fixed ratio, variable interval, or variable ratio.

MANAGER'S VOCABULARY

affiliation needs
autonomy
avoidance
critical psychological states
esteem needs
expectancy theory
experienced meaningfulness
experienced responsibility
extinction
extrinsic factors
feedback
fixed interval schedule
fixed ratio schedule
growth-need strength
hierarchy-of-needs model
hygiene factors
individual characteristics
intrinsic factors
instrumentality
job characteristics
job-enrichment model

knowledge of results
law of effect
motivation
motivator factors
needs
organizational characteristics
physiological needs
positive reinforcement
punishment
quality circle
reinforcement model
security needs
self-actualization needs
skill variety
task identity
task significance
two-factor model
variable interval schedule
variable ratio schedule

REVIEW QUESTIONS

1. From the manager's perspective, what three variables affect an employee's motivation to perform?

2. What are the categories of needs in the hierarchy-of-needs model, and how do these affect employees' motivation to perform?

3. State Herzberg's two-factor model. Why has it been so widely accepted by managers?

4. List the major factors in the job-enrichment model.

5. What assumptions form the basis of the expectancy model?

6. State how expectancy works.

7. What are the types of reinforcement techniques that can be used to motivate others? Which technique is most effective?

8. Identify and define four types of reinforcement schedules.

DISCUSSION QUESTIONS

1. Why is it so difficult to motivate others?

2. Evaluate the statement: "A satisfied worker is usually the most productive." Under what conditions is that true? false?

3. At the McCormick & Company, Inc., plant, what type of reinforcement schedule are the three workers on? If Tarland Beauchamp (the plant manager) wants to increase their performance, what type and schedule of reinforcement might be most appropriate?

4. According to the expectancy model, how do you choose a performance level to achieve?

5. What are the implications of the job-enrichment model for managers?

6. How has the reinforcement model been applied at Henry Butts Oldsmobile? What are some of the model's implications?

7. What implications does the expectancy model have for managers and organizations?

MANAGEMENT INCIDENTS AND CASES

Lincoln Electric Company

Lincoln Electric Company of Cleveland, Ohio, is the world market leader in arc-welding equipment. It is able to charge less today than it did in 1915 because of its outstanding productivity gains. Its 3624 workers earn an average of $21 an hour, including year-end profit sharing.

In the company's system of *incentive management,* workers are paid by the piece. If they can rearrange their work space or tasks to get a job done faster, they are free to do so. If they turn in a suggestion for restructuring their job, the piecework pay they lose will be offset by bonus points. Bonuses, awarded for teamwork and reliability, average close to 100 percent of base pay in most years, but vary widely from worker to worker. If employees are sick, they do not get paid. If someone lets a defective machine through, they fix it on their own time.

More than 80 percent of the stock in the 87-year-old company is owned by employees, retirees, or sympathetic Lincoln heirs. At $28.95, earnings per share have increased more than tenfold over the past two decades. The company has an employee-elected advisory board and does not hire executives from the outside.

The employees once voted down a dental insurance plan, fearing it would cut too deeply into profits and thus their bonus checks. For the same reason, they don't challenge the lack of air-conditioning. In peak years,

like 1981, overtime was mandatory. When orders are slack or machines broken, workers accept job reassignments by management. Sometimes the substitute assignment pays less than the regular one. There are no seniority rights.

Lincoln Electric has no central stockroom, and the company depends on a steady, reliable flow of supplies to be delivered to its factory. If there is a supply interruption, the purchasing department is penalized bonus points. The suppliers deliver directly to work areas through one of the many loading docks in the oblong factory, in which work flows crosswise. The suppliers are paid promptly. The company's unusual balance sheet shows no debt and cash in excess of all liabilities.

Regular employees with at least two years' service are guaranteed minimum employment of 30 hours a week. No one has been laid off in 30 years. In slack years, managers build inventory, and salespeople promote automated and solid-state products kept on hand for these periods. In boom years, management gives workers overtime instead of hiring more employees. Because of the employment guarantee, workers need not fear that productivity gains will cost them their jobs. The company has a turnover rate of only 6 percent a year, compared to the 36 percent average turnover rate in electric manufacturing companies nationwide.[25]

Questions

1. What are some individual, job, and organizational characteristics that influence employee productivity at Lincoln Electric?

2. What is Lincoln Electric's employee philosophy?

3. Why is Lincoln Electric so successful?

REFERENCES

1. Adapted and updated from S. Stewart, "Life in a Catsup Plant," *Dallas Times Herald,* October 18, 1981, p. J1.

2. "A Work Revolution in U.S. Industry," *Business Week,* May 16, 1983, p. 100ff; B. Reilly and J. Fuhr, "Productivity: An Economic and Management Analysis with a Direction Towards a New Synthesis," *Academy of Management Review,* 1983, 8:108–117.

3. D. Katz and R. Kahn, *The Social Psychology of Organizations,* 2nd ed. New York: John Wiley and Sons, 1978.

4. *Business Week,* June 30, 1980, pp. 99–100. *Also see* C. Derber and Wm. Schwartz, "Toward a Theory of Worker Participation," *Sociological Inquiry,* 1983, 53(1):71–78; G. Munchus, "Employer–Employee Based Quality Circles in Japan: Human Resource Policy Implications for American Firms," *Academy of Management Review,* 1983, 8:255–261.

5. L. Porter and R. Miles, "Motivation in Management." In J. McGuire (Ed.), *Contemporary Management: Issues and Viewpoints.* Englewood Cliffs, N.J.: Prentice-Hall, 1974, pp. 545–570.

6. A. Maslow, "A Theory of Human Needs," *Psychological Review,* 1943, 80:370–396.

7. For reviews of this literature, *see* J. Miner, *Theories of Organizational Behavior.* Hinsdale, Ill. Dryden, 1980, pp. 18–43.

8. A. Turner and P. Lawrence, *Industrial Jobs and the Worker.* Boston: Harvard University Press, 1965.

9. F. Herzberg, B. Mausner, and B. Snyderman, *The Motivation to Work.* New York: John Wiley & Sons, 1959.

10. For an excellent overview of this literature, *see* R. Griffin, *Task Design: An Integrated Approach.* Glenview, Ill.: Scott, Foresman, 1982; T. Taber, T. Beehr, and J. Walsh, "Relationship Between Job Evaluation Ratings and Self-Ratings of Job Characteristics," *Organizational Behavior and Human Performance,* 1985, 35:27–45.

11. J. R. Hackman and G. Oldham, *Work Redesign.* Reading, Mass.: Addison-Wesley, 1980.

12. A. Poza and M. Markus, "Success Story: The Team Approach to Work Restructuring," *Organizational Dynamics,* Winter 1980, pp. 3–25.

13. R. Griffin, "Objective and Social Sources of Information in Task Redesign: A Field Experiment," *Administrative Science Quarterly,* 1983, 28:184–200; M. Kiggundu, "Task Interdependence and Job Design: A Test of a Theory," *Organizational Behavior and Human Performance,* 1983, 31:145–172.

14. V. Vroom, *Work and Motivation.* New York: John Wiley & Sons, 1964.

15. D. Nadler, J. R. Hackman, and E. Lawler, *Managing Organizational Behavior.* Boston: Little, Brown, 1979, p. 32.

16. Adapted from Nadler, Hackman, and Lawler, *Managing Organizational Behavior,* p. 26; S. Rawlings, Marketing Research Department, American Airlines, D-FW Airport, Dallas, April 1984.

17. J. Wanous, T. Keon, and J. Latack, "Expectancy Theory and Occupational/Organizational Choices: A Review and Test," *Organizational Behavior and Human Performance,* 1983, 32:66–86; A. Harrell and M. Stahl, "Modeling Managers' Effort-Level Decisions for a Within-Persons Examination of Expectancy Theory in a Budget Setting," *Decision Sciences,* 1984, 15:52–73.

18. E. Pulakos and N. Schmitt, "A Longitudinal Study of a Valence Model Approach for the Prediction of Job Satisfaction for New Employees," *Journal of Applied Psychology,* 1983, 68:307–312.

19. B. F. Skinner, *Beyond Freedom and Human Dignity.* New York: Knopf, 1971.

20. For an expanded treatment of this material, *see* D. Hellriegel, J. Slocum, and R. Woodman, *Organizational Behavior,* 4th ed. St. Paul, Minn.: West, 1986, pp. 141–167.

21. For a list of rewards typically found in organizations, *see* F. Luthans and R. Kreitner, *Organizational Behavior Modification.* Glenview, Ill.: Scott, Foresman, 1984.

22. Prepared by A. Flavin, Cox School of Business, Southern Methodist University, Dallas, 1982.

23. C. Hamner, "Reinforcement Theory and Contingency Management in Organizational Settings." In H. Tosi and C. Hamner (Eds.), *Organizational Behavior and Management: A Contingency Approach.* Chicago: St. Clair, 1977, pp. 93–112.

24. F. Luthans and P. Smith, "Organizational Behavior Modification." In B. Karmel (Ed.), *Point and Counterpoint.* Hinsdale, Ill.: Dryden, 1980, pp. 45–93.

25. Adapted from W. Baldwin, "This Is the Answer," *Forbes,* June 5, 1982, 130(1):51–52.

Leadership

CHAPTER 13

PREVIEW CASE

PEOPLE EXPRESS AIRLINES, INC.

In 1980, Donald Burr left Texas International Airlines to start People Express Airlines. The airline uses Newark International Airport as a hub to offer low-priced destinations to 11 states and London. It offers no-frills service. Customers pay extra for baggage, coffee, meals, and can purchase their tickets while flying. When the company began, Burr started out with a simple functional structure and no formal hierarchy.

Since then, Burr has added one management level, but People Express still has no supervisors or vice presidents. There are also no secretaries because Burr believes that everyone should do their own letters.

The company seeks to maintain an environment in which employees are free to move around and grow. There is great emphasis on training and no rigid job slots. Employees are encouraged to look for the work they like best to do. The pilot who flies one day from Washington, D.C., to New York may be working the next day at Newark on marketing. The flight attendant who collects customers' fares on board may be working in scheduling the following week. According to Burr, every employee should be familiar with every job in the company. By having employees work at different jobs, People Express makes efficient use of its human resources; labor costs are 20 percent of their total expenses, compared to an industry average of 34 percent. Employees are highly motivated. This might help to explain why it was one of the

few airlines to make money since 1982. Only the maintenance work on the planes is contracted out.

Burr's managerial philosophy is that all employees should:

1. Work on meaningful jobs that are consistent with the objectives of the company.
2. Work on challenging jobs that create learning opportunities.
3. Work on jobs that provide feedback to the person and have standards for self-measurement.

Starting salaries at People Express are not high. In 1984, it was hiring reservations people for about $5 an hour and pilots for about $36,000 per year. All employees are required to be stockholders and to participate in a profit-sharing plan that pays up to 15 percent of the base salary of employees. There is also a special bonus plan under which the employee's purchase will be matched by the company.

Burr communicates frequently with all employees. There is an employee-stockholder meeting every three months. Since all employees are stockholders, Burr believes in keeping them informed and letting them share in the decision-making process.[1]

Source: People Express Airlines, Inc.

L ooking at People's experience, why has this airline been successful while others have lost money? How has Burr's managerial philosophy affected the day-to-day operations of People Express? This chapter will answer these and other questions about leadership by reviewing three approaches and describing how they can be applied by managers.

The chapter contains three major parts. First, we discuss the nature of leadership and the sources of power that leaders may have at their command to influence subordinates. Second, we present and discuss two traditional approaches to leadership. Finally, we discuss three contingency approaches to leadership.

IMPORTANCE OF LEADERSHIP

Leadership is the process of influencing the actions of a person or group to attain desired objectives.[2] It involves the behavior of the leader and followers in a specific situation. Since ancient times, various philosophers and other people have sought to advise leaders through their writings and teaching. Particularly influential were Confucius, Plato, Aristotle, contributors to the Bible, and Machiavelli. They told leaders to be wise, bold, good, willing to compromise, fair, and well-read.

Today many managers think that communication, motivation, and leadership are cure-alls that will solve the problems of their organizations. As a result, many of the more recent authors on leadership have found a ready and eager market for their cookbook answers, which have generated a number of leadership fads. These fads have been costly. Prescriptions—such as *be democratic* or *rule with an iron hand*—that have succeeded under one set of circumstances have been applied without much thought to other situations for which they were not well-suited. Managers have great incentive to find better ways to exercise leadership, not the least of which are the high-salary bonus rewards if their firm's annual profits increase.

The Role of Leader

A *leader* is someone whom others want to follow. Leaders are those who are able to command the trust, commitment and loyalty of followers—the great persons who capture and imagination and admiration of those with whom they deal. For example, young golfers admire and emulate Jack Nicklaus, Tom Watson, Carol Mann, or Jan Stephenson and try to copy the swings or style of dress or use clubs endorsed by these golfing professionals. When teaching children about our country's history, teachers in public schools usually point to George Washington, Abraham Lincoln, and others as great leaders. Such figures are often referred to as *born leaders*.

Most of the world's work is done by ordinary people who work on farms and in hospitals, insurance agencies, universities, steel mills, government offices and thousands of other types of jobs. Many of these people are leaders who take responsibility for planning, organizing, and communicating in order to reach certain organizational or community objectives. For example, Jane Smith works for a large university and has been elected chairperson of the local United Way drive. An important part of this job is to help prepare the budget, speak before groups, write letters, make phone calls, obtain volunteers, and perform many other duties that do not directly involve the supervision of others. *A leader is the person who communicates ideas to others and influences their behavior to achieve an objective.* Smith is an effective leader in this situation if she succeeds in influencing the behavior of others to achieve the United Way's financial and program objectives.

Even though leading is something a person does, it should not be confused with an individual's activity level. Aggressiveness and the constant direction of others do not necessarily indicate leadership. At times a good leader may hesitate before making a judgment or stay in the background so others may talk or act.

Leadership deals with the relationships between two or more persons. The dynamics of leadership include the leader, the follower, and the specific situation.[3] Figure 13.1 illustrates this point. Leadership cannot be studied in

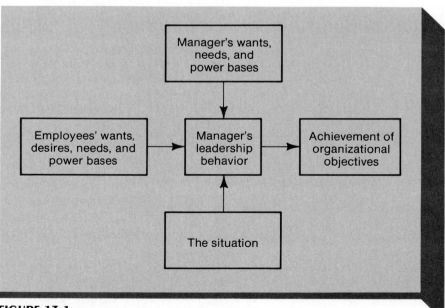

FIGURE 13.1
The Dynamics of Leadership

a vacuum; it must be studied in group settings. Effective leadership occurs only if the leader influences the activities of followers. Usually, a leader cannot threaten or force people into specific behavior over the long run. Leadership is the result of an *exchange* between followers and a leader and must satisfy both parties. In accepting a leader's way of doing things, followers voluntarily give up some of their freedom to make decisions. They permit the leader to make some decisions that affect them in specific situations. In return for permitting themselves to be influenced by a leader, followers want to receive certain intrinsic and extrinsic rewards in return. For example, the coach of a professional sports team demonstrates leadership abilities by guiding the team to a championship. The players follow the coach's advice on the field and suspend their own judgment because of the coach's ability to bring intrinsic and extrinsic rewards to them. Examples of intrinsic rewards include a sense of achievement from winning, media focus on the team, or the fulfillment of players' personal goals. Extrinsic rewards include the extra playoff money for winning a championship, opportunities to make commercial endorsements, TV appearances, and the like.

Motivation to Lead

Very few people can be forced to assume leadership positions against their will. Those who don't *want* to become leaders usually don't. Employees often decline promotions to supervisory and managerial positions. These people simply are not motivated to become leaders in the job situation.

Others want to become leaders. Some view leadership roles as having a great deal to offer and thus seek them out. If top executives hope to attract the best managers to perform leadership functions, they should know what attracts them to leadership roles.

There is little doubt that leadership positions can provide important extrinsic rewards. Steve Jobs, cofounder and former chairman of the board of Apple Computer, whose sales in 1983 were $983 million, has earned some $200 million in salary and other forms of compensation since 1976. Lee Iacocca, chairman of Chrysler, earned a salary of $1.19 million in 1984, while Phillip Caldwell, chairman of Ford, earned more than $1.57 million.[4] Few would argue that these men have not provided leadership as chief executive officers of their firms.

However, leadership is often sought when there are no monetary rewards. For example, the team captain, union steward, church leader, and PTA president are not paid for their positions. People who willingly occupy these positions usually exercise leadership. Why? Because these individuals can satisfy some of their esteem and self-actualization needs through such leadership roles, while helping an organization achieve its objectives.

Followers make it possible for leaders to satisfy some of these needs. Knowing that they can affect their own destiny and the destiny of others, or being recognized as the best in a given field, can be important intrinsic rewards for leaders. The leader receives rewards from the group, just as group members receive rewards from the leader.[5] To remain in a leadership position, the leader must help group members gain satisfactions that otherwise are beyond their reach.

SOURCES OF POWER

A leader has the power to offer or withhold resources from other people. In order to influence others, the leader must appeal to one or more of their needs. If you are holding a gun to my head and look as though you might fire it, chances are that I will do what you ask. However, history demonstrates that there are many situations in which people refuse to obey, even when faced with severe punishment. The implication for the leader is clear: Effective leadership depends as much on a follower accepting direction as on the leader giving it. Whether a leader can successfully influence others depends on how a follower answers the following questions:

1. Can I do what is asked of me without violating my beliefs and values?
2. What is the probability that I can achieve the objectives expected of me?
3. If I meet the objectives, what is the probability that the leader will reward me or withhold punishment?
4. What is the probability that the reward will satisfy my needs?
5. Does the leader have the power to make things happen?

Power and influence are central to the manager's job. Let's consider the bases of the leader's power, or the reasons why a subordinate will follow a leader.[6] One of the most useful frameworks for understanding them was developed by French and Raven.[7] They identify five different sources of power: (1) legitimacy, (2) control over rewards, (3) coercion, (4) referent or personal liking, and (5) expertise.

Legitimate power is based on a person's position in a hierarchy, the manager's formal authority. The corporation president has greater legitimate power than has the vice-president of manufacturing to make decisions about corporate policy. By the same token, the vice-president of manufacturing has more legitimate power than the first-line supervisor to decide issues of capital expenditures, scheduling overtime, and inventory levels.

Reward power depends on a leader's ability to reward subordinates (with valued intrinsic or extrinsic rewards) for their compliance. Subordinates comply with their supervisor's requests in the belief that their behavior will be rewarded. The supervisor may be able to reward them through favorable job assignments, vacation schedules, lunch breaks, promotions, and pay increases.

Coercive power is the ability of a person to punish others and obtain compliance through fear of punishment. Punishment might be in the form of official reprimands, less desirable work assignments, pay cuts, demotion, or firing. A manager who says, "I want these appliances shipped by June fifteenth or heads will roll," is using coercion. As a result, some workers may seek to avoid being reprimanded by falsifying performance reports rather than by changing the quality of their performance.

Referent power is the influence of others by virtue of their personal identification with the leader. This identification is often based on personal admiration and usually includes followers' desire to be like the leader. In other words, referent power usually is associated with people who possess admirable personal characteristics, charisma, or good reputations. A manager's referent power is increased by being considerate toward subordinates, showing concern for their needs and feelings, and defending their interests when dealing with superiors. Managers who use referent power indicate that they personally count on subordinates' support and cooperation.

Expertise power is the influence of others because of the leader's special knowledge. Street gangs usually assign expertise power to those who can fight the best; professors, to those colleagues who write journal articles and books or who are great teachers; workers, to the company president who invented a new product and successfully built a company to manufacture and market it. Expert power is narrow in scope, since a person's expertise generally is limited to specific task areas. For example, a star tennis player with high-expertise power on the courts may not possess such power in a chemistry class.

Power ultimately comes from subordinates' willingness to follow the directions of a leader and the leader's ability to satisfy subordinates' needs.[8] Access to resources and information and the ability to act quickly make it possible for the manager to accomplish more and to pass on rewards and information to subordinates. For this reason, people tend to refer to some managers as having *clout,* which is a person's pull or political influence in an organization. Some common examples of managerial clout are listed in Table 13.1. They indicate that a manager's power does not come from a style or skill so much as from the manager's position in the formal and informal

TABLE 13.1 ■ BENEFITS OF MANAGERIAL CLOUT

- A good job for a talented subordinate
- Approval for expenditures beyond the budget
- Above-average salary increases for subordinates
- Items on the agenda at meetings
- Access to top people in company
- Early information about decisions and policy shifts

Source: Reprinted by permission of the *Harvard Business Review.* Exhibit adapted from "Power Failure in Management Circuits" by Rosabeth Moss Kanter (Jult–August 1979). Copyright © 1979 by the President and Fellows of Harvard College; all rights reserved.

TABLE 13.2 ■ ORGANIZATIONAL FACTORS THAT CONTRIBUTE TO POWER OR POWERLESSNESS

FACTOR	GENERATES POWER WHEN FACTORS ARE	GENERATES POWERLESSNESS WHEN FACTORS ARE
Rules inherent in the job	few	many
Predecessors in the job	few	many
Established routines	few	many
Task variety	high	low
Rewards for unusual performance/ innovation	many	few
Flexibility around use of people	high	low
Approvals needed for nonroutine decisions	few	many
Physical location	central	distant
Publicity about job activities	high	low
Relation of tasks to current problem areas	central	peripheral
Interpersonal contact in the job	high	low
Contact with senior officials	high	low
Participation in programs, conferences, meetings	high	low
Participation in problem-solving task forces	high	low
Advancement prospects of subordinates	high	low

Source: Reprinted by permission of the *Harvard Business Review*. Exhibit adapted from "Power Failure in Management Circuits" by Rosabeth Moss Kanter (July–August 1979). Copyright © 1979 by the President amd Fellows of Harvard College; all rights reserved.

systems of the organization. Subordinates cooperate with a manager partly because they feel that the manager has the power to make things happen.

Some of the organizational factors that generate power or powerlessness are listed in Table 13.2. Power is most easily gained when a manager has a job that allows discretion (nonroutine tasks), results in recognition (visibility and notice), and is relevant (being central to major organizational problems and issues). Power comes to the manager who has relatively close contact with sponsors (higher-level managers who give approval, prestige, and backing). Power is also created through peer networks (circles of friends who provide information faster than the formal systems of communication). Subordinates who can be developed to relieve managers of some of their work and who can support the manager's plans with other employees are another source of power.

Uses of Power and Followers' Reactions

The manager's use of power can affect the behavior of subordinates. Three major behaviors affected by the use of power are: commitment, compliance, and resistance.[9] When subordinates are committed to a manager's objectives, they are enthusiastic about carrying out the manager's requests and make a maximum effort to do so. Simple compliance, on the other hand, means that subordinates will go along with a manager's plans or directions without necessarily accepting them. That is, they are not enthusiastic about the plans and may make only the minimal acceptable effort in carrying out the manager's requests. Resistance, in most cases, is clearly an undesirable behavior. Subordinates may reject a manager's plans, may pretend to comply, or may even intentionally delay or sabotage the plans. As Table 13.3 illustrates, expertise and referent power tend to result in subordinate commitment, legitimate and reward power tend to result in compliance, and coercive power tends to result in resistance.

Performance is usually better when subordinates are highly motivated to do a task. Expertise and referent power usually lead to high levels of performance. However, there are situations in which punishment is effective in getting subordinates to comply with rules and regulations. (See Chapter 12.) Similarly, when a manager legitimately asks a subordinate to perform a certain task that is within the subordinate's capabilities and job description, legitimate power is also effective in influencing others. Leaders are likely to use all five sources of power at one time or another. Leader effectiveness stems from knowing the appropriate type or combinations of power to use in each situation.

Guidelines for using managerial power

Managers need power to influence subordinates.[10] Leadership, in turn, depends on managers' ability to acquire and use the various sources of power.

TABLE 13.3 ■ BEHAVIORAL TENDENCIES BASED ON DIFFERENT SOURCES OF LEADER POWER

POWER SOURCE	COMMITMENT	COMPLIANCE	RESISTANCE
Legitimate	Possible	Likely	Possible
Reward	Possible	Likely	Possible
Coercive	Unlikely	Possible	Likely
Referent	Likely	Possible	Possible
Expertise	Likely	Possible	Possible

Source: Adapted from G. Yukl and T. Tabor, "The Effective Use of Managerial Power," *Personnel*, 1983, 60(2):39.

Thus effective managers:

- *Don't deny their formal authority.* They use their position to get things done. They act as the boss, but pay attention to the sensitivity and feelings of others. Rewards, punishments, and legitimacy are not guaranteed to work. They are necessary and important sources of power and are based on a manager's position in the organization.

- *Are not afraid to create a sense of obligation.* Some managers are highly skilled at doing favors that cost them very little but that others appreciate. As a result, these favors expand a manager's power bases.

INTERNATIONAL FOCUS

Pierre Dreyfus

Pierre Dreyfus rose to international fame as manager of the French automobile company, Renault, after World War II. Educated in an elite French institution, he began a brilliant career in the government bureaucracy. He was inspector general of industry and commerce and held other high positions, including, briefly, the presidency of the state-owned coal mines (Charbonnages de France). His great success with Renault came because of his ability to keep its management decisions relatively independent of government interference.

Under the Renault constitution as well as French law, the views of the company are considered in choosing a chairman but the government makes the decision. The government never makes such decisions lightly. The government knows that the most effective means of control is through the head of the company. Dreyfus was able to run Renault on comparatively loose reins as nationalized companies go. This is because the French government knew him, chose him, had confidence in him, and trusted him to keep Renault on a course that would be consistent with the government's objectives.

Dreyfus's book, *La Liberte de reussir* [The freedom to succeed], discloses fascinating details about his career and his strategies at Renault. The company's major goal was to grow to a position of great strength, first in the French market, then in the European, and finally in the international market. The government shared this goal—it wanted to minimize imports of foreign auto manufacturers and it wanted to encourage French exports. Dreyfus was successful in coaxing the government to give him the necessary capital to steadily expand output and establish Renault's dominance in the French market and to build its strength throughout Europe and the world.

Excerpted from: K. O. Walters and R. J. Monsen, "Managing the Nationalized Company," *California Management Review,* Summer 1983, pp. 21–22 (entire article is from: *Nationalized Companies.* Copyright © 1983 by R. Joseph Monsen and Kenneth D. Walters). Reprinted by permission of McGraw-Hill Book Company.

- *Create feelings of dependence.* The more people perceive themselves as dependent on their managers, the more inclined they will be to cooperate with them. Effective managers find ways to maintain this dependency by acquiring extra resources for their people or getting them higher raises or faster promotions.

- *Allow others the opportunity to identify with them as a person.* When others know and respect managers as people, they tend to behave in a manner consistent with their managers' desires. This requires regular and effective interpersonal communications between managers and their subordinates.

Still, the government often put pressure on Renault to do things that Dreyfus did not want to do. Dreyfus proved to be a skillful negotiator in such situations. He would never give the government a flat *non,* but would point out how other goals would suffer if Renault had to rescue too many companies, build plants in depressed and remote Brittany, and yet hold down prices. These conflicts were often resolved by Dreyfus talking the government into softening a proposed new control. He also knew how to avoid conflicts with the government by anticipating its views on issues. "I was never given a directive," he said when interviewed in his Paris apartment. What few conflicts did arise between Dreyfus and the French government were discreetly resolved between the president or the minister of finance and Dreyfus himself. They were not allowed to become open political squabbles which threatened both the government and Dreyfus's own career.

Another factor accounting for his success that Dreyfus himself stresses is the French educational system. The top government officials and industry leaders (including state industry executives) come from the same elite schools and know each other personally. This meant that he was able to deal with such men as De Gaulle, Pompidou, and Giscard D'Estaing on a highly personal level. Conflicts could be worked out pragmatically since there was mutual trust and respect. Dreyfus's personal connections within the government made him the most powerful and flexible manager in the history of France's state-owned firms. Indeed, among managers of state companies in France, his accomplishments and relative independence still remain unique.

TRADITIONAL APPROACHES TO LEADERSHIP

In Alfred Sloan's book, *My Years with General Motors,* the former chief operating officer of GM asks whether leadership is a characteristic of the individual or a term for describing relationships among members of a group.[11] And, for years, many people have tried to find out why some people are successful and others not. If there were simple answers, a person could simply try to develop the needed skills.

Three traditional approaches to leadership—trait, behavioral, and contingency—illustrate its complexity; they are shown in Fig. 13.2. Each of these approaches, or models, uses a different set of characteristics to describe and predict effective styles of leadership.

Leadership Traits Models

Many of the early studies of leadership were directed at identifying traits of leaders. Leadership **traits models** are based on the assumption that certain physical, social, personality, and other personal traits are inherent in leaders; that these traits can be used to distinguish leaders from nonleaders.

Common leadership traits

The traits commonly identified with leaders included the following.

- *Physical:* age, energy, appearance, height, weight.
- *Social Background:* education, social status, mobility.
- *Personality:* adaptability, aggressiveness, emotional balance, dominance, self-confidence.
- *Social Characteristics:* administrative ability, cooperativeness, interpersonal skills, tact, popularity.
- *Task-Related Characteristics:* drive to excel, drive for responsibility, initiative, task orientation.

There is some common-sense support for the notion that effective managers differ from less effective managers in terms of interests, interpersonal skills, and, perhaps also, some personality traits. However, traits models are not usually considered to be of much help in understanding leadership. There are no sets of leadership traits that can be used consistently as standards for designating individuals as either potential leaders or nonleaders.[12] This does not mean that individual traits have nothing to do with effective leadership, but rather that traits must be evaluated in relation to other factors.

Limitations of traits models

The major limitations of traits models are that they primarily focus on physical and personality traits. Physical traits have *not* been found to correlate

Questions

- Is leadership an individual characteristic?
- Why are some people more effective leaders than others?
- What is the best way to lead?

Answers

Traits models—focus on a leader's personal characteristics

Behavioral models—focus on a leader's behaviors

Contingency models—focus on matches between a leader's behaviors and characteristics of the situation

FIGURE 13.2
Three Approaches to Leadership

with successful leadership. In the military or police departments, for example, members must meet certain minimum standards of height and weight in order to perform their tasks effectively. These attributes may be helpful in the physical performance of some jobs. However, height and weight do not often relate to effective leadership.

Although some personality traits have been related to effective leadership, the results have not been consistent. For example, some of the personality traits found to relate to a salesperson's effectiveness (in terms of sales volume) include gregariousness, risk taking, impulsiveness, exhibitionism, and egocentrism. On the other hand, these traits are not commonly found among successful coaches of sports teams. They usually have personality traits of self-assertion, self-assurance, a strong need for power, and a low need for security. But there are successful salespeople and coaches who have personality profiles different from those mentioned.

Contributions of traits models

Despite their limitations, traits models should not be discarded too hastily. They have contributed to clarifying the nature of leadership. Most universities, for example, are run by educators who hold doctoral degrees and have educational experience; hospitals require the chiefs of their medical staffs to have medical degrees; and Supreme Court justices have legal backgrounds. These are considered to be social-background traits. Many managers argue that people with certain social-background traits are more likely to become leaders than others. Such traits may include an ability to verbalize feelings and concepts, above average intelligence (but not genius), sympathy for group members, some insight into group situations, tact, and flexibility in formulating new concepts and ideas. Although none of these traits is absolutely necessary, they may all help an individual to perform his or her leadership role.

The one essential personal trait for those who seek leadership roles is the *motivation to be a leader.*[13] In general, the stronger a person's motivation to be a leader, the more likely that person is to achieve a leadership position. Of course, the reasons for that motivation can vary widely: an urge to dominate others; devotion to the group and to the group's objectives; a high-level aspiration for either self or group; a need for prestige and esteem; and economic rewards.

To summarize, the idea that leadership effectiveness can be determined by personal traits has proved to be too simplistic. The dream of measuring traits, developing an optimal traits profile, and selecting individuals who fit the mold and will automatically become effective leaders has not been realized.

Behavioral Models

Although no single profile of traits distinguishes effective leaders from less effective leaders, some *behaviors* (styles of leadership) have been found to be more effective than others. Leadership **behavioral models** provide a way to distinguish effective from ineffective leaders by their different behavior profiles.

Interest in the behavior of leaders emerged during the 1930s. Research programs begun in the late 1940s at Ohio State University and Iowa State University strengthened this interest. Researchers at Iowa State University first conducted a study with small children to determine the effect of three different leadership styles on their performance.[14] Researchers labeled the leadership styles as autocratic, democratic, and laissez-faire (literally, *let it be*).

The **autocratic leader** led by command, and the commands were generally obeyed to avoid punishment. The leader was task-centered and tended to criticize when productivity slowed. The **democratic leader** permitted the group to discuss issues and make decisions. The leader encouraged group members to work with whomever they chose, and was supportive of the children's work. The **laissez-faire leader** allowed the group total freedom and exerted a minimal amount of personal influence.

The quantity of work produced was greatest in the autocratic groups. However, the quality of the work in the democratic groups was superior. When the autocratic leaders left the area, the children almost completely stopped working (a sign of job dissatisfaction). By contrast, the performance of those groups under democratic leaders decreased only slightly in the leaders' absence. In general, the laissez-faire style—complete permissiveness and indifference—was not effective in stimulating performance. Less work was done under laissez-faire leadership, and the work was of poorer quality than that of either the democratic or autocratic groups.

Ohio State University leadership models

From this early beginning, researchers at Ohio State University identified two basic styles of leadership: considerate and initiating structure.

Considerate style. A *considerate leadership style* is concerned with subordinates' well-being, status, and comfort. Considerate leaders seek to create a friendly and pleasant working climate. They assume that subordinates want to do their best and that their job is to make it easier for subordinates to achieve their own goals. Considerate leaders seek to gain acceptance by treating subordinates with respect and dignity. They tend to downplay both their formal position in the company and the use of coercive power. Some typical behaviors of considerate leaders include:

- expressing appreciation when subordinates do a good job;
- not demanding more than subordinates can do;
- helping subordinates with their personal problems;
- being friendly and easy to see; and
- rewarding subordinates for jobs well done.

Claims that the considerate leadership style is effective are based on its ready acceptance by subordinates. Advocates contend that highly considerate leader behavior generates goodwill among subordinates and leads to feelings of high job satisfaction. These positive attitudes lead to closer cooperation between leaders and subordinates, increase the work motivation of subordinates, create productive work groups, and result in low turnover and grievance rates.

Initiating-structure style. An *initiating-structure leadership style* is concerned with actively planning, organizing, controlling, and coordinating the activities of subordinates to reach departmental or organizational objectives. Typical behaviors of initiating-structure leaders include:

- assigning subordinates to particular tasks;
- establishing standards of job performance;
- informing subordinates of job requirements;
- scheduling work to be done by subordinates; and
- encouraging the use of uniform procedures.

Combinations of leadership behaviors. Figure 13.3 shows the four possible combinations of these two leadership styles. As might be expected, employee turnover rates were lowest and employee satisfaction was highest under leaders who were rated high in consideration and low in initiating structure. Conversely, leaders who were rated high in initiating structure and

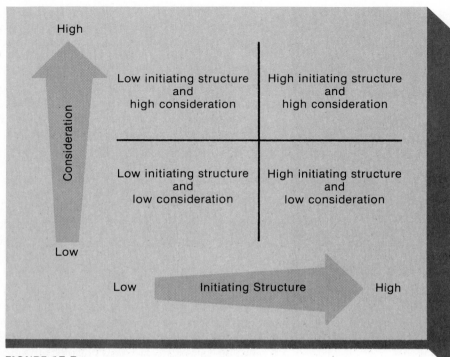

FIGURE 13.3
Combinations of Ohio State University Leadership Styles

low in consideration had high employee grievance and turnover rates. However, later research has suggested that effective leaders exhibit both consideration and initiating-structure behaviors.[15]

Managerial grid model

One of the more popular extensions of the Ohio State University work is the perspective developed by Blake and Mouton, called the ***managerial grid***.[16] The managerial grid identifies various combinations of concerns for production (initiating structure) and people (consideration), as shown in Fig. 13.4.

The vertical scale relates to concern for people, ranging from 1 (low concern) to 9 (high concern). The horizontal scale relates to concern for production, which also ranges from 1 (low concern) to 9 (high concern). At the lower left-hand corner (1, 1) is what can be called an impoverished style: low concern for both people and production. The primary job for such managers is to stay out of trouble; to simply pass orders along to subordinates, go along with the system, and make sure that they cannot be held accountable.

At the upper left-hand corner (1, 9) is the country club style: high concern for people, but low concern for production. Managers who use this style try to create a secure, comfortable, and family atmosphere and assume that, if this is done, their people will produce. High concern for production and low concern for people is found in the lower right-hand corner (9, 1). This is the produce or perish style. These managers see the personal needs of subordinates as irrelevant to achieving the organizational objectives. They use their formal authority and power to pressure subordinates to meet production quotas. In the middle of the grid (5, 5) is the middle-of-the-road manager. This person seeks to balance the needs of subordinates and the organization's productivity

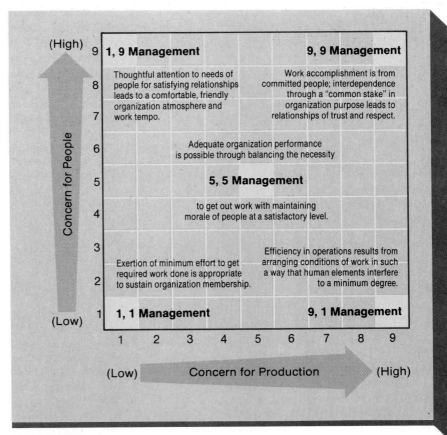

FIGURE 13.4
The Managerial Grid

objectives. In the upper right-hand corner (9, 9) is the team style: high concern for both people and production. Managers who use the team style attempt to develop cohesive work groups and committed people, so that both high rates of production and job satisfaction will result. Blake and Mouton believe that this is the most effective leadership style.

Let us consider briefly the leadership styles of William Howell, chairman and chief executive officer of the J. C. Penney Company. The various leadership characteristics and styles we identified are shown in parentheses following each type of behavior described.

IN PRACTICE
William R.
Howell,
J. C. Penney
Company

William Howell joined the J. C. Penney Company 26 years ago, right after graduating from the University of Oklahoma. His first job was as a trainee in Penney's Tulsa store. Subsequently, he held a variety of store management positions before being promoted to a district manager position in 1969. He transferred to New York as coordinator of small stores in 1971 and from that assignment moved to other executive jobs until assuming his present position of chairman and chief executive officer in September 1983.

Howell has been described by others as the kind of person they could speak to, not a big shot. He is approachable and not an autocrat (high consideration). Most people find that he possesses a wide-ranging intellect, a long-term vision, and a strong concern for the welfare of Penney's employees (high consideration). His leadership style reflects these. When visitors arrive at Penney headquarters in New York, Howell, not a secretary, comes out to greet them and usher them into his office. The company newspaper, *J. C. Penney Today*, emphasizes the family atmosphere by noting anniversaries, marriages, and how many second- and third-generation employees work there (high consideration). Howell says that people join J. C. Penney with the expectation that they will retire from the company, and that he is committed to help them do their best while working there.

Howell's day starts shortly after 6 A.M., and he arrives at headquarters at about 7:15. His day ends at 5:00 to 5:15 P.M., if he is not traveling. During each working day he is reminded of Penney's objectives (high initiating structure). The company does not position itself against Montgomery Ward, Sears, and Kmart. Rather, Howell believes that its competition is Kauffmann, Sanger-Harris, Burdine, or Macy's. To meet this competition, many of the newer stores in the 2000-store chain have dropped major appliances, paint, hardware, lawn and garden merchandise, and fabrics. The elimination of these lines of merchandise has left space to sell apparel and other softgoods. Some of this space has been devoted to Penney's operation of drug stores, J. C. Penney Financial Services, its insurance operations, and its development of shopping center offices. The wisdom of this restructuring has been reflected in sales. In 1984, sales rose to more than $13 billion, up from $11.4 billion in 1982.

Howell is a strong believer in Penney tradition of never referring to its people as employees (high consideration). When James Cash Penney opened the first store in 1902 in Kemmerer, Wyoming, he called employees *associates* and managers *partners*. Every year, all partners gather to initiate new partners. In 1980, for example, these initiations were held in 15 different cities at which time the newer managers were made partners. During this ceremony, the founding principles of the firm are restated, and at the conclusion, each new partner is given an HCSC pin, standing for Honor, Confidence, Service, and Cooperation (high consideration).

Howell believes that each employee has the ability to become a partner. Since all employees share in the profits of the entire operation, they are motivated to do their best to uphold the trust placed in them by Howell (task-related trait). To foster teamwork, Howell believes in promoting from within the organization (9, 9—team style). To prepare people for advancement, the company runs an intensive in-house training program. The bulk of this training takes place within the stores in order to reinforce the basic philosophy of the company and maintain the family atmosphere.[17]

CONTINGENCY APPROACHES TO LEADERSHIP

When we examine how Howell leads at J. C. Penney, we note that he changes his style according to the situation. When making decisions that affect the entire operation, he chooses an initiating-structure style, but when he presides over the ceremonies to initiate new partners, he chooses a considerate style. Obviously, Howell believes that situational factors are important to leadership style. This type of approach demonstrates that we cannot say with certainty that there are just a few leadership traits and behaviors that make effective leaders. As we saw through Howell's eyes, there are contingency approaches to leadership. The three most recent and well-known are Fiedler's contingency model, House's path–goal model, and Vroom–Yetton's decision model.[18]

FiedleR's ContiNgency Model

The first of the contingency models was developed by Fred Fiedler and his associates.[19] *Fiedler's contingency model* suggests that successful leadership depends on a good match between the style of the leader and the demands of the situation. Thus each leadership style is effective when it is used in the right situation. Fiedler's challenge to the manager is to (1) understand his or her own leadership style; (2) diagnose the situation; and (3) achieve a good match between the demands of the situation and the leadership style.

Leadership styles

The leadership styles used in this model are similar to the considerate and initiating-structure styles. What differentiates this model from others is the manner in which a leader's style is measured. The manager is asked to describe his or her *least preferred co-worker* (LPC), that is, the employee with whom the leader could work least well. The high-LPC person—one who describes the least preferred co-worker in a favorable light—perceives strong and positive emotional ties with subordinates as an important part of being an effective leader. This person is called a *relationship-oriented leader.*

A manager who describes his or her least preferred co-worker in an unfavorable light is called a low-LPC leader. A low-LPC, or *task-oriented leader,* is a person who initiates structure for subordinates, closely monitors their behaviors, and is minimally concerned with the human-relations aspect of the job. This manager simply wants to get the job done; how subordinates feel about his or her leadership style is not important.

Situational variables

Fiedler identified three variables in the work situation that help determine which leadership style will be effective: leader–member relations, task structure, and the leader's position power.

Leader–member relations.   The extent to which the leader is accepted or rejected by the group is reflected in *leader–member relations.* This is the most important influence on a leader's effectiveness. If a manager gets along well with subordinates and they respect the manager's expertise and ability to get things done, the manager may not have to rely on formal authority. On the other hand, if the manager is disliked or not trusted, cannot deliver, or appears to lack clout with upper management, the manager may have to rely on legitimate and coercive power bases to get subordinates to perform.

Task structure.   The nature of a task and the extent to which it can be defined is called the *task structure.* A simple and routine task is likely to have clearly defined performance standards (such as make a hamburger in 20 seconds) and detailed instructions on how to perform the work. Managers in such situations have a great deal of authority because there are clear guidelines by which to measure worker performance (the hamburger is prepared correctly or it isn't). The manager can back up instructions by referring to the standard operating procedures.

A complex and nonroutine task presents a manager and subordinates with alternative choices of how to get the job done and achieve objectives. Social workers, detectives, market researchers, engineers, and other professionals do work that requires a great deal of judgment and the knowledge of certain procedures. However, there are no clear guidelines that can be routinely applied to each new task. Under these conditions, subordinates can easily disagree with or question a manager's methods and instructions.

Leader-position power. The extent to which the manager has legitimate, coercive, and reward power is called *leader-position power.* As we indicated earlier, some positions in business organizations carry a great deal of formal power and authority, whereas leaders in most voluntary organizations have little position power over volunteer workers. High position power simplifies a manager's ability to influence subordinates, and low position power makes the manager's task more difficult. The types and sources of power for a manager were summarized in Tables 13.1 and 13.2.

MatchiNg situatioNs with leadership styles

The three situational variables that are most important in determining a leader's influence and control are whether (1) the work group accepts or rejects the leader (leader–member relations); (2) the task is relatively simple and routine or complex and nonroutine (task structure); and (3) the leader has high or low formal position power (position power). The more pleasant the leader–member relations, the more structured the task, and the greater the leader's position power, the more favorable the situation is for the leader.

Figure 13.5 shows Fiedler's contingency model of leadership. The three basic contingency variables are shown on the vertical axis. The eight numbered blocks represent combinations of the three variables and are arranged from the most favorable (block 1) to the least favorable (block 8) situation. A leader will have the most control and influence in block 1 situations. Here the leader is accepted and has high position power, and subordinates perform relatively structured tasks. A leader will have somewhat less control and influence in block 2 situations. The leader is accepted and has little position power, and the tasks are structured. In block 8 situations a leader's control and influence are very limited. The leader is not accepted and has little position power, and subordinates perform unstructured tasks.

Telephone offices, craft shops, meat departments, and grocery departments are typical of situations shown in blocks 1 and 5. Team sports and surveying parties are typical of situations shown in blocks 2 and 6. Situations involving general foremen, ROTC units, research chemists, and military planning groups are representative of blocks 3 and 7. Situations involving racially divided groups, disaster-relief groups, church groups, and mental health groups seem to be illustrated by blocks 4 and 8. The critical question is: What kind of leadership style is most effective in each of the different group situations?

EffectiVe leadership styles

As suggested in Fig. 13.5, task-oriented leaders perform most effectively in the most favorable situations (blocks 1, 2, and 3) and in the least favorable

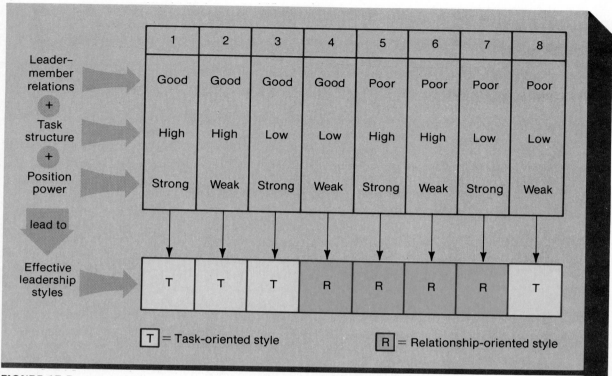

FIGURE 13.5
Combinations of Situational Variables

situation (block 8). In the most favorable situations, there is good group atmosphere, the leader's position power is high, and tasks are structured. In the least favorable situation (block 8), tasks are unstructured, the leader lacks group support, and the leader has low position power. The only hope for achieving any objective appears to be through the use of task-oriented leaders. Relationship-oriented leaders are most effective in moderately favorable situations (blocks 4, 5, 6, and 7). Blocks 4 and 5 describe situations in which (1) tasks are structured but the leader is disliked, or (2) the leader is liked but tasks are unstructured. In either case, the leader must depend on the willingness and creativity of the group's members to accomplish the tasks.

Managerial implications

There are several important managerial implications of this model.[20] Both relationship-oriented and task-oriented managers perform well under some situations but not others. For example, an outstanding salesperson who is promoted to district manager may fail because his or her task-oriented leadership style does not match the demands of the situation. The new position reflects a situational change for the person. Tasks probably have become more complex and nonroutine. Thus the task-oriented style of the new district manager no longer fits the situation. The new situation seems to call for a relationship-oriented style (block 4 in Fig. 13.5).

We cannot accurately label a manager as good or poor. Rather, we must think in terms of the manager who performs well in one situation but not in others. The effectiveness of a manager depends more on the three situational variables than on leadership style. Top management might try to improve a manager's effectiveness by attempting to change the manager's style but usually will be more successful if it modifies the situation to make it more favorable or shifts the manager to a situation that better matches the manager's style.

As with most managerial models, this one has limitations and is controversial.[21] Nevertheless, the Fiedler model is important because it was the first to recognize the importance of situational variables.

House's Path—Goal Model

Another useful contingency model is the one developed by Robert House.[22] It is called *House's path–goal model.* It states that effective leaders clarify the paths or means by which subordinates can attain both high job satisfaction and high performance. The leader does this by specifying what has to be done, reducing roadblocks to task achievement, and increasing opportunities for task-related personal satisfactions. The leader's function is to motivate and help subordinates reach their highly valued, job-related goals. The specific style of leader behavior should be determined by two contingency variables: employee characteristics and task characteristics. A simplified version of the path–goal model is shown in Fig. 13.6.

The path–goal model like the other two contingency models, does *not* provide a formula for the best way to lead. It is based on the premise that effective leadership involves selection of the style most appropriate to a particular situation and the needs of subordinates.

Leadership styles

House's model uses two styles of leadership: employee centered (similar to considerate) and task centered (similar to initiating structure). The employee-centered leader shows concern for the status, well-being, and needs of subordinates. This style of leadership is demonstrated by little things that the leader does to make work more pleasant, treat subordinates as equals, and be open. The task-centered leader defines tasks, schedules work, lets subordinates know what is expected of them, gives specific directions for doing tasks with a minimum of effort, and maintains definite standards of performance.

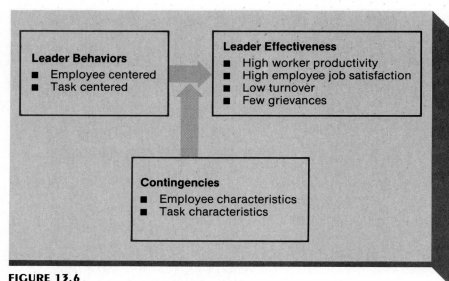

FIGURE 13.6
Path–Goal Model of Leader Effectiveness

Employee characteristics

The model states that a particular leadership style will be accepted by subordinates to the extent that they perceive it as an immediate source of job satisfaction or as necessary for future job satisfaction. For example, if employees have high needs for self-esteem and affiliation, an employee-centered leadership style may satisfy these needs. On the other hand, employees who have high needs for autonomy, responsibility, and achievement are more likely to be motivated by a task-centered leadership style.

Task characteristics

The second major contingency variable in House's model is task characteristics. When tasks are routine and simple, subordinates will regard close supervision as unnecessary. Under these conditions, a task-centered leader may increase performance by preventing "goofing off," but this also can decrease job satisfaction. Subordinates are likely to view such leadership as excessive and directed at keeping them working on unsatisfying tasks. An employee-centered leader is likely to have more satisfied employees if tasks are routine and simple. This style is likely to increase the worker's satisfaction with the supervisor and company policies, even if the tasks are unsatisfying.

On the other hand, when tasks are nonroutine and complex, a task-centered leadership style is appropriate. It helps subordinates to perform the task. A manager of an industrial-relations team who explains to a general foreman how to process a grievance for arbitration is trying to help the foreman to present the company's case as well as possible to the labor arbitrator.

Managerial implications

Figure 13.7 outlines the managerial dynamics of House's path–goal leadership model. An employee-centered manager will offer a wide range of rewards to subordinates—not only pay raises and promotion but also en-

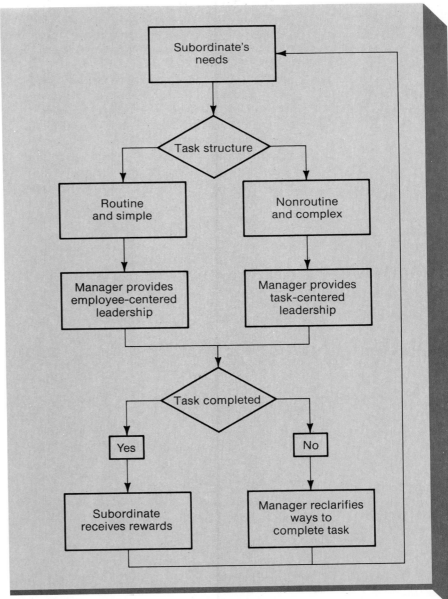

FIGURE 13.7
House's Path–Goal Leadership Model

couragement, pats on the back, and respect. In addition, this type of manager is likely to tailor rewards to the needs and desires of individual subordinates. A task-centered manager, on the other hand, will offer a narrower set of rewards based on the individual's performance—pay raises, bonuses, promotions. Subordinates of this type of manager will know exactly the productivity or performance level they have to reach to gain these rewards.

Because House's path–goal theory of leadership is fairly new, research evidence about its effectiveness is still inconclusive.[23] Some early findings indicate that workers on routine and simple jobs have reported higher job satisfaction when their manager uses an employee-centered rather than a task-centered leadership style. Workers performing nonroutine and complex tasks are more productive when their manager uses a task-centered style, but they do not necessarily report higher job satisfaction. This model is highly promising because it attempts to explain *why* a particular leadership style will be more effective in one situation than in another. J. W. Marriott, president of the Marriott Corporation, provides an example of how a manager who makes ample use of both employee- and task-centered leadership styles can be successful.

IN PRACTICE
J. W. MARRIOTT'S LEADERSHIP AT MARRIOTT CORPORATION

The Marriott Corporation began in 1928 as a mom-and-pop root-beer stand in downtown Washington, D.C. Today, Marriott is a multibillion-dollar-a-year business with interests ranging from fast-food restaurants to resort hotels, airline food catering, cruise ships, and family amusement parks. In 1983, Marriott Corporation earned $115 million in profits and employed more than 116,000 people. A share of Marriott stock purchased in 1953 has increased in value 30 times as a result of stock splits and dividends. The most spectacular growth has occurred in the 15 years since J. W. Marriott Jr. took over as president from his father. Annual sales were $85 million when he began as president. By 1984, annual sales had risen to almost $4 billion.

Marriott logs more than 100,000 air miles a year visiting each of the 46 company-owned or -managed hotels and 17 franchised inns. He calls at many of the 60 flight kitchens that provide food service to airlines throughout the world. He finds time to eat at Marriott's Big Boy coffee shops and Roy Rogers restaurants. He finds the time to inspect personally many of Marriott's other businesses, as well.

Marriott says, "This is a business of many details." There are few details that escape him. He delegates authority to his managers to run the restaurants (routine and simple tasks), but he gets deeply involved with the hotels and airline kitchens (nonroutine and complex tasks). He has a staff meeting every two weeks to find out what others are doing, allow staff people to find out what he is doing, and provide feedback to subordinates (task-centered leadership). Openness and communication are important aspects of his leadership style (employee-centered).

Marriott travels because he believes that he could not obtain the information and knowledge needed to make decisions if he stayed at his desk. He tries to provide a climate where "people can work together in harmony" (employee-centered leadership). He believes that people at *all* levels should be making decisions, and they should not be afraid to try new things or make mistakes. He says that he expects hard work and a dedication to excellence from Marriott people.

Because of the wide range of problems in the hotel and airline kitchen businesses, Marriott says that he spends a lot of time on details, clarifying what he wants done, and not enough time on broader issues (task-centered leadership). He tries to delegate more detail but admits, "I am still involved in an awful lot that I shouldn't be." He feels that, since he has been in the business longer than anyone who reports to him, he is more experienced at knowing what to do and what not to do.[24]

Vroom–Yetton's Decision Model

Vroom and Yetton have developed a decision model of leadership.[25] *Vroom–Yetton's decision model* focuses on the idea that managerial decisions are influenced by various situational problems, which can be solved by different leadership styles. Our discussion proceeds from a description of five leadership styles to eight diagnostic questions to combinations of decisions, situations, and leadership styles.

Five leadership styles

Vroom and Yetton identified five styles of leadership, ranging from highly autocratic to highly participative. These styles are described briefly in Table 13.4. The highly autocratic style is used when the manager has all the information needed to make a decision and simply announces it to the group. The group may accept the decision by virtue of the position the leader occupies (legitimate power), because the leader is an acknowledged expert (expertise power), or because the leader is strongly admired by the group (referent power). Under such conditions, it is not at all difficult for the leader to sell his or her decision to subordinates. The participative style is used when the group's acceptance and information are needed. It is the best means for permitting individuals to express their views.

Eight diagnostic questions

Eight diagnostic questions that managers should ask themselves are suggested. Managers can diagnose a problem situation quickly and accurately by answering them.

A. If the decision were accepted, would it make a difference which course of action was adopted?

TABLE 13.4 ■ FIVE LEADERSHIP STYLES

LEADERSHIP STYLES	DEGREE OF SUBORDINATE PARTICIPATION ENCOURAGED BY MANAGERS
	Low (Autocratic)
■ You solve the problem or make the decision yourself using information available to you at that time.	1
■ You obtain the necessary information from your subordinate(s), then decide on the solution to the problem yourself. You may or may not tell your subordinates what the problem is in getting the information from them. The role played by your subordinates in making the decision is clearly one of providing the necessary information to you, rather than generating or evaluating alternative solutions.	2
■ You share the problem with relevant subordinates individually, getting their ideas and suggestions without bringing them together as a group. Then you make the decision that may or may not reflect your subordinates' influence.	3
■ You share the problem with your subordinates as a group, collectively obtaining their ideas and suggestions. Then you make the decision that may or may not reflect your subordinates' influence.	4
■ You share a problem with your subordinates as a group. Together you generate and evaluate alternatives and attempt to reach agreement (consensus) on a solution. Your role is much like that of chairman. You do not try to influence the group to adopt "your" solution, and you are willing to accept and implement any solution that has the support of the entire group.	5
	High (Participative)

Source: Reprinted by permission of the publisher from "A New Look at Managerial Decision-Making," by Victor H. Vroom, *Organizational Dynamics*, Spring 1973, p. 67. Copyright © 1973 by AMACON, a division of American Management Association. All rights reserved.

B. Is there a quality requirement such that one solution is likely to be better than others?

C. Do I have sufficient information to make a high-quality decision?

D. Is the problem structured?

E. Is acceptance of the decision by subordinates critical to effective implementation?

F. If I were to make the decision by myself, is it reasonably certain that it would be accepted by my subordinates?

G. Do subordinates share the organizational goals to be obtained in solving this problem?

H. Is conflict among subordinates likely in preferred solutions?

After diagnosing the situation, the manager must choose a leadership style.[26] This assumes that a manager can change his or her leadership style depending on the situation.

Combinations of situations and leadership styles

The various combinations of problem situations and effective leadership styles are shown in Fig. 13.8, which indicates that there is more than one effective leadership style. The eight diagnostic questions are listed down the left-hand side of the figure. The numbers (1, 2, 3, 4, and 5) in the circles refer to each of the five leadership styles presented in Table 13.4. To use this diagram, start with question A and answer the question opposite each box as you come to it in working toward the bottom. When you reach a circle, the number in it tells you which style of leadership is most effective. Let us look at a concrete example.

Mark Rigg, Vice-President for Human Resources at Southland Corporation, is faced with a problem of high store-clerk turnover—about 300 percent a year. He investigated the problem and found that employee satisfaction is low because of a recent company policy change regarding pay. In this situation, group acceptance will be important in finding a solution to this problem. The Vroom–Yetton decision model indicates that Rigg can meet with individual clerks (leadership style 3 or 4) or with the entire group at once (leadership style 5). Rigg would choose leadership style 3 or 4 if he believed that conflict among the clerks concerning the preferred solutions is likely (situation H). Rigg would choose leadership style 5 if he believed that all clerks share his concern about solving this problem (situation G). In this case, Rigg probably should choose leadership style 5. Meeting with the entire group of clerks at once would be the ideal way to approach this problem and provide all the clerks with an opportunity to express their views.

Managerial implications

The selection of effective leadership styles depends on whether the manager *diagnoses* the problem situation correctly. To the extent that participation is desired, appropriate, and permitted by time, managers can choose leadership styles that are more participative. Employee participation often increases their commitment and avoids the problem of asking them to implement a decision for which they had no input. When subordinates have no input, they are likely to feel powerless and be less concerned about the outcome of the decision.

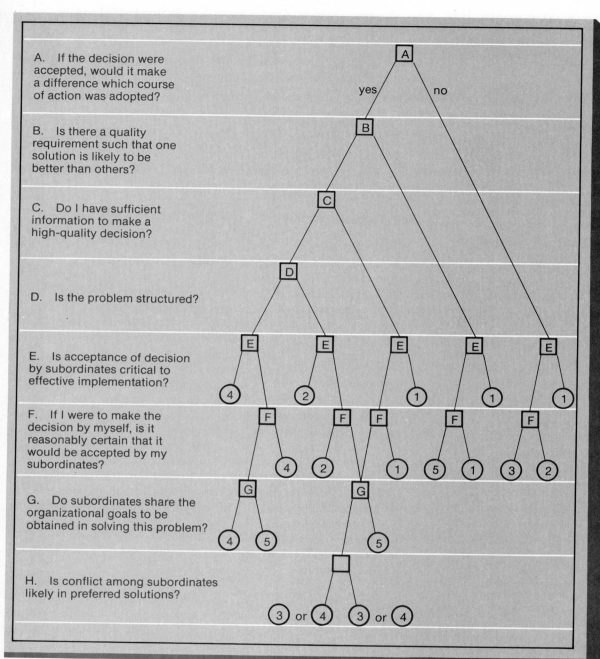

A. If the decision were accepted, would it make a difference which course of action was adopted?

yes   no

B. Is there a quality requirement such that one solution is likely to be better than others?

C. Do I have sufficient information to make a high-quality decision?

D. Is the problem structured?

E. Is acceptance of decision by subordinates critical to effective implementation?

F. If I were to make the decision by myself, is it reasonably certain that it would be accepted by my subordinates?

G. Do subordinates share the organizational goals to be obtained in solving this problem?

H. Is conflict among subordinates likely in preferred solutions?

FIGURE 13.8
Preferred Leadership Styles in Various Problem Situations

NOTE: *The preferred leadership style is circled. (See Table 13.4 for definitions.)*

Source: Reprinted by permission of the publisher from "A New Look at Managerial Decision-Making," by Victor H. Vroom, *Organizational Dynamics*, Spring 1973, p. 68. Copyright © 1973 by AMACON, a division of American Management Association. All rights reserved.

The Vroom–Yetton model has been used effectively to help managers diagnose their leadership styles and indicate when leadership styles might be modified to fit different situations.[27] Diagnose the following problem.

IN PRACTICE
General Foremen on the Alaska Pipeline

Each of the five general foremen has charge of a 20-man crew who lay sections of the oil pipeline in Alaska. They have to estimate their expected rate of progress in order to schedule material deliveries to their next field site.

They have been living in Alaska for the past five years and know the nature of the terrain. People at headquarters have the historical data needed for the foremen to compute the rate of travel over that type of terrain. Given these two variables, it is a simple matter to calculate the earliest and latest times at which materials and support facilities will be needed at the next site. It is important that the estimates be reasonably accurate. Underestimates result in idle foremen and workers, and an overestimate ties up material for a period of time before they are used.

Progress has been good, and the five foremen and other members of the gangs stand to receive substantial bonuses if the project is completed ahead of schedule. According to the Vroom–Yetton model, which style of leadership should the foremen choose? What are the characteristics of their situation? We believe the situation is described in row F in Fig. 13.8 The foremen should choose leadership style 1. Do you agree or disagree? Why?

You might be wondering how we arrived at our leadership style. Looking at Fig. 13.8, it will make a difference which decision was accepted because of the bonuses, etc., that are tied to the decision. If we answer *yes* to question A, we proceed to question B. The most appropriate solution can also be calculated on the basis of the facts and figures supplied by headquarters. Therefore, our answer to question B is *yes*. Once the data from headquarters have been received, the general foremen will probably have sufficient information to make a high quality decision. The answer to question C is *yes*. We also believe that subordinates must accept the decision. Thus, the answer to question E is *yes*. Thus, the most appropriate leadership style is 1: autocratic.[28]

Comparison of Contingency Models

An effective manager must be an effective leader, or someone who is able to direct the work of others so that they achieve both high productivity and job satisfaction. This sounds simple, but the three contingency models offer somewhat different advice about choosing an effective leadership style. Table 13.5 compares the elements of three models. Now, let us apply (and compare) these approaches to a problem that many of you might have encountered or will encounter.

TABLE 13.5 ■ A COMPARISON OF THREE LEADERSHIP CONTINGENCY MODELS

ELEMENT	FIEDLER'S CONTINGENCY MODEL	HOUSE'S PATH–GOAL MODEL	VROOM AND YETTON'S DECISION MODEL
Key situational variables	Task structure Leader–member relations Leader power	Task structure Subordinate characteristics	Eight diagnostic questions concerning time, quality, and acceptance
Leadership styles	Task oriented Relationship oriented	Task centered Employee centered	Five styles, ranging from autocratic to participative
Managerial implications	Match leader's style to situation. Change situation to fit leader. High or low control situations favor task-oriented leader. Moderate control situations favor relationship-oriented leader.	If tasks are routine and simple, an employee-centered style is best. If tasks are nonroutine and complex, task-centered style is best.	Effective leaders choose among the 5 styles, depending on situational characteristics.

SETTING THE STAGE

Tom Barry is a professor of marketing at Southern Methodist University. He teaches a course in advertising management and divides the class up into several student advertising agencies. Each agency is responsible for developing a detailed marketing and advertising campaign for a local financial or retailing client or a national client such as Dr. Pepper, *Sports Illustrated,* or *The Wall Street Journal.* Each client has three agencies competing for its account. Each agency consists of from four to six students with different responsibilities in marketing research, strategy, media focus, creative ideas, and account services. At the end of the semester, managers from the various clients attend class and listen to the agency pitches for their respective firms. They critically judge the presentations and then award the account to one of the agencies. The presentation heavily influences each student's grade for the class.

Suppose you are the account executive for one of the student agencies preparing a campaign for Sugar Free Dr. Pepper. Your objective is to win the competition for the account and you have to choose a style of leadership that will enable your agency to do so.

Apply the models

According to Fiedler's contingency model, the effectiveness of leadership depends on the match between the situation and your particular leadership style. The three situational variables to be considered are leader–member relations, task structure, and position power. You and your fellow students will probably develop good leader–member relations. Undoubtedly you were chosen because others in the group perceived you as trustworthy and as an easy person to work with. Your agency's task is relatively unstructured. You and your group might ask: "How should we do this? What's important? Does anybody's father work for Dr. Pepper? Who's the competition? Are we going to use movies, slides, or some other form of presentation to the client executive?" Your formal power to influence the members of the group to work on their assignments rather than to watch TV or go out for a beer is weak. That is, you have no formal power to tell the others what to do. Given these

Donald Burr's leadership of People Express challenged traditional barriers between management and subordinates. Breaking those barriers, Burr believes, allows employees to grow and broaden their skills.

Source: People Express Airlines, Inc.

conditions, what style of leadership is the Fiedler model likely to recommend? Look at Fig. 13.5 and find the block for contingency variable ratings of good, low, and weak, respectively. This is block 4, which indicates that relationship-oriented style is likely to work best.

According to House's path–goal model, a leader's major function is to provide a path for increasing the personal job satisfaction and productivity of subordinates. This is done by clarifying the nature of the task, increasing the opportunities of subordinates to obtain satisfaction from the work, and assisting members in completing the task. Again, the task is unstructured, for the reasons already stated. The group needs to perform well so that it will win the competition and each member will receive a high grade in the class. Given these conditions, which style of leadership would House's model recommend? Following the arrows in Fig. 13.7, you would choose a task-centered leadership style because it will enable you to give specific directions about what is supposed to be done when, where, by whom, and at what level of performance. If you can clarify the ways to complete the task for your group and guide the members in doing their parts, your agency can achieve its objective.

According to the Vroom–Yetton decision model, your assessment of the situation using the eight diagnostic questions will enable you to choose a leadership style. The questions and your probable answers are:

A. If the decision were accepted, would it make a difference which course of action was adopted?   *Yes.*

B. Is there a quality requirement such that one decision is likely to be better than others?   *Yes.*

C. Do I have sufficient information to make a high-quality decision?   *No.*

D. Is the problem structured?   *No.*

E. Is acceptance of the decision by subordinates critical to effective implementation?   *Yes.*

F. If I were to make the decision by myself, is it reasonably certain that it would be accepted by my subordinates?   *No.*

G. Do subordinates share the organizational goals to be obtained in solving this problem?   *Yes.*

H. Is conflict among subordinates likely in preferred solutions?   *Yes.*

Based on your diagnosis of the situation, which style of leadership would the Vroom–Yetton model recommend? Turn to Fig. 13.8 and follow the path that corresponds to the answers to the eight questions. The pattern of responses indicates that you should choose a highly participative style of leadership, or leadership style 5. Thus you should not try to get the group to adopt your solution but should try to rally the group around the best solution that all members can support.

Comparing and evaluating

These three contingency leadership models recommend different solutions. Vroom and Yetton suggest that a leader *can choose* a style, depending on the situation. This choice is based on two major factors: (1) the quality of the decision; and (2) the effective implementation of that decision by the group. Fiedler believes that a leader's style is *relatively fixed*. If you are a task-oriented leader, your group's performance would be low because your style does not fit the situation. Therefore this model suggests that you either change the situation to fit your style or that you not exercise leadership. House proposes that a leader's style reflect the task structure and subordinates' needs. Depending on the diagnosis of the situation, either an employee-centered or a task-centered leader would be most effective.

Clearly, the models cannot give you the answer about the best way to lead your group and win the competition. However, they can give you some useful ideas to consider in making a decision about how to lead the group and accomplish the objective.

CHAPTER SUMMARY

Leadership is one of the key interpersonal roles managers play in their organizations. This chapter focused on leadership as an *influence process*. Followers let themselves be influenced by a person so long as that person is able to satisfy their job-related needs. A leader's influence stems from the sources of power on which the leader has to draw: reward, coercive, legitimate, referent, and expertise. The means by which managers acquire power and how the bases of power affect followers' behaviors were reviewed.

Three approaches to the study of leadership were identified: traits, behavioral, and contingency. Traits models assume that individuals with a certain type of personality, physical characteristics, and social background, and task-related skills will be leaders. However, few studies have been able to consistently distinguish leaders from nonleaders or effective from ineffective leaders on the basis of traits alone.

Behavioral models focus on the styles that leaders use to influence their subordinates. From the Ohio State University leadership studies, two styles of leader behaviors emerged: considerate and initiating structure. A considerate manager seeks to create a friendly and pleasant working environment for employees by stressing good human relationships. An initiating-structure manager attempts to influence subordinates by planning, organizing, and controlling their work activities. One of the most popular models for understanding how leader behaviors affect subordinates was developed by Blake and Mouton. Called the *managerial grid,* this model identifies five different styles of management from a matrix of low to high concern for people and low to high concern for production.

The difficulty in trying to relate traits or styles to performance led researchers to try to determine how situational variables might cause one leadership style to be more effective than others. The three *contingency* models presented use various combinations of situational factors to predict which leadership style will be most effective in a given situation.

Fiedler's contingency model suggests that leader–member relations, task structure, and the leader's power position are the most important situational variables. It predicts which style of leadership (relationship or task oriented) will be the most effective in each of eight work situations. Fiedler suggests that, when leader–member relations are good, the task is structured, and the leader has high position power, a task-oriented style in leadership is most effective; that, when leader–member relations are poor, the task is unstructured, and the leader has low position power, a relationship-oriented leader performs best.

House's path–goal model suggests that the most important function of a manager is to provide a path for subordinates to achieve both high performance and job satisfaction. The most effective style of leadership (employee-centered or task-centered) depends on the structure of the task and the job-related needs of the subordinates. The leadership style that a manager uses will affect the types of rewards the manager offers and the specific activities subordinates must do in order to gain these rewards.

The Vroom–Yetton decision model focuses on the degree of participation that a leader should foster in a situation. After assessing a situation through the use of eight diagnostic questions, the manager should choose the style of leadership most appropriate to the situation. In diagnosing the situation, the manager evaluates the probable reactions of subordinates, especially if their acceptance of a decision is critical to the accomplishment of tasks and objectives.

MANAGER'S VOCABULARY

autocratic leader
behavioral models
clout
coercive power
considerate leadership style
democratic leader
expertise power
Fiedler's contingency model
House's path–goal model
initiating-structure leadership style
laissez-faire leader
leader
leader–member relations
leader-position power
leadership
least preferred co-worker (LPC)
legitimate power
managerial grid
referent power
relationship-oriented leader
reward power
task-oriented leader
task structure
traits models
Vroom–Yetton's decision model

REVIEW QUESTIONS

1. Define leadership.
2. What are the five sources of a leader's power?
3. What are the two basic leader behaviors found in the Ohio State University leadership studies?
4. What are the important dimensions in the *managerial grid*?
5. What are the important variables in Fiedler's contingency model? Explain how the model works?
6. What two variables in House's path–goal model determine the most effective leadership style?
7. What are the major characteristics of the Vroom–Yetton decision model?

DISCUSSION QUESTIONS

1. Comment on the statement: "Leaders are born, not made."
2. How does the source of a leader's power affect subordinates' behaviors?
3. What are the common themes of the three contingency leadership models?
4. How do the contingency models of Fiedler and House differ in their managerial implications?
5. How can the Vroom–Yetton decision model help managers to make better decisions?
6. Why are there so many answers to the question: What is the best way to lead?

MANAGEMENT INCIDENTS AND CASES

Budget Motors, Inc.

Plant Y was the largest and oldest of six assembly plants of Econocar division, a subsidiary of Budget Motors, Inc. It had close to 10,000 employees and was managed by Mr. Wickstrom. During the last few years, it fell behind all the other plants in performance. Not unexpectedly, headquarter management (HQM) started showing some uneasiness when there were signs that things would not improve in the foreseeable future. In its attempt to straighten things out, HQM has exerted steady pressure and issued specific directions for local plant management to follow.

Wickstrom was a respected and competent manager. He was not new to the responsibility of running a large plant. After all, he came up the hard way through the ranks and was well known for his ambition, technical competence, human-relations skills, and hard work. Moreover, he was a no-nonsense manager, well-liked by his subordinates. Under his leadership, plant Y had performed adequately until the energy and environmental crises teamed up to hit the auto industry really hard in the early 1970s. At that time, all six plants were in a panic to fill the sudden demand for compact cars, which are economical to run and environmentally safer to use. The speed of the assembly lines was stepped up, three-shift operations were begun, workers (mostly immigrants) were hired, and a large number of managers had to be placed in new jobs.

Although all the plants of the Econocar division had their share of the stress and strain inherent in the sudden changeover from bigger to smaller cars, the managers of these plants adapted differently to this new development in the market. Instead of comparing Wickstrom's adaptive behavior with that of his counterparts in other plants, we would rather concentrate on contrasting his style with that of Mr. Rhenman, his successor in the same plant. The following are some examples that illustrate how Wickstrom tried to cope with this crisis atmosphere.

One day, while making his regular plant tour, he personally ordered the foreman of a certain section to change the sequence of assembling instrument panels. He thought that this change would speed up the operation. When his production manager, Mr. Aberg, found out about the change, he got upset because it disrupted the schedule. He went to see Wickstrom in his office and to make a new suggestion about sequencing—one that coordinated Wickstrom's idea with his own. Much to Aberg's surprise, Wickstrom reacted rudely and told Aberg that things would remain the way he had ordered.

When Wickstrom read the weekly performance record of the body assembly line, he flew into a rage and called the foreman of this line, Mr. Jorgen, to his office and threatened to fire him if production was not speeded up. This tactic shook up Jorgen, who instantly thought of the incident two weeks before when his colleague, Ulf, had indeed been fired. He tried to justify the slow production by complaining that he was operating against overwhelming handicaps: antiquated and run-down equipment, inexperienced work force, and uninteresting and noninvolving job structure. Unfortunately, Wickstrom didn't care to listen to him.

One day the supply of electric power for the plant was reduced and the next day it was shut off completely.

This was due to a breakdown in the power station outside the plant. It was not Wickstrom's policy to run the plant by committee meetings but, faced with this crisis, he called a meeting of production managers and foremen. It was clear that the electric company would need at least a week to repair its network. The upshot of the meeting was a decision to shut down production and to seek union's support. When he submitted the minutes of this meeting to HQM, his decisions were vetoed immediately. The HQM argued that since compact cars sold almost as fast as they were rolled off lines, production should not stop and that a mobile auxiliary power unit should be brought in, no matter what its cost. This would be a very expensive proposition and it also would mean a lot of trouble for workers and managers alike. Wickstrom called a second meeting to inform his top aides of the instructions he had received from HQM; when word spread, some of his managers angrily protested this high-handed interference in their "domestic affairs." They said that this was but one more example of the HQM telling them how to run the show. Others, equally concerned, blamed Wickstrom for his inability to stand by his guns, take his case back to HQM, and challenge its excessive domination like other plant managers did. They felt they were being put on the defensive by HQM, which had no real feeling for what was going on in the plant. Some managers further complained that carrying out daily instructions from HQM had become Wickstrom's chief preoccupation. Managers in such staff services as accounting, quality control, materials control, and personnel also complained that they themselves were receiving too many specific orders from HQM. Like their line counterparts, they generally resented this controlling behavior on the part of HQM. They complained that they were no longer allowed to run their own departments or stations or to manage within their spheres of competence. This in turn, left them no choice but to withdraw legitimate authority from their immediate subordinates and interfere in the handling of the subordinates' affairs, thereby compounding the problem throughout the hierarchy.

In responding to the voices from below, HQM argued that the trouble with plant Y lay in Wickstrom's lack of control rather than in bad equipment, boring jobs, and inexperienced personnel.

With the intensification of the energy crisis caused by the sudden outbreak of the Mideast war of October 1973, the demand for compact cars far outstripped the available supply. Being dissatisfied with plant Y's performance, HQM decided to give Wickstrom early retirement and replace him with Mr. Rhenman. The latter accepted the job on condition that he should have "carte blanche" in running his own show for a reasonable period of time. This he got from HQM, which assured him that there would be no interference and that he was free to proceed in any manner he saw fit.

At the outset Rhenman indicated that, although HQM thought that deadwood should be removed from the staff, he disagreed and would give everyone ample opportunity to prove their worth. (It developed, in fact, that only a handful of people in an organization of 10,000 were dismissed during his regime.) He asked for money from HQM to modernize the plant, starting first with the cafeteria and washrooms used by blue-collar workers. Rhenman also went to the cafeteria during lunch hours, mingled with the workers, foremen, and lower-level managers. He not only listened to their complaints but also secured their cooperation and suggestions. He encouraged groups to meet regularly to solve common problems and, more important, to engage his long-range planning and consultation to prevent daily crises. His foremen often met informally, thereby increasing lateral communication. He structured an ongoing problem-solving dialogue between his staff and line personnel. Through this dialogue, staff personnel learned how irrelevant or self-defensive their services had been to line managers. He inspired confidence and loyalty and erased the fear-and-crisis syndrome that had prevailed. He did not change the formal organizational structure of the plant. He expected his managers to set goals for their units and be responsible for achieving them. He delegated the requisite authority to his managers and left them alone to perform their jobs.

Now, after about six months in his job, plant Y has started to rebound. Its performance record shows marked improvement. Rhenman was promoted within a year to a top executive job at HQ. Interestingly enough, plant Y is performing well without him.[29]

Questions

1. Compare and contrast the leadership styles of Wickstrom and Rhenman.

2. Who is to blame for Wickstrom's failure? Why did he lose his magic touch?

3. What caused plant Y to become an outstanding success?

4. Does it really make sense to talk about choosing your own leadership style?

REFERENCES

1. R. Levering, M. Moskowitz, and M. Katz, *The 100 Best Companies to Work for in America*. Reading, Mass.: Addison-Wesley, 1984, pp. 258–261.

2. B. Bass, *Stogdill's Handbook of Leadership*. New York: Free Press, 1981, p. 9.

3. G. Yukl, *Leadership in Organizations*. Englewood Cliffs, N.J.: Prentice-Hall, 1981.

4. Dallas Times Herald, June 1, 1985.

5. William K. Litzinger and Thomas Schaefer, "Leadership Through Followership," *Business Horizons*, September–October 1982, pp. 78–84; J. Wofford and T. Srinivasan, "Experimental Tests of the Leader-Environment-Follower Interaction Theory of Leadership," *Organizational Behavior and Human Performance*, 1983, 32(1):35–54.

6. P. Podsakoff and C. Schriesheim, "Field Studies of French and Raven's Bases of Power: Reanalysis, Critique, and Suggestions for Future Research," *Psychological Bulletin*, 1985, 97:387–411.

7. J. French and B. Raven, *The Bases of Social Power*. D. Cartwright (Ed.). Ann Arbor, Mich.: Institute for Social Research, 1959, pp. 150–167. For additional insights, *see* J. Pfeffer, *Power in Organizations*. Marshfield, Mass.: Pitman, 1981.

8. R. Kanter, "Power Failures in Management Circuits," *Harvard Business Review*, 1979, July–August 57:65–75; G. Salancik and J. Pfeffer, "Who Gets Power and How They Hold on to It: A Strategy-Contingency Model of Power," *Organizational Dynamics*, Winter 1977, pp. 3–25; D. Gioia and H. Sims, "Perceptions of Managerial Power as a Consequence of Managerial Behavior and Reputation," *Journal of Management*, 1983, 9:7–26.

9. G. Yukl and T. Taber, "The Effective Use of Managerial Power," *Personnel*, March–April, 1983, 60:37–44. *Also see* P. Podsakoff, "Determinants of a Supervisor's Use of Rewards and Punishments: A Literature Review and Suggestions for Future Research," *Organizational Behavior and Human Performance*, 1982, 29:58–83.

10. J. Kotter, "Acquiring and Using Power," *Harvard*

Business Review, July–August 1977, **55**:130–132; R. Kaplan, W. Drath, and J. Kofodimos, "Power-Getting Criticism," *Issues and Observation,* August 1984, 4:1ff.

11. A. Sloan, *My Years with General Motors.* New York: Macfadden, 1965.

12. For an excellent review of the trait literature, *see* B. Bass, *Stogdill's Handbook of Leadership.* New York: Free Press, 1981 (especially Chapters 4 and 5).

13. J. Miner, "Implications of Managerial Talent Projections for Management Education," *Academy of Management Review.* 1977, 2:412–440.

14. R. White and R. Lippett, "Leader Behavior and Member Reaction in Three 'Social Climates.' " In *Group Dynamics: Research and Theory,* 3rd ed. D. Cartwright and A. Zander (Eds.). New York: Harper & Row, 1967, pp. 318–336.

15. For an excellent survey of the Ohio State University leadership studies, *see* C. Schriesheim and S. Kerr, "Theories and Measures of Leadership: A Critical Appraisal of Current and Future Directions." In *Leadership: The Cutting Edge.* J. Hunt and L. Larson (Eds.). Carbondale, Ill.: Southern Illinois University Press, 1977, pp. 9–45, 51–56; S. Kerr, C. Schriesheim, C. Murphy, and R. Stogdill, "Toward a Contingency Theory of Leadership Based upon the Consideration and Initiating Structure Literature," *Organizational Behavior and Human Performance,* 1974, **12**:68–82; P. Podsakoff, W. Todor, and R. Schuler, "Leader Expertise as a Moderator of the Effects of Instrumental and Supportive Leader Behaviors," *Journal of Management,* 1983, 9(2):173–186.

16. R. Blake and J. Mouton, *The Managerial Grid.* Houston: Gulf, 1965.

17. Adapted from J. Hyde, "William R. Howell: Chairmen and CEO, J. C. Penney Company, Inc.," *Sky* May 1984, pp. 49–54; "Teamwork Pays Off at Penney's," *Business Week,* April 2, 1982, pp. 107–108.

18. For an overview of these models, *see* J. Hunt, D. Hosking, C. Schriesheim, and R. Stewart, *Leaders and Managers.* Elmsford, N.Y.: Pergamon, 1984.

19. F. Fiedler, *A Theory of Leadership Effectiveness.* New York: McGraw-Hill, 1967; F. Fiedler, M. Chemers, and L. Mahar, *Improving Leadership Effectiveness: The Leader Match Concept.* New York: John Wiley and Sons, 1976.

20. F. Fiedler and L. Mahar, "The Effectiveness of the Contingency Model Training: A Review of the Validation of Leader Match," *Personnel Psychology,* 1979, **32**:45–62.

21. For a review of these criticisms, *see* R. Rice, "Leader LPC and Follower Satisfaction: A Review," *Organizational Behavior and Human Performance,* 1981, **28**:1–26; B. Kabanoff, "A Critique of the Leader Match and Its Implications for Leadership Research," *Personnel Psychology,* 1981, **34**:749–764; R. Singh, "Leadership Style and Reward Allocation: Does Least Preferred Co-Worker Scale Measure Task and Relation Orientation?" *Organizational Behavior and Human Performance,* 1983, **2**:178–197.

22. R. J. House, "A Path–Goal Theory of Leadership," *Administrative Science Quarterly,* 1971, **16**:321–338.

23. For reviews of this literature, *see* J. Fulk and E. Wendler, "Dimensionality of Leader-Subordinate Interactions: A Path–Goal Investigation," *Organizational Behavior and Human Performance,* 1982, **30**:241–264; J. Schriesheim and C. Schriesheim, "A Test of the Path–Goal Theory of Leadership and Some Suggested Directions for Future Research," *Personnel Psychology,* 1981, **33**:349–370.

24. Abstracted and updated from: "The Marriott Corporation," *Nation's Business,* October 1979, pp. 51–56; *1984 Annual Report,* Marriott Corporation.

25. V. Vroom and P. Yetton. *Leadership and Decision Making.* Pittsburgh: University of Pittsburgh Press, 1973.

26. V. Vroom, "Can Leaders Learn to Lead?" *Organizational Dynamics,* Fall 1976, pp. 17–28.

27. W. Wedley and R. Field, "A Predecision Support System," *Academy of Management Review,* 1984, **9**:696–703.

28. V. Vroom and P. Yetton, *Leadership and Decision Making.* Pittsburgh: University of Pittsburgh Press, 1973, p. 41.

29. Adapted from case prepared by S. Kassem, University of Toledo, Toledo, Ohio.

COMMUNICATION IN ORGANIZATIONS

LEARNING OBJECTIVES

After studying this chapter, you should be able to:

- Explain the purpose of communication.
- Identify the six factors in the communication process.
- State the three types of nonverbal communications that people use.

- List the methods managers use to communicate with employees.
- List the barriers to communication and ways to overcome these.
- Identify the eight guidelines for effective communication.

CHAPTER OUTLINE

PREVIEW CASE

THE MOVIE SET

"Take number 64. Lights. Camera. Action!"

"Jane, I've missed you so much these past few weeks."

"I know, my darling, I've missed you too."

"We must make up for lost time."

"Cut, cut, cut! Tom, you're playing this scene like a frozen polar bear. This is a romantic love scene!" Helen screamed out in her loudest, shrillest voice. She continued, "You're supposed to play it with feeling and tenderness. You want to make people think you *love* Jane."

"Helen, I could play the part better if you'd just get off my back. I knew more about romance when I was a teenager than you do now," Tom shot back. Helen called out, "That's all for today, everybody. We can let our mechanical lover calm down and may get in a better mood for this scene tomorrow."

With that Tom stomped off the set, and everyone began to leave.

Helen Reardon is the producer and director of the film, "Going North." *Going North* was a novel that had stayed on the best-seller list for 16 months and was now being made into a movie. Helen was considered by many to be one of the best directors in Hollywood. She already had two Academy Awards to her credit and many hit motion pictures.

Tom Nesson was a young, promising actor. His most recent film, "The Western Express," was well received at the box office and had thrust him into the limelight. In fact, one of the reasons he was chosen to play the leading male part in "Going North" was his current popularity.

All had gone well on the set the first few weeks. But then problems began to arise. First came the arguments between the set-design staff and wardrobe. There were feelings that the sets and the costumes didn't match. The question was, "Whose fault was it?" Of course, each group blamed the other.

Later, the makeup staff walked off the job, claiming that they were being asked to work unreasonable hours. Helen had a knack for shooting movies at odd hours, particularly if the scene called for it. The makeup staff claimed that they had an informal agreement with studio manage-

Source: Harry R. Friedman, Dallas.

ment about the hours they would work and that this agreement had been violated. Although studio executives convinced them to return to work, the peace was an uneasy one.

The next day everybody was back on the set on time except Tom. He came in about ten minutes late. He explained that the makeup people were slow in getting his makeup on. No one questioned this, and they began where they had left off yesterday.

"Take number one. Lights. Camera. Action! . . . Take number 9. . . . Take number 19. . . . Take number 31. . . ." Finally Helen yelled, "Cut! Tom, we've got to find a way to get this right. What do you suggest?"

"I suggest you shoot it like it is. The scene was good. I've done it well several times, but you seem to keep finding small things wrong."

"Tom, do you really know what love is? Your acting doesn't show it."

With that Tom exploded. "Yes, I know what love is, but you obviously don't." He then left the set shouting, "I'm not coming back on the set until you're gone!"

Helen left the set immediately, going straight to the studio executive offices. She barged into the president's office and stated, "Either you get rid of Tom Nesson on this movie or I go!"

The studio executives were puzzled. They did not want to lose either Helen or Tom. Neither had a history of being difficult to work with. They were not sure what was causing the problem. They obviously needed to examine the entire operation surrounding the making of this movie.[1]

Whether in a movie studio, a bank, or at the local Burger King, communication is an ever-present necessity because it is the means by which people relate to one another in an organization. Communication to an organization is like the bloodstream is to a person. Just as a person can develop a hardening of the arteries that impairs physical efficiency, so too an organization can develop ineffective information channels that impair task efficiency. Just look at the problems in communication between Helen and Tom in the Preview Case.

Effective communication is important because managers can accomplish very little without it. Communication may take many forms: face to face, phone calls, notes posted on bulletin boards, memos, letters, reports, and presentations to employees. In this chapter, we will examine how communication takes place, some of the barriers to it, and ways to make it effective in organizations.

COMMUNICATION FUNDAMENTALS

Communication is the transfer of information and understanding from one person to another person. It is a way of reaching others with ideas, facts, thoughts, and values. Significantly, communication always involves two people: a sender and a receiver. One person alone cannot communicate; the receiver completes the communication link.

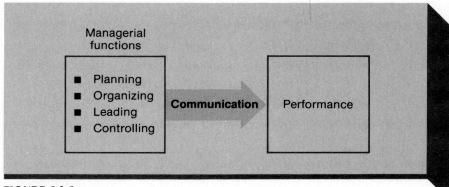

FIGURE 14.1
Management Functions and Communications

Source: Adapted from K. Davis, *Human Behavior at Work,* 6th ed. New York: McGraw-Hill, 1981, p. 400.

A sign posted on the bulletin board read, "NO SMOKING." The managers thought that they had communicated a message to employees, but this was only the start of the communication process. There are millions of messages on thousands of bulletin boards, but no communication occurs until one of those messages is read and understood.

IMPORTANCE of COMMUNICATION

Communication is the process by which management functions (planning, organizing, leading, and controlling) are carried out, as illustrated in Fig. 14.1. Relevant information must be communicated to managers so that they can make sound decisions—but until a manager's decisions are effectively communicated to others, they are worthless.

A large portion of a manager's time is spent communicating with others. Managers rarely spend time thinking alone at their desks. A manager's day is typically devoted to face-to-face communication with superiors, peers, and subordinates; writing memos, letters, or reports; or talking to others on the phone.

Henry Mintzberg, whose work we discussed in Chapter 1, described the manager's job in terms of three categories of roles.[2] Communication plays a vital part in each:

■ In *interpersonal roles,* managers act as figureheads and leaders of their organization. Mintzberg indicates that top managers spend about 45 percent of their contact time with peers, about 45 percent with people outside their company, and only about 10 percent with superiors.

- In *information roles,* managers seek information from peers, subordinates, and other personal contacts about anything that may affect their job and responsibilities. They give out interesting or important information in return. In addition, they provide suppliers, peers, and groups outside the organization with information about their organization.

- In *decision roles,* managers implement new projects, handle disturbances, and allocate resources. Some of the managers' decisions will be reached in private, but they will be based on information communicated to them. The managers, in turn, will have to communicate these decisions to others.

A MODEL OF THE COMMUNICATION PROCESS

Communication between people involves six factors.[3] These factors are:

1. Sender/encoder
2. Message
3. Channels
4. Receiver/decoder
5. Feedback
6. Perception

The way in which these factors are combined is illustrated in Fig. 14.2, a model of the communication process. This model also shows the variables

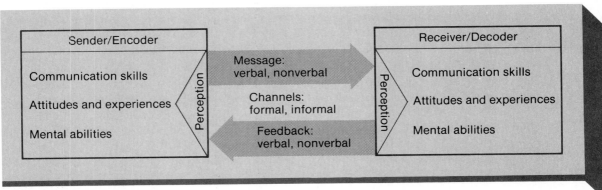

FIGURE 14.2
A Communication Model

Source: R. C. Huseman, J. M. Lahiff, J. M. Pence Jr., and J. D. Hatfield, *Business Communication: Strategies and Skills,* 2nd ed., 1985, p. 33. Copyright © 1985 by CBS College Publishing. Copyright © 1981 by the Dryden Press. Reprinted by permission of CBS College Publishing.

that a manager needs to be aware of and consider for successful communication.

Sender/Encoder

The *sender* is the source of information in the communication process. The sender must first picture the receiver and then choose communication channels that will enable the receiver to understand the message. On the movie set, Helen orally told Tom how the scene was supposed to be acted. When she used the phrase, "mechanical lover," she tried to communicate to Tom not to be so rigid but to be more spontaneous.

Encoding is the process of translating thoughts or feelings into messages. Imagine that you want to write a company about possible summer job openings. You have certain ideas you want to convey in that letter. For example, you will want to offer reasons why you chose that company. You will probably need to provide some background information about your qualifications for the job and how the job will help your career. When you put these ideas on paper, you are encoding.

Obviously, the sender/encoder is not going to get a response unless there is a receiver/decoder. The *receiver* is the person who gets the sender's message. *Decoding* is the process of translating messages into thoughts or feelings. For example, when you read a letter you have received, you are decoding.

There are five principles for increasing encoding accuracy. They apply to all forms of communication.

Relevancy

Make the message relevant for the receiver. In order to understand the message, the receiver must be able to relate this information to what he or she already knows. Therefore the message should be presented in a form that says to the receiver: "This is important and significant to you." This can be done by using words, symbols, or gestures that the receiver understands.

Simplicity

Reduce the message to the simplest possible terms. The sender should use as few words, symbols, or gestures as possible to communicate thoughts and feelings to the receiver. The simpler the message, the more likely it is to be understood.

Organization

Organize the message into a series of points. A well-organized message increases the receiver's understanding. A message can be organized into a series of points (thoughts or feelings), with completion of one point before introduction of the next. By developing one thought or feeling at a time, the sender will not overload the receiver.

Repetition

Repeat the key points of the message. Repetition is particularly important in oral communication, where words may not be clearly heard or fully understood the first time. The sender needs to use enough repetition to ensure an understanding of thoughts and feelings.

Focus

Focus on the essential aspects of the message. The reason for the message and its key points should be sharply focused. This will make the message clear and avoid losing the receiver in details. In oral communication the impact of significant points can be heightened by a different tone of voice, pauses, hand gestures, or facial expressions. In written communication this can be done by underlining or otherwise emphasizing key sentences, phrases, or words. You probably noticed that every key term in this book was set in boldface italic type.

IN PRACTICE
The Plumber

A plumber from New York developed what he thought was an excellent method for cleaning drains. He wrote the U. S. Bureau of Standards to say that he was using hydrochloric acid and to ask if it were harmless. The bureau replied, "The efficacy of hydrochloric acid is indisputable, but the chlorine residue is incompatible with metallic permanence."

The plumber wrote back, thanking the bureau for agreeing with him. Alarmed by his response, the bureau wrote another letter, saying, "We cannot assume responsibility for the production of toxic and noxious residues with hydrochloric acid, and suggest that you use an alternative procedure." The plumber wrote again, explaining how happy he was to learn that Washington still agreed with him.

At this stage, the bureau put the problem in simple terms: "Don't use hydrochloric acid. It eats the hell out of the pipes." Finally, the plumber understood.[4]

The plumber and the letter writer at the bureau both thought that they were communicating with each other. In fact, communication did not occur until the message from the bureau was sent in a form the plumber could understand. The goal of any manager should be to convey information—instructions, policies, rules, standards—that the receiver can both understand and use.

Message

The *message* part of the communication process contains the verbal and nonverbal symbols that represent the information we want to send to receivers.[5] It is important to remember that a message is like a coin: It has two sides. The message as seen by the sender/encoder and the message as seen by the receiver/decoder are not necessarily the same. The selection and interpretation of messages may differ greatly because of differences between the sender and the receiver or because the sender is sending more than one message at the same time. If you sent your resume off to a company asking for a summer job, was it typed or handwritten, neat or sloppy? If it was handwritten and contained misspelled words, this sends a message to the receiver that the job is not important to you and that you are not a neat person.

Managers use three types of messages: nonverbal, verbal, and written. Because the use of nonverbal communication has become extremely important, we give greater emphasis to this type of message than to the others.

Nonverbal messages

All messages that are not stated in words constitute **nonverbal communication.** Suppose that you are sitting in class, bored with a lecture that is deadly; in fact, it is one of those days when you really wish you had forgotten to set the alarm. For something to do, you glance around the room—and at the other end of your row a very attractive student of the opposite sex is staring at you.

You look away.

The other looks away quickly.

You glance back.

The other glances back.

You smile faintly.

You incline your head toward the professor and roll your eyes.

The other smiles wider and nods once.

You glance toward the door.

The other looks at you, then at the clock, then at the door.

Without saying a word, you set up a meeting place, a time, and an opening conversation with another student. This is nonverbal communication.

An understanding of nonverbal communication is essential because it can effectively reinforce or undermine the words we use when talking with someone. Of the many forms of nonverbal messages, we focus on three important types: how we communicate with space, how we communicate through dress, and how we communicate with our bodies.

Communicating with space. How close or far apart we and the other person are, where we sit or stand, or how we arrange our office can have a real impact on communication. Status or power is often communicated through spatial arrangements.[6] Top managers generally have larger offices, windows with better views, plusher carpeting, and higher quality furnishings.

Office space can be radically different for top and middle managers, even within the same organization.

Sources: Julie O'Neil/Stock, Boston (left); Tyrone Hall/Stock, Boston (right).

A personal secretary, seating arrangements at meetings, a chauffeured limousine, use of a private dining room, and summoning subordinates for discussion—all communicate messages through the use of space. Sometimes the use of space is expensive and requires time-consuming efforts of subordinates. The "refrigerator story" is an example of how managers at GM have been known to go to extremes.

IN PRACTICE
The Refrigerator Story

In preparing for the sales official's trip to this particular city, the Chevrolet zone salespeople learned from Detroit that the boss liked to have a refrigerator full of cold beer, sandwiches, and fruit in his room to snack on at night before going to bed. They lined up a suite in one of the city's better hotels, rented a refrigerator, and ordered the food and beer. However, the door to the suite was too small to accommodate the icebox. The hotel apparently nixed a plan to rip out the door and part of the adjoining wall. So the quick-thinking zone salespeople hired a crane and operator, put them on the roof of the hotel, knocked out a set of windows in the suite, and lowered and shoved the refrigerator into the room through this gaping hole.

That night the Chevrolet executive wolfed down cold-cut sandwiches, beer, and fresh fruit, no doubt thinking, "What a great bunch of people we have in this zone." The next day he was off to another city and, most likely, another refrigerator, while back in the city of his departure the zone people were once again dismantling hotel windows and removing the refrigerator by crane.[7]

Communicating with dress. Most of us have heard the saying, "Clothes make the person." John Molloy, a style consultant for major corporations, believes that the way a person dresses definitely communicates something to others. In his book, *Dress for Success,*[8] he presented answers to a series of questions about dress from more than 100 top executives. The following is a sample of these questions and the response.

1. He showed executives five pictures of men each wearing expensive, tailored, but high-fashion clothing. He asked the executives whether this is proper dress for a young business executive. Ninety-two said *no;* eight said *yes.*

2. He showed them five additional pictures of the same men neatly dressed in conservative clothing. He asked whether this is proper dress for a young executive. All said *yes.*

3. He showed them five more pictures of the same men obviously dressed in lower-middle-class attire and asked whether this is proper dress for a young executive. Forty-six said *yes;* 54 said *no.*

4. He then asked the executives whether they thought that the people dressed in the middle-class suit would succeed better in corporate life than those dressed in the lower-middle-class suit. Eighty-eight said *yes;* 12 said *no.*

Because dress affects *perceptions* of success, most people who are interested in climbing the corporate ladder must pay careful attention to what they wear on the job. In *Business Week's Guide to Careers,*[9] the dress code for men includes

■ conservative two-button suits in navy, gray, or pinstripes with narrow lapels;

■ contrasting ties or ties with small patterns;

■ basic wingtip, tassel, or lace-up shoes;

■ 100% cotton shirts with narrow pointed or button-down collars; and

■ a gold pen and a solid-color leather briefcase.

For women, the basic wardrobe includes

■ conservative blue, gray, black, and pinstripe suits;

■ a coatstyle dress with the look of a suit, accented with necklace or scarf;

■ a dress and jacket of all one color;

■ plain pump shoes with medium-heels in solid colors of black, navy, brown; and

■ a gold pen and a solid-color leather briefcase.

Communicating with our bodies. The body and its movements tell a lot about us, particularly the face and eyes, which are the most expressive means of body communication. Thus the ability to interpret facial meaning is an important part of communication. To test your ability to perceive facial expression, study the 10 photos in Fig. 14.3; then place the photo numbers in the appropriate blanks.

Eye contact is one of the most direct and powerful nonverbal ways people communicate. In the United States, social rules suggest that in most situations, eye contact is appropriate for a short period of time. Prolonged eye contact can be interpreted as a threatening symbol or a sign of romantic or sexual interest.

There are unspoken norms of eye contact—and other forms of nonverbal communication—that vary in different cultures. For blacks or Chicanos, looking away does not necessarily mean the same lack of attention that it might mean among whites. Consider the case of a young, white businessman who learned this lesson when he was managing a group of predominantly Chicano workers. The manager kept reprimanding a stock clerk, Carlos Martinez, for a repeated error in record keeping. As he tried to discuss the matter, Martinez kept averting eye contact. The manager became angry and said, "Look at me when I'm talking to you." To this manager, the lack of eye contact showed a lack of respect. For the stock clerk (following his own cultural norms), maintaining eye contact would have been a sign of disrespect to the person reprimanding him. It was only after the clerk became extremely upset that the manager realized that Martinez's behavior was not meant to communicate disrespect.[10]

A person's posture also communicates meaning, giving clues to a person's self-confidence or interest in what is being discussed. The more your interest in a subject, the more likely you are to lean toward the person you are talking with. Sitting back, on the other hand, may communicate a lack of interest in the subject and/or the person.[11] Good poker players watch the eyes of their fellow players as new cards are dealt. Pupil dilation will often show whether the card(s) just dealt improves the player's hand. Similarly, tension and anxiety typically show in a person's legs and feet. While people may be able to hide their tension from the waist up, they generally give themselves away by tightly crossing their legs and tapping their feet.

VERBAL MESSAGES

Managers communicate verbally (orally) more often than any other way. In fact, we showed in Chapter 1 that this is how managers spend most of their time. Oral communication takes place face-to-face and over the telephone. Face-to-face communication can involve more nonverbal communication than can telephone communication. This is why many managers prefer face-to-face communication. To get your meaning across on the telephone, you must choose your words and tone of voice more carefully.

Personal qualities required for effective oral communication can vary greatly depending on the nature of the communication and the situation.

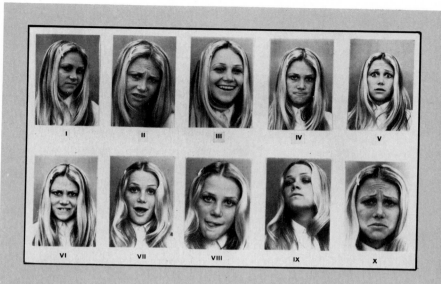

FACIAL MEANING SENSITIVITY TEST, PART 1

CLASS OF FACIAL MEANING	NUMBER OF EXPRESSION
Disgust	_____
Happiness	_____
Interest	_____
Sadness	_____
Bewilderment	_____
Contempt	_____
Surprise	_____
Anger	_____
Determination	_____
Fear	_____

The correct answers for Part I of the FMST are disgust = I; happiness = III; interest = VIII; sadness = X; bewilderment = II; contempt = IX; surprise = VII; anger = VI; determination = IV; and fear = V.

FIGURE 14.3
The Meaning of Facial Expressions

Source: Dale Leathers, *Nonverbal Communications Systems.* Copyright © 1976 by Allyn & Bacon, Boston. Reprinted with permission.

However, researchers have identified some common characteristics of effective oral communicators:[12]

self-confidence	reasoning	concern for listener
knowledge	sympathy	humor
articulation	open-mindedness	character
pleasing voice quality	honesty	tact
sincerity	personal appearance	friendliness

Effective verbal communication requires the sender to (1) encode the message in words (and nonverbal cues) that will convey it effectively to the receiver; (2) convey the message in a well-organized manner; and (3) try to eliminate distractions in the situation.

WRITTEN MESSAGES

The third type of message is written communication. Managers usually prefer verbal to written communication because it is quicker and the sender and receiver can interact. However, many forms of written messages (reports, memoranda, letters, newsletters) are used in business. They are most appropriate when information has to be distributed to a large number of people at scattered locations and when a record of what was said is needed. The following are some guidelines for good written communications.

- The message must be drafted with the receiver's needs clearly in mind.

- The facts of the message must be thought through *ahead of time*.

- The message should be as brief as possible. Eliminate all unnecessary words and ideas. Important messages should be prepared in draft form first, then corrected.

- If the message is long, include a summary of it on the first page. This summary should make the main points clear, with page references for details on each item.

- The message should be carefully organized. State the most important point first, then the next most important point, and so on. This way if the receiver reads only the first few points, the essentials of the message will get across.

- Make the subject clear by giving the message a title.

- Use simple words. Make the message more readable by using short, clear sentences.[13]

SELECTING THE BEST METHOD OF COMMUNICATION

In order to convey thoughts and feelings, a manager must choose between oral and written messages. The choice of sending an oral or written message depends on (1) the importance of the message; (2) whether a written record is needed; and (3) whether immediate feedback from the receiver is needed. Table 14.1 lists the methods most commonly used for communicating in organizations, along with the advantages and disadvantages of each method.

TABLE 14.1 ■ METHODS OF COMMUNICATION WITHIN ORGANIZATIONS

METHOD	ADVANTAGES	DISADVANTAGES
Telephone	Speed Permits questions and answers Convenient Two-way	No record of conversation Message might be misunderstood
Face to Face	Visual; personal contact Can "show" and "explain" Can set the mood Two-way	Timing may be inconvenient Requires spontaneous thinking May not be easy to terminate One person may feel subject to pressure by power or status Conversation may be heard by unintended receivers
Meetings	Visuals (charts graphs, films) can be used Involves several minds at once	Time consuming Timing may be inconvenient Can deteriorate into one-way communication
Memorandum	Brief Provides a record Can prethink the message	No control over receiver One-way
Formal Report	Complete; comprehensive Material organized at writer's leisure Can be disseminated widely	May require considerable time in reading Language may not be understandable Expense One-way

Source: Adapted and summarized from A. Uris, *The Executive Deskbook*. New York: Van Nostrand Reinhold, 1970, pp. 27–28.

Which method is most effective? It all depends upon the situation. Most managers who are concerned with protecting themselves believe the old saying, "get it in writing." But, in terms of retention, receiving information in writing is not superior to receiving it verbally. Research shows that verbal messages are more accurately remembered than written messages; that the accuracy of recall is best when information is received both orally and in writing.

Channels

The *channel* of communication is the path a message follows in going from the sender to the receiver.

Channels can be either formal or informal. **Formal channels** follow the hierarchical structure of the organization. Three kinds of formal channels are used by managers: downward, upward, and horizontal.

Downward channels

Management uses **downward channels** in sending orders, directives, objectives, policies, memoranda, and the like to employees at lower levels in the organization. Managers utilize downward channels to transmit

1. job instructions that pertain to performance of a certain task;
2. job descriptions that relate certain jobs to others in the organization;
3. policies and procedures that explain what is expected of employees and the organization's rules, regulations, and employee benefits;
4. feedback concerning an individual's job performance; and
5. indoctrination that identifies certain activities and events the company thinks are important for employees to participate in (charitable organizations, blood drive, and the like).

Downward communication is probably the most frequently used channel in organizations. It may also be the most misused, since some managers place little emphasis on upward communication. The basic problem with downward communication is that it's usually one-way: It does not provide for feedback from those who receive it.

Upward channels

Too many managers fail to see the value of encouraging employees to formally and fully participate in discussions of company objectives, plans, and policies. As a result, they do not provide clear channels for transmitting information upward through the company. **Upward channels** send information from subordinate to supervisor. They are the means that employees have for communicating with higher levels in the organization. Most of you complete a faculty evaluation survey at the end of a course. It asks you to rate the course, book, and instructor. This is an example of an upward communication channel.

Managers should encourage upward communication because it provides feedback on how well employees understand the messages they have received. It can also encourage employees to submit valuable ideas. For upward communication to be effective, it must be allowed to occur freely, not just at the whim of the manager. If effective, upward communication can provide an emotional release and, at the same time, give the employee a sense of personal worth and being listened to.

However, managers should be aware that certain failures may occur in upward communication.[14] First, few employees want their superiors to learn anything negative about them, so they usually screen out bad news. Most employees try to impress their superiors by indicating their contributions to the company. Some try to make themselves look better by pointing out how others in the department have not contributed. Second, an employee's personal anxieties, aspirations, and attitudes almost invariably color what he or she says. How many of you would tell the instructor that this course is terrible? Few would, because of the fear that the instructor would hold this against you when determining your grade. Finally, the employee may be competing for the manager's job and thus is willing to sit by and let the manager stumble. Politics are a way of life in most corporations.

Horizontal channels

Horizontal channels flow across departmental lines. They can be classified as formal or informal, depending on whether they follow the formal organizational structure. Horizontal channels frequently connect people on the same level in the company. Messages usually relate to coordinating activities, sharing information, and solving problems. Horizontal channels are extremely important in organizations that have adopted matrix structures because decisions need to be made quickly without following the formal lines of authority.

Informal channels

Although we have emphasized formal channels of communication, we should not underestimate the importance of *informal channels.* We know less about them, but we do know that the *grapevine* is one source of information for managers. The grapevine is the communication system of the informal organization.[15] The grapevine carries messages based on social interaction; it is fickle, dynamic, and is more hearsay and speculation than truth. Most of the information passed through the grapevine is incomplete, which can easily lead to misinterpretation and distortion. So, even when the grapevine carries the truth, it rarely is the entire truth.

Top managers also spend considerable time with peers and people outside the organization. They develop these relationships by forming informal networks. Networks provide the manager with close working relationships with talented people both inside and outside the organization. By creating these networks, managers try to make others feel obliged to them by doing favors and carefully using them for resources, career advancement, or other support. Lee Iacocca, chairman of the board and president of Chrysler Corporation, was able to gain support for his programs at Chrysler because of his contacts with suppliers, bankers, and government officials. These contacts formed a network of people whom he could call on for advice to help Chrysler solve its productivity and financial problems.

Receiver/Decoder

As we said earlier in this chapter, the receiver is the person who gets the sender's message. For the message to be clearly communicated, the receiver must decode the message. Decoding is the process by which receivers interpret messages and translate them into thoughts or feelings that are meaningful to themselves. This process is affected by the receiver's past experiences, intelligence, personality characteristics, and expectations about the sender. The plumber could not decode the message from the Bureau of Standards because the bureau at first used language the plumber could not understand. Two major processes affect the receiver: listening and feedback. We briefly discuss listening and more fully develop the feedback concept.

Listening

One of the major requirements of the receiver is that of listening. Managers can easily spend 75 percent or more of their time communicating. Of that time, about 50 percent is spent listening to others. Studies have shown that most people can recall only about 50 percent of what someone tells them immediately after they have heard it. Two months later, they can recall only 25 percent. Therefore becoming a better listener is an important way for managers to improve their communication skills. Several guidelines for effective listening are presented in Table 14.2.

Feedback

Since effective communication must be two-way, the receiver should provide *feedback* to the sender. Feedback is the receiver's response to the sender's message and is the best way to determine that a message has been received and how well it has been understood. Unfortunately, managers sometimes fail to recognize that they must have reliable feedback if they want effective communication. They should not assume that everything they say or write will be understood exactly as intended. All other things being equal, the manager who does not allow feedback will be less effective than the manager who encourages feedback.

TABLE 14.2 ■ GUIDELINES FOR EFFECTIVE LISTENING

- *Stop talking!* You cannot listen if you are talking. Polonius (*Hamlet*): "Give every man thine ear, but few thy voice."

- *Put the talker at ease.* Help a person feel free to talk. This is often called a permissive environment.

- *Show a talker that you want to listen.* Look and act interested. Do not read your mail while someone talks. Listen to understand rather than to oppose.

- *Remove distractions.* Don't doodle, tap, or shuffle papers. Will it be quieter if you shut the door?

- *Empathize with talkers.* Try to help yourself see the other person's point of view.

- *Be patient.* Allow plenty of time. Do not interrupt a talker. Don't start for the door or walk away.

- *Hold your temper.* An angry person takes the wrong meaning from words.

- *Go easy on argument and criticism.* These put people on the defensive, and they may "clam up" or become angry. Do not argue: Even if you win, you lose.

- *Ask questions.* This encourages a talker and shows that you are listening. It helps to develop points further.

- *Stop talking!* This is first and last, because all other guides depend on it. You cannot do an effective listening job while you are talking.

- Nature gave people two ears but only one tongue, which is a gentle hint that they should listen more than they talk.

- Listening requires two ears, one for meaning and one for feeling.

- Decision makers who do not listen have less information for making sound decisions.

Source: Adapted from K. Davis, *Human Behavior at Work: Organizational Behavior,* 6th ed. New York: McGraw-Hill, 1981, p. 413.

Effects of feedback

When a message is sent, the actions of the sender affect the reactions of the receiver. The reactions of the receiver, in turn, affect the subsequent actions of the sender. If the sender receives no response, this can mean that the message was never received or that the receiver chose not to respond for some reason. In either case the *lack* of feedback alerts the sender to the need to find out why the receiver did not respond. A sender who receives feedback that is rewarding will continue to produce the same kind of message. On the other hand, if the feedback is not rewarding, the message will eventually change.

Reactions of the receiver can also serve as feedback to tell the sender how well objectives or tasks are being accomplished. However, in this case the receiver exerts control over the sender by the kind of feedback given to the sender. It is necessary for the sender to rely on the receiver for accurate and complete information. This feedback assures the sender that things are going as planned or indicates that there are problems that have to be solved.

Characteristics of Effective Feedback

Procter & Gamble, Exxon, and other companies have established guidelines to help ensure that feedback in their organizations is effective. In general, these guidelines state that effective feedback has the following characteristics, which are summarized in Table 14.3.

1. It should be helpful. If the receiver of the message cannot provide feedback that adds to the information the sender already has, the feedback is not likely to be helpful.

2. It should be *descriptive rather than evaluative*. If the receiver responds in a descriptive manner to the effect of the message the feedback is more likely to be effective. If the receiver becomes evaluative (or judgmental), the feedback is likely to be ineffective or even cause a breakdown in communication.

3. It should be *specific rather than general*. The receiver needs to respond specifically to the points raised and questions asked in the message. If the receiver responds in generalities, the feedback may indicate evasion or lack of commitment.

4. It should be *well timed*. The reception—and thus the effectiveness—of feedback is affected by the situation in which it occurs. Giving feedback to a person during half-time of a football game or at a cocktail party is altogether different from giving the same person feedback in the office.

5. It *should not overwhelm*. This relates to how much feedback someone can absorb at one time. Oral communication requires heavy dependence on memory. Oral feedback is less effective than written feedback for large amounts of information. A person can rarely absorb more than three things at once and tends to tune in and out of conversations. Therefore a person often fails to grasp what the speaker is saying if the message is long and complex.[16]

TABLE 14.3 ■ SUMMARY OF CHARACTERISTICS OF GOOD FEEDBACK

- It is intended to help.
- It is specific rather than general.
- It is well defined.
- It is descriptive rather than evaluative.
- It does not overwhelm the receiver.

PERCEPTION

Perception is the meaning given a message by both sender and receiver, as was shown in Fig. 14.1. Perception determines behavior and is influenced by mental ability, past experiences, and attitudes.

Our perceptions are influenced by the objects we see, the ways in which we organize these objects in our memory, and the meanings we attach to them. The ability to perceive varies from person to person. Some people can enter a room only once and later can describe it in detail, whereas others can barely remember anything about it. Thus *mental ability* to discern differences is important. How we interpret what we perceive is also affected by our *past experiences*. A clenched fist raised in the air by a football player can be interpreted as an angry threat against the opposition or as an expression of team solidarity and accomplishment. The *attitude* we bring to a situation colors our perception of it. You can accept rejection of your application to graduate school because you partied too much as an undergraduate, or you can blame it on a biased admissions officer.

In all likelihood, the sender and the receiver of a message will bring different mental abilities, past experiences, and attitudes to the communication process. This is clearly illustrated by an actual incident, as related in the In Practice: President's Dinner.

IN PRACTICE
PRESIDENT'S
DINNER

The president of a major firm was considering promoting one of the upper-level managers to a top position in the firm. The prospective candidate was invited to the president's home for dinner. At the end of the main course, pie was served. The candidate made the mistake of putting the tines (prongs) of the fork straight into the pie instead of using the side of the fork. The president rejected the candidate because of the individual's lack of sophistication. The president told the personnel department that anyone so naive in his approach to such a simple matter as eating pie could not be trusted to make corporation-wide decisions.[17]

The president and the candidate had entirely different perceptions of what is important. To the candidate, how he ate the pie was of no consequence; to the president, it was a crucial indicator of style and performance.

Perception is a major cause of breakdowns in communication. One reason is that we do not carefully record what we perceive. For example, read aloud the following sentence.

Finished files are the result of years of scientific study combined with the experience of many years of experts.

How many times does the letter *f* appear? Many people count three; in fact, it appears seven times. Did you miss the four times the letter appears in the word *of*? Now, read aloud the sentences in the two triangles.

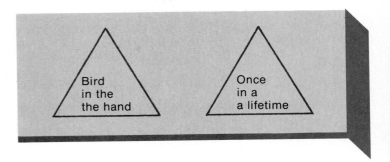

Did you notice that *the* appeared twice in the first triangle and *a* twice in the second? If not, it is because your past experience with these sayings controlled your ability to perceive and prevented you from reading accurately what was written.

In brief, our ability to encode and decode is based on our ability to perceive the situation accurately. People often perceive the same situation in different ways. The type of message they send, the channel of communication they use, and their ability to respond all depend on their perceptions.

BARRIERS TO EFFECTIVE COMMUNICATION

One of the first steps to communicating more successfully is identifying the barriers that stand in the way. These barriers hinder the sending and receiving of messages by distorting or sometimes even completely blocking intended meanings, as shown in Fig. 14.4. There are almost as many barriers as there are writers to list them.[18] For convenience, we divided them into organizational and individual barriers, although there obviously is some overlapping, and listed them in Table 14.4.

ORGANIZATIONAL BARRIERS

STRUCTURE

Whenever one person holds a higher position than another, communication problems are likely to occur. The more levels in the organization and the farther the receiver is from the sender, the harder it is for a message to be

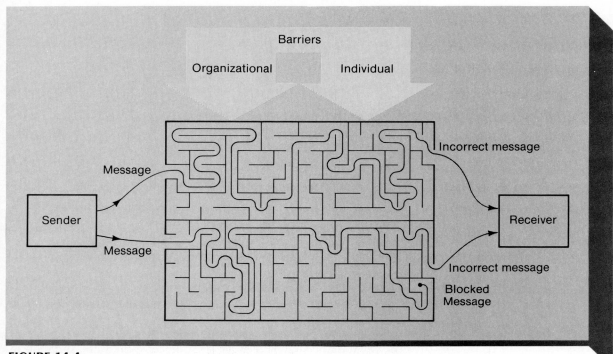

FIGURE 14.4
Communication Barriers

Source: Adapted from K. Davis, *Human Behavior at Work: Organizational Behavior,* 6th ed. New York: McGraw-Hill, 1981, p. 405.

TABLE 14.4 ■ BARRIERS TO COMMUNICATION

- Structure of the organization
- Specialization of task functions by members
- Different objectives
- Status relationships among members

INDIVIDUAL

- Conflicting assumptions
- Semantics
- Emotions
- Communication skills

effectively communicated. Figure 14.5 illustrates the loss of understanding as messages are passed down the hierarchy. Assuming that top management represents 100 percent understanding, by the time the message travels through another five levels, only 20 percent of the original message will be understood.

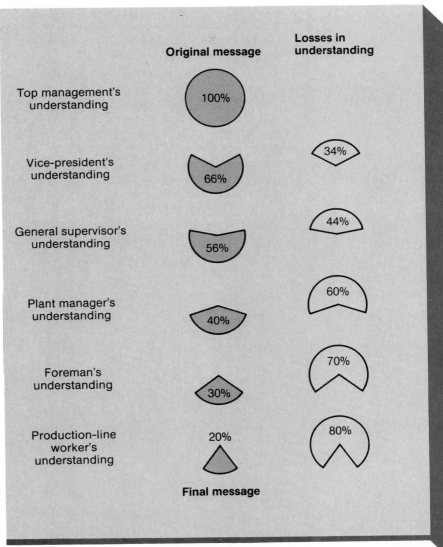

FIGURE 14.5
Levels of Understanding as Information Is Transmitted Down the Organization

Source: Adapted from E. Scannell, *Communication for Leadership*. New York: McGraw-Hill, 1970, p. 5. Reproduced with permission.

Specialization

As knowledge becomes more specialized professionals in a field develop their own jargon, or shorthand, to simplify communication among themselves. However, this makes communication with people in other fields increasingly difficult. We can easily understand how a tax accountant might find it hard to communicate successfully with a marketing research manager. Moreover, some people use the language of specialization to obscure and to attempt to make themselves indispensable.

Different objectives

Problems can arise because middle and first-line managers do not understand the general objectives of top management. Every department develops its own ideas about how to solve problems and reach its objectives. They exhibit tunnel vision and cannot see the long range needs of the organization. Attempts to work with other departments, except in times of crisis, are often avoided.

For the developer of a large office building, the objective is to get tenants into the new building as quickly as possible. To do this the developer has to hire an architect to draw plans and a construction company to erect the building. Unfortunately, the architect's objective may be to build a monument to architectural design. The incompatibility of these objectives can lead to delays throughout the project and cause each group to view the other as adversaries.

Status

Distinctions arise within groups because they enable people to focus on different characteristics and abilities of group members. *Status* is the social rank of a person in a group. Some typical symbols of status are shown in Table 14.5. Note that these are visible, external things that attach to a person or job and serve as evidence of social rank. They are most evident among different levels of managers because each higher level of management usually has the authority to give itself additional perquisites (perks).

Status is significant as a barrier to effective communication in three ways: (1) it is often used to insulate a manager from things he or she does not want

TABLE 14.5 ▪ TYPICAL SYMBOLS OF STATUS

- Furniture, such as leather chairs and large wooden executive desk
- Interior decorations, such as draperies, paintings and rugs
- Private secretary
- Office location, such as a top-floor, corner office
- Style of clothes worn
- Privileges, such as use of a company car, country club memberships, and company credit card.

to hear; (2) it influences the amount and kinds of information that subordinates channel upward; and (3) it encourages status seekers to misuse information in their drive to reach the top.

Individual Barriers

A manager must be able to send clear and effective messages. However, words, phrases, and references that may be clear to some employees may be puzzling and obscure to others. This kind of problem can be caused by conflicting assumptions, semantics, emotions, and lack of effective communication skills.

Conflicting assumptions

The sender of a message assumes that the receiver will interpret it as the sender intends. But a key word or phrase may mean one thing to the sender and something else to the receiver. For example, a sales representative of a large organization phoned in a special order and asked that it be shipped "as soon as possible." Five days later, the sales rep got a call from the upset customer wanting to know when the order would be delivered. On checking with the shipping department, the sales rep found that the order was being shipped that day. "I thought I told you to ship it as soon as possible," shouted the rep. "That's just what we're doing," yelled the person in the shipping department. To the salesperson, "as soon as possible" meant *now*. To the shipping department, which often received that kind of order from sales reps, it meant something totally different.

Semantics

The study of the way words are used and the maining they convey is called *semantics*. Improper word usage is a major source of communication failure. Most words in the dictionary have multiple meanings and some common words may have as many as 18 different meanings. One example of a common word with many meanings is *charge:*

Please put a charge on the battery.

Charge it.

You are charged with running a red light.

The charge for this service is $25.00.

Let's charge ahead on this new plan.

Another illustration is *run:*

Did you see that run by Eric Dickerson?

Run to the store and get a six-pack.

Who will run for president in 1988?

You have the run of the place.

When two people attribute different meanings to the same words and do not realize it, a barrier exists. Faculty members who say to their class, "This is an easy test," can mislead the students if the students do not know the faculty member's definition of an *easy* test.

Emotions

An *emotion* is a subjective reaction, a feeling. When we recall past experiences, we recall not only events but also the feelings that accompanied them. All communication has an emotional aspect. The sender's feelings influence encoding of the message. These feelings may be apparent to the receiver; if they are, they *and* the receiver's own feelings affect decoding of the message and the nature of the response.

Communication skills

The ability to communicate varies greatly. Some differences in communication skills result from education and training, while others stem from basic personality characteristics. For instance, articulate, persuasive, and confident people communicate more effectively than those who are less so. Some people are better listeners than others by virtue of education, training, personality characteristics, or physical (level of hearing) ability. Anxious people may be too preoccupied with personal problems or what they are going to say next to pay close attention to messages from other people. People under considerable stress may also be unable to listen properly.

Effectiveness of communication is also influenced by the *timing* of messages. Managers who relay important instructions to employees on the Friday afternoon before a holiday show poor timing. By that time, their attention has already shifted from work to what they are going to do over the long weekend. In contrast, the department manager who asks for new funds after the company has achieved its financial objectives for the year shows good timing. Under these circumstances, the department manager's superior is more likely to listen to the request.

Overcoming Barriers

Managers can overcome these barriers to effective communication. First, the manager must be aware that they exist and can cause serious organizational problems; then the manager must be willing to make the effort and spend the time necessary to overcome them. Several ways of overcoming barriers to communication are presented in Table 14.6

Regulate the flow of information

Managers can suffer from information overload when they receive too much information. Therefore managers should establish a system that permits priority messages to receive immediate attention. One such system is for

TABLE 14.6 ■ OVERCOMING BARRIERS TO COMMUNICATION

- Regulate the flow of information
- Encourage feedback
- Simplify message language
- Listen actively
- Restrain emotions
- Use nonverbal cues
- Use the grapevine

managers to instruct subordinates to bring them information only when there are significant deviations from objectives and plans (exceptions reporting). When everything is going as planned, the manager doesn't need a report. Second, messages should be condensed. Procter & Gamble recommends that all messages be limited to one page in length.

Encourage feedback

Managers should follow up to determine whether nonroutine messages are understood. The feedback will let the manager know that the subordinate understands the message accurately. Feedback does not have to be verbal, actions often speak louder than words. The sales manager who describes to his or her staff the changes desired in the monthly sales planning report will receive feedback when the report is turned in. If the report contains the proper changes, the manager has received feedback that the message was received. Similarly, when you talk to a group of people, look for the nonverbal feedback that tells you whether you are getting through to them.

Simplify message language

Since language can be a barrier, managers should choose words that subordinates will understand. They should avoid what happened between the Bureau of Standards and the plumber. Managers should not use jargon that people will not understand. Understanding is improved by simplifying the language used in relation to the intended audience.

Listen actively

Listening is an active search for the sender's meaning by the receiver. Managers need to become good listeners. Listening can be more tiring than talking because it demands mental concentration. The average person speaks at a rate of 150 words per minute but has the capacity to listen at the rate of more than 1000 words per minute. The difference between these rates leaves the brain idle time and opportunities for day-dreaming.

INTERNATIONAL FOCUS

International Blunders

Translation errors are the cause of a great number and variety of international business blunders. In fact, the largest number of promotional blunders has resulted from faulty translations. These blunders fall into three basic categories: carelessness, multiple meanings, and idioms.

CARELESSNESS

A Mexican magazine promotion for an American-brand shirt carried a message stating the exact opposite of what had originally been intended. The advertisement, instead of saying, "When I wore this shirt, I felt good," read "Until I used this shirt, I felt good."

Consider the experience of Otis Engineering Corporation when it participated in an exhibition held in Moscow. Initially, the company's representatives could not understand why its display won Soviet laughs as well as scorn. Much to their disappointment and embarrassment, it was discovered that a translator had made a sign that showed "completed equipment" as "equipment for orgasms."

An American manufacturer in the car business advertised its battery as "highly rated." Unfortunately, when the company introduced its car in Venezuela, the battery was described as "highly overrated." When "Body by Fisher" was translated into Flemish, it came out "Corpse by Fisher."

Finally, in an effort to attract tourists and foreign business people, a department store in Thailand made a sign which was supposed to read "Visit our bargain basement one flight up." The translation of the sign was: "Would you like to ride on your ass?"

MULTIPLE MEANINGS

The second category involves translated messages that can convey more than one meaning. The trials and tribulations of Parker Pen Company clearly illustrate this problem. In its advertisements destined for Latin America, Parker had hoped to use the word "bola" to describe its ballpoint pen. However, it

Source: Adapted from David Ricks and Vijay Mahajan, "Blunders in International Marketing: Fact or Fiction," *Long Range Planning*, 1984, 17(1):78–82, copyright 1984, Pergamon Press, Ltd.; David Ricks, *Big Business Blunders: Mistakes in Multinational Marketing*. Homewood, Ill.: Richard D. Irwin, 1983, pp. 74–95. Reprinted with permission.

Restrain emotions

Managers use emotions when communicating, but emotions can distort the content of the message. If a manager is emotionally upset, he or she is more likely to phrase the message poorly. If a subordinate is emotionally upset

was discovered that the word conveys multiple meanings in different Latin American countries. To some, "bola" conveys the intended meaning of ball, while in another country the translation means "revolution." "Bola" represents an obscenity in a third country, and yet in another it means a "lie." Fortunately, the company was able to stop this problem before it became a major blunder. A few years later, Parker decided to enter Latin America with its slogan, "Avoid embarrassment—use Parker Pens." The slogan was intended to show that Parker pocket pens would not leak once put in a shirt pocket. The company even posted metal signs featuring this short message on buildings in which the pens were sold, but the anticipated sales never materialized. What had gone wrong? The company had promoted a slogan which contained a multiple-meaning word. The Spanish word for embarrassment was also used to indicate pregnancy, so the Parker Pen Company was unknowingly promoting its pen as contraceptives!

Several U.S. tobacco companies have also experienced blunders. These firms advertised "low-tar" cigarettes in Spanish-speaking countries, but misused the word "brea." "Brea" literally translates to "tar," but it is the type of tar used in paving streets. Who would care to smoke a "low-asphalt" cigarette?

IDIOMS

Everyone in the United States has probably heard the advertisement for Pepsi-Cola as "Come alive with Pepsi." When the ad campaign was introduced in Germany, the company was forced to revise the ad because it discovered that the German translation of "come alive" became "come out of the grave." And in Asia, the same phrase translated to "Bring your ancestors back from the dead."

An American company advertised its product to a Spanish audience claiming that anyone who did not wear its brand of hosiery just "wouldn't have a leg to stand on." But when the copy was translated, it actually stated that the person would "only have one leg."

he or she is more likely to misinterpret the message. In the Preview Case, Helen and Tom's emotions got in the way of effective communication. The simplest answer in such a situation is to call a halt until the people involved can restrain their emotions, can be descriptive instead of evaluative.

Two keys to good communication between managers and employees are active listening, and taking advantage of the company grapevine.

Source: Christopher Morrow/ Stock, Boston.

Use nonverbal cues

Managers should use nonverbal cues to emphasize points and express feelings. We have already discussed methods of nonverbal communication and the importance of these messages. Managers also need to make sure that their actions reinforce their words so that they do not send mixed messages.

Use the grapevine

Managers cannot get rid of the grapevine in an organization. They should use it to send information rapidly, test reactions prior to a final decision, and obtain valuable feedback. We also noted that the grapevine often carries destructive rumors that can reduce employee morale and organizational effectiveness. Managers who are plugged into the grapevine can counteract this to a greater extent by making sure that relevant, accurate, and meaningful information gets to employees.

GUIDELINES FOR EFFECTIVE COMMUNICATION

In order to be effective communicators, managers must understand not merely the concepts presented in Fig. 14.2, but also the ways they can improve their communication skills. These concepts and methods were presented throughout the chapter, but we now pull them together and restate them as guidelines. We do this by presenting in Table 14.7 and then discussing the American Management Association's list of eight guidelines that managers can use to improve their communication.[19]

Clarify your ideas before communicating. The more you analyze a problem before communicating, the clearer it becomes in your mind. Some managers fail to communicate effectively because of inadequate message planning. Good message planning considers the objectives and attitudes of those who will receive the communication.

Examine the true purpose of the communication. Before you communicate, ask yourself what you really want to accomplish with the message. Do you want to obtain information, convey a decision, or persuade someone to take action?

Consider the setting in which the communication will take place. You convey meanings and intent by more than words alone. Attempting to communicate with a person in another office presents more difficulties than does communicating face-to-face with that person.

Consult with others, when appropriate, in planning communications. It is often desirable to seek the participation of those who will be affected by the message. They can often provide a viewpoint that you might not have considered.

Be mindful of the nonverbal messages you send. Your tone of voice, facial expression, eye contact, dress, and physical surroundings all influence the communication process. The receiver judges messages on the basis of the sender's words *and* nonverbal messages.

TABLE 14.7 ■ GUIDELINES FOR EFFECTIVE COMMUNICATION

- Clarify your ideas before communicating.
- Examine the true purpose of the communication.
- Consider the setting in which the communication will take place.
- Consult with others, when appropriate, in planning communications.
- Be mindful of the nonverbal messages you send.
- Take the opportunity to convey something of help to the receiver.
- Follow up the communication.
- Be sure your actions support your communication.

Take the opportunity to convey something of help to the receiver. Consideration of the other person's interests and needs frequently points up opportunities for the sender. Individuals can make their communication clearer by placing themselves in the other person's shoes. Effective communicators really try to see the message from the listener's point of view.

Follow up the communication. Your best efforts at communication can be wasted unless you succeed in getting your message across. It is often necessary to follow up and ask for feedback to know whether you succeeded. You cannot assume that the receiver understands; feedback in some form is necessary to tell you this.

Be sure your actions support your communication. In the final analysis, the most effective communication is not in what you say but in what you do.

CHAPTER SUMMARY

We defined communication as the process by which information is exchanged between two or more persons. Effective communication is important to achieve organizational objectives. As a result, top and middle managers spend up to 80 percent of their time communicating.

We then described the six basic elements in the communication process. The *sender/encoder* is the person who initiates the communication. The burden is on the sender to send the information accurately to the *receiver/decoder*. However, the receiver has an obligation to listen as actively as possible. There are three types of *messages:* nonverbal, verbal (oral), and written. Nonverbal messages involve the use of your voice (volume, speed, pitch), gestures, body, and facial expressions to convey information; most people are unaware of how they communicate nonverbally. Verbal or oral messages are sent and received over the telephone or face-to-face. Most managers prefer to communicate face-to-face because they can pick up nonverbal cues. Written messages include letters, memoranda, and reports; this form of communication provides a record of the message for future reference. We listed the advantages and disadvantages of the communication methods most commonly used by managers.

The *channel* is the path of communication. The downward channel (line of authority) and its potential advantages and problems were discussed. Highly bureaucratic organizations frequently rely on this channel to communicate with employees. The upward channel provides the subordinate with an opportunity to provide

feedback to superiors. We indicated that it is difficult to establish effective upward communication because employees usually do not like to have their superiors discover things that show them in a bad light. Finally, we described the informal channel, or grapevine, its potential for harm, and how managers can use it.

Feedback is vital if effective communication is to occur. We indicated five characteristics of effective feedback. It should be helpful, descriptive, specific, and well timed and should not overwhelm.

How the sender and receiver *perceive* the message is also important. The ability to perceive accurately the content of the message is affected by past experiences, personality, ability to discern differences, and expectations.

We briefly discussed some of the major organizational and individual barriers to communication and ways that managers can overcome them. We indicated some of the reasons why messages are not always understood by receivers and what can be done to correct this. In conclusion we presented eight guidelines for effective communication.

MANAGER'S VOCABULARY

channel
communication
decoding
downward channels
emotions

encoding
feedback
formal channels
horizontal channels
informal channels
message
nonverbal communication
perception
receiver
semantics
sender
status
upward channels

REVIEW QUESTIONS

1. State the six elements of the communication process.

2. List three types of nonverbal communication and give examples.

3. Identify the methods managers use to communicate with employees.

4. State the effective guidelines for listening.

5. Identify the major barriers to communication and ways managers can use to overcome them.

DISCUSSION QUESTIONS

1. Using the American Management Association's guidelines for effective communications, how would you improve communication between Helen and Tom in the Preview Case?

2. Visit a manager's office. What nonverbal cues are present in the office? How did these affect your communication with the manager?

3. How can managers control information in the grapevine?

4. Why do communication difficulties arise in large organizations?

5. The world is a busy and confusing place and people are constantly bombarded by multiple messages. People simplify these messages in order to handle this confusion. How do they do it?

6. An old song title goes, "Your lips tell me no, no, but there's yes, yes in your eyes." Describe another communication situation showing inconsistency between verbal and nonverbal communications.

MANAGEMENT INCIDENTS AND CASES

Xographics—PART A

Xographics was a division of a large telecommunications company. Ellen Bohn, the new production superintendent, had recently moved to Xographics from Rolm Communications where she had been a manager of a large office staff. The three line managers reporting to Ellen all had 20 or more years' experience with Xographics. They had seen it go from a productive company to one that was badly troubled with problem workers and poor performance.

In talking with one of the supervisors, Ellen learned that a good many of them were upset over the fact that they had to report any machine breakdown to the production manager or one of his assistants within 15 minutes of the breakdown. They felt that this did not give the workers the opportunity to repair the machine themselves. The breakdown report was forwarded to the production superintendent's office. The assistant told Ellen that the word was that once a worker got five reports, he or she was taken off the machine and given a lower paying job.

Questions

1. What should Ellen do?

2. What other problems (unidentified by Ellen) might be present?

3. What additional steps might the supervisors take?

PART B

One of the major problems that Ellen faced was that only about 40 percent of the jobs listed for scheduled maintenance shutdowns were ever performed. During an informal conversation with Ken Viet, Xographics personnel director, Ellen learned that the maintenance department was operating at about 30-percent efficiency. Ken also said that the maintenance workers had recently staged a slowdown in order to force the company to increase their wages. Ken also told Ellen that it had been a common practice for maintenance workers to quit about an hour early in order to wash up.

The head of the maintenance department had worked his way up through the ranks. He started with Xographics immediately after he graduated from high school and had been with the company 25 years. His reason for the "inefficiency" was that there were not many qualified maintenance people in the area and the personnel department sent him individuals who were not qualified to perform maintenance on the mill's machines. He did not have time to train each newly hired worker, but assigned this responsibility to other workers, usually those who had been around for a while.

Questions

1. How might Ellen approach the maintenance head?
2. Who else should Ellen talk to?

PART C

Two months after Ellen had joined Xographics, the company held its annual picnic at a local park. Most of the employees and their families were there. Ellen saw Ken at the picnic and handed him a beer. The following conversation then took place:

Ken: Hey, Ellen, got a minute?

Ellen: Sure. What's up?

Ken: Well, I was talking with one of your foremen that I know pretty well. You know, an off-the-record chart about the company.

Ellen: Yeah?

Ken: He told me that the company's management style is the mushroom style: Keep them in the dark and feed 'em a lot of manure. He said that nobody knew you were hired until you showed up at the plant. We heard that the guard didn't even know who you were.

Ellen: Yeah, I guess that's so.

Ken: This foreman said that he has been doing his job for ten years and has never received any performance appraisal. His raises are just added into his check. No one has pointed out his strong and weak points.

Ellen: Yeah, I guess that's so. But, I'm not totally sure. You know that I've been here only a few months myself.

Ken: Yeah, I know that, but listen to this. Tom Kerr, the new head of industrial engineering, has not talked to or even been introduced to anybody in the paper-machine area, and Tom has been on the job for three months.

Ellen: Ken, how widespread do you think this feeling is about the mushroom style of management?

Ken: I don't know, Ellen, but I think you ought to find out if you want this place to produce.

Questions

1. What steps can Ellen take?
2. What does this conversation tell you about the company? What organizational barriers to communication may exist?
3. What role has the informal communication channel played in this case?

REFERENCES

1. D. Middlemist and M. Hitt, *Organizational Behavior: Applied Concepts.* Chicago: SRA, Inc., 1981, pp. 293–294.
2. H. Mintzberg, *The Nature of Managerial Work.* New York: Harper & Row, 1973, pp. 58–93.
3. R. Huseman, J. Lahiff, and J. Hatfield, *Business Communication: Strategies and Skills,* 2nd ed. Hinsdale, Ill.: Dryden Press, 1985, p. 32.
4. E. Huse, *The Modern Manager.* St. Paul, Minn.: West, 1979, p. 246.
5. Huseman et al., *Business Communication . . . ,* p. 33.
6. J. Martin and C. Siehl, "Organizational Culture and Counterculture: An Uneasy Symbiosis," *Organizational Dynamics,* Autumn 1983, pp. 52–64; T. Davis, "The Influence of the Physical Environment in Offices," *Academy of Management Review,* 1984, 9:271–284.
7. J. Wright, *On a Clear Day You Can See General Motors.* New York: Wright Enterprises, 1979.
8. J. Molloy, *Dress for Success.* New York: Peter Wyden, 1975.
9. C. Lavington, "How to Establish Power Presence," *Business Week's Guide to Careers,* Fall/Winter 1983, pp. 68–70.

10. M. McCaskey, "The Hidden Messages Managers Send," *Harvard Business Review,* 1979, **57**(6):146–147.

11. R. Harrison, *Beyond Words: An Introduction to Nonverbal Communication.* Englewood Cliffs, N.J.: Prentice-Hall, 1974, pp. 132–133.

12. Huseman et al., pp. 382–405.

13. R. Lesikar, *Business Communication.* Homewood, Ill.: Richard D. Irwin, 1972; S. Axley, "Managerial and Organizational Communication in Terms of the Conduit Metaphor," *Academy of Management Review,* 1984, **9**:428–437.

14. C. O'Reilly and L. Pondy, "Organizational Communication." In *Organizational Behavior,* S. Kerr (Ed.). Columbus, Ohio: Grid, 1979, pp. 135–136.

15. K. Davis, "Business Communication and the Grapevine," *Harvard Business Review,* 1953, **31**(1):43–49; P. Gronn, "Talk as Work: The Accomplishment of School Administration," *Administrative Science Quarterly,* 1983, **28**:1–22.

16. J. Anderson, "Giving and Receiving Feedback." In *Managers and Their Careers: Cases and Readings.* J. Lorsch and L. Barnes (Eds.). Homewood, Ill.: Richard D. Irwin, 1972, pp. 260–267.

17. Abstracted from R. Powell, *Race, Religion and the Promotion of the American Executive.* Columbus, Ohio: Faculty of Administrative Studies, Ohio State University, 1979, No. AA-3.

18. For other barriers, *see* L. Porter and K. Roberts, "Communications in Organizations." In *Handbook of Industrial and Organizational Psychology.* R. Dubin (Ed.). Chicago: Rand McNally, 1976, pp. 1548–1585; C. O'Reilly, "Individuals and Information Overload in Organizations: Is More Necessarily Better?" *Academy of Management Journal,* 1980, **23**:685–696; T. Bonoma and G. Zaltman, *Psychology for Management.* Boston: Kent, 1981.

19. These are summarized from: *Ten Commandments of Good Communications.* New York: American Management Association, 1955.

Groups and Organizational Cultures

LEARNING OBJECTIVES

After studying this chapter, you should be able to:

- Answer five basic questions about groups: What is a group? What are the types of groups? How do individuals behave in groups? What are the assets and liabilities in the use of groups? What is an effective group?

- Use the group-process model to diagnose how groups operate.

- Describe how contingency variables—nature of groups, group size, and role of the leader—affect group processes.

- State how quality circles are intended to function in organizations.

- Define *organizational culture*.

- Outline how organizational cultures are created and transmitted.

- State four managerial implications of organizational cultures.

CHAPTER OUTLINE

PREVIEW CASE

New Product Groups at Whirlpool Corporation

"Historically, we have worked pretty much in a vacuum," confesses Jeryl I. Schornhorst, director of automatic washer engineering at Whirlpool Corporation, a major U.S. maker of home appliances. For years, he and his co-workers, who were involved in Whirlpool's product planning, worked on new designs without much contact with the people in manufacturing engineering. "We would design the parts and send prints out to manufacturing," explains Schornhorst. "Whatever it took to make things, it was their business."

Whirlpool senior management has established procedures aimed squarely at boosting productivity and quality by forcing the two disciplines to work together. They gave it its own acronym, TQA, for *Total Quality Assurance,* and started a rigorous engineering review process under which both new product designs, and, importantly, proposed manufacturing process designs are examined.

Unlike earlier practices in which manufacturing engineering did not start work until the product design was virtually finished, the two review processes now start off almost simultaneously and continue in parallel. "You don't just throw the design over the wall any more," says Alvin J. Elders, general manager of laundry engineering for Whirlpool. "This is a management system that brings people together to design for quality."

When a new product idea is approved by a business planning team, it is turned over to the appropriate product planning group. This group is assigned "ultimate responsibility until it is running smoothly down the line," says Schornhorst.

Just as in conventional systems, the product planners first develop the general concept. But as soon as they have the basic idea down, the process changes. Manufacturing, as well as other departments, now become involved. First, the design itself faces a committee made up of people selected from every department that has a stake in it—from manufacturing to purchasing to home economics. Second, once over this hurdle, a manufacturing team starts working on the production process for it. To further integrate departments, a separate, multidepartmental review committee is established to go over manufacturing plans. The total number of formal reviews varies, but major projects go through at least six full reviews, three

Source: Whirlpool Corporation.

of the project and three of the manufacturing processes.

To keep all this moving along, senior management assigns a manager to chair each review committee. The chairperson runs the review meetings, makes assignments for reports and for further study of any problems that emerge during this review. For objectivity, the chairperson is not directly involved in the particular project. That is sometimes hard to accomplish. "It's hard to find someone who doesn't have some axe to grind," says Joseph A. Gauer, director of manufacturing, laundry equipment division. "But so far, that has not caused an insurmountable problem."

In addition to these formal reviews, Whirlpool encourages informal ones. "One neat thing is that it causes a lot of interpersonal relationships to grow between product design engineers and the factory people," says Gauer. "We see product development people in our plant. They're much more attuned to our kinds of problems."

Despite some early hitches, Whirlpool's TQA program is breaking down barriers between departments. "It has been slow—it has taken more time to adapt to the Total Quality Assurance approach than we expected," admits Alan J. Koch, director of corporate quality and product safety. He adds: "As more and more people have been involved, it's running along more smoothly." Product designer Schornhorst agrees: "American industry has tended to compartmentalize engineering. Now we're thinking integration."[1]

As illustrated in the Preview Case, managers are increasingly recognizing the importance of formal and informal groups to make decisions, share information, improve coordination, build trust, and smooth interpersonal relations. The Whirlpool story suggests the role of groups—whether they be called teams, committees, task forces, or cliques—in linking different departments and levels of the organization.[2] One element of the TQA program at Whirlpool is bringing together in a group, early in the product design process, representatives of all the affected departments—from manufacturing to purchasing to home economics—to provide ideas and assessments of a proposed product as its design unfolds.

The importance of groups to organizations is partially indicated by the amount of time managers spend in group sessions (committee, task force, team, and informal get-togethers). Many top managers report spending up to 60 percent of their time in meetings. The time spent in group meetings varies between 25–60 percent for first-line managers.[3]

A survey of top and middle managers from nine nations, including the United States, ranked group meetings as the fourth-biggest time waster. The worst time waster was telephone interruptions, second was drop-in visitors, and third was ineffective delegation.[4] No one expects the use of groups to decline in organizations. Most of this chapter is intended to improve your understanding of groups and how they can be used effectively. The nature of formal and informal groups varies substantially with the broader organizational culture within which they operate. Thus the latter part of the chapter presents some basic ideas about how organizational cultures can shape group and individual behavior.

GROUPS

A *group* is two or more individuals who come into personal, meaningful, and purposeful contact on a relatively continuing basis.[5] If five strangers start playing basketball together just to pass a few spare minutes, they do not constitute a group. However, if five individuals play basketball together on a continuing basis, share a common goal of winning games, and communicate freely among themselves, they are a group.

Most of us belong to six or so groups. At work, we might be members of two or three groups. The formal work group is likely to consist of the immediate superior and fellow workers in our department. We also might belong to a union and informal social groups at work. An informal social group could be five or six workers who sit together every day during breaks to eat and play cards or who are members of the same bowling league. Away from work, we might belong to a church, PTA, community organization, and/or a political action committee.

Unlike five strangers who join in a playground game of basketball, players on professional teams need to be strongly united members of a group, with common goals and strategies.

Source: Ken Kaminsky/The Picture Cube.

Types of Groups

There are many types of groups in organizations. However, in the most basic sense, there are two major types: formal and informal.

Formal groups

A *formal group* is one whose objectives and activities relate directly to the achievement of stated organizational objectives. From the point of view of the organization, formal groups are generally used to pass along and share information, train people, or help make decisions.[6] Formal groups are part of the structure of an organization. They are represented as departments, sections, task forces, teams, project groups, quality circles, committees, and boards of directors.

Informal groups

An *informal group* is one that develops out of the day-to-day activities, interactions, and sentiments of the members for the purpose of meeting their own needs. A social group is one of the most common types of informal groups, in or out of organizations.

The purposes of informal groups are not necessarily related to formal organizational objectives.[7] However, the formal organization often influences considerably the development of informal groups—through the physical layout of work, the leadership practices of superiors, and the type of technology used.[8] For example, moving some people from one building to another is likely to have an impact on the membership of informal groups. The distance between them may make it difficult for them to continue to communicate face-to-face. Or, when taking over a department, a new manager might tell the members to shape up or ship out. With this type of threat, an informal group may form to unite its members against the new manager.[9]

Assets and Liabilities in the Use of Groups

Figure 15.1 shows some of the assets and liabilities of having some form of group decision making. Assets may include greater knowledge, more approaches, increased acceptance, and better understanding.[10]

Assets

Greater knowledge. A group's information and knowledge should be greater than that of any one member. If the group's members have various skills, knowledge, and sources of information in relation to their task, each might be able to fill gaps in the knowledge of others. For example, when Chrysler decided to produce its K-cars, people from departments such as marketing (customer acceptance), engineering (design), production (production feasibility), accounting (cost considerations), personnel (labor relations), and legal (safety and patent considerations), were brought together to solve the problems of making and marketing the K-cars.

More approaches. Individuals tend to develop tunnel-vision. That is, they regard only their own part of the problem as important. Even when individuals in a group have the same problem, their discussion can stimulate the search for more alternatives. By challenging one another's thinking, members of a group may arrive at a decision that takes all viewpoints into account to reach a consensus or workable compromise.

Increased acceptance. Group decision making may lead to increased acceptance of a decision by members and to more effective implementation of it. A person who has a chance to influence the group's decision may have a greater commitment to the decision and accept more responsibility for making it work than a person who is just told what to do. A high-quality solution that is handed down by a superior may not be as effective as a lower-quality solution that is arrived at more democratically. However, this conclusion is somewhat dependent on the relative power of the group to resist or implement a particular solution.[11]

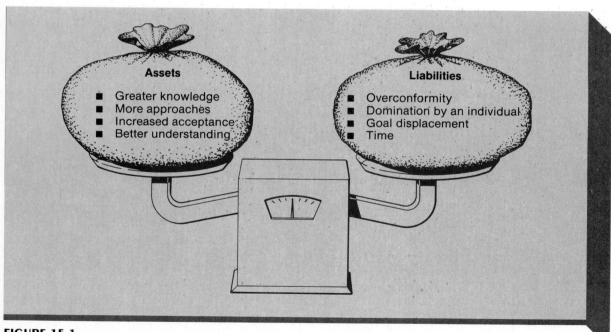

FIGURE 15.1
Assets and Liabilities in Group Decision Making

Better understanding. A person who solves problems alone usually has the additional task of persuading others to implement the solutions. Problems are often caused by the inadequate communication of decisions from superiors to subordinates or between co-workers. If those who must implement a decision have helped to make it, failure in communication is not so likely. They already know how and why the decision was made. Of course, this may be beneficial only so long as those who helped with the decision have some influence over how it is implemented.

Liabilities

The potential assets of group decision making are not guaranteed. Groups can also create liabilities in the form of overconformity, domination by an individual, goal displacement, and taking too much time.

Overconformity. Social pressures for maintaining friendships and trying to avoid disagreements can lead to conformity. Conformity is especially a problem when a solution should be based primarily on facts rather than on feelings or wishes. Moreover, a group's acceptance of a decision is not necessarily related to the quality of the decision. If a group is advisory, a superior can serve as a check on the group's decision or encourage the members to diagnose and analyze the group processes.

Domination by an individual. Group effectiveness can be reduced if one person dominates the discussion by talking too much, overusing persuasion, or being too persistent. These characteristics do not make a person a good problem solver. Some group leaders believe that it is their duty to control the group and provide the major input to decisions. Leaders need to be aware of their potential for domination of a group and the negative effects this can create. Even the best group members may be unable to upgrade and influence group decisions if they are not permitted—much less encouraged—to contribute.

Goal displacement. One major goal of a decision-making group is to find an effective solution. In order to accomplish this, members need to consider alternatives. Some members may be enthusiastic about one alternative and attempt to win support for it rather than find the best solution. This type of goal displacement can lower the quality of the decision. It probably would be better to go back to the beginning, generate new alternatives, and avoid evaluating them for the time being. If evaluation is clouded by a lack of facts, or controversy over them, the group session can be stopped until the facts can be clarified and supplemented.

Time. Time becomes a liability if decisions could be made just as effectively by individuals working alone. Time costs money. If we assume that the cost of a manager's time is $50 per hour, a meeting attended by 10 managers for two hours costs the organization $1000. Of course, this cost may be well worth it, but this cost is a liability if the managers could have better spent their time on other activities.

Individual Behavior in Groups

When joining a new group, employees often experience feelings of stress, anxiety, and frustration. Managers can help them deal with these emotions by reducing the problems of adjustment.[12] Managers can create a sense of belonging by introducing them to fellow employees, inviting them out to lunch with fellow employees, and chatting with them frequently during the first month or so to assist and reassure them.

Social and task behaviors

After individuals have become full-fledged members of a group, they generally exhibit different behaviors. Figure 15.2 presents a way of looking at different types of behaviors in groups. This framework was developed from a study of middle- and upper-level managers in problem-solving groups.[13] The vertical axis indicates the degree of *social behaviors* shown by the individual, from low to high. Social behaviors are actions such as joking, laughing, rewarding others, and agreeing with others. The horizontal axis represents the degree of *task behaviors,* also from low to high. Task behaviors are actions such as giving suggestions, providing information, analyzing problems, evaluating alternatives, and making decisions.

Four types of role behaviors

By cross-classifying the variables of social behaviors and task behaviors, four *pure* role types are identified: social specialists, stars, technical specialists, and the underchosen. They are positioned at the four corners of the grid in Fig. 15.2. As with any classification framework, many individuals are likely to fit some place between these four extremes. For example, the behaviors of individuals in two hypothetical work groups of seven members each are shown on the grid. Group A is likely to be ineffective and group B effective in performing work-related tasks based on the variations of the individual behaviors plotted.

In this particular study, the four role types showed little difference in their satisfaction with the way their groups operated. However, they differed widely in other respects.

Social specialists show a great deal of feeling and support for others. They avoid criticizing, disagreeing with, or showing aggression toward other group members. They are interested in keeping the group operating as one happy family.

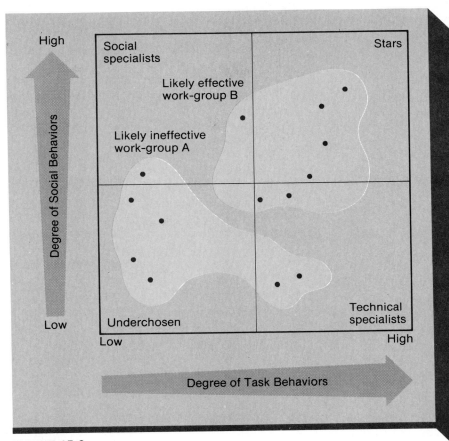

FIGURE 15.2
Role Behaviors of Individuals in Groups

Source: Adapted from D. Moment and A. Zaleznik, *Role Development and Interpersonal Competence: An Experimental Study of Role Performance in Problem-Solving Groups.* Boston: Division of Research, Graduate School of Business Administration, Harvard University, 1963, pp. 10–18.

Stars are active group members and exhibit a variety of behaviors. Stars let others know where they stand and show open, honest involvement without appearing too anxious. They address other members personally and do not emphasize only task behaviors or social behaviors. They exhibit different behaviors in different situations. As a rule, stars are likely to be more satisfied with group decisions than are the other three types.

Technical specialists show great concern with task-related problems and using their expertise to solve them. They often avoid confronting social and emotional problems and display little interpersonal expression. As seen by others, they are not supportive or hostile to group members. When they do speak at meetings, they tend to focus on task issues. Their limited desire for social contact is usually expressed through jokes that seem to meet personal rather than group needs.

Underchosen participants are not committed to the group and tend to show interest only in their personal needs. They are relatively serious, are the most aggressive and hostile of the four types, and are not the quietest. In group meetings, they talk more than the technical and social specialists but less than the stars. Their perceived lack of importance is due primarily to ineffectiveness.

Managerial implications

These roles have several implications for managers. First, it it unlikely that all individuals can or will play the same role.[14] Some people prefer to be technical specialists, others to be social specialists. The role group members play is a function of their personalities, communication styles, levels of need satisfaction, and leadership style of the group's leaders. Second, this framework provides a useful diagnostic tool for managers when their groups are operating poorly. Managers can ask: Is the group overbalanced with the underchosen, task specialists, or social specialists? Domination by any of these three roles may lead to ineffective performance. Groups can be more effective if more members are capable of performing the star role. Third, managers may use this framework to gain insight about their own behaviors in groups. For example, if managers wonder why no one ever questions their decisions and discussions are short-lived, it could be that they're acting out the underchosen role.

Group Effectiveness

Much of this chapter focuses on making groups more effective. Thus we need to know how to recognize effective and ineffective groups in the first place. In general, an effective group normally has the following characteristics.

- Members know why the group exists (they are striving to reach specific objectives).

- Members have approved guidelines or procedures for making decisions.

- Members have achieved honest and open communication among themselves.

- Members have learned to receive and give help to one another.

- Members have learned to accept and deal with conflict within the group.

- Members have learned to diagnose their processes and improve their own functioning.[15]

The degree to which one or more of these characteristics is not present determines whether—and to what extent—the group is ineffective.

GROUP-PROCESS MODEL

One of the more useful ways for describing and analyzing groups is the Homans systems model, developed by George Homans.[16] This model is useful because it

- provides some reasons why people act as they do within groups;
- provides managers with a means for diagnosing group processes within organizations;
- considers contingency factors likely to affect the processes and outputs of groups; and
- suggests how groups are likely to develop and change over time.

The Homans systems model consists of two major, but interrelated, parts: the internal system and the external system.

INTERNAL SYSTEM

The *internal system* includes the sentiments, activities, interactions, and norms that group members develop over time. Figure 15.3 suggests that these variables are interrelated; a change in one may result in a change in the others. Thus a group should be considered to be a system, not simply a sum of individual member behaviors. The way that members interact substantially influences their effectiveness as a group.

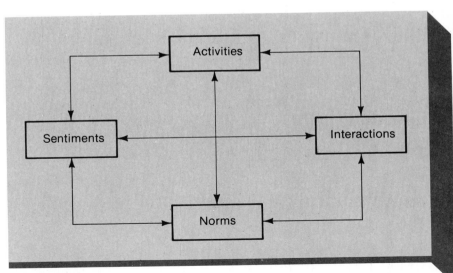

FIGURE 15.3
Internal System of a Group

ACTIVITIES

People engage in *activities* with others or with inanimate objects (machines and tools). In the Homans systems model, task behaviors—analyzing problems, evaluating alternatives, and making decisions—are part of the activities variable. In a business, task activities take up most of a manager's time. A civil engineer is likely to be most concerned with topography, soil conditions, drainage, and site preparation for construction of a building. In both cases social behaviors, such as playing cards or pitching pennies, are likely to be of secondary interest.

INTERACTIONS

Communication between two or more people involve *interactions.* This variable can be identified through such questions as:

- With whom do the group members talk?
- How often do they talk to one another?
- How long do they talk?
- Who starts the conversations?

Interactions occur in task behaviors and social behaviors.[17] By defining job responsibilities and communication channels, management strongly affects interactions in work groups. In the Preview Case, Whirlpool management created new groups that required interaction among the individuals and departments concerned with the introduction of new products, especially between those in product planning and manufacturing. Informal groups usually determine their own interaction patterns with respect to social behaviors.

SENTIMENTS

Day-to-day feelings (anger, happiness, sadness) as well as deeper feelings (openness and freedom) among group members comprise group *sentiments.* They can be thought of as the emotional climate of the group. The four sentiments most likely to influence group effectiveness and productivity are trust, openness, freedom, and felt interdependence. The more these sentiments are present, the more likely it is that the work group will be effective and productive.[18]

Assessing sentiments. Table 15.1 shows a simplified questionnaire for assessing trust, openness, freedom, and felt interdependence. Take a couple of minutes and complete this questionnaire for a work group or an informal group of which you have been a member. Circle the appropriate score for each description of the four variables; then score the questionnaire (possible range is 0–15 points for each variable).

- Trust: Add point values circled for statements 1–5 = _____.
- Openness: Add point values circled for statements 6–10 = _____.

TABLE 15.1 ■ GROUP SENTIMENTS QUESTIONNAIRE

Instructions: After each of the following statements, circle the number that corresponds to your degree of agreement or disagreement with that statement. The following scale is used: SD = strongly disagree; D = disagree; A = agree; SA = strongly agree.

STATEMENTS	SD	D	A	SA
Trust				
1. Members of this group trust each other very much	0	1	2	3
2. People are playing roles in this group and not being themselves	3	2	1	0
3. Some members are afraid of the group	3	2	1	0
4. The group treats each person in the group as an important member	0	1	2	3
5. Members seem to care very much for each other as individuals	0	1	2	3
Openness				
6. Members in this group are not really interested in what others have to say	3	2	1	0
7. Members of this group tell it like it is	0	1	2	3
8. Members often express different feelings and opinions outside of the group from those they express inside	3	2	1	0
9. Members of the group are afraid to be open and honest with the group	3	2	1	0
10. We don't keep secrets here	0	1	2	3
Freedom				
11. Members do what they ought to do in this group out of a personal sense of responsibility to the group	0	1	2	3
12. This group puts excessive pressure on each member to work toward group goals	3	2	1	0
13. When decisions are being made, members quickly express their thoughts	0	1	2	3
14. The group spends a lot of energy trying to get members to do things they don't really want to do	3	2	1	0
15. Members of this group are growing and changing all the time	0	1	2	3
Felt Interdependence				
16. Everyone in this group does his or her own thing with little thought for others	3	2	1	0
17. People in this group work together as members of a team	0	1	2	3
18. We need a lot of controls here to keep the group on track	3	2	1	0
19. There is little destructive competition in this group	0	1	2	3
20. You really need to have some power if you want to get anything done in this group	3	2	1	0

Source: Adapted from J. R. Gibb, "TORI Group Self-Diagnosis Scale." In J. E. Jones and J. W. Pfeiffer (Eds.), *The 1977 Annual Handbook for Group Facilitators,* San Diego: University Associates, 1977; J. R. Gibb, *Trust: A New View of Personal and Organizational Development.* Los Angeles: Guild of Tutors Press, 1978. Used with permission.

■ Freedom: Add point values circled for statements 11–15 = _____.

■ Felt interdependence: Add point values circled for statements 16–20 = _____.

■ Grand total: Add the sentiment totals (possible range of 0–60) = _____.

The higher the scores, the more likely the group is to be effective and productive. A score of five or less for one of the variables may suggest that it is blocking group effectiveness and should be worked on. Likewise, a grand total of 20 or less suggests severe problems with group sentiments.

Interpreting your score.   The following are some interpretations of what high or low scores for each sentiment might mean. A high score for *trust* might indicate: "I trust the group. I see the group climate as trusting and as a good environment for me and other members." A low score for trust might tell you: "I distrust the group. I see members as being impersonal and playing games. I see the group as a threatening and defensive environment for me and the other group members."

A high score for *openness* may suggest: "I see the group as open and spontaneous and the members as willing to share feelings with each other." A low score for openness may suggest: "I see the group as fearful, cautious, and unwilling to show feelings and opinions, particularly if they are negative or nonsupportive."

A high score for *freedom* could reveal that: "I see the group as allowing individual choice and as a good environment for directing my energies toward desired objectives." A low score for freedom might be saying: "I see the group creating great pressures on members to conform, to do things they don't want to do, and to work toward group objectives, regardless of the significance of those objectives."

Finally, a high score for *interdependence* may be saying: "I see the group as a smoothly functioning unit, which works effectively and cooperatively." A low score for interdependence might mean: "I see the group as unable to work well as a team, and missing significant ingredients necessary for effective functioning."

The sentiments identified in the Homans systems model have a critical influence on group effectiveness. Sentiments also affect norms, activities, and interaction. For example, negative sentiments by a work group toward higher management may result in a group norm to limit the productivity of individual members.

NORMS

The informal rules of behavior that are widely shared and enforced by members of the group are its **norms.** They set standards for member behaviors under specific circumstances. Norms of work groups may define how much and how little work should be done by members, what they wear, where they eat, what kinds of jokes are acceptable, how they should feel toward the organization, and how they deal with the boss.

Criteria for norms.   Group norms exist when three criteria have been met.[19] First, there must be standards of appropriate behavior for group members. For example, members of a work group may share a norm for the amount of work they should do on their shift. However, this norm would not apply to a member's part-time job with another company. Second, members must generally agree on the norms. This does not mean that all members of a group need to fully agree. But, if most of the members have significantly different opinions about how much work is enough, the group does not have a productivity norm. Third, the members must be aware that the group supports a particular norm through a system of rewards and punishments—rewards for compliance and punishments for violations.

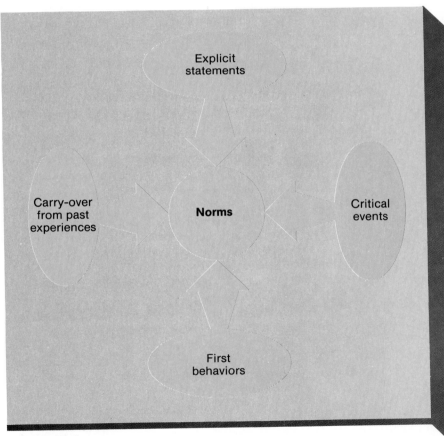

FIGURE 15.4
Development of Group Norms

Source: Adapted from D. C. Feldman, "The Development and Enforcement of Group Norms," *Academy of Management Review,* 1984, 9:50–52.

Development of norms.   Figure 15.4 suggests that most norms develop in one (or more) of four ways.[20] Superiors or co-workers may make *explicit statements* about what should or should not occur to increase the chances that the group will meet its objectives. For example, management might explicitly set a standard against smoking (except in designated areas) in a petroleum refinery because of the safety hazard. If group leaders and members accept and help enforce this standard, it becomes a group norm as well as a formal rule of the organization.

Critical events in the history of a group may lead to the formation of norms. Consider employees who are severely criticized or punished by their group after they blow-the-whistle on fellow workers or their superiors for poor quality or the misuse of the organization's assets for personal gain. The whistle-blowers are often viewed with scorn for having violated the norm of secrecy and norms concerning what may and may not be communicated to outsiders.

The *first behaviors* in new groups may emerge as norms that set future expectations and standards. For example, the initial seating arrangements of groups (committees, task forces, and quality circles) often lead to norms as to where each member is supposed to sit. This, in turn, can influence who talks to whom.

The *carry over* of behaviors that members have learned from past experiences influence the formation of norms in new situations. Students and professors do not have to create new norms as they go from class to class; they simply carry them over.

Power of norms.   The ability of a group to enforce its norms depends, in part, on the importance of the group's rewards and punishments to its members and the probability that they will be used on individual members.[21] These factors have to be considered from the point of view of group members. Individuals who value the rewards and recognize the punishments might still violate the norms if they believe they are not likely to be caught. This is especially true if they believe that the rewards for violating the norms are greater than the punishments. Take, for example, a salesperson whose work group punishes him or her (by not talking to this salesperson) for bringing in more orders than the norm. If the salesperson feels that there is little likelihood of being caught, while earning additional income, or that the norm has no personal importance, then that person will likely exceed the norm.

The importance of group rewards and punishments reflects the significance of the group to the individual. A deviant member often does not value the rewards or respect the punishments of the group and thus has little motivation to follow its norms. This is particularly true if the rewards and punishments are inconsistent with the individual's own standards. For example, a person who strongly identifies with management might be placed in a work group as part of a company's management training program. If this work group is hostile toward management and has a norm to keep production low, the trainee may still reject the norm. This individual's productivity could remain far above the norm, even though the group continues to try to punish the violator through harassment or the silent treatment.

GROUP SOCIAL STRUCTURE

As indicated by the two-directional arrows in Fig. 15.3, activities, sentiments, interactions, and norms are interrelated in a number of ways. The **group social structure** reflects the particular pattern of activities, sentiments, interactions, and norms among a group's members. The group social structure also indicates how task behaviors and social behaviors are likely to vary among the group members.

A group's social structure is determined primarily by the contribution of each member to the group's objectives, how much each member accepts the norms of the group, and the personal characteristics of each member. Figure 15.5 outlines the social structure of one group. Lori is the group leader, Dick is the deviant, four of the individuals are solid group members of equal status, and Sam is a marginal member, but not a trouble-making deviant. An analysis of a group's social structure requires an evaluation of the group leader, the group's communication patterns, and the status (differential ranking) assigned to members.

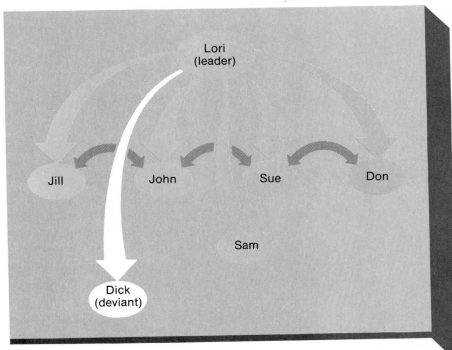

FIGURE 15.5
Group Social Structure

The impact of social structure in the day-to-day life of a group is illustrated by the following observations of group dynamics.

- An individual of higher social rank more often initiates communication with a person of lower social rank than vice versa.

- The higher an individual's social rank, the wider is the range of communication (interaction).

- The sentiments of the group leader carry greater weight than do those of the followers.

- The higher the rank of an individual within a group, the more nearly his or her activities conform to the norms of the group.

The social structure and norms of some work groups have created problems of discrimination for women and minorities. Sex-role or racial stereotyping by work groups may not give women or minorities a fair chance to demonstrate their abilities. Let us look at one flagrant case of hostile and negative racial norms.

IN PRACTICE
Ben Citchen

A black welder who endured years of racial harassment from his white co-workers was awarded a record $1.5 million in damages by the Michigan Civil Rights Commission in 1984.

One commission member said Ben Citchen's treatment at the defunct Firestone Steel Products auto-parts plant in suburban Wyandotte was "one of the most blatant and disgusting examples of discrimination" he had ever seen. The commission voted 7–0 to order Firestone to pay $1.5 million to Citchen for failing to stop the racial harassment despite his repeated pleas. Citchen, 55, now works for Ford Motor Company. In recommending approval of the award, Commission Chairman Alan May said Firestone did "little, if anything" to correct the situation.

Citchen filed his first complaint in 1971, four years after he was hired as the plant's first black. He filed a second complaint a year later, saying the harassment had grown even worse. He said at times he found dead rats, mice and fish in his locker at work, and once found nails in the shape of a cross. Twice, he said, nooses were hung in the plant, one with a note containing a racial slur. Plant officials refused to move them, so he finally did it himself.

In addition, racial slurs were scrawled on lavatory walls and other areas in the plant. Citchen's fellow employees and supervisors sometimes referred to him in racially derogatory terms, the commission report said. After he filed the first complaint, Citchen was placed on one-week disciplinary layoff for grabbing a white employee who had snapped him on the neck with a rubber band. The white employee was not disciplined. Citchen was demoted, then fired in 1976.[22]

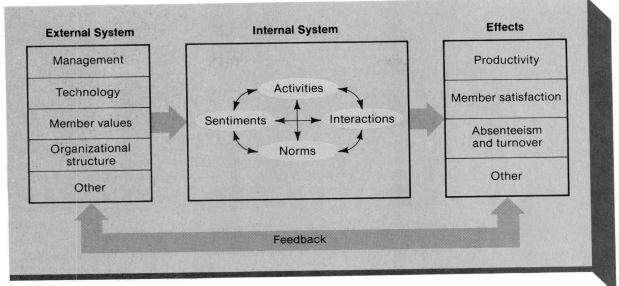

FIGURE 15.6
Basic Model of Group Process

External System

The second part of the Homans model is the external system. The *external system* includes outside conditions that existed before and after the group was formed, such as management leadership styles, technology used, member values, and organizational structure. These conditions will continue if the group ceases to function. Compared to that of gangs or friendship groups, the external system of work groups is relatively explicit.

Figure 15.6 summarizes the group-process model. It shows that the external system influences the development of the internal system. The internal system, in turn, directly impacts levels of productivity, member satisfaction, absenteeism, and turnover. These effects eventually provide feedback to the external system, which may result in action to modify the internal system. For example, low group productivity might motivate management to pressure a group for more output or to talk with group members about the productivity problem.

We can generalize about groups in the following manner, which is consistent with the group-process model.

■ If individuals continue to be together in a common situation, they develop activities, interactions, and sentiments that go beyond those that are required to do the job. Activities, interactions, and sentiments give rise to an internal system that has a social structure and norms.

■ Freedom to develop the internal system in a group is positively related to fulfillment of members' social needs, group morale, individual satisfaction, and commitment to the task.

■ Changes in the external system of a group generate changes in its internal system. The external system refers to the activities, interactions, and sentiments imposed by management and required for the group's survival.

We can illustrate the application of the group-process model with the results of a study of the sanitation department on the night shift of a food-processing plant. This study focused on the changes in the internal system of the group over a 15-month period and especially the impact of external system (management-initiated) changes on the internal system. This study is somewhat unique because it started very soon after the plant was opened and before informal groups had been formed.

IN PRACTICE
Sanitation Department of a Food-Processing Plant

EXTERNAL SYSTEM

The factory, which employed about 600 people, was the newest and most modern of those operated by a large national food corporation. The sanitation department work force varied between 50–65 employees and was divided into three work groups. We focus on one of the work groups, which had 12 members. The primary task of the department was to clean all equipment, floors, windows, and walls in the plant. The jobs were divided into two basic categories. The higher job category involved disassembling equipment for cleaning, washing the parts, and reassembling the equipment. The lower job category involved more cleaning tasks, including floors and windows. Eligibility for an assignment to the higher job category was based on seniority.

EMERGENCE OF INTERNAL SYSTEM

The new hires in the 12-person group were relatively similar—white males under 30 years of age. As they began to interact, the members became differentiated on an informal basis. Some of the members had military experience, others had traveled, one was known for his heavy drinking on weekends, and another for his self-proclaimed sexual exploits. In time, the relative skill and speed in job performance became the primary factors for placing individuals in the group's social structure. Gradually, the speed with which a member could perform his job became the dominant shared norm of the group. There was a continuing effort to improve speed, and members would even race to finish tasks. Eventually, most members could finish their work 30 minutes to an hour before quitting time. Fast workers were given high group status; slow workers, low status. Quality of work also emerged as an important basis for informal ranking. A reward for the speedy and high-quality workers was the free time at the end of the shift, when workers would relax and chat.

The supervisor did not object, so long as all of the work was done properly and the members did not flaunt their free time with other groups. Those who finished early often teased or joked in a friendly way about those not yet finished. During this initial period, the group's internal system encouraged a fairly high commitment to the job and also provided for the social needs of its members. This period lasted about six months and was characterized by a somewhat laissez-faire leadership style by the supervisor. In general, the sentiments of the group toward management were characterized by a reasonable degree of trust, openness, and freedom.

CHANGES IN EXTERNAL SYSTEM

After this initial period, several major changes in the external system disrupted the internal system and eventually led to a new internal system.

Supervisory Style Changes

A time-and-motion study was conducted on all jobs in the plant. During this study, workers tried to complete their work as fast as possible. New standards were put into effect. Top management pressured the immediate supervisor to become less considerate and more task oriented. For example, at the end of the shift, the supervisor would assign miscellaneous special projects (wiping grease off electric motors, scrubbing water hoses, cleaning light fixtures) to those who finished their regular jobs early. This change dramatically disrupted the informal social life of the group. The extra work projects were viewed as menial busy-work and extremely distasteful. The workers soon realized that speedy work was punished rather than rewarded. Workers in the higher job category complained especially bitterly.

Technological Changes

Following the change in leadership style, two technical changes were imposed by the external system. One change, developed by the quality-control department, simplified considerably the performance of certain tasks. The second change involved the installation of new equipment, which was to be cleaned by one person. Previously, two individuals were required to clean equipment. Because no time-and-motion studies had been done on cleaning this new equipment, the supervisor simply determined the time requirements by observing and questioning workers and then announced them to the group.

In response to this, the workers banded together and agreed to define the time requirements in the maximum terms they thought the supervisor would accept. The workers agreed that the cleaning of each piece of new equipment would take between one and two hours, depending on the condition of the machines. In reality, each machine could usually be cleaned within 30 minutes. However, the group was able to convince management of this time requirement and regain some of its previous freedom.

(continued)

NEW INTERNAL SYSTEM

From these informal adaptations to the external system, a new primary norm and ranking system developed within the group. This norm emphasized the need to pace the work so that it would be completed just before quitting time. The result was that very fast and very slow workers were given low informal status. Either of these patterns of work was seen as attracting unfavorable attention from the supervisor. Most of those who had been fast workers adapted successfully by slowing their pace and retaining their high status.

The new, informal patterns could not provide nearly so well for the purely social and recreational needs of the group. Group horseplay was practically eliminated, and the lively and boisterous conversations involving the entire group took place less often. The decline in morale and satisfaction was apparent. The sentiments of the group toward management definitely had shifted toward low levels of trust, openness, and freedom.[23]

MANAGERIAL IMPLICATIONS

Several managerial implications can be identified in the group process model and the sanitation department experience. The primary ones have to do with worker freedom, the need to diagnose both systems, and encouragement of constructive norms.

GIVE SOME FREEDOM

Individuals in industrial work groups may exert a greater effort to reach management's objectives if they are allowed some freedom in doing their jobs. Conversely, if group freedom is sharply curtailed, members may well reduce their commitment to formal organizational objectives. Groups may continue to perform satisfactorily but with minimal commitment, which does not result in productivity gains.

DIAGNOSE BOTH SYSTEMS

Managers can understand and predict the actions of a group only by diagnosing both the internal and external systems. The main contribution of the group-process model is that it provides a mental map for managers to use in making these diagnoses. The statements illustrating the relationships among sentiments, interactions, activities, and social structure are useful in suggesting the patterns of behavior to be expected in groups. For example, managers who issue orders that are inconsistent with group norms (such as changing the dress code of employees) may well face united groups demanding that the orders be changed. Or, if managers try to change or eliminate established communication patterns, the consequences may range from complaints to increased absenteeism and turnover.

Encourage constructive norms

Managers can provide effective leadership by encouraging the establishment of group norms that support organizational objectives. Where there is reciprocal interdependence (as on a basketball team), effective managers increase the use of group rewards rather than emphasize individual rewards. These rewards could be in the form of praise and recognition to the group as a whole or even a compensation system based on group production.

THREE KEY CONTINGENCIES

Three key contingencies warrant special attention from managers when they are considering whether a group approach is appropriate and, if so, the likelihood that the group will be effective. These contingencies are the nature of the task, group size, and role of the group leader.

Nature of Task

One of the most important factors in determining whether an individual or group approach should be used is the nature of the task. Some form of group process is desirable when one or more of the following conditions exists.

- Members have various bits of information that must be brought together to produce a solution, such as developing a new product.
- Members have skills and knowledge that need to be pooled in dealing with unstructured and complex tasks, such as how to reduce labor costs during the coming year.
- Members have different ideas about the best means for dealing with a problem or task, and their acceptance of the chosen solution is critical to effective implementation.

These conditions and others were presented as *diagnostic questions* in the discussion of the Vroom–Yetton decision model (Chapter 13). The belief that nonmanagerial employees can effectively contribute to such tasks through a group process has been recognized by the creation of quality circle programs in a number of firms.

Quality circles

A *quality circle* is usually a group of 3–12 employees from the same work area who voluntarily meet on a regular basis to identify, analyze, and solve problems related to their work.[24] Meetings are usually held once a week for about an hour during company time or on a paid overtime basis. The members of quality circles are normally given eight or more hours of formal training in decision making and group processes that apply to problems affecting their task assignments. Some of the guidelines for effective quality circles include:

- The circle should consist of a leader, a recorder, and members.
- The circle should have the authority to call on expert resource people from within the organization to help in its efforts at problem solving.
- The members should agree to set objectives for the coming year within three months of circle establishment and to revise these objectives on a yearly basis.
- Members should agree to contribute their leadership abilities to the circle.
- Decisions should be made by consensus, and enough time should be allowed to discuss all the issues thoroughly.
- All conflicts that may arise among members or between the circle and others should be discussed openly.[25]

Quality circles usually deal with the following types of issues: product and service quality, productivity, working conditions, safety, tools and equipment, work methods and procedures, communication, and the like. Quality circles normally do *not* discuss issues such as wages and salaries, personalities, hiring or firing, and disciplinary actions. The introduction of quality circles has been a rocky road in some companies.

IN PRACTICE
Quality Circles
at GM

Management and workers at the GM Chevrolet plant in Adrian, Michigan (southwest of Detroit), are now trying to make quality circles work for the third time. The factory supplies GM with plastic parts, such as fan shrouds and dashboards.

General Motors first attempted to introduce quality circles at Adrian in 1977. In the process, management broke most of the rules for how to get employees behind such a program. For starters, it failed to enlist the support of the local chapter of the United Auto Workers (UAW). It also neglected to train both workers and supervisors in how the circles were supposed to work. According to Charles Sower, president of the union local, workers soon quit the circles in disgust.

A second attempt to get the circles going began somewhat more auspiciously in 1979, with meetings for all employees at the local Holiday Inn. Meals and, on the last night, an open bar were inducements to a good turnout. However, this time management focused on what might, to dignify them, be called human-resource issues. Union official Sower describes the problem: "You might understand why your foreman was in a bad temper, but what were you supposed to do about it?" The circle meetings, to quote Sower, became "bitch sessions that discussed garbage like how far it was to walk to the parking lot." Predictably, this round of circles petered out, too.

It wasn't until 1981 that management and the UAW jointly presented a well-planned program with solid training for managers and workers on how to make employee participation groups, as they are known throughout GM, achieve practical results. Circle members were taught how to raise issues, how to discuss them amicably, and how to implement their ideas. Sower admits that he initially "thought it was a bunch of crap," and the new plant manager, Fred Meissinger, says he was more comfortable with the old-style, more adversarial approach, but both men decided to give it a chance. Instead of complaining about parking, workers sat down to discuss things like how to improve a troublesome conveyor belt. Two years later many of the original groups are still talking productively.

The only problem now is that the union is split over whether the circles should continue. While Sower wholeheartedly backs the experiment, two of the five members of the union's shop committee won office recently on a platform of old-style hostility to management. Sower now says he feels reluctant to show his face in the union office. The future of quality circles at the Adrian plant is by no means guaranteed.[26]

There have been many failures and successes in the use of quality circles. The preliminary research contrasting the successes and failures suggests that management style, commitment through all levels of management, and the broader organizational culture are the most important determinants of quality circle use and effectiveness.[27] Note the discussion of the evolution of Toyota's quality circles in the International Focus on pp. 540–541. At Toyota, quality circles are called quality-control circles. The contrasting forces that work against their effectiveness at GM and for their effectiveness at Toyota are obvious.

Group Size

The rationale for having a maximum of 12 members—preferably less—in quality circles is indicated by the second contingency factor: group size.

Effects of Size

As group size increases, a number of changes occur in group processes and performance. The critical points of change seem to be at from 7–12

INTERNATIONAL FOCUS

Evolution of Quality Circles at Toyota

Toyota's philosophy regarding the jobsite has changed a lot over the years. My father, Kiichiro Toyoda, founder of Toyota Motor Company, told me that in the days before Toyota moved into automobile production, skilled plant workers regarded themselves as craftsmen and would never share the secrets of their trade. Learning a trade was thus largely done by "stealing" the secrets of the skilled workers. That thinking gradually changed after the war, with the spread in Japan of the QC (quality control) policy first learned from the United States. QC circles comprised of workers from the same jobsite would meet, everyone would share ideas, and improvements would be discussed and introduced. This phenomenon was not limited to Toyota. It was a nationwide trend in Japan.

On the subject of Toyota's philosophy, let me mention Naoichi Saito, a former chairman of Toyota Motor Company. He was the first college graduate employed by Toyoda Automatic Loom Works. Up to then, Sakichi Toyoda, my grandfather and the founder of Toyoda Automatic Loom Works, felt that

Source: Excerpted from an interview with Toyota Motor Company president S. Toyoda. S. Yamamoto, "Emphasizing the Worker at the Jobsite: The Spirit of Autonomy and Reform," *Wheel Extended*, 1984, **14**(1):12–18.

members. In larger groups, it becomes increasingly difficult for the members to communicate (interact) with each other. In general, *as group size increases:*

- Demands on the leader are greater and the leader is more differentiated from the membership at large.

- The group's tolerance of direction from the leader is greater and the proceedings become more centralized.

- Ordinary members tend to inhibit their participation and the group's discussion becomes less exploratory and adventurous.

- The group atmosphere is less friendly, the actions are more impersonal, and the members in general are less satisfied.

- More subgroups (coalitions) form within the membership and the group's rules and procedures become more formalized.[28]

Managerial implications

These findings suggest that managers can influence group performance by controlling group size. For intensive decision making, the ideal size is from about 5–12 members.[29] If a group has 20 or more members, the manager should break it into smaller groups. This will help all members to share in

anyone with a college education was useless. Saito was hired not as a college graduate, but as one of the plant workers. In those days the foremen, men with long experience in plant operations, were more influential than college graduates. This might be called a characteristic of Toyota.

The situation in Toyota was pretty much like that when quality control thinking reached Japan from the United States after the war. Quality control primarily stressed that work scheduled to be done should be done well. At the same time the QC thinking was being assimilated in Japan, it was enhanced by the idea of making further quality improvements through talks by everyone at the jobsite. That idea led to the establishment of QC circle activities.

QC circles were thus first realized in Japan, although they have recently found their way back to the United States. It's interesting, though, that the idea of doing the work that has been chosen, and doing it right, did not describe the plants of Japan in earlier years. In fact, it's still not easy to have it done right, even now.

the process of analyzing task-related information. The larger group can then be used to discuss subgroup recommendations.

The manager of a large group needs to recognize the existence of several subgroups or cliques, each with its own informal leader. Although more potential resources may be available in large groups, these resources could have negative effects on overall group performance if each subgroup focuses on lobbying for its own solution. In addition, it usually is necessary to use some type of formal procedure, such as Robert's Rules of Order, to keep the agenda moving in large decision-making groups. Voting is often used to reach agreement in large groups. Unfortunately, merely voting may not reveal the intensity of member feelings, either positive or negative.

Large group meetings may be efficient when a manager's primary purpose is to communicate, interpret, or reinforce new policies, procedures, plans, and the like. With an adequate opportunity for questions and answers, the manager's objective to inform can be satisfied.

A manager's behavior in small-group sessions needs to be substantially different from that in large-group sessions. With small groups, a more person-centered style of leadership is effective. With large groups, a more directive, task-oriented style is necessary.

At annual sales meetings, organizations motivate members during large group sessions, while breaking into smaller groups to update members on shifts in corporate strategies.

Source: Richard Wood/The Picture Cube.

Role of the Leader

Group leaders should not reject or promote ideas according to their personal needs. They must be receptive and accept member contributions without evaluation. Good group leaders summarize information to facilitate integration, stimulate discussion, create awareness of problems, and detect when the group is ready to resolve differences and agree to a unified solution.[30] In terms of the Vroom–Yetton model, this behavior would represent the number 5 style of leadership. You may recall that member participation is extremely high under this leadership style.

This type of role may be strange to some managers. It certainly is not consistent with the popular image of what it means to be a leader.[31] Three important aspects of group leadership focus on management of disagreement, time, and change.

DISAGREEMENT

A skillful group leader can create an atmosphere for disagreement that stimulates innovative solutions. At the same time, the leader must minimize the risk that some members will leave the group with bitter feelings, especially if they are responsible for implementing group decisions. Disagreements can be managed if the leader permits differences within the group, delays the reaching of a decision, and separates idea generation from idea evaluation. This last technique makes it less likely that an alternative solution will be perceived as belonging to one individual rather than to the group.

TIME

A group leader must strike a proper balance between permissiveness and control. Rushing through a group session can prevent full discussion of the problems and lead to negative feelings. On the other hand, unless the leader keeps the discussion moving, members will become bored and arrive at poor solutions. Unfortunately, leaders often tend to push for an early solution because of time constraints. This often ends discussion before the full potential of the group has been realized.

CHANGE

When there are disagreements in a group, some members have to change their minds for the group to reach a consensus. This can be either an asset or a liability. If members offering the best alternatives are persuaded to change, the outcome suffers. The leader plays an important role in protecting individuals with a minority view by discouraging others from expressing hostility toward them. The leader also can give persons with a minority view the chance to influence the majority position. This can be done by keeping the minority view before the group, encouraging communication about that view, and reducing misunderstanding.

ORGANIZATIONAL CULTURE

Several of the basic notions about groups carry over to the concept of *organizational culture.* Organizational culture reflects the generally shared organization-wide patterns of: (1) values, norms, and sentiments; and (2) practices, activities, and interactions. They are demonstrated, reinforced, and communicated to current employees, new employees, and outsiders.[32] However, these patterns may be unstated and the members may even be unaware of them in the sense of being able to consciously verbalize them.[33] Let us take a look at the organizational culture of one firm—Trimac Limited—a trucking, energy, service, and construction company headquartered in Calgary, Alberta, Canada.

IN PRACTICE
Trimac Limited

Trimac Limited is Canada's largest hauler of bulk commodities and is a contract driller for oil and gas in Canada, the United States, and Europe. Its subsidiary companies are involved in waste management, construction, and energy investment. In 1984, Trimac had 4300 employees and was picked by *Canadian Business* magazine (based on an informal survey) as an exceptionally fine place to work and as a firm that was consistently as or more profitable than its competitors.

A big event for employees of Trimac is its annual Calgary Stampede bash. It starts with breakfast and music in the lobby of the company's luxurious 23-story headquarters, followed by lunch and a cabaret in a nearby hotel.

Such morale-boosting events are all very well when a firm is profitable. But what happens when the company is losing money, as Trimac did—to the tune of $1.7 million—last year? Trimac staged the $5,000 event anyway. Later that year, in the depths of Calgary's depression, it also picked up the $10,000 tab for the employees' Christmas party. And when layoffs swept the oil industry, Trimac tried to soften the impact by offering part-time jobs or lesser positions to some employees. Everyone took salary cuts, including top management.

Mervin Blahey, operations manager for M.B.I. Data Services Ltd., a Trimac subsidiary, notes that shareholders didn't get their usual free lunch at this year's annual meeting. He thinks it's typical that Trimac would rather cut out frills for the shareholders than trim employee benefits. "You get a feeling of togetherness here," he says.

Trimac president Tony Vanden Brink says his firm's pay scales are above the industry average. Trimac's policy is to be in the top 40 percent of the pay scale. "But pay alone doesn't tell the story," he says. "The key is participation. Everyone can be heard. Anyone in the company can talk to Bud McCaig [the chairman and CEO]."

When a Trimac employee is in trouble, the company usually goes out of its way to help. One employee, back in Calgary after an overseas posting, looked so ill that his co-workers feared that he was dying. Local efforts to diagnose his illness failed. Vanden Brink took one look at the employee and sent him, at company expense, to a tropical-disease clinic in England, where the bug was found and conquered.

But what employees really like about Trimac, even more than its Stampede bashes, is its policy of promoting from within. When Trimac needs to fill a vacant position, it looks first to its own staff. "When we go outside, it's an exception rather than the rule," says Vanden Brink. Thanks to that policy, Merrill Nelson is one of Calgary's few women contract administrators. She quit a go-nowhere job as a secretary to join Kenting Drilling, a Trimac subsidiary, in 1964. She started as a clerk-stenographer and worked her way up. So did payroll supervisor Judy Hart, who started as a payroll clerk. "We don't have any secretaries at Kenting," says Nelson, who, like everyone else, does her own typing. "They've given women opportunities in the company, and that's why they stay. The same applies out on the drilling rigs. We don't hire rig managers; we develop them through the system."

For managers, Trimac is a good place to work because its decision making is decentralized. For example, each of the 35 branch managers at Trimac Transportation Systems Ltd., the trucking subsidiary, is "running his own little business," says Bob Algar, vice-president of personnel and industrial relations for the trucking company. Algar left a good job at Alcan Aluminium Ltd. because he figured that in a smaller company he'd have a chance "to influence the bottom line."

"Work is work, but sometimes it feels like one big family here," says Theresa Munch, secretary to Vanden Brink and executive vice-president Donald Jackson. "I know what I do will get thanks from my bosses—and my raises reflect my accomplishments."[34]

The pattern of norms, sentiments, and interactions that cut across the hierarchy, departments, and strategic business units of Trimac show that it has a strong organizational culture. As in the case of small groups, organizational cultures don't just happen; they are cultivated by management, learned by employees, passed on to new employees, and change (but not easily) over time. Where well-developed organizational cultures exist, distinctions between formal and informal groups are often blurred; that is, there is much less separation between formal rules, activities, sentiments, and interactions and informally held norms, activities, sentiments, and interactions.

CREATION AND TRANSMISSION

We could write an entire book about how organizational cultures are created and transmitted. Thus we can only highlight here some of the ways that organizational cultures are created and transmitted. Table 15.2 highlights six of these ways. It also suggests that top management plays a pivotal role in

TABLE 15.2 ■ SOME WAYS OF CREATING AND TRANSMITTING ORGANIZATIONAL CULTURES

- Socialization (role modeling, teaching, and coaching) by leaders (especially top management).
- Importance of what leaders pay attention to, measure, and control.
- Leaders' reactions to critical incidents and organizational crises.
- Design of the social structure (choice of formal structure, allocation of power and rewards, perceived criteria for selection, promotion, and dismissal).
- Rites and ceremonials.
- Legends and stories about key people and events.

Source: Adapted from E. H. Schein, "The Role of the Founder in Creating Organizational Culture," *Organizational Dynamics,* Summer 1983, pp. 13–28.

determining whether and what type of organizational culture is created and transmitted.[35]

Organizational philosophy

Many companies that have well-developed organizational cultures have explicit statements of philosophy. It is often stated in a formal written charter or creed. Hewlett-Packard's philosophy is presented as a preamble to its statement of corporate objectives. (See the last In Practice in Chapter 4, entitled "Theory Z at Hewlett-Packard.") We also described the H-P philosophy and organizational culture in Chapter 2 to illustrate the behavioral viewpoint of management. Recall Dave Packard's comment: "The 'H-P Spirit' is one of the company's real strengths. It is the key to productivity and to leadership. It's the key to continuing progress and success in our company." The creed for Johnson & Johnson—a statement of organizational philosophy—was presented in Table 5.5. In both of these companies, employees view these organizational philosophies as value statements intended to guide their activities, interactions, and norms of behavior.

Socialization

Strong organizational cultures generally have well-developed methods for selecting the *right types* of employees and, once selected, to *mold* them. This molding of individually held and demonstrated norms, sentiments, activities, interactions, and practices takes place in a variety of ways. An obvious one is to show videotapes on the "H-P Way" to new employees at Hewlett-Packard. More powerful ones are the consistent role modeling, teaching, and coaching by managers—starting at the top and spreading through the organization.

Fortune magazine noted the relationship between socialization and organizational culture in these words:

> Many of the great American companies that thrive from one generation to the next—IBM, Procter & Gamble, Morgan Guaranty Trust—are organizations that have perfected their processes of socialization. Virtually none talk explicitly about socialization; they may not even be conscious of precisely what they are doing. Moreover, when one examines any particular aspect of their policy toward people—how they recruit or train or compensate—little stands out as unusual. But when the pieces are assembled, what emerges is an awesome internal consistency that powerfully shapes behavior.[36]

The socialization that takes place in an organization—explicitly and formally or implicitly and informally—can affect the types of organization-wide norms that develop. Table 15.3 presents examples of positive and negative organization-wide norms for five cluster areas of norms.

TABLE 15.3 ■ EXAMPLES OF POSITIVE AND NEGATIVE ORGANIZATION NORMS

	EXAMPLES	
CLUSTER AREA	*Positive Norm*	*Negative Norm*
Norms of organizational and personal pride	Around here people stand up for the company when others criticize it.	Around here people aren't really concerned with the company's problems.
Norms of performance/excellence	People always try to improve, even when they are doing well.	People are often satisfied with the routine or mediocre.
Norms of teamwork/communication	Around here people are good listeners and actively seek out the ideas and opinions of others.	Around here people talk about others behind their backs rather than confronting issues openly and constructively.
Norms of customer relations	Most of us feel that the customer is No. 1.	Most employees feel their convenience comes first. The customers can wait.
Norms of innovation and change	Around here you get a lot of recognition for new ideas.	Don't have an idea around here that your boss didn't have first.

Source: Adapted from R. F. Allen and S. Pilnick, "Confronting the Shadow Organization: How to Detect and Defeat Negative Norms," *Organizational Dynamics*, Spring 1973, pp. 2–18.

Rites and ceremonials

A *rite* refers to a relatively elaborate and planned set of dramatic expressions carried out through an event. A *ceremonial* is a system of several rites that take place at a single event.[37] For example, a commencement program at most universities and colleges is a ceremonial. A number of rites take place at commencement, including procession of faculty and honored guests, procession of graduates, invocation, statement of welcome, commencement speaker, awarding of diplomas (including calling off names, walking across stages, shaking of hands), and so on.

The Calgary Stampede bash and the Christmas party are two well-established ceremonies at Trimac Limited. You will recall that the company felt that these ceremonies were so important that they were held even during a year when the firm lost $1.7 million. These types of ceremonies are often used to build and reinforce positive sentiments and attitudes. Remember the comment of Mervin Blahey, a Trimac operations manager: "You get a feeling of togetherness here."

Legends and stories

A *legend* is a handed-down narrative of some great event that is based on historical fact but has been embellished with fictional details. A *story* is a narrative based on true events, often a combination of truth and fiction.[38] Legends and stories that are passed on by company storytellers help maintain cohesion and guidelines for employees to follow. These storytellers may even tell much of what it takes to get ahead in the organization.

IN PRACTICE
Legend of the Wild Ducks

Thomas Watson, Jr., son of IBM's founder, often told a story about a nature lover who liked watching the wild ducks fly south in vast flocks each October. Out of charity, he took to putting feed for them in a nearby pond. After a while, some of the ducks no longer bothered to fly south; they wintered in the pond on what he fed them. In time they flew less and less. After three or four years, they grew so fat and lazy that they found it difficult to fly at all. Watson had discovered this story in the writings of Danish philosopher Soren Kierkegaard. And he always ended it with the point that you can make wild ducks tame, but you can never make tame ducks wild again. Watson would further add that "the duck who is tamed will never go anywhere anymore. We are convinced that business needs its wild ducks. And in IBM we try not to tame them."

Watson told this story again and again to impress upon people the value of deviance and the tolerance for "outlaw heroes" in a company well known for its conformity and standardized ways. Once, however, an employee reportedly told Watson that "even wild ducks fly in formation." This rejoinder quickly became part of the wild-ducks story precisely because it makes another important point about the culture: we're all going in the same direction.[39]

Legends and stories can reveal and reinforce core values and norms of the organization. Consider the mostly true story about David Packard, co-founder of Hewlett-Packard. An engineer in the H-P Palo Alto lab constructed a prototype from inferior terminals. Dave Packard came upon the model after hours. He crushed the prototype to bits and left a note that stated: "That's not the H-P way. [signed] Dave." The story of this event spread rapidly. By the end of the next day, most of the people in H-P had heard the story.[40] This single event gave powerful reinforcement to H-P's belief in high quality.

Managerial Implications

Managers—especially top managers—are constantly faced with the need to determine which attributes of organizational culture should be preserved and which need modification. In Chapter 21, Organizational Change, we consider a variety of approaches and issues involved in changing organizations. Thus in this section we review only a few of the things that management can do to maintain or change organizational culture.[41]

Set the example

Top management cannot delegate responsibility for creating and transmitting an organizational culture *if* they desire one. The strongest influences on culture formation are the day-to-day activities, interactions, sentiments, and norms of top management as they are perceived throughout the organization.

Articulate values

In order to maintain or change organizational culture, it is usually desirable for managers to explicitly communicate and reinforce values, norms, and sentiments that are important to the organization. These are clearly communicated through promotions, awards, pay raises, appointments to key committees, and other visible expressions.

Socialize

Managers should be aware that it is possible to mold—within limits—how employees think, feel, and act within the organization. In the United States, with its emphasis on individualism, the process of socialization in firms like H-P and IBM blends the need for individuality with the need for a group and organizational consciousness. There is a strong effort to create a sense of unity without uniformity or blind conformity.

Don't underestimate

Don't underestimate the power of rites, ceremonials, legends, and stories in maintaining or changing organizational culture.[42] The cultural changes required as a result of AT&T's divestiture have been dramatic.[43] Many employees expressed feelings of anger and sorrow. The feeling of intense personal loss was noted by one employee in these words: "It was like waking up in familiar surroundings, but your family and all that you held dear were missing."[44] Such is the potential power of a strong organizational culture.

CHAPTER SUMMARY

Many of the decisions made by managers occur in group settings. Moreover, many of the problems and opportunities for managerial achievement occur within groups. Regardless of their personal preferences, managers must contend with groups—as leaders as well as members. The necessity of working with and through others in group settings at all levels of the organization is increasingly recognized by top managers. For example, "There is a definite trend these days toward fewer and fewer followers," says George S. Dively, honorary chairman of Harris Corporation and one of the business community's most respected elder statesmen. He adds, "Everyone wants to be part of the action."[45]

Informal and formal groups are inevitable in organizations. Their impacts on organizations and their own members' behaviors are wide-ranging. Groups can be a source of resistance and antagonism from the manager's point of view, or they can supplement the formal motivational and control system by reinforcing quality and quantity performance standards.

A number of guidelines were presented to help managers diagnose and use groups more effectively. These guidelines can be used to identify (1) the major factors that must be evaluated by managers when interacting with groups; and (2) the probable consequences of using different approaches to group decision making. The Homans systems model was suggested as an excellent aid for diagnosing groups. The interplay between the external and internal system of a group was demonstrated. The key variables in the internal system include activities, interactions, sentiments, and norms. Members of groups often do not engage in the same behaviors or have the same status. This was examined in the discussions of group social structure and four major types of individual roles within groups: so-

cial specialists, stars, technical specialists, and the underchosen.

Three key contingencies affect group processes and the appropriateness of using groups. These are the nature of the task, group size, and the role of the leader. Quality circles were examined as groups designed to bring the creativity and knowledge of nonmanagerial personnel to bear on problems and issues in their own task areas. We also noted the differences between the use of small and large groups.

The last major part of the chapter focused on the nature, development, and implications of organizational culture. Organizational culture is a broader and more complex concept than that of a group. However, they do have several similarities: both are concerned with norms, activities, interactions, sentiments, and social structure.

MANAGER'S VOCABULARY

activities
ceremonial
external system
formal group
group
group social structure
informal group
interactions
internal system
legend
norms
organizational culture
quality circle

REVIEW QUESTIONS

1. What are the four roles a group member can play?

2. What are the similarities and differences between a group and organizational culture?

3. What variables make up the internal system in the model of group process?

4. How can the external system impact on the internal system in the model of group process?

5. In what ways do the contingency factors of nature of the task, group size, and role of the leader impact on the process and outcomes of a group?

6. How are organizational cultures created and transmitted?

DISCUSSION QUESTIONS

1. Would you like to work in a firm with a strong and well-developed organizational culture? Why?

2. Do you think top management should try to explicitly shape and change the culture of an organization? Why?

3. On the basis of your personal experience, do you feel that the work groups to which you have belonged had desirable or undesirable effects on you and the organization? Explain.

4. How well did your last superior help you meet the emotional problems often experienced when entering a new group? What steps did he or she take or fail to take to reduce emotional problems?

5. Joe described his work group as ". . . friendly, just great. All the guys get along together, and we bowl and play softball after work." However, production records show that Joe's group is one of the poorest in the plant. Why might this be?

MANAGEMENT INCIDENTS AND CASES

DIANE'S NEW WORK GROUPS

Diane Hall is a 27-year-old graduate of a respected business school, married, with one six-year-old child. She has previously been employed by a clothing manufacturer in an administrative capacity and has recently changed jobs to accept a position as assistant production manager for a competitor. The company she is joining has a reputation for male dominance in managerial positions, and in fact she is the first woman that has been hired in a management capacity. She shares responsibility with Jim Booth, another assistant production manager and with him shares the services of a 41-year-old secretary, Penny Barrows. Both Diane and Jim report to Frank Murphy, the corporation Production Manager.

Upon her arrival Diane had been shown around the corporate headquarters, had a tour of the main plant, had her duties and responsibilities explained, and was told the normal administrative channels for report processing and the like. It was still her first day when Penny told her that Frank Murphy would like to see her in his office in fifteen minutes to welcome her to the company.

After reporting to Frank and surviving the momentary shared embarrassment of whether to shake hands or simply say hello (the alternative they took), Frank welcomed her to the firm, and told her of corporate goals and plans for the future. Frank had been cordial if a bit aloof, and as the interview was concluding made the following statement:

> Diane, as you must be aware, you are the first woman the company has hired at the management level. We really evaluated your qualifications in detail and are confident that we made the right choice. The fact that we have been under a great deal of pressure to hire women was not the deciding factor in your getting the job but I must advise you that you will be closely watched by your male associates. I'm sure you'll do a great job and will do well not only for the company but also will be the example the company needs to increase the number of women it employs. Good Luck.

Now, after seven months of employment, Diane has had the opportunity to evaluate where she is and where she is going. She feels she has performed well but is getting "bad vibes" about her position in the organization. She recalls that most of her associates tended to be politely helpful as she felt her way in the company but there was almost a condescending air about their actions. Jim Booth, her fellow assistant manager, seemed to be the point of contact for all production problems whether in his area or hers. Subordinates always went to Jim unless he was out of town. Diane felt she handled problems correctly when they were brought to her, but when Jim returned he was again the focal point. Subordinates always referred to Jim as "Mr. Booth" but Diane was always "Diane." She also sensed a feeling of coolness from her secretary, Penny. Penny was always cordial with Jim and seemed to be open with him discussing problems or the local rumors that circulated. While Penny was always efficient with Diane she was quite formal. She always addressed her as "Mrs. Hall" and never appeared to relax around Diane. When talking to other employees about Diane, she only referred to her as "she" or "her."

Diane has also noted that while Frank Murphy has been supportive, and not overcritical, he seems slightly ill at ease when he is around her. She has certainly been given enough meaningful work to keep her very busy, but the really complex problems that affect production goals and procedures invariably fall to Jim Booth regardless of who is responsible. Her dealings with outside plants have been isolated to those that are reasonably close with Jim pulling all the longer and more distant trips.

After considering all that has occurred, Diane feels that her career progression is being hindered. She is sure that sexual discrimination is standing in her way, and has made an appointment with Frank Murphy to discuss the situation. At the meeting Frank has commended her on the work she has done, told her how glad the company is to have her, and encourages her to continue to perform well. He then asks, "Well, Diane, what's on your mind?"[46]

Questions

1. To the extent possible, you should diagnose this case through the use of the group-process model. What are the indicators of the internal system in terms of activities, interactions, sentiments, norms, and social structure?

2. What is the external system in this case? Is this external system reinforcing or attempting to change the internal system?

3. What is the best way for Diane to present her case and feelings to Frank Murphy?

4. What can Diane do to change the group social structure in which she finds herself?

REFERENCES

1. Excerpted from "When Engineers Talk to Each Other—the Slow but Sure Payoff," *International Management*, July 1984, pp. 26–27. Reprinted with special permission from *International Management*. Copyright © by McGraw-Hill Publications Company. All rights reserved.

2. W. C. Swap and Associates (Eds.), *Group Decision Making*. Beverly Hills, Calif.: Sage, 1984; R. W. Napier and M. K. Gershenfeld, *Groups: Theory and Experience*, 3rd ed. Boston: Houghton Mifflin, 1985.

3. H. Meyer, "The Meeting-Goer's Lament," *Fortune*, August 1979, pp. 94–102; R. F. Vancil and C. H. Green, "How CEOs Use Top Management Committees," *Harvard Business Review*, January–February 1984, pp. 65–73.

4. Meyer, p. 95. *Also see:* G. W. Soden, "Avoid Meetings or Make Them Work," *Business Horizons*, March–April 1984, pp. 47–49.

5. G. Miller, "Living Systems: The Group," *Behavioral Science*, 1971, **16**:302–398; A Fuhreman, S. Dreschler, and G. Burlingame, "Conceptualizing Small Group Process," *Small Group Behavior*, 1984, **15**:427–440.

6. A. S. Grove, "How (and Why) To Run a Meeting," *Fortune*, July 1983, pp. 132–134ff; R. Wilkinson, "Is This Meeting Really Necessary?" *Industry Week*, September 3, 1984, p. 61.

7. P. Bernstein, "Workplace Democratization: Its Internal Dynamics," *Organization and Administrative Sciences*, 1976, 7:1–127.

8. N. Yamaki, "Productivity: Japanese Style—Small Group Activities in Mitsubishi Electric Corporation," *Management Japan*, Autumn 1984, pp. 10–18.

9. R. H. Guest, "Quality of Work Life: Japan and America Contrasted," *The Wheel Extended*, 1983, 13(4):8–14. *Also see:* A. Zander, "The Values Be-

longing to a Group in Japan," *Small Group Behavior,* 1983, **14**:3–14.

10. N. Maier, "Assets and Liabilities in Group Problem-Solving: The Need for an Integrative Function," *Psychology Review,* 1967, **74**:239–249; S. Hart, M. Boroush, G. Fink, and W. Hornick, "Managing Complexity through Consensus Mapping: Technology for the Structuring of Group Decisions," *Academy of Management Review,* July 1985, **10**:587–600; D. Tjosvold and R. H. Field, "Effects of Social Context on Consensus and Majority Vote Decision Making," *Academy of Management Journal,* 1983, **26**:500–506.

11. S. Stumpf, D. Zand, and R. Freedman, "Designing Groups for Judgmental Decisions," *Academy of Management Review,* 1979, **4**:589–600; S. Stumpf, R. Freedman, and D. Zand, "Judgmental Decisions: A Study of the Interactions among Group Membership, Group Functioning, and the Decision Situation," *Academy of Management Journal,* 1979, **22**:765–782.

12. J. P. Wanous, A. E. Reichers, and S. D. Malik, "Organizational Socialization and Group Development: Toward an Integrative Perspective," *Academy of Management Review,* 1984, **9**:670–683; C. R. Leana, "A Partial Test of Janis' Groupthink Model: Effects of Group Cohesiveness and Leader Behavior on Defective Decision Making," *Journal of Management,* 1985, **11**:5–17.

13. D. Moment and A. Zaleznik, *Role Development and Interpersonal Competence: An Experimental Study of Role Performance in Problem-Solving Groups.* Boston: Division of Research, Graduate School of Business Administration, Harvard University, 1963, pp. 10–18.

14. R. F. Bales, *Personality and Interpersonal Behavior.* New York: Holt, Rinehart, and Winston, 1970; S. L. Obert, "Developmental Patterns of Organizational Task Groups: A Preliminary Study," *Human Relations,* 1983, **36**:37–52.

15. L. Bradford and D. Mial, "When Is a Group?" *Educational Leadership,* 1963, **21**:147–151; K. A. Brown, "Explaining Group Poor Performance: An Attributional Analysis," *Academy of Management Review,* 1984, **9**:54–63; J. R. Hackman, *A Normative Model of Work Team Effectiveness.* Technical Report 2, Research Program on Group Effec-

tiveness, Yale School of Organization and Management, November 1983; J. Krantz, "Group Process Under Conditions of Organizational Decline," *Journal of Applied Behavioral Science,* 1985, **21**:1–18.

16. G. Homans, *The Human Group.* New York: Harcourt, Brace, 1950; G. Homans, *Social Behavior: Its Elementary Forms.* New York: Harcourt, Brace, 1961.

17. A. P. Hare, *Creativity in Small Groups.* Beverly Hills, Calif.: Sage, 1982; D. J. Brass, "Men's and Women's Networks: A Study of Interaction Patterns and Influence in an Organization," *Academy of Management Journal,* 1985, **28**:327–343.

18. J. Gibb, "TORI Theory and Practice." In J. W. Pfeiffer and J. Jones (Eds.), *The 1977 Annual Handbook for Group Facilitators.* La Jolla, Calif.: University Associates, 1977.

19. A. Athos and R. Coffey, *Behavior in Organizations: A Multidimensional View.* Englewood Cliffs, N.J.: Prentice-Hall, 1975.

20. D. C. Feldman, "The Development and Enforcement of Group Norms," *Academy of Management Review,* 1984, **9**:47–53. *Also see* J. L. Pearce and R. H. Peters, "A Contradictory Norms View of Employer–Employee Exchange," *Journal of Management,* 1985, **11**:19–30.

21. J. Davis, *Group Performance.* Reading, Mass.: Addison-Wesley, 1969.

22. "Man Wins $1.5 Million Bias Award," *Houston Chronicle,* May 24, 1984, Section 1, p. 6. *Also see:* J. Farley (Ed.), *The Woman in Management: Career and Family Issues.* Ithaca, N.Y.: ILR Press, 1983.

23. Adapted from: D. Johnson, "Social Organization of an Industrial Work Group: Emergence and Adaptation to Environmental Change," *Sociological Quarterly,* 1974, **15**:109–126.

24. H. B. Karp, "A Look at Quality Circles." In L. D. Goodstein and J. W. Pfeiffer (Eds.), *The 1983 Annual for Facilitators, Trainers, and Consultants.* San Diego: University Associates, 1983, pp. 157–163; G. Munchus III, "Employer–Employee Based Quality Circles in Japan: Human Resource Policy Implications for American Firms," *Academy of Management Review,* 1983, **2**:255–261; A. Korn, C. La Morte, M. K. Delmont, "Full Circle-Quality

Circle," *Journal of Creative Behavior*, 1984, 3:205–212.

25. L. Fitzgerald and J. Murphy, *Installing Quality Circles: A Strategic Approach*. San Diego: University Associates, 1982, pp. 113–115. *Also see:* S. G. Goldstein, "Organizational Dualism and Quality Circles," *Academy of Management Review*, July 1985, 10:504–517; G. W. Meyer and R. G. Scott, "Quality Circles. Panacea or Pandora's Box," *Organizational Dynamics*, Spring 1985, pp. 35–50.

26. Adapted from J. Main, "The Trouble with Managing Japanese-Style," *Fortune*, April 2, 1984, pp. 50–52ff. Copyright © Time, Inc. All rights reserved.

27. B. G. Dale and S. G. Hayward, "Quality Circle Failures in UK Manufacturing Companies—A Study," *OMEGA*, 1984, 12:475–484; J. D. Blair and C. J. Whitehead, "Can Quality Circles Survive in the United States?" *Business Horizons*, September–October 1984, pp. 17–23; R. E. Cole and D. S. Tachiki, "Forging Institutional Links: Making Quality Circles Work in the U.S." *National Productivity Review*, Autumn 1984, pp. 417–429; E. E. Lawler III and S. A. Mohrman, "Quality Circles after the Fad," *Harvard Business Review*, January–February 1985, pp. 65–71; M. O'Donnell and R. J. O'Donnell, "Quality Circles—The Latest Fad or a Real Winner?" *Business Horizons*, May–June, 1984, pp. 48–52; G. R. Ferris and J. A. Wagner III, "Quality Circles in the United States: A Conceptual Reevaluation," *Journal of Applied Behavioral Science*, 1985, 21:155–167.

28. B. Berelson and G. Steiner, *Human Behavior: An Inventory of Scientific Findings*. New York: Harcourt, Brace, 1964, p. 358. *Also see* R. Albanese and D. D. Van Fleet, "Rational Behavior in Groups: The Free-Riding Tendency," *Academy of Management Review*, 1985, 10:244–255.

29. G. Manners, "Another Look at Group Size, Group Problem-Solving and Member Consensus," *Academy of Management Journal*, 1975, 18:715–724.

30. N. Maier, "Assets and Liabilities in Group Problem-Solving . . . , p. 246.

31. F. Miner, "A Comparative Analysis of Three Diverse Group Decision Making Approaches," *Academy of Management Journal*, 1979, 22:81–93.

32. Adapted from H. M. Trice and J. M. Beyer, "Studying Organizational Cultures through Rites and Ceremonials," *Academy of Management Review*, 1984, 9:653–669. *Also see:* W. F. Joyce and J. W. Slocum Jr., "Collective Climate: Agreement as a Basis for Defining Aggregate Climates in Organizations," *Academy of Management Journal*, 1984, 27:721–742; Y. Allaire and M. E. Firsirotu, "Theories of Organizational Culture," *Organization Studies*, 1984, 5:193–226; N. C. Morey and F. Luthans, "Refining the Displacement of the Concept of Culture to Organizational Studies," *Academy of Management Review*, 1985, 10:219–229; L. Smircich, "Concepts of Culture and Organizational Analysis," *Administrative Science Quarterly*, 1983, 28:339–358.

33. V. Sathe, "Implications of Corporate Culture: A Manager's Guide to Action," *Organizational Dynamics*, Autumn 1983, pp. 5–23.

34. Adapted from D. Stoffman, "Great Workplaces and How They Got That Way," *Canadian Business*, September 1984, pp. 33–38.

35. E. H. Schein, "Coming to a New Awareness of Organizational Culture," *Sloan Management Review*, Winter 1984, pp. 3–16; D. R. Denison; "Bringing Corporate Culture to the Bottom Line," *Organizational Dynamics*, Autumn 1984, pp. 4–22.

36. R. Pascale, "Fitting New Employees into the Company Culture," *Fortune*, May 28, 1984, p. 28.

37. Trice and Beyer, "Studying Organizational Cultures . . . , p. 655.

38. Trice and Beyer, p. 655. *Also see:* J. Martin, M. S. Feldman, M. J. Hatch, and S. B. Sitkin, "The Uniqueness Paradox in Organizational Stories," *Administrative Science Quarterly*, 1983, 28:438–453; K. K. Smith, V. M. Simmons, "A Rumpelstiltskin Organization: Metaphors on Metaphors in Field Research," *Administrative Science Quarterly*, 1983, 28:377–392.

39. T. E. Deal and A. A. Kennedy, *Corporate Cultures: The Rites and Rituals of Corporate Life*. Reading, Mass.: Addison-Wesley, 1982, pp. 87–88.

40. T. E. Deal and A. A. Kennedy, "Culture: A New Look through Old Lenses," *Journal of Applied Behavioral Science*, 1983, 19:498–505.

41. S. M. Davis, *Managing Corporate Culture.* Cambridge, Mass.: Ballinger, 1984; F. Herzberg, "Mystery Systems Shape Loyalties," *Industry Week,* November 12, 1984, pp. 101–104; P. C. Nystrom and W. H. Starbuck, "Managing Beliefs in Organizations," *Journal of Applied Behavioral Science,* 1984, 20:277–287; W. D. Torrence, "Blending East and West: With Difficulties along the Way," *Organizational Dynamics,* Autumn 1984, pp. 23–34; A. L. Wilkins, "The Culture Audit: A Tool for Understanding Organizations," *Organizational Dynamics,* Autumn 1983, pp. 24–38; A. L. Wilkins and W. G. Ouchi, "Efficient Cultures: Exploring the Relationship between Culture and Organizational Performance," *Administrative Science Quarterly,* 1983, 28:468–481.

42. E. J. Koprowski, "Cultural Myths: Clues to Effective Management," *Organizational Dynamics,* Autumn 1983, pp. 39–51; J. Martin and C. Siehl, "Organizational Culture and Counterculture: An Uneasy Symbiosis," *Organizational Dynamics,* Autumn 1983, pp. 52–64.

43. W. B. Tunstall, "Cultural Transition at AT&T," *Sloan Management Review,* Fall 1983, pp. 15–26.

44. J. Main, "Waking Up at AT&T: There's Life After Culture Shock," *Fortune,* December 24, 1984, p. 67.

45. H. Meyer, "The Meeting-Goer's Lament," *Fortune,* August 1979, p. 94.

46. Case prepared by Dr. Kenneth A. Kovach, George Mason University. Used with permission. Copyright © 1981 by Kenneth A. Kovach.

Conflict and Stress Management

LEARNING OBJECTIVES

After studying this chapter, you should be able to:

- Describe the different views taken toward conflict.

- Diagnose four types of role conflict.

- Explain how the five interpersonal conflict styles influence a manager's effectiveness.

- State the major sources of job-related stress.

- List and give examples of five categories of the potential effects of severe negative stress.

- Describe the personal and organizational approaches for reducing negative stress and increasing a person's ability to cope with sources of stress.

CHAPTER OUTLINE

PREVIEW CASE

Pam McAllister Johnson

On a recent business trip, I read a magazine article entitled, "That's No Lady, That's My Boss." The first sentence asked, "What's more difficult than having a woman boss?" The second line answered: "Being one!" From my experience as the first black woman publisher of a general circulation newspaper, I can tell you that, while it may be difficult, it is also exciting and challenging.

As a woman executive, you have to be careful not to let others define you because they may, too often, define you in what they consciously or unconsciously think of as negative terms.* In order to be a successful executive, you have to have strong feelings of self-worth. It is especially important not to define yourself solely in terms of your job. Too many people over whom you have too little control can have a negative impact on you and your job.

A second important point is that you cannot be afraid of your own aggression or of getting angry. Sometimes women managers spend too much time worrying about hurting or alienating subordinates. Sometimes we have to be aggressive to bring about changes. But we have to learn to use our anger and our aggression constructively.

The corporation I work for has a slogan: "Do the right thing." When I first heard that, I said,

"You have got to be kidding." I could not believe that such a complex organization would have such a simplistic slogan. But people in my organization really do give one another that advice. Somebody says, "Hey, I've got a problem. What do you think I should do about it?" Some executive is likely to answer, "Do the right thing." And there is something to it. We have to look for solutions to problems in terms of what is right for the business and for us as individuals.

People constantly ask me what it is like to be black and a woman in a predominantly white male business world. In jest I reply, "I've been black for thirty-six years and a woman for thirty-six years

Source: Darlene Bordwell, Boston.

---

* I always try to keep in mind a phrase from "Desiderata": Do not compare yourself to others for you may become vain or bitter; there will always be greater and lesser persons than yourself.

and I have no problem with it." I try to explain how I feel about my "differences" by sharing the following anecdote. My first job as a journalist fifteen years ago was as a reporter for the *Chicago Tribune.* I found myself spending 75 percent of my time convincing my colleagues that it was all right for me to be a black, a female, and a reporter. I found I was letting others define and place me, placing me in a position to justify my very being. By defining myself I could be what I was hired and trained to be—a good reporter.

When I define myself as a black woman, I define those characteristics as positives, not as handicaps. I tell employers that I bring a larger perspective to the job than other people might. I have a strong and diverse educational, professional, and social background. How many publishers have worked for top print and broadcast companies? How many publishers have been totally immersed in different ethnic cultures? I have dealt with a more diverse group of people in more diverse situations than most managers. I went to an all-black elementary school, a Jewish junior high school, and a WASP high school. I had friends who were on welfare; I had some friends who were wealthy. So I would say to you that I hope you can define yourself in strong, positive statements and actions.[1]

These excerpts are from comments made by Pam McAllister Johnson, the publisher of the *Ithaca Journal,* during a conference on "Women in Management" held at Cornell University. She highlights some of the conflicts and stresses experienced in her work life and how she manages them. Johnson successfully handled a variety of work-related conflicts and stresses. This Preview Case captures two overriding themes of this chapter: (1) conflicts and stress in work, as in life, are inevitable; and (2) the employee and management play important parts in determining whether work-related conflicts and stress become destructive or are effectively managed. Work-related conflicts and stress are quite common and are dealt with in a variety of ways.

The chapter contains four major sections: (1) identification of attitudes taken toward conflict; (2) coverage of role conflict; (3) discussion of interpersonal styles of conflict; and (4) an overview of stress, including its sources, consequences, and management.

Conflict is the incompatible behaviors or interests between two or more individuals or *within* one individual. In the Preview Case, Pam McAllister Johnson implied that incompatible behaviors and interests are sometimes inevitable when she said, "Sometimes women managers spend too much time worrying about hurting or alienating subordinates." Conflicts within an individual refer to simultaneously opposing inner thoughts and sentiments to accept *and* reject something or someone—whether to get married or stay single, speak up or keep quiet, take a job or continue in school, express anger or be nice. The interplay of conflicts with others and conflicts within ourselves was conveyed by Johnson when she stated, "Sometimes we have to be aggressive to bring about changes. But we have to learn to use our anger and our aggression constructively."

Stress and anxiety are common reactions to excessive conflicts *and* other factors.[2] **Stress** is the nonspecific response of the body to any demand.[3] *Nonspecific response* simply refers to the idea that a person's body responds to a specific source of stress (heat, cold, pressure from the boss, fear) automatically (not consciously controlled). For example, heat produces sweating, cold produces shivering, and fear may produce a fight response or a flight response. Hans Selye, often regarded as the founder of stress studies, notes that stress is not something to be avoided. He comments that "Complete freedom from stress is death."[4] There are two major types of stress: *eustress* and *distress.* Eustress is pleasant or constructive stress (the positive emotions experienced after being congratulated for doing a good job). Distress is unpleasant, detrimental, or disease-producing stress. Most of the literature dealing with stress focuses on distress, as does this chapter. Some of the distress experienced by Pam McAllister Johnson in her managerial role is implied in her words, "On a recent business trip, I read a magazine article entitled, 'That's No Lady, That's My Boss.' The first sentence asked, 'What's more difficult than having a woman boss?' The second line answered: 'Being one!' From my experience as the first black woman publisher of a general circulation newspaper, I can tell you that, while it may be difficult, it is also exciting and challenging.

ATTITUDES TOWARD CONFLICT

Negative Attitude

To many people, the word *conflict* suggests negative situations—war, destruction, aggression, violence, and destructive competition. The traditional viewpoint of management typically holds that conflict is undesirable; that conflict could be reduced or eliminated through careful selection of people, training, detailed job descriptions, elaborate rules, and incentive systems. These prescriptions are still useful for reducing and preventing some undesirable conflicts but obviously are not the complete answer.

An employee who experiences frequent and high levels of conflict may show stress-based withdrawal psychologically (apathy and indifference) and physically (tardiness, absenteeism, and turnover). In other cases, aggressive and hostile behavior may result (stealing or damaging property).

From a decision-making standpoint, intense conflicts often lead to biased perceptions and gross distortions of reality.[5] In the heat of intense conflicts, we often forget to listen actively to the other person and concentrate on winning our own point, rather than mutually coming up with the best solution. The other person may come to be seen as an enemy in the conflict. These negative personal feelings can interfere with resolution of the issues that started the conflict.

Positive Attitude

Some people believe that the word *conflict* has primarily positive meanings—excitement, intrigue, adventure, and challenge. From a decision-making standpoint, conflict may result in better choices. When there are conflicting viewpoints, the reasons for each viewpoint are often better developed. Conflict can stimulate employees to search for ways to reduce or resolve their disagreements. This process often leads to innovation and change. Conflict can provide opportunities for monetary and personal rewards. For example, eustress may be experienced by employees who successfully handled conflict, achieved performance objectives, and received the related rewards.

From a control standpoint, conflict can indicate the need for adjustments in the managerial functions (planning, organizing, leading, and controlling). In addition, conflict provides managers with information about their operations and shows where corrective actions might be needed. The positive attitude toward conflict reflects the view that it is a necessary condition for the attainment of individual and organizational objectives.

Balanced Attitude

Most effective managers view conflict with a balanced attitude. They recognize that organizational conflict is a certainty; at times it may be highly desirable and at other times, destructive. These managers know that it is possible to prevent many conflicts but that many will occur and will need to be met and managed. These conflicts occur within the organization, with stakeholders, and with external individuals and groups.

Figure 16.1 illustrates the balanced attitude toward conflict. The vertical axis represents the consequences of conflict. These range from negative outcomes (loss of skilled employees, sabotage, low quality of work, personal distress) to neutral outcomes to positive outcomes (creative searches for alternatives, increased motivation and commitment, high quality of work, personal satisfaction).[6] The horizontal axis indicates the intensity of conflict experienced between individuals or *within* oneself. Intensity ranges from low to moderate to high. The horizontal dashed line approximates the division between positive and negative outcomes. The curve in Fig. 16.1 represents the general relationship between conflict outcomes and conflict intensity. This suggests that people and work settings can suffer from too little or too much conflict. *Conflict management* refers to interventions designed to reduce conflict if there is too much, or interventions to increase conflict if there is too little.[7]

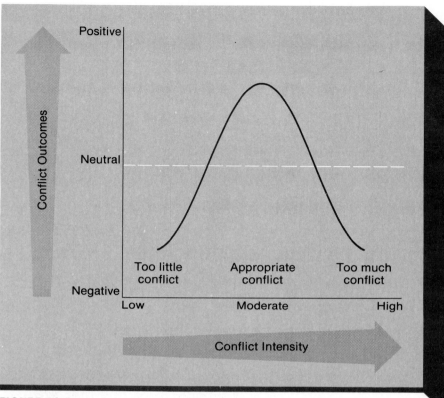

FIGURE 16.1
Balanced Attitude Toward Conflict

Source: Adapted from L. D. Brown, *Managerial Conflict at Organizational Interfaces.*
Reading, Mass.: Addison-Wesley, 1984, p. 8. Adapted and used with permission.

ROLE CONFLICT[8]

Role and Role Set

A *role* is a group of related activities carried out by an individual. Roles occur within organizations (superior, subordinate, peer) or outside of organizations (husband or wife, father or mother, female or male). Roles do not exist independently of the people who perform them. For example, the role of student involves the activities shown in Fig. 16.2.

A *role set* is a collection of roles that relate directly to the role of an individual. A press foreman in a plant that produces trim parts for automobiles has a role set consisting of 19 others: those of the general foreman, superintendent, sheet-metal foreman, inspector, shipping-room foreman and 14 press operators.[9] The people in these roles influence and are influenced by the press-foreman role.

Each member of a role set is influenced by his or her own performance and actions and those of the others. They may be rewarded or punished because of one person's behaviors and may require certain actions from that person in order to perform their own tasks. For a quarterback to complete a pass, for example, the line must block and the receivers must be able to hold on to the ball. Because the members of the offensive team are influenced by the quarterback's performance and actions, they develop attitudes about what the quarterback should and should not do. These attitudes are called *role expectations* and can vary from expectations about how a person should dress to how much or how little the person should produce on the job. Expectations are communicated by the members (*role senders*) of the role set to the individual (*focal person*) whose role is the focus of the set at any particular time. A role set for a student is suggested in Fig. 16.3.

Besides providing information, role senders may exert pressure on the focal person to meet their expectations. This is called *role pressure.* A professor who tells students that they must have an average of 90 or higher for an A is an example of a role sender creating role pressure. Pressures are exerted through the use of one or more types of power (reward, referent, coercive, or legitimate). The nature and intensity of role conflicts are influenced by the type of power used by those in conflict and by their relative power.[10] If two

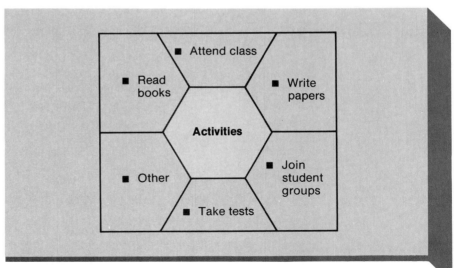

FIGURE 16.2
Student Role

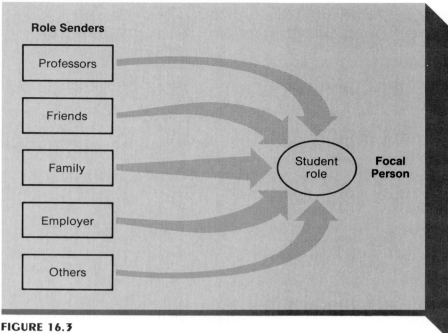

FIGURE 16.3
Student Role Set

people can reward each other in meaningful ways, they will probably be strongly motivated to seek a win–win resolution of their conflicts.

So far we have identified the role sender and the focal person as different people. Actually, one person can play both roles and often does. A person's *inner voice* provides the do's and don'ts for each role a person plays; internal role expectations and pressures can be just as great or greater than external ones. Thus John Doe's perception of his role as an ideal student might conflict with an awareness of his actual student role. If there is a large gap between the two and he cannot figure out how to reduce it, the role conflict can create severe distress. Figure 16.4 illustrates a gap and the resulting conflict between a student's ideal and actual roles.

Role-Episode Model

A *role episode* includes (1) attempts by one or more role senders to influence the behavior of a focal person; and (2) the responses of the focal person—which, in turn, influence the *future* expectations of the role sender(s). A simplified model of a role episode is provided in Fig. 16.5. For example, the expectations of a manager are translated into pressures that are communicated

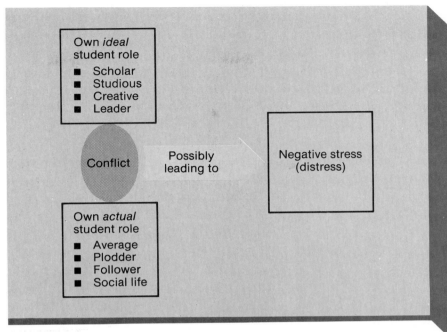

FIGURE 16.4
Student's Ideal versus Actual Role

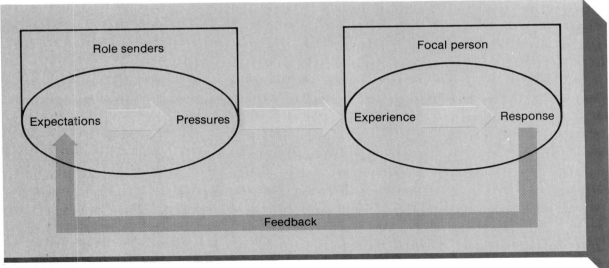

FIGURE 16.5
Role-Episode Model

to a subordinate. The subordinate responds both emotionally and cognitively to these pressures.

The *emotional response* is the subordinate's feelings about the pressures—good, angry, frustrated, happy, and so forth. The *cognitive response* is the subordinate's understanding of what the manager expects. These feelings and thoughts determine the way in which the subordinate responds to the manager. The response provides feedback to the manager; this feedback influences the manager's future expectations of the subordinate. A supervisor who responds with hostility to the pressures of the production manager will be thought of and handled differently than the supervisor who responds with submissive acceptance. If the supervisor shows signs of extreme distress from the expectations and their resulting pressures, the production manager may ease up or consider reassigning the supervisor.

Types of Role Conflict

Role conflict occurs when two or more incompatible pressures are placed on an individual, and by responding to one set of pressures it becomes more difficult for that person to respond to the other(s). The intensity of the role conflict depends mostly on the power of the role senders and the focal person's desire to meet their expectations. Insistence by two fellow workers to share information about a new product may be relatively easy to deal with. But the pressure of two managers asking a worker to complete different projects immediately and simultaneously may result in severe role conflict. In general, severe incompatible pressures lead to conflict and stress *within* the focal person and *with* one or more of the role senders.

There are four basic types of role conflict: intrasender role conflict, intersender role conflict, interrole conflict, and person–role conflict.

Intrasender role conflict

When the do's and the don'ts from a single role sender are incompatible, *intrasender role conflict* occurs. A manager might tell a subordinate that a particular task is to be completed today and then a short time later also assign another task to be completed today. If each task requires a full day to complete, conflict and distress will result. Figure 16.6 illustrates this intrasender role conflict situation for an employee. Another example is that of one spouse pressuring the other to cut expenditures for food and then complaining about the poor meals. A final example is that of professors assigning papers or cases to be completed and turned in during examination week.

Intersender role conflict

When the pressures from one role sender are incompatible with those of one or more other role senders, *intersender role conflict* occurs. For example,

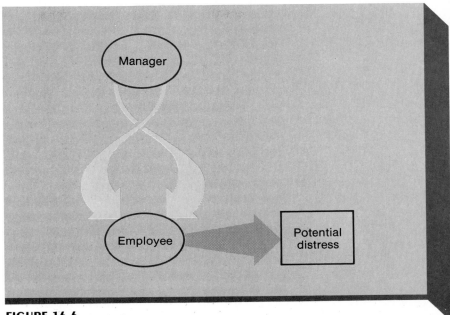

FIGURE 16.6
Intrasender Role Conflict

managers who must deal with multiple interest groups that place conflicting demands on the organization often face intersender role conflict. A study of directors of 67 federally supported manpower agencies indicated that they experienced conflicting pressures from three powerful interest groups: their own staffs, local community leaders, and the state and regional administrators who were responsible for providing program funds and evaluating results. Support from all three of these groups was needed to operate an effective manpower program.[11]

Figure 16.7 suggests an intersender role conflict situation for an employee. This type of conflict could be experienced by an employee in a work group that has norms different from those of management. The employee wants to have friendly relations with fellow employees but also wants to be a high performer—consistent with the manager's desires.

Interrole conflict

When role pressures associated with membership in one group or organization conflict with those stemming from membership in other groups or organizations, *interrole conflict* occurs. Pressures requiring overtime or take-home work may conflict with pressure to give more attention to family

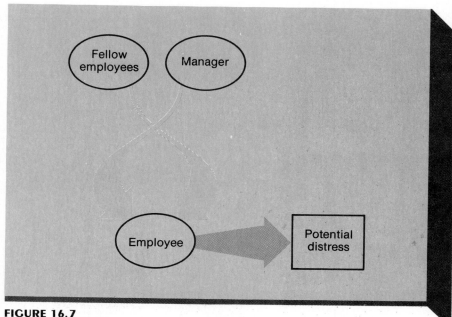

FIGURE 16.7
Intersender Role Conflict

matters. When this type of conflict becomes intense, individuals may withdraw from one of the roles. For example, in an extreme case a spouse might change jobs or get a divorce. Figure 16.8 shows a case of interrole conflict between the individual's role as an employee and his or her role in a family.

Interrole conflicts are quite common for single or married women who want a career.[12] Interrole conflicts and distress for women with children can be especially difficult. Joann Lublin, a professional journalist who returned to work three months after giving birth to a son, described her role conflicts and personal distress in a *Wall Street Journal* article entitled "Juggling Job and Junior."

IN PRACTICE
Joann Lublin

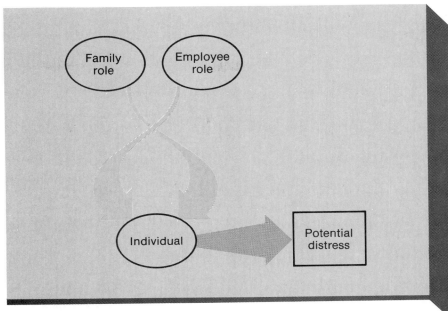

FIGURE 16.8
Interrole Conflict

of my male colleagues. "Where do you dump your kid every day?" asked one. Noticing my annoyance about a 20-minute wait for the bus home, another colleague cracked, "Well, Joann, you don't have to be here. You could be home rocking your baby in the rocking chair."

My first week back was the worst. I blew everything out of proportion. The scorecard reads: two stomach upsets, one anxiety attack, one episode of hysteria and two fights with my husband. When I got home from work those initial evenings, I carried Daniel around the house for hours in a baby carrier— just to be comforted by his warmth and to remind him I was still his mother.

The initial crises have passed, but little things continue to bother me.[13]

Person–role conflict

When differences arise between the pressures of the focal person's role(s) and his or her own needs, attitudes, values, or abilities, ***person–role conflict*** occurs. The college student who, because of parental pressures, enrolls as a management major rather than in the art program preferred by the student, may experience person–role conflict. Figure 16.9 illustrates a case of person–role conflict between the person's managerial role and the person's personality.

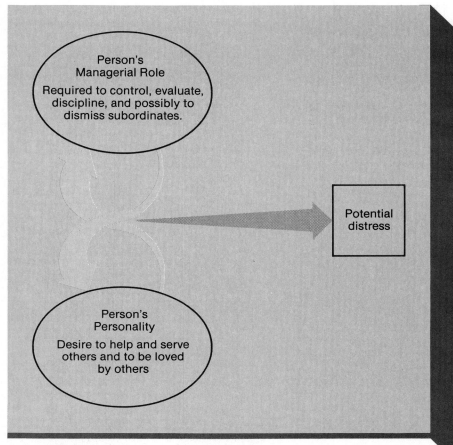

FIGURE 16.9
Person–Role Conflict

The In Practice about Jim Powell illustrates several role conflicts, especially person–role conflicts, he experienced. It relates the role conflicts and uncertainties that increased his level of distress. But you will also note that Jim experienced some positive reactions (eustress). Jim Powell was the general manager of a small plastics factory in Pennsylvania until nine months prior to this interview, when he was promoted to a staff position in the New York office. There he reports to a divisional vice-president on the executive committee. The interview began with Jim's statement that he was under intense pressure.

IN PRACTICE
Jim Powell

This company has a highly centralized management style. Most decisions, even the small ones, are made at the top. Members of the executive committee (Ex Com) must have accurate supporting material so that they can be on top of all issues and can make the best decisions. With a clear view from the top, they are in the best position to guide the company through troubled times like business in general is going through now. Accurate information requires good staff work and that's where I come in. I manage the staff work.

Since I came here, I haven't had more than a moment for my family. They are still in the old house. I'm waiting for time to look for a house near here so my family can join me. It's lonely living in a hotel during the week. It's also hard commuting such a long distance over the weekend, when I can get away, that is, when there isn't some super top priority emergency for-immediate-attention assignment that breaks on a Friday afternoon and requires a report for decision at the Ex Com meeting Monday morning.

My greatest source of tension comes from not being clear about exactly what is required of me because of the time pressure we are under. As top man at my plant, I could see the whole picture clearly. Here, I don't always have a clear picture of what the issues are, what information to collect, or what it will be used for. Some of the assignments are vague, ambiguous. Often I don't have the time to ask for clarification or my boss is not available to give it. As a result, my staff and I are often uncertain about what is required. We try to cover all bases, to make each report as complete as possible. The fear is enormous that something important will slip between the cracks just because we don't know about it. We compensate by trying to do everything, which occasionally turns out to be an enormous waste of time.

Even so, it really isn't the pressure of such unusually intense staff work or these special emergency projects that gets to me. It's that I can't find the time to do my own job, to meet my own objectives for the year. All this emergency work is extra. I'm very concerned that at the end of the year they'll tell me I haven't met my objectives—that they will forget or overlook the fact that I was pulled away from my own work so many times to take care of their top priority emergency assignments.

In my old job as head of the plastics factory I could control my own work, respond to my initiatives rather than to initiatives or pressure from others. I could do my own planning and feel sure that I had taken all factors into consideration, that nothing slipped between the cracks. I didn't have anyone sitting on top of me to please, day-by-day, memo-by-memo, rush special assignment by rush special assignment. I could afford to take a few risks. And if I made a mistake, it wasn't a potential catastrophe. Now I fear a mistake because of the possible consequences it might have.

But on balance this is a great job and a great place to work. The guy at the top is a genius. The Ex Com is getting us through the recession in good shape. We haven't had the layoffs experienced by other companies. My staff and I have confidence that the information we feed up to the top will be used

(continued)

constructively. We all feel part of a team that's winning a tough battle. It's exciting. It's all worth it.

I just hope this pace doesn't continue for too much longer. I have my personal life to put in order. My family doesn't have the same sense of excitement I do. They have a sense of inconvenience and uncertainty. One highly pressured week goes by like a day for me, like a month for those waiting for something different to happen.

I can foresee two types of problems developing in the near future. As an organization, we're taut, stretched thin, brittle in the sense that any new and important pressures may overload us. One more big pressure and something will have to give.

And my family is already giving off signals of impatience. I hope my wife does what she has always done, that is put my work first and allow her schedule to be determined by what I have to do to get ahead in my career. That's the way she felt when we made the decision to take this promotion and come to New York. I hope she doesn't sour on the deal.[14]

There is no single pattern used by individuals or organizations to manage intense role conflicts. The personality of the focal person and the types of interpersonal relationships with the role senders influence greatly the approaches used to manage role conflicts.

INTERPERSONAL CONFLICT-MANAGEMENT STYLES

Interpersonal conflict focuses on the communication, sentiments, and behaviors between the focal person and each role sender. *Interpersonal conflict* is broadly defined as (1) disagreements or incompatible interests over substantive issues (objectives, policies, means to accomplish objectives, and practices); and (2) incompatible behaviors and emotional issues involving negative sentiments (anger, distrust, fear, rejection, and resentment).[15] Although the two types of interpersonal conflict are often interrelated, they may require different strategies for resolution. The resolution of conflicts over substantive issues should emphasize problem solving (collaboration) and compromise (bargaining). The resolution of conflicts over incompatible behaviors and emotional issues should emphasize modification of views and increasing positive feelings among the people involved. Intervention by third parties can help in the management and resolution of both types of conflict. In union–management relations, the third party could be a mediator, arbitrator, or even a judge; in family matters, a counselor or lawyer. Various interpersonal styles of conflict management may be used when managers are parties to a conflict or in a conflict situation that involves two or more subordinates. The five major interpersonal styles for managing conflict are avoidance, smoothing, forcing, compromise, and collaboration.[16]

Avoidance Style

The *avoidance style* is the tendency to withdraw from or remain neutral in conflict situations. Managers who are unavailable for conferences, defer answering disturbing memos, and refuse to get involved in conflicts are using avoidance behaviors. Avoidance-prone managers may act merely as a communication link by sending messages between superiors and subordinates. When asked to take a position on controversial issues, these managers might say, "There has not been time to study the problem fully." or "I would need more facts before making a judgment." or "Perhaps the best way is to proceed as you think best." The avoidance style is symbolized as follows:

When unresolved conflicts affect the tasks for which managers are responsible, the avoidance style will lead to negative results for the organization. The avoidance style is desirable when

1. the issue is so minor or of passing importance that it is not worth the time or energy to confront the conflict;

2. a person's power is so low relative to the other's that there is little chance of causing change (such as major, top-level organization policies); and

3. others, such as subordinates themselves, can more effectively resolve the conflict than can the manager.[17]

Smoothing Style

The *smoothing style* is the tendency to minimize or suppress open recognition of real or perceived differences, while emphasizing common interests, in conflict situations. The smoothing-prone manager might state, "If it makes others happy, I try not to challenge their views." or "I always try not to say something that might hurt the feelings of others when discussing problems." or "Our friendship shouldn't be upset by this problem, so let's not worry too much about it; things will work out." The smoothing style is symbolized as follows:

When using the smoothing style, managers act as though the conflict will go away with time and appeal to the need for cooperation. These managers try to reduce tensions by reassuring and providing support to subordinates, co-workers, or superiors. There is some concern for the emotional aspects of the conflict, but there is little recognition of or interest in working on the substantive issues that are part of the conflict. The smoothing style simply encourages individuals to cover up and avoid expressing their feelings. Therefore, and not surprisingly, this style is generally ineffective. The smoothing style is effective on a short-term basis when

1. the individuals are in a potentially explosive emotional conflict situation, and smoothing is used to defuse it;

2. keeping harmony and avoiding disruption are especially important in the short run; and

3. the conflicts are based primarily on personality characteristics of the individuals and can't be dealt with in the prevailing organizational culture.[18]

Forcing Style

The *forcing style* is the tendency to use coercive and reward power to dominate another person by suppressing differences in conflict situations and requiring the other person to adopt or follow your position. The successful use of the forcing style produces outcomes that are satisfactory to only one of the parties involved. Forcing-prone managers may use such phrases as: "If you don't like the ways things are run, get out." or "If you can't learn to cooperate, I'm sure others can be hired who will." or "When people disagree with me, I try to cut them off to win my position." The forcing style is symbolized as shown in the margin.

Forcing-prone managers assume that conflicts involve win–lose situations.[19] When dealing with conflicts between subordinates or departments, these managers may threaten or actually use demotion, dismissal, poor performance evaluations, or other punishments. When conflicts occur between peers, an employee might try to get his or her own way by appealing to the supervisor. This represents an attempt to use the supervisor to force the decision on the opposing individual. The forcing style is most likely to be associated with personal outcomes of distress (negative stress).

Overreliance on forcing issues lessens the work motivation of the individual whose interests have not been considered. Furthermore, relevant information and other possible alternatives are ignored. However, there are some situations in which the forcing style may be necessary, such as when

1. there are extreme emergencies and quick action is necessary;

2. unpopular courses of action must be taken for long-term organizational effectiveness and survival (such as cost-cutting and dismissal of employees for unsatisfactory performance); and

3. others are trying to take advantage of someone, and the person needs to take quick action for self-promotion.[20]

Compromise Style

The *compromise style* is the tendency to partially sacrifice your interests in the process of making mutual concessions to reach an agreement. Compromise-prone managers often say: "I let other people have some of their positions, if they let me have some of mine." or "I try to find a fair combination of gains and losses for both of us." or "I try to find a position between theirs and mine." The compromise style is symbolized as follows:

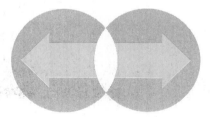

The compromise style is desirable when

1. the compromise agreement enables each party to be better off or, at least, not worse off than if no agreement were reached, but it is not possible to achieve a total win–win agreement;

2. more than one agreement could be reached; and

3. some of the parties' objectives are conflicting or their interests are opposed with regard to the different agreements that might be reached.

PREMATURE USE

Of primary concern is not that this style may be used, but that it may be used too early in conflict situations. There are several problems with the premature use of the compromise style. First, managers may be encouraging compromises on the stated issues rather than on the real ones. The early use of compromise often results in too little diagnosis and exploration of the real issues behind the conflict. The first issues raised are often not the real ones but are used merely as openers. For example, students telling professors that their courses are really tough and challenging may be trying to negotiate a better grade in the course. Second, it is easier to accept an initial position presented, rather than to search for additional alternatives that are more acceptable to all. Third, compromise may be inappropriate to all or part of the conflict situation. There may be better ways of resolving the conflict than those suggested by either party.

RELATIONSHIP TO NEGOTIATION

Compromise is a part of **negotiation.** Negotiation is a process in which two or more individuals or groups, who have both common interests and conflicting interests, present and discuss proposals for terms of a possible agreement.[21] The role of compromise in negotiation has been summed up this way:

> Despite its limitations, abuses, and hazards, negotiation has become an indispensible process in free societies. More effective than any alternative anybody has thought of so far, it enables us to realize common interests while we compromise conflicting interests. Since these are among the basic objectives of rational people, negotiation has to be counted among the greatest of human inventions.[22]

Collaborative Style

The **collaborative style** is the willingness to identify underlying causes of conflict, openly share information, and search for solutions considered to be mutually beneficial. Collaboration-prone managers might say: "I will try to deal with all concerns—theirs and mine." or "I will try to get all viewpoints and issues out in the open." or "If we don't have much agreement at first, let's spend some time thinking about the causes of the conflict and then look for an alternative that we can agree is the best we can do." With the collaborative style, conflicts are recognized openly and evaluated by all concerned. Sharing, examining, and assessing the reasons for the conflict lead to a more thorough development of alternatives that effectively resolves the conflict and is fully acceptable to all parties. The collaborative style is symbolized as follows:

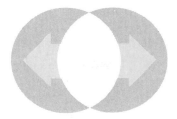

The collaborative style of conflict management is desirable when

1. the people involved have common objectives but are experiencing conflict over the *means* to achieve them;

2. a consensus should lead to the best overall solution to the conflict; and

3. there is a need to make high-quality decisions on the basis of the expertise and best information available.

Collaboration Guidelines

Guidelines for collaboration in managing interpersonal conflicts include the following.

■ Ask for and give feedback on the major points.

■ Consider compromise *after* analysis of the real problems and the generation of alternatives. Remember, the other person's view of reality may be just as valid as yours, even though it may differ from yours.

■ Never assume that you know what the other person is thinking until you have checked out the assumption in plain language.

■ Never put labels (*coward, neurotic,* or *child*) on the other person.

■ Forget the past and stay with the here-and-now. What either of you did last year or last month or yesterday morning is not as important as what you are doing and feeling now.[23]

These guidelines are easy to state but difficult to practice in a spontaneous and natural manner. Effective collaboration requires more than opening up to others; it also demands opening up to oneself and gaining self-insight.

The collaborative style has great potential for effectively managing conflicts, but those involved must be ready and willing to abide by the guidelines presented. Although collaboration is regarded as the best overall style, each style is useful in specific situations.[24] Those who are in conflict may need the assistance of third parties—external consultants or internal specialists in organizational behavior—to assist them in developing the skills and self-insights necessary for effective use of the collaborative style.

Barriers to Use

If collaboration is so effective, you might ask, why isn't it used more frequently? Some of the barriers to using the collaborative style include:

■ Time limits often inhibit direct confrontation of feelings and issues involved in a conflict.

■ Group norms, such as the belief that managers should not express negative feelings toward others.

■ Personal role concepts, such as the manager is able to engage in a conflict with a subordinate but nonetheless feels limited by his or her supervisory role.

The use of collaboration is influenced by the type of organizational culture and the leadership style used. Supportive and participative managers use the collaborative style more than autocratic managers. The collaborative style is more natural in open and supportive organizational cultures than in closed and autocratic organizational cultures. If external factors, such as the type of organizational culture or leadership style, do not prevent the use of collaboration, is it simply a matter of "opening up" and "going at it"? The answer is yes, but only when the conflicts are limited to plans, policies, and procedures. In these situations, the collaborative and compromise styles are most likely to lead to personal outcomes of eustress (positive stress). However, when volatile emotional issues are the focus of the conflict, collaboration can backfire and increase interpersonal conflicts.

WORK-RELATED STRESS

Earlier in the chapter, we presented the following definitions: (1) *stress* is the nonspecific response of the body to any demand; (2) *eustress* is pleasant or constructive stress; and (3) *distress* is unpleasant, detrimental, or disease-producing stress. The primary focus of this section is on distress (negative stress) as it relates to the work situation. For our purposes, **work-related stress** is a person's spontaneous physiological or psychological (thoughts and feelings) response to any organizational demand. A **stressor** is any physical or psychological demand experienced in the process of living.[25]

Sources of Work-Related Stress

Consistent with the definition of *stressor,* the potential sources of stressors at work are almost infinite.[26] Table 16.1 identifies four of the common sources of work-related stress: conflict and uncertainty, job pressure, job scope, and rapport with management. All of these factors have been found to create role

TABLE 16.1 ■ STRESS-ASSESSMENT QUESTIONNAIRE

Instructions: Listed below are various kinds of problems that may—or may not—arise in your work. Indicate to what extent you find each of them to be a problem, concern, or obstacle in carrying out your job duties and responsibilities.

FACTOR *This Factor is a Problem . . .*	RESPONSES				
	Never	*Sel-dom*	*Some-times*	*Usually*	*Always*
Conflict and Uncertainty					
1. Not knowing just what the people you work with expect of you	1	2	3	4	5
2. Feeling you have to do things on the job that are against your better judgment	1	2	3	4	5
3. Thinking that you will not be able to satisfy the conflicting demands of various people over you	1	2	3	4	5
Job Pressure					
4. Feeling you have too heavy a workload; one you can't possibly finish during an ordinary day	1	2	3	4	5
5. Not having enough time to do the work properly	1	2	3	4	5
6. Having the requirements of the job affect your personal life	1	2	3	4	5
Job Scope					
7. Being unclear on just what the scope and responsibilities of your job are	1	2	3	4	5
8. Feeling you have too little authority to carry out responsibilities assigned to you	1	2	3	4	5
9. Not being able to get the information you need to carry out your job	1	2	3	4	5
Rapport with Management					
10. Not knowing what your manager or supervisor thinks of you—how he or she evaluates your performance	1	2	3	4	5
11. Not being able to predict the reactions of people above you	1	2	3	4	5
12. Having ideas considerably different from those of your manager	1	2	3	4	5

Source: Adapted from A. A. McLean, *Work Stress*. Reading, Mass.: Addison-Wesley, 1979, pp. 131–132. Reprinted with permission.

conflicts that lead to work stress. We suggest that you use Table 16.1 to assess your level of work-related stress in a job you have now or have had in the past. The scoring directions for stress assessment are as follows:

1. Add the three numbers you circled in each of the four categories and enter the totals in the blanks.

   Conflict and uncertainty   _____

   Job pressure   _____

   Job scope   _____

   Rapport with management   _____

2. Add the four scores to obtain your overall total score.   _____

Scores in each of the four areas can range from 3–15. Scores of 9 or more suggest that the category presents a problem that deserves your attention. The overall total score can range from 12–60. Scores of 36 or more suggest a more-than-desirable amount of overall stress. This could be a reason for low job satisfaction or a desire to quit the job.

Effects of Distress

Distress is associated with a variety of potential effects.[27] Table 16.2 shows five categories of potential adverse effects: subjective, behavioral, cognitive, physiological, and organizational. These effects are not necessarily mutually exclusive; that is, a person or group experiencing distress may show adverse effects in more than one category. An individual or group will not necessarily experience effects in all these categories or all the specific effects within each category at the same time. Consider the following illustration of the potential effects of distress outlined in Table 16.2.

IN PRACTICE
Matt

Everyone talked about how we were the golden couple, how our marriage was so terrific, and I was buying that. . . . Then my wife told me she thought our marriage was rotten. That was the beginning of it. . . . I began to take her seriously when she was too depressed to get out of bed in the mornings. . . . It came as a shock to me that [my wife] questioned me, questioned her life. I thought I had that pretty well under control. The thing I learned is that you don't have a marriage and sort of put it away in a cabinet—now that's taken care of. See, I think that's the marital model we grew up with; you get married and put that behind you and get on with the important part of life, which is building the career. You have enough other things to worry about, your job and how much money you're making, and you put the marriage in the cabinet because it's more comfortable not to worry about it, and you polish it once a year on your anniversary because it's unsettling to have to think, gosh, you're in a relationship which might break up tomorrow.[28]

TABLE 16.2 ■ POTENTIAL EFFECTS OF DISTRESS

CATEGORY	POTENTIAL SPECIFIC EFFECTS
Subjective effects	Anxiety, aggression, apathy, boredom, depression, fatigue, frustration, guilt and shame, irritability and bad temper, moodiness, low self-esteem, threat and tension, nervousness, and loneliness
Behavioral effects	Accident proneness, drug use, emotional outbursts, excessive eating or loss of appetite, excessive drinking and smoking, excitability, impulsive behavior, impaired speech, nervous laughter, restlessness, trembling, and excessive sleeping or the inability to sleep
Cognitive effects	Inability to make decisions and concentrate, frequent forgetfulness, hypersensitivity to criticism, mental blocks, and denial
Physiological effects	Increased blood and urine catecholamines and corticosteroids, increased blood glucose levels, increased heart rate and blood pressure, dryness of the mouth, sweating, dilation of the pupils, difficulty in breathing, hot and cold spells, lump in the throat, numbness and tingling in parts of the limbs, hives and indigestion
Organizational effects	Absenteeism, poor industrial relations and low productivity, high accident and labor turnover rates, poor organizational climate, antagonism at work, and job dissatisfaction

Source: Adapted from T. Cox, *Stress.* Baltimore: University Park Press, 1978.

A heavy workload and the pressure of time constraints can cause work-related stress or burnout.

Source: George W. Gardner/ Stock, Boston.

Matt denied (cognitive effect) what was happening in his personal life until a crisis forced him to look at it. Once he looked, Matt appeared to experience a sense of threat and tension as well as nervousness (subjective effects) over the possibility that his marriage might break up. Matt's wife was experiencing even more distress effects: depression and apathy (subjective effects), excessive sleeping (behavioral effect), and possibly the inability to make decisions, which led to her questioning of Matt and her own life (cognitive effect).

Everyone is likely to experience distress from time to time, but it is not likely to become a severe problem unless experienced intensely and frequently. The International Focus about executive stress highlights how some managers from the United States and Brazil view the sources of stress in their jobs.

INTERNATIONAL FOCUS

Executive Stress Goes Global

The following information is based on an executive stress survey of subscribers to *International Management*. It is based on the summary findings for managers from two countries, the United States and Brazil. (Managers in 10 countries participated in the survey.)

UNITED STATES

"Pressure comes with the territory," remarked one U.S. manager, stating the general feeling that stress and being a manager go hand-in-hand. Overall, U.S. managers appear to have gained the upper hand in coping with distress. Presumably, the U.S. fetish with health, which to the rest of the world may seem a bit hypochondriacal, along with elaborate health facilities and stress counseling that many corporations now provide for executives, is paying dividends.

With respect to behavioral stress symptoms (such as pill-taking, smoking, and job dissatisfaction) U.S. managers fall near the 10-nation average. They score fairly high on alcoholic consumption, with 30.2 percent regularly taking one or more drinks a day.

As a group they diverge quite dramatically from the 10-country averages on what they believe to be their greatest sources of pressure at work. U.S. managers give the highest ratings to lack of power and influence (46.5 percent), an incompetent boss (30.2 percent), and beliefs that conflict with those of the organization (30.2 percent). These may indicate that the very top executives may not participate as much with managers at lower levels as we are often led to believe. Another rather surprising result, in view of the stereotyped ambitious, work-oriented U.S. executive, is that a higher-than-average percentage

Source: Excerpted and adapted from C. Cooper and J. Arbose, "Executive Stress Goes Global," *International Management*, May 1984, pp. 42–48.

BURNOUT

Some people who experience a high level of distress on a frequent basis suffer from **burnout.** This term applies to chronic emotional exhaustion and cynicism toward the job, which is experienced by some people in response to intense work stressors.[29] Burnout and distress don't just happen—they involve a complex interplay among personal, job, work setting, and organizational culture characteristics.[30] Individuals experiencing burnout seem to go through three stages of progression.

Stage 1: Puzzlement, confusion, and the appearance of frustration.

Stage 2: Experience of intense frustration and anger.

Stage 3: Apathy, withdrawal, and despair.[31]

---

of managers complain about having to work long hours and to take work home. (The average U.S. manager works an estimated 56.7 hours per week.)

BRAZIL

Brazil is a country with great potential for growth but is experiencing severe economic disruptions. These are due mainly to the lack of an educated group of managers and appropriate managerial processes to deal with rapid change. Hence, Brazilian managers are under extreme pressures. These show up in their mental-health-index scores, which are the second-lowest among the 10 countries surveyed. More than 40 percent of the managers gave responses that could indicate varying degrees of mental instability.

Drinking habits are irregular: Brazilian managers have the highest percentage of occasional drinkers in the 10-country survey and the second-lowest percentage of regular tipplers. They smoke less than the average executive but take slightly more sleeping pills and tranquilizers. Brazilian managers ranked the second-lowest in job satisfaction and most frequently stated that they are unhappy with their current posts.

Stressors affecting the performance of Brazilian managers ranged from time pressures and deadlines (61.8 percent) to having an unsympathetic boss (19.6 percent). Almost 28 percent find unrealistic objectives to be a major problem. This is not surprising in a country that experiences annual geometric increases in inflation. Brazilian managers appear to be highly work-oriented. Of all the managers surveyed, they complained least about work overload and long working hours. "It's easy to live, work, and love when you can see a light at the end of the tunnel," said one Brazilian manager.

The effects of distress and burnout have received widespread attention in recent years by the general public, business and health organizations, researchers, and the news media. Numerous prescriptions have been advanced for managing distress and avoiding burnout.

Managing Distress Effectively

The management of distress can be broken into various major, interrelated categories.[32] We consider several of these individual and organizational approaches for both preventing and reducing distress.

Individual approaches

Awareness of the causes of stress and self-awareness of our responses (behaviors, thoughts, and feelings) to stress are fundamental to individual stress-management approaches. Table 16.3 outlines a range of actions that a person can take to manage his or her own stress.

Reduce reactions to stressors.   People have considerable potential to control and reduce the various types of effects from distress. (See Table 16.2.) These include proper nutrition, meditation, R&R (rest and relaxation), physical exercise, proper sleep, biofeedback, and others. The control and reduction of severe effects from distress often require professional help.

TABLE 16.3 ■ ACTIONS FOR COPING WITH STRESS

- *Clarify your values.* It's important to run not on the fast track, but on *your* track.

- *Improve your "self-talks."* We all talk to ourselves, and many of our self-talks are needlessly negative. Discipline yourself not to overreact emotionally. Why be enraged when simple irritation will get your message across?

- *Learn how to relax.* All you need is a quiet room. Get comfortable. Then close your eyes, breathe rhythmically (preferably from your abdomen), and blot out distractions for 10 to 15 minutes. Do this twice a day.

- *Exercise regularly.* Try to exercise at least three times a week for 20 minutes at 75 percent of your maximum predicted heart rate. Make sure your doctor approves, and start gradually.

- *Get the leisure you need.* The best way to avoid burnout is to allow yourself proper leisure to renew your commitment to work and recharge your batteries. If you're a workaholic, consider: you owe it to yourself to take time off or else you jeopardize your chances of keeping on top of a rough job over the long haul.

- *Adopt dietary goals.* Maintain normal weight. Remember to eat a *real* breakfast.

- *Avoid "chemical haze."* One definition of stress is loss of control; the need to acquire control through artificial means accounts for the popularity of nicotine, alcohol, caffeine and drugs.

Source: Excerpted from *Is It Worth Dying For?* Copyright © 1984 by Robert S. Eliot and Dennis L. Breo; published by Bantam Books, Inc.

Alter behaviors and attitudes.   This approach assumes that experiences associated with some stressors relate more to personal attitudes and characteristics than to the stressors in the situation. For example, we can learn to make more use of the collaboration and compromise conflict-management styles and less use of the forcing and avoidance styles. This may serve to lessen the number of conflict incidents and to resolve more effectively the remaining conflict incidents that act as stressors. Learning to set reasonable objectives, carefully evaluating priorities, allowing more time for each activity, improving time management, and simply reducing the total number of activities—all may enable a person to go a long way toward avoiding and reducing distress. These prescriptions are especially important for the individual with a *Type A behavioral pattern.* The Type A behavioral pattern is that of a ". . . person who is aggressively involved in a chronic, incessant struggle to achieve more and more in less time, and if required to do so, against the opposing efforts of other things or other persons."[33] In contrast, the *Type B behavioral pattern* is that of a person who is often contemplative, nonaggressive, realistic in objectives pursued, and not hypercritical of themselves or others. Type A and Type B behavioral patterns have been contrasted as follows:

> The Type A individual is extremely competitive, constantly tending to challenge others—in sports, at work, and even in casual discussions. Type A people characteristically overreact and generally are hypercritical—both of themselves (to themselves) and of others (more openly). They might fume at something a Type B person would brush off as inconsequential.
>
> Type A's are said to have a great sense of urgency concerning time. They tend to thrive on deadlines and create them if none exist. Similarly, they establish difficult goals if none are set for them, and are quick to become impatient when goals and deadlines are not achieved. In contrast, Type B's are more contemplative. They take the time to ponder alternatives and usually feel there is plenty of time.[34]

Type A and B patterns represent extreme profiles. Many individuals fall between these extremes.

Withdrawal.   The simplest way of coping with distress is probably withdrawal (flight) from the stressors. This may involve a range of behaviors, including absenteeism, changing jobs, or even changing careers. Under certain circumstances, withdrawal may be an appropriate and healthy form of coping. However, withdrawal can also be an unhealthy means of attempting to escape reality.

Organizational approaches

Setting objectives.   A participative process of setting objectives (such as management by objectives) should help to reduce and resolve role conflicts and uncertainties. These factors are often major sources of distress and burnout.

Emotional support.   The empathy, caring, love, and trust that is displayed by others and that is perceived by the individual is termed *emotional support.*[35] Emotional and other forms of support in the work setting can be provided by superiors, co-workers, and subordinates. Emotional support appears to help individuals cope with sources of work stress.[36] Organizational cultures that convey a sense of caring, as described in Chapter 15, provide strong emotional support that helps employees successfully cope with expectations and pressures for high performance.

Others.   Counseling and "wellness" programs, physical fitness facilities, leadership training, team-building programs, structural and job redesign, and career development activities are some of the other steps that can be taken by organizations to prevent and reduce the distress experienced by employees.[37]

For example, Tenneco, Inc., has established a flextime program at its Houston headquarters. This program is aimed at assisting its employees in dealing with the stresses of urban commuting and traffic problems. Employees can apply for a daily schedule that starts between 7:00–9:00 A.M. (in 30-minute intervals) and ends between 3:45–5:45 P.M. Tenneco has also built an employee health and fitness center adjacent to the company's headquarters. The center operates from 6:00 A.M.–7:00 P.M. daily and is intended to promote employee health, including positive stress management, and physical fitness.[38]

CHAPTER SUMMARY

This chapter included material that should be helpful to the performance of a variety of managerial roles—especially the leader, disturbance-handler, and negotiator roles. Conflicts and work-related stress are not automatically good or bad in and of themselves. Situational factors such as the intensity and frequency of role conflicts, as well as the capabilities of individuals and organizations, play a significant part in determining whether the outcomes are positive or negative.

Role conflicts occur because of excessive, inconsistent expectations and pressure on a person. There are four types of role conflict: intrasender, intersender, interrole, and person–role. High levels of role conflict can lead to job stress and have negative effects, such as poor performance.

The causes of interpersonal conflict can range from disagreements over policies, practices, or plans to emotional issues. The interpersonal styles for managing conflicts are avoidance, smoothing, forcing, compromise, and collaboration. Severe role conflicts and other stressors (uncertainty about what is expected and how to

perform the job, feelings of too little authority and information to carry out the job, and poor rapport with higher management, co-workers, or subordinates) have the potential for creating severe distress. The potential effects of distress are classified as (1) subjective (aggression, apathy); (2) behavioral (excessive smoking and drinking, emotional outbursts); (3) cognitive (inability to make decisions, frequent forgetfulness); (4) physiological (increased heart rate and blood pressure, difficulty in breathing); and (5) organizational (excessive absenteeism and turnover, low productivity). Burnout was discussed as a potential outcome for some individuals who experience frequent high levels of distress.

Individual approaches for managing distress—withdrawal, altering behaviors and attitudes, and reducing negative reactions to stressors—were reviewed. The roles of Type A and Type B behavior patterns in influencing the response to stress by various individuals in the same objective environment were highlighted. The discussion of organizational approaches for preventing and reducing distress emphasized the importance of setting objectives and emotional support. Numerous other actions that can be taken by organizations—ranging from counseling and "wellness" programs to the provision of physical fitness facilities to training programs—were mentioned.

MANAGER'S VOCABULARY

avoidance style
burnout
cognitive response
collaborative style
compromise style
conflict
conflict management
distress
emotional response
emotional support
eustress
focal person
forcing style
interpersonal conflict
interrole conflict
intersender role conflict
intrasender role conflict
negotiation
person–role conflict
role
role conflict
role episode
role expectations
role pressure
role senders
role set
smoothing style
stress
stressor
Type A behavioral pattern
Type B behavioral pattern
work-related stress

REVIEW QUESTIONS

1. What is the role-episode model?
2. What are the four types of role conflict?

3. What are the five interpersonal conflict-management styles?
4. Under what conditions might each interpersonal conflict-management style be effective?
5. What are the major sources of work-related stress?
6. What are the major effects of negative stress?
7. What are some of the individual and organizational approaches for managing work-related stress?

DISCUSSION QUESTIONS

1. Why is conflict inevitable in organizations?
2. Drawing on your own experiences, give examples of intrasender, intersender, interrole, and person–role conflicts.
3. How would you describe yourself with respect to your relative use of the five interpersonal conflict-management styles?
4. Think of a current or past interpersonal relationship with someone who had much more power than you in the relationship. How would you describe this person's relative use of the five interpersonal conflict-management styles? How would you evaluate the effectiveness of this person's conflict-management profile?
5. Do you see yourself as characterized by or leaning toward the Type A or Type B behavioral pattern? What is the basis for this self-characterization? Do you think individuals that know you well would agree with this self-characterization?
6. What are the major stressors in your life at the present time? Do some of these stressors seem to create a sense of eustress and others a sense of distress? Explain.
7. What approaches, if any, do you usually use to manage negative stress? Are they usually effective? Explain.

MANAGEMENT INCIDENTS AND CASES

Conflict Style Incidents[39]

Instructions: Your task is to rank the five alternative courses of action in each of the following four incidents. Rank the sections from the most desirable or appropriate way of dealing with the conflict situation to the least desirable. Rank the most desirable course of action "l," the next most desirable "2," and so on, with the least desirable or least appropriate action as "5." Enter your rank for each item in the space next to each choice. Next, identify the conflict style being used with each of the possible courses of action, e.g., forcing, smoothing, avoidance, compromise, or collaboration.

Incident one

Pete is lead operator of a production molding machine. Recently he has noticed that one of the men from another machine has been coming over to his machine and talking to one of his men (not on break time). The efficiency of Pete's operator seems to be falling off, and there have been some rejects due to his inattention. Pete thinks he detects some resentment among the rest of the crew. If you were Pete, you would:

———— a. Talk to your man and tell him to limit his conversations during on-the-job time.

———— b. Ask the foreman to tell the lead operator of the other machine to keep his operators in line.

———— c. Confront both men the next time you see them together (as well as the other lead operator, if necessary), find out what they are up to, and tell them what you expect of your operators.

———— d. Say nothing now; it would be silly to make something big out of something so insignificant.

———— e. Try to put the rest of the crew at ease; it is important that they all work well together.

Incident two

Sally is the senior quality-control (Q-C) inspector and has been appointed group leader of the Q-C people on her crew. On separate occasions, two of her people have come to her with different suggestions for reporting test results to the machine operators. Paul wants to send the test results to the foreman and then to the machine operators, since the foreman is the person ultimately responsible for production output. Jim thinks the results should go directly to the lead operator on the machine in question, since he is the one who must take corrective action as soon as possible. Both ideas seem good, and Sally can find no ironclad procedures in the department on how to route the reports. If you were Sally, you would:

———— a. Decide who is right and ask the other person to go along with the decision (perhaps establish it as a written procedure).

———— b. Wait and see; the best solution will become apparent.

———— c. Tell both Paul and Jim not to get uptight about their disagreement; it is not that important.

———— d. Get Paul and Jim together and examine both of their ideas closely.

———— e. Send the report to the foreman, with a copy to the lead operator (even though it might mean a little more copy work for Q-C).

Incident three

Ralph is a module leader; his module consists of four very complex and expensive machines and five crewmen. The work is exacting, and inattention or improper procedures could cause a costly mistake or serious injury. Ralph suspects that one of his men is taking drugs on the job or at least showing up for work under the influence of drugs. Ralph feels he has some strong indications, but he knows he does not have a "case." If you were Ralph, you would:

———— a. Confront the man outright, tell him what you suspect and why and that you are concerned for him and for the safety of the rest of the crew.

———— b. Ask that the suspected offender keep his habit off the job; what he does on the job *is* part of your business.

———— c. Not confront the individual right now; it might either "turn him off" or drive him underground.

———— d. Give the man the "facts of life"; tell him it is illegal and unsafe and that if he gets caught, you will do everything you can to see that the man is fired.

———— e. Keep a close eye on the man to see that he is not endangering others.

Incident four

Gene is a foreman of a production crew. From time to time in the past, the product development section has tapped the production crews for operators to augment their own operator personnel to run test products on special machines. This has put very little strain on the production crews, since the demands have been small, temporary, and infrequent. Lately, however, there seems to have been an almost constant demand for four production operators. The rest of the production crew must fill in for these missing people, usually by working harder and taking shorter breaks. If you were Gene, you would:

_____ a. Let it go for now; the "crisis" will probably be over soon.

_____ b. Try to smooth things over with your own crew and with the development foreman; we all have jobs to do and cannot afford a conflict.

_____ c. Let development have two of the four operators they requested.

_____ d. Go to the development supervisor—or his or her foreman—and talk about how these demands for additional operators could best be met without placing production in a bind.

_____ e. Go to the supervisor of production (Gene's boss) and get him or her to "call off" the development people.

REFERENCES

1. Excerpted from P. McAllister Johnson, "Being a Manager in a Multicultural World." In Jennie Farley (Ed.), *The Woman in Management: Career and Family Issues.* Ithaca, N.Y.: ILR Press, 1983, pp. 37–39.

2. I. Janis and J. Mann, *Decision Making: A Psychological Analysis of Conflict, Choice, and Commitment.* New York: Free Press, 1977, p. 46.

3. H. Seyle, "The Stress Concept Today." In I. L. Kutash, L. B. Schlesinger, and Associates (Eds.), *Handbook on Stress and Anxiety.* San Francisco, Calif.: Jossey-Bass, 1980, pp. 127–143.

4. Seyle, "The Stress Concept Today," p. 128.

5. M. Deutsch, *The Resolution of Conflict: Constructive and Destructive Processes.* New Haven, Conn.: Yale University Press, 1973.

6. D. Dana, "The Costs of Organizational Conflict,"

Organizational Development Journal, Fall 1984, pp. 5–7; E. R. Kemery, A. G. Bedeian, K. W. Mossholder, and J. Touliatos, "Outcomes of Role Stress: A Multivariate Constructive Replication," *Academy of Management Journal,* 1985, **28**:363–375.

7. L. D. Brown, *Managing Conflict at Organizational Interfaces.* Reading, Mass.: Addison-Wesley, 1983; R. R. Blake and J. S. Mouton, *Solving Costly Organizational Conflicts: Achieving Intergroup Trust, Cooperation, and Teamwork.* San Francisco, Calif.: Jossey-Bass, 1984; N. M. Fraser and K. W. Hipel, *Conflict Analysis: Models and Resolutions.* New York: North-Holland, 1984.

8. Adapted from R. Kahn, D. Wolfe, R. Quinn, and J. Snoek, *Organizational Stress: Studies in Role Conflict and Ambiguity.* New York: John Wiley, 1964. *Also see:* V. Berger-Cross and A. I. Kraut, " 'Great Expectations': A No-Conflict Explanation of Role Conflict," *Journal of Applied Psychology,* 1984, **69**:261–271; S. E. Jackson and R. S. Schuler, "A Meta-Analysis and Conceptual Critique of Research on Role Ambiguity and Role Conflict in Work Settings," *Organizational Behavior and Decision Processes,* June 1985, **10**:16–78.

9. R. Merton, *Social Theory and Social Structure,* 2nd ed. Glenview: Free Press, 1957.

10. J. Nagel, *The Descriptive Analysis of Power.* New Haven: Yale University Press, 1975.

11. D. Whetten, "Coping with Incompatible Expectations: An Integrated View of Role Conflict," *Administrative Science Quarterly,* 1978, **23**:254–271; J. B. Shaw and J. A. Weekley, "The Effects of Objective Work-Load Variations of Psychological Strain and Post-Work-Load Performance," *Journal of Management,* 1985, **11**:87–98.

12. M. Davidson and C. Cooper, *Stress and the Woman Manager.* New York: St. Martin's Press, 1983; K. Bartol, "The Sex Structuring of Organizations: A Search for Possible Causes," *Academy of Management Review,* 1978, **3**:805–815; J. H. Greenhaus and N. J. Beutell, "Sources of Conflict Between Work and Family Roles," *Academy of Management Review,* 1985, **10**:76–88.

13. J. Lublin, "Juggling Job and Junior." *The Wall Street Journal,* 1980, **65**(57):23.

14. Adapted from L. Moss, *Management Stress.* Reading, Mass.: Addison-Wesley, 1981, pp. 58–60.

15. A. Filley, *Interpersonal Conflict Resolution*. Glenview, Ill.: Scott, Foresman, 1975.

16. R. Blake and J. Mouton, *The New Managerial Grid*. Houston: Gulf, 1978; M. Afzalur Rahim, "A Measure of Styles of Handling Interpersonal Conflict," *Academy of Management Journal*, 1983, **26**:368–376; R. Likert and J. G. Likert, *New Ways of Managing Conflict*. New York: McGraw-Hill, 1976.

17. K. Thomas, "Conflict and Conflict Management." In M. Dunnette (Ed.), *Handbook of Industrial and Organizational Psychology*. Chicago: Rand McNally, 1976, pp. 889–935.

18. K. W. Thomas and R. H. Kilmann, "The Thomas–Kilmann Conflict Mode Instrument." In O. W. Cole (Ed.), *Conflict Resolution Technology*. Cleveland: Organization Development Institute, 1983, pp. 57–64.

19. J. F. Gaski, "The Theory of Power and Conflict in Channels of Distribution," *Journal of Marketing*, 1984, **48**:9–29; B. Richardson, "The Zero-Sum Management Disease and the Von Thunen Prescription," *Business Horizons*, November–December 1984, pp. 15–20.

20. H. L. Ruben, *Competing: Understanding and Winning the Strategic Games We All Play*. New York: Lippincott and Crowell, 1980.

21. G. Holmes and S. Glaser, "Guidelines for Commercial Negotiations," *Business Horizons*, January–February 1984, pp. 21–25; R. L. Tung, "How to Negotiate with the Japanese," *California Management Review*, Summer 1984, pp. 62–77.

22. M. Ways, "The Virtues, Dangers, and Limits of Negotiation," *Fortune*, 1979, **99**:90.

23. R. R. Blake and J. S. Mouton, *The Versatile Manager: A Grid Profile*. Homewood, Ill.: Richard D. Irwin, 1981; R. R. Blake and J. S. Mouton, "Overcoming Group Warfare," *Harvard Business Review*, November–December 1984, pp. 98–108; H. B. Karp, "The Art of Creative Fighting." In L. D. Goodstein and J. W. Pfeiffer (Eds.), *The 1983 Annual for Facilitators, Trainers, and Consultants*. San Diego: 1983, pp. 214–222; G. F. Shea, *Creative Negotiating*. Boston: CBI Publishing, 1983.

24. H. Bernardin and K. Alvares, "The Managerial Grid as a Predictor of Conflict Resolution Method and Managerial Effectiveness," *Administrative Science Quarterly*, 1976, **21**:84–92; R. A. Baron, "Reducing Organizational Conflict: An Incompatible Response Approach," *Journal of Applied Psychology*, 1984, **69**:272–279; B. Schultz and J. Anderson, "Training in the Management of Conflict: A Communication Theory Perspective," *Small Group Behavior*, 1984, **15**:333–348.

25. J. C. Quick and J. D. Quick, *Organizational Stress and Preventive Management*. New York: McGraw-Hill, 1984, pp. 1–14.

26. Quick and Quick, *Organizational Stress . . .*, pp. 17–42; D. P. Boyd and D. E. Gumpert, "Coping with Entrepreneurial Stress," *Harvard Business Review*, March–April 1983, pp. 44–46ff; R. A. Cooke and D. M. Rousseau, "Stress and Strain From Family Roles and Work-Role Expectations," *Journal of Applied Psychology*, 1984, **69**:252–260; J. M. Ivancevich and M. T. Matteson, *Stress and Work: A Managerial Perspective*. Glenview, Ill.: Scott, Foresman, 1980; S. Parasuraman and J. A. Alutto, "Sources and Outcomes of Stress in Organizational Settings: Toward the Development of a Structural Model," *Academy of Management Journal*, 1984, **27**:330–350.

27. Quick and Quick, *Organizational Stress . . .*, pp. 43–94.

28. J. R. Kofodimos, "A Question of Balance," *Issues and Observations*. Greensboro, N.C.: Center for Creative Leadership. February 1984, pp. 1–8.

29. Adapted from C. Maslach, "Understanding Burnout: Definitional Issues in Analyzing a Complex Phenomenon." In W. S. Paine (Ed.), *Job Stress and Burnout: Research Theory and Intervention Perspectives*. Beverly Hills, Calif.: Sage Focus Editions, 1982, pp. 29–40; J. Gaines and J. H. Jermier, "Emotional Exhaustion in a High Stress Organization," *Academy of Management Journal*, 1983, **26**:567–586; J. M. Ivancevich, M. T. Matteson, and E. P. Richards III, "Who's Liable for Stress on the Job?" *Harvard Business Review*, March–April 1985, pp. 60–62ff.

30. D. N. Behrman and W. D. Perrcault Jr. "A Role Stress Model of the Performance and Satisfaction of Industrial Salespersons," *Journal of Marketing*, 1984, **48**:9–21; R. S. Bhagat, "Effects of Stressful Life Events on Individual Performance Effective-

ness and Work Adjustment Processes within Organizational Settings: A Research Model," *Academy of Management Review,* 1983, 8:660–671; J. I. Rooney and A. R. Cahoon, "The Challenge of Organizational Stress," *Organizational Development Journal,* Summer 1984, pp. 25–32; D. L. Nelson and J. C. Quick, "Professional Women: Are Distress and Disease Inevitable?" *Academy of Management Review,* 1985, 2:206–218.

31. M. Lauderdate, *Burnout: Strategies for Personal and Organizational Life/Speculations on Evolving Paradigms.* San Diego: University Associates, 1982; R. T. Golembiewski, R. Munzenrider, and D. Carter, "Phases of Progressive Burnout and Their Work Site Covariants: Critical Issues in OD Research and Praxis," *Journal of Applied Behavioral Science,* 1983, 19:461–481.

32. L. Levi, *Preventing Work Stress.* Reading, Mass.: Addison-Wesley, 1981; O. I. Niehouse, "Controlling Burnout: A Leadership Guide for Managers," *Business Horizons,* July–August 1984, pp. 80–85; D. P. Rogers, "Helping Employees Cope with Burnout," *Business,* October–December 1984, pp. 3–7; T. N. Martin and J. R. Schermerhorn Jr., "Work and Nonwork Influences on Health: A Research Agenda Using Inability to Leave as a Critical Variable," *Academy of Management Review,* 1983, 4:650–659.

33. M. Friedman and R. Roseman, *Type A Behavior and Your Heart.* New York: Alfred A. Knopf, 1974, p. 84.

34. A. A. McLean, *Work Stress.* Reading, Mass.: Addison-Wesley, 1979, p. 69. *Also see:* M. A. Diamond and S. Allcorn, "Psychological Barriers to Personal Responsibility," *Organizational Dynamics,* Spring 1984, pp. 66–77; M. T. Matteson, J. M. Ivancevich, and S. Y. Smith, "Relation of Type A Behavior to Performance and Satisfaction among Sales Personnel," *Journal of Vocational Behavior,* 1984, 25:203–214.

35. J. S. House, *Work Stress and Social Support.* Reading, Mass.: Addison-Wesley, 1981, pp. 23–24.

36. D. Etzion, "Moderating Effect of Social Support on the Stress–Burnout Relationship," *Journal of Applied Psychology,* 1984, 69:615–622; S. Jayaratne and W. A. Chess, "The Effects of Emotional Support on Perceived Job Stress and Strain," *Journal of Applied Behavioral Science,* 1984, 2:141–153; A. Seers, G. W. McGee, T. T. Servey, G. B. Graen, "The Interaction of Job Stress and Social Support: A Strong Inference Investigation," *Academy of Management Journal,* 1983, 26:273–284.

37. C. R. Stoner and F. L. Fry, "Developing a Corporate Policy for Managing Stress," *Personnel,* May–June 1983, pp. 66–76; R. L. Rose and J. F. Veiga, "Assessing the Sustained Effects of a Stress Management Intervention on Anxiety and Locus of Control," *Academy of Management Journal,* 1984, 27:190–198; P. H. Thompson, K. L. Kirkham, and J. Dixon, "Warning: The Fast Track May Be Hazardous to Organizational Health," *Organizational Dynamics,* Spring 1985, pp. 21–33.

38. Quick and Quick, *Organizational Stress . . . ,* pp. 278–279.

39. A. A. Zoll III, *Explorations in Managing.* Reading, Mass.: Addison-Wesley, 1974. Based on a format suggested by Allen A. Zoll III. Reprinted with permission.

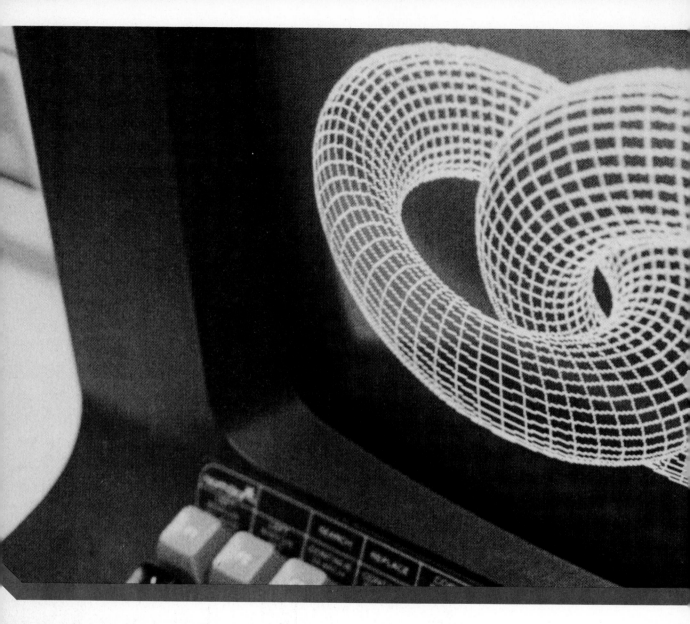

PART VI

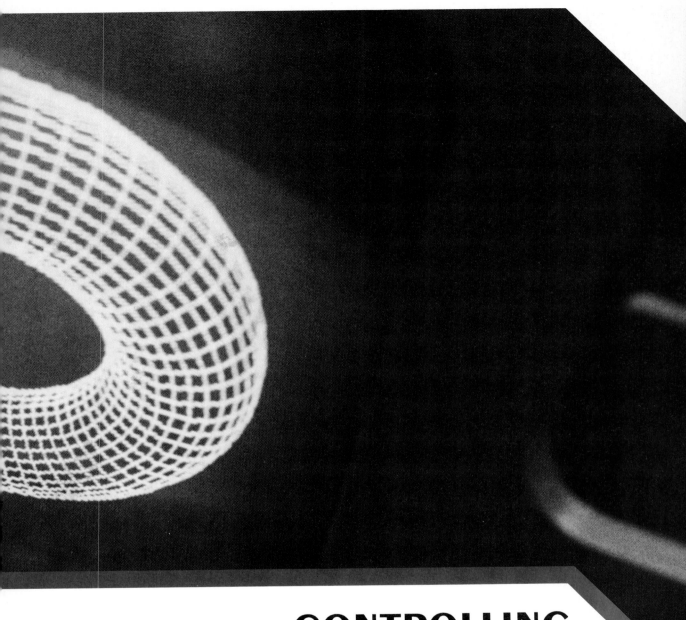

CONTROLLING

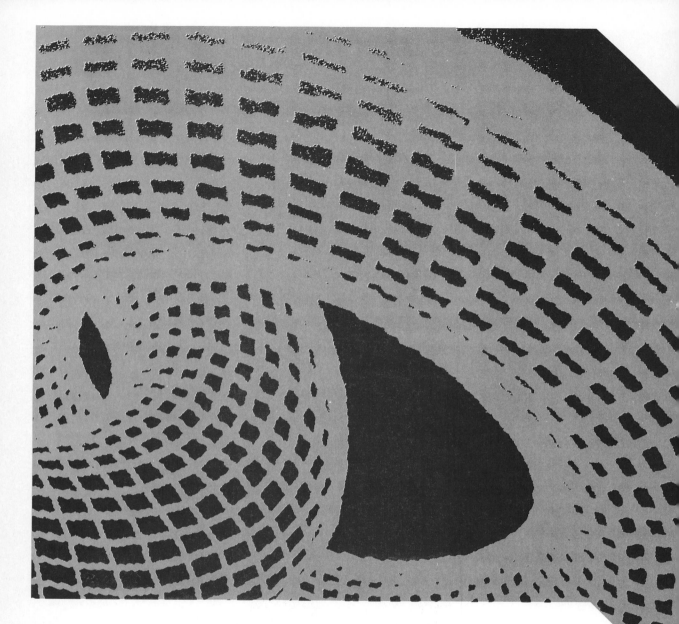

Managerial Control

LEARNING OBJECTIVES

After studying this chapter, you should be able to:

- Identify the types and sources of control.

- State the six steps included in the corrective-control model.

- Describe two controversial control methods—polygraph testing and security agents.

- Explain how performance-appraisal controls differ in mechanistic and organic management systems.

- Describe the six common managerial control strategies: staffing controls, performance-appraisal controls, formal-structure controls, policies and rule controls, financial controls, and machine controls.

CHAPTER OUTLINE

PREVIEW CASE

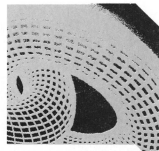

TEXAS COMMERCE BANCSHARES, INC.

To Ben F. Love, there is no great mystique about running a bank successfully. "Banking is a business," says the chairman of Texas Commerce Bancshares, Inc. That means (1) putting in place the controls and systems needed to run the business; and (2) identifying and analyzing other businesses that want to borrow money.

With that simple philosophy, Love has transformed Houston-based Texas Commerce Bancshares from a small, local operation into one of the nation's premier bank holding companies, with 67 banks across Texas and offices in eight foreign countries. The standards and controls for analyzing and monitoring loans introduced by Love are a lesson in managerial control.

This year the bank's loan officers will travel more than 1-million miles, mostly in Texas, making some 115,000 visits to potential and current customers. This extensive call program is designed both to seek out the best lending opportunities for the bank and to monitor corporate customers for trouble spots. "It may sound like what goes on at Procter & Gamble or 3M," Love says. "But I think that is the way to run any business, and a bank is no exception."

The loan officers must submit detailed reports on every one of their calls. To make sure that they are actually making all the calls they report, an internal-audit team examines the call reports from every bank in the system as carefully as they scru-

tinize financial data. Love takes pride in the strict standards of the audit team. "We don't have to wait for the federal regulators to tell us bad news," he says. "We know what is happening at each of our banks, and when we see a problem we take action immediately to correct it before the loan goes bad."

The system of checks and balances works right up the line. Every loan application must be approved or rejected by all the senior lending officers at the branch generating the business. One negative vote kills a loan application. Consequently, "Each of those officers must take responsibility for the loan," Love says. "There is no possibility that some lending officer might get out of control and make a bunch of questionable loans."

The board of directors of every Texas Commerce bank includes a number of the business leaders in its community. Each bank is able to keep close tabs on economic conditions and business activity in the area. That local expertise, analysts believe, has been particularly helpful in minimizing problem real-estate loans at Texas Commerce. "We like to personally know the people we are lending to," Love says, "especially in the real-estate area."

This control system, Love believes, allows Texas Commerce to be selective in making loans. "We stir up enough lending opportunities in the marketplace so that we don't have to grab at every

Source: Courtesy of Texas Commerce Bancshares, Inc.

opportunity we uncover," he says. "If we see a potential problem with a prospect, we will let some other bank make that loan."

Love does not rely only on controls to maintain the money-making machine at Texas Commerce. The human factor, he maintains, is equally important to its success. "We look for people who have not only intelligence but good work habits and who are accustomed to achieving and winning." With quality people operating within his strict system, Love confidently looks forward to continued growth for Texas Commerce.[1]

This account was taken from *Dun's Business Month,* which selected Texas Commerce Bancshares as one of the five best-managed companies in 1984. It captures an important theme. Decision making, planning, organizing, leading, and controlling must come together for successful management. A portion of Fig. 1.7 (Management as a Dynamic Process) is repeated in Fig. 17.1 as a reminder of this core theme. The Preview Case clearly illustrates the vital importance of planning, organizing, leading, and controlling in making good loan decisions. Ben Love's comment about the importance of "identifying and analyzing other businesses that want to borrow money" is certainly a part of the planning process. The decision to have a board of directors for every

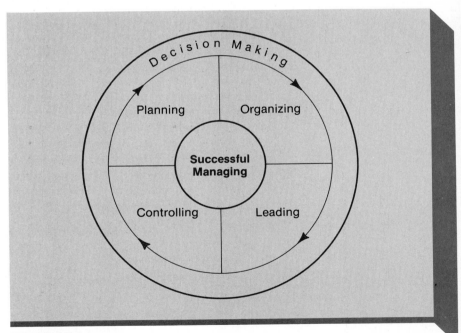

FIGURE 17.1
Basic Managerial Functions

Texas Commerce bank, each of which includes a number of local business leaders, is an example of the organizing process in action. Love's comments about the importance of the human factor to the bank's success and the sense of dynamism that he personally projects suggest a strong, innovative leadership process. Finally, Texas Commerce gives particular attention to the control process. This is indicated in a variety of ways: auditing of call reports, taking corrective actions before loans go bad, making each branch loan subject to the approval of *all* senior lending officers at the branch bank, and the like.

This chapter focuses on the basic issues, processes, and strategies of control internal to the organization. The types and sources of managerial control are covered in the first section of the chapter. The second section presents the six interconnected steps of the corrective-control model. The next section consists of two examples of controversial controls: the use of polygraph testing and security agents. The final section reviews six managerial control strategies.

TYPES AND SOURCES OF MANAGERIAL CONTROL

In its broadest sense, *control* is the process by which a person, group, or organization consciously determines or influences what another person, group, or organization will do.[2] Within U.S. and Canadian organizations and society in general, the reaction to the word *control* is usually negative. It is often interpreted to imply restraining, forcing, delimiting, directing, enforcing, watching, and manipulating. This is partially the result of deeply held values of individualism and democracy, which are somewhat inconsistent with the notion of strong external controls.

Managerial control is much narrower in scope than the general concept of control. Managerial control refers only to the strategies and actions taken by the organization to help ensure that employee behavior and performance conform as nearly as possible to the plans, structure, and rules of the organization.[3] Managerial control can be contrasted with planning in the following four ways.

1. Plans are the directions in which managers intend to lead the organization in order to achieve its objectives. Managerial controls are needed to ensure that outcomes are consistent with the plans.

2. Planning prescribes desired behaviors and results. Managerial controls can maintain or redirect actual behaviors and results.

3. Managers cannot effectively plan without information about the past and current status of each department, strategic business unit, product line, and the organization as a whole. Much of this essential information is obtained through the control process.

4. Managers cannot effectively control the organization unless there are plans to indicate the purposes to be served by the control process. Thus the planning and control processes complement and support one another.[4]

Types of Control

The two major types of managerial control are *preventive controls* and *corrective controls.* Both types are needed and used within an organization. Preventive controls are intended to prevent costly and time-consuming actions. Their use requires an understanding of critical points in processes and operations, anticipation of problems, and a keen awareness of human nature. The more commonly used corrective controls reflect the fact that managers often hesitate to think that trust will be betrayed. Also, managers find it easier to impose controls after something has gone wrong than it is to anticipate the problem.

Preventive controls

Preventive controls are designed to avoid missteps and thereby minimize the need for taking corrective action. For example, some laws serve to limit the control of one group or institution by another. The Bill of Rights acts as a restraint to limit (control) the authority of the federal government over U.S. citizens. However, it is not self-enforcing; the legal system is the control mechanism required to guarantee citizens of these back rights.

Rules and regulations, selection procedures, and training-and-development programs function primarily as preventive controls. For example, rules and regulations direct and limit the behaviors of employees. It is usually assumed that if employees comply with these restrictions, the objectives of the organization are likely to be achieved. Again, control mechanisms have to be used to make sure that the rules and regulations are working and are being followed.

In the Preview Case, we learned that Texas Commerce makes effective use of preventive controls. Loan officers at the branch banks know that an internal-audit team at corporate headquarters examines their detailed call reports. This team also checks with customers on a sample basis to verify the information contained in the call reports. The widespread knowledge of this audit process among loan officers serves as a preventive control by reducing the likelihood that they will file inaccurate, misleading, or even fraudulent call reports.

Corrective controls

The more common view of managerial control emphasizes the corrective approach. Corrective controls are intended to return behavior and performance to predetermined and expected levels. For example, management might believe that theft by some employees has increased to an unacceptable level.

To change this situation, management posts a security guard and requires all employees to enter and leave the building through a common entry and exit area in the hope of reducing theft.

At Texas Commerce the auditing process also increases management's ability to take quick corrective action against loan officers who might file inaccurate, misleading, or fraudulent call reports. Recall Ben Love's comment: "We know what is happening at each of our banks and when we see a problem we take action immediately to correct it before the loan goes bad."

Sources of Control

There are three sources of control for most organizations.[5] *Formal organization controls* are those control strategies and mechanisms intentionally created and designed by managers. Rules, budgets, and auditing departments are examples of formal organization-control mechanisms. *Group controls* are based on the shared norms and values of group members and are typically developed and maintained through informal socialization, reward, and punishment. *Individual self-control* refers to the preventive and corrective control mechanisms that operate consciously or unconsciously within individuals.[6] An unconscious (automatic), corrective control mechanism is sweating when you are exposed to excessive heat. A conscious, preventive control mechanism is your unwillingness to steal money or goods from the company because of internally held values of honesty, not simply because you are afraid of getting caught. Table 17.1 provides examples of the three sources of control in

TABLE 17.1 ■ SOURCES AND TYPES OF CONTROLS IN ORGANIZATIONS

| SOURCE | TYPE AND EXAMPLES | |
	Preventive Control	*Corrective Control*
Formal organization controls	Using budgets to guide expenditures	Disciplining an employee for violating a "No Smoking" safety regulation in a hazardous area
Group controls	Advising a new employee about group's norm in relation to expected level of output	Harassing and socially isolating a worker who doesn't conform to the group norms
Individual self-controls	Deciding to skip lunch because you are running behind schedule in getting a project completed	Quitting a job that you find too stressful and unrewarding

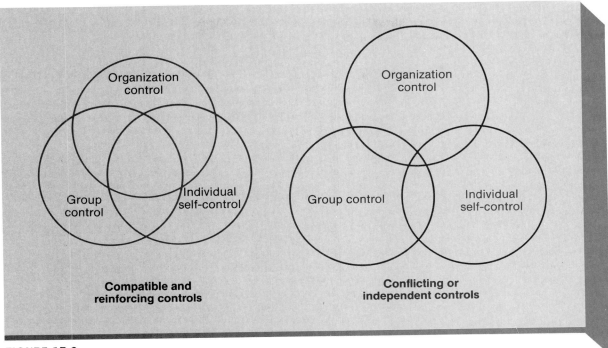

FIGURE 17.2
Illustrative Control Patterns

relation to the two types of control that are likely to be found in most organizations.

Compatibility and conflict

The three sources of control can conflict with each other or operate somewhat independently of each other.[7] Thus the direct authority that managers have over formal organization controls is usually not adequate for achieving effective organizational control.[8] Strong organizational cultures usually result in considerable compatibility and reinforcement between formal organization controls, group controls, and individual self-controls. On the other hand, the sources of control generally operate at odds and/or independently of each other in organizations that exhibit extreme internal conflict or indifference.

The potential extremes in the patterns of overall control found in organizations are illustrated in Fig. 17.2. A strong organizational culture fosters reinforcement and overlap among the three sources of control; there are no sharp differences between formal and informal control processes. However, the pattern for conflicting or independent controls indicates much less connection between formal organization controls and group controls and individual self-controls. In the chapters dealing with motivation, leadership, groups, and conflict, we presented some of the issues and ways managers can achieve greater compatibility among these three sources of organizational control. We want to reemphasize that management cannot achieve an effective pattern of organizational control by only focusing on formal organization controls.[9] However, because managers can most directly influence the establishment and change of formal organization controls, we now turn to consideration of ways that they can be used effectively.

Uses of formal controls

Some general uses of formal organization controls have already been suggested. In addition, formal controls are used to

- *standardize performance,* which is accomplished by supervisory inspections, written procedures, or production schedules;

- *protect an organization's assets* from theft, waste, or misuse, which involves record-keeping requirements, auditing procedures, and division of responsibilities;

- *standardize the quality* of products or services sold to customers, which is done through employee training, inspections, statistical quality control, and incentive systems;

- *limit the amount of authority* that can be exercised by managers and employees by means of job descriptions, policy directives, rules, and accounting requirements; and

- *measure and direct employee performance* through merit-rating systems, direct supervisory observation, and reports on output or scrap loss per employee.[10]

Formal controls have many other uses besides those listed. Such controls are needed to ensure profitability and survival, and are utilized throughout most organizations.

Effectiveness of formal controls

Formal controls should be recognized as *means* to help an organization achieve its objectives. The costs of formal control systems must be compared with their benefits. Analysis of the effectiveness of control systems involves three basic questions:

1. What are the costs versus the benefits of various amounts of formal control?

2. What are the cost–benefit relationships of alternative controls for the same activity?

3. At what point or for what activities should controls be used?

The effectiveness of a formal control system is the difference between its costs and the expected improvement in behaviors and results. For example, when the quality of output is unsatisfactory, is it more effective to reduce the span of control (that is, have more supervision of fewer subordinates); give workers more pay as the quality of their work increases; substitute machines for people; or relocate controls to detect errors earlier?

Cost–benefit model. A cost–benefit model of formal control-system effectiveness is shown in Fig. 17.3. This model suggests that managers must consider trade-offs when making decisions about the amount of emphasis to place on formal controls. The horizontal axis indicates the amount of formal

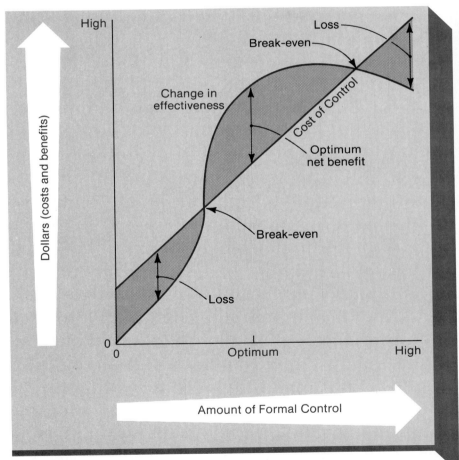

FIGURE 17.3
Cost–Benefit Model of Formal Control

control, ranging from low to high. The vertical axis indicates the dollar costs or benefits of a control decision, ranging from zero to high. For purposes of illustration, the cost-of-control curve is shown as a direct function of the amount of formal control.

With too little control, the formal control system is so weak that the costs exceed its benefits, and it is ineffective. As the amount of formal control increases, so does its effectiveness—but only up to a point. Beyond that point, continued increases in the amount of formal control result in a loss. For example, an organization might benefit from reducing the span of control of supervisors from 20 to 15 employees. However, to further reduce the span of control from 15 to 8 employees would mean paying more supervisors, and the costs might outweigh the benefits. It could also create hostility among workers who might feel oversupervised and under too much pressure to produce. This could lead to lower job satisfaction, high absenteeism, and higher turnover.

Two break-even points are shown in Fig. 17.3. They indicate where the amount of formal control begins to result in a net benefit or returns to a loss for the organization. The *optimum* amount of control (Fig. 17.3) is very difficult to achieve, but successful managers can probably come close to it.[11]

IN PRACTICE
Internal Bleeding

Internal controls cover a range of activities from simple computerization of inventories, to voucher systems that prevent low-level staffers from making high-level purchases, to cross-checks that prevent one employee from shipping goods without another employee making sure the bills are going out. Such systems also do far more than keep employees honest. Tight accounting is essential to successful management.

Many of the abuses that managers are most eager to stop stem from pressures they create. Tell a guy in your Phoenix office his job depends on higher sales, and you run the risk he will falsify orders to keep from being fired. In essence, that's what happened at J. Walter Thompson (JWT) when the advertising agency announced in 1982 that it would have to take a $30.4 million writeoff. The company's Phoenix office had been overstating its profits and revenues regularly to keep up with steadily climbing objectives. Nothing was stolen, but when the falsified sales were discovered and reported, the company's stock dropped 20%.

In the aftermath, JWT restructured its control system. "The primary difference is that we now have one general ledger system and one chart of accounts," says Herbert Eames Jr., executive vice president for finance. "We don't have a multitude of charts, accounts and systems. As a result, it's easier for the auditors to go through one account process and one set of audit materials."

Formal controls can be expensive. There's no point in spending $1 million in accountants' salaries to find a mere $500,000 in misplaced inventories. "You get into cost-benefit tradeoffs," says John Collins, a partner at Peat Marwick. "In a fast food place, what's the cost-benefit tradeoff of making sure that every hamburger gets rung up, versus the cost of making certain that 98% of the hamburgers get rung up?"

The cost of internal controls often can't be measured in dollars alone. Frequently, the question relates more to lost productivity and creativity. "It begins with a person who has a good idea for a product, and it's going to cost $10,000 to start development," says Bob Kavner, a partner with Coopers & Lybrand. "In a highly bureaucratic company, that requires a senior vice president's approval. Then it has to go to several other committees. Pretty soon the young champion who had the idea gets exhausted from trying to get approvals. After going through all this once, he decides it just isn't worth the fight next time."

At General Electric managers are wary of controlling executives to the point where they can't get anything done. "We've lowered the level at which certain activities can be authorized, so we run as a smaller company," says James Costello, GE's comptroller. "Some executives can approve expenditures of over $10 million. That's probably double what it was three or four years ago."

What's unfortunate about all this is that every time a company has a major financial breakdown, there is a tendency to overreact. Controls must be tight enough to keep the crooks out, but loose enough to encourage creativity. Such balancing is difficult, and much too important to be left solely to the accountants.[12]

CORRECTIVE-CONTROL MODEL

The *corrective-control model* is the process of detecting and correcting deviations from preestablished objectives or standards.[13] It relies heavily on feedback and reaction to what has already happened.[14] As shown in Fig. 17.4, a corrective-control model requires six interconnected steps:

1. Define the subsystem (an individual, a department, or a process);

2. Identify characteristics to be measured;

3. Set standards;

4. Collect information;

5. Make comparisons; and

6. Diagnose situation and implement corrections.

Define the Subsystem

A formal control process might be created and maintained for an employee, a department, or an entire organization.[15] The controls could focus on specific inputs, production processes, or outputs. Even rewards like incentive-pay systems can motivate employees to engage in corrective self-control.[16] Controls on *inputs* often place limitations on how much the raw materials used

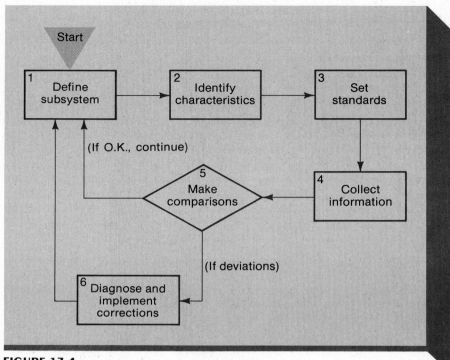

FIGURE 17.4
Corrective-Control Model

in the production process can vary from company standards. This reduces uncertainty about the quality and quantity of inputs into the production process. For example, at Stroh's breweries, elaborate controls (including personal inspections and laboratory testing) are used to make sure that the water and grains used in the production of its beer meet predetermined standards.

Many controls are applied to the *production* process. For Stroh's these include the length of time for cooking the brew, temperature in the vats, sampling of the brew, laboratory testing of the brew at each stage of the process, visual inspection of the beer prior to final packing, and others.

Finally, controls on the *output* of goods and services are maintained. At Stroh's these range from specifying the levels of inventories to be maintained to monitoring consumer attitudes toward the company's goods and services.

Identify Characteristics

The types of information that can and should be obtained about the subsystem must be identified. Establishment of a formal corrective-control process requires early determination of (1) the characteristics that can be measured; (2)

the economic costs of obtaining information on each characteristic relative to the expected benefits; and (3) whether variations in each characteristic affect the performance objectives of the subsystem.

After identifying the characteristics that can be measured, managers must be selective in choosing those to be measured. The *principle of selectivity,* also known as Pareto's law, states that in any series of elements to be controlled, a small number of elements always accounts for a large number of effects.[17] In brewing beer, for example, three of the critical characteristics that influence the quality of the beer are water quality, temperature, and length of brewing time. The control aspect of a management-by-objectives (MBO) system is based on this principle. The direct control of objectives makes possible the control of the few, but vital, elements that can account for major variations in results.

Set Standards

Managers should set standards for each characteristic measured. *Standards* are the criteria for evaluating the activities undertaken in the subsystem and are often interrelated. A considerable amount of coordination among organizational departments is required in setting standards. For example, a consulting firm whose objective is to provide only the highest-quality services must have strict standards for screening its personnel. These personnel-selection standards might include a minimum of a master's degree, three years of industrial experience, ability to express oneself in writing and orally, and the ability to act independently.

Increasingly, managers are developing control systems based on performance standards (performance objectives). There are many possible types of performance standards. The following are examples of standards in five performance areas.

- *Inventory:* Monthly finished goods inventory should be maintained at the unit sales forecasted for the following two-month period.

- *Accounts receivable:* Monthly accounts receivable should be no more than the dollar value of the previous 1.5-months' sales.

- *Sales productivity:* The dollar value of sales per salesperson should be $1000 greater than the comparable month for the previous year and $12,000 greater on an annual basis.

- *Employee turnover:* The turnover of field sales personnel should be no more than 5 per 100 salespersons per month and no more than 30 per 100 salespersons on an annual basis.

- *Production scrap:* Scrap should amount to no more than $50 per month per full-time production worker and no more than $600 per full-time production worker on an annual basis.[18]

Collect Information

The collection of information is a means of obtaining measurements for each of the designated characteristics. Information can be collected by people or by mechanical means, such as a counting device used by libraries. Information may be collected by the individual or group whose performance is to be controlled. However, in some cases, this can result in a loss of valid information.

Employees are likely to be motivated to distort or conceal information if negative information is used primarily as a basis for criticizing or punishing them. Moreover, when formal controls put too much emphasis on punishment to correct poor behaviors and performance, strong group controls often develop to distort the information that is reported to higher management; this makes the pinpointing of responsibility difficult.

Top managers create special departments to act as information monitors and collectors by auditing certain activities of other departments. A personnel department collects data in order to determine whether standards regarding pay raises are being met or that affirmative action guidelines are being followed. Similarly, a controller's department collects and analyzes information in order to ascertain that the recording of income and expenditures is done according to certain accounting standards. Recall that, in the Preview Case, Texas Commerce uses an internal-audit team to monitor and review the call reports of branch-bank loan officers.

Make Comparisons

In order to make comparisons, managers must find out whether there is a difference between what *is* happening and what *should be* happening. This means that they must compare their information about results with performance standards. These standards might be contained in written rules, computer programs, or carried in the manager's memory. Making comparisons occurs when a professor's graduate assistant

1. obtains the output of student scores on a multiple-choice test from the college's computer center;

2. compares these scores with the professor's standards;

3. determines the extent to which the students' scores (performances) differ from the standards; and

4. gives these analyses to the professor for evaluation of the results if they are not consistent with the established standards for grading.

If there is no apparent difference between what is happening and what should be happening, the individual or department normally continues to function without any change. Table 17.2 illustrates steps 3–5 of the corrective-control model for the standards in five performance areas previously listed for a four-month period. The first column shows the standards (that is, what should be happening in each area). The information-collected columns show what has happened for the previous month and year-to-date. The comparisons-made columns show whether performance in each area is at, above, or below standard for the previous month and year-to-date. Control information is often collected and compared on a monthly (January, February, . . . December) and year-to-date (January–March, January–October) basis.

TABLE 17.2 ■ STANDARDS, INFORMATION, AND COMPARISONS IN THE CORRECTIVE-CONTROL MODEL FOR FOUR-MONTH PERIOD

PERFORMANCE AREA AND STANDARD	INFORMATION COLLECTED		COMPARISON MADE	
	Previous Month	*Year-to-Date*	*Previous Month*	*Year-to-Date*
Inventory Monthly finished goods inventory should be maintained at the unit sales forecasted for the following 2-month period.	Inventory at 3.5 months	Inventory at 3 months	1.5 months below standard	1 month below standard
Accounts Receivable Monthly accounts receivable should be no more than the dollar value of the previous 1.5-months' sales.	Receivables at 2 months	Receivables at 2.5 months	0.5 month below standard	1 month below standard
Sales Productivity The dollar value of sales per salesperson should be $1000 greater than the comparable month for the previous year and $12,000 greater on an annual basis.	$1100 greater	$4400 greater	$100 better than standard	$400 better than standard
Employee Turnover The turnover of field sales personnel should be no more than 5 per 100 salespersons per month and no more than 60 per 100 salespersons on an annual basis.	8	20 (standard: 20 year-to-date)	3 better than standard	At standard
Production Scrap Scrap should amount to no more than $50 per month per full-time production worker and no more than $600 per full-time production worker on an annual basis.	$45	$185 (standard: $200 year-to-date)	$5 better than standard	$15 better than standard

Diagnose Situation and Implement Corrections

Diagnosis involves assessing the types, amounts, and causes of *deviations*. Then action is needed to eliminate those deviations. As shown in Table 17.2, management should take action to correct deviations for inventory levels and accounts receivable. A careful diagnosis of the causes of these deviations should be followed by quick actions to correct these deviations. On the other hand, management is likely to be pleased with the better than standard sales productivity of the field sales personnel and the lower than expected production scrap per full-time production worker.

The fact that a characteristic can be controlled does not necessarily mean that it should be controlled. The five performance areas and their standards used in Table 17.2 illustrate the principle of selectivity. The comparison of actual results to standards provides a framework by which managers can concentrate on the control of deviations or exceptions. This makes overmanaging less likely and encourages the more efficient use of a manager's time.

CONTROVERSIAL CONTROLS

Companies are increasingly using two controversial controls: polygraph testing and security agents. These methods supplement the more common preventive and corrective controls that we have discussed.

Polygraph Testing

Polygraph testing is used by some firms to screen job applicants (preventive control), to check on current employees for possible theft and fraud (preventive and corrective control), and to investigate specific thefts or irregularities (corrective control). For example, the Jack Eckerd Corporation, a diversified drug company, requires periodic polygraph testing of *all* employees, from the chairman of the board and president down. By requiring all employees to take polygraph tests, a company lessens the likelihood that a group of employees will feel that they are being singled out or are under more suspicion than any other group. The use of polygraph testing as a preventive control assumes that, if employees know they must take these tests on a regular basis, it will serve as an effective deterrent to theft.

Contrary to popular opinion, a polygraph machine itself cannot detect lies. A *polygraph machine* simply measures a number of physiological characteristics—pulse rate, blood pressure, rate and depth of breathing, resistance of the skin to electricity, and skin temperature—at the same time.[19]

In theory, individuals experience emotional responses such as guilt, anxiety, or fear when they lie. These emotions can cause involuntary changes in physiological processes (changes in heart rate, skin temperature, and so on). The polygraph only records physiological changes, if any, that follow answers to questions. Any lie-detection assessment must be done by the person administering the test, who interprets the output of the polygraph machine.

A polygraph test consists of two major types of questions. *Relevant* (critical) questions are expected to trigger stress—and thus fluctuations in physiological responses—if the person being tested lies. *Information* (neutral) questions are used to establish normal physiological response patterns. The examiner(s) attempt to detect abnormal patterns in response to relevant questions based on the normal patterns established through responses to informational questions. Abnormal patterns in response to relevant questions are usually considered evidence of lying. Let us consider a set of polygraph questions that might be asked of a current employee who is being investigated to help determine whether he stole $1000.

IN PRACTICE
Polygraph
Questions for the
$1000 Theft

Information Questions:

1. Is your name John?

2. Is your last name Smith?

Relevant Question:

3. Do you know who took the $1000 now missing from register no. 1?

Information Question:

4. Were you born in 1943?

Relevant Question:

5. Did you make any plan to steal that $1000 now missing from register no. 1?

Information Question:

6. Did you attend the University of Alabama?

Relevant Question (relive the crime):

7. Did you take the $1000 now missing from register no. 1?

Information Question:

8. Are you now 41 years old?

Control Question:*

9. During the first 30 years of your life do you remember stealing anything of value?

---

* A control question is a general question that inquires about a similar but unrelated event. The question is designed so that the examinee will probably lie in responding. This question is used to interpret the chart.[20]

(continued)

Information Question:

10. Is your address 1927 Fox Run?

Relevant Question (evidence connecting):

11. At the time the $1000 was stolen, were you there?

Control Question:

12. Between the ages of 10 and 30 do you remember stealing anything of value?

Relevant Question (most serious issue—relive crime):

13. Are you the person who stole the missing $1000?

Information Question:

14. Are you married?

Relevant Question (confirming issue):

15. Do you know where the missing $1000 is now?

We do not intend to suggest that polygraph testing be used as a part of managerial control. There are major ethical and right-to-privacy implications associated with its use. Moreover, there is considerable controversy over its accuracy.[21]

Security Agents

On-the-job *employee theft* is estimated at about $50 billion per year in the United States.[22] Employee theft is the unauthorized taking, control, or transfer of money and/or property of the organization by an employee.[23] The forms of employee theft are wide-ranging and include pilferage (repeatedly stealing in small amounts); kickbacks, bribery, securities theft and fraud; embezzlement (taking assets entrusted to one's care); arson, burglary, and vandalism (malicious destruction of assets); and shoplifting, insurance fraud, check fraud, and credit-card fraud. Although the news media have played up the role of outsiders in computer-related crime, most of it is committed by employees.[24] The primary reason for the growth in internal security staffs and outside security firms (Pinkerton, Burns, Wachenhut, Guardsmark) is management's need to bring the increasing rate of employee theft under control.

Companies are increasingly using undercover agents to control employee theft. This has become a controversial control tactic, but not as controversial as the use of polygraph testing. Undercover security seems to be tolerated and generally accepted—both legally and socially—so long as there is no hint of entrapment. *Entrapment* is the luring of an individual into a compromising or illegal act.

Pinkerton and other security firms provide companies with undercover security agents, often in response to the feeling that theft is taking place. For example, a Pinkerton undercover agent went to work as a production employee at a manufacturing company. The agent discovered that the inventory shrinkage of 1 percent year after year was due to widespread pilfering.[25] Since pilferage means stealing in small amounts, the employee norms apparently supported stealing in small amounts.

Security agents may go through fairly involved steps to prevent and correct employee theft. The tactics reported by an actual security manager (in his own words) to check employee honesty and document his suspicions are presented in the In Practice "The Honesty Test." Some people feel that these tactics border on entrapment. Do you agree?

IN PRACTICE
The Honesty Test

Another honesty test we do is we'll put a check, let's say a $20 personal check, into the back of the register drawer. Along with that check, I'll put a $10 or $20 bill, depending on what they like to take. Some people like to take $20 at a time, some people take $10 at a time, or $5, whatever, but generally what their pattern is. So along with that check at the back of the register, I'll put a $10 bill and record the serial numbers. When that employee I suspect is up there working, I'll be observing from a blind or somewhere and I'll have credit or another investigator call and say there's a check missing in register so-and-so, could you check it out. "Open up the drawer and look back there and see if it's back there." Here I'm presenting another opportunity for them. I know it sounds like entrapment, but it isn't. It's perfectly legal and I've prosecuted people on this. It just goes to show that anybody's capable of it. This person probably was good for $200 in cash and he was smart. Okay, he'd just finished four years of school. I had him go back to the register. Sure enough, he looked, took the ten, folded it up and put it in his pocket right away. This is my leverage. So we called him in. I interviewed him and all he'd admit to was stealing that $10 bill. That's all he'd admit to. He would not admit to the $120 that I had him charted out for that I know he'd stolen but I couldn't prove it. I didn't have him on tape. Another method we use is videotape recorder with a camera over the register so I can record stealing. I've caught nine people this way in automotive and over in paint. I've got them on tape.[26]

MANAGERIAL CONTROL STRATEGIES

The more common internal organization-control strategies used by managers include staffing, performance-appraisal, formal-structure, policies and rules, financial, and machine controls. Figure 17.5 reflects the idea that these internal

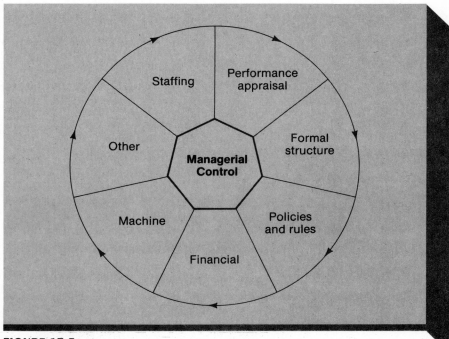

FIGURE 17.5
Common Internal Managerial Control Strategies

control strategies are not mutually exclusive. In fact, in an effective formal organizational control system, they are closely linked. The control of many activities usually requires that two (or more) of these strategies be used at the same time. In other words, a combination of strategies gives managers greater control than if each strategy were used separately. For example, use of a budget as a financial control is often linked to the performance appraisal of managers. Managers are expected to operate within their budgets and the appraisal of their performance is partially determined by their deviation from those budgets.

We present each of these strategies here briefly. Our emphasis is on their strategic, rather than tactical, use in the managerial control function.

Staffing Controls

Organizational effectiveness improves when managers control undesirable and unwanted employee behaviors and attitudes. The two primary means of doing this involve selection and socialization and training. Personnel selection techniques screen people for initial employment and for later promotions and transfers. Socialization and training programs mold the behaviors and attitudes of employees toward their jobs and the organization. If an organization is to be successful, selection and socialization and training controls are needed.

Selection

Selection controls focus on who is hired, promoted, or transferred within an organization. In a tight labor market, few candidates are available and a company may find it necessary to lower its standards to obtain new workers. When this happens, the quality of the work is likely to suffer unless training efforts are increased.

The extent of selection controls used is influenced by the type of position for which a person is being considered. Two aspects of the position are especially important: (1) how much the person's decisions can harm or help the organization; and (2) how much leeway the person would have to allocate and use the organization's resources. For example, compared to the controls used in selecting marketing executives who develop sales strategies, control budgets, and supervise others, the selection controls used in hiring file clerks are minimal.

Socialization and training

Socialization and training involve planned attempts to shape the attitudes and behaviors of employees.[27] Company orientation and socialization programs are usually designed to foster attitudes (sentiments) that are consistent with the needs of the organization. These programs, in contrast to technical and skill training, are often intended to develop a sense of commitment to the philosophy and objectives of the organization.[28] All employees are likely to be exposed to such programs in companies that are committed to creating or maintaining a strong organizational culture, such as Hewlett-Packard, Toyota, and IBM. Some people have expressed concern about the possible dangers of excessive socialization efforts, feeling that some organizations may subtly manipulate and brain wash employees.[29]

The effort an organization puts into shaping individual attitudes depends on the results desired, which may range from relative indifference to intensive indoctrination. (See Fig. 17.6.) Chaos and instability might result if managers and employees hold highly incompatible goals, values, and attitudes. At the other extreme is absolute conformity, represented by the organization-man stereotype.

In companies in the United States, Canada, the U.K., and other Western nations, the ideal socialization program might employ deliberate conditioning to create unity without conformity.[30] Management by objectives programs can provide the means of achieving this. Recall that, in MBO programs, open discussion of objectives is encouraged; then an effort is made to reach agreement on which objectives should be pursued; and finally, people are given some discretion in how they work toward those objectives. The International

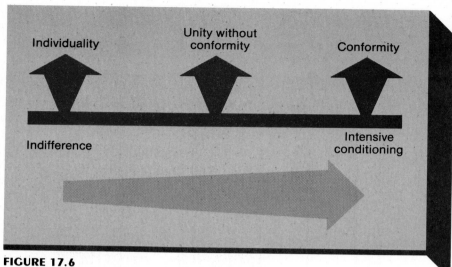

FIGURE 17.6
Formal Organization Socialization Continuum

INTERNATIONAL FOCUS

Hell Camp

The 140 executives are in the 10th day of a 13-day training cycle. It is 5 A.M., the beginning of a day that will not end until 9 P.M., and it is easy to see why the Japanese managers shivering in the biting mountain air call this retreat in the foothills of Fuji the "hell camp." Stripped of the pinstripes and other badges that mark them as men on the way up, they are here to learn humility and how to concentrate on detail under exquisitely applied stress.

As the light rises and the mountains begin to turn from black to green, you see there is scarcely anyone wearing fewer than a dozen of the 16 blue "ribbons of shame" pinned to their white uniform shirts at the initiation ceremony that began the training cycle. At that ceremony the trainees made a pledge to one another and to the school. The heart of the pledge was a willingness to admit serious flaws in themselves and a deep commitment to correct them.

The 16 ribbons of shame spoke of shortcomings in basics: reading, writing, speech, pronunciation, good manners and dealing with others. Most of the 24,000 or so managers who have gone through the school since it was founded five years ago are from small to middle-size companies. Take Sam Yamada, University of Oregon business school '55 ("Gosh, was it that long ago?"), who handles administration for Konan Asco Co., Ltd., a joint venture partly owned by the Automatic Switch Co., in Florham Park, N.J. "I'm here because my

Focus describes the operation of one organization that specializes in socializing and training managers from small and middle-sized Japanese companies; its approach probably would be rejected by managers in most Western societies.

Performance-Appraisal Controls

Formal performance appraisals are another control strategy for preventing or correcting unwanted employee behaviors and performance; their forms and effectiveness vary greatly. A range of reward and punishment combinations are likely to result from performance appraisal systems.[31]

In a mechanistic management system, managers attempt to control employees through performance appraisal by emphasizing extrinsic rewards for desired performance: wages, pension plans, status symbols (size of office, access to information), and job security. At times, performance-appraisal control relies on certain forms of punishment, such as suspension, demotion, and dismissal.

In an organic management system, by contrast, formal performance appraisal acknowledges that employee behavior and performance are determined

president asked me to come," says Yamada, who switches easily from Japanese to good English. "And besides, as a social psychology major, I wanted to see how the group worked."

One reason for the success of the program—it costs participating companies the equivalent of about $1100 per trainee per cycle—is the fear among many of the Japanese top brass that prosperity makes for soft management. Most of those picked to go through Kanrisha are slated for promotion.

The ribbons of shame are removed, one by one, only after the sweating managers have passed a rigorous test in each of the subjects the ribbons represent. One trainee, reading a speech about the need to look after the health of subordinates, has the paper snatched from his hands. "You won't have a piece of paper in your hand when you're giving a speech at the office," snaps his instructor. Yukio Harumi, testing another recruit on voice projection, wraps a big pair of hands around the student's diaphragm and squeezes. "It's got to come from the stomach," he shouts.

The final twist of the psychological knife is that less than 30% of this class—like most others—will shed its ribbons fast enough to pass through the solemnity of graduation on the appointed 13th day. That's the final humilia-

(continued)

tion—to kneel in a sweat-stained shirt still weighted with those accusing ribbons while the graduates, natty in pinstripes, step forward to receive their diplomas.

It took Sam Yamada and other rejects another 48 hours of testing to get rid of their ribbons. Yamada came out of the hell camp saying, "I sort of enjoyed it. They taught me how to make a speech, and that's something." What it also taught him, of course, is something else quintessentially Japanese: Part of the price of success is almost always endless attention to detail.

Source: Excerpted from R. Phalon, "Hell Camps," *Forbes,* June 18, 1984, p. 56–58.

by intrinsic rewards (satisfying work), self-control (personal sense of responsibility for work), group control (attitudes and norms of the work group), and extrinsic rewards (pay raises, promotions). An organic management system is generally characterized by a strong and well-defined organizational culture, which may not be the case in a mechanistic management system.

Formal-Structure Controls

Formal structures help top management to control the organization by establishing the pattern of authority, flow of communication, and span of control.[32]

Pattern of Authority

Organizations typically have formal, written job descriptions that describe the authority and responsibilities of each position. In mechanistic management systems, job descriptions will be very specific. In organic management systems, job descriptions are likely to be broader and may consist of only the major responsibilities and authority of the position. In either case, job descriptions set limits on the formal authority of each individual.

Flow of Communication

Formal structures help to establish control by prescribing the flow of communication. Formal communication systems frequently follow the organization's hierarchy. The hierarchy specifies lateral and diagonal communication and coordination points as well. This is most apparent in the matrix form of organization as well as with staff departments, such as personnel, auditing, legal, and planning. For example, the personnel department may be responsible for certain activity controls, such as affirmative action or exercising varying degrees of authority. A personnel department that has a high degree of control over affirmative action can make decisions in this particular activity area that are binding on all departments.

Span of control

Another structural variable affecting formal control is the span of control (the number of people reporting to a superior). Changing a manager's span of control influences how he or she controls subordinates. A narrow span of control increases control over the activities of subordinates by having fewer subordinates report to a superior. A wider span of control usually prevents managers from supervising subordinates too closely, creating too much subordinate dependence, and becoming too personally involved with subordinates.

Policies and Rules Controls

Policies and rules are also important ways for exercising control over many organizational activities and functions. They help to define the discretion and required actions of individuals and departments.

A *policy* is a guide for actions. It is general rather than specific and expresses a condition to be reached. The policy manual at Brooklyn Union Gas states: "Promotions will be based on merit."

A *rule* specifies a course of action that must be followed. It is established to create uniformity of action and may or may not be a prohibition. An example of a rule is: "Courses may be dropped by the student through the third week of classes without a grade being assigned."

The basic difference between policies and rules is the amount of flexibility allowed. Policies are made by top managers as guides for more specific rule making, which occurs at all management levels.[33] Policy making at GM, for example, is the responsibility of the executive and finance committees. These committees include representatives from all the company's major divisions and departments. These committees also frequently develop rules to implement the firm's general policies.

Effectiveness of rules

Formal rules are not always effective and they can have both desirable and undesirable consequences for an organization. Rules *reflect formal authority*. They help structure relationships among people and departments and ensure action consistent with the organization's purposes. For example, rules may define the relative authority of the personnel department and other managers in the organization with respect to the hiring of employees.

By defining minimum acceptable work standards for subordinates, rules may *reinforce apathy*. For example, a rule may specify that employees who do not average 300 units of output per week will be subject to a disciplinary layoff. This type of rule may simply motivate employees to produce 300 units and no more.

Rules may inadvertently result in a *means–end reversal*. That is, a rule may become an end rather than a means to an end. For example, a rule may state that the organization will stop serving customers at 5:00 P.M. When one of the authors was standing in line at a library on a Saturday afternoon, the clock struck 5:00 P.M. Even though several people protested, the clerk cited the rule and refused to check out any more books.

Rules can have a *domino effect* (rules lead to more rules). This may occur as managers attempt to deal with hostile worker groups. For example, rules may specify the number of vacation days employees receive based on number of years worked. Conflict might arise between management and workers over how this vacation time should be taken—all at once or spread out. If specific requests cannot be worked out cooperatively and with some give and take on both sides, an elaborate network of formal rules may be developed to specify how vacation time can be taken.

Financial Controls

Financial controls include a wide range of techniques and procedures that are intended to (1) prevent the misallocation of financial resources; and (2) provide timely feedback of economic information so that corrective action can be taken. Entire courses are offered on these methods, techniques, and procedures. Therefore, we will only highlight two of the more essential financial controls: comparative financial analysis and budgeting. For many companies the monitoring and control aspects of these financial controls are most often performed by external auditors (certified public accounting firms like Arthur Anderson and Price Waterhouse), internal auditing departments, accounting departments, controller departments, and treasury departments. The primary responsibility of external auditors is to the stockholders. Their control role is to assure stockholders that the firm's financial statements present fairly its financial position and are in conformity with generally accepted accounting principles that have been consistently applied.

Comparative financial analysis

A **comparative financial analysis** is the economic evaluation of the firm and its departments for two or more time periods or between other similar firms and departments when such information exists. Industry trade associations often collect information from their members and publish it in a consolidated form. Publicly owned firms publish income statements, balance sheets, and other financial statements. These sources are often used by management and external groups to assess changes in certain of the firm's financial indicators over time and compare them with other firms in the same industry. Companies that have multiple and similar production plants (GM, Ford, Exxon, IBM), retail outlets (Kmart, Walmart, Sears, Penney, Foley's), restaurants (McDonald's, Wendy's, Red Lobster, Bennigan's), and hotels (Hilton, Holiday Inn, Ramada Inn) make financially based comparisons among units for control purposes.

The most common method for making such comparisons is through *ratio analysis.* Ratio analysis involves selecting two significant figures, expressing their relationship as a proportion or fraction (percentage, rate per hundred), and comparing them over time/or with those of similar departments or organizations.

Figure 17.7 shows a pyramid of ratios used to assess various aspects of return on investment (ROI). They identify changes in the firm over time and trigger the need for corrective actions. These ratios are also used by management and stockholders to compare a firm's financial position with that of other firms. For example, management might judge that competitors seem to

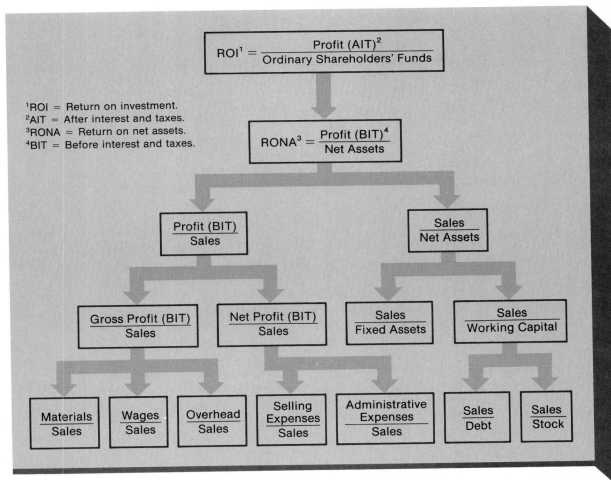

FIGURE 17.7
Typical Pyramid of Ratios in Return on Investment Tree

be getting a higher return on investment and that corrective actions are needed; or stockholders might judge that the firm is slipping and needs new management or that they should sell their stock.

Let us examine some possible uses of these ratios. Sales could be increasing rapidly but, if profits are constant or falling, the profit margin will decrease (profit before interest and tax ÷ sales). This might indicate the need for stricter cost controls. Net assets may not be producing as high a level of sales as they have done historically (sales ÷ net assets). This might suggest problems of asset management.[34] In addition to those shown in Fig. 17.7, a number of other financial ratios are useful to managers. One of the more important ones compares current assets with current liabilities: current assets ÷ current liabilities.

Although ratio analysis is an important control tool, it must be coupled with sound managerial judgment. The use of ratios for making comparisons simply reports continuity or deviations; the ratios do not automatically tell management that all is well or that changes are needed. Managerial judgment is required to determine whether corrections are required and, if so, which type would be most effective.

Budgeting

Proposed expenditures are defined and linked with desired objectives in *budgets*.[35] They are usually expressed in the dollar costs of various activities. For example, production budgets may be derived from hours of labor per unit produced, machine downtime per thousand hours of running time, wage rates, and similar historical information. In budgeting for completely new activities, managers may have to assign dollar costs based on rough estimates. Budgets for established activities are usually easier to determine because historical cost data are available. In either case, the individuals who prepare budgets must exercise judgment in the use of historical data and their knowledge of each resource category, in combination with forecasts of changing conditions and costs. Budgets are often developed for a one-year period and then broken down by month. This enables managers to track their progress in meeting the budget as the year unfolds. The major budget categories usually include labor (human effort), materials and supplies, and facilities (property, buildings, equipment).

Purposes of budgeting.   Budgeting serves three main purposes: (1) it aids managers in planning their work more effectively; (2) it aids managers in planning the best way to allocate resources; and (3) it aids managers in controlling and monitoring the resources being used during the budget period. When managers place dollars and cents on the specific resources needed, they sometimes realize that their objectives aren't worth the cost. When this occurs, managers can modify or abandon objectives and plans or come up with new ones.

Close budget control allows managers to plan work, allocate resources, and monitor progress toward attainment of objectives.

Source: Elizabeth Hamlin/Stock, Boston.

Use of budgeting as a control. The control aspect of budgeting may be either corrective or preventive. When budgeting is used as a corrective control, the emphasis is on identifying *deviations* from the budget. Deviations serve as a basis for subsequent managerial action to identify and correct the causes of the deviations or to decide whether the budget itself should be changed.[36]

The power of a budget, especially when used as a preventive control, depends on whether managers and employees view it as an informal contract to which they have agreed. One study investigated this and other issues by mailing a questionnaire to first-line managers in order to obtain their views about how their company budgets were used.[37] They were asked: "Do you feel that frequently budgets or standards are a club held over the head of the supervisor to force better performance?" Twenty percent of the 204 respondents replied *yes* and 68 percent answered *no*.

Most managers who must live by budgets usually accept their use by top management as a control mechanism. Others, however, view budgets with fear and hostility.[38] This usually occurs when an organization enforces budget controls by excessive use of punishment and the threat of punishment.

Types of budgets. There is no single classification system for budgets. Specific individuals, sections, projects, teams, committees, departments, divisions, and strategic business units could all be assigned budgets within which they are expected to operate. However, the following are among the most common types of budgets found in business organizations.[39]

- *Sales budget:* A forecast of expected revenues, generally stated by product line on a monthly basis and revised at least annually.

- *Materials budget:* Expected purchases, generally stated by specific categories, which may vary month-to-month on the basis of seasonal variations and inventory levels.

- *Labor budget:* Expected staffing, generally stated by number of individuals and dollars for each job category (electrical engineers, carpenters, secretaries).

- *Capital budget:* Targeted spending for major tangible assets (new or renovated headquarters building, new production plant, major equipment) that often requires a time horizon beyond one year.[40]

- *Research and development budget:* Targeted spending for the refinement or development of production or services, materials, and processes.

- *Cash budget:* Expected flow of monetary receipts and expenditures, generally developed at least once a year for each month of the year.

The types of budgets and budget categories are strongly influenced by the philosophy of top management and the structure of the organization. For example, a functional structure (marketing, production, finance, personnel) will usually have a primary budget for each functional category. On the other hand, a product structure will usually have a budget for each product line. For example, PepsiCo uses product-line budgeting with its product structure (Wilson Sporting goods, Pizza Inn, North American Van Lines, and others).

Zero-base budgeting. Although there are several different types of budgeting processes that can be used for planning and control purposes, we will discuss only one: *zero-base budgeting* (ZBB). This is a system of justifying activities and programs in terms of efficiency and organizational priorities and by treating them as if they were entirely new.[41] The objective of ZBB is to assist managers in allocating (and moving) resources to their most cost-effective uses. As a planning technique, it aids in the achievement of strategic objectives in response to proven needs and perceived threats, risks, or opportunities. As a control technique, it forces managers to examine their functions and operations thoroughly.[42] The U.S. Department of Agriculture (USDA) developed this method in the early 1960s. It has since been refined and used by USDA, other government agencies, and many firms (such as Texas Instruments, Eastern Airlines, Owens-Illinois, and New York Telephone).

Zero-base budgeting is essentially a "bottom-up" system that includes two major parts. The first part is a *decision package*—a verbal description of what is needed in order to accomplish each major objective for a manager's unit. Developed by analyzing and describing specific objectives, decision packages generally include the following.

1. Objective of the activity.
2. Description of the activity.
3. Alternative ways of achieving the objective.
4. Consequences of not performing the activity.
5. Advantages of retaining the activity.
6. The personnel, equipment, space, and other resources required during the current budget year.
7. The resources needed for the activity during the next budget period.[43]

The second major part in ZBB involves the *ranking* of decision packages.[44] This may be accomplished through a variety of means from complicated cost-benefit assessments to subjective evaluation by a superior. Sometimes the rankings include a voting process in which key managers rate activities on a scale from "essential" to "would be nice to have."

Zero-base budgeting is consistent with management by objectives. In fact, ZBB serves as a particularly useful tool within the action-planning and objective-setting steps of an MBO system. The departments that can most easily use ZBB are legal, traffic, public relations, advertising, production control, personnel and human resources, and credit and financial management. All these departments provide service, advice, control, or information to other departments. Managers of departments for which profit-related objectives can be established—such as production or marketing—may find that other budgeting techniques are better.[45] In sum, ZBB weaves together the planning and control processes.[46]

Machine Controls

Stages of development

Machines have developed through several major stages.[47] They first increased worker productivity by giving individuals better and easier physical control over certain activities; next, workers and machines responded to information from each other, creating a mutual control system.

A new threshold was reached with **automation.** Automation refers to processes that are primarily self-regulating and are able to operate independently of humans in a wide range of conditions. Automation usually involves joining machines that perform work with other machines.

Now, machines (computers) controlling other machines, as in the case of robots, perform part of the managerial control function, and participate with managers in the control process. For example, computers in oil refineries are used to monitor and make automatic adjustments in refinery processes. These adjustments are based on data collected by the computer from numerous stages in the refining of oil.

USE IN PRODUCTION

There has been a steady shift toward machine controls in production operations. The shift was initially from human to machine control of non-human resources (using automatic sensors instead of visual inspection in the production of steel). With the advent of assembly-line, mass-production technology, machines supplemented rules and regulations for directly controlling production workers. In continuous-process or robotic operations, machines control machines.

There are many instances of advanced machine control in the automobile industry. Chevrolet installed in its brake plant at Saginaw, Michigan, an automated system that controls four cranes, records inventory, directs five miles of conveyors, and diagnoses tool problems for the maintenance staff. Chrysler's computer-controlled system in its Syracuse, New York, plant expands or contracts a boring tool to adjust for the temperature and wear condition of the tool. The system feeds the exact diameters of finished pistons to the machines bearing the cylinder blocks so they can adjust their bits.[48]

The impact of automatic machine control on management has been reported in a number of studies. One researcher found that the introduction of an advanced automated system in one large factory reduced the number of middle-management jobs by 34 percent.[49]

CHAPTER SUMMARY

This chapter focused on managerial control methods that involve application of the managerial roles of disturbance-handler, monitor, and leader. Formal controls are used by managers to help them achieve objectives and serve to prevent and correct unwanted deviations from objectives and standards. Increasing the amount of formal control does not necessarily lead to a more effective organization because (1) controls cost money and may not pay for themselves; (2) controls, unless carefully designed, can lead to negative reactions by those who must abide by them; and (3) group controls and individual self-control are not necessarily consistent with formal controls. Successful managers recognize the interplay among the three major sources of control found in organizations: formal organization controls, group controls, and individual self-controls.

Preventive controls reduce the number and severity of problems that require corrective action. Such controls include orientation, training, and socialization of new employees in order to reduce the chances that they will make performance errors or engage in unacceptable job-related behaviors. The corrective-control model probably represents the most common view of the formal control process. The basic steps in this process are used to correct deviations from defined standards through feedback. Two of the more controversial controls increasingly being used by business firms are polygraph testing and security agents. The use of undercover security agents can be especially controversial if it appears that their activities involve some form of entrapment.

The chapter provided an overview of six managerial control strategies: (1) the control of personnel through staffing systems; (2) the use of performance-appraisal systems; (3) the formal structure, which helps establish control through position descriptions, specification of communication flow, the creation of special auditing units, and the span of control; (4) the development of policies and rules, which are used to guide behavior and decision making; (5) the use of budgeting; and (6) the application of machine controls. These strategies are interrelated and managers usually employ them in combination to achieve the level of control desired.

MANAGER'S VOCABULARY

automation
budgets
capital budget
cash budget
comparative financial analysis
control
corrective-control model
corrective controls
employee theft
entrapment
financial controls
formal organization controls
group controls
individual self-control
labor budget
managerial control
materials budget
policy
polygraph machine
preventive controls
principle of selectivity
ratio analysis
research and development budget
rule
sales budget
standards
zero-base budgeting

REVIEW QUESTIONS

1. What are the types and sources of control?

2. What are the uses of formal controls?

3. When are formal controls effective?

4. What are the six steps in the corrective-control model?

5. What are the six common managerial control strategies?

DISCUSSION QUESTIONS

1. Control has been defined as a superior dominating the work life of his or her subordinates. Discuss this statement in the light of your new knowledge of the control function.

2. How might the controls applied to your instructor by the Dean differ from those applied to sales clerks at the local McDonald's by its manager?

3. How might the control function in a marketing research department differ from that in a production department that bags potato chips?

4. Drawing on your own work experience, develop an example of the application of the corrective-control model. Try to identify each of the steps in the corrective-control model as shown in Fig. 17.4.

5. Evaluate this statement: "The fewer the controls in an organization, the greater the likelihood the organization will be effective."

MANAGEMENT INCIDENTS AND CASES

First-Line Supervisor: In the Middle

Background
RICH's, a national supermarket chain headquartered in Boston, consists of over 150 stores located throughout the country. Decentralized control of the stores is delegated from the Headquarter's top management level down to the district level. Each district, consisting of approximately 30 stores, is under the control of a District Manager. Each district is further divided into sub-districts under the direction of District Supervisors. Each District Supervisor deals directly with the Store Managers and Assistant Store Managers within his or her geographic area of responsibility. During the monthly visits to the stores, the District Supervisor evaluates the store's overall financial condition, cleanliness, quality of customer service, record keeping, displays,

and compliance with company policies and procedures. All discrepancies are immediately brought to the attention of the Store Manager for correction. Each department within the store (Dairy, Meat, Produce, etc.) has its own manager who is directly responsible to the Store Manager. The remainder of the employees are primarily high school students or recent graduates who perform most of the physical labor, such as unloading trucks, stocking shelves, and mopping the floors. All employees, from the Assistant Manager on down, must become Union members in a certain number of days after being hired.

Internal pressure

Top management establishes profit quotas for each store based on the total sales potential projected for each district. Pressure to meet these quotas is passed to the District Managers who impose it on the District Supervisors who exert pressure on the Store Managers to achieve their profit targets. Although no written policy exists, it is not uncommon for both the Store Manager and the District Supervisor to be fired when quotas are not met.

The buck stops here

One of the Store Managers, Mr. Dinkel, believes that the best way to manage is to be a member of the team. He personally opens and closes the store every day, and frequently assists the employees with much of the physical work. Mr. Dinkel treats them fairly, and in return, they respect him and work additional hours without pay. Although they were aware of the pressure on Mr. Dinkel to meet the profit quotas, they never felt direct pressure since he assumed total responsibility. As a result, the store enjoyed the highest profits in the district. However, a few of the more "important" customers began complaining to the District Manager that Mr. Dinkel was never available in his office, and that he seemed to prefer unloading trucks to managing. Consequently, both Mr. Dinkel and the District Supervisor were fired.

The buck stops there

The first thing Mr. Pearce did when he replaced Mr. Dinkel was to delegate the responsibility of opening and closing the store each day to the Assistant Manager. Additional pressures were placed on the employees to meet the profit target for each store. Employees began competing with each other for fear of losing their jobs. Ironically, they also performed only the minimum amount of work required to get the job done. During absences of Mr. Pearce, the Assistant Manager would frequently reverse Mr. Pearce's directives, which further increased employee tension. The employees filed a complaint with their Union, but received little satisfaction. During the next visit by the District Supervisor, he noticed an increase in loss and damage to inventory, as well as the amount of sick-time being taken by employees. Mr. Pearce told the District Supervisor that there was no apparent explanation.[50]

Questions

1. Is decentralization the best method of control in this case?

2. What are the advantages and disadvantages of Mr. Dinkel and Mr. Pearce's techniques of controlling?

3. What controls, other than pressure and punishment, could top management have used to attain high profits?

REFERENCES

1. Adapted and excerpted from "Texas Commerce: Master of Controls," *Dun's Business Month,* December 1984, pp. 40–41. Copyright © 1984 by Dun & Bradstreet Publications Corporation. Used with permission.

2. G. Giglioni and A. Bedeian, "A Conspectus of Management Control Theory: 1900–1972," *Academy of Management Journal,* 1974, **17**:292–305. *Also see:* T. Heller, "Changing Authority Patterns: A Cultural Perspective," *Academy of Management Review,* July 1985, **10**:488–495.

3. Adapted from W. H. Newman, "Managerial Control." In J. E. Rosenzweig and F. E. Kast (Eds.), *Modules in Management Series.* Chicago: Science Research Associates, 1984, pp. 1–42.

4. K. J. Euske, *Management Control: Planning, Control, Measurement and Evaluation.* Reading, Mass.: Addison-Wesley, 1984, pp. 18–19; D. Rhodes, M. Wright, and M. Jarrett, "Management Control for Effective Corporate Planning," *Long Range Planning,* August 1984, pp. 115–121; P. Lorange, "Strategic Control: Some Issues in Making it Operationally More Useful." In R. B. Lamb

(Ed.), *Competitive Strategic Management.* Englewood Cliffs, N.J.: Prentice-Hall, 1984, pp. 247–271; P. Lorange and M. S. Morton, *Strategic Control Systems.* St. Paul, Minn.: West, 1986.

5. G. W. Dalton, "Motivation and Control in Organizations." In G. W. Dalton and P. R. Lawrence (Eds.), *Motivation and Control in Organizations.* Homewood, Ill.: Richard D. Irwin, 1971, pp. 1–35.

6. For a discussion of self-perceived control *see* E. J. Langer, *The Psychology of Control.* Beverly Hills, Calif.: Sage, 1983; R. E. Walton, "From Control to Commitment in the Workplace," *Harvard Business Review,* March–April 1985, pp. 77–84; G. A. Walter, "Organizational Development and Individual Rights," *Journal of Applied Behavioral Science,* 1984, **20:**423–439.

7. R. Butler, "Control of Workflow in Organizations: Perspectives from Markets, Hierarchies, and Collectives," *Human Relations,* 1983, **36:**421–440; W. G. Ouchi and J. B. Johnson, "Types of Organizational Control and Their Relationship to Emotional Well Being," *Administrative Science Quarterly,* 1978, **23:**293–317; R. Albanese and D. D. Van Fleet, "Rational Behavior in Groups: The Free-Riding Tendency," *Academy of Management Review,* 1985, **10:**244–255.

8. L. D. Parker, "Control in Organization Life: The Contribution of Mary Parker Follett," *Academy of Management Review,* 1984, **9:**736–745; R. E. Walton, "From Control to Commitment in the Workplace," *Harvard Business Review,* March–April 1985, pp. 76–84.

9. R. L. Daft and N. B. Macintosh, "The Nature and Use of Formal Control Systems for Management Control and Strategy Implementation," *Journal of Management,* 1984, **10:**43–66; G. R. Jones, "Forms of Control and Leader Behavior," *Journal of Management,* 1983, **9:**159–172.

10. W. Jerome III, *Executive Control: The Catalyst.* New York: John Wiley, 1961.

11. J. Emery, *Organizational Planning and Control Systems: Theory and Technology.* New York: Macmillan, 1969; H. Tosi, "The Organizational Control Structure," *Journal of Business Research,* 1983, **11:**271–279.

12. Excerpted from R. Greene, "Internal Bleeding," *Forbes,* February 27, 1984, pp. 121–122.

13. E. Lawler III, and J. Rhode, *Information and Control in Organizations.* Pacific Palisades, Calif.: Goodyear, 1976; K. A. Marchant, *Control in Business Organizations.* Boston: Pitman, 1984.

14. G. Hofstede, "The Poverty of Management Control Philosophy," *Academy of Management Review,* 1978, **3:**450–461.

15. W. G. Astley and P. S. Sachdeva, "Structural Sources of Intraorganizational Power: A Theoretical Synthesis," *Academy of Management Review,* 1984, **9:**104–113; A. T. Cobb, "An Episodic Model of Power: Toward an Integration of Theory and Research," *Academy of Management Review,* 1984, **9:**482–493; J. A. Klein, "Why Supervisors Resist Employee Involvement," *Harvard Business Review,* September–October 1984, pp. 87–95.

16. M. Mrowca, "Ohio Firm Relies on Incentive-Pay System to Motivate Workers and Maintain Products," *Wall Street Journal,* August 12, 1983, p. 23.

17. R. Boyce, *Integrated Management Controls.* London: Longman's, Green, 1967.

18. "Staying in Control: Making the Right Decisions Requires the Right Data," *Small Business Report,* August, 1984, pp. 37–39.

19. H. T. Steele, G. E. Summers, and M. J. Welsh, "The Impact of Polygraph Testing on Internal Control," *Internal Auditor,* December 1984, pp. 28–33.

20. Steele, Summers, and Welsh, "The Impact of Polygraph Testing . . . ," p. 32. Reprinted with permission of Institute of Internal Auditors.

21. M. A. Coghill, *The Lie Detector in Employment.* Ithaca, N.Y.: Cornell University Press, 1968; B. Kleinmuntz, "Lie Detectors Fail the Truth Test," *Harvard Business Review,* July–August 1985, pp. 36–37ff; L. Saxe, D. Dougherty, and T. Cross, "The Validity of Polygraph Testing: Scientific Analysis and Public Controversy," *American Psychologist,* 1985, **40:**355–366.

22. J. Perham, "Growing Role for Undercover Agents," *Dun's Business Month,* August 1984, p. 35.

23. G. Robin, "White Collar Crime and Employee Theft," *Crime and Delinquency,* 1974, **20:**251–262.

24. "Computer Security: What Can Be Done?" *Business Week,* September 26, 1983, pp. 126–130.

25. J. Perham, "Growing Role . . . ," p. 35.

26. R. C. Hollinger and J. P. Clark, *Theft By Employees.* Lexington, Mass.: D. C. Heath, 1983, p. 89.

27. G. Inzerilli, "Culture and Organizational Control," *Journal of Business Research,* 1983, 11:281–292; D. C. Feldman, "The Multiple Socialization of Organization Members," *Academy of Management Review,* 1981, 6:309–318; G. R. Jones, "Psychological Orientation and the Process of Organizational Socialization: An Interactionist Perspective," *Academy of Management Review,* 1983, 8:464–474; J. P. Wanous, A. E. Reichers, and S. D. Malik, "Organizational Socialization and Group Development: Toward an Integrative Perspective," *Academy of Management Review,* 1984, 9:670–683.

28. W. Scott, "Executive Development as an Instrument of Higher Control," *Academy of Management Journal,* 1963, 6:191–203. *Also see:* K. E. Kram, *Mentoring at Work: Developmental Relationships in Organizational Life.* Glenview, Ill.: Scott, Foresman, 1985; G. M. Logan, "Inspiring Loyalty and a Sense of Purpose," *California Management Review,* Fall 1984, pp. 149–156.

29. R. Howard, "High Technology and the Reenchantment of the Work Place," *National Productivity Review,* Summer 1984, pp. 255–264; J. J. Sullivan, "A Critique of Theory Z," *Academy of Management Review,* 1983, 8:132–142.

30. F. Kast and J. Rosenzweig, *Organization and Management: A Systems and Contingency Approach,* 3rd ed. New York: McGraw-Hill, 1979, pp. 451–454.

31. J. M. Beyer and H. M. Trice, "A Field Study of the Use and Perceived Effects of Disciplines in Controlling Performance," *Academy of Management Journal,* 1984, 27:743–764; L. L. Cummings, "Compensation, Culture, and Motivation: A Systems Perspective," *Organizational Dynamics,* Winter 1984, pp. 33–44; D. W. Ewing, *Do It My Way or You're Fired.* New York: John Wiley, 1983; A. Grimes, "Authority, Power, Influence and Social Control: A Theoretical Synthesis," *Academy of Management Review,* 1978, 3:724–735; J. S. Kim,

"Effect of Behavior Plus Outcome Goal Setting and Feedback on Employee Satisfaction and Performance," *Academy of Management Journal,* 1984, 27:139–149; D. N. Campbell, R. L. Fleming, and R. C. Grote, "Discipline without Punishment—At Last," *Harvard Business Review,* July–August 1985, pp. 62–64ff.

32. R. L. Daft, *Organization Theory and Design,* 2nd ed. St. Paul, Minn.: West, 1986; H. Mintzberg, *Power in and Around Organizations.* Englewood Cliffs, N.J.: Prentice-Hall, 1983.

33. R. Stewart, *Choices for the Manager.* Englewood Cliffs, N.J.: Prentice-Hall, 1982.

34. J. T. Shorrock and S. Dobson, "Planning and Control in the Eighties: The Role of Financial Analysis in Measuring Relative Performance," *Director,* December 1979, pp. 40–43.

35. A. Wildavsky, *Budgeting: A Comparative Theory of Budgetry Processes.* Boston: Little, Brown, 1975; N. C. Churchill, "Budget Choice: Planning vs. Control," *Harvard Business Review,* July–August 1984, pp. 150–152ff.

36. A. Stedry, *Budget Control and Cost Behavior.* Englewood Cliffs, N.J.: Prentice-Hall, 1965, pp. 46–50.

37. B. Sord and G. Welsch, *Managerial Planning and Control.* Austin: University of Texas, Bureau of Business Research, 1964, pp. 93–99.

38. C. Argyris, *The Impact of Budgets on People.* New York: Controllership Foundation, 1952.

39. H. Swan, "Improving Operating Performance Through the Use of Operations Budgets." In T. S. Dudick and R. V. Gorski (Eds.), *Handbook of Business Planning and Budgeting for Executives with Profit Responsibilities.* New York: Van Nostrand Reinhold, 1983, pp. 412–435.

40. H. Bierman Jr. and S. Smidt, *The Capital Budget Decision,* 6th ed. New York: Macmillan, 1984.

41. P. Pyhrr, *Zero-Base Budgeting: A Practical Management Tool for Evaluating Expense.* New York: John Wiley, 1973.

42. "Zero-Base Budgeting: Justifying All Business Activity from the Ground Up," *Small Business Report,* November 1983, pp. 20–25.

43. G. Odiorne, *MBO II: A System of Managerial Leadership for the 80's*. Belmont, Calif.: 1979, pp. 210–217.

44. M. Dirsmith and S. Jablonsky, "Zero-Base Budgeting as a Management Technique and Political Strategy," *Academy of Management Review*, 1979, 4:555–565.

45. L. Cheek, *Zero-Base Budgeting Comes of Age*. New York: AMACOM, 1977.

46. J. Camillus and J. Grant, "Operational Planning: The Integration of Programming and Budgeting," *Academy of Management Review*, 1980, 5:369–379.

47. A. Toffler, *The Third Wave*. New York: William Morrow and Co., 1980.

48. "The Smart Machine Revolution," *Business Week*, July 5, 1976, pp. 38–44. *Also see:* R. E. McGarrah, "Ironies of Our Computer Age," *Business Horizons*, September–October, 1984, pp. 34–41.

49. T. Whisler and C. Meyers, *The Impact of Computers on Management*. Cambridge: M.I.T. Press, 1967. *Also see:* D. Davis, "SMR Forum: Computers and Top Management," *Sloan Management Review*, Spring 1984, pp. 63–67; H. C. Lucas and J. A. Turner, "A Corporate Strategy for the Control of Information Processing," *Sloan Management Review*, Spring 1982, pp. 25–36; W. P. Patterson, "Surviving the Micro Attack: As the Invasion Spreads, Will CEO's Lose Control?," *Forbes*, June 11, 1984, p. 39ff.

50. Case developed by Dr. Kenneth A. Kovach, George Mason University. Used with permission. Copyright © 1981 by Kenneth A. Kovach.

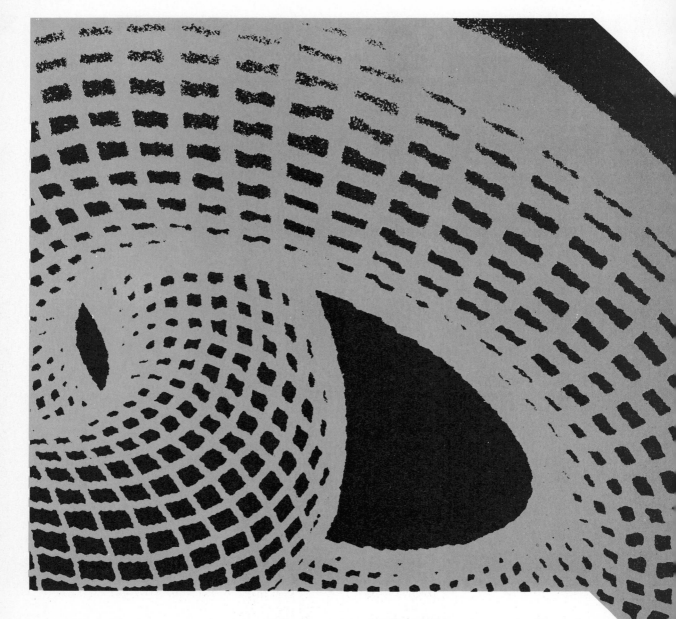

Control Through Staffing and Performance Appraisal

CHAPTER 18

LEARNING OBJECTIVES

After studying this chapter, you should be able to:

- Identify the components of the staffing function.

- Name two tools of use in human-resource planning and forecasting.

- List five external recruitment sources.

- Discuss several types of tests used in selecting new employees.

- Identify five uses of performance appraisals.

- Name at least three problems with performance appraisals.

- List several methods of appraising performance.

- Discuss the activities critical for an effective performance review.

CHAPTER OUTLINE

This chapter was contributed by Jeff Weekley, the Zale Corporation.

PREVIEW CASE

Alice Johnson

Alice Johnson completed her B.A. in marketing near the top of her class. Because she lived in a smaller city and for a variety of reasons was unable to move, Alice had a difficult time finding a marketing job. After a couple of months of unsuccessful job hunting, Alice began to panic. Consequently, she began to pursue job opportunities in areas other than marketing, even jobs requiring considerably less skill than she possessed. She eventually was offered, and accepted, a job as an administrative assistant in the Personnel Department of a small retail chain headquartered in the city.

As an administrative assistant, Johnson's tasks were varied and many. They included typing and filing, scheduling meetings, coordinating programs, and generally handling the work assigned to her by her boss, the personnel director. When she took the job, Alice did so with the intention of working hard, demonstrating her ability, and then moving into the marketing department as soon as possible. After a year, it became apparent

to Johnson that she would never get to move into the marketing department. Disillusioned at the thought of not being able to use the skills she had acquired in school, Johnson became uninterested in her administrative assistant's job and quit the company. Although out of work again, she was determined to keep looking until she found a marketing position. The company, in turn, began again the process of hiring another administrative assistant.

Source: Darlene Bordwell, Boston.

An effective organization must have the right people in the right jobs. It must also be able to reward outstanding performance and help to develop people who need to improve their skills. Consider the case of Alice Johnson. She may have been the right person placed in the wrong job. The company she went to work for did not do a good job of evaluating Alice's skills and talents in relation to those required by the job and thus everyone lost. Alice lost because she became so frustrated at not being able to do what she was trained to do that she quit her job. The organization lost because it had to go to the expense of filling that job a second time. The company also lost a potentially valuable employee. If the company had more carefully considered the skills required by the position it had open, it might have been more successful at hiring someone with the right skills and training.

The Preview Case shows that evaluation is an important function in personnel management. Organizations must evaluate both their human-resource needs and candidates for job openings; only then can sound decisions be made about matching people and jobs. The *staffing process* includes planning for future human-resource needs, recruiting and selecting candidates to meet these needs, and then orienting them to their new jobs and the organization.[1] After a person is placed in a job, the employee's supervisor must also evaluate how well he or she is performing that job. *Performance appraisal* is the method by which employees are evaluated. Performance appraisal is essential if the organization is to reward good performers more than poor performers, provide poorer performers with training to improve their job performance, and when necessary to let completely inadequate performers go. Despite its importance, many organizations do not manage personnel well.

In this chapter we will take a look at how some companies have tackled the difficult, yet vital, staffing process. The first part of the chapter considers the staffing process, from planning to recruiting to selection and orientation. The second half of the chapter examines the performance appraisal function, why it is necessary, and how some companies use performance appraisals.

THE STAFFING PROCESS

Of the many different ways that an organization may seek to control and direct the actions of its employees, staffing is one of the more subtle. How *does* an organization guide employee actions through its staffing policies and procedures? It does so by attracting, selecting, and retaining certain types of people; that is, people having certain characteristics and backgrounds. We are all familiar with organizations that have stereotypical employees. For example, IBM was for years known for its conservative culture in which its marketing and sales employees wore white shirts and black shoes. Similarly, Electronic Data Systems, a division of GM (see Chapter 11), is noted for its preference in employing people with prior experience in one of the branches of the military. By hiring employees with similar beliefs, values, and attitudes, the organization is better able to manage the work of individuals in the pursuit of common objectives.[2] Staffing is not synonymous with hiring; it encompasses a range of activities affecting employees as they flow through the organization.

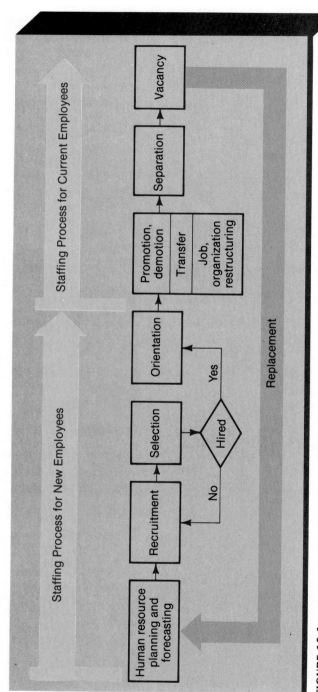

FIGURE 18.1
The Staffing Process

Overview

As Fig. 18.1 illustrates, staffing can be viewed as an input/output flow process. Staffing includes not only the movement of individuals into an organization, but also their movement through (promotion, job rotation, transfer) and out (termination, retirement) of the organization. Like other organizational resources, human resources may become (1) more valuable with time; (2) obsolete because of technological change; or (3) totally exhausted, in the case of employees who work with a company until retirement.

Figure 18.1 highlights the distinct components of the staffing process. Human-resource plans and forecasts are useful guides for recruitment and development efforts. By predicting human-resources requirements, an organization can determine the types of skills and the number of employees it will need. Knowing the number and types of employees needed and already employed, the organization can then plan its recruitment effort more effectively. After recruiting candidates for available positions, the organization must next select for each position the person deemed most likely to meet the organization's needs.

Once selected, new employees must be oriented by the organization. Orientation programs include both formal and informal communications regarding organization: what to do, what not to do, and what to expect. Having completed the orientation period, the individual may still participate in the staffing process. Transfers, promotions, demotions, and separation are all part of staffing; they complete one staffing assignment and stimulate another (the person promoted fills one vacancy and creates another).

Staffing is made more difficult by the complex, changing, and confusing regulatory environment. As a society, we have decided that equal opportunity in all aspects of employment is worthy and just. To achieve this end, a number of laws have been passed and several regulatory agencies have been created. The influence of these laws and their application by regulatory agencies have profoundly affected staffing methods and decisions. We will consider briefly the major equal employment laws before examining the components of the staffing process in more detail.

Impact of equal opportunity laws

Table 18.1 summarizes the U.S. equal employment opportunity laws and executive orders that significantly affect the staffing process in organizations.[3] The major focus of these laws is to prohibit discrimination in all phases of employment on the basis of race, color, religion, sex, age, or national origin (except where such a factor constitutes a valid occupational qualification). It is unlawful for employers to discriminate not only in hiring, but also in promotions, compensation, benefits, and terminations. If an organization provides different terms of employment for individuals on the basis of their sex, race, age, or other characteristics, it must demonstrate a strong business

TABLE 18.1 ■ KEY EQUAL EMPLOYMENT OPPORTUNITY LEGISLATION AND EXECUTIVE ORDERS

LAW/EXECUTIVE ORDER	OBJECTIVE	ENFORCEMENT AGENCY
Title VII, Civil Rights Act (1964)	Prevent discrimination on the basis of race, sex, religion, color, or national origin	Equal Employment Opportunity Commission
Equal Pay Act (1963)	Prohibit unequal pay for males and females with equal skills, effort, and responsibility working under similar working conditions	Equal Employment Opportunity Commission
Age Discrimination Act (1967)	Prevent discrimination against persons 40–65 years of age	Equal Employment Opportunity Commission
Rehabilitation Act (1973)	Prevent discrimination against persons with physical and/or mental handicaps	Equal Employment Opportunity Commission
Executive Order 11478 (1969)	Prevent discrimination in federal agencies on the basis of race, color, religion, sex, or national origin	Equal Employment Opportunity Commission
Executive Orders 11246 (1965); and 11375 (1966)	Prevent discrimination by federal contractors and subcontractors with contracts of more than $50,000 on the basis of race, color, sex, religion, and national origin	Office of Federal Contract Compliance

necessity for doing so. Understandably, the courts have taken a very narrow view of what constitutes business necessity. While age may be a criterion justified by business necessity for long-haul bus drivers, sex is not a criterion defensible as a business necessity for an airline cabin attendant.[4]

Of the equal employment debates currently going on, probably none is more important than that surrounding the notion of *comparable worth*. The Equal Pay Act requires equal pay for men and women, but only where they perform the same work. However, advocates of comparable worth want equal pay for jobs of **equal worth** regardless of whether or not the work performed is the same. Advocates of comparable worth argue that traditionally female occupations (teacher, secretary, nurse) are undervalued relative to traditionally male occupations (laborer, truck driver). That is, pay for these jobs is less than they are actually worth. Opponents of comparable worth point out that there is no agreed-on means of determining the worth of a job and that wages for various occupations are set in accordance with the going rate in the labor market. Comparable worth is a difficult issue and probably one that will not be resolved any time soon.[5]

Although brief, this review of major equal employment opportunity legislation emphasizes several important points.

1. The law prohibits discrimination on the basis of a number of characteristics other than race and sex.

2. Discrimination in all terms of employment, not just hiring, is unlawful.

3. Exceptions to the laws and their implementing regulations are possible but are rare.

4. Debates, such as that over comparable worth, point out the ambiguities that can exist.

The laws and regulations covering equal employment opportunity are not always clear cut and many of the issues raised in their enforcement have to be finally settled in the courts. With these points in mind, we now turn to consideration of the various components of an integrated staffing process.

Human-Resource Planning and Forecasting

Human-resource planning and forecasting is the function of anticipating future human resource needs as determined by future business demands.[6] Organizations that can accurately predict their future human-resource needs are in a much better position to meet these needs effectively than those that do not plan. For example, knowing that about 20 sales managers will be needed over the next three years, a company can begin to provide sales representatives with the training and development they will need to become successful sales managers. Further, if there are not enough qualified internal candidates—those considered by the company to be potentially successful—the company will be able to determine its recruiting needs for sales managers. Even somewhat inaccurate forecasts of future human-resource needs are better than none and assist a company in its attempt to meet its needs.

Reasons for human-resource planning

One of the main reasons for human-resource planning is that it improves an organization's chances of recruiting qualified people. For example, by knowing approximately how many electrical engineers it will need and when, Hewlett-Packard can get the jump on its competition in recruiting top candidates from the best schools. In short, planning increases the odds that an organization will get the right people in the right job at the right time. Another advantage of human-resource planning is that it requires clear statements of organizational and departmental objectives. These objectives must be set before human-resource requirements can be determined adequately. Finally, human-resource planning increases an organization's control, particularly in the face of change. The company whose management is thinking about entering a new business should carefully consider the human-resource needs of the business, how they might be met, and how they would impact the present organization.

Tools and techniques

Skills inventory. A number of tools and techniques are used for planning and forecasting personnel needs and availability.[7] One such tool is called the **skills inventory.** It is a detailed file on each employee, which includes his or her level of education, training, experience, length of service, job title, salary, performance history, and various demographic characteristics like age, race, or sex. Many organizations have computerized information systems for the storage and easy retrieval of this important job-related information. The start-up costs of such systems can be large; keeping the information current can be even more costly. However, significant savings also can result from the installation and use of the system. For example, assume that Corning Glass Works needs a Spanish-speaking college graduate with five years' manufacturing experience to work in its plant in Monterrey, Mexico. Before going outside to recruit for this position, the personnel office would probably scan its information system for a current employee who meets those requirements. If Corning can find such an employee, the company will save time and money by not having to recruit from outside and orient them to the company.

Job analysis. The use of a skills inventory requires, among other things, knowledge of the specific skills, abilities, and experience required by the job to be filled. This knowledge is generated by a **job analysis.**[8] A thorough job analysis has two parts: (1) a **job description,** which specifies the tasks, duties, and responsibilities of the job and which should be updated every year or so to keep them current; and (2) the **job specification,** which identifies the personal characteristics, skills and abilities, and experience necessary for effective performance of the job. Table 18.2 reproduces part of a job description and part of a job specification for a sales position at the Zale Corporation. The job description specifies duties, with behavioral statements, while the job specification identifies the personal characteristics that are needed for the work.

For filling a vacant position, the job specification is most useful. By knowing the skills, abilities, and work experiences that are important for success on a job, the personnel administrator and department manager will be much more successful in identifying the right candidate for the job. The job description is used more often in the development of sound compensation and performance-appraisal systems but is also helpful in recruitment. For example, recruiters often take copies of job descriptions with them when visiting campuses. The job description allows the recruiter to describe realistically the vacant job to potential candidates. Given a clear understanding of the job in question, potential candidates can then decide more readily whether they are interested in it. Just as an organization must decide if the candidates fit the job, the candidates must decide if the job and the organization fit their needs.

TABLE 18.2 ■ JOB DESCRIPTION AND JOB SPECIFICATION STATEMENT FOR A SALES ASSOCIATE POSITION AT THE ZALE CORPORATION

JOB TITLE

Sales Associate

Job Description

Primarily responsible for selling merchandise to customers who enter the store. Additional responsibilities include certain merchandising and housekeeping duties. Examples of duties required include:

■ Handles repairs, including providing estimates, maintaining repair records, sending merchandise to repair shop, following up on overdue repairs.

■ Straightens and cleans display and understock merchandise, cases, and windows; sets up merchandise displays; and otherwise maintains store appearance.

■ Asks questions of customer to determine what he or she is looking for in terms of merchandise type, style, cost, etc.

■ Makes suggestions on how to mix methods of payment in financing a purchase.

■ Attempts to close a sale several times.

Job Specification

Personal characteristics important to success include:

■ Previous sales experience.

■ Maturity.

■ Well-groomed and neat appearance.

■ Aggressive and persistent demeanor.

■ High school education.

Basic personnel activities. Job analyses and skills inventories are tools that aid in forecasting both the internal and external demand for and supply of human resources. When demand and supply are not equal, certain basic personnel actions should be taken. For example, when demand is less than supply, the supply can be reduced through termination, layoffs, and planned or early retirement. When demand is greater than supply, job training, external recruiting, and adjustment of job descriptions can be used. In forecasting the expected supply of human resources from within, the organization's internal information system is relied on. Because such systems contain hire dates, salary increases, departmental transfers, and so on, the human-resource planner is capable of tracking the movement of employees through the organization. For example, by analyzing employment records from the past five years, a human-resource planner might estimate that 30 percent of all trainees become managers after four years. Of the remaining 70 percent, 40 percent quit the company, 10 percent transfer into another job within the company,

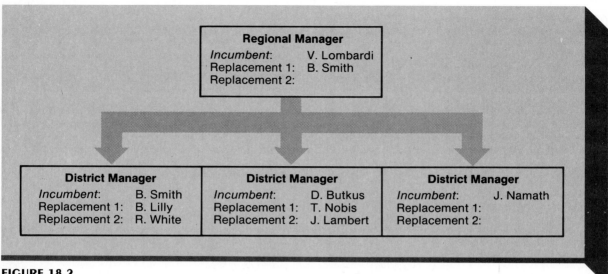

FIGURE 18.2
Replacement Chart

and 20 percent remain trainees. Based on this knowledge, the planner can predict that of the 200 trainees hired in 1986, 60 will be managers or manager candidates by 1990. The others will either no longer be with the company or not be in managerial jobs.

The replacement chart.   An approach commonly used in relation to professional and managerial jobs involves the use of a *replacement chart.* It shows each position in the management hierarchy. Beneath the name of each incumbent are listed the names of individuals who are considered eligible to replace the incumbent. Figure 18.2 shows a replacement chart for four positions in a company.

As can be seen in Fig. 18.2, incumbents for lower-level positions may or may not be considered as potential replacements for upper-level jobs. It also indicates that there are no suitable replacements currently available for one of the positions. This is not uncommon and, in such cases, the gaps in the chart point to the need for management development or possibly external recruiting. Replacement charts provide a simple means of forecasting future internal human-resource supplies.

Forecasting demand.   When forecasting demand, the human-resource planner typically relies on business plans and productivity ratios.[9] Assume that the planner has been able to determine that an average production worker is capable of assembling and testing 4000 fishing reels a year. Based on strategic business plans and forecasts of expected sales, the planner also knows that the company expects to manufacture and sell 1,000,000 fishing reels. This is a 200,000-unit increase over the previous year. Based on these data, and assuming no major change in technology, the planner is able to forecast that the company will have to add 50 new employees to meet its production objective (200,000 ÷ 4000 = 50).

Although oversimplified, this example illustrates how future human resource demands can be estimated, using the company's business plans, sales forecast, and productivity records. It also points out the need for managers to integrate the staffing and strategic planning processes.

RECRUITMENT

A forecast of demand can be compared with the organization's expected supply of internal candidates. Where there are not enough internal candidates to meet the demand, the organization must look outside for the necessary talent. *Recruitment* is the search for new employees outside the organization. An important objective is to obtain highly qualified employees at the lowest effective cost. One strategy is to pay high wages in order to attract quality applicants while minimizing search costs. Alternatively, companies can choose to pay lower wages and engage in little recruitment but spend considerable sums of money on management training and development. The point is that recruitment can be a trade-off for other personnel activities that may achieve the same outcome.

For most companies, recruitment is an important function in the staffing process. However, employers generally are not able to recruit as they please.[10] They face a number of restrictions, some of which are highlighted in Table 18.3.

CURRENT EMPLOYEES

Current employees have a significant impact on recruiting practices. Most organizations attempt to promote from within at levels above the entry level; to do otherwise would severely erode morale and reduce employee motivation. Why should employees work hard if they have little chance for promotion? Recall that internal recruiting usually involves scanning the organization's skills inventory for qualified candidates.

TABLE 18.3 ■ RESTRICTIONS ON ORGANIZATIONAL RECRUITING

- Current employees
- Governmental regulations
- Labor unions
- Labor market

Governmental regulations

A second type of restriction on an organization's recruiting policies and procedures is that of laws, executive orders, governmental regulations, and court rulings. The Equal Employment Opportunity Commission (EEOC) requires employers to maintain records on the number of applicants and the people they hire for various job categories (broken down by race, sex, and other characteristics). If a company is underutilizing members of a designated minority (in the opinion of the regulating agency), the government may require special recruiting and training efforts of the company. Ideally, the characteristics of a company's work force will match those of the people in the surrounding community. Thus, if a community is composed of 60 percent white, 30 percent black, and 10 percent of other races, the organization's work force ideally should be 60 percent white, 30 percent black, and 10 percent other. Where the work-force characteristics are not similar to those of the surrounding community, the company may be required to make special hiring plans. These plans, known as *affirmative action* plans, generally involve a commitment to make special efforts to recruit members of an underrepresented class or classes of people for designated job categories.

Labor unions

Another restriction on recruiting comes from labor unions. Some states permit a *union security clause* in management–labor contracts. Union security clauses typically require all new employees of a company covered by the contract to be union members or to join the union shortly after being hired. Thus a company is prevented from diluting the union's influence by hiring only candidates with antiunion sentiments. The UAW, for example, has made union security a key issue in its negotiations with GM, Ford, and Chrysler.

Labor market

The labor market itself greatly influences recruiting efforts. If the local supply of qualified workers in a job category exceeds the local demand, wages will be depressed and recruitment will be minimal. On the other hand, if the local supply of qualified workers is less than the demand, recruiting efforts intensify. For example, following deregulation of prices in the oil industry in the late 1970s, oil companies increased exploration for new sources. This resulted in heavy competition for petroleum engineers. As the demand and price for oil dropped in the 1980s, the demand for petroleum engineers dropped sharply.

Methods of recruitment

Faced with the restrictions on the recruiting function, organizations attempt to identify and attract the right kind of person, so that they will not have to repeat the effort too often. How is the actual recruitment of people carried out in organizations? Typically, when a position becomes vacant, the manager of the department in which the opening has occurred submits a requisition to the personnel department. The requisition states the title of the job to be filled, the salary range for the job, the department in which the opening exists, and so on. Most importantly, the requisition usually contains the job specifications. That is, the requisition tells the personnel department of the personal requirements and qualifications necessary for someone to perform the job. This information is essential if the department is to identify qualified applicants.

If there are no qualified candidates internally, a recruiter begins the task of locating potential candidates. In doing so, recruiters use a variety of external sources; the more common sources are listed in Table 18.4. Some of these sources are relatively low cost (walk-ins, write-ins), whereas others may be

TABLE 18.4 ■ COMMON SOURCES OF RECRUITMENT FOR JOB CANDIDATES

SOURCE	COMMENT
Educational institutions	High schools can be an excellent source for office, clerical, and secretarial employees. Likewise, trade and vocational schools provide many machinists, mechanics, paraprofessionals, and the like. Colleges and universities provide most management trainees and professionals.
Public employment services	Many states and the federal government provide employment services at no charge. Such services deal primarily with the unemployed and to a lesser extent with those seeking a job change. The military also provides some placement assistance for veterans.
Private employment services	These services differ according to who pays for them. Search consultants or "headhunters" are paid by the organization and tend to focus on upper-level professionals and managers. Employment agencies, on the other hand, collect their fees from job seekers.
Unsolicited applications	Many jobs are filled by walk-in or write-in candidates. While walk-ins tend to seek lower-level jobs, many professionals mail in unsolicited résumés.
Employee referrals	One of the best and most consistently used sources of new employees is referral of candidates by current employees. However, reliance on employee referrals may act to perpetuate past discrimination, if the work force is homogeneous. A predominantly white male work force may refer mostly white males, thereby inviting an EEOC investigation.
Advertisements	Newspapers carry many help-wanted ads, particularly in their Sunday editions. Availability of professional positions that require specialized backgrounds are advertised in many professional journals (ad for a chemist in a chemistry journal).

relatively expensive (executive search firms). Which of these sources is the best? The answer is that it all depends.[11]

The best source for recruitment is often dictated by the type of job to be filled. For example, a job at Squibb or Johnson & Johnson that requires an organic chemist with a Ph.D. will be more readily filled through on-campus recruiting efforts (at those schools with a doctoral program in organic chemistry) than through a classified ad in the Sunday paper. Some research shows that newspaper ads and college placement offices are, in general, poorer sources of employees than professional journal ads or self-initiated contacts for research scientists.[12] For other jobs, such as clerical or typing jobs, there may be a number of potential sources for candidates. In order to determine which source is best, many organizations conduct evaluations of cost effectiveness. By evaluating the performance and tenure of employees hired through various sources, an organization can often determine which one is the best source of employees for specific types of jobs.

The recruiting function of the staffing process is complete when candidates have been found and have applied for the job. The next step in the staffing process is to fill the position from among those candidates (or to resume recruitment if none is acceptable to the person responsible for hiring).

Personnel Selection

A number of sources of information are available to managers to assist them in making selection decisions. Some of these information sources are more costly than others, and many organizations rely on the less expensive ones to narrow the choice of candidates.

Résumés

One inexpensive source of information comes from applicants' résumés. A well-written résumé will contain educational qualifications, work experience, personal information, and interests. A résumé should be one or two pages at most in length. It should be clear, concise, easy to read, and easy to understand. The sample résumé in Table 18.5 contains five key pieces of information: (1) name, address, and telephone number; (2) education, including GPA; (3) highlights of extracurricular activities; (4) job experience; and (5) personal information. Remember, neither line and staff managers nor personnel administrators have time to read long, involved descriptions. However, if a résumé does not contain sufficient relevant information, the candidate might be eliminated from further consideration.

Reference checks

Because résumés can easily be falsified, managers should request references and conduct reference checks. Many companies routinely verify educational qualifications, including schools attended, degrees, dates, and major areas of

TABLE 18.5 ■ A SAMPLE RÉSUMÉ

Richard Pinchot
1425 Patricia Lane
Columbus, OH 43201
Telephone (814) 422-3130

OBJECTIVE	A challenging college internship or entry-level position offering on-the-job-training in the field of accounting, finance, or economics
EDUCATION	The Ohio State University, Columbus, Ohio Candidate for B.S. in Business Administration, June 1986 Major: Finance GPA: 2.8 GPA in Major: 3.5 Oxford University, Oxford, England Summer Study Program Curriculum, Eighteenth Century Art, Literature, and History Hanover High School, Hanover, New Hampshire Graduated, 1982
COLLEGE ACTIVITIES	Phi Kappa Tau Fraternity Treasurer, 1985: Managed financial affairs of fraternity under a $90,000 annual budget, made a significant contribution in eliminating a $4000 deficit. Vice-president of rush, 1984: Organized and coordinated the recruitment program, which was highlighted by "formal rush" involving 500 rushees. Representative to Interfraternity Council, 1984: Acted as liaison between fraternity presidents and executive boards.
JOB EXPERIENCE	April–June 1982 TGI Friday's, 454 Kenny Road, Columbus, Ohio 43212 Full-time work on dayshift Summer 1981 and 1982 Chieftain Motel, Lyme Road, Hanover, New Hampshire 03755 Manager on evening shift November 1977–September 1981 Mary Hitchcock Memorial Hospital, Manor Street, Hanover, New Hampshire 03755 Worked in transportation department as an orderly full-time summers and part-time during the school year
PERSONAL	Age: 23 Height: 5'8" Weight: 148 lb. Health: Excellent Marital Status: Single
REFERENCES	Available on request

study. Previous employers are often reluctant to provide subjective evaluations of former employees, but many will confirm factual information such as dates of employment, salary, and position held. Therefore, when calling an applicant's former employer, many personnel administrators will only verify job-related facts provided by the applicant.

Job Applications

Another inexpensive source of information that can be used to screen employees is the *job application.* Almost all organizations require candidates for jobs to fill out an application. It is a form that asks for personal information such as education, work experience, address, phone number, and the like. In many cases, the job application serves the same purpose as a résumé and also can be used by the employer to gather information for government reporting purposes. One common misconception is that it is against the law for an employer to ask questions about an applicant's sex, race, age, marital status, and national origin. It is *not* against the law to ask these questions and, in fact, in some cases the employer is required by the government to ask them. What *is* against the law is for an employer to use such information in a discriminatory manner. In order to lessen concern over how such information is used, most organizations (unless otherwise required) do not ask these questions until after a person has been hired. Beyond the obvious questions about race and sex, other questions may raise suspicions of discrimination. Table 18.6 contains a sample of such less obvious, yet potentially sensitive questions. These are called *problem questions* in EEOC and affirmative-action literature. None of these questions is essentially job-related and consequently, most organizations are able to avoid them in the selection process.

Realistic Job Previews

Résumés, reference checks, and applications are relatively simple, and usually inexpensive, screening techniques. A screening technique that is gaining in popularity is the *realistic job preview.*[13] In a realistic job preview, the

TABLE 18.6 ■ POTENTIALLY SENSITIVE INTERVIEW QUESTIONS

TYPE OF QUESTION	POSSIBLE TYPES OF SELECTION BIAS
Height or weight	May indicate sexual bias.
Eye or hair color	May indicate racial bias.
Birthplace	May indicate national-origin bias.
Marital status	May be used to discriminate against women planning to have children.
Birthdate	May be used to discriminate on the basis of age.
Child-care plans	May be used to discriminate against women.

candidate is told about "how it really is," the good points of the job and the bad. In many cases, realistic job previews have reduced the turnover rate for those hired. One explanation for this is the technique's *self-selection* effect. That is, applicants likely to be dissatisfied with the job, and therefore quit, select themselves out of the job before being hired.

INTERVIEWS

After candidates have been screened and their number narrowed down to the finalists, someone must still choose one of the remaining candidates to fill the job that is open. In making a final selection decision, most organizations rely on some combination of interviews and tests. Typically, there are three interviews for someone who is graduating from college: on-campus, plant or office, and final selection. Let us find out how *not* to interview job candidates.

IN PRACTICE
STEVE COX

Steve Cox was recently promoted to the position of plant manager from his previous position as foreman. As plant manager, one of Steve's new responsibilities is to interview applicants for some of the "skill" jobs in the plant. In his old job, Steve never had to formally interview anyone. The first time he had to fill a position, it was for a Senior Mechanic job. This job requires extensive knowledge of diesel engine repair and maintenance. The plant personnel manager narrowed the number of applicants down to three from which Steve had to make the final decision.

In conducting the interviews, Steve had no real plan of action. He thought it best to allow each interview to take its natural course. The first applicant seemed all right. She answered the questions well enough but seemed a little nervous. The second applicant was a disaster. He would answer most questions with a "yes" or a "no" and would not say anything more. Steve tried to ask the second applicant the same questions he asked the first, but he couldn't remember some of them. Finally, he interviewed the third applicant. The last applicant was very outgoing and talked quite easily. In comparison with the second applicant, the third seemed very bright and friendly.

After completing the interviews, Steve sat down to ponder and make a decision. In doing so, he realized immediately that he had forgotten most of what the first applicant had said. The second applicant had been such a poor speaker that Steve never found out whether he really knew anything about diesel mechanics. The final applicant had been such a good speaker, compared to the second, that the interview lasted quite some time. In contrasting the third applicant's responses, Steve soon recognized that they had little to do with mechanical ability. Also, because they had been talking so easily and naturally, Steve had forgotten to ask the third applicant several important questions. In the end, Steve decided he *liked* the third applicant the best but did not know who would make the *best mechanic*. Steve asked the personnel manager to make the selection decision.

Interviews, although commonly used, are relatively poor predictors of performance.[14] Most people have no trouble staying alert and being pleasant for a 30-minute interview. Their behavior during the interview does not necessarily indicate how well they can perform a job, relate to co-workers, and accept direction day after day.

Interviewers are subject to errors in judgment. One common type of error is the **contrast error** that is, rating an interviewee as particularly good or bad in contrast with the preceding candidate. Recall that Steve Cox liked the third applicant but that interview came right after the second, during which the applicant would not or could not express himself well. Another common error is the **similarity error,** or bias in favor of certain applicants because they look and act like the interviewer. Research has also shown that interviewers tend to make decisions early in the interview and spend the rest of the time seeking information to support that decision. Another type of judgment error is the tendency to give negative information too much weight. A single bit of negative information is often enough to sway the interviewer and lead to making a negative decision.[15]

Despite these judgment errors, the interview remains the most popular selection technique. The reasons for its continued popularity vary, but an interview does serve useful purposes. The interview is a convenient time to exchange information. Not only does the interviewer learn what the applicant has to offer, but the applicant also learns what the organization has to offer. Although interviews do not necessarily indicate whether someone will perform well, they may indicate how well the applicant will fit in with the other workers in the work group. Finally, human nature is such that most people will not hire someone they have not met; both the employer and the applicant expect an interview.

The several *Do's* and *Don'ts* of interviewing are listed in Table 18.7. Particular care should be exercised to ask job- and company-related questions. Had Steve Cox followed these simple guidelines, he would have been in a better position to make a valid selection decision. For example, Steve could have evaluated the candidates more fairly if he had asked each the same questions. By taking notes, he also would not have forgotten what the first candidate said. Although they are simple, these interviewing guidelines are all too often ignored.

Testing

In addition to interviews, many organizations use tests to help screen and select candidates. Tests may be oral, written, or performance-based. In fact, an interview can be considered to be an oral test. Most people, however, think of questionnaires to be filled out when they think of tests. A commonly used type, called **cognitive ability tests,** measures general intelligence, verbal ability, numerical ability, reasoning ability, and so on. They have been found to be relatively good predictors of success for certain types of jobs.[16] **Personality**

TABLE 18.7 ■ DO'S AND DON'TS OF INTERVIEWING

DO	DON'T
1. Read the job description prior to interview.	1. Interrupt the candidate or be sarcastic, "cute," or otherwise rude. The applicant deserves respect.
2. Structure the interview based on the job analysis. Make sure that questions are job-related and prepared ahead of time.	2. Let first impressions control. Reserve judgment until the end of the interview.
3. Compare the interviewee's personal characteristics with the requirements of the job, not with those of previous interviewees.	3. Talk too much. Let the applicant do most of the talking. Try to guide the discussion, not lead it.
4. Take notes and write down what the interviewee says. Let him or her know ahead of time that you will be taking notes.	4. Overemphasize negative information. Remember, everyone has strengths and weaknesses.
5. Leave time between interviews to review notes and make a judgment about the candidate.	

tests and ***interest inventories,*** unlike cognitive ability tests, have no right or wrong answers. Personality tests measure a person's tendency toward introversion–extraversion, assertiveness–passivity, and so on. Interest inventories attempt to assess a person's occupational interests. Personality tests and interest inventories are poor predictors of job performance; responses can be faked easily, and interpretation is difficult. Another common type of test in industry is the performance test. ***Performance tests*** simulate all or part of an actual job. A typing test for a secretary or a code-writing test for a computer programmer are examples of performance tests.

Regardless of the job to be filled, all tests should meet two basic criteria. First, they should meet the criterion of ***reliability.*** A reliable test provides consistent measures. For example, if you stepped on a bathroom scale and it read 150 pounds and then you reweighed yourself one minute later and it read 140 pounds, the scale would not be reliable. The second criterion is that of ***validity.*** A valid test is one that measures what it is supposed to measure. A valid test to measure product knowledge for a jeweler would not contain questions regarding mechanical principles of gasoline engines. Unless a test is both reliable and valid, the organization using it will not be getting a good return on its testing investment. Also, an invalid test that results in discrimination against a minority group is indefensible. A test that is not job related *and* that acts to reject a disproportionate number of members of a protected class (women, veterans, those between the ages of 40 and 70) is considered to be discriminatory.

ASSESSMENT CENTERS

The selection techniques discussed so far are used primarily as aids in filling office, production, and some professional positions. Selection of individuals for managerial positions often involves the use of another technique: the *assessment center.* The assessment center is not a place, but a technique first used in World War II to select spies. Assessment centers simulate situations that would be faced on the job. One common situational test is the in-basket test. In an in-basket exercise, the candidate is given a stack of letters, notes, memos, and other materials that have supposedly collected in his or her in-basket. The individual responds to these materials by writing letters, scheduling meetings, delegating assignments, and other role plays as if actually on the job. Other common situational tests include leaderless group discussions

INTERNATIONAL FOCUS

Reducing Turnover of Overseas Managers

Multinational corporations have attracted much of the world's frustration over the economic and social conditions of poor people living in Third-World countries. Third-World people know that they are poor and that most U.S. managers on assignment to their countries are not. They see Americans on television, read about the good life in the United States in newspapers, and see first-hand how managers of U.S. companies and their families live.

For the most part, employees selected to go overseas have not been trained to perform their duties successfully in another country. Few companies have training programs that prepare the expatriate (a person who leaves his or her country to live in another country) for business and cultural problems, and even fewer address the trials of the spouse and children of the expatriate manager. In addition, most training programs do not deal with the critical problems of reentering the United States at the end of a foreign assignment. Because adequate preparations have not been made prior to taking an overseas assignment, a significant number of expatriate families return to the United States before the end of their overseas assignments. This does not take into consideration the "brownout" families, those who remain abroad but are not high performers.

According to Ronald Marston, vice-president of Hospital Corporation International, it is reasonable to assume that recruiting and relocating an individual and his or her family for an international assignment costs about $75,000–$100,000. If a company has 250 people overseas and a turnover rate of 40 percent per year, that turnover is costing the company about $7.5 million per year. What can companies do to stop this high turnover? According to Bob

and problem analyses. In most cases, the candidate's performance is evaluated by trained observers. After the individual has performed all the tests, the observers exchange observations and evaluations until a consensus is reached. This overall evaluation is then used to predict if the candidate is likely to succeed in the managerial position for which he or she is being considered.[17]

Orientation

After selection, the new employee must be oriented. *Orientation* provides the new employee with information about the company, the job, and what is expected of the employee. The extent to which companies provide formal orientation varies greatly. At one extreme are those organizations, such as Burger King, that provide no formal orientation for waiters, bus boys, and most kitchen help. At the other extreme, organizations such as IBM and Citicorp have lengthy programs to prepare people for stepping into manage-

Lanier, president of Overseas Briefing Association, a company should do seven things.

PREVISIT

If time and money permit, a previsit to the country for the manager and spouse is worth the cost. During the trip, the couple should not be given special treatment but should be allowed to meet and talk with other expatriate managers about schools, shopping, clubs, and the like. It is most helpful if the families already living there will freely discuss the emotional shocks, disappointments, frustrations, and successes that the new family will probably meet. Having some knowledge of the kinds of emotional stress of "culture shock" will greatly assist the new family adapting in their new country.

LANGUAGE

Only about 7 percent of the Americans who have not started studying a second language before arrival overseas work at it after getting there. Even 20–30 hours of basic language instruction will help an employee get over the first hurdle. The employee and family should be able to buy necessities, order a meal, make simple comments, read signs, ask directions, and the like in the language of the country in which they are living.

(continued)

INTENSIVE AREA STUDY

Managers should study the culture of the country, concentrating on habits, attitudes, religious beliefs, sensitivities, and the like. Company briefings should also provide a clear, but concise, idea of the current political situation and the state of the economy. It is important to know current problems and be aware of national pride.

COUNTRY-SPECIFIC HANDBOOK

Such a handbook should explain how the law works when you have an accident, how to find and handle household help, how the telephone system works, and company policy regarding holidays, medical plans, tax plans, and travel allowances. The family also wants to know about the kind of housing generally available and whether it's well-heated and/or air-conditioned, how it compares with their present house, and how close it is to schools, shopping, the manager's job, and other expatriate families.

IN-COMPANY COUNSELING

Managers need to be briefed about the firm's compensation policies, rules and regulations, and the move itself. They should also talk with a higher-level manager about their future with the company after they have finished the overseas assignment.

MEETING RETURNEES

Out-going families should spend time with families who have returned from the same location. However, they should choose returning families who had good experiences, if possible.

ON ARRIVAL

Someone from the personnel office should meet the new family at the airport upon arrival and help them through customs, open a bank account, get started on house hunting, work out transportation problems, and obtain driver's licenses. In addition, a spouses' committee should assist the spouse in meeting other families, enrolling children in school, shopping, and enrolling in a language class.

Sources: This material was compiled from M. Harvey, "The Multinational Corporation's Expatriate Problem: An Application of Murphy's Law," *Business Horizons,* January–February 1983, **26**(1):71–78; R. Marston, "Orientation of Internal Expatriates for Middle East Assignments," *Personnel Administrator,* August 1979, pp. 21–24; B. Lanier, "Selecting and Preparing Personnel for Overseas Transfers," *Personnel Journal,* March 1979, **58**(3):160–163; M. Harvey, "Executive Family: An Overlooked Variable in International Assignments," *Columbia Journal of World Business,* 1985; M. Mendenhall and G. Oddou, "The Dimensions of Expatriate Acculturation: A Review," *Academy of Management Review,* 1985, **10**:39–47.

ment and other positions in the company. The orientation efforts of most organizations probably fall somewhere in between.

A typical formal orientation program may last a day or less. During this time, the new employee is provided with information about the organization, its history, and its current structure; the benefits for which he or she is eligible; and the organization's policies and procedures. Also covered are the more routine things a newcomer must learn, such as the location of the restrooms, break rooms, parking, and cafeteria (if available). Most organizations attempt to provide only basic information during the formal orientation program.

If formal orientation programs provide only minimal factual information, how do new employees "learn the ropes" in an organization? They do it through a process called *socialization.* Socialization is the informal and, occasionally, the formal orientation processes through which newcomers learn how things really work. Newcomers learn how to behave, how to dress and talk, who to go to for answers, and how to interact with co-workers and supervisors. Though usually informal, socialization is a very powerful means of controlling the behavior of individuals.[18] To the extent that all newcomers are taught the unwritten "rules of the game," the organization does not have to invest much of its resources in writing rules and regulations. The same could be said of the entire staffing process. By planning for human-resource needs, by recruiting and selecting people to meet those needs, and by orienting those selected in the ways of the organization, the need for other forms of control is lessened. Another form of control is performance appraisal, which, like staffing, involves evaluation.

PERFORMANCE APPRAISAL

Performance appraisal is "the systematic description of the job-relevant strengths and weaknesses of employees."[19] Performance appraisal continues to be one of the most important human-resource management issues. There are at least two reasons for this emphasis. First, the accurate evaluation of each individual's performance is very important because this information can be used in many different ways and can affect many important decisions; it is crucial that such information be as accurate and fair as possible. Second, only a few organizations have been able to develop and implement completely satisfactory appraisal systems.

Over the years, researchers have tried to overcome these problems. Their approach has typically been to try and devise new methods for rating performance.[20] However, these efforts have not been totally successful. Part of the reason is because performance appraisals profoundly affect individuals. Imagine yourself as a supervisor. One of your duties is to rate the performance of your employees. You know that your ratings will determine the amount of the pay raise each person will get. You also know that you will have to tell each of your subordinates how you rated them, how you arrived at your ratings, and what this means to them in terms of a pay increase. All this must be done on the basis of your own opinions and judgment. Your employees can and probably will disagree with you. Finally, you have to continue to work with them, even if they do not like your ratings. The easiest thing to do, of course, would be to give everyone good ratings. That way everyone would get a large pay raise; you would be happy and your employees would be happy. Everyone would be pleased except top management.

Performance appraisals are useful for many purposes, the primary one being the extent that they help distinguish between better and poorer performers. Before considering some of the uses of performance-appraisal information, let us consider Jacob Wilson's experiences with a performance-appraisal system.

IN PRACTICE
Jacob Wilson

Jacob Wilson is a sales representative for an electronics manufacturing firm. Among its many product lines, the company manufactures and sells to retailers a line of personal computers and related accessories (such as printers). The company also sells this personal computer line directly to businesses, which is Wilson's area of responsibility. He has a particular region of the country in which he contacts business people for purposes of selling them the company's personal computer line. The company has decided that customers prefer to deal with only one representative, so they also require their sales representatives to provide service after the sale. Thus Wilson is also responsible for servicing existing accounts; that is, when customers who have bought personal computers run into problems with them or when they simply have questions, he must see to it that their concerns are satisfied. Of course, when Wilson has to service existing accounts, he is unable to spend that time attempting to open new accounts or to make new sales.

The personal computer market is extremely competitive. The company decided that it would be better able to achieve its sales and growth objectives if it provided generous incentives for new sales. This was particularly true, the company reasoned, in those parts of the country where the personal computer market was still up for grabs. Moreover, sales volume represented an objective measure of each sales representative's sales performance. This made it easy to measure each sales representative's performance and to pay him or her accordingly. Consequently, the company began paying its sales reps on a commission-only basis. That is, sales reps were paid a flat percentage of their monthly sales volume.

Soon after implementing its new sales-based pay system, both Wilson and the company noticed some disturbing changes. For Wilson, whose territory included the area around "silicon valley" in California, the change was a loss in earnings relative to his peers. Not only was his territory the home of many competitors, but also a great percentage of the potential customers already owned personal computers. However, sales reps in other parts of the country worked in far less competitive markets where the degree of penetration by other manufacturers was not large. As might be expected, these sales reps were able to sell much more and, consequently, make much more money.

The company also noticed some changes. Foremost among them was a rapid decline in service to customers after sales. Increasingly, customers were calling corporate headquarters to complain about slow service from the sales representatives. The company soon realized, as the sales reps did earlier, that it actually cost the sales representatives income to provide service. Since they were paid solely on the basis of their sales performance, as measured in sales volume, the sales reps were devoting all of their time and energy to creating new sales. Naturally, service deteriorated. Because of the importance of customer service in the computer industry, the company soon dropped its sales commission and reverted to its old way of measuring and rewarding performance.

Uses of Performance Appraisals

Performance-appraisal information is invaluable in making many kinds of personnel-management decisions. Figure 18.3 indicates some of the varied and important uses of this information.

Pay, bonus, and other reward decisions

Most organizations attempt to base pay, bonuses, and other types of financial rewards on performance as an incentive for employees. In the case of Jacob Wilson, for example, the company attempted to motivate its sales representatives to sell more by paying them on the basis of how much they sold. The incentive was so successful that the sales representatives quit performing their other major duty, that of providing service after the sale.

Movement of personnel

Performance-appraisal information is also useful to managers in making a variety of decisions regarding the movement of personnel. Who does the organization promote? Who does it demote? In times of economic crisis, which many companies experienced during the early 1980s, layoffs or reductions in force become necessary. In such circumstances, who does the company terminate? These decisions may be relatively easy in small organizations or where a manager must make only a single decision (for example, when a manager has to choose the one person to be promoted). On the other hand, as the decision-making process becomes more complex, the availability of good

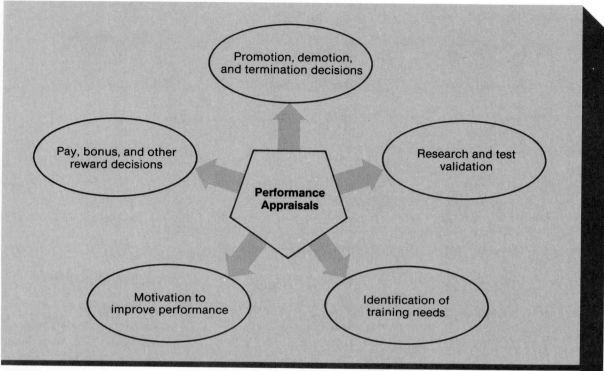

FIGURE 18.3
Uses of Performance Appraisals

performance-appraisal information becomes increasingly important. The human-resources manager of a 3000-employee organization would find the task of deciding which 150 employees to lay off much easier (though no more pleasant) if there were good performance evaluations available to help in the decision-making process.

Motivation to improve performance

Another use of performance appraisals is to motivate employees to improve their performance. Many organizations require their managers to conduct annual or semiannual appraisals and discuss them with employees. These evaluations provide feedback to employees about their specific strengths and weaknesses in performing their jobs and working toward both departmental and organizational objectives. In addition, the manager must also provide some guidance about what the employee needs to do in order to perform better. The employee is then expected to begin working on the weaknesses identified.

IdentificatioN of traiNiNG NEEds

Performance-appraisal information can also be used to identify training needs. For example, if a secretary is rated *satisfactory* in filing and dictation but *below average* in typing, the organization can provide training to improve the employee's typing skills. In other words, by identifying areas of poor performance, the manager also identifies job duties in need of developmental training.

PErsoNNEl REsEARch ANd TEsT ValidatioN

The final major use for performance-appraisal information is to provide criteria for personnel research. Recall that employment tests should be job related. The best way to demonstrate the job relatedness of a test is to show a relationship between test scores and job performance. Obviously, in order to demonstrate such a relationship, valid measures of job performance are needed. Job performance can also be of use in other research projects. Many organizations monitor employee turnover rates. By studying voluntary and involuntary turnover rates of good and poor performers, the organization can decide if turnover is working for or against the company. Where turnover is high among poor performers and low among good performers, turnover may be working in favor of the company by allowing the replacement of poor performers with potentially good performers.

PRoblEMs witH PERfoRMANcE AppRAisals

The performance-appraisal system used to measure the performance of Jacob Wilson had several flaws. Four of these, which are typical problems, are shown in Table 18.8. Let us look at them in some detail.

DEficiENcy

Recall that the performance of sales representatives was measured only in terms of sales volume. The other major duty, that of providing service after the sale, wasn't considered at all. In short, the performance-appraisal system used to evaluate and reward Jacob Wilson considered only part of his job. This problem is known as *deficiency*. Deficiency is the extent to which an

---

TABLE 18.8 ■ TYPICAL PROBLEMS WITH PERFORMANCE APPRAISALS

- Deficiency
- Contamination
- Leniency/severity
- Halo error

appraisal system fails to include all major performance dimensions in the evaluation process. An organization that measures only part of job performance will not be able to monitor and control performance on those parts not measured. Deficient appraisal systems are also likely to be considered unfair by the person being evaluated. If performance evaluations are considered to be unfair and inaccurate, they are not going to be as useful for the purposes for which they are intended.[21]

CONTAMINATION

Whereas deficiency concerns the omission of major duties, *contamination* refers to the biasing effects of extraneous variables. In Jacob Wilson's case, the measure of sales volume was contaminated by the extraneous variable, territory. His territory was highly competitive and a large percentage of potential customers already owned personal computers. However, some of Wilson's co-workers had territories in which there was far less competition. These people were able to sell much more than Wilson could, even though they had no more ability or tried no harder. Contamination can also occur when employees are evaluated on performance dimensions they really are not expected to perform. For example, if Wilson were rated on the quality of repair work performed for his customers but he was not responsible for actually performing the repairs, his evaluation would be contaminated by a non-job related factor.

LENIENCY/SEVERITY

The problems of deficiency and contamination are serious and can occur with seemingly fair and objective measures of performance. For most jobs, objective measures of performance are not available. In such cases, the only alternative is for managers to use subjective evaluations of performance. Unfortunately, these evaluations are susceptible to a number of biases in addition to deficiency and contamination. One such bias is called *leniency,* which refers to the providing of ratings that are consistently higher than deserved. The opposite of leniency is called *severity,* which occurs when ratings that are all consistently lower than deserved are given.

The reasons for leniency error are varied, but many have to do with the motive of the person making the ratings. For example, everyone in a work group may receive high ratings because the rater feels that (1) all poor performers have already been discharged; (2) poorly performing subordinates would reflect negatively on his or her managerial skills; or (3) high ratings will win better pay raises and promotions for the subordinates and improve the reputation of the manager as a good person for whom to work. Also, many raters assign high ratings simply to avoid having to confront people with the fact that their performance needs improvement. Confronting subordinates with performance problems can be very difficult to do.

IN PRACTICE
Your Turn

Think of a friend you currently have (if not your best friend, then at least someone with whom you enjoy interacting). Imagine that you are your friend's boss. You are a middle manager in a small manufacturing concern, and your friend has been working for you for six months. It's company policy to provide all new employees a six-month performance review. You now have to rate the performance of your friend and determine how much of a merit-pay raise he or she will receive. In addition, you have to conduct a formal performance review with your friend. In this review, you have to explain how you arrived at your ratings (if you even know) and you have to suggest ways your friend can improve his or her performance. Unfortunately, it has become apparent to you lately that your friend is not performing very well. Your friend does not complete many assigned tasks on time and, when he or she does, they are done poorly. What would you do? Would you rate your friend as honestly as you possibly could? If you did, would you be able to sit down with your friend and explain why he or she received a low rating (and therefore a low merit-pay increase)? Or, would you rate your friend higher than deserved and hope his or her performance would improve? What would you do if your friend challenged the ratings you made as being too low? How would you defend your ratings?

Halo error

The *halo error* is the practice of rating employees at more or less the same level (high, average, or low) across all performance dimensions. Some people argue that halo errors occur because raters make their evaluations on the basis of an overall impression. Others suggest that halo errors result from the rating of all performance dimensions based on the rater's knowledge of the person's performance on a single dimension. Thus, if Jacob Wilson's supervisor knew he was good at sales, the supervisor might also rate him high on service after the sale without really having observed this dimension of his performance. In any event, the halo error occurs when ratings do not differ across performance dimensions. In some cases, the halo error may not be an error at all. It is entirely conceivable that some employees perform at the same level on all dimensions. However, most people will do some things better than others, and thus their ratings should differ somewhat from one performance dimension to another.[22]

Managerial implications

There are other problems with the use of performance appraisals, particularly in the area of subjective ratings. However, the problems presented serve to illustrate how difficult it is for managers to evaluate the performance of subordinates. Most attempts to solve these problems have focused on finding new methods of performance appraisal. As a result, there are many different types of rating-scale formats and evaluation techniques. Unfortunately, none of these methods is clearly superior to the others.

Evaluating employee performance objectively can be difficult, and rating biases (such as severity) often occur.

Source: Sarah Putnam/The Picture Cube.

Methods of Performance Appraisal

In the discussion so far, we have suggested two general approaches to evaluating performance: objective and subjective. *Objective measures* apply to things that can be counted, such as sales volume, units produced, amount of scrap, tonnage transported, number of accidents, number of times a person is late, and so on. Because such items can be counted easily, their measurement tends to be very accurate. However, this does not mean that such measures of performance are also fair. Objective measures such as sales volume can be contaminated by factors beyond the salesperson's control. Moreover, objective measures are often deficient. Imagine, for example, being evaluated on the basis of your absenteeism record only.

Because objective measures have deficiencies, it is wise to supplement objective performance measures (where available) with subjective ones. There are many different subjective methods of appraising performance. However, we will focus on two general types—ranking and ratings—of methods for making subjective performance appraisals.

Ranking

The various *ranking* methods comprise the first of these approaches. In simple ranking, the rater simply rank orders people from best to worst. A variation of this is called alternation ranking. This type of ranking requires the rater to select the best employee, the worst, the second best, the second worst, and so on. Ranking methods are easy to use. They also have the advantage of effectively combating leniency: The rater can't give everyone a high evaluation.

Because of these advantages, ranking methods are very effective for some performance-appraisal uses. For example, rankings are particularly useful in making defensible promotion or termination decisions. The manager has only to select from the top down on the ranking list until all promotion vacancies are filled; or, conversely, from the bottom up until all necessary reductions in force have been accomplished.

Ranking also has some disadvantages, which limit its usefulness for other performance-appraisal purposes. Rankings tend to be based on overall performance. This limits their usefulness in providing feedback on various dimensions of performance. To know that you are ranked fourth out of 10 people, for example, does not tell you what you need to do to become the top-ranked employee. Also, rankings do not indicate how much better the performance of one person is than that of another. For example, the top-ranked person may produce 20 percent more than the second-ranked person who, in turn, may produce 5 percent more than the third-ranked person. Because such rankings tell you that one person is better than another but not by how much, they are limited for compensation purposes. In order to determine equitable pay raises, a manager has to know something about the size of the difference among those evaluated. Another problem with ranking is that the rater has to be familiar with the performance of all the employees being ranked. This usually limits the number of employees that can be evaluated using ranking methods.

Rating

The second general approach to evaluating performance subjectively includes the various **rating** methods. With such methods, the performance dimension of the job to be evaluated is presented along with some form of rating scale. A typical rating scale may range from 1–5, where 1 represents poor performance and 5 represents outstanding performance. The remaining scale points, of course, represent levels of performance in between. Table 18.9 illustrates three common rating scales that might be used to evaluate a salesperson's service performance. The rater uses these scales to indicate how well the person is performing each aspect (dimension) of the job.

Returning to Jacob Wilson, his supervisor might be required to rate his *sales performance* and *service performance* using 5-point scales. Table 18.9 shows that scales can be more or less explicit regarding what constitutes average, above average, and below average performance. The more clearly

TABLE 18.9 ■ THREE TYPES OF SCALES FOR EVALUATING SERVICE PERFORMANCE

■ Service Performance:

5	4	3	2	1
Outstanding	Above average	Average	Below average	Poor

■ Service Performance:

5—Always provides timely, courteous, and efficient service to all customers.

4—Service to most customers is almost always timely, courteous, and efficient.

3—Usually provides timely, courteous, and efficient service to most customers.

2—Service to many customers is untimely, discourteous, or inefficient.

1—Provides service that is typically late and inefficient; often rude to some customers.

■ Service Performance:

9 8 7	6 5 4	3 2 1
Excellent	Average	Unsatisfactory

and explicitly the scales are defined the better. Similarly, the more clearly the performance dimension being rated is defined the better.[23] For example, it is always a good idea to state clearly and precisely what is meant by sales performance or service performance.

In an effort to clearly define various aspects of a job, some organizations are using **behavior-anchored rating scales** (BARS). Behavior-anchored rating scales are used to evaluate whether the employee has performed certain job behaviors and how frequently. Table 18.10 illustrates a behavior-anchored scale, which contains 11 statements that could be used to describe a nurse's job knowledge and ability.

In the past, a considerable amount of research was conducted on various behavior-anchored rating scales. That research suggests that different forms do not result in different ratings of performance. What *is* important, it seems, is whether the job dimensions (such as sales, service performance, organizational ability) and the scales (ranging, for example, from 1–5 or 1–7) are clearly defined. If the job dimensions are clear, there should be good agreement among raters on the aspect of performance that is being rated. If the scales are clear, there should be good agreement about what constitutes outstanding performance, average performance, and poor performance.

Managerial implications

The best method of appraising performance depends on the use to which the appraisal will be put.[24] Compared to rankings, rating methods have a number of advantages and disadvantages. In terms of disadvantages, rating scales typically do not control leniency error very well. It is not impossible or even unusual, for example, for everyone to be rated in the highest one or two

TABLE 18.10 ■ BEHAVIOR-ANCHORED RATING SCALE

CLINICAL KNOWLEDGE

Nurse possesses the clinical knowledge and exercises good judgment in fulfilling her job duties in a competent fashion.

My observations of this nurse's job knowledge and judgment include:

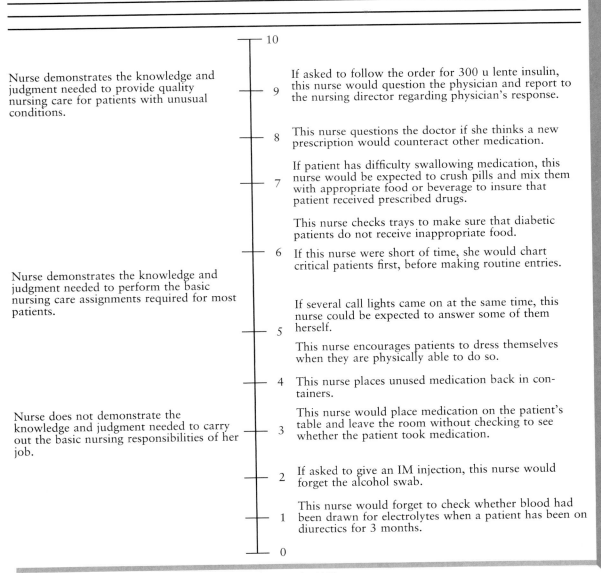

Nurse demonstrates the knowledge and judgment needed to provide quality nursing care for patients with unusual conditions.

10 —

9 — If asked to follow the order for 300 u lente insulin, this nurse would question the physician and report to the nursing director regarding physician's response.

8 — This nurse questions the doctor if she thinks a new prescription would counteract other medication.

7 — If patient has difficulty swallowing medication, this nurse would be expected to crush pills and mix them with appropriate food or beverage to insure that patient received prescribed drugs.

This nurse checks trays to make sure that diabetic patients do not receive inappropriate food.

6 — If this nurse were short of time, she would chart critical patients first, before making routine entries.

Nurse demonstrates the knowledge and judgment needed to perform the basic nursing care assignments required for most patients.

5 — If several call lights came on at the same time, this nurse could be expected to answer some of them herself.

This nurse encourages patients to dress themselves when they are physically able to do so.

4 — This nurse places unused medication back in containers.

Nurse does not demonstrate the knowledge and judgment needed to carry out the basic nursing responsibilities of her job.

3 — This nurse would place medication on the patient's table and leave the room without checking to see whether the patient took medication.

2 — If asked to give an IM injection, this nurse would forget the alcohol swab.

1 — This nurse would forget to check whether blood had been drawn for electrolytes when a patient has been on diurectics for 3 months.

0 —

Source: John Sheridan, Texas Christian University, Fort Worth, 1985.

categories. When this happens, the ratings may be worthless to the manager for use in making promotion or termination decisions. That is, if everyone is rated highly, how would you select the person to promote (or terminate)?

In terms of advantages, rating scales can be an exceptionally good way for a manager to provide performance feedback to employees. For example, with the use of behavior-anchored rating scales, the manager is able to tell a subordinate exactly what improvements he or she needs to make. Ratings also indicate how much better one employee is than another. Thus they can be used in allocating merit-pay raises, bonuses, and other rewards.

Design of Performance-Appraisal Systems

When designing a performance-appraisal system, managers should be aware of the many options available to them and the important decisions that have to be made about them. These decisions concern the methods to be used, who will perform the evaluations, and how often evaluations should be conducted.

Selection of methods

Selection of a method of performance appraisal depends on several factors, one of which is the use to which the appraisal information will be put. At least two other important criteria must be considered: (1) accuracy of information and (2) fairness. For an organization that has various levels of responsibility, types of jobs, and both line and staff functions, different methods or systems of performance appraisal may, in fact, be necessary for different purposes and for groups or classes of employees. For example, the Southland Corporation has separate appraisal systems for compensation and promotion purposes. The method or methods to be used should be selected to yield the most accurate information and fairest employee evaluations for the levels of responsibility occupied and the types of jobs performed by the employees to be evaluated.

Selection of evaluators

Another important decision concerns who will provide the evaluations.[25] In most organizations, this is the immediate supervisor's responsibility. However, it is also possible to have peers, subordinates, outsiders, or even the employee provide the ratings. Research indicates that raters with different roles (supervisors, peers, subordinates) often produce different evaluations of the same person.[26] Although different raters may produce different evaluations, none is necessarily wrong; they may simply be reporting what they observe from different perspectives. Students evaluate a faculty member's performance on instructional competence, while department heads and deans evaluate the same person not only on instruction but also on research and service. Students may rate the faculty member as an exceptional teacher, but he or she may still receive a small salary increase because of poor performance on other dimensions.

Ideally, the person who is in the best position to observe the employee's performance should make the performance evaluation. Thus ratings for compensation and promotion decisions are almost always provided by supervisors. Peer ratings have been found to be good predictors of success after a person has been promoted.[27] Subordinates may be the best source of information about a manager's leadership abilities. However, peers and subordinates generally do not view the evaluation of co-workers, particularly for compensation or promotion purposes, to be a legitimate part of their roles. Those organizations that do utilize peer or subordinate evaluations, or self-ratings, generally limit their uses to identification of employee-development or training needs.

Selection of Frequency

Designers of performance-appraisal systems must also determine how often to evaluate employees. Most organizations require that employee evaluations be conducted either every six or 12 months. However, when organizations have multiple appraisal systems for different purposes, the evaluations are conducted as often as is necessary to meet the needs of each system.

The Performance-Appraisal Interview

For performance appraisals to motivate an employee to improve performance, the person who made the evaluation must effectively communicate the results to the employee. During the performance-appraisal interview, supervisor and employee should exchange information and ideas about the employee's strengths and weaknesses and about ways to improve performance. This is one of the most important steps in the performance-appraisal process. An accurate and fair evaluation of an employee's performance can be wasted if it is not communicated or communicated poorly to the employee. The case of Susan Wheeler illustrates what not to do when conducting a performance review.

IN PRACTICE
Susan Wheeler

Susan Wheeler's supervisor was showing her the ratings she had received in her latest performance review. In going through the ratings, the supervisor was talking quickly, pausing only periodically to ask questions such as, "You don't have any problems with that assessment, do you?" After going through the ratings, he immediately moved to the objectives he wanted her to accomplish before the next performance review. Handing Wheeler a typed list of objectives, the supervisor asked her to read through them to make sure she understood them. As he got up to leave, explaining that he was late for another meeting, the supervisor reminded her to sign the evaluation form and asked her to give it to the departmental secretary.

Wheeler's supervisor obviously was ill at ease and anxious for the appraisal interview to end. Consequently, he moved quickly, did all the talking, and unilaterally set objectives for future improvement without asking for her input. This type of appraisal interview is likely to generate feelings of resentment and distrust of the performance-appraisal process, and little commitment to assigned performance objectives on the part of the employee. Most experts agree that there are a number of activities that should occur before, during, and after the appraisal interview.[28]

Prior to interview

Prior to actually conducting an interview, effective managers will probably

1. communicate frequently with subordinates;
2. evaluate their own managerial performance; and
3. encourage subordinates to engage in a self-evaluation of performance.

It is often said that there should be no surprises during an appraisal interview. If subordinates express surprise at the ratings they receive, it may mean that the manager has done a poor job of communicating and has not provided enough feedback to subordinates about their performance since the previous evaluation.

Subordinates are more capable of contributing to a discussion of their performance if they have taken the time to analyze it relative to their own expectations and to examine the problems they have encountered. To make future comparisons easier, the manager should ask subordinates to rate themselves, using the same form that the manager used. In this way, both the manager and subordinates will be able to discuss their performance in the same terms.

During appraisal interview

During the appraisal interview, managers should

1. encourage participation;
2. evaluate performance and not personality;
3. be specific;
4. listen; and
5. set mutually agreeable objectives.

Unlike Susan Wheeler's supervisor, effective managers will actively encourage participation by the subordinate. If a person is allowed to present feelings, evaluations, and ideas, he or she will tend to feel that the interview is fair, helpful, and worthwhile.

It is also important for the manager to focus only on job-related performance measures and avoid discussing personality, mannerisms, habits, and so on that don't affect job performance. In discussing the evaluation, managers should be as specific as possible; they should take care to point out specific actions that were effective and ineffective. Because it is difficult for most people to remember many specific details over a rating period, managers should keep a diary of incidents of good and poor performance. They can then refer to the diary before conducting interviews and provide specific feedback.

It is essential for the manager to listen actively to the subordinate during the appraisal interview. Listening and responding assures the subordinate that his or her position is understood and valued. One way to do this is to periodically repeat and reaffirm what the subordinate has said.

Finally, it is important for the manager and subordinate to set mutually agreeable performance-improvement objectives. Recall that Wheeler's supervisor gave her an already prepared list of objectives without giving her a chance to participate in setting them. Participation in the establishment of objectives is one way to increase an employee's commitment to reaching those objectives. Consequently, Wheeler's supervisor should not be surprised if she is not particularly committed to accomplishing the objectives he set for her. After all, they are his objectives, not hers.

After the interview
After appraisal interviews have been conducted, managers should

1. monitor subordinates' progress toward the accomplishment of objectives; and

2. reward subordinates for performance improvements.

By monitoring subordinates' progress, managers can provide directive feedback and coaching to help them accomplish objectives. It is just as important for managers to communicate with subordinates about their performance after the appraisal interviews as it is before the interviews. By making valued rewards (merit pay, praise) contingent upon accomplishment of objectives, managers increase subordinates' motivation to accomplish them. Unless subordinates are rewarded for meeting objectives, they may exert little effort toward accomplishing them.

CHAPTER SUMMARY

In this chapter, we noted that evaluation underlies both staffing and performance appraisal. By evaluating candidates and positions, the organization is better able to select people capable of performing the tasks that need to be done. One way to control performance is to ensure an appropriate match between the requirements of the job and the qualifications of the selected candidate. Performance appraisal also serves an important control function. By promoting certain individuals and not others, or by rewarding some actions and outcomes but not others, managers can influence people to behave in ways consistent with the organizational objectives.

To achieve an effective match between the individual and the organization, several types of action are required. These constitute the components of the staffing process. The first is to forecast and make plans for meeting the organization's future human-resource needs (demand). These needs should accurately reflect the business strategy of the firm. If the internal supply of candidates is expected to be insufficient to meet the demand, the organization must recruit externally. Regardless of the source of the recruits, the organization ultimately can select only one per job opening. Several different selection techniques are commonly used: the job application, realistic job previews, interviews, testing, and assessment centers. Having made a selection decision, the manager must orient the new employee to the job and to the organization's culture.

The performance-appraisal process assesses the strengths and weaknesses of the employee in relation to the job. Performance appraisals can be used in many different ways. All appraisal methods have certain shortcomings and none of the methods is more successful for most situations than any other. Objective measures are used when performance units can be counted and measured. Subject appraisal methods have to be used most of the time and include two general types: ranking and rating.

Managers must make decisions about the method or methods of appraisal to use, who will make the appraisals, frequency of appraisal, and the purposes of the appraisal when designing an appraisal system. After making a performance evaluation, a manager should discuss the results with the person being evaluated, follow up to check on performance improvement, and reward the person for achievements.

MANAGER'S VOCABULARY

affirmative action
assessment center
behavior-anchored rating scale
cognitive ability tests
contamination
contrast error
deficiency
equal worth
halo error
human-resource planning and forecasting
interest inventories
job analysis
job application
job description

job specification
leniency
objective measures
orientation
performance appraisal
performance tests
personality tests
ranking
rating
realistic job preview
recruitment
reliability
replacement chart
severity
similarity error
skills inventory
socialization
staffing process
union security clause
validity

REVIEW QUESTIONS

1. Define the two basic criteria all tests should meet.

2. Describe the two components of a thorough job analysis.

3. Define contamination, deficiency, and halo error.

4. Name three techniques used by managers to narrow the choice of candidates for a job.

5. Describe three different subjective methods of performance appraisal.

6. State three things a manager should do before conducting a performance appraisal.

7. Describe two approaches to forecasting human-resource supply.

DISCUSSION QUESTIONS

1. Describe a skills inventory. What information does it contain? How is this information used in planning? In recruitment? In selection?

2. What are the major laws regarding equal employment opportunity? What do these laws mean for employers? How do they affect staffing? Performance appraisal?

3. Identify the various sources of external recruitment. Which are likely to be most effective for office and secretarial employees? For skilled trades? For professional and managerial employees?

4. Describe the various types of tests used for selection. Which are likely to be most effective? Which are likely to cause the most resentment from job applicants? The least resentment?

5. Discuss the various methods of appraising performance. Which is likely to be best for each of the uses? Which are least susceptible to the various problems? Most susceptible?

6. How should a performance appraisal interview be conducted? What should the manager do before, during, and after the review? What should the employee do?

MANAGEMENT INCIDENTS AND CASES

Who Wants to Play God?

Thomas Reynolds sat at his desk looking at the performance appraisal form he had just completed on Ellen Jackofsky, one of his insurance underwriters. Ellen was on her way to Tom's office for her annual review session. Tom dreaded these performance appraisal sessions, even when he did not have to confront his subordinates with negative feedback on their performance.

A few years ago, Canyon Creek Insurance Company, which had experienced rapid growth in sales and profits, had decided to implement a formal appraisal system. All of the supervisors had been presented with the new appraisal form. People from the personnel department had instructed all supervisors on how to complete the form. All insurance underwriters were to be rated on five job dimensions: job knowledge, supervision needed, and quantity, quality, and dedication to work. Supervisors were asked to rate employees on each dimension using a scale that ranged from unacceptable (a value of 1) to exceptional (a value of 5). They were also advised by people from the personnel department to maintain a file on each of their subordinates during the year. Supervisors would use these files as documentation when completing the appraisal form. Supervisors were told by the personnel department that they could give a rating of 1 or 5 only if they had substantial documentation to back up their rating. Tom had never given one of these ratings, and he wasn't too careful

about keeping detailed records of actual behaviors. He believed that the people in the personnel department were just making work for managers, who had other things to do. A couple of people in Tom's department had deserved a 5 rating, but so far had not complained about the appraisals they received from Tom.

Ellen was one of Tom's best performers. He could recall several specific incidents of how Ellen's exceptional performance saved the company time and money. These incidents, unfortunately, were not written down because of Tom's belief that writing them down was just a waste of time. "Oh, well," Tom said to himself, "I'll just give her 3's and 4's. The personnel department doesn't require me to justify those numbers." One of the five performance dimensions was dedication to work. Tom had never really understood what that meant or whether it was even relevant for the job of an insurance underwriter. Therefore he checked 3 (meaning satisfactory) for Ellen, as he did for all his subordinates. Tom understood the other dimensions, although he was not sure of the difference between a 3 (satisfactory) and a 4 (above average).

Ellen knocked on Tom's office door and came in. Tom looked up and said, "Hi, Ellen. Sit down. I guess it's my time to play God."

Questions

1. Does Tom feel very comfortable giving Ellen her performance appraisal?

2. What problems do you see with the appraisal system that Tom is using?

3. What do you think Ellen's reactions will be when Tom tells her that she has scored mainly 3's and 4's, even though Tom thinks she's one of the best workers?

4. What suggestions do you have for improving this performance-appraisal system?

REFERENCES

1. L. E. Albright, "Staffing Policies and Strategies." In D. Yoder and H. G. Heneman Jr. (Eds.), *Staffing Policies and Strategies*. Washington, D.C.: BNA, 1974. For those interested in the relationship between corporate strategy and human resources, *see* C. Fombrun, N. Tichy, and M. DeVanna, *Strategic Human Resource Management*. New York: John

Wiley & Sons, 1984; G. Odiorne, *Strategic Management of Human Resources.* San Francisco: Jossey Bass, 1984.

2. B. Schneider, "An Interactionist Prospective on Organizational Effectiveness." In K. S. Cameron and D. A. Whetten (Eds.), *Organizational Effectiveness: A Comparison of Multiple Models.* New York: Academic Press, 1983.

3. K. L. Sovereign, *Personnel Law.* Reston, Va.: Reston, 1984.

4. W. P. Murphy, J. G. Getman, and J. E. Jones, *Discrimination in Employment.* Washington, D.C.: BNA, 1979.

5. E. R. Livernash, *Comparable Worth: Issues and Alternatives.* Washington, D.C.: Equal Employment Advisory Council, 1980.

6. B. Schneider, *Staffing Organizations.* Pacific Palisades, Calif.: Goodyear, 1976.

7. J. W. Walker, *Human Resource Planning.* New York: McGraw-Hill, 1980.

8. E. J. McCormick, *Job Analysis: Methods and Applications.* New York: AMACOM, 1979.

9. E. H. Burack and N. J. Mathys, *Human Resource Planning: A Pragmatic Approach to Manpower Staffing and Development.* Lake Forest, Ill.: Brace-Park, 1979.

10. W. F. Cascio and E. M. Awad, *Human Resource Management: An Information Systems Approach.* Reston, Va.: Reston, 1981.

11. P. F. Wernimont, "Recruitment Policies and Procedures." In D. Yoder and H. G. Heneman Jr. (Eds.), *Staffing Policies and Strategies.* Washington, D.C.: BNA, 1974.

12. J. Breaugh, "Relationships Between Recruiting Sources and Employee Performance, Absenteeism and Work Attitudes," *Academy of Management Journal,* 1981, **24:**142–147. *Also see:* M. S. Taylor and D. W. Schmidt, "A Process-Oriented Investigation of Recruitment Source Effectiveness," *Personnel Psychology,* 1983, **36:**343–354; G. Powell, "Effects of Job Attitudes and Recruiting Practices on Applicant Decisions: A Comparison," *Personnel Psychology,* 1984, **37:**721–732.

13. J. P. Wanous, *Organizational Entry: Recruitment, Selection and Socialization of Newcomers.* Reading, Mass.: Addison-Wesley, 1980; R. Dean and J. Wanous, "Effects of Realistic Job Previews on Hiring Bank Tellers," *Journal of Applied Psychology,* 1984, **69:**61–68.

14. J. E. Hunter and R. F. Hunter, "Validity and Utility of Alternative Predictors of Job Performance," *Psychological Bulletin,* 1984, **96:**72–98; R. Arvey and J. Campion, "The Employment Interview: A Summary and Review of Recent Research," *Personnel Psychology,* 1982, **35:**281–322; J. Goodale, *The Fine Art of Interviewing.* Englewood Cliffs, N.J.: Prentice-Hall, 1982.

15. W. F. Cascio, *Applied Psychology in Personnel Management.* Reston, Va.: Reston, 1982.

16. F. L. Schmidt, J. E. Hunter, and K. Pearlman, "Task Differences as Moderators of Aptitude Test Validity in Selection: A Red Herring," *Journal of Applied Psychology,* 1981, **66:**166–185; L. James, R. Demaree, and S. Mulaik, *A Note on Validity Generalization Procedures.* Arlington, Va.: Office of Naval Research, 1985, Report No. GT-ONR-7.

17. G. C. Thornton and W. C. Byham, *Assessment Centers and Managerial Performance.* New York: Academic Press, 1982.

18. C. D. Fisher and J. A. Weekley, *Socialization in Work Organizations.* Office of Naval Research Technical Report TR-ONR-1, 1981.

19. R. Schuler, *Personnel and Human Resource Management.* St. Paul, Minn.: West, 1984, p. 236.

20. F. J. Landy and J. L. Farr, *The Measurement of Work Performance: Methods, Theory, and Applications.* New York: Academic Press, 1983.

21. S. J. Tannenbaum and M. J. Kavanagh, "Rater–Ratee Differences, Interview Processes, and Acceptance of Performance Evaluations." Paper presented at the annual meeting of the American Psychological Association, Toronto, Ontario, 1984.

22. W. H. Cooper, "Ubiquitous Halo," *Psychological Bulletin,* 1981, **90:**218–244.

23. S. J. Carroll and C. D. Schneier, *Performance Appraisal and Review Systems: The Identification, Measurement, and Development of Performance in Organizations.* Glenview, Ill.: Scott, Foresman, 1982; C. Banks and L. Roberson, "Performance Appraisers as Test Developers," *Academy of Man-*

agement Review, 1985, **10**:128–142; B. Nathan and R. Alexander, "Role of Inferential Accuracy in Performance Rating," *Academy of Management Review,* 1985, **10**:109–115.

24. H. J. Bernardin and R. W. Beatty, *Performance Appraisal: Assessing Human Behavior at Work.* Boston: Kent, 1984. *Also see* K. Williams, A. DeNisi, A. Blencoe, and T. Cafferty, "The Role of Appraisal Purpose: Effects of Purpose of Information Acquisition and Utilization," *Organizational Behavior and Human Decision Processes,* 1985, **35**:314–339; C. Hobson and W. Gibson, "Policy Capturing as an Approach to Understanding and Improving Performance Appraisal: A Review of the Literature," *Academy of Management Review,* 1983, **8**:640–702.

25. F. J. Landy and J. L. Farr, "Performance Rating," *Psychological Bulletin,* 1980, **87**:72–107; and S. Silverman and K. Wexley, "Reactions of Employees to Performance Appraisal Interviews as a Function of Their Participation in Rating Scale Development," *Personnel Psychology,* 1984, **37**:703–710.

26. M. K. Mount, "Supervisor, Self-, and Subordinate Ratings of Performance and Satisfaction with Supervision," *Journal of Management,* 1984, **10**:305–320; M. Mount, Psychometric Properties of Subordinate Ratings of Managerial Performance, *Personnel Psychology,* 1984, **37**:687–702.

27. R. A. Ash and K. D. Jones, "Reliability and Validity of Peer Assessments: Results of a Meta-Analysis." Paper presented at the annual meeting of the American Psychological Association, Toronto, Ontario, 1984.

28. Adapted from W. F. Cascio and E. M. Awad, *Human Resources Management: An Information Systems Approach.* Reston, Va.: Reston, 1981; M. Sashkin, *Assessing Performance Appraisal.* San Diego: University Associates, 1981.

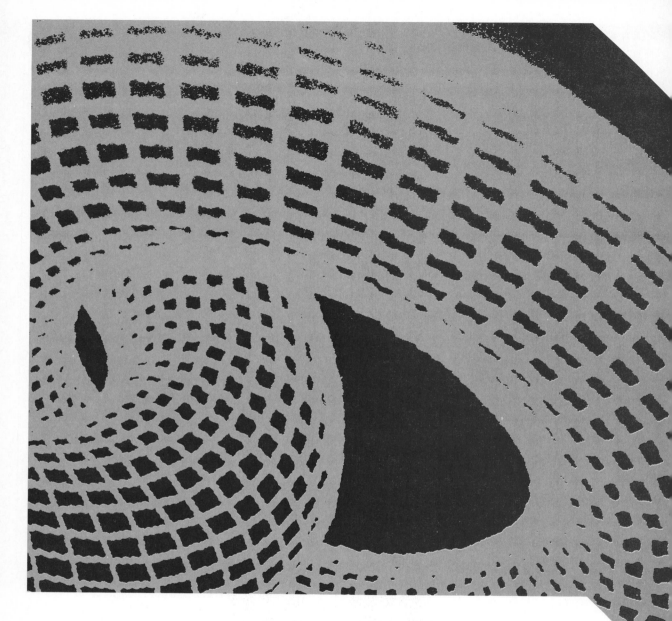

Production and Operations Management

LEARNING OBJECTIVES

After studying this chapter, you should be able to:

■ Describe production and operations management as a system.

■ State the role of manufacturing strategy as part of overall organizational strategy.

■ Identify the two basic types of production systems.

■ State the significance of productivity and product quality in manufacturing.

■ Describe some of the ways for improving quality control in manufacturing operations.

■ Explain how inventory control is a part of materials-requirement planning and the just-in-time concept.

CHAPTER OUTLINE

PREVIEW CASE

Windsor Assembly Plant

Just-In-Time Concept

Chrysler's Windsor, Ontario, assembly plant for T-wagons (Dodge Caravan, Plymouth Voyager, and Mini-Ran Van) uses a new concept to make these wagons. Called just-in-time (JIT), it refers to producing and delivering (1) finished goods just in time to be sold; (2) subassemblies just in time to be assembled into finished goods; (3) fabricated parts just in time to go into subassemblies; and (4) purchased materials just in time to be transformed into fabricated parts. Like perfect quality, absolute just-in-time performance is never achieved, but represents an ideal that can be pursued.[1] At Chrysler Windsor, JIT applies to subassemblies produced in the plant as well as to parts provided by suppliers. The assembly plant, containing 2.5 million square feet of space, was converted to a whole new way of automobile manufacturing in 1984. The system was designed with a maximum capacity of approximately 70 vehicles per hour. In 1985, the plant was operating with two shifts per day and 3000 workers per shift.

Chrysler Windsor, like virtually every other new auto plant, uses flow-through production as well as just-in-time quality and materials-control techniques. Sheet metal parts are received almost hourly in returnable racks from nearby plants. Engines come from as far away as Mexico and Japan, sometimes twice a week, sometimes daily. Depending on their sizes and quantities, trim parts are received on an hourly to a weekly basis.

The fact that the whole plant is filled with production equipment leaves very little room for storage of the thousands of parts used in the T-wagons. It was planned that way. If you operate on a JIT system for a few high-value parts, you might as well operate that way for all parts. This is especially true when the suppliers' plants are close by. The only time storage must be used as a hedge against delivery problems is for items that take a long time to arrive at the plant, such as engines.

Conveyors Pace the Flow

Innovative conveyor systems tie the production processes together and provide movement for the vehicles throughout the plant to a point almost out the door. The most significant new conveyor handling approach is the inverted-power and free-conveyor system. More than 10,000 feet of inverted-power and free conveyor and some linear-motor-powered, transfer-free trolley lines are used in the Body-in-White Division. This area of the assembly operation is where the main body panels are welded together.

Robotic Welding, Lifting, and Conveying

Floor pans, for instance, are welded on one robotic spot-weld line and then picked up by a robot and hung on a loop of power and free overhead

Courtesy of Chrysler Corporation.

conveyor, which forms a buffer between pan welding and the beginning of the body assembly system. [*Robots* are reprogrammable, multifunctional manipulators. The robot frame is a substitute for the human arm and its microprocessor (computer) takes the place of the human brain. Robots have been programmed to perform numerous tasks such as welding, assembly, spray painting, lifting, dipping, inspecting and carrying parts.][2]

A second robot removes the pans in sequence and places them onto a sequencing conveyor to be joined to the engine compartment. The pans then advance to another robot where they are joined by the side aperture panels and precisely aligned and tack welded. The tack-welded body then heads for the "Turkey Farm" where a line of spot-welding robots on both sides of a conveyor apply hundreds of additional spot welds. The roof is also added and welded here by robots mounted overhead. Optical laser gauging is used to control the fit of every vehicle body.

After welding, the bodies are transferred to carriers on an overhead P&F conveyor that takes them through an eight-stage, full-immersion phosphate system to assure rust protection inside and out. The bodies with all panels in place then rise to a second-floor paint area.

Robotic Painting

Gun-applied sealer from 475-gallon tanks is added at the rate of about 110 lineal feet per chassis. The bodies are then automatically transferred by conveyor through the paint system. Robots paint the bodies inside and out. The painting robots are programmed by vehicle: Any robot can paint any body any color; any skipped part of a painting program will be picked up by the following robot. Production flow does not run in color batches. Every body may be a different color, and the robots can change quickly from one color to another. The bodies are indexed through the paint booths, stopping at the programmed robot stations. At the end of the color painting stage, two high-voltage–electrostatic spray heads apply the final clear-gloss overcoat that gives the paint its deep shine.

Trim and Final Assembly

After being painted, the bodies are lowered to the first-floor level by mechanical carriers for trim and final assembly. These carriers move quickly back and forth between floor levels to make the assembly operations as easy as possible. In the Trim Division, 4800 feet of conveyors handle the bodies as interior parts and exterior trim are added. A conveyor with special carriers brings the engine and front-wheel–drive assembly and the rear axle and suspension up under the bodies. An air lift holds the assemblies in place while they are secured.

The last parts added while the vehicles are in the air are the wheels and tires. The overhead conveyor then brings the van in for a landing on a synchronized flat-top, floor-level conveyor.

Versatile Conveyor System

Chrysler stated that the conveyor system is the most versatile it has tried to date. The more than 10 miles of advanced conveyors are an industry first, the company believes. The conveyor permits improved housekeeping, provides a disciplined working environment, and makes many assembly jobs easier.

On-Line Sequencing

The plant is a North American first in the way vehicles are scheduled, from the parts that make up the floor pan and the holes that are punched in it for seat belts right through the smallest options. Once a body emerges from the Body-In-White operations, it will remain in sequence to the end of the flat-top conveyor at the end of the line.

For materials-handling purposes, with 1849 vehicles in the system at one time, the supply of parts to various operations can be determined by the hour or day or for several days. Special equipment can be scheduled ahead; only the quantity needed is placed on the line at the correct station.

Guided Vehicle System

Several loops of guide wire take driverless trains of incoming parts to the operations in the plant. There are 27 drop zones, plus the vehicle battery charging area and the rail dock. Fourteen trains pull three trailers each. The trains stop in the area where they are to be unloaded. Lift-truck operators servicing that area remove the parts to stock the assembly line or place loads on nearby, two-level racks. Empty pallets, containers, and refuse are returned on the same trains.

Risks and Track Record

The just-in-time philosophy has had a major impact on this plant because it is a new way of operating. Everyone is aware that this plant, with its more than 3000 workers per shift, could come to a grinding halt if key components, such as seats, are not received on time. There are no areas to store unfinished vehicles, empty wire baskets, racks, or even trash for that matter. With single-line, continuous flow of mixed styles, colors, and options, the system either works or the whole plant shuts down.

About 80 percent of the vehicles coming off the line meet all quality standards with no re-working required. The aim, of course, is 100 percent, but Chrysler believes the present rate is excellent. However, the smallest quality problem keeps the vehicle from rolling out the door.[3]

Before continuing, you should reread the Preview Case. It describes many of the latest concepts and techniques for improving manufacturing productivity and the quality of goods produced, which are two important issues in both domestic and international competition. Moreover, in presenting key topics in this chapter, such as quality control and inventory control, we repeatedly refer back to the Preview Case.

Production and operations management refers to the transformation of inputs (labor, capital, materials) into outputs (goods, services, waste products) and the managerial activities that direct and control the process of transformation. Production and operations management is necessary in all organizations and involves the use of various technologies—from the federal government (processing a social security check) to private firms (producing T-wagons) and from municipal governments (collecting and disposing of garbage) to private retail and service operations (making McDonald's hamburgers or cutting hair).[4] In this chapter we focus primarily on production and operations management in manufacturing plants, giving special emphasis to manufacturing processes and control techniques.

SYSTEMS VIEW

The specifics of production and operations management systems can vary widely within the same organization and from one organization to another. For example, the system used to produce vascular X-ray equipment at GE is substantially different from the one Chrysler uses to produce T-vans. While different, these two production and operations management systems have certain basic common elements: environmental factors, inputs, transformation, and outputs. Figure 19.1 provides a systems view of production and operations management and its elements.

Environmental Factors

Many environmental factors influence production and operations management. In previous chapters, you read about the Japanese emphasis on collectivism and how this leads to extensive group decision making involving all employees—an example of how values influence the production process. Strategic planning becomes an environmental factor in the production and operations management system. Strategic plans determine the types of goods and services that will be marketed by the firm. These decisions affect the types of inputs and transformation processes to be used to create the desired goods and services.

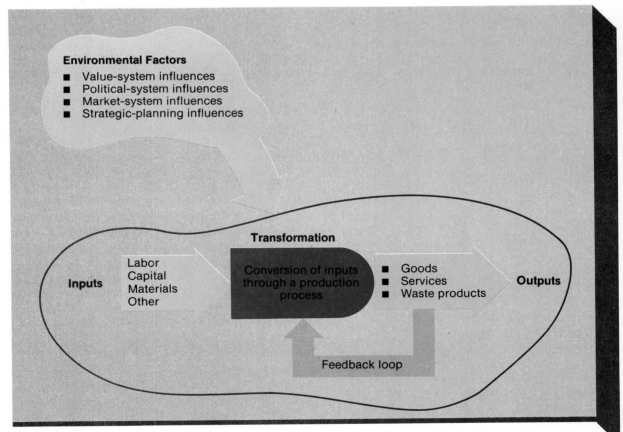

FIGURE 19.1
Systems View of Production and Operations Management

INPUTS

Labor refers to the human resources (employees) of an organization. Production and operations management is typically most concerned with employees directly involved with the production process. The 6000 employees (3000 per shift) at the Chrysler Windsor plant are directly involved in the transformation process.

Capital is the money, machinery, equipment, buildings, and other assets of an organization. Capital at the Windsor plant includes the building, conveyor systems, robotic welders, optical laser equipment, robotic painting equipment, driverless trains, and the like. The amount of capital per production employee at the Windsor plant is much higher than at older assembly plants; capital (such as robots) is used to improve productivity and quality.

Materials are the physical items used directly in creating the desired products or services. At the Windsor plant, these include the thousands of parts and materials used in the production of T-wagons (such as engines, seats, paint, floor pans, radios, carpet, windows, and tires).

TRANSFORMATION

Labor, capital, and materials are the three main inputs to transformation. *Transformation* is the conversion of inputs, through a production process, into outputs. Transformation is more extensive and dramatic in some industries and production processes than in others. For example, production plants in the aluminum industry transform a whitish powder, bauxite, into aluminum ingots with the use of electric furnaces. The input does not in any way resemble the output. At the Windsor plant, transformation focuses on the assembly of parts that were created at other plants (engines, windows, seats, tires) and various finishing activities (sanding of rough spots, painting).

OUTPUTS

Outputs are the goods, services, and waste products created by transformation. Outputs include goods and services such as vans at the Windsor plant, government social security checks, and waste products (garbage, air pollution, water pollution).

Feedback

Vital information regarding characteristics of its outputs is provided to the transformation part of the system by *feedback loops.* The T-wagons coming off the assembly line at the Windsor plant are tested to make sure that they run and that all the equipment works as it should. In addition, the warranty provided to T-wagon purchasers by Chrysler provides another method of collecting information on the quality of the wagons. When owners take their wagons to be repaired under the warranty, this information is fed back to corporate headquarters. Each wagon has a code number that enables management to determine when it was assembled and the supplier of the defective parts. The information on defects is then sent to the assembly plant or the parts supplier to avoid the same problems in the future.

BASIC MANUFACTURING ISSUES

Four basic manufacturing issues—manufacturing strategy, production systems, productivity, and quality—are important in production and operations management. Managers are continually called on to make decisions concerning these issues.

Manufacturing Strategy

Manufacturing strategy should flow from organizational strategy or strategic business unit strategy. Organizational strategy defines the desired competitive advantages of the products or services to be offered, the types of customers to be served, and the geographic areas in which the products or services are to be marketed. Thus a manufacturing strategy specifies how it will help achieve the desired competitive advantage and complement other functional strategies (marketing, human-resource, research and development).[5]

Chrysler's Windsor plant is testimony to top management's belief that improved manufacturing productivity and high quality were essential to Chrysler's survival in the face of intense international competition. It recognized that a new line of products was not enough; that is, the new products must also be efficiently produced and be seen by customers as matching or beating the competition in terms of quality.

Table 19.1 identifies eight decision categories that comprise a manufacturing strategy. Strategic questions associated with each decision category and answers for the Chrysler Windsor plant are also shown. The eight decision categories are capacity, technology, vertical integration, work force, quality, production planning, materials control, and organization. The specific technology selected will be strongly influenced by the type of production system needed to produce the desired goods.

Types of Production Systems

There are two major types of production systems—process-focused and product-focused—with a range of less important types between them.[6]

Process-focused systems

Process-focused systems are highly flexible manufacturing operations designed to meet the varying requirements of custom-made products. Job shops, such as a machine shop, commonly organize equipment and other physical

TABLE 19.1   DECISION CATEGORIES COMPRISING MANUFACTURING STRATEGY

CATEGORY	STRATEGIC QUESTION	EXAMPLES OF ANSWERS FOR WINDSOR PLANT
Capacity	How much capacity should be provided?	70 wagons per hour
	When should new capacity be added?	Next year, five years from now
	What type of capacity is needed?	To produce T-wagons
Technology	What type of equipment should be used?	Robotic welders
	How much should the plant be automated?	Move parts on power- and computer-controlled conveyors
Vertical integration	Which parts should be provided by suppliers and which self-manufactured?	Manufacture own engines but purchase tires and windows from suppliers for assembly
Workforce	What skill levels, pay policies, and security programs are to be offered?	Described in collective bargaining agreement between Chrysler and the United Auto Workers
Quality	How are quality defects to be prevented?	Inspection of incoming parts
	How are quality defects to be monitored?	All employees plus inspectors responsible for checking for defects
Production planning	How centralized are production decisions?	Corporate headquarters makes primary decisions as to the specific types and numbers of wagons to be produced
Materials control	Who is to order materials and parts and determine their sources?	Corporate headquarters makes primary decisions
Organization	What will be the organizational structure of the plant, including reporting levels and support groups?	Described in Chrysler's policy manual for this plant

Source: Adapted from S. C. Wheelwright, "Manufacturing Strategy: Defining the Missing Link," *Strategic Management Journal,* January–February 1984, p. 84. Reprinted by permission of John Wiley & Sons, Ltd.

facilities by the nature of the processes: milling machines, lathes, drill presses, and so on. The flow of items through the shop is dictated by the requirements of the individual products.

Product-focused systems

Product-focused systems are manufacturing operations that produce highly standardized products on a relatively continuous basis. The steps and sequencing of a process is adapted completely to the product (the Windsor plant was designed to produce variations of Chrysler's T-Wagons only). The flow of raw materials may also be continuous as in a petroleum refinery.

Produce to inventory or to order

For a variety of reasons, companies might make a strategic manufacturing decision to produce items to maintain an inventory or in response to orders; this decision constitutes the company's finished-goods inventory policy. Until Chrysler's crisis in the late 1970s, it produced cars to inventory. Lee Iacocca, Chrysler CEO, changed this policy. Chrysler now produces cars and T-wagons in response to orders from dealers. The Chrysler dealers, of course, purchase many cars to maintain or increase their inventory stock. But, the dealers, not Chrysler Corporation, take the risk of maintaining inventories of finished cars and T-wagons.

Four production combinations

As shown in Fig. 19.2, the two major types of production systems and the two major finished-goods inventory policies (produce to inventory or produce in response to orders) result in four strategic manufacturing combi-

	Produce to Inventory	Produce to Order
Product-focused	Word processors Office copiers TV sets Calculators Gasoline	Cars Construction equipment Buses, trucks Experimental chemicals Textiles
Process-focused	Medical instruments Test equipment Electronic components Some steel products Molded plastic parts	Boeing 747s Nuclear submarines Space shuttle Ships Corporate headquarters building

Production System

Inventory Policy

FIGURE 19.2
Four Production Combinations

nations. The inventory policies directly impact on production planning, control, and scheduling. A produce-to-order policy requires more complex controls than does a produce-to-inventory policy. For example, the managers at the Windsor plant must be able to respond to Chrysler's marketing personnel when dealers make inquiries concerning the progress of their orders, to quote delivery dates, and to control orders as they go through the plant in order to make sure the right number of T-wagons come off the line in the right colors and with the proper extras.

Productivity

Productivity measures the relationship between outputs (amounts of goods and services produced) and inputs (quantities of labor, capital, and materials used to produce the outputs).[7] Productivity in the United States and Canada has become a major concern for businesses in general and manufacturing firms in particular. Two different and important productivity problems have been identified: (1) the slowdown in the rate of productivity growth in the United States and Canada, which began in the latter part of the 1960s; and (2) a much lower rate of U.S. and Canadian productivity growth throughout the past two decades in comparison with Japan, Korea, Italy, France, Sweden, West Germany, and other industrialized countries.[8]

Measuring productivity

Two indices are commonly used to measure productivity: *labor productivity* and *total-factor productivity.* Labor productivity measures output per hour (based on hours worked or hours paid for) in a plant, an industry, or a nation. Total-factor productivity includes labor inputs plus plant and equipment (capital) inputs, energy inputs, and materials inputs. Outputs are divided by the sum of these inputs to obtain a productivity measure. When output is measured on a *value-added basis,* only *capital and labor inputs* are included in the total-factor productivity measure; all other inputs are excluded. When output is measured as *gross output* (or physical units of output), all *purchased inputs* are included in the productivity measure. Most studies recognize inputs as including labor, capital, energy, and materials (usually includes all other purchased services).[9]

Chrysler's Windsor plant was designed to substantially increase labor productivity. The amount of labor required to assemble each T-wagon is significantly less than would have been required at the older type of assembly plant. The use of robots, computer-controlled conveyors, the just-in-time inventory approach, preventive and real-time quality control methods, and changed management practices have all helped to raise labor productivity. The new plant requires about 40 percent fewer workers to produce the same number of T-wagons, but of higher quality, than would Chrysler's old type of assembly plant.

At the Windsor plant, Chrysler invested much more capital (an input) per plant worker than at its older assembly plants. This capital was used to purchase robots, modern conveyor systems, computers used to track and control orders, and the like. Thus total-factor productivity at the plant did not increase as much as labor productivity, but it is still a substantial increase.

Productivity is generally expressed in the form of ratios. Many of the financial ratios discussed in Chapter 17 are used as capital-productivity ratios. The following are several of the many productivity ratios used.[10]

$$\frac{\text{Units produced per day, week, or month}}{\text{Kilowatt hours of electricity per day, week, or month}}$$

$$\frac{\text{Units produced per day, week, or month}}{\text{Direct production labor hours per day, week, or month}}$$

$$\frac{\text{Units produced per month}}{\text{Average dollar value of inventory in production process per month}}$$

$$\frac{\text{Units produced per day, week, or month}}{\text{Defective units produced per day, week, or month}}$$

Importance of productivity

Is all the concern about productivity justified? One comprehensive study of productivity gives this response:

> Productivity has a direct influence on a nation's standard of living. As long as the ratio of the employed labor force to overall population does not change, and as long as hours of labor per worker remain constant, it follows mathematically that movements in per capita income must precisely follow those in average output per worker. If output per worker increases, per capita income can go up likewise and workers can benefit from increased productivity growth. Conversely, any economy whose labor-productivity growth lags persistently behind that of others must eventually experience a relatively (although not absolutely) lower standard of living. An example of this is the United Kingdom, whose per capita income is now only slightly more than half that in Sweden, West Germany, the Netherlands, France, and a number of other European countries.[11]

Improving the productivity of U.S. and Canadian manufacturing operations is a key to maintaining and restoring their international competitive positions in a variety of industries, such as automobiles, electronic equipment, bicycles, motorcycles, cameras, small appliances, and steel.[12] Some productivity experts forecast that the improvement in rates of growth in U.S. productivity that began in about 1983 will continue into the 1990s. The expected 3 percent annual rate of productivity increases is in sharp contrast to no productivity increases from 1978–1982 and the less than 2 percent annual rate of increase from 1970–1977.[13]

PRODUCT QUALITY

DIMENSIONS OF QUALITY

Unfortunately, there is no single set of characteristics that effectively defines *product quality.* It can variously mean performance, features, reliability, conformance, serviceability, aesthetics, and perceived quality.[14] Table 19.2 explains each of these dimensions and applies them to Chrysler's line of T-wagons (Dodge Caravan, Plymouth Voyager, and Mini-Ram Van) assembled at the Windsor plant. Some of these dimensions are closely related, such as performance and features. Aesthetics and perceived quality are based on consumer perceptions and attitudes rather than physical measurements.

TABLE 19.2 ■ DIMENSIONS OF PRODUCT QUALITY

DIMENSION	EXPLANATION	SAMPLE APPLICATION TO CHRYSLER T-WAGONS PRODUCED AT WINDSOR PLANT
Performance	Primary operating characteristics	Acceleration, handling, safety, cruising speed, comfort
Features	Secondary characteristics supplementing the product's basic function	Control of road noise, instrument panel readability, radio/stereo sound system
Reliability	Probability of product failure within a specified period of time and/or for a specified amount of use	Chrysler's 5-year, 50,000-mile warranty on certain parts
Conformance	Degree to which product design and operation match preestablished standards	80% of vehicles coming off the line meet all quality standards with no reworking required; aim is 100%.
Serviceability	Ease, speed, courtesy, and competence of repair	Designed to enable easy access to parts most likely to need repair; monitor dealers to see that service standards are maintained.
Aesthetics	Consumer perceptions of how a product looks, feels, sounds, tastes, or smells	Consumer research prior to offering T-wagons
Perceived quality	Image, reputation, name of product	Advertising, comparative claims, use of guarantees (warranty) to influence perceived quality

Source: Part of this table was adapted from: D. A. Garvin, "What Does 'Product Quality' Really Mean?" *Sloan Management Review,* Fall 1984, p. 25.

IMPORTANCE OF QUALITY

Product quality is increasingly important in international competition. Chrysler with its 5-year, 50,000-mile warranty and Ford with its company-wide campaign of "quality is job one" are both trying to overcome consumer perceptions that U.S. and Canadian cars are of poor quality compared to Japanese and many European cars.[15] Harold Sperlich, president of Chrysler, comments: "We thought we were competitive, and we were, in a limited, protected way. But we were club tennis players, we had a terrific game going every weekend. And then when we ran into the Japanese, it was as if Jimmy Connors and John McEnroe walked on the court."[16]

Japanese manufacturers have gained market share in the United States, in part, because of the consumer's perception their products are of high quality. The quality superiority of Japanese cars has been principally in fit and finish. In the quality dimensions that relate to safety and corrosion resistance, U.S. car manufacturers are claimed to have been superior.[17]

For years, U.S. manufacturers focused on the costs of maintaining or increasing product quality. However, product quality and costs are being seen increasingly as inversely related. That is, the costs of improving quality may be less than the resulting savings in reworking, scrap, warranty expenses, product liability, and the like. This, in turn, suggests that improving quality could be a way to increase productivity. This belief is widely held among Japanese manufacturers and explains much of their dedication to the goal of continuous improvements in product quality and, ultimately, zero defects.[18]

Total quality costs typically include expenditures in the following categories: (1) prevention (quality planning, worker training, and supplier education); (2) appraisal (product inspection and testing); (3) internal failures (reworking and scrap); and (4) external failures (warranty and product liability).[19] In 1983, auto-industry sources estimated that as much as 25 percent of the price of a car was attributable to poor quality (scrappage, reject parts, extra inspection and repair, warranty costs, and product liability).[20] Chrysler managers believe that the major capital investment in the Windsor plant is offset by the reduction of substantial costs previously caused by lower quality.

QUALITY CONTROL

Quality control used to be thought of as mainly the inspection activity that would take place during or, most often, at the end of the production process. The responsibility for quality control was often assigned to a particular department—such as a quality-control department—and a relatively small group of inspectors and, possibly, lab technicians. But times have changed, and the emphasis on product quality has increased.

Total Quality Control

Total quality control has emerged as an important management philosophy, concept, and practice. It is the agreed-on company and plant-wide operating philosophy and systems for guiding and using employees, machines, and information to ensure customer satisfaction with quality and economic costs of quality.[21] Total quality control includes planning for quality, preventing quality defects, correcting quality defects, and a philosophy of continuous efforts to build into products increased quality to the extent economically and competitively feasible.[22]

IN PRACTICE
Signetics
Corporation

Charles C. Harwood, president of Signetics Corporation (a manufacturer of more than 3000 types of integrated circuits) changed the firm's operating philosophy from the traditional concept of quality control to the concept of total quality control. The shifts in the operating philosophy for Signetics were as follows:

From Traditional Quality Control $\longrightarrow$	To Total Quality Control
Screen for quality. $\longrightarrow$	Plan for quality.
Quality is the responsibility of the quality and reliability department. $\longrightarrow$	Quality is everybody's responsibility
Some mistakes are inevitable. $\longrightarrow$	Zero defects is possible.
Quality means inspection. $\longrightarrow$	Quality means conformance to requirements
Scrap and reworking are the major costs of poor quality. $\longrightarrow$	Scrap and reworking are only a small part of the costs of non-conformance
Quality is a tactical issue. $\longrightarrow$	Quality is a strategic issue.
Production units are where quality should be measured. $\longrightarrow$	Individual accountability is where quality should be measured.

Harwood indicates that the process of moving toward total quality control started in 1979 but that its foundation was not solid until 1984, a five-year journey with many obstacles. Some of the bottom-line results from Signetics' program of total quality control are: (1) $12 million in savings from quality efforts in 1983, for a total of $20 million in savings since 1980; (2) on-time deliveries increased 50 percent since 1980; and (3) returns for all reasons decreased by 90 percent since 1980.

Harwood states: "People ask me, 'What is important to you, what do you stand for?' I say, What we stand for is 'People Committed to Quality' . . . and that starts with me."[23]

The concept of total quality control involves building in and ensuring quality from product planning to design and design evaluation through pre-production, purchasing, and production to sales and services.[24] The International Focus briefly describes Toyota's application of total quality control to mass production manufacturing. Quality control at Chrysler's Windsor plant includes most of the practices described for Toyota. Toyota first introduced quality-control procedures in 1950, following visits to Japan by Dr. W. Edwards Deming, an American quality-control expert. Deming has made a series of visits to Japan since 1950 to consult and conduct training courses in quality control.[25]

INTERNATIONAL FOCUS

Toyota's Quality Control

The essence of quality control in mass production manufacturing at Toyota is correct materials processing, parts processing and parts fitting, combined with regular quality checks and process evaluation. Problems must be solved quickly and permanently. The following types of measures, and the careful application of standards and process control, are used for continuous quality assurance.

MEASURES FOR REDUCING VARIATIONS IN QUALITY

It takes time to set up dies, jigs, and other types of machine tools; measurement errors invariably occur. To prevent such errors and to reduce set-up time, easy-on, easy-off tool holders were designed. Cutter holders are stored near the production line, and precision adjustments are made in such a way that cutters can be changed simply by exchanging holders. Measurements are taken regularly, and control charts are used to monitor quality variations on a daily basis.

MEASURES FOR PREVENTING PROCESSING ERRORS

Measures were developed to prevent errors in fitting parts and in nonstandard operations.

MEASURES FOR REDUCING OPERATIONS ERRORS

Options in work operations lead to misassembly and related errors. To prevent these types of errors, care is taken to make sure that all workers are thoroughly familiar with the tasks they perform.

(continued)

MEASURES TO ENSURE QUALITY CHECKS

Depending on the importance of a part and its production volume, quality checks are performed either on all parts or on a representative sample. For sampling checks the line is stopped at prescribed intervals, and an accurate count is kept of the number of parts checked. The time of each check and the number of the part are recorded; this record is kept at the line for a fixed period of time, which allows the supervisor to determine at a glance how quality checking is being carried out.

MEASURES TO PREVENT DEFECTIVE PARTS FROM MOVING TO LATER PRODUCTION RECORDS

These measures are of the mechanical, foolproof type. In the case of hole-boring operations, for example, an automatic inspection station at the next point on the line ensures that parts have been bored properly.

Source: Excerpted and adapted from S. Sekiya, "Quality Control at Toyota Motor Corporation," *Wheel Extended,* 1984, 14(1):101–116. (S. Sekiya was General Manager of Toyota Motor Company's Quality Assurance Department from 1977–1982 and is currently a Director of Toyota Motor Corporation.)

DEMING'S PRESCRIPTIONS

In 1985, W. Edwards Deming was 85 years old. He, more than anyone else, is regarded as the man who taught the Japanese about quality control. He designed a four-day seminar for Japanese executives in 1950 and subsequently became almost a guru to Japanese industry. To honor his contributions, Japanese industry created the Deming Prize in 1951, which annually recognizes the Japanese company that has attained the highest level of quality; the prize is revered in Japan.[26]

Until 1980, his work received relatively little notice by top management of U.S. industry. In June 1980, NBC did a TV documentary that contrasted Japanese product quality with American product quality. Deming was prominently featured on the program and was presented as the major authority on quality control in the world. He soon was in demand everywhere and signed long-term consulting contracts with Ford and GM. Deming strongly asserts that "We in America will have to be more protectionist or more competitive. The choice is very simple. If we are to become more competitive, then we have to begin with quality."[27]

Deming believes that poor quality is 85 percent a management problem and 15 percent a worker problem. His prescription for total quality control is deceptively simple:

- Accept the doctrine that poor quality is flatly unacceptable. Defective materials, workmanship, products, and service will not be tolerated.

- Use statistical evidence of quality *during* the process, not at the end of the process. The earlier an error is caught, the less it costs to correct it.

- Rely on suppliers that have historically provided quality, not on sampling inspections to determine the quality of each delivery. Instead of many suppliers, select and stay with a few sources that furnish consistently satisfactory quality.

- Depend on training and retraining of employees in skills to use statistical methods in their jobs, not on slogans, to improve quality. Employees should feel free to report any conditions that detract from quality.

- Supervisors should be guided by statistical methods to help people do their work better, not on production-work standards. Statistical techniques detect *sources* of poor quality. Teams of designers, supervisors, and workers can then eliminate the sources of poor quality.[28]

There is a point at which continuous increases in the quality of the product may need to be reflected in higher prices. Consider the case of Maytag.

IN PRACTICE
MAYTAG

Maytag, the manufacturer of washers, dryers, and other appliances, boasts of keeping their repairmen "the loneliest men in town" by maintaining extremely high quality. Their president, Sterling O. Swanger, has maintained quality as an important principle in the firm. He has held the line on quality when other appliance manufacturers did not. As a result, Maytag is producing a more reliable machine than ever. In the mid-1950s, the company's late president, Fred Maytag II, laid down a standard of ten years of trouble-free operations for the company's products. At that time, the company's average automatic washer was three years short of the target. Today, objective quality-control tests show that a new Maytag washing machine should run 14 years without serious trouble.[29] This commitment to extraordinary quality has its cost. Maytags are probably the most expensive (in terms of purchase price) appliances on the market. Of course, the Maytag salesperson would argue that it is the least expensive over the long haul.

The Quality-Control Process

Decision making to ensure quality control generally focuses on four functions: measurement, inputs, work-in-process, and outputs. Together, these functions comprise the quality-control process.

MEASUREMENT

The seven dimensions of product quality (Table 19.2) must be measured in order to achieve effective quality control. *Measurement* is the means used to determine the amount or degree of specific characteristics and is fundamental to quality control. The more accurate the measurement, the easier it is to compare desired results (standards) against actual results (outputs).

Quality control generally measures characteristics either by variable or by attribute. *Measuring by variable* refers to the assessment of characteristics for which there are specific standards, such as the physical characteristics of length, diameter, height, weight, and temperature. *Measuring by attribute* refers to the assessment of characteristics that must fall within specified upper and lower limits. Measuring by attribute is usually easier than measuring by variable; it provides acceptable quality so long as the goods or services fall within the stated upper or lower limits. For example, door manufacturers generally ship their doors so long as they are plus or minus one-quarter inch of the predetermined size. However, setting quality limits is not usually simple. Several years ago, a new kind of bus—called the Flexible Bus—was produced. The trade-off between strength needed in the bus frame and the light weight needed to improve fuel consumption was misjudged. Several cities purchased this proclaimed new generation bus and experienced numerous problems with it, including cracked frames.

INPUTS

Traditional quality control generally begins with the inputs—especially raw materials and parts—used in transformation. Automobile assembly plants, like Chrysler's Windsor plant, could not function if parts and other raw materials did not fall within the upper and lower limits of predetermined standards. Inspectors at the Windsor plant sample each new batch of inputs to make sure that they meet the standards that have been set. Fierce foreign competition has caused all automakers to both toughen and more vigorously enforce input standards.

WORK-IN-PROCESS

Quality-control inspections are also used between successive stages of production. Work-in-process inspections can result in reworking or rejecting an item before additional transformation work is done on it.

The use of quality-control circles, as discussed in Chapter 15, is one of the new approaches for improving work-in-process quality control. In 1980, Chrysler and the United Auto Workers developed the first agreement in the U.S. and Canadian auto industry that gave assembly-line workers a role in controlling the quality of cars they make. Workers at two of the assembly lines producing Chrysler's K cars gained the right to demand that defects be corrected as they occurred at each stage of assembly. Workers were promised no reprisals for calling attention to shoddy quality. Marc Stepp, a UAW vice-president, commented:

> If a foreman tells a worker to "forget it"—as has sometimes happened in the past—we will expect that worker to make a report, and if plant supervision doesn't blow the whistle on that foreman, the union will, and we will go straight to the top of the corporation.[30]

High quality was needed if the K cars were to compete successfully, especially with Japanese imports. The union and workers obviously had a vested interest in helping the Chrysler K cars succeed in the marketplace, which they did.

Finished goods or services

The most recognizable form of quality control is the test made after a product has been completed or a service provided. In the case of a product, quality-control tests take place before the items are shipped to customers. Of course, goods returned by customers because of shoddy workmanship or other problems are also part of the overall quality-control process. U.S. and Canadian automobile manufacturers are now more prone to return parts or ma-

Part of the quality-control process is a series of quality tests to ensure a product's endurance, safety, and reliability. These Sony engineers test the Trinitron television for a minimum of 300 hours per set.

Source: John Launois/Black Star

terials, if they find them lacking in some respect, to suppliers. In the case of services, barbers and hairdressers, for example, usually involve their customers in checking quality by handing them a mirror and asking them if everything is okay. The satisfactory provision of a service is often more difficult to measure than the satisfactory manufacture of a product.

Our ability to measure product quality does not tell us what the quality level should be. Desired quality levels are strongly influenced by company strategy (Maytag) and by competition (Chrysler's K cars and T-wagons). The importance of management strategy and attitudes toward quality-control decisions cannot be overstated. Stephen Moss of the Arthur D. Little consulting firm has worked with corporations in both Japan and the United States; he made the following observation in 1980.

> The U.S. manager sets an acceptable level of quality and then sticks to it. The Japanese are constantly upgrading their goals. The American assumes a certain rate of failure is inevitable, while the Japanese shoots for perfection and sometimes gets close.[31]

Fortunately, the marketplace is operating. U.S. and Canadian industries have actively geared up since 1980 to meet the new standards of quality set by the Japanese and others.[32]

INVENTORY CONTROL

Inventory is the amount and type of raw materials, parts, work-in-process (partially finished goods), supplies, and finished goods not yet shipped to customers. *Inventory control* is concerned primarily with (1) setting maximum, optimum, and minimum levels of inventory; (2) maintaining feedback about the changes in inventory levels; and (3) signaling the need for action to avoid going above or below the predetermined levels. Controlling the amount of inventory has enormous implications for the amount of capital required and the productivity of the firm's capital. Everything else being equal, if a firm can cut its average inventory from $10 million to $8 million, it can operate with $2 million less in capital or borrowed funds, on which interest has to be paid. This reduction in the amount of money tied up in inventory has the effect of increasing the productivity of the $8 million for inventory by 20 percent.

Relation to Materials-Requirement Planning

Inventory control is often a part of *materials-requirement planning* (MRP). This is a management scheduling and control system designed to minimize inventory investment, to maximize production and operations efficiency, and to improve customer service.[33] It is usually implemented with a computerized information system, which is based on the demand for finished goods. The demand for finished goods generates the requirements for raw materials, parts, subassemblies, and so on. The amount and timing of orders for materials to be used as inputs is taken from the amount and timing for the finished goods.

Materials-requirement planning helps to meet three basic information needs in production and operations management: (1) What is needed? (2) How much is needed? and (3) When is it needed? In order to respond to these questions, managers need a planning and reporting system that consists of three primary parts:

- *Master schedule,* which shows what finished goods are desired, when, and in what quantities.

- *Bill of materials,* which describes the inputs for each finished good—raw materials, parts, subassemblies.

- *Inventory-record file,* which shows the inventory on hand and on order for each stock item by time period (day, week, and/or month) and also includes information on lead time, lot (order) size, and suppliers.[34]

Materials-requirement planning involves the calculation of gross and net requirements for inputs by time period.[35] The financial impact that a computer-based MRP system can have is suggested by the experience at Holley Carburetor of Warren, Michigan.

IN PRACTICE
Computer-Based MRP at Holley Carburetor

Too much inventory and too little control prompted Holley Carburetor, a division of Colt Industries, Inc., to seek new solutions. "In analyzing our problems, it was obvious that we had too many dollars tied up in inventory," recalls Michael D. Hecker, Holley's inventory-management director. "Even so, we had problems with parts shortages. We often had to fly in parts from all over the country."

But the $200-million-a-year manufacturer of fuel-delivery systems decided that off-the-shelf computer software packages would not meet its needs. So it persuaded a software company to modify its materials-requirement planning (MRP) module.

In just two years, Holley has reduced its inventory from $30 million to $20 million. These savings, alone, paid for the initial $250,000 software investment, Mr. Hecker notes.

To implement the system, Mr. Hecker suggested that top management spend three days absorbing ideas at a manufacturing software seminar. After the senior executives had been convinced, representatives were assembled from

(continued)

the 6000-employee firm's 15 functional areas and the overall plan was explained. Mr. Hecker and the 35-person data-processing staff gave the representatives 120 hours of instruction. They, in turn, instructed others in their departments.

When the system is fully implemented, Mr. Hecker says, "It will give anyone in the organization the ability to log onto the computer and see where we are with respect to satisfying a customer order—where we are in the production process, the status of inventory, what's on order, and the like."

Despite the benefits, there were concerns about acceptance. "We have to be careful not to force too much change on people too quickly," Mr. Hecker explains. The change has already affected Holley's suppliers. Each was told to adopt statistical quality-control methods to ensure both quality and inventory accuracy. "One vendor told us flat out that we were crazy," Mr. Hecker notes, "and that the cost would have to be passed on to us." But, 11 months later, that vendor reported to his amazement that his scrap had been reduced by 40 percent.

In the future, Holley expects to reap other benefits associated with computer-integrated manufacturing—including "just-in-time" production scheduling.[36]

From an inventory-control perspective, materials-requirement planning appears to have the greatest application to process-focused production systems (Fig. 19.2). In contrast, the just-in-time concept has relatively more potential as a means of tighter inventory control for product-focused production systems. This is especially true where there is high-volume and repetitive production of a few models, as with autos.[37]

Relation to Just-in-Time Concept

In the Preview Case, the *just-in-time* (JIT) *concept* was described as providing and delivering: (1) finished goods just-in-time to be sold; (2) subassemblies just-in-time to be assembled into finished goods; (3) fabricated parts just-in-time to go into subassemblies; and (4) purchased materials just-in-time to be transformed into fabricated parts.[38] At each stage of the production process, JIT means delivery of the smallest possible quantities at the latest possible time and the elimination of as much inventory as possible.

Like Chrysler's use of it at the Windsor plant, General Motors has implemented the just-in-time concept for delivery and production. Between 1982 and 1984, GM reportedly slashed the *annual* costs of holding inventory from $8 billion to $2 billion. Most of this reduction is attributed to its introduction of the just-in-time concept.[39]

JIT, like materials-requirement planning, is much more than an inventory-control system. It requires fundamental changes in the relationships between a manufacturer and its suppliers. The conflict-management styles used shift from a combination of forcing and compromise styles to collaboration and compromise styles. Table 19.3 outlines the major implications of the JIT concept with respect to quantities purchased, quality expectations, suppliers used, and shipping practices. There are a number of other aspects of the JIT concept, which are beyond the scope of this chapter.[40]

TABLE 19.3 ■ SELECTED JUST-IN-TIME PURCHASING AND INVENTORY IMPLICATIONS

IMPLICATIONS FOR QUANTITIES

- Study output rate by manufacturer
- Frequent deliveries in small quantities to manufacturer
- Long-term contracts, blanket orders with suppliers
- Delivery quantities variable from delivery to delivery but fixed for overall contract term
- Little or no overage or underage acceptable in deliveries

IMPLICATIONS FOR QUALITY CONTROL

- Suppliers helped to meet quality requirements by manufacturer
- Close relationships between buyer and suppliers' quality-control people
- Suppliers encouraged to use controls at each step in their production process, instead of just inspecting outputs

IMPLICATIONS FOR SUPPLIERS USED

- Few suppliers
- Nearby suppliers
- Repeat business with same suppliers
- Competitive bidding mostly limited to new parts
- Suppliers encouraged to extend JIT buying to *their* suppliers

IMPLICATIONS FOR SHIPPING

- Scheduling inbound freight by manufacturer
- Gaining control of shipping by use of company-owned or contract shipping, contract warehousing, and trailers for freight consolidation/storage where possible, instead of common carriers

Source: Adapted from R. J. Schonberger, *Japanese Manufacturing Techniques: Nine Hidden Lessons in Simplicity.* New York: Free Press, 1982, pp. 159–161.

Chrysler first used the JIT concept to control inventory levels at its Windsor plant and has extended the use of JIT company-wide. Chrysler is considered to be one of the leaders in the use of JIT in North America.

IN PRACTICE
JIT at Chrysler

Chrysler operates 13 JIT manufacturing facilities, of which five assembly plants receive JIT deliveries (including two major facilities: Windsor, Ontario, and Sterling Heights, Michigan). Chrysler stipulates when carriers must arrive at a supplier's dock, when they will arrive at a company plant, and what the carrier will be hauling. The traffic department coordinates with the carrier and the supplier and obtains from the carrier an agreement covering precise service standards.

Chrysler uses its own private fleet for moving two-thirds of its parts among its plants within the Detroit area. Outside carriers account for the remaining one-third of its freight-hauling needs. The automaker is now considering reducing the outside third even further. For now, Chrysler organizes JIT transportation by dividing the country into three regions east of the Mississippi, where the majority of its suppliers are located. By doing so, Chrysler may assign one trucking company responsibility for all shipments within a given geographic region.[41]

INVENTORY COSTS

Inventory costs are the expenses associated with maintaining an inventory. Four basic types of costs are incurred in maintaining an inventory: (1) ordering costs; (2) carrying costs; (3) shortage costs; and (4) set-up costs. Managers should consider all these costs when making decisions about how much inventory to keep on hand. Let us briefly consider each of the four specific types of costs.

- *Ordering costs* are the expenses of actually preparing the purchase order. These costs are generally not very large.

- *Carrying costs* are the expenses of holding goods in inventory. These costs include such items as obsolescence, insurance, storage facilities, depreciation, taxes, breakage, pilferage, and the cost of capital.

- *Shortage costs* are the expenses that occur when a customer orders a product, but there is none in inventory. The customer must either wait until the inventory is replenished or cancel the order. It is difficult to determine the costs resulting from a customer's decision to cancel an order and place future orders elsewhere.

- *Set-up costs* are the expenses of changing over to make a different product. These include the time required to get new raw materials, make equipment changes, make changes in the sequence of production processes, and clear out in-process inventories of other items. They also include the costs of additional administrative time, employee training, idle time, and overtime. These costs may be difficult to pinpoint but should be estimated as accurately as possible.

Purposes of Maintaining Inventory

Inventories serve many purposes, even though they may create high costs. Five of the more important purposes are to (1) maintain independent operations; (2) allow flexibility in the production schedule; (3) provide a safeguard against problems that can arise when input materials have different delivery times; (4) meet variations in product demand; and (5) take advantage of economic purchase-order size. Let us look at the impact on production and operations management of each of these purposes.

In order to provide some independence for work stations a supply of needed materials must be available at each station. If the operators at one station are delayed or slow, they will not delay operators at all the following work stations. *In-process inventory* includes these input materials and the goods that are partially completed, which will have additional labor and materials added to obtain a finished good.

Inventories allow flexibility in the production schedule. An inventory of finished goods lessens the pressure to produce goods by a particular date and provides for longer lead times. *Lead time* is the amount of time between the placement of an order and the actual receipt of that order by the customer. Longer lead time permits smoother work flows and the production of economical order sizes.

Inventories provide a safeguard against problems that can be caused by variations in the delivery of raw materials. An operations manager cannot always count on arrival of an order for raw materials on a specific date. Reasons for possible delays include labor problems, transportation holdups, and late shipments. Without a safety-stock inventory of raw materials, even slight delays can shut down an entire operation. Managers recognize this as a risk in using the JIT concept.

Inventories help meet variations in market demand for the firm's outputs. It is seldom feasible for a company to produce the number of items needed to exactly match market demand. A common practice is to maintain a safety or buffer inventory. This inventory will absorb the increases in demand that are caused by unanticipated market conditions. Inventories may also be increased to meet seasonal changes in demand, such as in swimsuits.

Inventories enable management to take advantage of economic purchase-order size. It costs money to order materials and to carry the materials in inventory. These costs—and any offsetting supplier discounts for quantity ordering—are important in determining the most economic size of an order.

Inventories may also serve other purposes, such as stabilizing employment, hedging against inflation, reducing the risk of possible future shortages, and eliminating the need for possible future overtime. It simply is not possible for us to cover all the developments in inventory and production management and their implications in this book.[42]

Two Basic Inventory-Control Models

Specific inventory purposes and costs are part of the control process for determining desirable inventory levels and the ideal size of orders to replace inventories. "How much do I order?" is a practical decision and control problem that every manager responsible for inventory levels must face. The order size for inventory replacement, where the just-in-time concept is not used, is usually based on one of two basic inventory control models: the fixed-order quantity model or the fixed-order period model.

Fixed-order quantity model

The *fixed-order quantity model* is a method for determining the standard number of items to be ordered when the inventory reaches a predetermined level. The amount of the order is always the same, but the timing of the order varies. Figure 19.3 identifies the typical cost tradeoffs in determining ideal inventory levels. The vertical axis shows the average annual costs associated with different reorder quantities and different carrying costs; the horizontal axis shows the reorder quantities. The total-cost curve is simply the sum of reorder costs and carrying costs at each possible quantity level. Managers must know these costs in order to use the fixed-order quantity model.

Figure 19.3 suggests that, as the quantity ordered increases, the ordering cost per unit decreases. However, as the order quantity and average inventory level increases, the carrying cost of the inventory also increases. This is because more money and space are tied up in the inventory. The optimum inventory level is simply the quantity that provides the lowest total inventory costs. This is shown as Q_1 in Fig. 19.3 and influences the optimal reorder quantity. Figure 19.3 is used to help you visualize these cost relationships, but it is not precise. For precision, we can use the equation for the fixed-order quantity model:

$$FOQ = \sqrt{\frac{2DO}{C}},$$

where

$$FOQ = \text{fixed order quantity;}$$
$$D = \text{average annual demand;}$$
$$O = \text{cost per order; and}$$
$$C = \text{carrying cost per unit.}$$

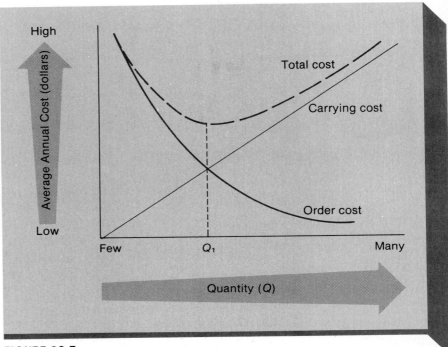

FIGURE 19.3
Cost Tradeoffs for Determining Inventory Levels

Figure 19.4 shows graphically the inventory level for the basic fixed-order quantity model; Q_1 represents the fixed-order quantity. Inventory will have to be reordered when it reaches the reorder level shown by the dashed horizontal line. This level of inventory is based on the assumption that the new inventory will be received before the current inventory is used up. The time between placing and receiving the order is the lead time. Because unexpected events could affect the time of delivery, management might want to maintain a "safety stock" of inventory. In this case, the reorder level would be set somewhat higher than that shown in Fig. 19.4

Fixed-order period model

The *fixed-order period model* is a method for determining the number of items, up to a predetermined maximum level, to be ordered at fixed time intervals. The period of time between orders is always the same, but the amount of the order varies. Most supermarkets use this model. It is triggered by specific dates—such as each Friday, the first of the month, or the beginning of a quarter—rather than by a particular level of inventory.

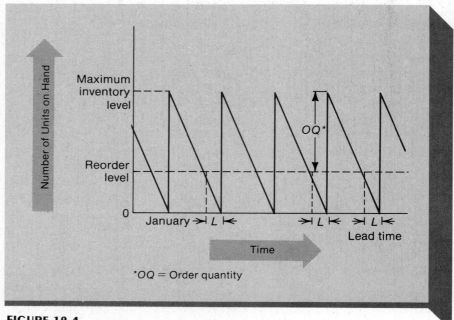

FIGURE 19.4
Fixed-Order Quantity Model

The equation for the fixed-order period model is

$$T = \sqrt{\frac{2O}{DC}},$$

where

T = the optimal time period between replenishing inventory;

O = cost per order;

D = average annual demand; and

C = carrying cost per unit.

Figure 19.5 shows the fixed-order period model in schematic form. Note that there is, again, a maximum inventory level; the vertical and horizontal axes are the same as for the fixed-order quantity model; but there is no reorder level; orders are placed at time intervals. For example, a local soft-drink distributor wants to maintain a maximum inventory of 1000 cases of Pepsi-Cola. On the reorder date, the inventory of Pepsi is only 400 cases, so an order would be placed for 600 cases. On the next reorder date, if the inventory level is 700 cases, a reorder for only 300 cases would be placed.

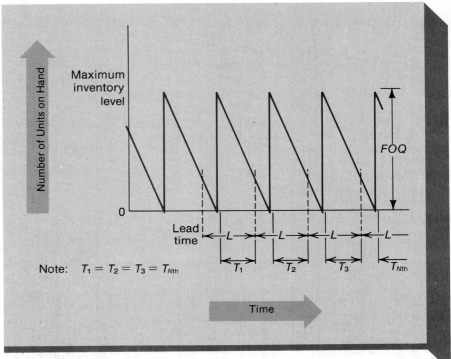

FIGURE 19.5
Fixed-Order Period Model

CHAPTER SUMMARY

Production and operations management focuses on inputs, transformation, and outputs. Knowledge of production and operations management is necessary for performance of the decision roles of *monitor* and *resource allocator*. The monitor role focuses on scanning the environment. The section on basic manufacturing issues suggests the skills needed for effective monitoring of the environment in order to improve productivity and product quality. The resource-allocator role involves making choices for the effective allocation and use of resources. The discussions of inventory control and quality control indicate the skills needed for those purposes in production and operations management.

Production and operations management is vitally concerned with preventive control and corrective control. A manufacturing strategy must address questions about plant capacity, technology, degree of vertical in-

tegration, work force needed in manufacturing operations, the prevention and correction of quality defects, production planning and materials (inventory) controls, and organizational structure for manufacturing operations.

Two major types of production systems were explained: process-focused systems and product-focused systems. Process-focused systems are flexible operations designed to produce custom-made products (nuclear submarines, new corporate headquarters buildings, Boeing 747s). Product-focused systems usually produce highly standardized products on a relatively continuous basis (Chrysler's T-wagons, Exxon gasoline, Apple microcomputers).

The importance of productivity and typical productivity measures were reviewed. The importance of product quality and seven dimensions of quality—performance, features, reliability, conformance, service-ability, aesthetics, and perceived quality—were reviewed.

The concepts of traditional quality control and total quality control were presented and contrasted. The gradual shift toward a management attitude and set of actions associated with total quality control by U.S. and Canadian manufacturers was noted. Quality-control decisions are influenced by the available means and costs of measurement. Quality-control models usually focus on inputs, work-in-process, and outputs. Outputs are the finished goods or services provided to the marketplace. The quality-control discussion covered guidelines and issues rather than specific techniques.

The importance of inventory control for the purpose of reducing capital requirements and thereby increasing the productivity of the company's capital was explained. The place of inventory control within the broader systems of materials-requirement planning and the just-in-time (JIT) concept was developed. Four specific inventory costs and five purposes of inventory were explained. Two of the commonly used inventory-control models—fixed-order quantity model and fixed-order period model—were presented as aids to controlling inventory.

MANAGER'S VOCABULARY

bill of materials
capital
carrying costs
feedback loops
fixed-order period model
fixed-order quantity model
in-process inventory
inventory
inventory control
inventory costs
inventory-record file
just-in-time concept
labor
labor productivity
lead time
manufacturing strategy
master schedule
materials
materials-requirement planning

measurement
measuring by attribute
measuring by variable
ordering costs
outputs
process-focused systems
product-focused systems
product quality
production and operations management
productivity
quality control
robots
set-up costs
shortage costs
total-factor productivity
total quality control
total quality costs
transformation

REVIEW QUESTIONS

1. What is the systems view of production and operations management?

2. What is a manufacturing strategy?

3. What are the two types of production systems?

4. What are the two ways that productivity can be measured?

5. What are the dimensions of product quality?

6. What is total quality control?

7. How does inventory control fit in to materials-requirement planning and the just-in-time concept?

8. What are the differences between the fixed-order quantity and period models of inventory control?

DISCUSSION QUESTIONS

1. For a service industry and a manufacturing industry, give an example of each of the following: (a) inputs, (b) transformation process, (c) outputs, (d) feedback loops.

2. What types of problems should management anticipate with the increasing introduction of robots in manufacturing?

3. Why is the just-in-time concept not useful in all types of production operations?

4. It is claimed by some that U.S. and Canadian industry is losing its competitive edge because the quality of foreign-made products selling at the same price is superior. Do you agree? Why? Can you cite specific personal experience for your feelings?

5. Jackson Hole Manufacturing has an annual demand for its product of 6300 units, while ordering costs are $19.00 and holding costs are $3.00 per unit, respectively. What is the economic-order quantity? What happens when demand increases to 7500 units per year? to 13,850 units per year?

6. What happens if the data from question 5 are used in a fixed-order period model?

7. Is total quality control realistic? Explain.

MANAGEMENT INCIDENTS AND CASES

Bridal, Inc.

In June of 1980 Mr. LeBrun, newly hired production manager of Bridal, Inc. of Canada, was considering the possibility of a new process layout in the company's only factory. Since being at Bridal, he thought that possibly the addition of an assembly line technique would work more efficiently than the current layout of the factory. Because Bridal was losing money and their current customers, something had to be done. Mr. LeBrun thought that adding an assembly line to transfer work from one station to the next would reduce costs and thereby increase profits.

Present layout of Bridal

Bridal, Inc. is a factory located in 3-Rivers, Quebec. It consists of a basement and three floors. It manufactures women's gowns. In the basement, the dresses are cut and then sent by elevator to the third floor where they are bundled. There are also cutters on the third floor. From the third floor, the work is sent to the first floor where beads and lace are placed on the dresses. From the first floor, the work is then sent to the second floor where the pieces of the dress are stitched, pressed and packed. From there, the work is sent back to the first floor where it is ready to be shipped out.

At Bridal, Inc., each machine works independently of the other. There is flexibility with the system. The product is a non-standardized product and the layout is arranged according to the type of work performed. There are many types and styles of products with an emphasis on special orders. The general problem with the layout is the assignment of a set of facilities to various locations within limited space. This is one reason Mr. LeBrun was thinking of moving to an assembly line layout. He figured that because of the limited space, the assembly line would be more economical and feasible. By using the assembly line, he also thought productivity in the manufacture of gowns would increase.

The following is a detailed analysis of the observations Mr. LeBrun made of the flow of work in the current process layout at Bridal, Inc. Layouts of each of the floors can be referred to in Figs. 19.6, 19.7, 19.8, and 19.9.

The work starts in the basement at the cutters table, areas Bb and Bc. Two cutters walk from the cutters table Bc to where the fabrics are kept, area C. The distance between the cutters table and where the fabric is kept is approximately 9 feet. Total walking distance for both of the workers is approximately 36 feet. The number of times these two workers go back and forth in a day depends on the number of gowns they are required to cut. When there is a sufficient amount of

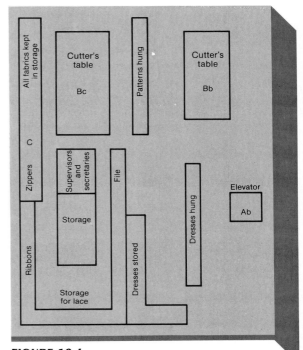

FIGURE 19.6
Basement Production Layout for Bridal, Inc.

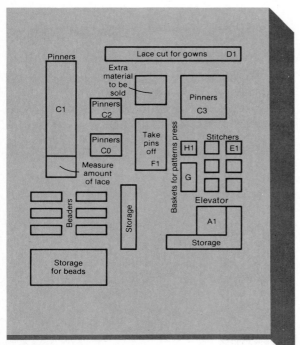

FIGURE 19.7
First Floor Production Layout for Bridal, Inc.

when needed to be matched to the pieces of gown material. The boss then travels approximately 20 feet to the pinners where the lace is pinned to the pieces of gown material. Depending on the amount of work to be distributed, the boss travels to tables C1, C2, and C3.

After the lace is pinned to the pieces of material, the boss goes from C1 to C0 to C2 to C3 and then to area E1, the stitchers. Here the lace is stitched to the pieces of material. The distance traveled is about 55 feet. When the stitchers are finished, they place their output in storage baskets. From the storage baskets, the work is taken to area F1. Here, the pins are taken off and the material is sent to be pressed at area H1. From H1 the work is taken 30 feet to the storage area. It is here that the pieces of material with lace are matched with their lining and brought to the second floor.

When the gowns arrive on the second floor, they are taken to the stitchers. After stitching, the gowns are hung and then distributed among the hand workers, where the finishing touches are made. The gowns are

work on the cutters table and when the work is needed upstairs on the third floor, an employee places the cut work in a carriage and brings it up on the elevator to the third floor. The distance covered by this employee is roughly 45 feet. This is usually done twice a day. The total distance traveled is 90 feet.

Once the cut work reaches the third floor, the same employee takes it from the elevator and places it on the bundlers table. Another employee makes the bundles. From the bundlers table, bundled pieces are brought down to the first floor where they are placed in storage. The transport of work to the storage area is done by one person who travels about 10 feet. This takes place about two times a day.

Once the work reaches the first floor, a new process begins. The amount of lace required for the gown pieces is measured from rolls of lace at area C1. This lace is then taken by the boss who travels about 40 feet to where the lace is cut in pieces for the gowns, area D1. From area D1, the boss takes the pieces of lace and puts them in storage. The lace is then taken out of storage

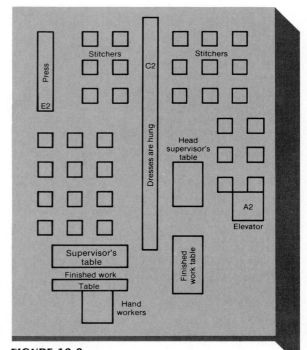

FIGURE 19.8
Second Floor Production Layout for Bridal, Inc.

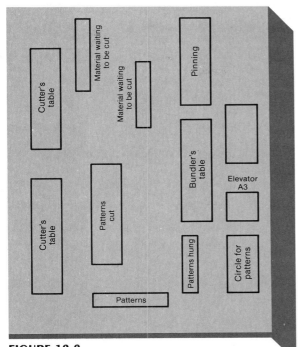

FIGURE 19.9
Third Floor Production Layout for Bridal, Inc.

then taken to be pressed (E2). After pressing, they are then taken to the supervisors table for packing. The packed gowns are sent to customers.

The equipment used is rather generalized. There is only one specialized machine. It is the sewing machine used to make ruffles. The hand rack on the third floor does not rotate. The gowns are moved manually.[43]

Questions

1. Mr. LeBrun asked himself whether there is a more efficient layout for the production of gowns. Mr. LeBrun thought that an assembly line could be the answer. Do you agree? Why?

2. Could the factory be rearranged to cut down on traveling time? How?

3. Could Bridal, Inc., use the just-in-time concept? Why?

4. What inventory control practices should be adopted by Bridal, Inc.?

5. Should Bridal, Inc., adopt the concept of total quality control? Why?

6. Could a team concept of production be used? What changes would be needed?

REFERENCES

1. R. J. Schonberger, *Japanese Manufacturing Techniques: Nine Hidden Lessons in Simplicity.* New York: Free Press, 1982, p. 16.

2. F. K. Foulkes and J. L. Hirsch, "People Make Robots Work," *Harvard Business Review,* January–February 1984, pp. 94–102; J. Baranson, *Robots in Manufacturing: Key to International Competitiveness.* Mt. Airy, Md.: Lomand Publications, 1983; E. M. Knod Jr., J. L. Wall, J. P. Daniels, H. M. Shane, and T. A. Wernimount, "Robotics: Challenges for the Human Resources Manager," *Business Horizons,* March–April 1984, pp. 38–46; C. J. Hollon and G. N. Rogol, "How Robotization Affects People," *Business Horizons,* May–June 1985, pp. 74–80.

3. Adapted from G. Schwind, "Chrysler Windsor: A Plant in a Hurry to Turn Out Vans in a Hurry," *Materials Handling Engineering,* November 1984, pp. 50–54.

4. E. E. Adam Jr., "Towards a Typology of Production and Operations Management Systems," *Academy of Management Review,* 1983, 8:363–375; E. E. Adam Jr. and R. J. Ebert, *Production and Operations Management: Concepts, Models and Behavior,* 2nd ed. New York: Prentice-Hall, 1982; R. B. Chase and N. J. Aquilano, *Production and Operations Management: A Life Cycle Approach,* 4th ed. Homewood, Ill.: Richard D. Irwin, 1985.

5. S. C. Wheelwright, "Manufacturing Strategy: Defining the Missing Link," *Strategic Management Journal,* January–March 1984, pp. 77–91; W. Skinner, "Reinventing the Factory: A Manufacturing Strategy Response to Industrial Malaise." In R. Boyden (Ed.), *Competitive Strategic Management.* Englewood Cliffs, N.J.: Prentice-Hall, 1984, pp. 520–529; G. Bylinsky, "America's Best-Managed Factories," *Fortune,* May 28, 1984, pp. 16–24; S. C. Wheelwright, "Restoring the Competitive Edge in U.S. Manufacturing," *California Management Review,* Spring 1985, pp. 26–42.

6. E. S. Buffa, *Meeting the Competitive Challenge: Manufacturing Strategy for U.S. Companies.*

Homewood, Ill.: Dow Jones–Irwin, 1984; T. E. Hendrick and F. G. Moore, *Production/Operations Management,* 9th ed. Homewood, Ill.: Richard D. Irwin, 1985; G. B. Northcraft and R. B. Chase, "Managing Service Demand at the Point of Delivery," *Academy of Management Review,* 1985, 10:66–75.

7. Committee for Economic Development, *Productivity Policy: Key to the Nation's Economic Future.* New York: Committee for Economic Development, 1983; P. Mali, *Improving Total Productivity: MBO Strategies for Business, Government, and Not-For-Profit Organizations.* New York: John Wiley, 1978; J. W. Hendrick, *Improving Company Productivity: Handbook with Case Studies.* Baltimore: Johns Hopkins University Press, 1984.

8. Hendrick, *Improving Company Productivity . . . ,* pp. 69–81; K. Nishino, "Why Productivity of Japanese Industry is High," *Management Japan,* Spring 1983, pp. 19–25; B. N. Slade and R. Mohindra, *Winning the Productivity Race.* Lexington, Mass.: Lexington Books, 1985.

9. J. R. Norsworthy, testimony on Recent Productivity Trends in the U.S. and Japan before the Subcommittee on Employment and Productivity, Senate Committee on Labor and Human Resources (97th Congress, 2nd session, 2 April 1982). For further information, *also see* U.S. Senate, Committee on Labor and Human Resources, *Productivity in the American Economy: Report and Findings,* Washington, D.C.: U.S. Government Printing Office, 1982.

10. J. L. Riggs and G. H. Felix, *Productivity by Objectives.* Englewood Cliffs, N.J.: Prentice-Hall, 1983; H. S. Gitlow and P. T. Hertz, "Product Defects and Productivity," *Harvard Business Review,* September–October 1983, pp. 131–141; D. M. Miller, "Profitability = Productivity + Price Recovery," *Harvard Business Review,* May–June 1984, pp. 145–153.

11. Committee for Economic Development, *Productivity Policy . . . ,* p. 23.

12. W. J. Kaydos, "Manufacturing Market. Share," *Business Horizons,* May–June 1984, pp. 37–39; P. Pascarella, "Rolling Out a Rusty Weapon: Manufacturing is Regaining its Strategic Role," *Industry*

Week, October 29, 1984, pp. 33A ff; E. J. Poza, "Twelve Actions to Build Strong U.S. Factories," *Sloan Management Review,* Fall 1983, pp. 27–38; B. J. Reilly and J. P. Fuhr Jr., "Productivity: An Economic and Management Analysis with Direction Towards a New Synthesis," *Academy of Management Review,* 1983, 8:108–117.

13. "The Revival of Productivity," *Business Week,* February 13, 1984, pp. 92–95ff; H. D. Sherman, "Improving the Productivity of Service Businesses," *Sloan Management Review,* Spring 1984, pp. 11–23.

14. D. A. Garvin, "What Does 'Product Quality' Really Mean?" *Sloan Management Review,* Fall 1984, pp. 25–39. *Also see* T. E. Vollman, W. L. Berry, and D. C. Whybark, *Manufacturing Planning and Control Systems.* Homewood, Ill.: Richard D. Irwin, 1984.

15. H. Takeuchi and J. A. Quelch, "Quality Is More than Making a Good Product," *Harvard Business Review,* July–August 1983, pp. 139–145.

16. D. Halberstam, "Yes We Can," *Parade Magazine,* July 8, 1984, p. 5.

17. J. Reddy and A. Berger, "Three Essentials of Product Quality," *Harvard Business Review,* July–August 1983, pp. 153–159.

18. R. E. Cole, "Improving Quality Through Continuous Feedback," *Management Review,* October 1983, pp. 8–12; D. A. Garvin, "Quality on the Line," *Harvard Business Review,* September–October 1983, pp. 65–75.

19. J. Capannella and F. J. Corcoran, "Principles of Quality Costs," *Quality Progress,* April 1983, pp. 17–21.

20. "Quality: The U.S. Drives to Catch-Up," *Business Week,* November 1, 1982, pp. 66–69 ff.

21. C. Pavsidis, "Total Quality Control: An Overview of Current Efforts," *Quality Progress,* September 1984, pp. 28–29; M. H. Sinha and W. O. Willborn, *Essentials of Quality Assurance Management.* New York: John Wiley & Sons, 1986.

22. P. Crosby, *Quality is Free: The Art of Making Quality Certain.* New York: McGraw-Hill, 1979; H. M. Wadsworth, K. S. Stephens, and A. B. Godfrey, *Quality Control.* New York: John Wiley & Sons, 1986.

23. Adapted from C. C. Harwood, "The View From the Top," *Quality Progress,* October 1984, pp. 26–30.

24. S. Sekiya, "Quality Control at Toyota Motor Corporation," *Wheel Extended,* 1984, **14**(1):101–116.

25. H. Kume, "Quality Control in Japan's Industries," *Wheel Extended,* 1984, **14**(1):56–63.

26. C. Mozer, "Total Quality Control: A Route to the Deming Prize," *Quality Progress,* September 1984, pp. 30–33.

27. Halberstam, "Yes We Can!," p. 5.

28. J. L. Riggs and G. H. Felix, *Productivity By Objectives.* Englewood Cliffs, N.J.: Prentice-Hall, 1983; J. M. Juran and F. M. Gryna Jr., *Quality Planning and Analysis,* 2nd ed. New York: McGraw-Hill, 1980; M. Sinha and W. O. Willborn, *The Management of Quality Assurance.* New York: John Wiley & Sons, 1985.

29. E. Faltemayer, "Lonely Maytag Repairmen," *Fortune,* September 1979, pp. 190–195.

30. M. Feinsilber, "Chrysler Gives Workers Voice in Controlling Quality of K Cars," *Houston Chronicle,* June 28, 1980, Section 1, p. 21.

31. J. Main, "The Battle for Quality Begins," *Fortune,* December 24, 1980, p. 29.

32. O. C. Boileau, "Improving Quality and Productivity at General Dynamics," *Quality Progress,* August 1984, pp. 16–20; J. T. Hagan, "The Management of Quality: Preparing for a Competitive Future," *Quality Progress,* December 1984, pp. 21–25.

33. J. F. Cox and S. J. Clark, "Material Requirement Planning Systems," *Computer and Industrial Engineering,* 1978, **2**:123–139.

34. C. H. Davis, F. Raafat, and M. H. Safizadeh, "Production and Inventory Information Processing: Material Requirements Planning," *Journal of Small Business Management,* July 1983, pp. 25–35.

35. S. J. Clark, J. F. Cox, R. R. Jesse Jr., and R. W. Smud, "How to Evaluate Your Material Requirements Planning System," *Production and Inventory Management,* 3rd Quarter 1982, pp. 15–34; D. W. Dobler, L. Lee Jr., and D. N. Burt, *Purchasing and Materials Management: Text and Cases,* 4th ed. New York: McGraw-Hill, 1984; J. J. Kanet, "Inventory Planning at Black and Decker," *Production and Inventory Management,* 3rd Quarter 1984, pp. 9–21.

36. W. P. Patterson, "The Software Solution: Forging Manufacturing's Missing Link," *Industry Week,* September 17, 1984, pp. 92ff. Excerpted and reprinted with permission.

37. R. J. Schonberger, "Selecting the Right Manufacturing Inventory System: Western and Japanese Approaches," *Production and Inventory Management,* 1983, **24**:33–44.

38. Schonberger, "Selecting the Right . . . ," p. 36.

39. D. Whiteside and J. Arbose, "Unsnarling Industrial Production: Why Top Management is Starting to Care," *International Management,* March 1984, pp. 20–26.

40. Schonberger, pp. 15–45; G. W. Connell, "Quality at the Source: The First Step in Just-in-Time Production," *Quality Progress,* November 1984, pp. 44–45; G. Schwind, "MAN Arrives Just In Time to Save Harley-Davidson," *Material Handling Engineering,* August 1984, pp. 28ff; R. D. Shapiro, "Get Leverage From Logistics," *Harvard Business Review,* May–June 1984, pp. 119–126.

41. B. S. Moskal, "Delivering Just In Time," *Industry Week,* October 1, 1984, pp. 44ff; B. S. Moskal, "Just In Time: Putting the Squeeze on Suppliers," *Industry Week,* July 9, 1984, pp. 59ff.

42. N. L. Hyer and V. Wemmerlöv, "Group Technology and Productivity," *Harvard Business Review,* July–August 1984, pp. 140–149; M. Jelinek and J. D. Goldhar, "The Strategic Implications of the Factory of the Future," *Sloan Management Review,* Summer 1984, pp. 29–37; L. P. Ritzman, B. E. King, and L. J. Kraiewski, "Manufacturing Performance—Pulling the Right Levers," *Harvard Business Review,* March–April 1984, pp. 143–152; W. H. Slautterback and W. B. Werther Jr., "The Third Revolution: Computer-Integrated Manufacturing," *National Productivity Review,* 1984, **8**:367–374.

43. Case material prepared by Professor Joel Corman, Suffolk University, as a basis for class discussion. Cases are not designed to present illustrations of either correct or incorrect handling of problem. Copyright © 1982 by Suffolk University, Boston.

PART VII

CHANGE

CAREER DEVELOPMENT

LEARNING OBJECTIVES

After studying this chapter, you should be able to:

- Identify the personal and organizational factors that affect career decisions.

- Describe reality shock and how it impacts a person's career.

- List the four stages people normally go through in their career.

- State the central activities and psychological issues associated with each career stage.

- Name the six critical flaws preventing managers from achieving successful careers.

- Identify the tactics for a successful career.

CHAPTER OUTLINE

PREVIEW CASE

Charles Schwab

After graduating from high school, Charles started to work at Republic Bank of Denver as an errand boy. He left after one year to get his college degree. During the summers, he worked as a summer intern for a division of the bank in Boulder. By the time he completed his undergraduate degree, he had developed an interest in marketing and received several job offers. He chose Republic Bank because he was familiar with the bank, did not have to relocate to a strange city, his wife could keep her marketing job at IBM, and he felt that Republic Bank offered the combination of financial analysis, computer applications, and marketing that he wanted. His first job with the bank involved financial analysis work with the Loan Department. He was given the opportunity to work on the microcomputer banking task force to consider installing these machines in each branch. This was Charles's first contact with Sue Wilson, another member of the task force from the Retailing Department.

Charles worked on this task force for three years and was promoted to assistant manager in the process. Since it was a task force, it was to be disbanded upon the successful installation of these machines in the bank's 14 branches. It meant that the members of the task force needed to find other positions in the bank. While working with the task force, he developed good relationships with people in the Commercial Credit Department. They offered him a job. He was also offered an opportunity to manage the Retail Banking Department

in a small branch office, which he turned down. "I didn't want to manage a branch or even a group of branches. I figured that Retail Banking was probably the fastest way to the top, but I didn't want that job." The position that Charles accepted involved new services development work for VISA, MasterCard, and the bank's own card, Impact. His new boss was Sue Wilson.

Charles reported to Sue Wilson through an intermediate boss who was in charge of two new service developments. Charles's responsibilities were to develop the service concept, prepare a test market, and coordinate the marketing efforts with customer-services and computer-systems managers. The goal of his group was the quick development of new services which would be handed over to the branches as soon as possible.

Source: Darlene Bordwell, Boston.

The service concept Charles worked on for a year was one of the bank's successes. It provided consumers with opportunities to use any one of their three credit cards at most retail stores in the Denver area. His performance was rewarded by his assuming responsibility for one of the four new service concepts Republic had defined, but had yet to market. Charles indicated that he felt good about his new role, but would really like to get promoted to a manager's job by the end of the year. This desire was made more important by an unsolicited offer from Chemical Bank for a manager in the Consumer Services Department. The offer would be a promotion and would include a 25 percent increase in salary and "the promise of additional responsibility in the next eighteen months in the Retailing Bank Department." "But I didn't want a job in that department forever. I like new-services development and want to progress in management along these lines. I might like to run a bank someday, but not by working my way up from the production floor through production positions. I talked to Sue about this. She thinks that it's possible to advance in Republic Bank to a VP level in services, but she is not optimistic about promotion to senior VP. Sue has worked with some high-level people at Republic Bank and knows what she's talking about. Yet, the bank is so large it's hard to know what career information is really important to me. Sue may not have the power to get things to really happen for me. My wife and I are expecting our first child shortly and we've been thinking of buying a house. That 25 percent salary increase could really come in handy. Chemical Bank doesn't have the prestige of Republic in the business community, and it would be difficult for me to return to Republic."[1]

Charles's career concerns will probably face most of you. What is the best career path for good people like Charles? He has the ability to be a top-level manager in Republic, but chooses not to take the conventional route of working in the Retailing Bank Department. His promotion would be a reward for high performance and possibly attract other good people into New Services Department. However, it might be difficult to move into a senior VP job without experience in retail banking. Yet, he has been at the bank for 10 years, has done an outstanding job, and believes he deserves the opportunity to become an Assistant VP.

Most managers have experiences like Charles's. Sometimes we feel successful and other times we do not. A *career* is a set of attitudes and behaviors associated with work experiences and activities that span a person's life.[2] A career includes those changes over time that reflect a person's needs, motives, and aspirations, as well as societal and organizational expectations and constraints. Few of us have detailed career goals and no one has complete control over career opportunities. With changing economic and social conditions, management of a career has increased in importance. Managing careers is a joint process involving people and their organizations.[3] When individual and organizational responsibilities are clearly stated, individuals are better able to manage their careers effectively and organizations are better able to manage their human resources profitably.

This chapter focuses on (1) how individual and organizational factors affect careers; (2) the career problems that young managers are likely to face; (3) four career stages that people—especially managers—normally progress through and the problems associated with each stage; and (4) how individuals can take an active role in managing their careers.

FACTORS AFFECTING CAREER DECISIONS

Whereas a career used to mean little more than a steady paycheck, today it means much more. The career plays an important part in the way we view ourselves: It is an integral part of our sense of identify, achievement, satisfaction, and self-worth. In order to make a decision, we need to know and understand the factors that often affect career decisions. These factors fall into two major groups: individual and organizational.

Individual Factors

Many individual factors affect career decisions, some of which are illustrated in Fig. 20.1. An individual's personality may influence the type of career chosen. For example, artistically creative people can express their emotions more easily and are more likely to choose careers in art, music, dance, and

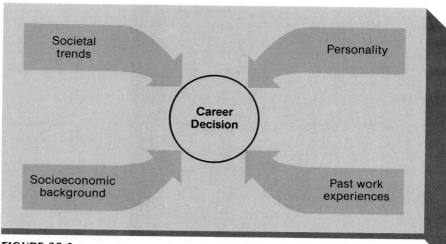

FIGURE 20.1
Individual Factors Affecting Career Decisions

Source: Adapted from M. London and S. Stumpf, *Managing Careers*, Reading, Mass.: Addison-Wesley, 1982, p. 7.

education than those who find it difficult to express emotions. Likewise, enterprising people will tend to choose careers as managers and lawyers because of the opportunity to influence others and to attain power.[4]

Societal trends also affect career choices. As we pointed out in Chapters 3 and 4, a variety of forces in the environment shape values and cultures; some of these same forces influence career decisions. During the 1980s, impressive amounts of money were given to universities to train people to become engineers and management-information–systems analysts. People who are computer literate are in great demand by companies such as GE, GM, Ford, and Kmart. The increased use of personal computers and public demands for energy conservation and pollution control created many new job opportunities in these fields and starting salaries shot up. Enrollments at many schools increased, and more young people chose to enter occupations in these fields.[5]

Parents' socioeconomic class can also influence career choice. Their occupational and educational attainments strongly influence the type of career their children choose and the educational level they attain. For example, a person born to parents who have formal educations and do skilled work is most likely to choose an occupation requiring those or similar skills. There are notable exceptions, which are due in part to the expectations parents hold for us and to the significant others (teachers, friends) we meet in everyday life.[6]

Past work experiences also provide self-knowledge about career opportunities in various fields. Most of us have had summer jobs that gave us some knowledge about what a career in that field would be like. Schools that have co-op and intern programs give students an opportunity to experience actual work situations in their major field. In sum, career decisions are not viewed as isolated events, but need to be considered in relations to our life experiences.[7]

Organizational Factors

Organizational factors that influence career decisions are shown in Fig. 20.2. Chapter 4 compared types of organizations and how each type develops specific patterns of behaviors. In the typical Japanese firm, promotions are slow, employment is long term, career paths are nonspecialized, and performance evaluations are subjective. Some U.S. companies (Alcoa, Hewlett-Packard, Westinghouse, Hershey Foods, and others) emphasize teamwork, worker participation, and informality. However, the more typical American firm encourages rapid promotions, short-term employment (the average person changes companies four times during a career), highly specialized career paths, and quantitative measures of performance. The differences in these organizations lead to different career opportunities and limitations.[8]

In Chapter 18 we discussed how various human-resource practices (selection, staffing, performance appraisal, training, development) influence the

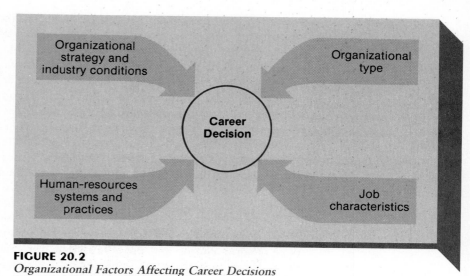

FIGURE 20.2
Organizational Factors Affecting Career Decisions

Source: Adapted from M. London and S. Stumpf, *Managing Careers.* Reading, Mass.: Addison-Wesley, 1982, p. 10.

types of persons recruited and retained by a firm. At Tandem Computers, Inc., human-resources programs stress values (styled after the Japanese) and organizational needs. Xerox, 3-M, Travelers Insurance, and AT&T, among others, use assessment centers to identify areas (human, technical, conceptual) in which the employee needs to improve and jobs that will likely fit the individual's career path.

In Chapter 12 we discussed how job characteristics can influence motivation to perform. Since jobs are a major source of stimulation, career decisions are products of the stimulation provided by a person's current job and previous jobs. Jobs that present a sense of challenge, variety, autonomy, feedback, and visibility to top management provide more varied career decisions than those which lack these characteristics. The industry and a company's strategy can affect careers.[9] If the firm is operating in a mature industry (construction machinery, glass containers, textile, steel, paper, rubber), opportunities for promotion are less than if the firm is operating in a growing industry (microcomputers, transportation, telecommunications, chemicals, food and/or beverage). In mature industries, people may be laid off by companies to enable the entire industry to regain its competitive position in the marketplace. In expanding industries, new companies are forming, promotions are often rapid, and there is a general shortage of trained people. Similarly, if the company strategy (Chapter 8) emphasizes personnel development (Tandem, IBM, PepsiCo) career concerns are likely to be more important to top management than in companies such as Gulf + Western and Alco Standard, where employee development is not so highly valued.

Career decision making is a complicated process. It involves looking both at ourselves and at the organization. Just as we have several aspects to our identities, so do organizations. Organizational factors are often defined by the type of work performed; the rules, policies, and decision-making methods used; and the type of business strategy chosen by top management. Part of managing a career involves matching individual and organizational factors.

Matching Individual and Organizational Factors

Many young people (especially college graduates) are often very disappointed during their first weeks or months on a job. Some of the reasons may reflect a lack of preparation and information about the job, city, living arrangements, and social life. Others involve the unrealistic expectations created during interviewing sessions. Recruiters and managers have been known to inflate the attractiveness of jobs to attract highly qualified candidates. They do this by giving jobs fancy titles (administrative assistant instead of secretary) and promising rapid promotions and pay hikes, which cannot be delivered. Job candidates may overstate their abilities and understate their limitations to improve their chances of getting an interview and, ultimately, the job. Thus, when each side tells only half the story before a person starts to work, a mismatch is likely.

The process leading to matches or mismatches and some of their consequences are shown in Fig. 20.3. A new employee may soon learn that the initial job is not as challenging and exciting as he or she was led to believe. Older employees may resent any preferential treatment shown to a new employee. The employee's ability to perform without much close supervision may not be as fully developed as the employer was led to believe. When these situations occur, the number of mismatches increases; job satisfaction, performance, and commitment to the organization decline. While in school, students often learn the latest techniques and methods to solve problems. When they go to work, they find that the application of these approaches lags behind in the real world. Many recent graduates, especially during their first six-to-nine months on the job, have trouble accepting the fact that the newest technique they learned is not being used. An instant reaction may be: "Why don't they do it right?" If a newcomer is being managed by someone who is not as knowledgeable or well-trained as the newcomer, the problem becomes more complex.

Individuals whose expectations are inconsistent with the realities of their new jobs are likely to experience *reality shock.* This is the realization by newcomers that they must conform to the established norms and procedures

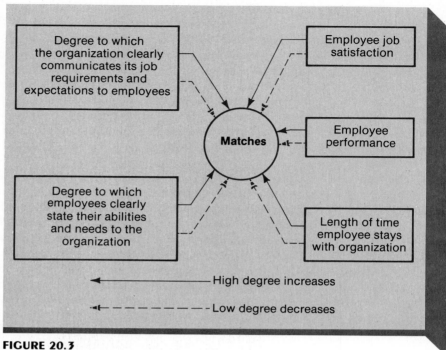

FIGURE 20.3
Matching Individual and Organization Factors

of their organizations far more than they were led to believe during recruitment.[10] Reality shock is unmet expectations and surprises; it is not being prepared for the day-to-day routine activities of the company. Organizations such as Texas Instruments, Prudential Life Insurance, and Johnson & Johnson have attempted to overcome these problems by telling newcomers about both the positive and the negative aspects of the company and its jobs. At Cleveland Trust, for example, career workshops are an integral part of the orientation program. During these workshops, the company discusses the requirements of their jobs. If new employees do not find them desirable, the bank provides an outplacement service to help them find more suitable jobs elsewhere.[11]

IN PRACTICE
Jan Adams

Jan Adams enjoyed working with people. Her choice of psychology as a major seemed consistent to her as a way of furthering her understanding of and interest in people. However, she soon learned that most companies were interested in students who had some business knowledge and/or experience. So, she took course work in the business school.

Upon graduation, Jan was offered jobs from two companies as a "management trainee." There were differences between the two positions in terms of location, starting salary, general reputation as a desirable company for new college graduates, and initial job assignment. After weighing all these factors, Jan accepted the position with a large multinational company that sold business machines. She began her sales-training program about two weeks after graduation.

The first phase of the training program lasted three months and was held in a campuslike setting away from the main office. Most of the people that Jan met were either new college grads or members of the Human Resources Department. Although the program was interesting and well-organized, Jan felt that she still hadn't learned "how things really work." The next eight months of initial sales experience helped change this feeling. During this period, she was under the supervision of an experienced sales person.

After another year, Jan was on her own in the field. Up to this point, she had received feedback about her performance in the training sessions from her boss and the salesperson with whom she worked. Now, however, things were different. She was on a straight commission basis. The formula for computing the commission was complicated and had one unique feature. If a company renting the machine decided not to renew the contract, a portion of the lost revenue was charged back to the sales division and subtracted from Jan's commissions on other sales. This was designed to motivate salespeople to give good service to current customers. In practice, however, some decisions to terminate were completely out of the control of the salesperson and they were not the result of poor service. This meant that her income was not as predictable as it had been. She soon discovered that the charge-back system was considered a threat by many new sales reps and was resented by others. She also learned that promotions to assistant manager were not based on sales but on loyalty, seniority, "fitting in," and personal relationships formed in college. Since she had not been in a sorority or a member of other social clubs, she felt uneasy. The pressure to maintain customers and generate new ones meant that she was spending 55–60 hours per week at work and didn't have time to pursue many leisure activities. The challenge of trying to meet a customer's problem to avoid a charge-back entailed a lot of routine paperwork and reading over mountains of legal contracts. After about seven months, she quit.[12]

Jan Adams's experience illustrates several points about reality shock. First, companies often promise people challenging jobs in order to attract them. However, many organizations start college graduates on relatively easy projects and gradually increase the level of job difficulty as the employees receive training and gain experience. Thus, for many college graduates, their immediate expectations of challenging work are not fulfilled. Second, most organizations promise feedback on how well the newcomer is doing while in training. Actually, many newcomers are on their own and are left in a state of confusion about how well they are doing and what they need to do to improve. Third, many recruiters promise growth and rapid promotions to high-performing people. However, in some organizations rewards may depend more on conformity to its customs, methods, and social networks than on performance.

STAGES IN CAREER DEVELOPMENT

Our working lives may be reviewed as a series of stages. Each stage is characterized by changes in values, developmental needs, career concerns and activities, and type of job. These stages emerge as we grow older. However, unlike stages of childhood and youth that are well-defined by grade school, high school, graduation, and driving age, changes that affect a career are more difficult to identify. Lawyers, dentists, or surgeons who open practices after years of formal schooling will probably be concerned with establishing themselves in their profession, whether they are 30 or 40 years old. However, the 40-year-old will probably have a different set of career concerns than the 30-year-old.

There are a number of ways of looking at careers and the relationship between careers and age.[13] The model we have chosen to use was developed by Donald Super and his associates at Columbia University.[14] Figure 20.4 identifies the four career stages most people will pass through. Each of these stages is described in terms of the central activities that individuals usually accomplish, the primary working relationships that they establish, and the major career issues they face. The ***exploration and trial stage*** usually occurs between the time that people graduate from school and reach 25 years of age. During this time, people try various jobs, companies, and life interests in an attempt to find an occupation that matches their self-concept. Having found appropriate occupations, people enter the ***establishment and advancement stage*** themselves in their chosen field. These are the most creative years for most people and the period when they establish families. Having made a place for themselves in the company, people enter the ***maintenance stage*** where they try to hold on to what they have achieved. While career growth is still possible, people often become more interested in other satisfactions that life can offer. During this stage, people can still get promoted or stay in the same job. If their career progress has not lived up to their expectations, a ***mid-life crisis*** may result. Feelings of resentment and frustration may cause a decline in performance and overall career growth. As their physical and mental powers fade, people enter the ***disengagement stage*** of their careers. Sometime late in the maintenance stage, the pace of work slackens, job duties are shifted, or the nature of the work is redefined to suit the person's career.

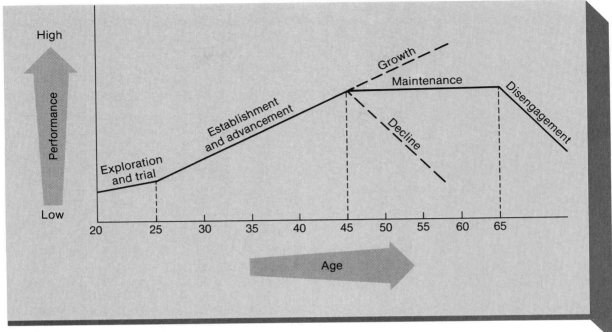

FIGURE 20.4
Stages of Career Development

Source: D. Hall, *Careers in Organizations.* Santa Monica, Calif.: Goodyear, 1976, p. 57.

Try to look ahead at possible directions and events in your career. This may not be easy because ideas about what people think and feel when they are over 60 years of age might seem foreign. Therefore we will discuss the disengagement stage only briefly. More attention will be given to the other three stages for two additional reasons: (1) you are likely to work and talk with many people who are experiencing career concerns in these first three stages (parents, friends, relatives, fellow workers, first supervisor); and (2) all of us will be better managers if we have some knowledge and understanding about the career concerns of others.

Exploration and Trial Stage

When first joining an organization, a person is immediately faced with several challenges. Some of them were illustrated in the problems facing both Charles Schwab and Jan Adams. First, the new employee must learn to perform at least some tasks of the work competently and to learn which tasks are essential and which require less attention. Meanwhile, the newcomer must also learn how to get things done, using both formal and informal communication channels. Finally, the employee must do these things while being closely watched by a supervisor for competency and indications of future potential. Because many new college graduates lack knowledge about the organizations, they are usually assigned to an experienced person, as in Jan Adams's case, and begin by helping someone else do their work.

Central activities

The lack of job challenge is a major contributor to reality shock. Much of a new employee's work in the exploration and trial stage involves fairly routine duties. It is important for a person not to become completely bogged down in this detail work, but to show some initiative and be innovative in finding solutions to problems. New employees are typically assigned a part of a larger project that is being directed by a superior, which many people find frustrating. Such an attitude is understandable, but those who try to escape this subordinate position too quickly will miss an important aspect of career development. They will fail to learn what others have gained by experience. More importantly, by undertaking tasks for which they are not prepared, the newcomer may acquire the reputation of being a mediocre performer, a reputation that is hard to overcome.

Studies of college graduates who left companies, as well as those who remained, cited lack of job challenge as the major cause of dissatisfaction with their organization.[15] The degree of challenge in a first job relates to successful performance of subsequent assignments and career advancement. Successful accomplishment of even routine tasks in this career stage leads a person to develop high performance standards and to work harder on future tasks. In addition, successful task accomplishment causes the manager's expectations to increase so that the employee is given increasingly difficult and challenging tasks. People who are given unchallenging tasks and perform poorly, generally do not receive more challenging assignments because their superiors do not come to expect high performance.

Primary relationship

At this stage the employee's primary relationship is that of a subordinate to a superior. Effectiveness at managing this relationship may be critical to building an effective career. An employee's first supervisor represents the organization's pluses and minuses. Ideally, the newcomer will be assigned to a mentor who knows the organization, is successful, and has been trained to work with newly hired people. A *mentor* is a person who will sponsor you and speak to his or her boss about your accomplishments.[16] The mentor suggests what to do and what not to do and supplies judgments about organizational life that are not found in textbooks. At Jewel Companies, each trainee is assigned to a mentor. The mentor helps the employee gain the skills, experience, and visibility necessary for advancement in the company. Donald

A mentor provides subordinates with a sympathetic ear to turn to with questions ranging from company policies and procedures to the best methods of socializing with other employees.

Source: Richard Wood/The Picture Cube.

Perkins, the president of Jewel Companies, states: "I don't know that anyone has ever succeeded in any business without having some unselfish mentorship. . . . Everyone who succeeds has had a mentor or mentors."[17]

Mentoring is relatively prevalent in most well-run organizations. A recent survey of 1250 top executives found that about 70 percent of them had a mentor during the trial stage of their careers. The effective mentors of these executives were knowledgeable about the company and how to use power effectively, were good counselors and were willing to share their knowledge and experience. In contrast to executives who did not have mentors, those with mentors earned more money, had more graduate degrees, had engaged in career planning prior to seeking a mentor, and were more satisfied with their careers and their work.[18]

In Chapter 13, we discussed how expectations of supervisors affect employees' attitudes and performance. Regardless of their abilities, people want to please their boss. If, for example, supervisors look upon newcomers as potentially outstanding performers, they will treat them accordingly by encouraging them to do their best. Conversely, supervisors who expect newcomers to perform poorly will communicate these expectations directly or indirectly, thereby triggering poor performance.[19]

IN PRACTICE
Jay Parke

My first two years at the company were a disaster. I worked for a person that I disliked and did not respect. The person provided me with very little assistance or guidance. As a result, I made little or no progress in terms of salary raises or promotions. Then I began to work with another engineer who could get things done in the company. She protected me from the flack coming down from above. She provided a climate that I enjoyed and was willing to go to bat for me to get above-average raises and some visibility with her boss. When she got promoted, she requested that I join her new group, where I became an informal leader. Later, she recommended me for a promotion.

Jay's experience points out some of the benefits of having a good mentor in the early stages of a career, as well as some of the problems of having a poor one. Jay's second boss knew the right people and could show Jay how the system worked: how to lay out the job, obtain needed equipment, process travel funds, get extra computer time, and so on. A good mentor becomes a model to follow whenever an employee is unsure about how to approach a situation.[20]

Psychological issues
The psychological adjustments required during the exploration and trial stage are as important as the tasks performed or the relationships established with superiors. One of the basic psychological problems is the adjustment to the role of subordinate. Many young people look forward to completing their education so that they can be free from the demands of their professors and gain the independence they believe their years in school earned them. According to Ross Webber, there are three types of problems: (1) political insensitivity; (2) loyalty demands; and (3) personal anxiety.[21] An awareness of these problems can minimize their potentially damaging results.

Political insensitivity.   Political alliances are an organizational reality. Managers seek to influence their subordinates to perform certain activities and often seek power in order to protect and/or expand their department's influence in the organization. Managers who are skilled politicians are often better able to maintain or increase the resources available to their departments than those who lack this ability. Politically skilled managers can also enlist the cooperation of others through informal, as well as formal, communication channels.

Newcomers often believe that problems are solved rationally. As Jan Adams discovered, the salespersons with the highest sales figures were not always those who got the largest salary increases or quickest promotions. Promotions and salary increases may depend on the employee's mentor. Facing these realities, newcomers frequently become disenchanted with the system. Instead of trying to understand what is happening and forming their own political connections, they may only concentrate on narrow job specialties and thus find that their careers are drifting.

As political awareness develops, an employee is less inclined to bet his or her future on any one mentor or connection. Such a relationship often boomerangs when the mentor gets passed over for a promotion or leaves the organization. A broad base of working connections is preferable. From these connections, the employee can adapt more quickly to the organization and take a more active interest in managing his or her career.

Loyalty demands. A new employee faces various demands from superiors. Webber describes five common ways in which these demands can be defined by a superior.

1. *Obey me.* Managers have a right to expect that their legitimate orders will be carried out. Disobedience, if carried too far, will prevent the organization from reaching its objectives. However, unquestioning obedience on the part of subordinates can lead to poor decisions. Subordinates who know, for example, that a superior's instructions are inappropriate but who proceed to obey them out of loyalty are doing their superior and the organization more harm than good. Sometimes, loyalty may even call for disobedience of an order that is unethical or that was given in haste or anger.

2. *Protect me and don't make me look bad.* Managers are responsible for and ultimately judged by the actions of their subordinates. They therefore have a right to expect that subordinates consider their superiors' reputation as they carry out their work activities and interact with those outside their departments. However, this demand for loyalty can lead subordinates to avoid taking necessary risks or to cover up mistakes.

3. *Work hard.* In the eyes of many managers, the best proof of loyalty to the organization is the willingness to work long and hard. However, if unrealistic standards of performance are demanded, morale may drop and subordinates' performance decline.

4. *Be successful.* "Get the job done no matter what" and "I don't care what you do so long as the bottom line shows a profit" are often implicit (if not explicit) in managers' instructions to their subordinates. This may cause subordinates to feel a conflict between organizational loyalty and their own ethical codes. If they disobey instructions, their careers might suffer; if they violate their ethics (or the law), guilt or scandal might result.

5. *Tell me the truth*. Obviously, it is important for superiors to be told about problems in their departments—not only so that they can take steps to deal with the problem, but also so that they can prepare to deal with their own superiors. All too often, though, reporting a problem—especially when it is in the subordinate's area of responsibility—may cause the subordinate to be blamed or punished. In such situations, newcomers often learn to apply their loyalty selectively, putting self-protection before the needs of their superiors or the organization. As a consequence, failures may not be reported until it is too late to minimize their consequences.

As we approach the age of 30, most of us feel a greater commitment to the organization than we did when we were 21. Managers recognize this and use **golden handcuffs** to retain valued employees. These are the salary, perks (country club memberships, company car), and fringe benefits (deferred compensation plans, stock options) that companies use to tie employees to the company. The independence sought by the college student has now been replaced by a growing commitment to and dependence on the organization. The manner in which this tradeoff between independence and dependence is resolved has a major influence on how a person's career progresses.

Personal anxiety

Edgar Schein has described three ways in which an employee can respond to an organization's efforts to enforce compliance with its values and expectations.

1. *Conformity:* complete acceptance of all the organization's norms and values. Total conformity represents a loss both for the individual and the organization. Employees lose their sense of identity and initiative, while the organization loses access to the diversity of opinion and ideas that its long-term success requires.

2. *Rebellion:* complete rejection of the organization's values and expectations. Rebellious, extremely individualistic people either cause the organization to change or, more likely, voluntarily leave the organization or are dismissed.

3. *Creative individualism:* acceptance of the organization's important, constructive values and neglect of those that are trivial or inappropriate. Obviously, this response is difficult to maintain. A decision about which norms are important may not be accurate, and an employee may be criticized for violating even unimportant norms. Moreover, with each lateral transfer or promotion, new norms come into play while others lose their relevance. For example, the values of an employee's superior in the research department are likely to be somewhat different from those of his or her superior in the sales department. Therefore people have to

TABLE 20.1 ■ EXPLORATION AND TRIAL CAREER STAGE FACTORS

- Central activity: helping, learning, and following directions
- Primary relationship: being an apprentice and finding a mentor
- What people need from a boss: coaching, feedback, protection, and acceptance
- What a boss needs from people: technical and psychological support
- Major psychological issues: political insensitivity, loyalty demands, and personal anxiety

Source: Adapted from G. Dalton, P. Thompson, and R. Price. "The Four Stages of Professional Careers—A New Look at Performance by Professionals," *Organizational Dynamics,* Summer 1977, pp. 19–42; L. Baird and K. Kram, "Career Dynamics: Managing the Superior/Subordinate Relationship," *Organizational Dynamics,* Summer 1983, pp. 46–64.

make many choices about which values to accept over the course of their careers.[22]

Summary. The factors involved in the exploration and trial career stage are highlighted in Table 20.1. This stage requires time for adjustment to the reality of the job, orientation to the organization, and establishment of a mentoring relationship with a supervisor. Being able to complete routine jobs successfully can lead to early success and more challenging assignments in the future. To the extent that a good mentor provides help, the difficulties of learning the ropes can be minimized.

Establishment and Advancement Stage

The second career stage often involves new experiences: special assignments, transfers and promotions, offers from other organizations, chances for visibility to senior management, and establishing value to the organization. Feedback on performance becomes critical to development of feelings of success or failure. This stage is also for establishing professional credentials and developing a level of expertise that is valuable to the organization and contributes to self-esteem.

Central activities

With greater self-confidence and knowledge of the organization, people are more likely to be concerned about promotion and advancement than about their ability to get the work done. With a track record developing, they will be looking ahead to having their own projects. This does not mean that they will be allowed to work alone; most projects still must be coordinated with other activities of the organization. It does mean that the person is no longer closely supervised or given specific methods to use in getting the job done, and is likely to be responsible for the work of several subordinates.[23]

The important decision to be made is how much to specialize in one area. One strategy involves a deliberate choice of an area in which to specialize (marketing research, tax accounting, training and development, industrial engineering, computer programming). Specializing in one area allows a person to become an expert in it; the potential danger, though, is that of being pigeonholed in that area. For example, if a movie director wanted a person to play a cowboy role, who would be chosen? Prior to his death, why John Wayne, of course. When Wayne was asked why he didn't play different roles, he said he was never asked. The other strategy is to develop a set of specialized skills and apply them to a variety of problems. For example, a computer scientist can find skill applications in marketing, accounting, personnel, and finance. The risk here is of becoming a jack of all trades, and a master of none.

During this stage, potential for advancement in an organization generally becomes apparent. Those who are seen to have high potential by supervisors are given jobs that allow competition for promotions to higher levels. Those who are good performers, but do not have the potential for top or middle management positions, start to resign themselves to the fact that their career hopes for rapid advancement may never be realized in this company.

We can help our own careers to progress in several ways. For example, we can try to be at the right place at the right time by volunteering for visible assignments, challenging tasks, and developing ourselves for key management positions. We can also take initiative in the management of our own careers rather than relying on others to promote them.

Primary relationships

Peer relationships take on great importance. As a person relies less and less on mentors for direction and advice, they turn to the peer group. It provides an outlet for discussion of the inequities of the system, such as who did and didn't get promoted and why, the size of pay increases, and the like.

This transition from using a superior as a mentor to relating to a peer group is not easy. Peer group members often exploit flaws of others in the group to promote themselves when the opportunity arises. As we discussed in Chapter 15, people turn to their peer group for support, especially when things do not go well. For example, if you are turned down for a promotion, you turn to your peer group for support. You hope that they will agree that the wrong person was promoted and offer advice that will boost your self-esteem. However, some of them may secretly be glad that you were not promoted because this opens opportunities for them to get promoted faster. Once you have been passed over, your chances for being considered again decrease.[24] Similarly, newcomers in the exploration and trial stage of their careers are not likely to want you to mentor them; few of us want to work for a person who cannot advance our careers.

Psychological issues

Since most people want to move from a state of dependence to one of independence, the transition should be easy. Unfortunately, this is not so.

An employee's mentoring gradually becomes less important once the employee has established strong peer relationships. At that point, the focus shifts from familiarizing oneself with the day-to-day operation of the organization to seeking approval and support from a select group of co-workers.

Source: Frank Siteman/The Picture Cube.

From first grade through college, most of us have been dependent on others. To ensure a good grade, we did what the teacher wanted; in our first job, in order to get promoted, we rely on the advice of our superior and then act on it.

In the establishment and advancement stage, people must break that dependence and develop their own ideas and standards of behavior. Some help might be available from an old mentor and peers, but individual judgment is needed in deciding when to apply which standards.

IN PRACTICE
Judy Sullivan

Judy Sullivan worked with Kay Bartol, her boss, on various accounting projects for three years at a large accounting firm before she developed enough confidence to submit a plan to a customer on her own. But she found that her confidence was short-lived. She had been used to checking with Kay, who actually made the final decision, and asking Kay's advice on how to present the proposal to the customer. Now she had her own project, but lacked the confidence to make many of the important and necessary decisions about it. Kay was unavailable for six months, and Judy feared that if she asked for help from her fellow workers, they would take this as a sign of inadequacy. Eventually, she discovered that she could get opinions from others outside her department and use their advice when making decisions. Eventually, Judy became a very successful accountant.

It is important to Kay, also, that Judy establish herself as a highly competent person. Kay's future with the company is based, to a large extent, on the performance of subordinates. If Kay has a track record of developing *stars,* she will have proved herself to upper management as a good developer of people. If Judy actively supports Kay by producing good work and using her expertise to make the entire department look good, it will reflect well on Kay's managerial competence.

During this stage, a person's struggles to make decisions at work are compounded by struggles to make important personal decisions. Such decisions are often interrelated, such as whether to take a promotion with its possible effects (relocating, longer hours, a lot more travel, increased stress) on a person's personal life (buying a home and, perhaps, starting a family). Whether to stay with an organization and become increasingly committed to it is another question. Most college graduates will change jobs on the average of four times during their careers, and many people change jobs during this career stage.[25]

SUMMARY

The factors that affect individuals during the establishment and advancement career stage are shown in Table 20.2. The important activity is that of establishing a professional standing and developing a specialized field of knowledge. As the potential for advancement is either realized or not, self-esteem and the probability of future advancement are determined. The peer group becomes the means through which work-related issues are discussed. Being recognized as an independent contributor is important.

MAINTENANCE STAGE

Development in this stage depends on the direction a career has taken during the first two stages. Those who have been picked by the organization as management stars will continue to receive more promotions, new job assign-

---

TABLE 20.2 ■ ESTABLISHMENT AND ADVANCEMENT CAREER STAGE FACTORS

- Central activity: specialization, independent contributor
- Primary relationship: peers
- What people need from a boss: exposure, challenging work, sponsorship
- What a boss needs from people: loyalty, competence
- Major psychological issues: independence, career–personal-life conflicts

Source: Adapted from G. Dalton, P. Thompson, and R. Price, "The Four Stages of Professional Careers—A New Look at Performance by Professionals," *Organizational Dynamics,* Summer 1977, pp. 19–42; L. Baird and K. Kram, "Career Dynamics: Managing the Superior/Subordinate Relationship," *Organizational Dynamics,* Summer 1983, pp. 46–64.

ments, greater responsibility, and higher status.[26] These people feel that they have almost made it. This does not mean that they can rest on the strength of past successes. Fear of stagnation may lead them to continue to reach for the top, or it may lead to a reevaluation of career goals.

Many employees are **solid citizens.** They are reliable and do good work but, for one reason or another, have little chance for a promotion within the organization. They may lack the technical skills needed to move to a higher position, lack the desire for further promotion, or be too valuable in their present positions for the organization to move them to another job. Managers who have these characteristics constitute the largest group of managers in most organizations and accomplish most of its work. Regardless of the reasons, they may continue to be effective until they retire.

Other managers, **deadwood,** have little chance of promotion. They are often given staff jobs that top managers have labeled *dead-end positions.* The performance of these managers is likely to decline to a point where it becomes marginal.

Central activities

Special assignments and expanded mentoring roles are critical to stars.[27] These special assignments may entail dealing with others outside the organization, such as governmental agencies and large-customer accounts. Managers are several levels removed from production work themselves but act as mentors for newcomers by being professionally competent managers. Since managers may lack the technical skills of newcomers, they become the behind-the-scenes persons who get things done or the persons to whom newcomers turn when problems are politically sensitive.

Managers who are considered to be solid citizens are satisfied with the way their careers have developed and will continue to work effectively and take pride in their achievements. By the time we have reached 40, we probably have been married, have had children, and have made our career choices. As solid citizens, we know that a **career plateau** has been reached. Although we often cannot forsee any major job changes, we can stay alert by learning new techniques and sharpening decision skills. A career plateau is the level at which the likelihood of additional promotions is very low.[28] Plateauing does not ordinarily lead to poor performance. A plateau is reached in most cases simply because there are far more qualified people for higher-level positions than there are positions available. Since openings at higher levels are scarcer, even the most successful managers will eventually reach a plateau. This does not mean that a career is a failure. How many people are president of GM, RCA, or GE? One at a time.

Managers who are deadwood simply try not to make mistakes that will result in their getting fired. By accepting positions out of the mainstream of decision making, they hope to hang on until retirement. Few people come to them for advice, and they are involved less and less in the organization.

*The ability to elicit cooper-
ation from subordinates is
essential to successfully
handling many managerial
responsibilities.*

Source: Sarah Putnam/The
Picture Cube.

Primary relationships

Stars use their primary relationships to attempt to take care of others in
the organization; they assume greater accountability for the work of others.
Upon receiving an assignment that depends on the cooperation of others, they
quickly tap the others for their advice. Interpersonal skills in setting objectives,
delegating tasks, and supervising others become important. Stars must also
learn to handle the proverbial man-in-the-middle role. That is, they have
responsibilities to top management to get results and to subordinates to retain
their loyalties and gain them visibility to top management. Unless they have
strong influence in both directions, they will become ineffective in dealing
with the people they supervise. Finally, stars are expected to motivate the solid
citizen and deadwood.

The solid citizens are faced with doing the same job for many years, with
few meaningful changes in responsibility. Some may become mentors to others,
passing on expertise and showing newcomers the ropes. This activity involves
being patient, trying not to overreact to mistakes, and helping newcomers
learn from their mistakes. Others may develop outside interests; community
and family activities become important to these people.

The deadwood have few relationships at work. Because they lack influence
in the organization, any attempts at mentoring fail. They do not receive

challenging assignments, and salary increases are minimal. The way that organizations typically manage deadwood is described in the Don Johnston story.

IN PRACTICE
Don Johnston

Don Johnston, 57, had been one of the most successful sales managers during his first 20 years with the company. Reputed to be an excellent motivator, year after year he took young college graduates and trained them to be successful salespersons. About 17 years ago things began to fall apart in his territory.

His monthly sales meetings, usually run very well, became rambling lectures of questionable business value. Don's unsolicited advice on everything from politics to dress shirts became increasingly difficult for subordinates to handle, destroying his rapport with the new college grads. Accounts were lost, sales declined, turnover increased, and finally Don was reassigned to a small territory in a branch office located some distance from the home office. Don's trips to the home office were so infrequent that most of the office staff did not know his name. He was seldom asked to attend seminars or weekend staff retreats.

Psychological issues

Moving into the maintenance stage is often associated with a number of personal changes. Thirty-five percent of today's managers will probably experience mid-life crisis. A mid-life crisis is when a person's behavior changes radically between the ages of 39–44.[29] Feelings of resentment, sadness, and frustration about a career that has not lived up to a person's dreams may cause that person to lose his or her emotional balance. The crisis may lead to quitting a stable, good paying job and taking a less secure one, becoming a middle-aged hippie, experiencing family troubles, or getting divorced. Look at what happened to George Flowers.

IN PRACTICE
George Flowers

At 43, George left his production job at Digital Equipment for a challenging marketing job at Optigraphics. As George described it, "The same job for twenty years and damn near the same thoughts for twenty years. Twenty more years of the same wasn't very attractive. I decided it was time to do something new." Not only did George leave Digital, he purchased a 1000 cc Honda motorcycle. He got five speeding tickets in the next six months and was involved in one near-fatal accident. George also saw his influence eroding within his family. His son decided not to get his MBA but to work as an assistant golf pro at the local country club; his daughter graduated from college and planned to marry a man that George did not approve of; and his wife decided to return to school.[30]

While there are many debates about why mid-life crises occur, some of the more important ones are:

■ *Empty nest.* As we reach 40, children leave the home and the spouse may return to work or school. As this happens, the focus shifts away from the home. We may see the spouse and children as less dependent on us and less subject to our influence. They are less available as sources of ego support.

■ *Limits to life.* A physical exam for an insurance policy, a major illness, or a parent or friend's death raise the inevitability of our own death. This realization can lead us to come to grips with the fact that we will not be able to accomplish all we had wanted to do; there isn't time.

■ *Physiological changes.* Changes in hair, skin, and physical stamina come more rapidly after 40. Our hair begins to gray, our skin to wrinkle, tennis and handball strain our bodies.

■ *The dream.* In the middle years, we may perceive that the stability achieved in family, work, and community is stagnating. Routines at home and the office become ruts, lack challenge, and offer little opportunity for excitement.[31]

More people in their 40's or 50's are taking risks, retraining, changing jobs if the old one is a compromise, starting new businesses, or launching second careers after retirement. Many civil servants can retire after 25 years of service with a comfortable pension. When life expectancies were shorter, facing disappointments and unfinished dreams at 40 might have been an invitation to depression. Now people may shift their fulfillment by starting new careers because they still have many working years ahead of them.

INTERNATIONAL FOCUS

MYTHS AND TRUTHS ABOUT INTERNATIONAL CAREERS

North American business is no longer domestic. By 1984, foreigners had bought U.S. businesses that generate sales of more than $250 billion. In less than 25 years, the percent of gross national product (GNP) exported from the United States to other countries has more than doubled. Foreign investment by U.S. companies in other countries has continued to grow at 10 percent per year. Given the importance of international business, many managers are predicting that the next generation of executives will have to have experience in a foreign assignment to reach the top.

One notable characteristic of U.S. managers on foreign assignment is that they are overwhelmingly men. In a survey of 686 U.S. and Canadian corporations with overseas operations, only 3 percent were using women managers. Similarly, most women managers in European countries were sent from Eastern Block countries, not the United States or Canada.

SUMMARY

The maintenance career stage is a period of time when most people review their career progress. As shown in Table 20.3, the central activity for most managers at this stage involves being a mentor to younger employees. Primary relationships depend on the career path: star, solid citizen, or deadwood. Stars continue to grow within the company and mentor younger managers who have high-performance potential. Solid citizens are satisfied with their careers, demonstrate loyalty to the company, and can serve as mentors for newcomers. Deadwood are assigned duties that are out of the mainstream of the organization. The major issue facing a manager at the maintenance career stage is coping with a possible mid-life crisis. For more and more people, a series of different careers is beginning to make sense because their productive and energetic years are being prolonged.

TABLE 20.3 ■ MAINTENANCE CAREER STAGE FACTORS

- ■ Central activity: training
- ■ Primary relationship: mentoring
- ■ What people need from a boss: autonomy, opportunities to develop others
- ■ What a boss needs from people: opportunities to mentor
- ■ Psychological issues: mid-life crisis, assuming responsibility for others

Source: Adapted from G. Dalton, P. Thompson, and R. Price. "The Four Stages of Professional Careers—A New Look at Performance by Professionals," *Organizational Dynamics,* Summer 1977, pp. 19–42; L. Baird and K. Kram, "Career Dynamics: Managing the Superior/Subordinate Relationship," *Organizational Dynamics,* Summer 1983, pp. 46–64.

What are some of the reasons that cause people to reject international assignments? First was location. Almost 60 percent of a sample of more than 1100 college graduates indicated that they would turn down an assignment if the country were seen as politically unstable or too "uncivilized," or if it had extreme poverty. Second were job and career concerns. Thirty-five percent of these people did not see a foreign assignment as good for their long-term career strategies. They saw a higher risk of failure, being isolated from the U.S.-based company, and getting "lost in the company hierarchy" as major reasons. Third were spouse and family. International assignments were turned down if it would put too much strain on a marriage, if children needed special care, or if the other spouse was working and couldn't relocate.

(continued)

How do women's chances of success compare with those of men? Men were seen as having significantly more opportunities than women to succeed in their overseas jobs. Eighty-three percent believed that men's chances of being selected for an international assignment were better than those of women and that these successes lead to higher job satisfactions, greater company recognition and faster promotions; 63 percent believed that men's chances of being effective were better than women's.

What factors influence these results? There are four barriers to women in international management. More than 80 percent of this sample said that *foreigners' attitudes* are the biggest obstacle facing women who moved into management positions. North American managers generally accept women as equals, whereas sending a woman on an overseas assignment would offend foreigners because foreign women do not have equal status with men. The second barrier is a company's reluctance to *select women for these assignments*. The company's reluctance is based on the belief that the woman manager would encounter resistance from superiors, peers, and clients. According to a senior manager of human resources at Mobil Oil Company, "The real problem exists in the minds of those who make decisions regarding who shall make business trips abroad and who shall be offered overseas assignments." The third barrier is the *dual-career marriage*. Many managers believe that women do not want to move their families. If the woman gets an overseas job, her husband will not be willing or able to transfer overseas. Fourth, women are *not interested in international assignments*. Women have traditionally avoided international management because it has been stereotyped as a career for men, and there are few women role models.

What should companies do? Since many of the women in the sample would like an overseas assignment, managers are urged to take one of three actions. First, companies should be aware of women's interest in international careers and consider them, as well as men, as candidates for overseas assignments. Second, companies should realize that foreigners do not treat women managers in the same ways that they treat local women. Women managers should be sent selectively to countries in which there are very few local women managers. Third, companies should be aware that men perceive that international work leads to greater organizational rewards than do women. They should be careful to make sure that rewards for equal work are equivalent.

Source: Adapted from Nancy Adler, "Women Do Not Want International Careers and Other Myths about International Management," *Organizational Dynamics,* 1984, 13(2):66–79.

DISENGAGEMENT STAGE

This stage occurs for most people when they reach about 60 years of age. Many managers who have been around an organization for a long time can bring together the resources and people to push new ideas to a successful conclusion, playing the role of maverick or internal entrepreneur. These roles are legitimate so long as they can be played successfully. A person's identity as a maverick or entrepreneur can often be established on the basis of a solid reputation in the company, which has benefited from the individual's past achievements.

It is important for older managers to establish mentor relationships with younger managers in a firm. Many will spend considerable time and energy in the development of key people to replace themselves upon their retirement. They learn to think about the needs of the organization beyond the time of their involvement in it. Others will dedicate time to establishing relationships outside their organizations (representing the company on community organizations, such as the Rotary and Chamber of Commerce, serving on municipal advisory boards and commissions).

CAREER MANAGEMENT

Many organizations (IBM, Mobil, Gulf Oil, Tenneco, SmithKline, GE, Xerox, Travelers Insurance Company, and others) have programs that help employees to manage their careers. The objectives and methods of career planning, development and management are illustrated by the program at Arthur Young.

IN PRACTICE
Career Planning
and Development
at Arthur Young

Arthur Young, a big eight accounting firm, believes that people can grow when they are aware of their progress in the firm. To this end, employees are given every opportunity during their careers to realize the full potential of their own professional goals and aspirations. The realization of this broad objective is implemented through a Career Planning and Development program.

The Career Planning and Development program has two objectives:

1. To ensure that you are clearly aware of your progress in the firm and to assist you in developing the necessary resources to improve your performance; and

2. To encourage, guide, and assist you in the formulation of your career objectives by setting specific goals and by monitoring progress toward the achievement of these goals.

To help people reach these objectives, each person is assigned to a counselor. In most offices managers or principals do the counseling. In career planning the role of the counselor is to assist people in structuring their career path at Arthur Young by setting specific career-development goals. For example, if a person has a goal to transfer to the tax department from the auditing department in a year, a specific program that will increase the person's tax knowledge should be established.

(continued)

In order to help people make career decisions, the counselor's job is to keep them informed about the opportunities in the firm. The typical career path to partnerships in both auditing and tax accounting ranges from 9–13 years; 2–3 years as a staff accountant, 2–3 years as a senior accountant, 3–4 years as a manager, and 2–3 years as a principal. At each level, the firm expects employees to be exposed to a variety of professional experiences and challenges that will enhance their professional development. For example, staff accountants are expected to demonstrate the ability to communicate well; to display personal characteristics of integrity, independence, and commitment; and to have a professional appearance and manner. The firm also expects that most staff accountants will pass the Certified Public Accountant (CPA) examination during this stage of their careers.

The managers at Arthur Young believe that it is important for their people to become involved in civic activities of the community and to expand the services it provides to existing clients. The latter provides the firm with additional work and exposure.[32]

However, career management is the individual's responsibility. Just as successful corporations develop business strategies, people who succeed are likely to use a number of tactics to increase the likelihood of success. There are two reasons for this. First, people who have career goals can focus their time and energy on specific activities and jobs, rather than drifting from one job to the next without any ultimate goal. They are less likely to choose jobs that will not help them reach their goals. Second, those who have set goals and have plans for reaching them are likely to be sought out by others; they are perceived by others to be more motivated and goal directed.

Although politics plays an important role in organizational decisions, an individual's flaws can just as easily short-circuit a career. Let us review these flaws and then consider some tactics that are recommended for use to advance a career.

Managerial Flaws

When asked what sealed the fate of managers who had fallen short of their ultimate career goals, a group of high-level managers consistently named the six factors shown in Table 20.4.[33]

Insensitivity to others

Those who failed often deliberately poked fun at others. Common subordinate reactions were: "She made me feel so stupid;" or "He wouldn't give you the time of day unless you were a star." When under stress, these managers became abrasive and did not permit subordinates to voice different opinions.

Although the managers might be brilliant, they were too tough and insensitive to others, which eventually led subordinates to not want to work for them.

Overly ambitious

Derailed managers were also overly ambitious and seemed always to be thinking about the next assignment. They failed to give subordinates enough guidance and encouragement in current projects. They attempted to please upper management by being a jump ahead, when they should have been paying more attention to assignments they had already been given.

Specific performance problems

Managers who failed usually had a series of performance problems. They did not meet profit objectives, were lazy, and demonstrated that they could not handle certain kinds of work (usually work involving strategic decision making). Sixty-six percent of the executives reported that at some point in their careers they had accepted a position for which they lacked the training and experience and had floundered for a year or so.

Betrayal of trust

Some managers committed what, perhaps, is the only unforgivable sin: the betrayal of trust. This does not refer to honesty but rather to the failure to follow through on promises made. For instance, one manager did not implement a decision as he had promised to do, thus causing a series of conflicts between his company's marketing and production departments.

Overdependence on a mentor

When a mentor falls from favor, so do his or her proteges. Even if the mentor still remained in power, people questioned the protege's ability to

TABLE 20.4 ■ REASONS FOR DERAILMENT

REASON	PERCENT AGREEING
Insensitivity to others	100
Overly ambitious	75
Specific performance problems	75
Betrayal of trust	50
Inability to adapt to a new boss	50
Failure to delegate	50

Source: M. Lombardo and M. McCall. "Great Truths that May Not Be," *Issues and Observations,* February 1983, 3:1–4; "What Makes a Top Executive," *Psychology Today,* November 1982, pp. 82–86.

make independent decisions. For example, one manager worked for the same executive for 15 years, following him from assignment to assignment. When top management changed and his mentor no longer fit in, the manager was viewed merely as a spokesperson of his mentor and was passed over for a promotion.

Failure to delegate

Managers fail to delegate for a number of reasons. (See Chapter 10.) Generally, managers whose careers aren't as successful as they might be are insecure. That is, they are accountable for their subordinates' actions, which makes them reluctant to take chances and delegate assignments. Or the manager may fear a loss of power if subordinates do a good job. Managers who fail to develop subordinates severely limit their own upward mobility.

Tactics for Career Success

A number of popular books discuss tactics for career success, including *What Color is Your Parachute,*[34] *Getting Yours,*[35] *Career Strategies: Planning for Personal Growth,*[36] *Career Success/Personal Failure,*[37] and *Executive Career Strategy.*[38] The following tactics are recommended for advancing a career. Their use depends on the particular organization and the person's career stage.

Do excellent work

High performance and excellent work are the basics of a successful career. While political ability can by itself cause an average performer to be promoted faster than those with a better track record, corporate politics can backfire. As a general rule, the better the work, the greater are the chances of being promoted and given greater authority and responsibility.

Become visible

One of the problems facing Charles Schwab in the Preview Case was that he did not want to take a job in the Retail Banking Department. People in that department were visible to senior management and thus more likely to be promoted. A visible job has these characteristics:

- Few rules and regulations
- Many rewards for unusual and/or innovative performance
- High publicity about job activities
- Many contacts with senior management
- Relationships that cross departmental lines
- Opportunities for participation in conferences and problem-solving task forces.[39]

Promotion and praise depend partly on an employee's visibility to upper manage-ment. Those left behind because they fail to demand—or deserve—attention often wind up in dead-end positions.

Source: Nancy Wasserman/The Picture Cube.

Be mobile

Those who want a top-management job must be prepared to move. Experience in different functional departments (accounting, marketing, pro-duction, engineering, human resources) will help a person to develop the variety of skills he or she will need to become a general manager. The *type* of job is important, not the *content*. For example, a job that requires turning around an unprofitable division is likely to lead the manager to an understand-ing of organizational structure and control systems. This job might reg changes in product lines, reporting relationships, accounting syst ntion personnel.[40] Managers at IBM had a saying: "IBM means I've P some costs. Experience at different geographical locations within the as an understanding of the organization as a whole and nonal plans call for, of top management. Remember, though, that mobbs with other companies

In order to advance their careers faster ve percent of college graduates many younger employees find it advis rather than wait for promotions change employers within the first three years after graduation. During the trial and establishment phase, many people leave their jobs because the jobs offer no challenge. Joining another company requires establishment of a whole new set of contacts and relationships, but if the move presents the needed challenges and experiences, it can further a career.

Find a mentor

A higher-level manager can be a powerful ally. Most successful managers have had several mentors and have learned valuable lessons from each. Having more than one mentor also minimizes the danger that an individual will be identified too closely with a single mentor. (Remember that having a single mentor was one reason why executives failed to advance.) A variety of mentors helps a person learn how to motivate various types of people and develop a sensitivity to their needs. Notably, managers most often learn what *not* to do from their mentors.

Avoid deadwood

Incompetent supervisors can hinder a career because they might not appreciate a person's abilities. They also will not have their recommendations taken seriously, since they have been bypassed. Asking for a transfer to escape deadwood can be ineffective in some companies because it is considered to be a sign of disloyalty. A more effective method is for the employee to let a superior in another department know of his or her work and availability and let that manager arrange the transfer.

CHAPTER SUMMARY

Gaining an understanding of why certain events occur somewhat predictably over the course of a career has been the focus of this chapter. Individual and organizational factors affect our choice of a career, as well as the probability that we will choose the one in which we might be successful. Individual factors include personality, societal trends, socioeconomic class, and past ⁓rk experiences. Organizational factors include the betw̶rganization, its human-resources practices and is more lik̶ly̶ ̶teristics of the job, the type of industry, performer, and dev̶ ̶ ̶ ̶ ̶ ̶ trategy. When there is a good match When this matching proces̶ ̶ e organization, the employee with the job, be a high ̶ ̶ ̶tment to the firm. ̶ ̶ ̶wcomer may

experience reality shock. The absence of initial challenge, low job satisfaction, and a lack of understanding about what really constitutes good performance all contribute to reality shock.

Your working life can be broken down into four career stages. Each of these stages poses certain problems that you will have to resolve. In the exploration and trial stage, you will be expected to follow orders and perform routine tasks well. During this stage, you should also find mentors who will sponsor you. Some of the psychological issues you will face during this stage are: (1) political insensitivity; (2) loyalty demands; and (3) personal anxiety.

After passing through the exploration and trial stage, you will move into the establishment and advancement stage. The central activity involves specialization and making an independent contribution. Instead of relying solely on a mentor for sponsorship, you will likely turn to your peer group for encouragement and support. Psychological issues revolve around trading off work activities with social and family activities and the need to become independent.

As you approach 40, you probably will enter the maintenance stage of your career. During this stage, you may follow one of three paths. You might be labeled a star and continue to receive assignments that involve responsibility, authority, and high visibility. Or, you might become known as a solid citizen. You will probably not be promoted further because you will have reached your career plateau, but will continue to perform well. (The majority of managers in organizations are "solid citizens.") Or, you could become deadwood. If you plateau but let your performance slip and become indifferent you will be bypassed and cut off from mainstream decision making. (Most of us will plateau sometime during our careers because of the scarcity of higher-level managerial jobs.) Depending on your career path, you are likely to handle a mid-life crisis differently.

In the disengagement career stage, you will begin to withdraw from the day-to-day decision-making processes of the firm. You might play the maverick role, while others spend time establishing relationships outside the organization. As you proceed through this final stage, you would begin to feel the loss of power (influence) and would have to learn not to second guess subordinates when they make operating decisions.

In the final section of this chapter, we presented some guidelines for managing a career. Individual career management includes the ability to spot and correct personal flaws and to choose tactics that can be used to advance a career. Some of the tactics identified were: doing excellent work, becoming visible, being mobile, and finding mentors.

MANAGER'S VOCABULARY

career
career plateau
deadwood
disengagement stage
establishment and advancement stage
exploration and trial stage
golden handcuffs
maintenance stage
mentor
mid-life crisis
reality shock
solid citizens
stars

REVIEW QUESTIONS

1. What is reality shock? How does it influence a person's behavior at work?

2. What are the important personal and organizational factors that affect a person's career decision?

3. What are the important activities, relationships, and psychological issues that people face in the trial and exploration stage of their careers?

4. What are the important activities, relationships, and psychological issues that people face in the establishment and advancement stage of their careers?

5. What are the important activities, relationships, and psychological issues that people face in the maintenance stage of their careers?

6. Name the flaws that can derail a person's upward mobility.

DISCUSSION QUESTIONS

1. In what career stage is Charles Schwab? What are the major questions that he must resolve at this stage in order to be an effective manager?

2. What can organizations do to minimize the impact of reality shock?

3. Why is a mentor important? How can obtain a mentor?

4. Discuss the ways that a person classes of problems that newcomers to an org

5. Why do so ma crisis? Wh to sur

6. How does a manager's career get derailed? What kinds of mistakes has this person likely made? What tactics should a manager use to avoid getting derailed?

MANAGEMENT INCIDENTS AND CASES

Christina Vila

Christina Vila, a woman in her late thirties, was unsure about whether to continue at BayCity Trust Company. All through her MBA program she had been excited about the possibility of employment at BayCity in the marketing department and working directly with Steven Sykes. But, her current situation was not what she had expected it to be.

Right after college, armed with her degree in mathematics, Christina began working as a computer programmer for Crocker National Bank in San Francisco. She progressed quickly from programmer to systems analyst. She enjoyed the detail and problem-solving nature of her position and was most satisfied with the opportunities she had had to work on challenging and important projects. Yet, at 29, Christina suddenly felt the need for something more.

Christina was the sole support of a young daughter and when approached by Systems Analysts, Inc., a leading computer consulting firm in the San Francisco area, she jumped at the opportunity. Christina was sure that the variety of projects to which she would be assigned would give her the chance to learn more about business in general, not just banking.

However, because of her knowledge of banking, SAI placed Christina on a project at BayCity Trust Company. Christina was to head the project team responsible for the development of the software for the automatic teller machines. Her client was to be Steven Sykes.

Even before Christina actually met Steven, she had heard of his reputation as the brightest star on the BayCity horizon. At 45, Steven was everything a manager should be. He knew how to motivate and excite his subordinates, set realistic yet challenging objectives, [ta]lor his managerial responses to the situation. She [se]emed to have an instant rapport. She spent [time] with Steven discussing her current [bus]iness perspective and her disap[pointing] assignment. Steven en-

couraged Christina to "get the proper perspective on business" through an MBA. And, if she decided to go into marketing, he was sure that BayCity would have a place for her.

So, right after Christina completed the programming for the automated teller machines, she left SAI and San Francisco to study for an MBA. Her program was exciting, but demanding. She retained her sense of humor, often joking with classmates that the lowest grade she received was in the marketing of financial services course.

When Christina graduated, Steven kept his word and offered her a lucrative position as the marketing manager for the automated teller machine network and charged her with establishing a marketing campaign for the new ATM system, which was being expanded into all suburban locations. She viewed this as her first true managerial experience.

Christina's MBA training had given her the overall business knowledge and confidence that she had sought. She no longer needed to look to Steven for answers and advice as she had before, but he seemed to want to oversee her work, checking with her constantly. At first, she enjoyed the renewed attention, but she was now becoming resentful. What was once much appreciated support and encouragement she now saw as interference and lack of autonomy. She and Steven began to disagree about how to market the ATM product. Christina wanted her way and was not a good team player, or so she heard from Steven who constantly reminded her that marketing was different from systems. She had built a good working relationship with John Tennyson, who like Christina, was another new marketing manager in commercial accounts and a recent MBA program graduate. She found herself appreciating his suggestions more than Steven's.

Steven, however, was not the only person with whom Christina was having difficulty. The bank's management-training program had assigned Christina a trainee, Shiela Taylor, a young college graduate who was rotating through various departments at the bank. This was Shiela's first assignment in marketing. According to Christina, Shiela was constantly commenting about the routineness of assignments she was given, and Christina felt that Shiela just wouldn't follow directions. Christina couldn't get Shiela to do what she was supposed to do.

Mark Henderson, a veteran bank employee of almost 40 years was also assigned to Christina. Mark loved to tell stories of what banking was like "back in the beginning," before all this "new fangled gadgetry." Although Mark, now 59, would be retiring in several years, he had made it quite clear that he would not retire early. Mark's experience with the company was truly rich, for he had seen BayCity change from a small storefront operation to a multinational financial institution with assets of billions of dollars. Christina felt that Mark didn't have much to offer, and he actually made Christina uncomfortable.

In all, Christina's first few months were not going well. She was questioning her decision to work for the bank and was wondering about whether she should leave. She wasn't a quitter, but she simply didn't know how to alter her situation.[41]

Questions

1. What career stage is Christina presently in? What career issues is she presently experiencing? What issues has she encountered in the past?

2. What mistakes has Christina made in adapting to her managerial situation?

3. If Christina decides to stay, how might a knowledge of career stages and issues help Christina adapt better to her situation?

REFERENCES

1. Adapted from M. London and S. Stumpf, *Managing Careers*. Reading, Mass.: Addison-Wesley, 1982, pp. 15–22.

2. D. Hall, *Careers in Organizations*. Pacific Palisades, Calif.: Goodyear, 1976, p. 4.

3. D. Super, "A Life-span, Life-space Approach to Career Development," *Journal of Vocational Behavior*, 1980, 16:282–298.

4. For a list of personality characteristics that can influence one's career decisions, *see* J. Holland, *Making Vocational Choices: A Theory of Careers*. Englewood Cliffs, N.J.: Prentice-Hall, 1973; J. Latack, "Person/Role Conflict: Holland's Model Extended to Role-Stress Research, Stress Management and Career Development," *Academy of Manage-*

ment Review, 1981, 6:89–103; A. Spokane, "A Review of Research on Person–Environment Congruence in Holland's Theory of Careers," *Journal of Vocational Behavior*, 1985, 26:306–343.

5. S. Ross, "Entry-Level Jobs with a Future," *Business Week's Guide to Careers*, February–March 1984, pp. 35–37ff.

6. P. Blau, J. Gustad, R. Jesson, H. Parnes, and R. Wilcox, "Occupational Choices: A Conceptual Framework," *Industral Relations*, 1956, 9:531ff.

7. M. Lewis, B. Posner, and G. Powell, "The Availability and Helpfulness of Socialization Practices," *Personnel Psychology*, 1983, 36:856–866.

8. A. Howard, K. Shudo, and M. Umeshima, "Motivation and Values among Japanese and American Managers," *Personnel Psychology*, 1983, 36:883–898; R. Pascale and A. Athos, *The Art of Japanese Management: Applications for American Executives*. New York: Simon and Schuster, 1981.

9. J. Slocum, Wm. Cron, R. Hansen, and S. Rawlings, "Business Strategy and the Management of the Plateaued Performer," *Academy of Management Journal*, 1985, 28:133–154.

10. M. Louis, "Surprise and Sense Making: What Newcomers Experience in Entering Unfamiliar Organizational Settings," *Administrative Science Quarterly*, 1980, 25:226–251.

11. E. Huse and T. Cummings, *Organizational Development & Change*, 3rd ed. St. Paul, Minn.: West, 1985.

12. Abridged from London and Stumpf, *Managing Careers*, pp. 65–67.

13. M. London, "Toward a Theory of Career Development," *Academy of Management Review*, 1983, 8:620–630; J. Sonnenfeld and J. Kotter, "The Maturation of Career Theory," *Human Relat*, 1982, 35:19–46; S. Rhodes and M. Doe, Integrated Model of Career Change, *Management Review*, 1983, 8:6

14. D. Super and M. Bohn, O, Belmont, Calif.: Wad, *Psychology of C*, Brothers, 19

15. D. Berl

agers: Effects of Expectations on Performance," *Administrative Science Quarterly,* 1966, **11:**207–223; E. Schein, "The First Job Dilemma," *Psychology Today,* March 1968, **1:**22–37.

16. K. Kram, "Phases of the Mentor Relationship," *Academy of Management Journal,* 1983, **26:**608–625; K. Kram and L. Isabella, "Mentoring Alternatives: The Role of Peer Relationships in Career Development," *Academy of Management Journal,* 1985, **28:**110–132.

17. E. Collins and P. Scott, "Everyone Who Makes It Has a Mentor," *Harvard Business Review,* July–August 1978, **56:**100.

18. G. Roche, "Much Ado about Mentors," *Harvard Business Review,* January–February 1978, **56:**14–28.

19. J. Livingston, "Pygmalion in Management," *Harvard Business Review,* July–August 1969, **47:**81–89.

20. L. Baird and K. Kram, "Career Dynamics: Managing the Superior/Subordinate Relationship," *Organizational Dynamics,* Spring 1983, pp. 46–64.

21. R. Webber, "The Three Career Dilemmas of Career Growth," *MBA,* May 1974, pp. 41–48; R. Webber, "Career Problems of Young Managers," *California Management Review,* 1976, **18**(4):11–33.

22. E. Schein, "Organizational Socialization and the Profession of Management," *Industrial Management Review,* Winter 1968, **9:**1–16.

23. G. Dalton, P. Thompson, and R. Price, "The Four Stages of Professional Careers: A New Look at Performance by Professionals," *Organizational Dynamics,* Summer 1977, pp. 19–42.

24. J. Rosenbaum, "Tournament Mobility: Career Patterns in a Corporation," *Administrative Science Quarterly,* 1979, **24:**220–241.

25. J. Slocum and Wm. Cron, "Job Attitudes and Performance During Three Career Stages," *Journal of Vocational Behavior,* 1985, **26:**126–145.

T. Ference, J. Stoner, and E. Warren, "Managing reer Plateau," *Academy of Management Re-* 2:602–612; J. Stoner, T. Ference, E. Christensen, *Managerial Career* Center for Research on Ca-

reer Development, Columbia University, 1980; J. Veiga, "Plateaued versus Nonplateaued Managers: Career Patterns, Attitudes and Path Potential," *Academy of Management Journal,* 1981, **24:**566–578.

27. A. Korman and R. Korman, *Career Success/Personal Failure.* Englewood Cliffs, N.J.: Prentice-Hall, 1980; B. Greiff and P. Munter, *Trade-offs: Executive, Family and Organizational Life.* New York: New American Library, 1980.

28. J. Carnazza, A. Korman, T. Ference, and J. Stoner, "Plateaued and Nonplateaued Managers: Factors in Job Performance," *Journal of Management,* 1981, **7:**7–27.

29. M. McGill, "Facing the Mid-Life Crisis," *Business Horizons,* November 1977, pp. 5–13; M. McGill, *The 40-to-60 Year-Old Male.* New York: Simon and Schuster, 1980.

30. Abridged from McGill, "Facing the Mid-Life Crisis," 1977, p. 5.

31. McGill, "Facing the Mid-Life Crisis," 1977, pp. 5–9.

32. Compiled from brochures distributed by Arthur Young, August 1985, and conversations with Stan Scott, retired partner, Arthur Young.

33. M. McCall and M. Lombardo, "What Makes a Top Executive?" *Psychology Today,* November 1982, pp. 82–86.

34. R. Bollos, *What Color is Your Parachute?* Berkeley, Calif.: Ten Speed Press, 1972. *Also see* P. Cochran and S. Wartick, "Golden Parachutes: A Closer Look," *California Management Review,* 1984, **26**(4):111–120.

35. L. Pogrebin, *Getting Yours: How to Make the System Work for the Working Woman.* New York: McKay, 1975.

36. A. Souerwine, *Career Strategies: Planning for Personal Growth,* New York: AMACOM, 1978.

37. A. Korman and R. Korman, *Career Success/Personal Failure.* Englewood Cliffs, N.J.: Prentice-Hall, 1980.

38. F. Schoonmaker, *Executive Career Strategy.* New York: American Management Association, 1978.

39. R. Kanter, "Power Failure in Management Circuits," *Harvard Business Review,* July–August 1979, **67**:65–75.

40. J. Veiga, "Mobility Influences During Managerial career Stages," *Academy of Management Journal,* 1983, **26**:64–85; J. Latack, "Career Transitions Within Organizations: An Exploratory Study of Work, Nonwork, and Coping Strategies," *Organizational Behavior and Human Performance,* 1984, **34**:329–340; J. Raelin, "An Examination of Deviant/Adaptive Behavior in the Organizational Careers of Professionals," *Academy of Management Review,* 1984, **9**:413–427.

41. Case prepared specifically for this book by L. Isabella. Used with permission of Professor Lynn A. Isabella, Edwin L. Cox School of Business, Southern Methodist University, Dallas.

Organizational Change

LEARNING OBJECTIVES

After studying this chapter, you should be able to:

- Describe the basic objectives of planned organizational change.

- State the eight phases of the organizational change model.

- Explain the reasons why people and organizations may resist change.

- Describe ways that managers can overcome resistance to change.

- State the four strategies for achieving organizational change.

CHAPTER OUTLINE

PREVIEW CASE

Levi Strauss & Co.

A family-run business for more than 134 years, Levi Strauss had built its reputation on two principles: adherence to quality and one big happy corporate culture. As the company grew, its managers concentrated on manufacturing enough jeans to satisfy the market. The jeans industry grew 15 percent annually for the past 20 years. Retailers could sell all the jeans they received. But that focus left Levi unequipped to deal with the slowdown in jeans sales growth and the market's shift toward more fashionable apparel.

One problem was that Levi was perceived as aloof and inflexible in its dealings with retailers. The company spent little money on advertising and did not support in-store promotions. When the demand for jeans slacked off, Levi lacked the support from retailers to carry the new Levi products. Retailers instead chose companies such as VF (with its Lee brand) or Blue Bell (with its Wrangler line) that had provided them with service.

In an attempt to win customers, Levi tried to broaden its product base. In 1980, it introduced a new line, David Hunter, that was supposed to compete against designer labels, such as Ralph Lauren's Polo brand. But Levi's advertising program did not convince customers that clothing from Levi was comparable to designer lines.

Levi reported a dip in sales in 1982—$2.57 billion, down from $2.85 billion in 1981. Sales rose to $2.73 billion in 1983, a result of retailers' restocking empty inventories and Levi's large or-

ders from Sears, Roebuck and Company and J.C. Penney Company. Some retailers were angry that Levi's could be purchased from these large mass merchandisers, and dropped the Levi line from their specialty stores. The company felt the impact in 1984, when Levi reported an 8 percent dip in sales and a 79 percent drop in net income.

In response to these figures, President Robert Haas, the great-great-grandnephew of founder Levi Strauss, made some dramatic changes in late 1984. First, he expanded Levi's local advertising budget and its participation in special promotions. Levi co-sponsored a local track meet with Seattle's Bernie's, a marketing technique that was unheard of several years ago. Second, Haas recruited a management team that he hopes will be more responsive to the frequent shifts in the apparel in-

Source: Courtesy of Levi Strauss & Co.

dustry. Because the hot market today is high priced fashions made in relatively small quantities, Haas believes that Levi needs to become more of a marketing company and less of a production company. To implement this change, Haas has created a new strategic business unit called Battery Street Enterprises. The major objective of this strategic business unit is to make a push into the fashion market. Battery Street Enterprises is so independent from Levi Strauss that the employees' paychecks do not carry Levi's name. To respond quickly to fashion shifts, Battery Street Enterprises has fewer layers of middle managers than the jeans company. The president of this company told his managers

that they would be spending most of their time with the retailer, traveling with salespeople, and just listening to what retailers want.

Haas is trying to make the jeans company more market-oriented and flexible. He is searching for people with marketing, as opposed to manufacturing backgrounds, to join the executive team. To increase Levi's profitability, Haas reduced the company's production capacity by 15 percent, closing 14 U.S. plants and five in international locations. This action resulted in a loss of jobs for about 5,300 employees, reducing Levi's work force to 37,000. Levi offered generous severance and retraining benefits to all discharged workers.[1]

t's far too early to tell if Haas's changes are only temporary or whether these changes will have a major impact on the company. How can a company go from one of the best-managed companies cited in Peters and Waterman's 1982 book, *In Search of Excellence,* to one that has declining profits and management problems?

The answer is that organizations are never static. In Chapter 1, we highlighted the eight basic characteristics of successfully managed companies identified by Peters and Waterman. According to a follow-up article in *Business Week* (November 5, 1984) at least 14 of the 43 "excellent" companies cited by Peters and Waterman have reported declines in profits since that time. In addition to Levi Strauss, Atari, Avon, Caterpillar Tractor, Chesebrough Pond, and Delta Air Lines have all experienced a decline in profits during 1984. For example, Delta Air Lines, which reported record profits by minimizing debt and maintaining a close-knit culture to keep labor costs low, was unable to adapt fast enough to the new competitive, deregulated environment. The Atlanta-based carrier was slow in recognizing the importance of computers for keeping track of ticket prices in different markets. Consequently, Delta failed to meet competitors' lower prices as quickly as some other airlines did. This partially accounted for Delta's $86.7 million loss in 1983. Even successful companies must effectively adjust to broad business, regulatory, and economic trends.

Successful companies are not forever successful. As we discussed in Chapters 3, 4, and 8, shifts in consumer preferences, technologic   throughs, and demands from diverse groups in society are some   underlie the need for organizational change. Most of us   employees, managers, or consultants, are involved with o changing. If we are to be effective managers, we must learn how to deal creatively with the conditions that require organizations to change and with the tensions and frustrations of change in our daily lives. One of the purposes of this chapter is to focus on the ways that organizations can survive in our changing world.

THE IMPACT OF CHANGE

Change is an integral part of our society. Many types of change, of course, are beyond the control of an organization, like industry deregulation. Other changes can be created and guided by the organization. One author has stated:

> Change has always been a part of the human condition. What is different now is the pace of change, and the prospect that it will come faster and faster, affecting every part of life, including personal values, morality, and religion, which seem almost remote from technology. . . . So swift is the acceleration, that trying to "make sense" of change will become our basic industry.[2]

In his penetrating book, *Future Shock,* Alvin Toffler argued that humanity is now a part of an environment so unfamiliar and complex that it is threatening millions with **future shock.**[3] Future shock occurs when the types of changes and their speed of introduction overpower the individual's capacity to adapt to them. The problem is not that a particular change is too difficult to handle; rather it is that so many things are changing at the same time that a new kind of society, the *temporary society,* has emerged and new ways of dealing with it are needed. This new society is characterized by the temporary nature of housing, jobs, friendships, and neighborhoods. Although people have always faced change in their environment, it is the ever-accelerating *rate* of change that causes problems. Events move so quickly that long-term stability is threatened, and even values may become a victim of a "throw-away" society. The relative rates of change in six areas of our lives over the past 100 years are shown in Fig. 21.1.

The Challenge for Management

Change has become so rapid that we scarcely have time to adjust before more change takes place. The decades of the 1970s and 1980s have been called the *explosion* decades; explosions in knowledge, technology, communications, and global competition. The dramatic changes that have affected youth, women, minority groups, values, morals, and politics contribute to the challenge of the 1980s. The lesson is clear for today's organization: Yesterday's corporate successes mean very little in a world of rapidly changing markets, products, values, and life-styles. Managers must recognize when change is necessary, and, above all, they must be able to make changes when required to do so. Some companies have created specialized strategic planning or venture departments whose primary purpose is to help their firms innovate (Chapter 8). These departments spend a great deal of time assessing, developing, and implementing new programs to improve the performance of their organizations.

Executives today are bombarded by constantly changing information and work. No managerial functions appear to be immune from the knowledge explosion. Personnel, organizational development, and training managers are faced with many new employment, training, and safety acts (Chapter 18). There is an ever-increasing demand for human-relations programs to cope with changes in the attitudes and expectations of the work force. People involved in production, research and development, maintenance, and transportation are faced with tremendous technological advances in the fields of communications and electronics. Financial managers must cope with new accounting procedures, changes in tax and corporate laws, and fluctuations of the money markets.

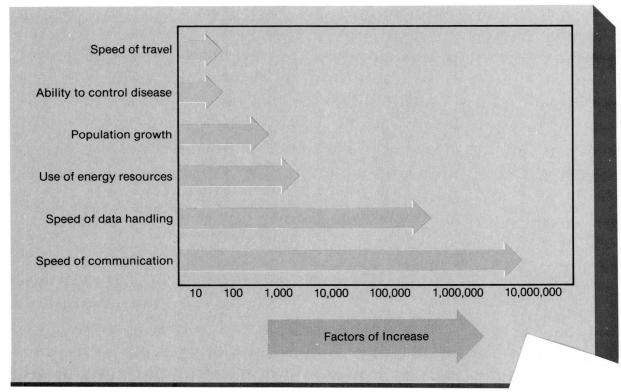

FIGURE 21.1
Rates of Change over the Past 100 Years

An important part of the manager's job is to achieve stability in the face of constant interruptions. For example, a conductor must coax acceptable music from a symphony orchestra, some of whose members may be preoccupied with personal problems, while stage hands are having trouble with the lighting and the air-conditioning system is changing the auditorium into a giant freezer. Like the conductor of an orchestra, managers must bring a degree of order to the system.

Managers can deal constructively with change and stability in two ways. First, managers can react to changes as needed. This approach is often called

INTERNATIONAL FOCUS

World Banking

Walter Wriston's vision of the future is shaped by what he calls the "convergence of the technologies of telecommunications and the computer." Together, they have created an "information society" in which vast amounts of intelligence whip around the world at incredible speed. To Wriston, this flow of information has become an elemental force in the modern world. "I can't think of anything that you do, literally, that isn't tied to that flow," the recently retired chairman of Citicorp says.

Wriston's vision is no mere wishful thinking. It powerfully influenced the direction in which he took Citicorp—and indeed, he believes, the technologies have created an entirely new system of world finance. Every business is based on comparative advantage, Wriston explains, and the banking industry's comparative advantage "since the dawn of time" has been the confidential information it has about its customers. With that knowledge, bankers are able to grant loans with the reasonable expectation that the money will be repaid. Other potential lenders who don't share that information are at a big disadvantage because they can't judge, for instance, how risky a particular loan would be or what the terms should be.

In recent years, of course, large corporations have been publishing "incredible amounts" of information about themselves. In a paper-based society, however, it was difficult for an individual or company to assemble all this available information. But, when the delivery system for information changed from paper-based to electronic, and giant data bases were compiled, the information became available to anyone with a computer terminal on his desk. A person isn't interested in finding out in five days what his balance is in Denver. He wants it now. Likewise with his balances in Paris, London, Rome and wherever.

To satisfy that demand, Citibank has spent more than a half-billion dollars on telecommunications, computers, software and the rest. "OK, we're pretty

Source: Clem Morgello, "The World of Banking According to Wriston," *Dun's Business Month*, February 1985, pp. 61–62. Reprinted with permission of *Dun's Business Month*. Copyright © 1985 by Dun & Bradstreet Publications Corporation.

fire fighting. Every time a problem appears, small changes are sought to solve the immediate problem. Second, managers can develop a program of ***planned organizational change.*** The planned-change approach requires managers to deal not only with present problems, but also with anticipated problems.

REACTIVE CHANGE

The first approach—fire-fighting—is relatively simple and inexpensive. It was appropriate when the pace of change was slower, competition was not as severe, and when organizations were smaller and less complicated. Today,

good at it," says Wriston. "But who are our competitors?" His own answer: Reuters, the Dow Jones news service, IBM and the telephone companies, "all of whom have a comparative advantage over financial institutions." They have been in the technology business a long time, have enormous resources and long experience with various aspects of gathering, packaging and distributing information. And the digitized information that rides the stream of electrons up to a communications satellite and back to earth goes at the same speed and for the same price whether it's news of wars, elections, tennis matches or a corporate balance sheet.

How will bankers survive in this radically new environment?

It's "very, very clear" to Wriston what they must do. To begin with, they must know the cost of the various services they provide. Surprisingly, many bankers don't. "They're professionals with other people's money," says Wriston, "but amateurs with their own." He confesses that when he took over as Citicorp chairman his board "didn't have a clue" as to what things cost.

Second, banks will have to develop fee-based business in areas where they have a comparative advantage—"what we call investment banking. Others call it merchant banking—mergers and acquisitions, financial advice, trading and so forth."

The third segment of Wriston's bank of the future is the consumer business, because, he says, echoing bank robber Willie Sutton, "that's where the money is." He doesn't believe that banks can fund their operations over an extended period in the professional market because it isn't large enough, "but there's a trillion-and-a-half dollars out there in the consumer's pocket."

Summing up the changes he sees for banking, Wriston comments, "I'm not saying that we're going to be doing things a lot differently tomorrow than we did yesterday. And if you sit around longing for the way things were yesterday, there isn't going to be any tomorrow."

fire-fighting is appropriate only for minor adjustments that are integral parts of managers' day-to-day jobs, not in response to systematic, long-term changes in the environment. Here are two examples of reactive change: (1) Jerry Cooper, vice-president of human resources for Henry C. Beck Company, designed a new performance-appraisal form to take into consideration the rising cost of job-related injuries on construction sites; and (2) Jerry Nash, plant manager of a Xerox parts-distribution service center modified a sales form because the old form led to many errors. These are small changes and can be handled quickly by an effective manager.

Planned change

The second approach—planned organizational change—is found more often in today's organizations than in the past. It is the deliberate attempt to modify the functioning of the total organization or any of its major departments in order to increase effectiveness.[4] Planned change usually is more extensive than fire-fighting and involves a greater commitment of time and resources. It requires more skills and knowledge for successful implementation and can lead to serious problems if implementation is unsuccessful.

When the editors of *Fortune* magazine studied companies that were successful innovators, they found a zest for letting a "thousand flowers bloom" with a disdain for the status quo. For example, in the late 1970s, General Electric was one of the nation's 10 largest industrial corporations.[5] Most of its sales came from relatively slow-moving products. When John Welch became the chief executive officer of GE in 1981, he told the company's managers to concentrate on faster-growing fields, many in high tech. Any product line that didn't fit the plan would be sold. Within a year, Welch sold off more than 100 product lines, from small appliances to air conditioners. To keep products flowing, GE encourages its managers to find new ways to revitalize their businesses. For example, when the courts decided that companies could generate their own electricity from the heat produced in manufacturing, GE's managers responsible for the electrical-equipment line jumped at this opportunity. They devised a whole new method of building, financing, and operating generating systems for their customers.

PROCESS OF PLANNED ORGANIZATIONAL CHANGE

Figure 21.2 presents an eight-step process of planned organizational change. These eight steps represent how a planned change program should proceed; ideally, each step should be taken in sequence. Although the actual introduction of change in many organizations may not follow this logical, step-by-step sequence, success is likely to be greater when managers follow it as closely as possible.

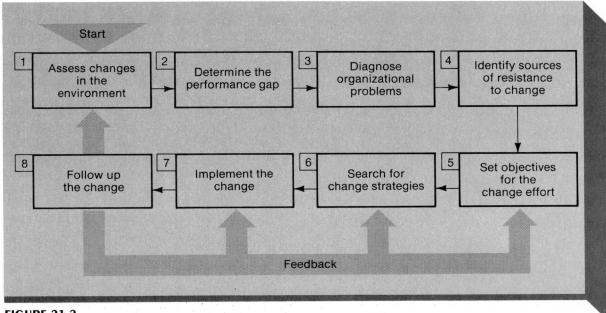

FIGURE 21.2
Process of Planned Organizational Change

Assess Changes in the Environment [1] *

An organization's external environment is in a constant state of flux. Major contributing forces include those of competition, technology, politics, and culture (Chapters 3–5). One of the primary functions of managers is to cope with these forces and the changes they cause so that the organization can function effectively.

The market for a company's goods or services may be stable (with respect to price, materials, supplies, suppliers, customers, governmental regulations, and so on), or it may be unstable. Relatively stable markets can be found in the brewing, insurance, and commercial baking industries. Within each of these industries, the products, customers, suppliers, methods of distribution, and price are similar. Extensive advertising campaigns are carried on by firms in these industries to differentiate products and create a demand. Miller Brewing Company makes "Lite®" beer and Stroh's sells Schlitz "Light" beer. These two firms compete for the same beer drinkers, charge similar prices, negotiate with the same international union, and face similar distribution problems. Insurance premiums of the large insurance companies, suc`    ` State

---

* Note that the numbers in boxes in this section correspond to the steps in the p'
Fig. 21.2.

Farm, Allstate, Prudential, Travelers, and Hartford, are very similar. The difference among these firms is in the service that each insurance agent promises to give to the policyholder.

In Chapter 8, we discussed the strategic-planning problems facing companies that operate multiple businesses, which sell unrelated products. Some firms that have adopted this strategy include W. R. Grace, ITT, Gulf + Western, and Alco Standard. For example, W. R. Grace is a diversified, worldwide company that operates 2400 plants in 47 states and 43 countries and employs 78,000 people.[6] Grace had operations in six different businesses and reported sales of over $6 billion in 1985. Each of these businesses represents different challenges to Grace's management in terms of governmental regulations, competitors, and customers. In the food business, it operates four types of restaurants: (1) dinnerhouses, such as Houlihan's Old Place, Baxter's and R.J.'s; (2) Mexican, such as Tequila Willi's, El Torito, and LaFiesta; (3) family style, such as Coco's and Jojo's; and (4) fast food, such as T. J. Applebee's and Del Taco. The problems faced by managers of these restaurants are vastly different from those of managers running Grace's retail businesses (J. B. Robinson Jewelers, Herman's sportswear, Handy Dan House Works). Grace's top-management team faces a real challenge in trying to keep all of these diverse businesses profitable.

Another problem for companies is the rapid rate of technological change. An interesting fact is that 93 percent of all scientists who have ever lived are alive today. Most industries have undergone tremendous technological advances since World War II. In some industries, the technology of 20 years ago is now outdated. Consider, for example, the rapid increase in the use of computers and related management information systems in the insurance industry. Before the development of computers, most records were posted by hand or with the aid of elementary accounting machines. In response to the computer and electronic processing methods, most insurance firms have undergone several structural and job-design changes. High rates of obsolescence have encouraged many companies to adopt a short-term payback period, so that they will not be caught with outmoded equipment. New technology can reduce costs and improve quality, and those companies that are slow in adopting it run the risk of declining profits.

DETERMINE THE PERFORMANCE GAP   2

The next step in the change process is to determine the *performance gap.* This is the difference between what the organization could do and what it actually does to take advantage of its opportunities. The gap might be positive as in the case of new marketing opportunities resulting from changes in consumer tastes, or it might be negative if a market is lost because of new competition.

A performance gap may occur when new technical breakthroughs are made and may persist for some time before it is recognized. (In fact, it may never be recognized.) When recognized it must also be thought to have significant consequences for the firm, if it is to be narrowed or bridged. Consider the performance gap experienced by Nike.

IN PRACTICE
Nike

Nike's victories at the 1984 summer Olympic games were bitter-sweet. Athletes wearing its shoes were promised money if they got medals. What Nike did not count on was the number of medals won. Nike wound up paying its athlete-promoters more than $2 million. If the Russians and other countries had not boycotted these games, the payout might have been less. The result was a 65% decline in earnings.

Founded in 1972 by University of Oregon runner Philip Knight, Nike grew rapidly. When jogging peaked around 1982, Nike did not adapt to the changes in the market. Nike was forced to sell running shoes below market value and reported a $27 million loss. Nike has been slow to develop a footwear franchise system and it was late to enter the fast-growing market for shoes worn by Jane-Fonda-style aerobics. To maintain its profits during the sales slump, Nike diversified into apparel and established overseas distributors. While Nike apparel accounted for 21% of the company's sales in 1984, profits have been disappointing.

Nike's problems have been reflected in the number of top management who have left the company. Because of Knight's fondness for recruiting athletes, often other Oregon alumni, the management at its Beaverton, Oregon, plant resembles a fraternity. In 1984, Knight replaced Robert Woodell as president and put in Neil Goldschmidt. Both are Oregon alumni. Woodell now manages new product lines for Knight.

Industry observers believe that Knight should bring in non-Oregon people to help run this $92 million company. These observers do not believe that Knight has the ability to solve Nike's problems. Because of Nike's problems, Knight's stock is worth $130 million less than it was in 1983. However, despite these problems, Knight signed Michael Jordan, the Chicago Bull's basketball star, to a five-year, $2.5 million contract just to wear Nike shoes.[7]

Diagnose Organizational Problems 3

The change process often gets underway early in the diagnostic step, depending on who does the diagnosis and the methods chosen for analyzing the problem. The objective of this step is to identify the nature and extent of the problem before taking action. The caution *diagnosis should precede action* may seem obvious, but its importance is often overlooked or ignored. Hard and results-oriented managers often impatiently push for solutions problem itself is clear.

Most organizational problems have multiple causes; there is seldom one simple and obvious cause for a problem. Assuming that Phil Knight wanted you to help him solve Nike's problems, what would you do? As part of the diagnosis step, you might begin by asking him these questions:

1. What are the specific problems you believe have to be corrected?
2. What are the causes of these problems?
3. What must be changed to solve these problems?
4. What forces are likely to work for and against these changes?
5. What are the objectives of these changes and how will they be measured?

A variety of data-gathering techniques have been used successfully—attitude surveys, conferences, informal interviews, and team meetings—to diagnose problems. The central concern of these approaches is to gather data that are not biased by a few dominant persons in the organization or by consultants. In order for Knight to answer your five questions, he might have to hold a series of meetings with his staff and gather information from throughout the organization.

Interpersonal problems usually require extensive attitude surveys, which may involve the use of outside consultants to conduct interviews and analyze the data. Attitude surveys usually tap the feelings of employees effectively. This method may enable management to evaluate employee attitudes about pay, types of work, and working conditions. Survey responses should be recorded anonymously so that employees can express their real feelings without fear of reprisal from management. Because attitude surveys can provide insight into many potential problems, managers or their consultants should formulate relevant questions covering a wide variety of work-related factors.[8]

Identify Sources of Resistance to Change [4]

Although few organizational changes are complete failures, few also go as smoothly as managers would like. Most changes encounter resistance; as a result, they often take longer than expected and desired, they sometimes hurt morale, and they often cost a great deal in terms of management time and emotional upheaval. Some managers do not initiate needed changes because they are afraid that they are incapable of successfully carrying them off.

Organizational change efforts often run into various forms of resistance, and experienced managers are generally all too aware of them. Yet, surprisingly few managers take the time to think through the reasons that might cause people to resist change. Instead, they often charge right into implementing change, using their past experiences as guidelines. The forms of resistance that managers might experience can be separated into two categories: individual and organizational.

Individual RESISTANCE

Some people resist change because they fear they will not be able to develop the new skills and behaviors required of them. Peter Drucker has stated that the major obstacle to organizational change is managers' inability to change their own attitudes and behaviors as rapidly as their organizations require. Even when managers understand the need for change, they sometimes are unable to make the change called for. Figure 21.3 shows four reasons why people tend to resist change.[9]

Self-interest.   People often resist change because they think they will lose something of value; that is, self-interest becomes dominant. People focus on their own best interests and not on those of the total organization. Internal political alliances form and attempt to influence change efforts before, during, and after implementation. When the self-interests of powerful or vocal individuals or groups are threatened, political action resembles armed camps publicly fighting over the spoils of battle. This happened when Mesa Oil Corporation tried to buy Gulf Oil in 1984 and when Bendix Corporation attempted to buy Martin Marietta Corporation. However, in most cases, self-interest does not lead to such extreme and public displays of resistance.

Misunderstanding or lack of trust.   People resist change when they do not understand its implications, which may occur because of misunderstanding or a lack of trust. Unless managers quickly bring these misunderstandings to the surface and clarify them, resistance can build. This type of resistance often takes managers by surprise, especially if they assume that people resist change only when it is not in their best interests. For example, the manager of a 200-person office recently attended a seminar on improving the quality of work life. During the seminar, the concept of flextime had been discussed. When

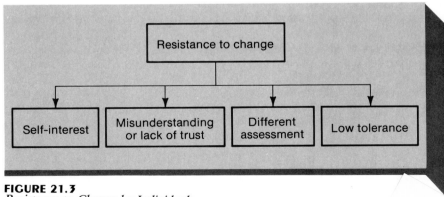

FIGURE 21.3
Resistance to Change by Individuals

she returned to her office, she discussed the concept with several vice-presidents, then announced the decision to implement flexible work hours to her employees. Because few of her employees had ever heard of this approach, the rumor mill got into high gear. One rumor, for instance, was that flexible working hours meant that most people would have to work whenever their supervisors asked them to work, including evenings and Saturdays. The local union president called a meeting and the members voted to send the manager a letter demanding that the flextime concept be dropped. The manager, completely surprised by this reaction, dropped the idea.

Different assessment. Another common reason for resistance to change is that people may assess the situation differently from their managers. Managers sometimes initiate change believing that they have all the relevant information needed. They believe that anyone with the same information would make the same decision. Unfortunately, neither assumption is correct. The president of a steel company was shocked to learn that verification of a large order had been lost in the factory. If not discovered, this loss could have severely hurt the company's profitability. Within a week, the president outlined a new set of communication and coordination procedures to link marketing, sales, and manufacturing. Because of the sensitivity of the issue, the president told only the senior vice-presidents. When they were announced the changes immediately ran into massive resistance from employees in sales and marketing who had assessed the problem differently. Several managers in the sales and marketing departments threatened to quit if the reorganization were implemented.

Low tolerance. Some people have a low tolerance for any change and may resist a change even when they think it is a good one. For example, a person who receives a promotion will probably be very happy. But this person might also feel uneasy and resist giving up certain aspects of the current situation. A new and different job will require new and different behavior and relationships, as well as a loss of some currently satisfactory activities and relationships. In Chapter 1, we discussed the different job activities required for successful first-line and middle managers. For example, the worker who is promoted from the ranks to a first-line manager's job will probably have to stop drinking with the gang, being a member of their bowling team, and the like. The new job requires that person to relate to other managers and establish some distance from former fellow workers. If changes are too great and an individual's tolerance for change is low he or she is likely to resist the changes.

Organizational resistance

Most organizations are designed to restrict innovation. That is, they customarily are designed to do a certain few things and to do them consistently

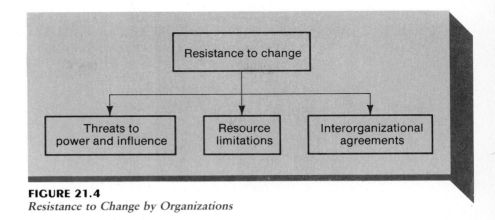

FIGURE 21.4
Resistance to Change by Organizations

and well. To ensure stability and consistency, an organization may create strong defenses against change. Three types of organizational resistance are illustrated in Fig. 21.4.

Threats to power and influence. Organizations resist change primarily because they want stability. While this is understandable, it is the manager's job to balance the need for stability against the need for change. The typical bureaucratic organization defines jobs narrowly, spells out lines of authority and responsibility, and emphasizes the hierarchical flow of information and orders from the top down. It stresses discipline through the use of rewards and punishments. Novel ideas and new uses of resources may be perceived as threats to the internal distribution of power and status. This type of resistance to change can be seen at Texas Instruments.

IN PRACTICE
TEXAS INSTRUMENTS

Texas Instruments (TI) is a large, high-tech company in the electronics industry. It has about 68,000 employees in 45 plants in 18 countries. In the early 1960s, the company found itself facing a changing environment, with rapid product obsolescence, explosive markets, and increasing competition. TI recognized these changes and developed a plan aimed at innovating while maintaining tight control over production costs. Attempts to implement the plan encountered extreme difficulties, however. The major problem was the firm's technical system. While it was designed to control production costs, it seemed to stifle innovation. The company was structured into different product customer centers. Each was geared to improving the production processes for a particular product. Managers focused on short-term efficiency with little attention to

(continued)

long-term innovation. They attended to their own products and customers, while ignoring the broader interactions needed for long-range projections and innovations at TI. Other departments supported this short-run production orientation. Participation by middle managers was low, communication was mainly top down, and there was little feedback to the various managerial levels.[10]

Resource limitations. Although some organizations emphasize stability, others would change if they had the resources necessary to implement a change. Let us consider the plight of the asbestos industry. Efforts by Congress to set up a fund that would compensate workers suffering from asbestos-related diseases has had a tremendous impact on companies in this industry. Symptoms of asbestos disease do not show up until long after exposure, but some insurance companies have refused to compensate workers unless symptoms began to occur during employment with the company. Currently, there are more than 23,000 claims for compensation pending in the courts. Manville Corporation, a major manufacturer of asbestos, was forced into bankruptcy in 1982 when workers and their families filed a $2 billion lawsuit against the company. In December 1984, Congress authorized the Asbestos Claims Facility, an organization of producers and their insurers to settle workers' claims out of court. To join the claims facility, a company must agree to pay a person or family up to $95,000 regardless of when the first symptoms of asbestos disease appear. Proponents say that this award is about what victims could expect to win from juries, but that the victims will receive their awards much more quickly.[11] Without congressional help, many asbestos companies would go out of business.

Another example is the decline of central business districts in cities. Many retailers watch their customers desert them for the greater convenience of suburban shopping centers. Yet, these retailers usually are unable to raise the funds needed to provide the parking facilities and rapid transit systems required and to modernize their stores in order to counter this trend.

Resource limitations are not confined to organizations that lack assets. Asset-rich organizations may find themselves hard pressed for cash because they have invested much of their capital in fixed assets (equipment, buildings, land). They may be locked into the present by their assets. These past investments are called ***sunk costs.*** Companies may decide to terminate or sell off all or part of a business rather than put new money into it. That is exactly what International Harvester did in 1984 when it sold its line of agricultural equipment products to Tenneco. Tenneco owns J. I. Case, another agricultural equipment manufacturer. By merging the two companies, Tenneco's top management feels that excess capacity can be eliminated from the industry by closing down the least efficient J. I. Case and International Harvester plants.

The marketing and physical distribution departments will be merged to further improve efficiency. Although eligible for many termination benefits, the 13,000 persons thrown out of work showed understandable resistance to this change.

Interorganizational agreements.   Interorganizational agreements can create obligations that limit future options. Labor contracts are the most common examples. Some actions that were once considered major rights of management (right to hire and fire, assignment of personnel to jobs, promotions) have now become subjects of negotiation. Other kinds of contracts and commitments can also create obligations for management. Advocates of change may find their plans delayed because of arrangements with competitors, commitments to suppliers, pledges to public officials in return for licenses or permits, or promises to contractors. Although agreements are sometimes ignored or violated, the legal costs for settlement can be expensive; lost customers might be hesitant to buy the product again and a declining credit rating can be disastrous.

Overcoming resistance to change

Not all resistance is bad; it can bring some benefits. Resistance may encourage management to reexamine its proposals for change to be sure that they are appropriate. In this way, employees can operate as a check-and-balance to ensure that management properly plans and implements change. If justifiable resistance causes management to screen its proposed changes more carefully, it may encourage more careful management decisions.

Does it follow, then, that managers must expect strong resistance when trying to change organizations or individuals? Our answer is no. Resistance to change will probably never stop completely, but managers can learn to succeed and to minimize resistance by planning change more carefully. Kotter and Schlesinger have identified four methods commonly used by managers in overcoming resistance to change; they are summarized in Table 21.1.[12]

Education and communication.   One of the most common ways to overcome resistance to change is to inform and educate people about change before it happens. Communication of ideas helps people to understand the need for and the logic of change. This method is ideal when (1) resistance is based on inadequate or inaccurate information and analysis; and (2) the managers proposing the change need the resistors to implement it.

Use of this method requires a good relationship between the initiators of the change and the resistors. If there is a poor relationship, the resistors may not believe what they hear. The Preview Case in Chapter 8 highlighted how Lee Iacocca at Chrysler put together a series of presentations that explained the changes required to keep Chrysler alive and the reasons for them. He asked for union and nonunion personnel to make wage concessions that would save Chrysler $1.2 billion. He also cut the work force from 160,000 to

TABLE 21.1 ■ METHODS FOR DEALING WITH RESISTANCE TO CHANGE

METHOD	COMMONLY USED IN SITUATIONS	ADVANTAGES	DRAWBACKS
Education + communication	Where there is a lack of information or inaccurate information and analysis	Once persuaded, people will often help with the implementation of the change.	Can be very time-consuming if lots of people are involved.
Participation + involvement	Where the initiators do not have all the information they need to design the change, and where others have considerable power to resist.	People who participate will be committed to implementing change, and any relevant information they have will be integrated into the change plan.	Can be very time-consuming if participators design an inappropriate change.
Negotiation + agreement	Where someone or some group will clearly lose out in a change, and where that group has considerable power to resist.	Sometimes it is a relatively easy way to avoid major resistance.	Can be too expensive in many cases if it alerts others to negotiate for compliance.
Manipulation + cooptation	Where other tactics will not work, or are too expensive.	It can be a relatively quick and inexpensive solution to resistance problems.	Can lead to future problems if people feel manipulated.

Source: Adapted from J. Kotter and L. Schlesinger, "Choosing Strategies for Change," *Harvard Business Review*, March–April 1979, 57:111.

Over a six-month period, Iacocca made this presentation at all 40 Chrysler production plants and to numerous government and banking officials. Iacocca made his case believable.

Participation and involvement. If managers who are proposing change involve potential resistors in some aspect of its design and implementation, they can often forestall or at least minimize resistance. Figure 21.5 shows the inverse relationship between participation and resistance: the greater the participation, the less the resistance.

Many managers have strong feelings about participation. Some managers feel that change efforts should always include participation, while others feel that this is a mistake. Participation works best when those proposing change need information from others in order to design and implement the change or when they need a major commitment from others to make implementation successful. Research has found that participation leads to commitment. Nevertheless, participation does have its drawbacks. (See Chapter 15 for a vivid description of these drawbacks.) If it is not carefully managed, participation can lead to a poor solution. It can also be enormously time-consuming. When change must be made quickly and will probably be resisted in any event, the involvement of others may simply not be worth it.

Negotiation and agreement. Another way to deal with resistance is to offer incentives or rewards to potential or active resistors. This method of dealing with resistance is particularly appropriate when it is clear that someone is going to lose out as a result of the change. For example, Lee Iacocca convinced workers at Chrysler that the corporation could survive only if both union and management employees agreed to wage and benefits concessions. Many people lost their jobs when Chrysler cut its management staff in half and closed 19 obsolete plants. However, those who remained were committed to the changes that Iacocca proposed to save Chrysler.

Manipulation and cooptation. In some situations, managers may also resort to manipulation in their attempts to influence others. This normally

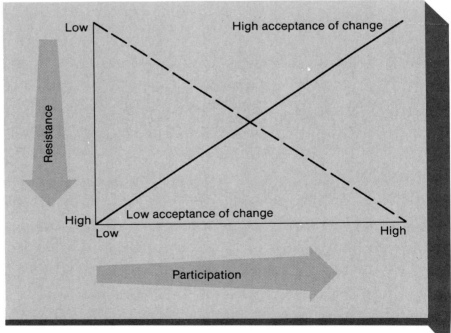

FIGURE 21.5
Effect of Participation on Resistance to Change

involves the selective use of information and the careful construction of events. One common form of manipulation is cooptation. We discussed this concept in Chapter 3 as a political method that organizations use to handle disturbances. Coopting individuals usually involves giving them desirable roles in the design and implementation of the change process. Coopting a group involves giving one of its leaders a role in the change process. This is not a form of participation because those who are proposing the change do not really want advice from the coopted people, but merely their endorsement and lack of resistance.

Cooptation can be a relatively inexpensive and easy way to gain an individual or group's support, but it has some drawbacks. If people feel that they have been tricked into not resisting, are not being treated fairly, or are being lied to, they may respond very negatively to the change. Many managers have found that, by initially coopting subordinates, they have ultimately created more resistance to the change than if they had chosen another method. If those who were coopted then use their ability and influence to propose changes that are not in the best interests of the organization, the manager faces another set of problems.

Choosing a method to overcome resistance

The method that a manager should use to overcome resistance to change depends on the four situational factors shown in Table 21.2. These situational factors should not be thought of individually but as interrelated parts of the existing situation.[13]

Amount and kind of resistance anticipated.   All other things being equal, the greater the anticipated resistance, the more difficult it will be simply to overcome it. The negotiation-and-agreement and manipulation-and-cooptation methods are probably less appropriate for combatting strong resistance than are the education or participation methods.

Power of resistors.   The greater the power of resistors with respect to others in the organization, the more the proponent of change must involve

TABLE 21.2 ■ SITUATIONAL FACTORS INVOLVED IN CHOOSING A METHOD TO OVERCOME RESISTANCE

- Amount and type of resistance anticipated
- Power of potential or active resistors
- Location of needed information and commitment
- Stakes involved
- Short-term and long-term effects

the resistors. Conversely, the stronger the proponent's position, the greater is the opportunity to use negotiation or manipulation.

Location of needed information and commitment.   The more that change initiators anticipate the need of information and commitment from others to help design and implement change, the more they should use the education and participation methods. Gaining vital information and commitment from others requires time and their involvement.

Stakes involved.   The greater the short-run potential for risks to the organization's performance and survival if the situation is not changed, the greater is the likelihood that managers should try to negotiate and/or use manipulation to overcome resistance.

Short-term and long-term effects.   Accurate assessment of these four factors still leaves the manager with the choice between short- and long-term effects. Forcing change on people can have many negative effects, both for the short and long term. Using the education-and-communication and the negotiation-and-agreement methods can overcome initial resistance and lead to long-term benefits. The participation and involvement method can minimize both short- and long-term resistance. The manipulation and cooptation method may be expedient in the short run but can lead to long-term resistance.

Let us look at the types of resistance William Buehler of AT&T met when he attempted to change AT&T General Business Systems and his lack of success in overcoming them. Buehler's experience at AT&T illustrates the difficulties managers face when attempting organizational change. Although most managers are not faced with the same problems, the types of resistance Buehler faced are familiar to all managers.

IN PRACTICE
AT&T General Business Systems

In recent years, AT&T has been trying to shift its strategy and culture from a service-oriented utility to a market-driven communications business. This strategic change is largely in response to rapidly growing opportunities in the communications/information industry and the recent divestiture of its Bell operating companies. A key part of the change was the creation on January 1, 1983 of AT&T Information Systems as the unregulated equipment-marketing unit of the company. Information Systems was organized into two parts. General Business Systems, headed by newly appointed vice president William Buehler, sells smaller systems at high volume. National Business Systems, run by Robert Casale, markets to large accounts. The following recounts how Buehler created a highly successful corporate culture at General Business Systems, and how the large corporation responded to that success.

(continued)

In creating a new market-oriented culture, Buehler drew heavily from Peters and Waterman's bestseller, *In Search of Excellence*. He developed and gave to the sales force a sheet of marching orders titled: "What We Aspire to Be." It contained verbatim phrases from the book like: "customer is king," "reward results, not process," "staff supports the line," and "keep it simple." This list was the only guide given the workforce; there were no detailed plans or directives. Buehler stated: "I wanted the team to know from the start that this was an entrepreneurial venture, and they were to abide by these points in a way that worked best for them."

Also from the start, Buehler was highly visible. He was a charismatic leader who loved the limelight and constantly dominated meetings and conversations with his market-oriented, performance-driven message. Putting aside his family life and hobbies, Buehler began working 16 hour days. He traveled to all 27 branches to meet employees. For many, this was the first time they had seen an AT&T vice president. During these visits, Buehler often had lunch (e.g., hoagie sandwiches) with the lowest-level staff. This was a radical departure from standards practiced at AT&T.

Buehler instituted a number of organizational changes to support the new culture. He dropped AT&T's endless memos, meetings, strict chain of command, detailed planning manuals, and threw out employee tests. He put salespeople on the highest commission plan in AT&T's history. Buehler posted individual sales monthly in a prominent place in each sales office. Then, each month he got rid of those who couldn't meet his tough quotas. In the first year, about one-third of the salesforce quit, were transferred, or were fired.

In moving General Business Systems to the new culture, Buehler demanded strict obedience from his team. When managers disagreed with his decisions, he often told them to support the decisions as if they were their own. Buehler bluntly stated: "If I found one of my managers trying to sabotage any decision I made, I'd cut his neck off."

Buehler's salespeople had trouble at first picking up the new culture and achieving results. Few sales were made in the first quarter, while the more traditional National Business Systems was meeting its quota. Equally troublesome was the reception Buehler's group was getting from the rest of AT&T. He recalled: "Employees in different parts of the company enjoyed seeing us fail." About the same time, Buehler's boss and major supporter, Archie McGuill, left the company. McGuill, a former IBM executive had been brought in to reshape AT&T's business marketing. Like Buehler, McGuill was the antithesis of the traditional Bell manager. He was combative and performance-driven, and encouraged his managers to be entrepreneurs. Insiders suggested that McGuill had left AT&T rather than take a lesser job because higher-ups found him difficult to control.

Shortly after McGuill's departure, General Business Systems caught "Buehler fever" and started bringing in the sales. Salespeople were exceeding quotas, and managers were growing accustomed to the new, free-wheeling culture. Sales began putting demands on Buehler to speed things up. He responded by guaranteeing faster delivery of equipment, streamlining the sales contract, and speeding up approval of customer designs and bids. As one account executive put it: "Decisions that would have taken two years in the Bell system were made in days by Bill Buehler." The results were impressive, and the Buehler group soon outperformed its traditionally run rival, National Business Systems.

But 12 months after starting the new culture in General Business Systems, Buehler was removed from his job and transferred to an obscure planning position. This weakened the culture, and as one account executive put it: "We're all upset and worried that we'll lose our new culture." There is a difference of opinion at AT&T about why Buehler lost his job. Charles Marshall, chairman of AT&T Information Systems, explains the move as a means of having small-systems sales report up the same channels as the large systems unit. To others, however, Buehler was removed because he was too threatening to the traditional AT&T culture. Despite his success, he was viewed more as a maverick than as a visionary.[14]

Set Objectives for the Change Effort   5

If change is to be effective, objectives must be set before the change effort is started. If possible, objectives should be stated in measurable terms and should be (1) based on realistic organizational and employee needs; (2) stated clearly; (3) consistent with the organization's policies; and (4) attainable. For example, if an objective of a change program is to help foremen reduce machine downtime, one of the organization's obligations is to train foremen adequately and then delegate maintenance procedures to them. If the change program cannot do this, it should not be undertaken. Many change efforts have failed because their objectives were not stated clearly or understood by all the people involved.

Managers generally use two classes of objectives—internal and external—against which to assess the effectiveness of organizational change. *Internal objectives* refer to changes that occur within the individual (changes in attitudes, improved decision-making ability, increased work motivation, greater job satisfaction). *External objectives* (turnover, grievances, absenteeism, profits, new customers, rate of production) reflect the anticipated effects of internal changes, or how the change program is expected to affect job behavior and performance. Changes in attitudes, for example, should be expressed directly in improved performance before a manager can call the change a success; that is, changes in attitudes do not necessarily lead to achievement of external objectives. If the objectives of a change effort are spelled out in this fashion, a sequence of learning activities can be planned, and the most appropriate change strategy can be adopted by the organization. A clear statement of objectives also gives the manager the indicators to use in determining whether the strategy was successful.

Search for Change Strategies 6

The sixth step is to look for change strategies that can be used. Successful change can be accomplished only by modifying certain forces in an organization. The four interrelated forces—technology, structure, task, and people—involved in organizational change are shown in Fig. 21.6. A change in any one of these forces usually affects others. For example, at GM, Chrysler, and Ford, robots are used to spray-paint cars, weld parts of chassis together, load and unload materials from storage bins, and inspect engine blocks. By 1990, GM intends to have installed computerized systems that will completely integrate design and manufacturing, along with robots that will inspect parts and guide and repair other robots. This strategy has several important change implications:

1. Robots are able to perform repetitive tasks more efficiently than people.

2. As the cost of labor rises, it is often cheaper for a company to buy a robot than to hire people.

3. A new breed of employee—robotic engineers, hydraulic and electronic experts—is increasingly needed. According to one GM official, this new breed of employee must be able to communicate with "people who wear bowling shirts and baseball caps."

4. Many jobs will be redesigned to take advantage of what robots can do.[15]

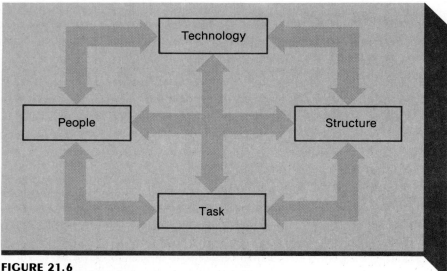

FIGURE 21.6
Forces in Organizational Change

Source: From H. Leavitt, "Applied Organizational Change in Industry: Structural, Technological and Humanistic Approaches." In *Handbook of Organizations*, J. March (Ed.). Chicago: Rand McNally, 1965, p. 1145. Used with permission.

TABLE 21.3 ■ STRATEGIES FOR ORGANIZATIONAL CHANGE

FORCE	STRATEGY
Technology	Modification of production methods
	Modification of machinery
	Automation
Structure	Change of position descriptions
	Modification of authority and responsibility relationships
	Modification of formal reward systems
Task	Job enrichment
	Job simplification
	Team development
People	On-the-job training
	Management development courses
	Organizational development programs

Source: Adapted from H. Carlisle, *Management Concepts and Situations*. Chicago: Science Research Associates, 1976, p. 450.

Some of the change strategies that can be used are shown in Table 21.3. A *technology strategy* focuses on change in workflows, methods, materials, and information systems. This will occur at GM with the use of robots. An *organization-structure strategy* emphasizes the internal structural changes that can be brought about by managers: creation or realignment of departments; changes in the locations of decision making; installation of a new compensation system; and the merger or reorganization of departments that sell the company's products.[16] A *task strategy* concentrates on changing specific job activities to increase both the quality of the work experience for employees and their job performance. A *people strategy* is usually directed toward improving individual skills and organizational effectiveness by means of training and development programs.

Implement the Change 7

The next step in the change process is to implement and reinforce change over a period of time. The change process should be designed so that a specific change can be sustained over a period of time. The ability to sustain change depends primarily on how well the organization reinforces newly learned behaviors during and after the change effort.

Effective implementation requires that the new behaviors acquired by employees be properly rewarded. Organizational rewards can enha⸝ ⸍he implementation process in two ways: (1) a combination of money and pats-on-the-back can reinforce new behaviors; and (2) new behaviors should persist to the extent that employees view the rewards as equitable. When new behaviors are fairly compensated, people are likely to develop and maintain preferences for those behaviors.

Effective implementation is enhanced when the people who have been asked to change their behaviors have participated in the design and implementation of the change program. Managers should not unilaterally decide that a change program is good for their employees. Freedom of employees to ask questions prior to the implementation of a change usually leads to commitment. However, if employees are not asked to participate, they may comply with the program but will not be committed; people will use subtle tactics to make sure that the program fails.

Follow Up the Change $\boxed{8}$

In the eighth, or follow-up, step, the manager faces the problem of deciding whether the change process has been a success. This depends on the trend in improvement over a period of time, which has three dimensions: (1) the level of satisfaction, productivity, new-product development, and market share before the change process begins; (2) the magnitude of the improvement or decline; and (3) the duration of the improvement or decline. Before a change program is implemented, management should have established the internal and external objectives and current benchmark levels to use in measuring the program's success (step 5). Now, achievement of the internal objectives (job satisfaction) should be measured and related to the level of achievement of the external objectives (job performance). If this is not done, misleading conclusions about the success of the change effort could be reached. For example, in a large insurance company, the jobs of many of the clerks were enriched. (See Chapter 12 for a full discussion of this.) The employees indicated greater job satisfaction, but their productivity did not increase. Therefore the manager could not conclude that the change was entirely successful. Thus the effectiveness of a change program should not be determined by measuring only attitudes or measuring only performance against objectives. A composite index made up of both attitudinal and performance objectives and accomplishments should be used.

Ideally, managers should monitor the effectiveness of a change continuously. However, this is usually too costly and time-consuming, so managers usually make assessments at predetermined time intervals. One measurement should be made immediately after a change is implemented. For example, if a people strategy were used, changes in employee attitudes, knowledge, skills, and job satisfaction would be compared against the predetermined objectives for these characteristics. To avoid a potentially faulty assessment based on only temporary changes in attitudes, another measurement should be made later, after the immediate effect of change has worn off. This second measurement will often indicate attitudinal changes that the first one did not reveal. At the time of the first measurement, the organization had not yet had the opportunity to reinforce (or try to eliminate) newly developed employee attitudes. Participants in a human-relations training program might show an initial increase in their sensitivity to others. Unless the organization reinforces this behavior over a period of time, through various rewards and managerial behaviors, the sensitivity acquired in the training program is not likely to last.

When does a manager decide that the change program is a failure? Let us go back to the Preview Case for one answer. Levi Strauss decided that, when it introduced its jeans into large department stores and profits did not increase, a new tactic was needed. Robert Haas, the president, decided to reevaluate Levi's decision against advertising and local-store promotional campaigns. Haas and his key managers made the decision to cosponsor local events that store managers thought were important. Similarly, Levi formed a new division, Battery Street Enterprises, that is attempting to capture a share of the fashion market. These decisions were the result of Levi's failure to successfully change its profitability when it made the decision to sell its jeans to large mass merchandisers such as Sears, J.C. Penney, and others.

STRATEGIES FOR ORGANIZATIONAL CHANGE

The methods for changing organizations and employees that we present in this section are representative of the methods shown in Table 21.3. Some of these methods were woven into previous chapters (job enrichment in Chapter 12, structural changes in Chapter 11) and thus will not be discussed at length here. There is no ready-made or agreed-on formula for determining which strategies, or methods within each strategy, to use. However, managers can get clues from the way an organization responds to its environment and how the behaviors of its employees change generally. One key managerial concern should be the nature of the problem faced. With this in mind, each of the change strategies is illustrated by only one or two change methods.

TECHNOLOGY STRATEGY

There have always been two fundamental ways to increase business profits: (1) increasing sales demand for the product; or (2) by reducing per-unit costs. During the 1960s, when new market horizons seemed boundless, corporations put much of their effort into marketing. Now corporate managers are paying increased attention to reducing per-unit costs. Changing the technology of an organization is a commonly used strategy, which can have far-reaching effects

Changes in an organization's technology—for example, placing personal computers at work spaces for all managers and staff—can greatly influence productivity and morale.
Source: Ellis Herwig/The Picture Cube.

on costs and personnel throughout the organization. Not only are production people and costs affected by the change; marketing, industrial engineering, and financial systems are also often affected. Let us look at what happened when Corning Glass changed technologies.

IN PRACTICE
Corning Glass Works

In 1880, when Thomas A. Edison asked Corning to make him up a batch of glass envelopes that he could fashion into light bulbs, glassmaking was a handcraft. By 1926, a "ribbon" machine was invented to replace hand blowing, and Corning's per unit costs dropped dramatically. Recently, Corning has developed an all-electric furnace that has resulted in further cost reductions.

Thomas MacAvoy, president of Corning, says that most of the gains have come from technology. Productivity in the glass industry has been growing at a three-percent rate throughout the 1970s, but Corning has its productivity growth up to six percent. According to MacAvoy, "We are always trying to redesign jobs, motivate people, and what not, but frankly I don't think people are basically lazy and ineffective. I don't think it's possible to get them to work 20 percent harder. To get them to work smarter is different, and that involves the application of technology."

In Corning's Pressware plant, where laminated glass dinnerware is made, there is a control panel next to the long kilns in which the dinnerware is fired. Because the kiln operators work together rather than in separate stations, they are able to control the flow of production smoothly. Further down the line, there are three sets of traffic lights hanging from the ceiling. A green light means that the line is running smoothly. Amber advertises the fact that the line needs close inspection because defects were found in some dinnerware. Red indicates a shutdown. The signals are regulated by quality-control inspectors. They used to hand-check each plate, but now only a sample of plates are checked. This new method has led to better quality control and much faster production.

White collar productivity is also crucial at Corning since the company depends heavily on bright, innovative scientists and engineers. The company hopes to improve the productivity of the corporate engineering people by bringing them together under one roof in a new building. The coffee lounges are equipped with blackboards to encourage engineers to talk out technical problems. Escalators facilitate movement from floor to floor and make face-to-face communication easier.

The company's new computerized accounting system enables Corning management to regularly measure productivity at each of Corning's 39 plants. This program tells managers exactly how much productivity they are getting out of labor, capital, energy, and materials. These more refined productivity data should help Thomas Howitt, energy expert, control Corning's energy costs. In 1972, Corning's total energy cost was $18 million. If Corning had been operating the same way in 1978, even allowing for a substantial increase in volume, its energy bill would have been $80 million. However, because of technological innovations, its bill was only $56 million. The $24 million savings was achieved mostly through conversion of glass melting furnaces from natural gas or oil to electric. More energy was saved by such measures as removing fluorescent bulbs in offices and monitoring room temperatures.[17]

ORGANIZATION-STRUCTURE STRATEGY

Another strategy for improving the effectiveness of an organization is by changing the organization's structure. In Chapter 11, we highlighted the restructuring of General Motors' Automotive Division. In that instance, GM changed the bases of departmentalization and coordination.

Managers of some companies have given the following reasons for using a structural change strategy.

■ The pressure of competition on profits, which puts a premium on an efficient organizational structure. Overlapping departments have to be combined, product divisions consolidated, and marginal functions eliminated.

■ The booming international trade market, which requires a change to export departments to international divisions, to establish regional management groups, and to restructure the corporate staff.

■ Mergers and acquisitions, which generate strong pressures for reorganization in parent companies as well as in newly acquired subsidiaries.

■ New developments in technology, which often require new organizational arrangements to realize its ultimate potential for improving corporate performance.

The restructuring of a large Chicago bank, First Chicago Corporation, was based on several of these reasons.

IN PRACTICE
First Chicago Corporation

Deregulation has challenged virtually all U.S. banks with the large task of overhauling their organizational structures, picking their market niches, and turning managers into marketers and strategic planners. When Barry F. Sullivan, chairman of First Chicago, took over this bank in 1980, its financial performance was poor, and executive turnover was almost 13% a year.

Sullivan built a new management team by recruiting more than 300 officers and created a product development and planning department. While initiating these changes, he reorganized the bank into 145 strategic business units in an attempt to push responsibility for strategic planning and marketing down the management ranks. Some of these strategic business units sell specific products and services while others market a broad line of services within a specific region. This was a major departure from First's traditional dependence on specialty groups catering to individual industries, such as housing, energy, transportation, and real estate.

Sullivan's efforts have clearly created a more entrepreneurial corporate culture. This corporate culture enabled First to penetrate investment banking markets, such as corporate finance, trade financing, and leasing. According to one vice president, "We have a mission to run a freestanding business that generates a profit of its own." The manager of one strategic business unit has seen his budget increase 27% during one year and his unit's ranking among competitors rise from number 11 to number 1 in less than two years. According to another vice president, "Under the old organization, First could have six different people making calls in Minneapolis according to their business. The result was a lot of plane trips by people who never got to know the Minneapolis market. We were missing a lot of good prospects because they didn't happen to be a large company in one of our specialities."[18]

While its chairman, Barry F. Sullivan, has managed to turn the bank's performance around and cut down executive turnover to 5 percent per year, some problems remain. The proliferation of different strategic business units has created confusion about who is in charge of planning, who reports to whom, and which strategic business unit is expected to sell which products and services to which customers. Sullivan admits that "melding those strategic business units together remains a major challenge."

Task Strategy

Whenever a job is changed—whether because of new technology, internal reorganization, or managerial whim—task redesign takes place. When specific jobs are changed with the intent of increasing both the quality of the employees' work experience and their productivity, it is referred to as "job enrichment." The basic method was described in Chapter 12; therefore we will review briefly only its major points and present another example.

There are four unique aspects to job enrichment. First, job enrichment changes the basic relationship between employees and what they do on the job. It enables workers to break out of the givens in their jobs. Job enrichment is based on the assumption that work itself may be a very powerful influence on employee motivation, satisfaction, and productivity. Where work may be satisfying only the lower-order needs (or hygiene factors) of employees, job enrichment provides a method for them to move toward satisfaction of higher-order needs (or motivator factors).

Second, job enrichment directly changes behavior. The basic objective of job enrichment is to change the behaviors of employees in ways that gradually lead to more positive attitudes about the work, the organization, and their own self-image. Because enriched jobs usually increase feelings of autonomy and personal freedom, employees are likely to develop attitudes that are supportive of their new job-related behaviors.

Third, job enrichment offers numerous opportunities for initiating other organizational changes. Technical problems are likely to develop when jobs are changed, which offers management an opportunity to refine the technology. Interpersonal issues almost inevitably arise between supervisors and subordinates and sometimes among co-workers who have to relate to each other in different ways. These issues offer opportunities for developing new supervisory skills and teamwork.

Finally, job enrichment can humanize an organization. Job enrichment can help individuals to experience the high that comes from developing competence in their work and doing a job well. Individuals are encouraged to grow and push themselves.

With the advent of personal computers, more than 70 companies, such as Aetna Life and Casualty, American Express, Blue Cross-Blue Shield, and Control Data have experimented with a new form of task redesign. Called the *cottage system,* this system permits workers to work at home. The workers, mostly women who have small children at home, are able to transmit data from a personal computer to a central computer by telephone. They can process the work according to their own personal schedules.

IN PRACTICE
Control Data
Corporation

Control Data Corporation started its cottage program in Dallas, Texas, in October 1983. The company trained workers for six weeks on how to code data, operate a personal computer, and transmit these data to Control Data's central computer. All the workers who joined this program were women, ranging in age from 25 to 35, and had small children at home. Batches of claims are delivered to their door every week by a company driver. Workers are paid according to the number of insurance claims they process correctly. Each properly processed claim is worth $0.50. Incorrect claims are returned to the worker for corrections. Control Data has no fringe benefits, such as life insurance, vacations, or retirement plans, for these workers. The average cottage worker earns $225.00 per week. A full-time claims processor working in Control Data's Computer Center is paid $1300 a month for working 38 hours a week and correctly processing 150 claims per week. However, the full-time employee is responsible for communicating with the claimant either by phone or letter and answering questions about claims. The cottage worker is not required to do these tasks. Similarly, the cottage worker does not have to worry about commuting, office clothes, day-care, and other expenses incurred by the full-time employee.

What have been the results? Most cottage workers favor the program. According to one worker, "I put in my 40 hours, but it's my own schedule. Sometimes I work until 2 A.M. to finish my claims. After the kids go to bed, I'll key information into the computer. In an odd way, it's great because it gives me something to do. Besides, I have the freedom to take my dog for a walk or do some cleaning and then go back to work. I can take whatever kind of breaks I want." Another worker commented, "I prefer working alone, rather than being thrown into a working environment where there's a lot of commotion and a lot of people who really don't mean anything to me." Control Data management thinks that the program works really well. Productivity is higher than expected (95 percent of the claims are properly coded), and, since it does not have to pay for fringe benefits, the company saves on labor expense.[19]

If we examine the various characteristics of the job (variety, autonomy, task completion, task significance, feedback, and interpersonal relations), we find that the cottage program permits workers a lot of autonomy, task significance and feedback. However, it does not offer the employees a chance to use a variety of skills or communicate with co-workers.

People Strategy

Technological, structural, and task strategies attempt to improve organizational performance by changing the work. They are based on the belief that by creating the appropriate work situation, employees will become more productive. A people strategy, on the other hand, attempts indirectly to change

In the 1980s, many women executives have successfully continued their careers after, and even during, childrearing. The "cottage system" allows them to work at home, yet remain current in their professions.

Source: David Burnett/Woodfin Camp & Associates.

the behavior of employees by focusing on their skills, attitudes, perceptions, and expectations. These new attitudes, skills, and expectations may, of course, encourage employees to seek changes in the organization's structure, technology, or tasks.

Methods to change employee job-related behavior and attitudes can be directed at individuals, groups, or the entire organization. Many of the methods used to change behaviors or attitudes are commonly grouped under the broad label of *organization development* (OD) methods.[20] Organization development is a planned, long-range, behavioral-science strategy for understanding, changing, and developing organizations to improve their effectiveness. Although OD methods frequently include structural, technological, and task changes, their primary focus is on changing people. Many OD practitioners believe that those affected by the change process should actively participate in developing methods to achieve change, which usually leads to greater commitment than does lack of participation. Typical OD methods include survey feedback, team building, problem solving, conflict resolution, interpersonal relations, and the like. These methods can be used in attempts to resolve problems and conflicts within a work group or between work groups.

OD cHARACTERISTICS ANd vAlUES

An OD program is tailored to meet the specific needs of an organization. Thus the emphasis placed on different organizational characteristics and values will vary. Organization development emphasizes three major sets of values that make it a unique approach to achieving organizational change: values toward people, groups, and organizations.[21]

Values toward people.   People have a natural desire for growth and development. If people are permitted to grow and develop, they have the potential to make greater contributions to an organization. Organization development aims to overcome obstacles to individual growth. It encourages treating people with dignity and respect, stresses genuine behavior while downplaying game playing, and strives for open communication.

Values toward groups.   It is important for people to be accepted by their work group. Collaboration and involvement in group problems leads to expression of feelings and perceptions. If members of a work group hide these feelings or are not accepted as members of their group, the individual's willingness to solve problems constructively will diminish. While the encouragement of openness can be risky, it can usually help people plan and implement ways to solve problems.

Values toward organizations.   The way that groups are linked has a strong influence on their effectiveness. Organization development is a top-to-bottom change method that recognizes the importance of starting change at the top of an organization and gradually introducing it throughout the rest of the organization. As one manager put it: "Successful change is like a waterfall. It cascades from the top to the bottom." The link between the top and the bottom is the group.

OD METHods foR AcHiEViNG cHANGE

There are many OD methods that can be utilized to achieve organizational change. We have chosen to highlight three of the more commonly used approaches: survey feedback, team building, and managerial grid.

Survey feedback.   Accurate feedback from others about behavior and job performance is one of the primary characteristics and values on which OD is based. *Survey feedback* is a method whereby managers and employees provide feedback about the organization and receive feedback about their own behaviors.[22] This feedback provides the basis for group discussion and the stimulus for change.

The survey-feedback method involves three stages: (1) a questionnaire is developed, as illustrated in Table 21.4, usually with the active participation of people who will fill it out; (2) the questionnaire is distributed to employees, who complete it and turn it in anonymously; (3) data are summarized, and results of the questionnaire are fed back to those who completed it. Usually a consultant or someone from the company's human-resources department summarizes the data, which are then used in group problem-solving activities. Group meetings are chaired by the manager, whose job is to (1) help the group to interpret what the data mean; (2) help the group to make plans for constructive change; and (3) help the group make plans to distribute the results to others in the organization. If the manager and subordinates decide that additional data are needed, another questionnaire might be developed.

Team building. Every organization depends on the cooperation of a number of people if its work is to be done effectively. Teams or groups of people must work together on a permanent or temporary basis to accomplish

TABLE 21.4 ■ SURVEY-FEEDBACK QUESTIONS

Instructions: The questions in this survey are answered on a number scale from 1 to 7. Please indicate your answer by circling the *one* number which best represents how you feel about the particular statement. *You may use any of the numbers from one to seven.* Please read each statement carefully and circle the one number which best represents *your* opinion on the subject. THERE ARE NO RIGHT OR WRONG AN-SWERS—THE ONLY REAL ANSWER IS YOUR OWN FRANK OPINION. Please read each statement and answer it. It is not necessary to spend a lot of time thinking about each one. Your first reaction is probably the best response. PLEASE DO NOT SIGN YOUR NAME TO THE SURVEY.

To what extent is this organization responsive to changes in its business environment?

TO A VERY GREAT EXTENT   7 6 5 4 3 2 1   TO A VERY LITTLE EXTENT

Overall, how would you rate the opportunities for promotion within the organization?

EXTREMELY GOOD   7 6 5 4 3 2 1   EXTREMELY POOR

To what extent are managers free to take independent actions that are necessary to carry out their job responsibilities?

TO A VERY GREAT EXTENT   7 6 5 4 3 2 1   TO A VERY LITTLE EXTENT

Goals in this organization tend to be:

VENTURESOME   7 6 5 4 3 2 1   CAUTIOUS

Decision making in this organization tends to be:

AT APPROPRIATE LEVELS   7 6 5 4 3 2 1   AT INAPPROPRIATE LEVELS

To what extent do the various persons within your unit truly cooperate with one another?

TO A VERY LITTLE EXTENT   1 2 3 4 5 6 7   TO A VERY GREAT EXTENT

When a management vacancy exists, the search within the organization to fill that vacancy tends to be:

VERY BROAD   7 6 5 4 3 2 1   VERY NARROW

To what extent are managers held personally accountable for the end results they produce or fail to produce?

TO A VERY GREAT EXTENT   7 6 5 4 3 2 1   TO A VERY LITTLE EXTENT

Source: Harry Sutherland, Assistant Manager, Human Resources Department, Brooklyn Union Gas Company, 1985.

organizational objectives. Managers often create teams to solve problems but must take care to define the problem and identify to the extent possible its relationship to other problems. The principal objective of **team building** is to help teams operate more effectively by evaluating and improving their structure, processes (leadership, communication, conflict resolution), and member satisfaction.[23] Team building normally begins at the top of an organization and extends downward. Ideally, it focuses on solving intragroup problems. Team-building sessions may last from a half day to several days, depending on group needs and the manager's skill as a group leader; they should be held away from the office setting; and usually address:

- Climate building. The meeting purpose and objectives are discussed. People share information about themselves and state what they would like to accomplish.

- Process and structure evaluation. The group evaluates the strengths and weaknesses of its group processes. The group may evaluate (1) its policies and structure; (2) how decisions are made; (3) how communications take place; (4) the norms of the group; and (5) how each person could be a more effective team member.

- Problem solving. The group identifies its major strengths and weaknesses and develops alternatives for overcoming weaknesses. The focus is on developing solutions to problems.

- Setting objectives and planning. Team objectives are agreed on and plans are made for reaching these objectives.

- Training. Team-building sessions include some form of training that is helpful to the group, such as improving communication skills, learning how to run meetings effectively, or diagnosing leadership styles.

- Closure. Closure involves summarizing what has been accomplished and by assigning follow-up responsibilities.

In Chapter 15, we discussed the three skills of effective groups: (1) the ability to gather relevant information about a problem; (2) the ability to make sound decisions; and (3) the ability to obtain member commitment to implementing the decisions. Team-building efforts focus on developing such skills in an organization.

The managerial grid.   Since the early 1960s, the **managerial grid** has been used in OD by nine of the 10 largest corporations in the world and has widespread application throughout the world.[24] This method assumes that managers can maximize concerns both for production and for people; that is, organizational and individual objectives can be compatible rather than at odds.

As you will recall from Chapter 13, the grid is a graphic representation of five managerial styles. The two key variables—concern for people and concern for production—and some of their possible combinations are shown in Fig. 21.7 (presented previously as Fig. 13.4). A rating of 1 on each scale represents a minimum concern, whereas a rating of 9 represents a maximum concern.

Thus the lower left-hand corner (1, 1) represents minimum concern for both people and production. The manager is simply a communication link between subordinates and higher management. Production will be limited. The assumptions are that people don't want to work and that little reward is attached to work accomplished with others.

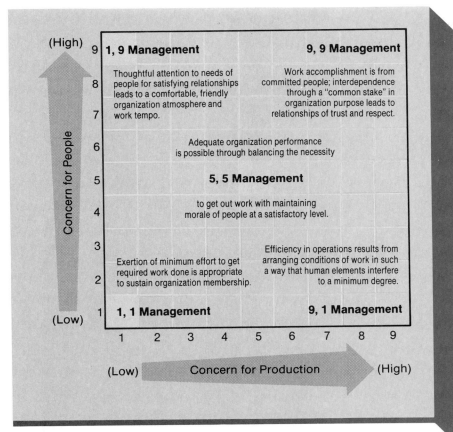

FIGURE 21.7
The Managerial Grid

The upper left-hand (1, 9) corner represents minimum concern for production and maximum concern for people. Human relationships are ends in themselves; that is, if people are made comfortable and secure, production will take care of itself.

The lower right-hand corner (9, 1) represents maximum concern for production and minimum concern for people. This management style is also based on the assumption that people resist working. The manager exerts heavy pressures and controls on people to get high production.

The center point (5, 5) represents a management style that balances concern for production and people. The assumption here is that the needs of people and production conflict. The manager resolves this conflict through compromise.

The upper right-hand corner (9, 9) represents maximum concern for both production and people, or the ideal managerial style. The assumptions are that people are basically mature and responsible and, if given rewarding work to which they are committed, that they will produce at maximum level. This, of course, conflicts with other theories, which indicate that in certain settings a (9, 1) or (1, 9) manager might be more effective.

When used as an OD method, the managerial grid involves the group process and six phases of learning, assessment, and implementation. The educational content of phase 1 includes the use of self-evaluation forms, placing oneself on the grid, and organizational problem-solving exercises. The problem-solving exercises attempt to simulate organizational conditions in which interpersonal behavior affects task performance. Teams are formed from the participants; each team meets separately and is responsible for developing solutions and improving its own problem-solving effectiveness; effectiveness is measured against objective standards. After the teams have been informed of their performance, they meet separately again and critique their operational effectiveness. Weaknesses and strengths are identified and analyzed; plans for increasing effectiveness are introduced.

Phases 2 and 3 concentrate on the application of behavioral-science knowledge to intragroup development and intergroup teamwork; that is, on improving relationships among people at the same level, between superiors and subordinates, and between groups. The most common barriers to increasing team effectiveness are failures to communicate fully, plan properly, listen to others' opinions, and resolve interpersonal friction. In these two phases, each member analyzes the team climate and problems and proposes solutions. Members evaluate their own job performance and that of others on the team. The team then discusses these problems and develops solutions.

Phase 4 stresses organizational objectives that require commitment at all levels of the organization. Objectives discussed in this phase pertain to union–management relations, basic policy development, safety, promotions, and determining the proper structure of the organization. The specific objectives to be introduced are identified by the teams.

The success of phase 5, implementation of a corporate model for effectiveness, is based on the quality and character of the achievements resulting from the preceding phases. Ideally, behavioral theories have been understood, communication roadblocks removed, and a full understanding of and commitment to corporate excellence obtained. The manager's primary goal is to help achieve the objectives set during phase 4 and also to recognize previously undefined problems.

The final phase of the OD process is stabilization. During this phase, the organization must be supportive of the changes introduced in the earlier phases. These changes are assessed and reinforced so that the chances of returning to the original condition will be minimal.

The effectiveness of basing an OD program on the managerial grid concept is open to question.[25] Many corporations (British-America Tobacco Company, Texas Instruments, Pillsbury, Charles Pfizer and Company, Union Carbide and Company, and Honeywell, among others) have utilized this method. However, its effectiveness has not been tested rigorously. In many of the studies of the use of this approach, the exact causes of organizational change were not reported, nor was the effect of any particular phase of the program evaluated for its contribution to the change that occurred. Productivity, profits, and attitudes improved in some companies where the executives participated in the program. In these companies, considerable time was spent on team problem solving, which concentrated on making managers more aware of the alternatives available to them. Similarly, subordinates have reported that their managers became more understanding of their problems. Changes in attitudes and knowledge of behavioral concepts do not necessarily lead to improved performance but, with them, the chances of improved performance are much greater.

CHAPTER SUMMARY

This chapter focused on the organizational-change process. Organizational change has two objectives: adapting to the environment and changing the behavior of employees. We presented an eight-step model for organizational change that shows how managers can systematically analyze a company's external environment, its internal structure, and its organizational culture. The starting point is an analysis of changes in the organization's environment, including opportunities that can be seized. Managers often become aware of the need for change because of a performance gap, or the difference between what the organization could do with its market opportunities and what it actually does with them. Organizational problems that prevent taking full advantage of the opportunities and possible solutions have to be identified. Change efforts may be resisted by employees and even by an entire organization and have to be anticipated insofar as possible. Once the reasons for resistance have been explored, management must set objectives for the change effort and select a change strategy among those that are available. Implementation of change requires reinforcement of newly learned behaviors. Finally, change has to be monitored and evaluated for effectiveness.

We identified four types of change strategies. A technology strategy focuses on change in workflows, methods, materials, and information systems. The organization-structure strategy emphasizes the internal changes that managers make when playing the decisional role, to increase the organization's effectiveness. A task strategy focuses on specific job activities that can be changed to increase both the quality of employee work experience and job performance. A people strategy is usually directed toward improving communications and relations among individuals and groups. Survey feedback, team building, and the managerial grid are three organization development (OD) methods commonly used to change people's job-related behaviors and attitudes.

The way in which managers diagnose problems and how accurately they recognize the need for change influence the success of a change. Success also depends largely on the current level of dissatisfaction within the firm, support by top management for the change effort, and the correct diagnosis of sources of resistance to the change effort. Change can alter individual objectives, corporate cultures, and economic rewards. Thus, in successful programs, those directly affected by the change are generally involved in the process from the start.

MANAGER'S VOCABULARY

cottage system
external objectives
fire fighting
future shock
internal objectives
managerial grid
organization development
organization-structure strategy
people strategy
performance gap
planned organizational change
sunk costs
survey feedback
task strategy
team building
technology strategy

REVIEW QUESTIONS

1. What are the four factors requiring managers to change the way they operate in order to be successful in today's business world?

2. What are the eight steps in the change-process model?

3. What are the four reasons why people resist change?

4. What are the three reasons why organizations resist change?

5. State the methods that managers can use to overcome resistance to change.

6. What are four strategies that managers can use to achieve change?

DISCUSSION QUESTIONS

1. Evaluate the following comment: "We trained hard, but it seemed that every time we were beginning to form up into teams, we would be reorganized. We tend to meet any new situation by reorganizing, and what a wonderful method it can be for creating the illusion of progress while producing confusion, inefficiency, and demoralization." (Petronius, 210 B.C.)

2. Evaluate the following quote from Peanuts to Snoopy based on your knowledge of the ways that people and organizations resist change: "Once a dog, always a dog."

3. How can the major obstacles to change be overcome?

4. What are the similarities and differences of the four change strategies? When should each strategy be used?

5. How do the assumptions and values of OD affect changes in organizations?

6. According to Tom Peters, co-author of *In Search of Excellence,* whenever anything is being changed, it is being done by a monomaniac with a mission. What implications does this have for achieving change in organizations?

MANAGEMENT INCIDENTS AND CASES

FINANCIAL SYSTEMS, INC.

Financial Systems, Inc., of Memphis, Tennessee, had begun operations in the check processing business in November 1977 when its current president, Earl Roberts, agreed to join the firm on a full-time basis. Prior to that time Roberts had been acting as a consultant to the firm. In that capacity, he assisted management in arranging for a series of small loans that were needed to maintain operations. The company had been attempting, with little success, to develop and market check-processing equipment for the commercial banking industry. No sales had actually been made because the product design efforts had encountered serious technical problems.

When asked why he had agreed to join the firm, Roberts replied that "Even though the future for Financial Systems, Inc., was very uncertain in 1977, I felt that the technical problems with the product could be solved and I felt certain that a good market existed for a product of this type if we could just get into production and begin selling."

By the end of 1978, after scrapping the original product design and starting with a new approach, the engineering staff had developed a product that could be manufactured. Several of the units were sold toward the end of 1978 and shipped to customers. Revenues totaled $13,000 and $209,000 for 1977 and 1978, respectively. The initial success of the product in the customers' installations indicated that the new design was a good one and that a substantial market existed.

Early in 1978, it became apparent that the company would need new outside financing for the expansion of marketing, manufacturing, and engineering efforts. Roberts approached private investors and persuaded them to invest a total of approximately $300,000, for which they received stock and warrants. With these new funds, a staff of three key managers was recruited to head up the functional areas of marketing, manufacturing and engineering, and accounting. These three individuals and Roberts, formed the initial management team. In 1984, all three were vice-presidents of Financial Systems. These individuals, along with Roberts, had been responsible for the growth and success of the company (Fig. 21.8).

Marketing organization

Art Bellamy joined Financial Systems in February 1978, after working for several years as an industry marketing manager for a large facilities management firm. Although he lacked extensive direct selling experience, he was a tireless, dynamic individual with an excellent background in computer operations in the banking industry. Upon arrival at the company, Bellamy's efforts were directed entirely to selling. His sales success was impressive. In 1979, with the introduction

ASSETS	1984 (000's)	1977 (000's)
Cash and near cash	$1531	$ 21
Accounts receivable	2419	16
Inventories	970	15
Prepaid expenses	76	3
Total current assets	4996	55
Equipment	1586	59
Furniture and fixtures	103	8
Less: Depreciation	(233)	(2)
Total Fixed Assets	1456	65
Total Assets	$6452	$ 120
LIABILITIES		
Accounts payable	$1100	$ 82
Notes payable	50	44
Accrued liabilities	1035	21
Total current liabilities	2185	147
Common equity at par	26	26
Paid-in-surplus	1271	318
Retained earnings	2970	(371)
Total Liabilities and Equity	$6452	$ 120

FIGURE 21.8
Comparative Balance Sheet

of a second product, he began to recruit a small staff of salespeople, and by 1983 he had hired a staff of eight. Each salesperson had previous experience, and each was assigned to a specific geographic territory. The salespeople lived in their territories and communicated with Bellamy and others at the home office primarily by telephone. A secretary served as a communication link among the salespeople, Bellamy, and the home-office staff. In addition she typed correspondence and prepared trip itineraries. All official company correspondence and sales proposals were prepared at the home office and mailed to users and prospective customers. This was necessary because the salespeople did not have typing services available to them and because Bellamy approved all customer and prospect communications. As a result, the salespeople spent a great deal of time dictating and reviewing proposal contents by telephone prior to finalization by Bellamy.

Bellamy maintained a heavy travel schedule; he felt that "Whenever one of my salespeople has an account that is ready to sign a contract, I want to be there. I want to be certain that nothing goes wrong at the last minute, and also I am the only person, except Mr. Roberts, who can negotiate contract terms with a customer."

In addition to salespeople, Bellamy had a home-office staff of six software specialists. They were scheduled by Bellamy to assist customers in equipment-related operational problems at their facilities. Two administrative assistants also reported to him. They prepared equipment demonstrations, scheduled trade-show activities, and maintained contract and customer records. Contract review and signing, as well as equipment shipment schedules, were Bellamy's responsibility.

Markets served

Financial Systems' primary marketplace is the domestic commercial-banking industry. Specifically, the firm manufactures, markets, and supports automated computer-based systems and associated supplies for check processing. Current and planned future products are directed at fulfilling the needs of the 500 largest U.S. banks whose check-processing centers, either directly for their own customers or indirectly through correspondent relationships with smaller area banks, process a major portion of the estimated 40 billion checks written annually in the United States.

In addition to processing checks, there are many other bank document-processing applications that can be handled by the company's products. These applications include return items (checks that cannot be processed due to insufficient funds, closed accounts, invalid signature), lockbox, remittance processing, and bank card drafts (MasterCard, Visa). Each of these applications represents a major market for the company.

Outside the commercial banking industry, only a few customers currently use Financial Systems' equipment. However, document-processing applications that are compatible with the company's products offer significant potential in the insurance, energy-utility, retail-credit, and government markets.

Market potential

Since 1978, when the company began actively marketing its products, penetration into the commercial-banking market and acceptance of the company's products have progressed rapidly. Continued growth in the volume of checks has been forecasted (55 billion checks by 1989) by industry sources, assuring a large and growing market for present and future products. The additional commercial-banking applications and the on-going sales of equipment supplies significantly extend the potential sales for current products to a total of more than $150 million over the next five years. One large bank initially installed eight systems for check processing and now has a total of 31, which are used for a variety of processing applications.

New banking-system products, available for delivery in late 1984, combine to provide additional potential over the next five years of approximately $200 million. These new systems represent a significant technological advance over equipment that is presently available from other firms, which has reached its maximum level of effectiveness for most banks. The new technology will provide for significant gains in cost reduction, processing time, accuracy, and new products and services that banks can offer to both commercial and individual customers.

Competition

Companies with whom Financial Systems, Inc., competes in the commercial-banking industry are the large data-processing firms such as Burroughs, NCR, and IBM. However, Financial Systems has successfully segmented the market by addressing applications for which its present products offer clear operational (speed, accuracy) and financial advantages (lower product cost) over those of its competitors. These applications are traditionally labor-intensive clerical functions that lend themselves to automation, yet are small enough to avoid the concentrated attention of large competitors.

The versatility of the company's products in meeting a variety of processing needs, in addition to the primary application for which they are purchased, has been a key element to Financial Systems' success. Operational and financial gains that are available to customers, in addition to the expertise and service orientation of the sales and support staff, provide a significant competitive advantage in the selected market segments. Future products have been similarly targeted at market segments where they can enjoy price and operational advantages.

Manufacturing and engineering

Jim Lawrence, vice-president of manufacturing and engineering, is one of the original group of key employees who joined Financial Systems in 1978. Previously, he had been a division manager for a medium-sized instrument company, and was responsible for engineering, research, and manufacturing. A quiet, low-key individual, Lawrence relied on procedures, rules and regulations, structures, and job definitions, rather than dynamic personal leadership, to manage his department. He preferred to give only broad, general advice to his managers, and to allow them to make their own decisions within their defined areas of responsibility.

Manufacturing operations are limited in scope and require only 25 employees. Most major components for the company's products are bought from outside vendors under long-term purchase agreements. However, some components and subunits are assembled in Houston, and are shipped directly to a customer's facility along with those parts purchased from outside suppliers. Final system configuration assembly and checkout is performed at the customer's facility. A customer-engineering department, consisting of 50 service engineers reporting to Lawrence (Fig. 21.9), is responsible

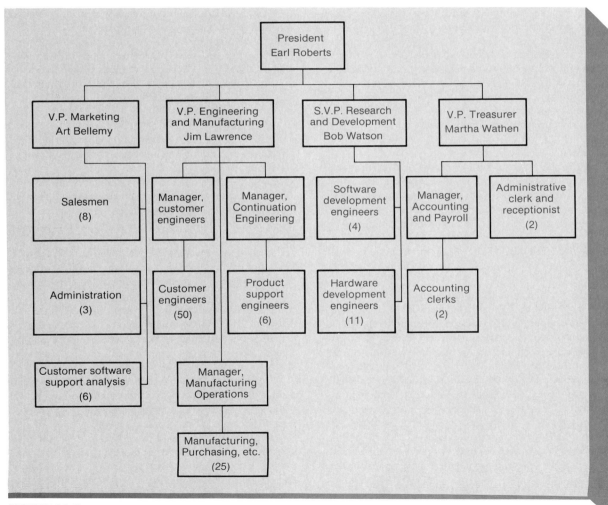

FIGURE 21.9
Company Organization Chart, 1983

for final assembly and checkout of equipment and for the ongoing maintenance of all equipment that has been sold. Equipment maintenance is provided to each customer under a renewable, one-year contract. Prior to 1983, maintenance had been provided by a third-party contractor. During the past year, Lawrence was given the responsibility for organizing, staffing, and managing the conversion to the present maintenance system. According to Roberts, Lawrence handled this new responsibility well.

A small continuation engineering group also reports to Lawrence. Its function is to provide technical support to the assembly and customer-engineering groups. The staff is comprised of senior engineers with broadly based experience; they design engineering solutions to technical problems on short notice and provide minor product improvements and/or modifications, when necessary, to meet unique customer requirements. They are also responsible for maintaining engineering standards and documentation, as well as providing the technical interface with outside vendors.

Finance

Financial Systems is a privately held corporation whose stock is owned by a small group of institutional and individual investors. These investors are very active in the management of the company, either as members of the board of directors or as corporate officers. The total amount of invested capital is slightly more than $1 million. (See Fig. 21.8.) Since early 1982, growth had been entirely financed with internally generated funds.

The finance and accounting department employs four people whose primary functions include accounts payable, accounts receivable, payroll, and preparation of quarterly and annual statements. Martha Wathen, another of the original group of employees, is responsible for the finance department. Before joining the company, she had performed accounting services for small local companies. Although she had no formal training in accounting or finance, she had been an assistant to the chief financial officer of a medium-sized computer firm and had gained practical experience before joining Financial Systems. Roberts had also served as a financial officer in the past and participated in setting financial policy for the firm.

Research and development

Early in 1983, Financial Systems acquired, by merger, a small firm that was actively involved in the development of an advanced bank data-processing system. According to Roberts, the merger extends the company's product line. The owner and president of the acquired firm, Bob Watson, and a small group of competent developmental engineers now comprise Financial Systems' research and development department. Prior to the merger, product development activities had been the responsibility of the engineering/manufacturing group headed by Lawrence. These two groups now share some resources, such as test equipment and technicians, often resulting in conflict over assignment of resources and priorities.

As a result of the merger, Watson became the major stockholder in Financial Systems, a senior vice-president, and a member of the board of directors. Having earned both an engineering degree and an MBA, and as a result of his experience as a founder of an electronics firm, he is well-qualified in both the technical and business aspects of the company's operations.

Current status

The rapid growth of the company caused some internal stress and inefficiencies that concerned Roberts. He felt that the product strategy adopted by Financial Systems, the acceptance of the company's products in the marketplace, and the growing size of the market all indicated that continued rapid growth was possible. Sales of $25 million with profits of $6 million were forecast for 1984 and were expected to grow to $100 million and $30 million, respectively, by 1989. Further, the board of directors was considering a public offering of the company's stock sometime in 1984. The president was very much involved in analyzing the structure, strategy, and personnel requirements necessary to ensure that the company would be capable of meeting the demands of continued rapid growth. Additionally, he wanted to position the company for a public offering if one were made.

Roberts was involved on a day-to-day basis in the management of each functional department. He and Art Bellamy had several lengthy conversations regarding the need to hire subordinate managers and to allow salespeople more flexibility and discretion in their jobs. He felt that these actions were necessary, since it was clear to him that Bellamy was having problems maintaining control over the growing marketing operations and that many of the more experienced salesmen were unhappy with Bellamy's management style. Bellamy strongly resisted these ideas; he felt that the company's past success was a result of his direct involvement in all sales activity.

Their conversations tended to digress: They talked about conflicts between marketing and finance or manufacturing; such things as control over product-shipping schedules and commission payments; or other operating decisions that Bellamy felt he should participate in. The communication problem was compounded by his heavy travel schedule.

Because Roberts's time was being consumed more and more with day-to-day activities, he was concerned that corporate management functions were being neglected. Furthermore, departmental managers were used to operating in a hands-on role and were not able to give adequate attention to planning.[26]

Questions

1. Identify the external factors facing this company. What are the causes of the conflicts between the functional departments and within marketing?

2. What action(s) should Roberts take regarding the organization's structure? What would be the likely short- and long-term effects?

3. How would you implement your recommendations if you were in Roberts's position? How would you feel about making changes to the organization if you were Roberts?

4. What sources of resistance might you encounter in implementing your recommendations? How would you handle these?

REFERENCES

1. "Who's Excellent Now?" *Business Week,* November 5, 1984, pp. 76–88.

2. M. Ways, "The Era of Radical Change," *Fortune,* 1964, 79:113.

3. A. Toffler, *Future Shock.* New York: Random House, 1970. For an insightful update, *see* G. Colvin, "What the Baby Boomers Will Buy Next," *Fortune,* October 15, 1984, pp. 28–34.

4. E. Huse and T. Cummings, *Organization Development and Change.* St. Paul, Minn.: West, 1985; N. Tichy, *Managing Strategic Change.* New York: John Wiley & Sons, 1983.

5. S. Sherman, "Eight Big Masters of Innovation," *Fortune,* October 15, 1984, pp. 66–70.

6. R. Loeb, "Integrating Mechanisms Used by W. R. Grace & Company at the Holding Company Level." Unpublished term paper, Southern Methodist University, Dallas, 1984.

7. E. Tracy, "Nike Loses Its Footing on the Fast Track," *Fortune,* November 12, 1984, p. 74; S. Antilla, "Nike Hopes Revamp Has It Back on Track," *U.S.A. Today,* July 25, 1985, pp. B-1–B-2.

8. R. Dunham and F. Smith, *Organizational Surveys.* Glenview, Ill.: Scott, Foresman, 1979.

9. J. Kotter and L. Schlesinger, "Choosing Strategies for Change," *Harvard Business Review,* March–April 1979, 57:106–114.

10. N. Tichy, *Managing Strategic Change,* pp. 175–178ff.

11. A. Cifelli, "Asbestos Defendants Try a New Approach," *Fortune,* November 12, 1984, p. 165.

12. Kotter and Schlesinger, "Choosing Strategies for Change," pp. 106–114.

13. Several excellent books describe how managers can overcome resistance to change, some of which are: R. Kilmann, *Beyond the Quick Fix.* San Francisco, Jossey-Bass, 1984; G. Zaltman and R. Duncan, *Strategies for Planned Change.* New York: John Wiley Interscience, 1977; L. Hrebiniak and Wm. Joyce, *Implementing Strategy.* New York: Macmillan, 1984, pp. 217–242.

14. M. Langley, "Wrong Number: AT&T Manager Finds His Effort to Galvanize Sales Meets Resistance," *Wall Street Journal,* December 16, 1983, 1ff.

15. P. Ingrassia and D. Darlin, "Cincinnati Milacron, Mainly a Metal Bender, Now a Robot Maker," *Wall Street Journal,* April 7, 1983, 1ff.

16. For an insightful look into how one man transformed ITT from an aging dinosaur into a diversified giant, *see* H. Geneen, *Managing.* New York: Doubleday, 1984.

17. E. Meadows, "How Three Companies Increased Their Productivity," *Fortune,* March 10, 1980, pp. 92–101.

18. "The New Challenge at First Chicago: Maintaining the Momentum," *Business Week,* December 5, 1983, pp. 140–143.

19. D. Martinez, "Job Characteristics as a Measure of Job Enrichment: Example of the 'Cottage Program' at Control Data Corporation." Unpublished term

paper, Southern Methodist University, Dallas, 1984.

20. D. Warrick, "Managing Organization Change and Development." In *Modules in Management*. J. Rosenzweig and F. Kast (Eds.). Chicago: Science Research Associates, Inc., 1984, p. 6.

21. M. Sashkin and Wm. Morris, *Organizational Behavior: Concepts and Experiences*. Reston, Va.: Reston Publishing Company, 1984, pp. 376–380; W. French and C. Bell, *Organization Development: Behavioral Science Interventions for Organization Improvement*. Englewood Cliffs, N.J.: Prentice-Hall, 1984, pp. 45–53.

22. For excellent overviews of this approach, *see* D. Nadler, *Feedback and Organization Development*. Reading, Mass.: Addison-Wesley, 1977; J. Gavin, "Survey Feedback: The Perspectives of Science & Practice," *Groups and Organization Studies*, 1984, 9:29–70; E. Conlon and L. Short, "Survey Feedback as a Large-Scale Change Device: An Empirical

Investigation," *Groups and Organization Studies*, 1984, 9:399–416.

23. Much of this section is abstracted from Wm. Dyer, *Team Building: Issues and Alternatives*. Reading, Mass.: Addison-Wesley, 1977.

24. R. Blake and J. Mouton, *The Managerial Grid*. Houston: Gulf, 1965.

25. Sashkin and Morris, *Organizational Behavior*, pp. 386–387; French and Bell, *Organization Development*, pp. 278–279; J. Nicholas, "The Comparative Impact of Organizational Development Interventions on Hard Criteria Measures," *Academy of Management Review*, 1982, 7:531–542; J. Porras and P. Berg, "The Impact of Organizational Development," *Academy of Management Review*, 1978, 3:249–266.

26. Case prepared by G. Clark, Cox School of Business, Southern Methodist University, Dallas, under the direction of J. W. Slocum Jr.

Author Index

Author Index

Subject Index

Subject Index